Fingerprints of the Gods

Graham Hancock is a former East African
correspondent for *The Economist* and
has travelled widely around the world.
He is the author of *The Sign and the Seal*
and *Lords of Poverty*.

Fingerprints
of the Gods

A Quest for the Beginning and the End

GRAHAM HANCOCK

Photographs by Santha Faiia

SEAL BOOKS
McClelland-Bantam, Inc.
Toronto

FINGERPRINTS OF THE GODS

A Seal Book
published by arrangement with Graham Hancock

First published in Great Britain 1995
by William Heinemann Ltd

Seal edition 1996

Canadian Cataloguing in Publication Data applied for

Hardback ISBN 0-385-25475-X
Paperback ISBN 0-770-42725-1

Typeset by Deltatype Ltd, Ellesmere Port, Cheshire
Printed and bound in Great Britain by Cox & Wyman Ltd, Reading, Berkshire

Seal Books are published by McClelland-Bantam, Inc.
Its trademark, consisting of the words "Seal Books" and the
portrayal of a seal, is the property of McClelland-Bantam, Inc.
105 Bond St., Toronto, Ontario M5B 1Y3, Canada. This
trademark has been registered in the Trademark Office of
Canada. The trademark, consisting of the words "Bantam
Books" and the portrayal of a rooster, is the property of
and is used with the consent of Bantam Books, Inc.,
1540 Broadway, New York, N.Y. 10036. This trademark
has been duly registered in the Trademark Office of Canada
and elsewhere.

For Santha . . . . for being there.
With all my love.

Contents

x   Contents

Acknowledgements

Fingerprints of the Gods could not have been written without the generous, warm-hearted and sustaining love of my partner Santha Faiia – who always gives more than she takes and who enriches the lives of everyone around her with creativity, kindness and imagination. All the photographs in the book are her work.

I am also grateful for the support and encouragement of our six children – Gabrielle, Leila, Luke, Ravi, Sean and Shanti – each one of whom I feel priviledged to know.

My parents, Donald and Muriel Hancock, have been incredibly helpful, active and involved through this and many other difficult times and projects. Together with my uncle James Macaulay they have also patiently read the drafts of the evolving manuscript, offering a wealth of positive suggestions. Thanks, too, to my oldest and closest friend, Peter Marshall, with whom I have weathered many storms, and to Rob Gardner, Joseph and Sherry Jahoda, Roel Oostra, Joseph and Laura Schor, Niven Sinclair, Colin Skinner and Clem Vallance, all of whom gave me good advice.

In 1992 I suddenly found that I had a friend in Lansing, Michigan. His name is Ed Ponist and he got in touch with me soon after the publication of my previous book, *The Sign and the Seal*. Like a guardian angel he volunteered to devote a hefty chunk of his spare time to helping me out in the US with research, contacts and the collection of documentary resources of relevance to *Fingerprints of the Gods*. He did a brilliant job, always sending me the right books just when I needed them and finding references that I didn't even know existed. He was also an accurate weather-vane on the quality of my work, whose judgement I quickly learned to trust and respect. Last but not least, when Santha and I went to Arizona, to the Hopi Nation, it was Ed who came with us and who opened the way. . .

Ed's initial letter was part of an overwhelming deluge of mail that I received from around the world after writing *The Sign and the Seal*. For a while I tried to answer all the letters individually. Eventually, however, I got swamped with the new work on *Fingerprints* and had to stop replying. I feel bad about this, and would like to take this opportunity to thank everybody who wrote to me and to whom I did not write back. I'm intending to be more systematic in the future because I enormously value this correspondence and appreciate the high-quality information that it frequently turns out to contain. . .

Other researchers who have helped me on *Fingerprints of the Gods* have been Martin Slavin, David Mestecky and Jonathan Derrick. In addition I would like to thank my Anglophone editors on both sides of the Atlantic, Tom Weldon at Heinemann, Jim Wade at Crown and John Pearce at Doubleday Canada, as well as my literary agents Bill Hamilton and Sara Fisher, for their continuing commitment, solidarity and wise counsel.

My warmest appreciation also to those co-researchers and colleagues who have become my friends during the course of this investigation: Robert Bauval in Britain (with whom I shall be co-authoring two future books on related subjects), John Anthony West and Lew Jenkins in the United States, Rand and Rose Flem-Ath and Paul William Roberts in Canada.

Finally I want to pay tribute to Ignatius Donnelly, Arthur Posnansky, R.A. Schwaller de Lubicz, Charles Hapgood and Giorgio de Santillana – investigators who saw that something was badly wrong with the history of mankind, who had the courage to speak out against intellectual adversity, and who pioneered the momentous paradigm shift that is now irrevocably under way.

Part I

Introduction
The Mystery of the Maps

Chapter 1

A Map of Hidden Places

8 RECONNAISSANCE TECHNICAL SQUADRON (SAC)
UNITED STATES AIRFORCE
Westover Airforce Base
Massachusetts

6 July 1960

SUBJECT: Admiral Piri Reis World Map

To: Professor Charles H. Hapgood,
Keene College,
Keene, New Hampshire.

Dear Professor Hapgood,

Your request for evaluation of certain unusual features of the Piri Reis World Map of 1513 by this organization has been reviewed.

The claim that the lower part of the map portrays the Princess Martha Coast of Queen Maud Land Antarctica, and the Palmer Peninsula, is reasonable. We find this is the most logical and in all probability the correct interpretation of the map.

The geographical detail shown in the lower part of the map agrees very remarkably with the results of the seismic profile made across the top of the ice-cap by the Swedish-British Antarctic Expedition of 1949.

This indicates *the coastline had been mapped before it was covered by the ice-cap*.

The ice-cap in this region is now about a mile thick.

We have no idea how the data on this map can be reconciled with the supposed state of geographical knowledge in 1513.

HAROLD Z. OHLMEYER
Lt Colonel, USAF
Commander

Despite the deadpan language, Ohlmeyer's letter[1] is a bombshell. If Queen Maud Land was mapped before it was covered by ice, the original cartography must have been done an extraordinarily long time ago.

How long ago exactly?

Conventional wisdom has it that the Antarctic ice-cap, in its present extent and form, is millions of years old. On closer examination, this notion turns out to be seriously flawed – so seriously that we need not assume the map drawn by Admiral Piri Reis depicts Queen Maud Land as it looked millions of years in the past. The best recent evidence suggests that Queen Maud Land, and the neighbouring regions shown on the map, passed through a long ice-free period which may not have come completely to an end until about six thousand years ago.[2] This evidence, which we shall touch upon again in the next chapter, liberates us from the burdensome task of explaining who (or what) had the technology to undertake an accurate geographical survey of Antarctica in, say, two million BC, long before our own species came into existence. By the same token, since map-making is a complex and *civilized* activity, it compels us to explain how such a task could have been accomplished even six thousand years ago, well before the development of the first true civilizations recognized by historians.

Ancient sources

In attempting that explanation it is worth reminding ourselves of the basic historical and geological facts:

1 The Piri Reis Map, which is a genuine document, not a hoax of any kind, was made at Constantinople in AD 1513.[3]
2 It focuses on the western coast of Africa, the eastern coast of South America and the northern coast of Antarctica.
3 Piri Reis could not have acquired his information on this latter

region from contemporary explorers because Antarctica remained undiscovered until AD 1818,[4] more than 300 years after he drew the map.

4 The ice-free coast of Queen Maud Land shown in the map is a colossal puzzle because the geological evidence confirms that the latest date it could have been surveyed and charted in an ice-free condition is 4000 BC.[5]

5 It is not possible to pinpoint the *earliest* date that such a task could have been accomplished, but it seems that the Queen Maud Land littoral may have remained in a stable, unglaciated condition for at least 9000 years before the spreading ice-cap swallowed it entirely.[6]

6 There is no civilization known to history that had the capacity or need to survey that coastline in the relevant period: between 13000 BC and 4000 BC.[7]

In other words, the true enigma of this 1513 map is not so much its inclusion of a continent not discovered until 1818 but its portrayal of part of the coastline of that continent under ice-free conditions which came to an end 6000 years ago and have not since recurred.

How can this be explained? Piri Reis obligingly gives us the answer in a series of notes written in his own hand on the map itself. He tells us that he was not responsible for the original surveying and cartography. On the contrary, he admits that his role was merely that of compiler and copyist and that the map was derived from a large number of source maps.[8] Some of these had been drawn by contemporary or near-contemporary explorers (including Christopher Columbus), who had by then reached South America and the Caribbean, but others were documents dating back to the fourth century BC or earlier.[9]

Piri Reis did not venture any suggestion as to the identity of the cartographers who had produced the earlier maps. In 1963, however, Professor Hapgood proposed a novel and thought-provoking solution to the problem. He argued that some of the source maps the admiral had made use of, in particular those said to date back to the fourth century BC, had themselves been based on even *older* sources, which in turn had been based on sources originating in the furthest antiquity. There was, he asserted, irrefutable evidence that the earth had been

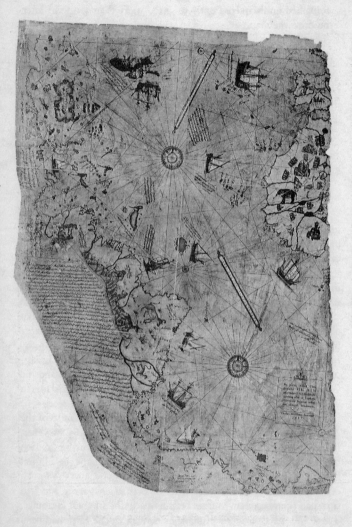

Left Piri Reis map (original). *Above* Redrawing to show detail.

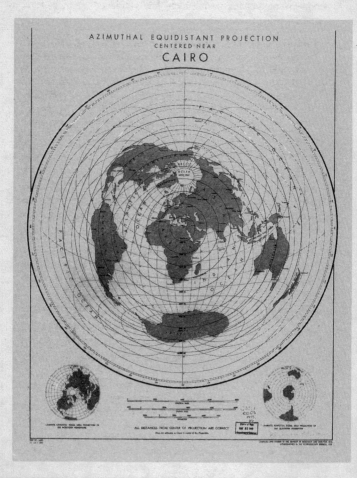

The US Airforce map shows the probable projection that governed the layout of the ancient Piri Reis map.

comprehensively mapped before 4000 BC by a hitherto unknown and undiscovered civilization which had achieved a high level of technological advancement:[10]

> It appears [he concluded] that accurate information has been passed down from people to people. It appears that the charts must have originated with a people unknown and they were passed on, perhaps by the Minoans and the Phoenicians, who were, for a thousand years and more, the greatest sailors of the ancient world. We have evidence that they were collected and studied in the great library of Alexandria [Egypt] and that compilations of them were made by the geographers who worked there.[11]

From Alexandria, according to Hapgood's reconstruction, copies of these compilations and of some of the original source maps were transferred to other centres of learning – notably Constantinople. Finally, when Constantinople was seized by the Venetians during the Fourth Crusade in 1204, the maps began to find their way into the hands of European sailors and adventurers:

> Most of these maps were of the Mediterranean and the Black Sea. But maps of other areas survived. These included maps of the Americas and maps of the Arctic and Antarctic Oceans. It becomes clear that the ancient voyagers travelled from pole to pole. Unbelievable as it may appear, the evidence nevertheless indicates that some ancient people explored Antarctica when its coasts were free of ice. It is clear, too, that they had an instrument of navigation for accurately determining longitudes that was far superior to anything possessed by the peoples of ancient, medieval or modern times until the second half of the eighteenth century.
> This evidence of a lost technology will support and give credence to many of the other hypotheses that have been brought forward of a lost civilization in remote times. Scholars have been able to dismiss most of that evidence as mere myth, but here we have evidence that cannot be dismissed. The evidence requires that all the other evidence that has been brought forward in the past should be re-examined with an open mind.[12]

Despite a ringing endorsement from Albert Einstein (see below), and despite the later admission of John Wright, president of the American Geographical Society, that Hapgood had 'posed hypotheses that cry aloud for further testing', no further scientific research has ever been undertaken into these anomalous early maps. Moreover, far from being applauded for making a serious new contribution to the debate about the antiquity of human civilization, Hapgood until his death was cold-shouldered by the majority of his professional peers, who couched their discussion of his work in what has accurately been described as 'thick and unwarranted sarcasm, selecting trivia and factors not subject to verification as the bases for condemnation, seeking in this way to avoid the basic issues'.[13]

A man ahead of his time

The late Charles Hapgood taught the history of science at Keene College, New Hampshire, USA. He wasn't a geologist, or an ancient historian. It is possible, however, that future generations will remember him as the man whose work undermined the foundations of world history – and a large chunk of world geology as well.

Albert Einstein was among the first to realize this when he took the unprecedented step of contributing the foreword to a book Hapgood wrote in 1953, some years before he began his investigation of the Piri Reis Map:

> I frequently receive communications from people who wish to consult me concerning their unpublished ideas [Einstein observed]. It goes without saying that these ideas are very seldom possessed of scientific validity. The very first communication, however, that I received from Mr Hapgood electrified me. His idea is original, of great simplicity, and – if it continues to prove itself – of great importance to everything that is related to the history of the earth's surface.[14]

The 'idea' expressed in Hapgood's 1953 book is a global geological theory which elegantly explains how and why large parts of Antarctica could have remained ice-free until 4000 BC, together with many other anomalies of earth science. In brief the argument is:

1 Antarctica was not always covered with ice and was at one time much warmer than it is today.

2 It was warm because it was not physically located at the South Pole in that period. Instead it was approximately 2000 miles farther north. This 'would have put it outside the Antarctic

Circle in a temperate or cold temperate climate'.[15]

3 The continent moved to its present position inside the Antarctic Circle as a result of a mechanism known as 'earth-crust displacement'. This mechanism, in no sense to be confused with plate-tectonics or 'continental drift', is one whereby the lithosphere, the whole outer crust of the earth, 'may be displaced at times, moving over the soft inner body, much as the skin of an orange, if it were loose, might shift over the inner part of the orange all in one piece'.[16]

4 During the envisaged southwards movement of Antarctica brought about by earth-crust displacement, the continent would gradually have grown colder, an ice-cap forming and remorselessly expanding over several thousands of years until it attained its present dimensions.'[17]

Further details of the evidence supporting these radical proposals are set out in Part VIII of this book. Orthodox geologists, however, remain reluctant to accept Hapgood's theory (although none has succeeded in proving it incorrect). It raises many questions.

Of these by far the most important is: what conceivable mechanism would be able to exert sufficient thrust on the lithosphere to precipitate a phenomenon of such magnitude as a crustal displacement?

We have no better guide than Einstein to summarize Hapgood's findings:

> In a polar region there is continual deposition of ice, which is not symmetrically distributed about the pole. The earth's rotation acts on these unsymmetrically deposited masses, and produces centrifugal momentum that is transmitted to the rigid crust of the earth. The constantly increasing centrifugal momentum produced in this way will, when it has reached a certain point, produce a movement of the earth's crust over the rest of the earth's body . . .'[18]

The Piri Reis Map seems to contain surprising collateral evidence in support of the thesis of a geologically recent glaciation of parts of Antarctica following a sudden southward displacement of the earth's crust. Moreover since such a map could only have been drawn *prior* to 4000 BC, its implications for the history of human civilization are staggering. Prior to 4000 BC there are supposed to have been no civilizations at all.

At some risk of over-simplification, the academic consensus is broadly:

- Civilization first developed in the Fertile Crescent of the Middle East.
- This development began after 4000 BC, and culminated in the emergence of the earliest true civilizations (Sumer and Egypt) around 3000 BC, soon followed by the Indus Valley and China.
- About 1500 years later, civilization took off spontaneously and independently in the Americas.
- Since 3000 BC in the Old World (and about 1500 BC in the New) civilization has steadily 'evolved' in the direction of ever more refined, complex and productive forms.
- In consequence, and particularly by comparison with ourselves, all ancient civilizations (and all their works) are to be understood as essentially primitive (the Sumerian astronomers regarded the heavens with unscientific awe, and even the pyramids of Egypt were built by 'technological primitives').

The evidence of the Piri Reis Map appears to contradict all this.

Piri Reis and his sources

In his day, Piri Reis was a well-known figure; his historical identity is firmly established. An admiral in the navy of the Ottoman Turks, he was involved, often on the winning side, in numerous sea battles around the mid-sixteenth century. He was, in addition, considered an expert on the lands of the Mediterranean, and was the author of a famous sailing book, the *Kitabi Bahriye*, which provided a comprehensive description of the coasts, harbours, currents, shallows, landing places, bays and straits of the Aegean and Mediterranean Seas. Despite this illustrious career he fell foul of his masters and was beheaded in AD 1554 or 1555.[19]

The source maps Piri Reis used to draw up his 1513 map were in all probability lodged originally in the Imperial Library at Constantinople, to which the admiral is known to have enjoyed privileged access. Those sources (which may have been transferred or copied from even more ancient centres of learning) no longer exist, or, at any rate, have not been found. It was, however, in the library of the old Imperial Palace at Constantinople that the Piri Reis Map was rediscovered, painted on a gazelle skin and rolled up on a dusty shelf, as recently as 1929.[20]

Legacy of a lost civilization?

As the baffled Ohlmeyer admitted in his letter to Hapgood in 1960, the Piri Reis Map depicts the *subglacial topography*, the true profile of Queen Maud Land Antarctica *beneath* the ice. This profile remained completely hidden from view from 4000 BC (when the advancing ice sheet covered it) until it was revealed again as a result of the comprehensive seismic survey of Queen Maud Land carried out during 1949 by a joint British-Swedish scientific reconnaissance team.[21]

If Piri Reis had been the only cartographer with access to such anomalous information, it would be wrong to place any great weight on his map. At the most one might say, 'Perhaps it is significant but, then again, perhaps it is just a coincidence.' However, the Turkish admiral was by no means alone in the possession of seemingly impossible and inexplicable geographical knowledge. It would be futile to speculate further than Hapgood has already done as to what 'underground stream' could have carried and preserved such knowledge through the ages, transmitting fragments of it from culture to culture and from epoch to epoch. Whatever the mechanism, the fact is that a number of other cartographers seem to have been privy to the same curious secrets.

Is it possible that all these map-makers could have partaken, perhaps unknowingly, in the bountiful scientific legacy of a vanished civilization?

Chapter 2

Rivers in the Southern Continent

In the Christmas recess of 1959–60 Charles Hapgood was looking for Antarctica in the Reference Room of the Library of Congress, Washington DC. For several consecutive weeks he worked there, lost in the search, surrounded by literally hundreds of medieval maps and charts.

> I found [he reported] many fascinating things I had not expected to find, and a number of charts showing the southern continent. Then, one day, I turned a page and sat transfixed. As my eyes fell upon the southern hemisphere of a world map drawn by Oronteus Finaeus in 1531, I had the instant conviction that I had found here a truly authentic map of the real Antarctica.
>
> The general shape of the continent was startlingly like the outline of the continent on our modern maps. The position of the South Pole, nearly in the center of the continent, seemed about right. The mountain ranges that skirted the coasts suggested the numerous ranges that have been discovered in Antarctica in recent years. It was obvious, too, that this was no slapdash creation of somebody's imagination. The mountain ranges were individualized, some definitely coastal and some not. From most of them rivers were shown flowing into the sea, following in every case what looked like very natural and very convincing drainage patterns. This suggested, of course, that the coasts may have been ice-free when the original map was drawn. The deep interior, however, was free entirely of rivers and mountains, suggesting that the ice might have been present there.[1]

Closer investigation of the Oronteus Finaeus Map by Hapgood, and by Dr Richard Strachan of the Massachusetts Institute of Technology, confirmed the following:

1 It had been copied and compiled from several earlier source maps drawn up according to a number of different projections.[2]

2 It did indeed show non-glacial conditions in coastal regions of Antarctica, notably Queen Maud Land, Enderby Land, Wilkes Land, Victoria Land (the east coast of the Ross Sea), and Marie Byrd Land.[3]

3 As in the case of the Piri Reis Map, the general profile of the terrain, and the visible physical features, matched closely seismic survey maps of the *subglacial* land surfaces of Antarctica.[4]

The Oronteus Finaeus Map, Hapgood concluded, appeared to document 'the surprising proposition that Antarctica was visited and perhaps settled by men when it was largely if not entirely non-glacial.

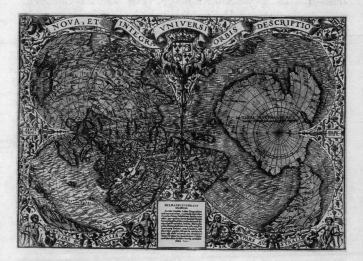

The Oronteus Finaeus map, showing Antarctica with ice-free coasts, mountains and rivers.

It goes without saying that this implies a very great antiquity . . .
[Indeed] the Oronteus Finaeus Map takes the civilization of the
original map-makers back to a time contemporary with the end of the
last Ice Age in the northern hemisphere.'[5]

Ross Sea

Further evidence in support of this view arises from the manner in
which the Ross Sea was shown by Oronteus Finaeus. Where today
great glaciers like the Beardmore and the Scott disgorge themselves
into the sea, the 1531 map shows estuaries, broad inlets and
indications of rivers. The unmistakable implication of these features is
that there was no ice on the Ross Sea or its coasts when the source
maps used by Oronteus Finaeus were made: 'There also had to be a
considerable hinterland free of ice to feed the rivers. At the present
time all these coasts and their hinterlands are deeply buried in the
mile-thick ice-cap, while on the Ross Sea itself there is a floating ice-
shelf hundreds of feet thick.'[6]

The Ross Sea evidence provides strong corroboration for the
notion that Antarctica must have been mapped by some unknown
civilization during the extensively ice-free period which ended
around 4000 BC. This is emphasized by the coring tubes used, in 1949,
by one of the Byrd Antarctic Expeditions to take samples of sediment
from the bottom of the Ross Sea. The sediments showed numerous
clearly demarcated layers of stratification reflecting different environmental conditions in different epochs: 'coarse glacial marine',
'medium glacial marine', 'fine glacial marine', and so on. The most
surprising discovery, however, 'was that a number of the layers were
formed of fine-grained, well-assorted sediments, such as are brought
down to the sea by rivers flowing from temperate (that is, ice-free)
lands . . .'[7]

Using the ionium-dating method developed by Dr W. D. Urry
(which makes use of three different radioactive elements found in sea
water[8]), researchers at the Carnegie Institute in Washington DC were
able to establish beyond any reasonable doubt that great rivers
carrying fine-grained well-assorted sediments had indeed flowed in
Antarctica until about 6000 years ago, as the Oronteus Finaeus Map

showed. It was only after that date, around 4000 BC, 'that the glacial kind of sediment began to be deposited on the Ross Sea bottom . . . The cores indicate that warm conditions had prevailed for a long period before that.'[9]

Mercator and Buache

The Piri Reis and Oronteus Finaeus Maps therefore provide us with a glimpse of Antarctica as no cartographer in historical times could possibly have seen it. On their own, of course, these two pieces of evidence should not be sufficient to persuade us that we might be gazing at the fingerprints of a lost civilization. Can three, or four, or six such maps, however, be dismissed with equal justification?

Is it safe, or reasonable, for example, for us to continue to ignore the historical implications of some of the maps made by the sixteenth-century's most famous cartographer: Gerard Kremer, otherwise known as Mercator? Best remembered for the Mercator projection,

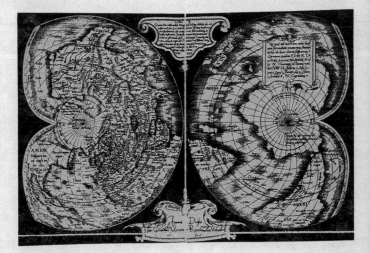

The Mercator map, showing Antarctica's mountains and rivers covered by ice.

still used on most world maps today, this enigmatic individual (who paid an unexplained visit to the Great Pyramid of Egypt in 1563[10]) was reportedly 'indefatigable in searching out . . . the learning of long ago', and spent many years diligently accumulating a vast and eclectic reference library of ancient source maps.[11]

Significantly, Mercator included the Oronteus Finaeus map in his *Atlas* of 1569 and also depicted the Antarctic on several he himself drew in the same year. Identifiable parts of the then undiscovered southern continent on these maps are Cape Dart and Cape Herlacher in Marie Byrd Land, the Amundsen Sea, Thurston Island in Ellsworth Land, the Fletcher Islands in the Bellinghausen Sea, Alexander I Island, the Antarctic (Palmer) Peninsula, the Weddell Sea, Cape Norvegia, the Regula Range in Queen Maud Land (as islands), the Muhlig-Hoffman Mountains (as islands), the Prince Harald Coast, the Shirase Glacier as an estuary on Prince Harald Coast, Padda Island in Lutzow-Holm Bay, and the Prince Olaf Coast in Enderby Land. 'In some cases these features are more distinctly recognisable than on the Oronteus Finaeus Map,' observed Hapgood, 'and it seems clear, in general, that Mercator had at his disposal source maps other than those used by Oronteus Finaeus.'[12]

And not only Mercator.

Philippe Buache, the eighteenth-century French geographer, was also able to publish a map of Antarctica long before the southern continent was officially 'discovered'. And the extraordinary feature of Buache's map is that it seems to have been based on source maps made earlier, perhaps *thousands of years earlier*, than those used by Oronteus Finaeus and Mercator. What Buache gives us is an eerily precise representation of Antarctica as it must have looked *when there was no ice on it at all*.[13] His map reveals the subglacial topography of the entire continent, which even we did not have full knowledge of until 1958, International Geophysical Year, when a comprehensive seismic survey was carried out.

That survey only confirmed what Buache had already proclaimed when he published his map of Antarctica in 1737. Basing his cartography on ancient sources now lost, the French academician depicted a *clear waterway* across the southern continent dividing it

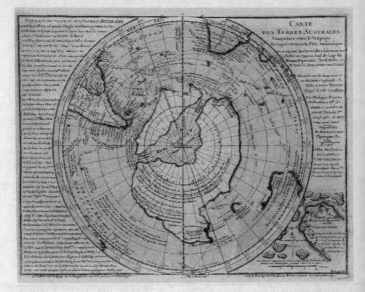

The Buache map, with landmasses which show Antarctica very much as it would have looked before it became covered by ice.

into two principal landmasses lying east and west of the line now marked by the Trans-Antarctic Mountains.

Such a waterway, connecting the Ross, Weddell and Bellinghausen Seas, would indeed exist if Antarctica were free of ice. As the 1958 IGY Survey shows, the continent (which appears on modern maps as one continuous landmass) consists of an archipelago of large islands with mile-thick ice packed between them and rising above sea level.

The epoch of the map-makers

As we have seen, many orthodox geologists believe that the last time any waterway existed in these ice-filled basins was millions of years ago. From the scholarly point of view, however, it is equally orthodox to affirm that no human beings had evolved in those remote times, let alone human beings capable of accurately mapping the landmasses of the Antarctic. The big problem raised by the Buache/IGY evidence is that those landmasses *do* seem to have been mapped when they were free of ice. This confronts scholars with two mutually contradictory propositions.

Which one is correct?

If we are to go along with orthodox geologists and accept that millions of years have indeed elapsed since Antarctica was last completely free of ice, then all the evidence of human evolution, painstakingly accumulated by distinguished scientists from Darwin on, must be wrong. It seems inconceivable that this could be the case: the fossil record makes it abundantly clear that only the unevolved ancestors of humanity existed millions of years ago – low-browed knuckle-dragging hominids incapable of advanced intellectual tasks like map-making.

Are we therefore to assume the intervention of alien cartographers in orbiting spaceships to explain the existence of sophisticated maps of an ice-free Antarctica? Or shall we think again about the implications of Hapgood's theory of earth-crust displacement which allows the southern continent to have been in the ice-free condition depicted by Buache as little as 15,000 years ago?[14]

Is it possible that a human civilization, sufficiently advanced to have mapped Antarctica, could have developed by 13,000 BC and later disappeared? And, if so, how much later?

The combined effect of the Piri Reis, Oronteus Finaeus, Mercator and Buache Maps is the strong, though disturbing, impression that Antarctica may have been *continuously surveyed* over a period of several thousands of years as the ice-cap gradually spread outwards from the interior, increasing its grip with every passing millennium but not engulfing all the coasts of the southern continent until around 4000 BC. The original sources for the Piri Reis and Mercator Maps must therefore have been prepared towards the end of this period, when only the coasts of Antarctica were free of ice; the source for the Oronteus Finaeus Map, on the other hand, seems to have been considerably earlier, when the ice-cap was present only in the deep interior of the continent; and the source for the Buache Map appears

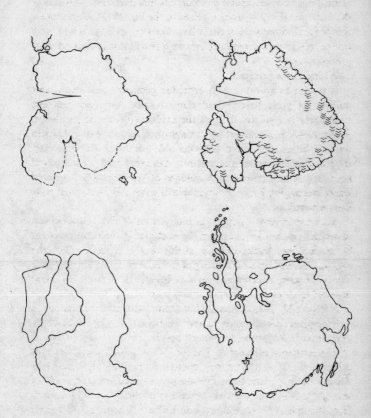

Above left and right Redrawings of the Mercator and Oronteus Finaeus maps showing the progressive glaciation of Antarctica. *Below left* Redrawing of the Buache map. *Below right* The subglacial topography of Antarctica, according to modern seismic surveys.

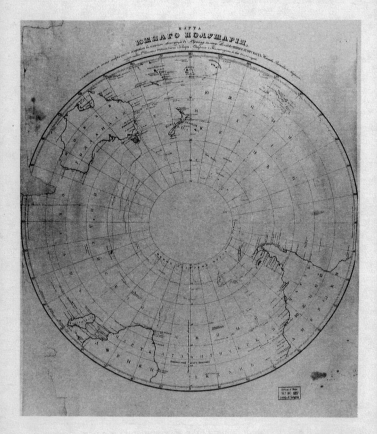

An early nineteenth-century Russian map showing that the existence of Antarctica was at that time unknown. The continent was 'discovered' in AD 1818. But could it have been mapped thousands of years earlier than that by the cartographers of an as yet unidentified high civilization of prehistory?

to originate in even earlier period (around 13,000 BC), when there was no ice in Antarctica at all.

South America

Were other parts of the world surveyed and accurately charted at widely separated intervals during this same epoch; roughly from 13,000 BC to 4000 BC? The answer may lie once again in the Piri Reis Map, which contains more mysteries than just Antarctica:

- Drawn in 1513, the map demonstrates an uncanny knowledge of South America – and not only of its eastern coast but of the Andes mountains on the western side of the continent, which were of course unknown at that time. The map correctly shows the Amazon River rising in these unexplored mountains and thence flowing eastwards.[15]

- Itself compiled from more than twenty different source documents of varying antiquity,[16] the Piri Reis Map depicts the Amazon not once but *twice* (most probably as a result of the unintentional overlapping of two of the source documents used by the Turkish admiral[17]). In the first of these the Amazon's course is shown down to its Para River mouth, but the important island of Marajo does not appear. According to Hapgood, this suggests that the relevant source map must have dated from a time, perhaps as much as 15,000 years ago, when the Para River was the main or only mouth of the Amazon and when Marajo Island was part of the mainland on the northern side of the river.[18] The second depiction of the Amazon, on the other hand, *does* show Marajo (and in fantastically accurate detail) despite the fact that this island was not discovered until 1543.[19] Again, the possibility is raised of an unknown civilization which undertook continuous surveying and mapping operations of the changing face of the earth over a period of many thousands of years, with Piri Reis making use of earlier and later source maps left behind by this civilization.

- Neither the Orinoco River nor its present delta is represented on the Piri Reis Map. Instead, as Hapgood proved, 'two estuaries extending far inland (for a distance of about 100 miles) are shown close to the site of the present river. The longitude on the grid would be correct for the Orinoco, and the latitude is also quite accurate. Is it possible that these estuaries have been filled in, and the delta extended this much, since the source maps were made?'[20]

- Although they remained undiscovered until 1592, the Falkland Islands appear on the 1513 map at their correct latitude.[21]
- The library of ancient sources incorporated in the Piri Reis Map may also account for the fact that it convincingly portrays a large island in the Atlantic Ocean to the east of the South American coast where no such island now exists. Is it pure coincidence that this 'imaginary' island turns out to be located right over the sub-oceanic Mid-Atlantic Ridge just north of the equator and 700 miles east of the coast of Brazil, where the tiny Rocks of Sts Peter and Paul now jut above the waves?[22] Or was the relevant source map drawn deep in the last Ice Age, when sea levels were far lower than they are today and a large island could indeed have been exposed at this spot?

Sea levels and ice ages

Other sixteenth-century maps also look as though they could have been based on accurate world surveys conducted during the last Ice Age. One was compiled by the Turk Hadji Ahmed in 1559, a cartographer, as Hapgood puts it, who must have had access to some 'most extraordinary' source maps.[23]

The strangest and most immediately striking feature of Hadji Ahmed's compilation is that it shows quite plainly a strip of territory, almost 1000 miles wide, connecting Alaska and Siberia. Such a 'land-bridge', as geologists refer to it, did once exist (where the Bering Strait is now) but was submerged beneath the waves by rising sea levels at the end of the last Ice Age.[24]

The rising sea levels were caused by the tumultuous melting of the ice-cap which was rapidly retreating everywhere in the northern hemisphere by around 10,000 BC.[25] It is therefore interesting that at least one ancient map appears to show southern Sweden covered with remnant glaciers of the kind that must indeed have been prevalent then in these latitudes. The remnant glaciers are on Claudius Ptolemy's famous Map of the North. Originally compiled in the second century AD, this remarkable work from the last great geographer of classical antiquity was lost for hundreds of years and rediscovered in the fifteenth century.[26]

Ptolemy was custodian of the library at Alexandria, which contained the greatest manuscript collection of ancient times,[27] and it was there that he consulted the archaic source documents that enabled him to compile his own map.[28] Acceptance of the possibility that the original version of at least one of the charts he referred to could have been made around 10,000 BC helps us to explain why he shows glaciers, characteristic of that exact epoch, together with 'lakes . . . suggesting the shapes of present-day lakes, and streams very much suggesting glacial streams . . . flowing from the glaciers into the lakes.'[29]

It is probably unnecessary to add that no one on earth in Roman times, when Ptolemy drew his map, had the slightest suspicion that ice ages could once have existed in northern Europe. Nor did anyone in the fifteenth century (when the map was rediscovered) possess such knowledge. Indeed, it is impossible to see how the remnant glaciers and other features shown on Ptolemy's map could have been surveyed, imagined or invented by any known civilization prior to our own.

The implications of this are obvious. So, too, are the implications of another map, the 'Portolano' of Iehudi Ibn Ben Zara, drawn in the year 1487.[30] This chart of Europe and North Africa may have been based on a source even earlier than Ptolemy's, for it seems to show glaciers much farther south than Sweden (roughly on the same latitude as England in fact)[31] and to depict the Mediterranean, Adriatic and Aegean Seas as they might have looked before the melting of the European ice-cap.[32] Sea level would, of course, have been significantly lower than it is today. It is therefore interesting, in the case for instance of the Aegean section of the map, to note that a great many more islands are shown than currently exist.[33] At first sight this seems odd. However, if ten or twelve thousand years have indeed elapsed since the era when Ibn Ben Zara's source map was made, the discrepancy can be simply explained: the missing islands must have been submerged by rising sea levels at the end of the last Ice Age.

Once again we seem to be looking at the fingerprints of a vanished civilization – one capable of drawing impressively accurate maps of widely separated parts of the earth.

What kind of technology, and what state of science and culture, would have been required to do a job like that?

Chapter 3

Fingerprints of a Lost Science

We saw that the Mercator World Map of 1569 included an accurate portrayal of the coasts of Antarctica as they would have looked thousands of years ago when they were free of ice. Interestingly enough, this same map is considerably *less* accurate in its portrayal of another region, the west coast of South America, than an earlier (1538) map also drawn by Mercator.[1]

The reason for this appears to be that the sixteenth-century geographer based the earlier map on the ancient sources which we know he had at his disposal, whereas for the later map he relied upon the observations and measurements of the first Spanish explorers of western South America. Since those explorers had supposedly brought the latest information back to Europe, Mercator can hardly be blamed for following them. In so doing the accuracy of his work declined: instruments capable of finding longitude did not exist in 1569, but appear to have been used to prepare the ancient source documents Mercator consulted to produce his 1538 map.[2]

The mysteries of longitude

Let us consider the problem of longitude, defined as the distance in degrees east or west of the prime meridian. The current internationally accepted prime meridian is an imaginary curve drawn from the North Pole to the South Pole passing through the Royal Observatory at Greenwich, London. Greenwich therefore stands at 0° longitude while New York, for example, stands at around 74° west, and Canberra, Australia, at roughly 150° east.

It would be possible to write an elaborate explanation of longitude and of what needs to be done to fix it precisely for any given point on the earth's surface. What we are concerned with here, however, is not so much technical detail as the accepted *historical* facts about humanity's growing knowledge of the mysteries of longitude. Among these facts, this is the most important: *until a breakthrough invention in the eighteenth century, cartographers and navigators were unable to fix longitude with any kind of precision.* They could only make guesses which were usually inaccurate by many hundreds of miles, because the technology had not yet been developed to allow them to do the job properly.

Latitude north or south of the equator did not pose such a problem: it could be worked out by means of angular measurements of the sun and stars taken with relatively simple instruments. But to find longitude equipment of an altogether different and superior calibre was needed, which could combine position measurements with time measurements. Throughout the span of known history the invention of such equipment had remained beyond the capacities of scientists, but by the beginning of the eighteenth century, with rapidly increasing sea traffic, a mood of impatience and urgency had set in. In the words of an authority on the period, 'The search for longitude overshadowed the life of every man afloat, and the safety of every ship and cargo. Accurate measurement seemed an impossible dream and "discovering the longitude" had become a stock phrase in the press like "pigs might fly".'[3]

What was needed, above all else, was an instrument that would keep the time (at the place of departure) with perfect accuracy during long sea journeys despite the motion of the ship and despite the adverse conditions of alternating heat and cold, wet and dry. 'Such a Watch', as Isaac Newton told the members of the British government's official Board of Longitude in 1714, 'hath not yet been made'.[4]

Indeed not. The timepieces of the seventeenth and early eighteenth centuries were crude devices which typically lost or gained as much as

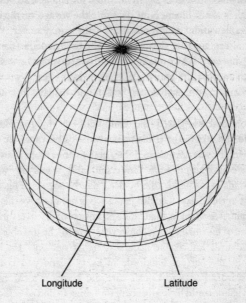

Longitude   Latitude

a quarter of an hour *per day*. By contrast, an effective marine chronometer could afford to lose or gain that much only over several years.[5]

It was not until the 1720s that the talented English clockmaker John Harrison began work on the first of a series of designs which resulted in the manufacture of such a chronometer. His objective was to win the prize of £20,000 offered by the Board of Longitude 'for the inventor of any means of determining a ship's longitude within 30 nautical miles at the end of a six weeks' voyage'.[6] A chronometer capable of fulfilling this condition would have to keep time to within three seconds per day. It took almost forty years, during which several prototypes were completed and tested, before Harrison was able to meet these standards. Finally, in 1761, his elegant Chronometer No. 4

left Britain on board HMS *Deptford* bound for Jamaica, accompanied by Harrison's son William. Nine days into the voyage, on the basis of longitude calculations made possible by the chronometer, William advised the captain that they would sight the Madeira Islands the following morning. The captain offered five to one that he was wrong but agreed to hold the course. William won the bet. Two months later, at Jamaica, the instrument was found to have lost just five seconds.[7]

Harrison had surpassed the conditions set by the Board of Longitude. Thanks to the British government's bureaucratic dithering, however, he was not awarded the £20,000 prize money until three years before his death in 1776. Understandably, it was only when he had the funds in his hands that he divulged the secrets of his design. As a result of this delay, Captain James Cook did not have the benefit of a chronometer when he made his first voyage of discovery in 1768.[8] By the time of his third voyage, however (1778–9), he was able to map the Pacific with impressive accuracy, fixing not only the correct latitude but the correct longitude of every island and coastline.[9] Henceforward, 'thanks to Cook's care and Harrison's chronometer . . . no navigator could have an excuse for failing to find a Pacific island . . . or for being wrecked on a coastline appearing from nowhere.'[10]

Indeed, with their accurate longitudes, Cook's Pacific maps must be ranked among the very first examples of the precise cartography of our modern era. They remind us, moreover, that the making of really good maps requires at least three key ingredients: great journeys of discovery; first-class mathematical and cartographic skills, sophisticated chronometers.

It was not until Harrison's chronometer became generally available in the 1770s that the third of these preconditions was fulfilled. This brilliant invention made it possible for cartographers to fix longitude precisely, something that the Sumerians, the Ancient Egyptians, the Greeks and the Romans, and indeed all other known civilizations before the eighteenth century were supposedly unable to do. It is therefore surprising and unsettling to come across vastly older maps which give latitudes and longitudes with modern precision.

Precision instruments

These inexplicably precise latitudes and longitudes are found in the same general category of documents that contain the advanced geographical knowledge I have outlined.

The Piri Reis Map of 1513, for example, places South America and Africa in *the correct relative longitudes*,[11] theoretically an impossible feat for the science of the time. But Piri Reis was candid in admitting that his map was based on far earlier sources. Could it have been from one of these sources that he derived his accurate longitudes?

Also of great interest is the so-called 'Dulcert Portolano' of AD 1339 which focuses on Europe and North Africa. Here latitude is perfect across huge distances and the total longitude of the Mediterranean and Black Seas is correct to within half a degree.[12]

Professor Hapgood comments that the maker of the original source from which the Dulcert Portolano was copied had 'achieved highly scientific accuracy in finding the ratio of latitude to longitude. He could only have done this if he had precise information on the relative longitudes of a great many places scattered all the way from Galway in Ireland to the eastern bend of the Don in Russia.'[13]

The Zeno Map[14] of AD 1380 is another enigma. Covering a vast area of the north as far as Greenland, it locates a great many widely scattered places at latitudes and longitudes which are 'amazingly correct'.[15] It is 'unbelievable', asserts Hapgood, 'that anyone in the fourteenth century could have found accurate latitudes for these places, to say nothing of accurate longitudes'.[16]

The Oronteus Finaeus World Map also commands attention: it successfully places the coasts of Antarctica in correct latitudes and relative longitudes and finds a remarkably accurate area for the continent as a whole. This reflects a level of geographical knowledge not available until the twentieth century.[17]

The Portolano of Iehudi Ibn Ben Zara is another map notable for its accuracy where relative latitudes and longitudes are concerned.[18] Total longitude between Gibraltar and the Sea of Azov is accurate to half a degree, while across the map as a whole average errors of longitude are less than a degree.[19]

These examples represent only a small fraction of the large and challenging dossier of evidence presented by Hapgood. Layer upon layer, the cumulative effect of his painstaking and detailed analysis is to suggest that we are deluding ourselves when we suppose that accurate instruments for measuring longitude were not invented until the eighteenth century. On the contrary, the Piri Reis and other maps appear to indicate very strongly that such instruments were *rediscovered* then, that they had existed long ages before and had been used by a civilized people, now lost to history, who had explored and charted the entire earth. Furthermore, it seems that these people were capable not only of designing and manufacturing precise and technically advanced mechanical instruments but were masters of a precocious mathematical science.

The lost mathematicians

To understand why, we should first remind ourselves of the obvious: the earth is a sphere. When it comes to mapping it, therefore, only a globe can represent it in correct proportion. Transferring cartographic data from a globe to flat sheets of paper inevitably involves distortions and can be accomplished only by means of an artificial and complex mechanical and mathematical device known as map projection.

There are many different kinds of projection. Mercator's, still used in atlases today, is perhaps the most familiar. Others are dauntingly referred to as Azimuthal, Stereographic, Gnomonic, Azimuthal Equidistant, Cordiform, and so on, but it is unnecessary to go into this any further here. We need only note that *all successful projections require the use of sophisticated mathematical techniques of a kind supposedly unknown in the ancient world* [20] (particularly in the deepest antiquity before 4000 BC when there was allegedly no human civilization at all, let alone one capable of developing and using advanced mathematics and geometry).

Charles Hapgood submitted his collection of ancient maps to the Massachusetts Institute of Technology for evaluation by Professor Richard Strachan. The general conclusion was obvious, but he wanted to know *precisely* what level of mathematics would have been required to draw up the original source documents. On 18 April 1965 Strachan replied that a very high level of mathematics indeed would have been necessary. Some of the maps, for example, seemed to express 'a Mercator type projection' long before the time of Mercator himself. The relative complexity of this projection (involving latitude expansion) meant that a trigonometric coordinate transformation method must have been used.

Other reasons for deducing that the ancient map-makers must have been skilled mathematicians were as follows:

1 The determination of place locations on a continent requires at least geometric triangulation methods. Over large distances (of the order of 1000 miles) corrections must be made for the curvature of the earth, which requires some understanding of spherical trigonometry.
2 The location of continents with respect to one another requires an understanding of the earth's sphericity, and the use of spherical trigonometry.
3 Cultures with this knowledge, plus the precision instruments to make the required measurements to determine location, would most certainly use their mathematical technology in creating maps and charts.'[21]

Strachan's impression that the maps, through generations of copyists, revealed the handiwork of an ancient, mysterious and technologically advanced civilization, was shared by reconnaissance experts from the US Airforce to whom Hapgood submitted the evidence. Lorenzo Burroughs, chief of the 8th Reconnaissance Technical Squadron's Cartographic Section at Westover Air Base, made a particularly close study of the Oronteus Finaeus Map. He concluded that some of the sources upon which it was based must have been drawn up by means of a projection similar to the modern Cordiform Projection. This, said Burroughs:

> suggests the use of advanced mathematics. Further, the shape given to the Antarctic Continent suggests the possibility, if not the probability, that the original source maps were compiled on a stereographic or gnomonic type of projection involving the use of spherical trigonometry.
>
> We are convinced that the findings made by you and your associates are valid, and that they raise extremely important questions affecting geology and ancient history . . .'[22]

Hapgood was to make one more important discovery: a Chinese map copied from an earlier original on to a stone pillar in AD 1137.[23] This map incorporates precisely the same kind of high quality information about longitudes as the others. It has a similar grid and was drawn up with the benefit of spherical trigonometry. Indeed, on close examination, it shares so many features with the European and Middle Eastern maps that only one explanation seems adequate: it and they must have stemmed from a *common source*.[24]

We seem to be confronted once again by a surviving fragment of the scientific knowledge of a lost civilization. More than that, it appears that this civilization must have been at least in some respects as advanced as our own and that its cartographers had 'mapped virtually the entire globe with a uniform general level of technology, with similar methods, equal knowledge of mathematics, and probably the same sorts of instruments'.[25]

The Chinese map also indicates something else: a *global legacy* must have been handed down – a legacy of inestimable value, in all probability incorporating much more than sophisticated geographical knowledge.

Could it have been some portion of this legacy that was distributed in prehistoric Peru by the so-called 'Viracochas', mysterious bearded strangers said to have come from across the seas, in a 'time of darkness', to restore civilization after a great upheaval of the earth?

I decided to go to Peru to see what I could find.

Part II

Foam of the Sea
Peru and Bolivia

Chapter 4

Flight of the Condor

I'm in southern Peru, flying over the Nazca lines.

Below me, after the whale and the monkey, the hummingbird comes into view, flutters and unfolds her wings, stretches forward her delicate beak towards some imaginary flower. Then we turn hard right, pursued by our own tiny shadow as we cross the bleak scar of the Pan-American highway, and follow a trajectory that brings us over the fabulous snake-necked 'Alcatraz': a heron 900 feet long conceived in the mind of a master geometer. We circle around, cross the highway for a second time, pass an astonishing arrangement of fish and triangles laid out beside a pelican, turn left and find ourselves floating over the sublime image of a giant condor with feathers extended in stylized flight.

Just as I try to catch my breath, another condor almost close enough to touch materializes out of nowhere, a real condor this time, haughty as a fallen angel riding a thermal back to heaven. My pilot gasps and tries to follow him. For a moment I catch a glimpse of a bright, dispassionate eye that seems to weigh us up and find us wanting. Then, like a vision from some ancient myth, the creature banks and glides contemptuously backwards into the sun leaving our single-engined Cessna floundering in the lower air.

Below us now there's a pair of parallel lines almost two miles long, arrow straight all the way to vanishing point. And there, off to the right, a series of abstract shapes on a scale so vast – and yet so precisely executed – that it seems inconceivable they could have been the work of men.

The people around here say that they were not the work of men, but of demigods, the Viracochas,[1] who also left their fingerprints elsewhere in the Andean region many thousands of years ago.

The riddle of the lines

The Nazca plateau in southern Peru is a desolate place, sere and unwelcoming, barren and profitless. Human populations have never concentrated here, nor will they do so in the future: the surface of the moon seems hardly less hospitable.

If you happen to be an artist with grand designs, however, these high and daunting plains look like a very promising canvas, with 200 square miles of uninterrupted tableland and the certainty that your masterwork won't be carried away on the desert breeze or covered by drifting sand.

It's true that high winds do blow here, but by a happy accident of physics they are robbed of their sting at ground level: the pebbles that litter the pampa absorb and retain the sun's heat, throwing up a protective force-field of warm air. In addition, the soil contains enough gypsum to glue small stones to the subsurface, an adhesive regularly renewed by the moistening effect of early morning dews. Once things are drawn here, therefore, they tend to stay drawn. There's hardly any rain; indeed, with less than half an hour of miserly drizzle every decade, Nazca is among the driest places on earth.

If you are an artist, therefore, if you have something grand and important to express, and if you want it to be visible for ever, these strange and lonely flatlands could look like the answer to your prayers.

Experts have pronounced upon the antiquity of Nazca, basing their opinions on fragments of pottery found embedded in the lines and on radiocarbon results from various organic remains unearthed here. The dates conjectured range between 350 BC and AD 600.[2] Realistically, they tell us nothing about the age of the lines themselves, which are inherently as undatable as the stones cleared to make them. All we can say for sure is that the most recent are at least 1400 years old, but it is theoretically possible that they could be far more ancient than that –

for the simple reason that the artefacts from which such dates are derived could have been brought to Nazca by later peoples.

The majority of the designs are spread out across a clearly defined area of southern Peru bounded by the Rio Ingenio to the north and the Rio Nazca to the south, a roughly square canvas of dun-coloured desert with forty-six kilometres of the Pan-American highway running obliquely through it from top-centre to bottom right. Here, scattered apparently at random, are literally hundreds of different figures. Some depict animals and birds (a total of eighteen different birds). But far more take the form of geometrical devices in the form of trapezoids, rectangles, triangles and straight lines. Viewed from above, these latter resemble to the modern eye a jumble of runways, as though some megalomaniac civil engineer had been licensed to act out his most flamboyant fantasies of airfield design.

It therefore comes as no surprise, since humans are not supposed to have been able to fly until the beginning of the twentieth century, that the Nazca lines have been identified by a number of observers as landing strips for alien spaceships. This is a seductive notion, but Nazca is perhaps not the best place to seek evidence for it. For example, it is difficult to understand why extra-terrestrials advanced enough to have crossed hundreds of light years of interstellar space should have needed landing strips at all. Surely such beings would have mastered the technology of setting their flying saucers down vertically?

Besides, there is really no question of the Nazca lines ever having been used as runways – by flying saucers or anything else – although some of them look like that from above. Viewed at ground-level they are little more than grazes on the surface made by scraping away thousands of tons of black volcanic pebbles to expose the desert's paler base of yellow sand and clay. None of the cleared areas is more than a few inches deep and all are much too soft to have permitted the landing of wheeled flying vehicles. The German mathematician Maria Reiche, who devoted half a century to the study of the lines, was only being logical when, she dismissed the extra-terrestrial theory with a single pithy sentence a few years ago: 'I'm afraid the spacemen would have gotten stuck.'

If not runways for the chariots of alien 'gods', therefore, what else

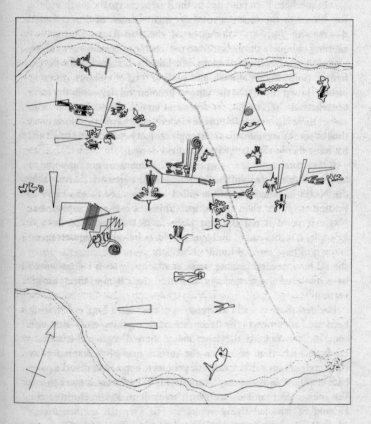

The principal figures of the Nazca plateau.

might the Nazca lines be? The truth is that no one knows their purpose, just as no one really knows their age; they are a genuine mystery of the past. And the closer you look at them the more baffling they become.

It's clear, for example, that the animals and birds antedate the geometry of the 'runways', because many of the trapezoids, rectangles and straight lines bisect (and thus partly obliterate) the more complex figures. The obvious deduction is that the final artwork of the desert as we view it today must have been produced in two phases. Moreover, though it seems contrary to the normal laws of technical progress, we must concede that the *earlier* of the two phases was the more advanced. The execution of the zoomorphic figures called for far higher levels of skill and technology than the etching of the straight lines. But how widely separated in time were the earlier and later artists?

Scholars do not address themselves to this question. Instead they lump both cultures together as 'the Nazcans' and depict them as primitive tribesmen who unaccountably developed sophisticated techniques of artistic self-expression, and then vanished from the Peruvian scene, many hundreds of years before the appearance of their better-known successors, the Incas.

How sophisticated were these Nazcan 'primitives'? What kind of knowledge must they have possessed to inscribe their gigantic signatures on the plateau? It seems, for a start, that they were pretty good observational astronomers – at least according to Dr Phillis Pitluga, an astronomer with the Adler Planetarium in Chicago. After making an intensive computer-aided study of stellar alignments at Nazca, she has concluded that *the famous spider figure was devised as a terrestrial diagram of the giant constellation of Orion*, and that the arrow-straight lines linked to the figure appear to have been set out to track through the ages the changing declinations of the three stars of Orion's Belt.[3]

The real significance of Dr Pitluga's discovery will become apparent in due course. Meanwhile, let us note that the Nazca spider also accurately depicts a member of a known spider genus – *Ricinulei*.[4] This, as it happens, is one of the rarest spider genera in the world, so rare indeed that it has only been found in remote and inaccessible parts of the Amazon rainforest.[5] How did the supposedly primitive Nazcan artists travel so far from their homeland, crossing the formidable barrier of the Andes, to obtain a specimen? More to the point, why should they have wanted to do such a thing and how were they able to duplicate minute details of *Ricinulei*'s anatomy normally visible only under a microscope,[6] notably the reproductive organ positioned on the end of its extended right leg?

Such mysteries multiply at Nazca and none of the designs, except perhaps the condor, really seems quite at home here. The whale and the monkey are, after all, as out of place in this desert environment as the Amazonian spider. A curious figure of a man, his right arm raised as though in greeting, heavy boots on his feet and round eyes staring owlishly forward, cannot be said to belong to any known era or culture. And other drawings depicting the human form are equally peculiar: their heads enclosed in halos of radiance, they do indeed look like visitors from another planet. Their sheer size is equally noteworthy and bizarre. The hummingbird is 165 feet long, the spider 150 feet long, the condor stretches nearly 400 feet from beak to tail-feathers (as does the pelican), and a lizard, whose tail is now divided by the Pan-American highway, is 617 feet in length. Almost every design is executed on the same cyclopean scale and in the same difficult manner, by the careful contouring of a single continuous line.

Similar attention to detail is to be found in the geometrical devices. Some of these take the form of straight lines *more than five miles long*, marching like Roman roads across the desert, dropping into dried-out river beds, surmounting rocky outcrops, and never once deviating from true.

This kind of precision is hard, but not impossible, to explain in conventional commonsense terms. More puzzling by far are the zoomorphic figures. How could they have been so perfectly made when, without aircraft, their creators could not have checked the progress of their work by viewing it in its proper perspective? None of the designs is small enough to be seen from ground level, where they appear merely as a series of shapeless ruts in the desert. They show their true form only when seen from an altitude of several hundred feet. There is no elevation nearby that provides such a vantage point.

Linemakers, map-makers

I'm flying over the lines, trying to make sense of it all.

My pilot is Rodolfo Arias, lately of the Peruvian Airforce. After a career in jet fighters he finds the little Cessna slow and uninspiring and treats it like a taxi with wings. Once already we've been back to the airstrip at Nazca to remove a window so that my partner Santha can point her cameras vertically down at the alluring glyphs. Now we're experimenting with the view from different altitudes. At a couple of hundred feet above the plain Ricinulei, the Amazonian spider, looks like he's going to rear up and snatch us in his jaws. At 500 feet we can see several of the figures at once: a dog, a tree, a weird pair of hands, the condor, and some of the triangles and trapezoids. When we ascend to 1500 feet, the zoomorphs, hitherto predominant, are revealed merely as small scattered units surrounded by an astonishing scribble of vast geometric forms. These forms now look less like runways and more like pathways made by giants – pathways that criss-cross the plateau in what seems at first a bewildering variety of shapes, angles and sizes.

As the ground continues to recede, however, and as the widening perspective on the lines permits more of an eagle's-eye view, I begin to wonder whether there might not after all be some *method* to the cuneiform slashes and scratches spread out below me. I am reminded of an observation made by Maria Reiche, the mathematician who has lived at Nazca and studied the lines since 1946. In her view

> The geometric drawings give the impression of a cipher-script in which the same words are sometimes written in huge letters, at another time in minute characters. There are line arrangements which appear in a great variety of size categories together with very similar shapes. All the drawings are composed of a certain number of basic elements . . . [7]

As the Cessna bumps and heaves across the heavens, I also remember it is no accident that the Nazca lines were only properly identified in the twentieth century, after the era of flight had begun. In the late sixteenth century a magistrate named Luis de Monzon was the first Spanish traveller to bring back eyewitness reports concerning these mysterious 'marks on the desert' and to collect the strange local traditions that linked them to the Viracochas.[8] However, until commercial airlines began to operate regularly between Lima and Arequipa in the 1930s no one seems to have grasped that the largest piece of graphic art in the world lay here in southern Peru. It was the development of aviation that made the difference, giving men and women the godlike ability to take to the skies and see beautiful and puzzling things that had hitherto been hidden from them.

Rodolfo is steering the Cessna in a gentle circle over the figure of the monkey – a big monkey tied in a riddle of geometric forms. It's not easy to describe the eerie, hypnotic feeling this design gives me: it's very complicated and absorbing to look at, and slightly sinister in an abstract, indefinable way. The monkey's body is defined by a continuous unbroken line. And, without ever being interrupted, this same line winds up stairs, over pyramids, into a series of zig-zags, through a spiral labyrinth (the tail), and then back around a number of starlike hairpin bends. It would be a real *tour de force* of draughtsmanship and artistic skill on a sheet of notepaper, but this is the Nazca desert (where they do things on a grand scale) and the monkey is at least 400 feet long and 300 feet wide . . .

Were the linemakers map-makers too?

And why were they called the Viracochas?

Chapter 5

The Inca Trail to the Past

No artefacts or monuments, no cities or temples, have endured in recognizable form for longer than the most resilient religious traditions. Whether expressed in the Pyramid Texts of Ancient Egypt, or the Hebrew Bible, or the Vedas, such traditions are among the most imperishable of all human creations: they are vehicles of knowledge voyaging through time.

The last custodians of the ancient religious heritage of Peru were the Incas, whose beliefs and 'idolatry' were 'extirpated' and whose treasures were ransacked during the thirty terrible years that followed the Spanish conquest in AD 1532.[1] Providentially, however, a number of early Spanish travellers made sincere efforts to document Inca traditions before they were entirely forgotten.

Though little attention was paid at the time, some of these traditions speak strikingly of a great civilization that was believed to have existed in Peru many thousands of years earlier.[2] Powerful memories were preserved of this civilization, said to have been founded by the Viracochas, the same mysterious beings credited with the making of the Nazca lines.

'Foam of the Sea'

When the Spanish *conquistadores* arrived, the Inca empire extended along the Pacific coast and Andean highlands of South America from the northern border of modern Ecuador, through the whole of Peru, and as far south as the Maule River in central Chile. Connecting the far-flung corners of this empire was a vast and sophisticated road system: two parallel north–south highways, for example, one running for 3600 kilometres along the coast and the other for a similar distance through the Andes. Both these great thoroughfares were paved and connected by frequent links. In addition, they exhibited an interesting range of design and engineering features such as suspension bridges and tunnels cut through solid rock. They were clearly the work of an evolved, disciplined and ambitious society. Ironically, they played a significant part in its downfall: the Spanish forces, led by Francisco Pizarro, used them to great effect to speed up their ruthless advance into the Inca heartland.[3]

The capital of the Inca empire was the city of Cuzco, a name meaning 'the earth's navel' in the local Quechua language.[4] According to legend it was established by Manco Capac and Mama Occlo, two children of the Sun. Here, though the Incas worshipped the sun god, whom they knew as *Inti*, quite another deity was venerated as the Most Holy of all. This was Viracocha, whose namesakes were said to have made the Nazca lines and whose own name meant 'Foam of the Sea.'[5]

No doubt it is just a coincidence that the Greek goddess Aphrodite, who was born of the sea, received her name because of 'the foam [*aphros*] out of which she was formed'.[6] Besides, Viracocha was always depicted uncompromisingly as a *male* by the peoples of the Andes. That much about him is known for certain. No historian, however, is able to say how ancient was the cult of this deity before the Spanish arrived to put a stop to it. This is because the cult seemed always to have been around; indeed, long before the Incas incorporated him into their cosmogony and built a magnificent temple for him at Cuzco, the evidence suggests that the high god Viracocha had been worshipped by *all* the civilizations that had ever existed in the long history of Peru.

Citadel of Viracocha

A few days after leaving Nazca, Santha and I arrived in Cuzco and made our way to the site of the Coricancha, the great temple dedicated to Viracocha in the pre-Colombian era. The Coricancha was of course long gone. Or, to be more exact, it was not so much gone as *buried* beneath layers of later architecture. The Spanish had kept its superb Inca foundations, and the lower parts of its fabulously strong walls, and had erected their own grandiose colonial cathedral on top.

Walking towards the front entrance of this cathedral, I remembered that the Inca temple that had once stood here had been covered with more than 700 sheets of pure gold (each weighing around two kilograms) and that its spacious courtyard had been planted with 'fields' of replica corn also fashioned out of gold.[7] I could not help but be reminded of Solomon's temple in far-off Jerusalem, also reputed to have been adorned with sheets of gold and a marvellous orchard of golden trees.[8]

Earthquakes in 1650 and again in 1950 had largely demolished the Spanish cathedral of Santo Domingo which stood on the site of the temple of Viracocha, and it had been necessary to rebuild it on both occasions. Its Inca foundations and lower walls survived these natural disasters intact, thanks to their characteristic design which made use of an elegant system of interlocking polygonal blocks. These blocks, and the general layout of the place, were almost all that was now left of the original structure, apart from an octagonal grey stone platform at the centre of the vast rectangular courtyard which had once been covered with 55 kilograms of solid gold.[9] On either side of the courtyard were ante-chambers, also from the Inca temple, with refined architectural features such as walls that tapered upwards and beautifully-carved niches hewn out of single pieces of granite.

We took a walk through the narrow, cobbled streets of Cuzco. Looking around, I realized it was not just the cathedral that reflected Spanish imposition on top of an earlier culture: the whole town was slightly schizophrenic. Spacious, balconied, pastel-shaded colonial homes and palaces towered above me but almost all of them stood on Inca foundations or incorporated complete Inca structures of the same beautiful polygonal architecture used in the Coricancha. In one alleyway, known as Hatunrumiyoc, I paused to examine an intricate jigsaw puzzle of a wall made of countless drystone blocks all perfectly fitted together, all of different sizes and shapes, interlocking in a bewildering array of angles. The carving of the individual blocks, and their arrangement into so complicated a structure could only have been achieved by master craftsmen possessed of very high levels of skill, with untold centuries of architectural experimentation behind them. On one block I counted twelve angles and sides in a single plane, and I could not slip even the edge of a piece of thin paper into the joints that connected it to the surrounding blocks.

The bearded stranger

It seemed that in the early sixteenth century, before the Spanish began to demolish Peruvian culture in earnest, an idol of Viracocha had stood in the Holy of Holies of the Coricancha. According to a contemporary text, the *Relacion anonyma de los costumbres antiquos de los naturales del Piru*, this idol took the form of a marble statue of the god – a statue described 'as to the hair, complexion, features, raiment and sandals, just as painters represent the apostle Saint Bartholomew'.[10] Other accounts of Viracocha likened his appearance to that of the Saint Thomas.[11] I examined a number of illustrated ecclesiastical manuscripts in which these two saints appeared; both were routinely depicted as lean, bearded white men, past middle age, wearing sandals and dressed in long, flowing cloaks. As we shall see, the records confirmed this was exactly the appearance ascribed to Viracocha by those who worshipped him. Whoever he was, therefore, he could not have been an American Indian, they are relatively dark-skinned people with sparse facial hair.[12] Viracocha's bushy beard and pale complexion made him sound like a Caucasian.

Back in the sixteenth century the Incas had thought so too. Indeed their legends and religious beliefs made them so certain of his physical type that they initially mistook the white and bearded Spaniards who arrived on their shores for the returning Viracocha and his demigods,[13] an event long prophesied and which Viracocha was said in all the legends to have promised. This happy coincidence gave Pizarro's *conquistadores* the decisive strategic and psychological edge that they needed to overcome the numerically superior Inca forces in the battles that followed.

Who had provided the model for the Virachochas?

Chapter 6

He Came in a Time of Chaos

Through all the ancient legends of the peoples of the Andes stalked a tall, bearded, pale-skinned figure wrapped in a cloak of secrecy. And though he was known by many different names in many different places he was always recognizably the *same* figure: Viracocha, Foam of the Sea, a master of science and magic who wielded terrible weapons and who came in a time of chaos to set the world to rights.

The same basic story was shared in many variants by all the peoples of the Andean region. It began with a vivid description of a terrifying period when the earth had been inundated by a great flood and plunged into darkness by the disappearance of the sun. Society had fallen into disorder, and the people suffered much hardship. Then

> there suddenly appeared, coming from the south, a white man of large stature and authoritative demeanour. This man had such great power that he changed the hills into valleys and from the valleys made great hills, causing streams to flow from the living stone . . .[1]

The early Spanish chronicler who recorded this tradition explained that it had been told to him by the Indians he had travelled among on his journeys in the Andes:

> And they heard it from their fathers, who in their turn had it from the old songs which were handed down from very ancient times . . . They say that this man travelled along the highland route to the north, working marvels as he went and that they never saw him again. They

say that in many places he gave men instructions how they should live, speaking to them with great love and kindness and admonishing them to be good and to do no damage or injury one to another, but to love one another and show charity to all. In most places they name him Ticci Viracocha . . .[2]

Other names applied to the same figure included Huaracocha, Con, Con Ticci or Kon Tiki, Thunupa, Taapac, Tupaca and Illa.[3] He was a scientist, an architect of surpassing skills, a sculptor and an engineer: 'He caused terraces and fields to be formed on the steep sides of ravines, and sustaining walls to rise up and support them. He also made irrigating channels to flow . . . and he went in various directions, arranging many things.'[4]

Viracocha was also a teacher and a healer and made himself helpful to people in need. It was said that 'wherever he passed, he healed all that were sick and restored sight to the blind.'[5]

This gentle, civilizing, 'superhuman', samaritan had another side to his nature, however. If his life were threatened, as it seems to have been on several occasions, he had the weapon of heavenly fire at his disposal:

> Working great miracles by his words, he came to the district of the Canas and there, near a village called Cacha . . . the people rose up against him and threatened to stone him. They saw him sink to his knees and raise his hands to heaven as if beseeching aid in the peril which beset him. The Indians declare that thereupon they saw fire in the sky which seemed all around them. Full of fear, they approached him whom they had intended to kill and besought him to forgive them . . . Presently they saw that the fire was extinguished at his command, though stones were consumed by fire in such wise that large blocks could be lifted by hand as if they were cork. They narrate further that, leaving the place where this occurred, he came to the coast and there, holding his mantle, he went forth amidst the waves and was seen no more. And as he went they gave him the name Viracocha, which means 'Foam of the Sea'.[6]

The legends were unanimous in their physical description of Viracocha. In his *Suma y Narracion de los Incas*, for example, Juan de Betanzos, a sixteenth-century Spanish chronicler, stated that according to the Indians, he had been 'a bearded man of tall stature clothed in a white robe which came down to his feet and which he wore belted at the waist'.[7]

Other descriptions, collected from many different and widely separated Andean peoples, all seemed to identify the same enigmatic individual. According to one he was

> A bearded man of medium height dressed in a rather long cloak. He was past his prime, with grey hair, and lean. He walked with a staff and addressed the natives with love, calling them his sons and daughters. As he traversed all the land he worked miracles. He healed the sick by touch. He spoke every tongue even better than the natives. They called him Thunupa or Tarpaca, Viracocha-rapacha or Pachac-can . . .[8]

In one legend Thunupa–Viracocha was said to have been a 'white man of large stature, whose air and person aroused great respect and veneration'.[9] In another he was described as a white man of august appearance, blue-eyed, bearded, without headgear and wearing a *cusma*, a jerkin or sleeveless shirt reaching to the knees'. In yet another, which seemed to refer to a later phase of his life, he was revered as 'a wise counsellor in matters of state' and depicted as 'an old man with a beard and long hair wearing a long tunic'.[10]

Civilizing mission

Above all else, Viracocha was remembered in the legends as a teacher. Before his coming, it was said, 'men lived in a condition of disorder, many went naked like savages; they had no houses or other dwellings than caves, and from these they went forth to gather whatever they could find to eat in the countryside.'[11]

Viracocha was credited with changing all this and with initiating the long-lost golden age which later generations looked back on with nostalgia. All the legends agreed, furthermore, that he had carried out his civilizing mission with great kindness and as far as possible had abjured the use of force: careful instruction and personal example had been the main methods used to equip the people with the techniques and knowledge necessary for a cultured and productive life. In particular, he was remembered for bringing to Peru such varied skills as medicine, metallurgy, farming, animal husbandry, the art of writing (said by the Incas to have been introduced by Viracocha but later forgotten), and a sophisticated understanding of the principles of engineering and architecture.

I had already been impressed by the quality of Inca stonework in Cuzco. As my research in the old town continued, however, I was surprised to discover that by no means all the so-called Inca masonry could be attributed with any degree of archaeological certainty to the Incas. It was true that they had been masters in the manipulation of stone, and many monuments in the Cuzco area were indisputably their work. It seemed, however, that some of the more remarkable structures routinely attributed to them could have been erected by earlier civilizations; the evidence suggested that the Incas had often functioned as the restorers of these structures rather than their original builders.

The same appeared to be true of the highly developed system of roads connecting the far-flung parts of the Inca empire. The reader will recall that these roads took the form of parallel highways running north to south, one along the coast and the other through the Andes. All in all more than 15,000 miles of surfaced tracks had been in regular and efficient use before the time of the Spanish conquest, and I had assumed that the Incas had been responsible for all of them. I now learned that it was much more likely that they had inherited the system. Their role had been to restore, maintain and unify a pre-existing network. Indeed, though it was not often admitted, no expert could safely estimate how old these incredible highways were or who had built them.[12]

The mystery was deepened by local traditions which stated not only that the road system and the sophisticated architecture had been 'ancient in the time of the Incas', but that both 'were the work of white, auburn-haired men' who had lived thousands of years earlier.[13]

One legend described Viracocha as being accompanied by 'messengers' of two kinds, 'faithful soldiers' (*huaminca*) and 'shining ones' (*hayhuaypanti*). Their role was to carry their lord's message 'to every part of the world'.[14]

Elsewhere there were phrases such as: 'Con Ticci returned . . . with a number of attendants'; 'Con Ticci then summoned his followers, who were called viracocha'; 'Con Ticci commanded all but two of the viracocha to go east . . .'[15]; 'There came forth from a lake a Lord named Con Ticci Viracocha bringing with him a certain number of people . . .'[16]; 'Thus those viracochas went off to the various districts which Viracocha had indicated for them . . .'.[17]

The work of demons?

The ancient citadel of Sacsayhuaman lies just north of Cuzco. We reached it late one afternoon under a sky almost occluded by heavy clouds of tarnished silver. A cold grey breeze was blowing across the high-altitude tundra as I clambered up stairways, through lintelled stone gates built for giants, and walked along the mammoth rows of zig-zag walls.

I craned my neck and looked up at a big granite boulder that my route now passed under. Twelve feet high, seven feet across, and weighing considerably more than 100 tons, it was a work of man, not nature. It had been cut and shaped into a symphonic harmony of angles, manipulated with apparent ease (as though it were made of wax or putty) and stood on its end in a wall of other huge and problematic polygonal blocks, some of them positioned above it, some below it, some to each side, and all in perfectly balanced and well-ordered juxtaposition.

Since one of these astonishing pieces of carefully hewn stone had a height of twenty-eight feet and was calculated to weigh 361 tons[18] (roughly the equivalent of *five hundred* family-sized automobiles), it seemed to me that a number of fundamental questions were crying out for answers.

How had the Incas, or their predecessors, been able to work stone on such a gargantuan scale? How had they cut and shaped these cyclopean boulders so precisely? How had they transported them tens of miles from distant quarries? By what means had they made walls of them, shuffling the individual blocks around and raising them high above the ground with such apparent ease? These people weren't even supposed to have had the wheel, let alone machinery capable of lifting and manipulating dozens of irregularly shaped 100-ton blocks, and sorting them into three-dimensional jigsaw puzzles.

I knew that the chroniclers of the early colonial period had been as perplexed as I was by what they had seen. The respected Garcilaso de la Vega, for example, who came here in the sixteenth century, had spoken with awe about the fortress of Sacsayhuaman:

> Its proportions are inconceivable when one has not actually seen it; and when one has looked at it closely and examined it attentively, they appear to be so extraordinary that it seems as though some magic had presided over its construction; that it must be the work of demons instead of human beings. It is made of such great stones, and in such great number, that one wonders simultaneously how the Indians were able to quarry them, how they transported them . . . and how they hewed them and set them one on top of the other with such precision. For they disposed of neither iron nor steel with which to penetrate the rock and cut and polish the stones; they had neither wagon nor oxen to transport them, and, in fact, there exist neither wagons nor oxen throughout the world that would have sufficed for this task, so enormous are these stones and so rude the mountain paths over which they were conveyed . . .[19]

Garcilaso also reported something else interesting. In his *Royal Commentaries of the Incas* he gave an account of how, in historical times, an Inca king had tried to emulate the achievements of his predecessors who had built Sacsayhuaman. The attempt had involved bringing just one immense boulder from several miles away to add to the existing fortifications: 'This boulder was hauled across the mountain by more than 20,000 Indians, going up and down very steep hills . . . At a certain spot, it fell from their hands over a precipice crushing more than 3000 men.'[20] In all the histories I surveyed, this was the only report which described the Incas actually building, or trying to build, with huge blocks like those employed at Sacsayhuaman. The report suggested that they possessed no experience of the techniques involved and that their attempt had ended in disaster.

This, of course, proved nothing in itself. But Garcilaso's story did intensify my doubts about the great fortifications which towered above me. As I looked at them I felt that they could, indeed, have been erected before the age of the Incas and by some infinitely older and more technically advanced race.

Not for the first time I was reminded of how difficult archaeologists found it to provide accurate dates for engineering works like roads and drystone walls which contained no organic compounds. Radiocarbon was redundant in such circumstances; thermoluminescence, too, was useless. And while promising new tests such as Chlorine-36 rock-exposure dating were now being developed their implementation was still some way off. Pending further advances in the latter field, therefore, 'expert' chronology was still largely the result of guesswork and subjective assumptions. Since it was known that the Incas had made intensive *use* of Sacsayhuaman I could easily understand why it had been assumed that they had *built* it. But there was no obvious or necessary connection between these two propositions. The Incas could just as well have found the structures already in place and moved into them.

If so, who had the original builders been?

The Viracochas, said the ancient myths, the bearded, white-skinned strangers, the 'shining ones', the 'faithful soldiers.'

As we travelled I continued to study the accounts of the Spanish adventurers and ethnographers of the sixteenth and seventeenth centuries who had faithfully recorded the ancient, pre-contact traditions of the Peruvian Indians. What was particularly noticeable about these traditions was the repeated emphasis that the coming of the Viracochas had been associated with a terrible deluge which had overwhelmed the earth and destroyed the greater part of humanity.

Chapter 7

Were There Giants Then?

Just after six in the morning the little train jerked into motion and began its slow climb up the steep sides of the valley of Cuzco. The narrow-gauge tracks were laid out in a series of Z shapes. We chugged along the lower horizontal of the first Z, then shunted and went backwards up the oblique, shunted again and went forward along the upper horizontal – and so on, with numerous stops and starts, following a route that eventually took us high above the ancient city. The Inca walls and colonial palaces, the narrow streets, the cathedral of Santo Domingo squatting atop the ruins of Viracocha's temple, all looked spectral and surreal in the pearl-grey light of a dawn sky. A fairy pattern of electric lamps still decorated the streets, a thin mist seeped across the ground, and the smoke of domestic fires rose from the chimneys over the tiled roofs of countless small houses.

Eventually the train turned its back on Cuzco and we proceeded for a while in a straight north-westerly direction towards our destination: Machu Picchu, the lost city of the Incas, some three hours and 130 kilometres away. I had intended to read, but lulled by the rocking motion of the carriage, I dropped off to sleep instead. Fifty minutes later I awoke to find that we were passing through a painting. The foreground, brightly sunlit, consisted of flat green meadows sprinkled with little patches of thawing frost, distributed on either side of a stream across a long, wide valley.

In the middle of my view, dotted with bushes, was a large field on which a handful of black and white dairy cows grazed. Nearby was a scattered settlement of houses outside which stood small, dark-skinned Quechua Indians dressed in ponchos, balaclavas and colourful woollen hats. More distant were slopes canopied in fir trees and exotic eucalyptus. My eye followed the rising contours of a pair of high green mountains, which then parted to reveal folded and even more lofty uplands. Beyond these soared a far horizon surmounted by a jagged range of radiant and snowy peaks.

Casting down the giants

It was with understandable reluctance that I turned at last to my reading. I wanted to look more closely at some of the curious links I thought I had identified connecting the sudden appearance of Viracocha to the deluge legends of the Incas and other Andean peoples.

Before me was a passage from Fr Jose de Acosta's *Natural and Moral History of the Indies*, in which the learned priest set out 'what the Indians themselves report of their beginning':

> They make great mention of a deluge, which happened in their country . . . The Indians say that all men were drowned in the deluge, and they report that out of Lake Titicaca came one Viracocha, who stayed in Tiahuanaco, where at this day there are to be seen the ruins of ancient and very strange buildings, and from thence came to Cuzco, and so began mankind to multiply . . .[1]

Making a mental note to find out more about Lake Titicaca, and the mysterious Tiahuanaco, I read the following passage summarizing a legend from the Cuzco area:

> For some crime unstated the people who lived in the most ancient times were destroyed by the creator . . . in a deluge. After the deluge the creator appeared in human form from Lake Titicaca. He then created the sun and moon and stars. After that he renewed the human population of the earth . . .[2]

In another myth

> The great Creator God, Viracocha, decided to make a world for men

to live in. First he made the earth and sky. Then he began to make people to live in it, carving great stone figures of giants which he brought to life. At first all went well but after a time the giants began to fight among themselves and refused to work. Viracocha decided that he must destroy them. Some he turned back into stone . . . the rest he overwhelmed with a great flood.[3]

Very similar notions were, of course, found in other, quite unconnected, sources, such as the Jewish Old Testament. In Chapter six of the *Book of Genesis*, for example, which describes the Hebrew God's displeasure with his creation and his decision to destroy it, I had long been intrigued by one of the few descriptive statements made about the forgotton era before the Flood. According to the enigmatic language of that statement, 'There were giants in the earth in those days . . .'.[4] Could the 'giants' buried in the biblical sands of the Middle East be connected in some unseen way to the 'giants' woven into the fabric of pre-Colombian native American legends? Adding considerably to the mystery was the fact that the Jewish and Peruvian sources both went on, with many further details in common, to depict an angry deity unleashing a catastrophic flood upon a wicked and disobedient world.

On the next page of the sheaf of documents I had assembled was this Inca account of the deluge handed down by a certain Father Molina in his *Relacion de las fabulas y ritos de los Yngas*:

In the life of Manco Capac, who was the first Inca, and from whom they began to boast themselves children of the Sun and from whom they derived their idolatrous worship of the Sun, they had an ample account of the deluge. They say that in it perished all races of men and created things insomuch that the waters rose above the highest mountain peaks in the world. No living thing survived except a man and a woman who remained in a box and, when the waters subsided, the wind carried them . . . to Tiahuanaco [where] the creator began to raise up the people and the nations that are in that region . . .[5]

Garcilaso de la Vega, the son of a Spanish nobleman and an Inca royal woman, was already familiar to me from his *Royal Commentaries of the Incas*. He was regarded as one of the most reliable chroniclers of the traditions of his mother's people and had done his work in the sixteenth century, soon after the conquest, when those traditions had not yet been contaminated by foreign influences. He, too, confirmed what had obviously been a universal and deeply impressed belief: 'After the waters of the deluge had subsided, a certain man appeared in the country of Tiahuanaco . . .'[6]

That man had been Viracocha. Wrapped in his cloak, he was strong and 'august of countenance' and walked with unassailable confidence through the most dangerous badlands. He worked miracles of healing and could call down fire from heaven. To the Indians it must have seemed that he had materialized from nowhere.

Ancient traditions

We were now more than two hours into our journey to Machu Picchu and the panorama had changed. Huge black mountains, upon which not a trace of snow remained to reflect the sunlight, towered darkly above us and we seemed to be running through a rocky defile at the end of a narrow valley filled with sombre shadows. The air was cold and so were my feet. I shivered and resumed reading.

One thing was obvious amid the confused web of legends I had reviewed, legends which supplemented one another but also at times conflicted. All the scholars agreed that the Incas had borrowed, absorbed and passed on the traditions of many of the different civilized peoples over whom they had extended their control during the centuries of expansion of their vast empire. In this sense, whatever the outcome of the historical debate over the antiquity of the Incas themselves, nobody could seriously dispute their role as transmitters of the ancient belief systems of all the great archaic cultures – coastal and highland, known and unknown – that had preceded them in this land.

And who could say just *what* civilizations might have existed in Peru in the unexplored regions of the past? Every year archaeologists come up with new finds which extend the horizons further and further back in time. So why shouldn't they one day discover evidence of the penetration into the Andes, in remote antiquity, of a race of civilizers who had come from overseas and gone away again after completing their work? That was what the legends seemed to me to be suggesting, legends that most of all, and most clearly, had immortalized the memory of the man/god Viracocha striding the high windswept byways of the Andes working miracles wherever he went:

> Viracocha himself, with his two assistants, journeyed north . . . He travelled up the cordillera, one assistant went along the coast, and the other up the edge of the eastern forests . . . The Creator proceeded to Urcos, near Cuzco, where he commanded the future population to emerge from a mountain. He visited Cuzco, and then continued north to Ecuador. There, in the coastal province of Manta, he took leave of his people and, walking on the waves, disappeared across the ocean.[7]

There was always this poignant moment of goodbye at the end of every folk memory featuring the remarkable stranger whose name meant 'Foam of the Sea':

> Viracocha went on his way, calling forth the races of men . . . When he came to the district of Puerto Viejo he was joined by his followers whom he had sent on before, and when they had joined him he put to sea in their company and they say that he and his people went by water as easily as they had traversed the land.[8]

Always this poignant goodbye . . . and often a hint of science or magic.

Time capsule

Outside the window of the train things were happening. To my left, swollen with dark water, I could see the Urubamba, a tributary of the Amazon and a river sacred to the Incas. The air temperature had warmed-up noticeably: we had descended into a relatively low-lying valley with its own tropical micro-climate. The mountain slopes rising on either side of the tracks were densely covered in green forests and I was reminded that this was truly a region of vast and virtually insuperable obstacles. Whoever had ventured all this way into the middle of nowhere to build Machu Picchu must have had a very strong motive for doing so.

Whatever the reason had been, the choice of such a remote location had at least one beneficial side-effect: Machu Picchu was never found by the *conquistadores* and friars during their days of destructive zeal. Indeed, it was not until 1911, when the fabulous heritage of older races was beginning to be treated with greater respect, that a young American explorer, Hiram Bingham, revealed Machu Picchu to the world. It was realized at once that this incredible site opened a unique window on pre-Colombian civilization; in consequence the ruins were protected from looters and souvenir hunters and an important chunk of the enigmatic past was preserved to amaze future generations.

Having passed through a one-horse town named Agua Caliente (Hot Water), where a few broken-down restaurants and cheap bars leered at travellers from beside the tracks, we reached Machu Picchu Puentas Ruinas station at ten minutes past nine in the morning. From here a half-hour bus ride on a winding dirt road up the side of a steep and forbidding mountain brought us to Machu Picchu itself, to the ruins, and to a bad hotel which charged us a nonsensical amount of money for a not very clean room. We were the only guests. Though it had been years since the local guerrilla movement had last bombed the Machu Picchu train, not many foreigners were keen to come here any more.

Machu Picchu dreaming

It was two in the afternoon. I stood on a high point at the southern end of the site. The ruins stretched out northwards in lichen-enshrouded terraces before me. Thick clouds were wrapped in a ring around the mountain tops but the sunlight still occasionally burst through here and there.

Way down on the valley floor I could see the sacred river curled in a hairpin loop right around the central formation on which Machu Picchu was based, like a moat surrounding a giant castle. The river showed deep green from this vantage point, reflecting the greenness of the steep jungle slopes. And there were patches of white water and wonderful sparkling gleams of light.

I gazed across the ruins towards the dominant peak. Its name is Huana Picchu and it used to feature in all the classic travel agency posters of this site. To my astonishment I now observed that for a hundred metres or so below its summit it had been neatly terraced and sculpted: somebody had been up there and had carefully raked the near-vertical cliffs into a graceful hanging garden which had perhaps in ancient times been planted with bright flowers.

It seemed to me that the entire site, together with its setting, was a monumental work of sculpture composed in part of mountains, in part of rock, in part of trees, in part of stones – and also in part of water. It was a heartachingly beautiful place, certainly one of the most beautiful places I have ever seen.

Despite its luminous brilliance, however, I felt that I was gazing down on to a city of ghosts. It was like the wreck of the *Marie Celeste*, deserted and restless. The houses were arranged in long terraces. Each house was tiny, with just one room fronting directly on to the narrow street, and the architecture was solid and functional but by no means ornate. By way of contrast certain ceremonial areas were engineered to an infinitely higher standard and incorporated giant blocks similar to those I had seen at Sacsayhuaman. One smoothly polished polygonal monolith was around twelve feet long by five feet wide by five feet thick and could not have weighed less than 200 tons. How had the ancient builders managed to get it up here?

There were dozens of others like it too, and they were all arranged in the familiar jigsaw puzzle walls of interlocking angles. On one block I was able to count a total of thirty-three angles, every one intermeshed faultlessly with a matching angle on an adjoining block. There were massive polygons and perfect ashlars with razor-sharp edges. There were also natural, unhewn boulders integrated into the overall design at a number of points. And there were strange and unusual devices such as the Intihuatana, the 'hitching post of the sun'. This remarkable artefact consisted of an elemental chunk of bedrock, grey and crystalline, carved into a complex geometrical form of curves and angles, incised niches and external buttresses, surmounted at the centre by a stubby vertical prong.

Jigsaw puzzle

How old is Machu Picchu? The academic consensus is that the city could not have been built much earlier than the fifteenth century AD.[9] Dissenting opinions, however, have from time to time been expressed by a number of more daring but respectable scholars. In the 1930s, for

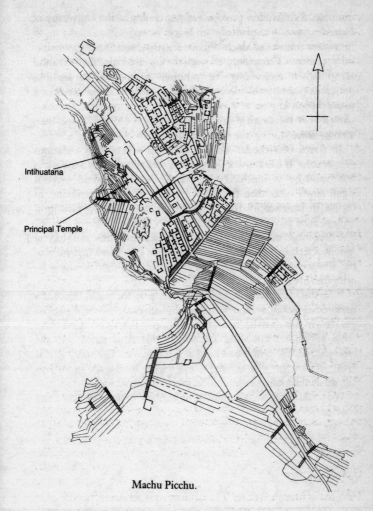

Intihuatana

Principal Temple

Machu Picchu.

example, Rolf Muller, professor of Astronomy at the University of Potsdam, found convincing evidence to suggest that the most important features of Machu Picchu possessed significant astronomical alignments. From these, through the use of detailed mathematical computations concerning star positions in the sky in previous millennia (which gradually alter down the epochs as the result of a phenomenon known as precession of the equinoxes), Muller concluded that the original layout of the site could only have been accomplished during 'the era of 4000 BC to 2000 BC'.[10]

In terms of orthodox history, this was a heresy of audacious proportions. If Muller was right, Machu Picchu was not a mere 500 but could be as much as 6000 years old. This would make it significantly older than the Great Pyramid of Egypt (assuming, of course, that one accepted the Great Pyramid's own orthodox dating of around 2500 BC).

There were other dissenting voices concerning the antiquity of Machu Picchu, and most, like Muller, were convinced that parts of the site were thousands of years older than the date favoured by orthodox historians.[11]

Like the big polygonal blocks that made up the walls, this was a notion that looked as though it might fit with other pieces of a jigsaw puzzle – in this case the jigsaw puzzle of a past that didn't quite make sense any more. Viracocha was part of that same puzzle. All the legends said his capital had been at Tiahuanaco. The ruins of this great and ancient city lay across the border in Bolivia, in an area known as the Collao, twelve miles south of Lake Titicaca.

We could get there, I calculated, in a couple of days, via Lima and La Paz.

Chapter 8

The Lake at the Roof of the World

La Paz, the capital city of Bolivia, nestles in the uneven bottom of a spectacular hole in the ground more than two miles above sea level. This plunging ravine, thousands of feet deep, was carved in some primeval age by a tremendous downrush of water that carried with it an abrasive tide of loose rocks and rubble.

Provided by nature with such an apocalyptic setting, La Paz possesses a unique though slightly sleazy charm. With its narrow streets, dark-walled tenements, imposing cathedrals, garish cinemas and hamburger bars open till late, it generates an atmosphere of quirky intrigue which is oddly intoxicating. It's hard going for the pedestrian, however, unless equipped with lungs like bellows, because the whole of the central district is built up and down the sides of precipitous hills.

La Paz airport is almost 5000 feet higher than the city itself on the edge of the Altiplano – the cold, rolling uplands that are the dominant topographical feature of this region. Santha and I landed there well after midnight on a delayed flight from Lima. In the draughty arrivals hall we were offered coca tea in little plastic cups as a prophylactic against altitude sickness. After considerable delay and exertion, we extracted our luggage from customs, hailed an ancient American-made taxi, and clanked and rattled down towards the dim yellow lights of the city far below.

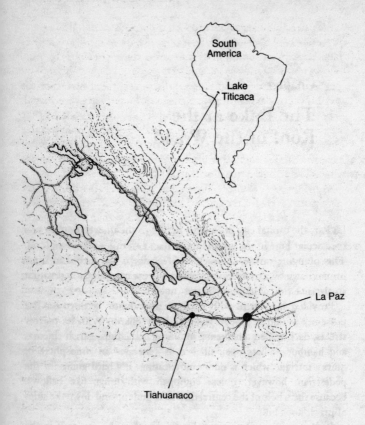

Lake Titicaca.

Rumours of a cataclysm

Around four o'clock the next afternoon we set off for Lake Titicaca in a rented jeep, fought our way through the capital's incomprehensible permanent rush-hour traffic-jams, then drove up out of the skyscrapers and slums into the wide, clear horizons of the Altiplano.

At first, still close to the city, our route took us through a zone of bleak suburbs and sprawling shantytowns where the sidewalks were lined with auto-repair shops and scrap yards. The more distance we put between ourselves and La Paz, however, the more attenuated the settlements became, until almost all signs of human habitation ceased. The empty, treeless, undulating savannahs, distantly bordered by the snow-covered peaks of the Cordillera Real, created an unforgettable spectacle of natural beauty and power. But there was also a feeling of otherworldliness about this place, which seemed to float above the clouds like an enchanted kingdom.

Although our ultimate destination was Tiahuanaco, we were aiming that night for the town of Copacabana on a promontory near the southern end of Lake Titicaca. To reach it we had to cross a neck of water by improvised car ferry at the fishing town of Tiquine. Then, with dusk descending, we followed the main highway, now little more than a narrow and uneven track, up a series of steep hairpin bends and on to the shoulder of a mountain spur. From this point a contrasting panorama unfolded: the dark, dark waters of the lake below appeared to lie at the edge of a limitless ocean drowned in sombre shadows, and yet the jagged peaks of the snow-capped mountains in the distance were still drenched in dazzling sunlight.

From the very beginning Lake Titicaca seemed to me a special place. I knew that it lay some 12,500 feet above sea level, that the frontier between Peru and Bolivia passed through it, that it covered an area of 3200 square miles and was 138 miles long by about 70 miles wide. I also knew it was deep, reaching almost 1000 feet in places, and had a puzzling geological history.

Here are the mysteries, and some of the solutions that have been proposed:

1 Though now more than two miles above sea level, the area around Lake Titicaca is littered with millions upon millions of fossilized sea shells. This suggests that at some stage the whole of the Altiplano was forced upwards from the sea-bed, perhaps as part of the general terrestrial rising that formed South America as a whole. In the process great quantities of ocean water, together with countless myriads of living marine

creatures, were scooped up and suspended among the Andean ranges.[1] This is thought to have happened not more recently than about 100 million years ago.[2]

2 Paradoxically, despite the mighty antiquity of this event, Lake Titicaca has retained, until the present day, 'a marine icthyofauna'[3], in other words, though now located hundreds of miles from any ocean, its fish and crustacea feature many oceanic (rather than fresh-water) types. Surprising creatures brought to the surface in fishermen's nets have included examples of *Hippocampus* (the seahorse).[4] In addition, as one authority has pointed out, 'The various species of *Allorquestes* (*hyalella inermis*, etc.) and other examples of marine fauna leave no doubt that this lake in other periods was much saltier than today, or, more accurately, that the water which formed it was from the sea and that it was damned up and locked in the Andes when the continent rose.'[5]

3 So much, then, for the events which may have created Lake Titicaca in the first place. Since its formation this great 'interior sea', and the Altiplano itself, has undergone several other drastic and dramatic changes. Of these by far the most notable is that the lake's extent appears to have fluctuated enormously, indicated by the existence of an ancient strandline visible on much of the surrounding terrain. Puzzlingly, this strandline is not level but *slopes* markedly from north to south over a considerable horizontal distance. At the northernmost point surveyed it is as much as 295 feet higher than Titicaca; some 400 miles farther south, it is 274 feet lower than the present level of the lake.[6] From this, and much other evidence, geologists have deduced that the Altiplano is still gradually rising, but in an unbalanced manner with greater altitudes being attained in the northern part and lesser in the southern. The process involved here is thought to have less to do with changes in the level of Titicaca's waters themselves (although such changes have certainly occurred) than with changes in the level of the whole terrain in which the lake is situated.[7]

4 Much harder to explain in such terms, however, given the very long time periods major geological transformations are supposed

to require, is irrefutable evidence that *the city of Tiahuanaco was once a port, complete with extensive docks, positioned right on the the shore of Lake Titicaca.*[8] The problem is that Tiahuanaco's ruins are now marooned about twelve miles south of the lake and *more than 100 feet higher* than the present shoreline.[9] In the period since the city was built, it therefore follows that one of two things must have happened: either the level of lake has fallen greatly or the land on which Tiahuanaco stands has risen comparably.

5 Either way it is obvious that there have been massive and traumatic physical changes. Some of these, such as the rise of the Altiplano from the floor of the ocean, certainly took place in remote geological ages, before the advent of human civilization. Others are not nearly so ancient and must have occurred after the construction of Tiahuanaco.[10] The question, therefore, is this: *when* was Tiahuanaco built?

The orthodox historical view is that the ruins cannot possibly be dated much earlier than AD 500.[11] An alternative chronology also exists, however, which, although not accepted by the majority of scholars, seems more in tune with the scale of the geological upheavals that have occurred in this region. Based on the mathematical/astronomical calculations of Professor Arthur Posnansky of the University of La Paz, and of Professor Rolf Muller (who also challenged the official dating of Machu Picchu), it pushes the main phase of construction at Tiahuanaco back to *15,000 BC*. This chronology also indicates that the city later suffered immense destruction in a phenomenal natural catastrophe around the eleventh millennium BC, and thereafter rapidly became separated from the lakeshore.[12]

We shall be reviewing Posnansky's and Muller's findings in Chapter Eleven, findings which suggest that the great Andean city of Tiahuanaco flourished during the last Ice Age in the deep dark, moonless midnight of prehistory.

Chapter 9

Once and Future King

During my travels in the Andes I had several times re-read a curious variant of the mainstream tradition of Viracocha. In this variant, which was from the area around Lake Titicaca known as the Collao, the deity civilizing-hero had been named Thunupa:

> Thunupa appeared on the Altiplano in ancient times, coming from the north with five disciples. A white man of august presence, blue-eyed, and bearded, he was sober, puritanical and preached against drunkenness, polygamy and war.[1]

After travelling great distances through the Andes, where he created a peaceful kingdom and taught men all the arts of civilization,[2] Thunupa was struck down and grievously wounded by a group of jealous conspirators:

> They put his blessed body in a boat of totora rush and set it adrift on Lake Titicaca. There . . . he sailed away with such speed that those who had tried so cruelly to kill him were left behind in terror and astonishment – for this lake has no current . . . The boat came to the shore at Cochamarca, where today is the river Desguardero. Indian tradition asserts that the boat struck the land with such force it created the river Desguardero, which before then did not exist. And on the water so released the holy body was carried many leagues away to the sea coast at Arica . . .[3]

Boats, water and salvation

There are curious parallels here to the story of Osiris, the ancient Egyptian high god of death and resurrection. The fullest account of the original myth defining this mysterious figure is given by Plutarch[4] and says that, after bringing the gifts of civilization to his people, teaching them all manner of useful skills, abolishing cannibalism and human sacrifice, and providing them with their first legal code, Osiris left Egypt and travelled about the world to spread the benefits of civilization to other nations as well. He never forced the barbarians he encountered to accept his laws, preferring instead to argue with them and to appeal to their reason. It is also recorded that he passed on his teachings to them by means of hymns and songs accompanied by musical instruments.

While he was gone, however, he was plotted against by seventy-two members of his court, led by his brother-in-law Set. On his return the conspirators invited him to a banquet where a splendid coffer of wood and gold was offered as a prize to any guest who could fit into it exactly. Osiris did not know that the coffer had been constructed precisely to his body measurements. As a result, when the assembled guests tried one by one to get into it they failed. Osiris lay down comfortably inside. Before he had time to get out the conspirators rushed forward, nailed the lid tightly closed and sealed even the cracks with molten lead so that there would be no air. The coffer was then thrown into the Nile. It had been intended that it should sink, but it floated rapidly away, drifting for a considerable distance until it reached the sea coast.

At this point the goddess Isis, wife of Osiris, intervened. Using all the great magic for which she was renowned, she found the coffer and concealed it in a secret place. However, her evil brother Set, out hunting in the marshes, discovered the coffer, opened it and, in a mad fury, cut the royal corpse into fourteen pieces which he scattered throughout the land.

Once more Isis set off to save her husband. She made a small boat of papyrus reeds, coated with pitch, and embarked on the Nile in search of the remains. When she had found them she worked powerful spells to reunite the dismembered parts of the body so that it resumed its old form. Thereafter, in an intact and perfect state, Osiris went through a process of stellar rebirth to become god of the dead and king of the underworld – from which place, legend had it, he occasionally returned to earth in the guise of a mortal man.[5]

Although there are huge differences between the traditions it is bizarre that Osiris in Egypt and Thunupa-Viracocha in South America should have had all of the following points in common:

- both were great civilizers;
- both were conspired against;
- both were struck down;
- both were sealed inside a container or vessel of some kind;
- both were then cast into water;
- both drifted away on a river;
- both eventually reached the sea.

Are such parallels to be dismissed as coincidences? or could there be some underlying connection?

Reed boats of Suriqui

The air was Alpine cold and I was sitting on the front of a motor launch doing about twenty knots across the icy waters of Lake Titicaca. The sky above was clear blue, reflecting aquamarine and turquoise tints inshore, and the vast body of the lake, glinting in copper and silver tones, seemed to stretch away for ever . . .

The passages in the legends that spoke of vessels made of reeds needed to be followed up because I knew that 'boats of totora rush' were a traditional form of transport on this lake. However, the ancient skills required to build craft of this type had atrophied in recent years and we were now headed towards Suriqui, the one place where they were still properly made.

On Suriqui Island, in a small village close to the lakeshore, I found two elderly Indians making a boat from bundled totora rushes. The elegant craft, which appeared to be nearly complete, was approximately fifteen feet long. It was wide amidships, but narrow at either end with a high curving prow and stern.

I sat down for a while to watch. The more senior of the two builders, who wore a brown felt hat over a curious peaked woollen cap, repeatedly braced his bare left foot against the side of the vessel to give additional leverage as he pulled and tightened the cords that held the bundles of reeds in place. From time to time I noticed that he rubbed a length of cord against his own perspiring brow – thus moistening it to increase its adhesion.

The boat, surrounded by chickens and occasionally investigated by a shy, browsing alpaca, stood amid a litter of discarded rushes in the backyard of a ramshackle farmhouse. It was one of several I was able to study over the next few hours and, though the setting was unmistakably Andean, I found myself repeatedly overtaken by a sense of *déjà vu* from another place and another time. The reason was that the totora vessels of Suriqui were virtually identical, both in the method of construction and in finished appearance, to the beautiful craft fashioned from papyrus reeds in which the Pharaohs had sailed the Nile thousands of years previously. In my travels in Egypt I had examined the images of many such vessels painted on the walls of ancient tombs. It sent a tingle down my spine to see them now so colourfully brought to life on an obscure island on Lake Titicaca – even though my research had partially prepared me for this coincidence. I knew that no satisfactory explanation had ever been given for how such close and richly detailed similarities of boat design could occur in two such widely separated places. Nevertheless, in the words of one authority in ancient navigation who had addressed himself to this conundrum:

> Here was the same compact shape, peaked and raised at both ends with rope lashings running from the deck right round the bottom of the boat all in one piece . . . Each straw was placed with maximum precision to achieve perfect symmetry and streamlined elegance, while the bundles were so tightly lashed that they looked like . . . gilded logs bent into a clog-shaped peak fore and aft.[6]

The reed boats of the ancient Nile, and the reed boats of Lake Titicaca (the original design of which, local Indians insisted, had been given to them by 'the Viracocha people'[7]), had other points in common. Both, for example, were equipped with sails mounted on peculiar two-legged straddled masts.[8] Both had also been used for the long-distance transport of exceptionally heavy building materials: obelisks and gargantuan blocks of stone bound for the temples at Giza and Luxor

and Abydos on the one hand and for the mysterious edifices of
Tiahuanaco on the other.

In those far-off days, before Lake Titicaca became more than one
hundred feet shallower, Tiahuanaco had stood at the water's edge
overlooking a vista of awesome and sacred beauty. Now the great port,
capital city of Viracocha himself, lay lost amid eroded hills and empty
windswept plains.

Road to Tiahuanaco . . .

After returning from Suriqui to the mainland we drove our hired jeep
across those plains, raising a cloud of dust. Our route took us through
the towns of Puccarani and Laha, populated by stolid Aymara Indians
who walked slowly in the narrow cobbled streets and sat placidly in
the little sunlit plazas.

Were these people the descendants of the builders of Tiahuanaco,
as the scholars insisted? Or were the legends right? Had the ancient
city been the work of foreigners with godlike powers who had settled
here, long ages ago?

Chapter 10

The City at the Gate of the Sun

The early Spanish travellers who visited the ruined Bolivian city of Tiahuanaco at around the time of the conquest were impressed by the sheer size of its buildings and by the atmosphere of mystery that clung to them. 'I asked the natives whether these edifices were built in the time of the Inca,' wrote the chronicler Pedro Cieza de Leon, 'They laughed at the question, affirming that they were made long before the Inca reign and . . . that they had heard from their forebears that everything to be seen there appeared suddenly in the course of a single night . . .'[1] Meanwhile another Spanish visitor of the same period recorded a tradition which said that the stones had been lifted miraculously off the ground, 'They were carried through the air to the sound of a trumpet.'[2]

Not long after the conquest a detailed description of the city was written by the historian Garcilaso de la Vega. No looting for treasure or for building materials had yet taken place and, though ravaged by the tooth of time, the site was still magnificent enough to take his breath away:

> We must now say something about the large and almost incredible buildings of Tiahuanaco. There is an artificial hill, of great height, built on stone foundations so that the earth will not slide. There are gigantic figures carved in stone . . . these are much worn which shows their great antiquity. There are walls, the stones of which are so enormous it is difficult to imagine what human force could have put

them in place. And there are the remains of strange buildings, the most remarkable being stone portals, hewn out of solid rock; these stand on bases anything up to 30 feet long, 15 feet wide and 6 feet thick, base and portal being all of one piece . . . How, and with the use of what tools or implements, massive works of such size could be achieved are questions which we are unable to answer . . . Nor can it be imagined how such enormous stones could have been brought here . . .[3]

That was in the sixteenth century. More than 400 years later, at the end of the twentieth century, I shared Garcilaso's puzzlement. Scattered around Tiahuanaco, in defiance of the looters who had robbed the site of so much in recent years, were monoliths so big and cumbersome yet so well cut that they almost seemed to be the work of super-beings.

Sunken temple

Like a disciple at the feet of his master, I sat on the floor of the sunken temple and looked up at the enigmatic face which all the scholars of Tiahuanaco believed was intended to represent Viracocha. Untold centuries ago, unknown hands had carved this likeness into a tall pillar of red rock. Though now much eroded, it was the likeness of a man at peace with himself. It was the likeness of a man of power . . .

He had a high forehead, and large, round eyes. His nose was straight, narrow at the bridge but flaring towards the nostrils. His lips were full. His distinguishing feature, however, was his stylish and imposing beard, which had the effect of making his face broader at the jaws than at the temples. Looking more closely, I could see that the sculptor had portrayed a man whose skin was shaved all around his lips with the result that his moustache began high on his cheeks, roughly parallel with the end of his nose. From there it curved extravagantly down beside the corners of his mouth, forming an exaggerated goatee at the chin, and then followed his jawline back to his ears.

Above and below the ears, on the side of the head, were carved odd representations of animals. Or perhaps it would be better to describe

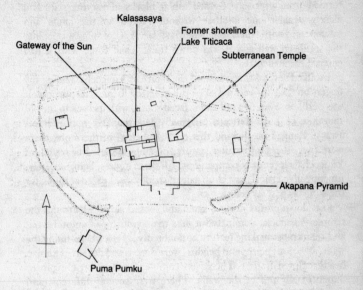

Tiahuanaco.

these carvings as representations of *odd* animals, because they looked like big, clumsy, prehistoric mammals with fat tails and club feet.

There were other points of interest. For example, the stone figure of Viracocha had been sculpted with the hands and arms folded, one below the other, over the front of a long, flowing robe. On each side of this robe appeared the sinuous form of a snake coiling upwards from ground to shoulder level. And as I looked at this beautiful design (the original of which had perhaps been embroidered on rich cloth) the picture that came into my mind was of Viracocha as a wizard or a sorcerer, a bearded, Merlin-like figure dressed in weird and wonderful clothes, calling down fire from heaven.

The 'temple' in which the Viracocha pillar stood was open to the sky and consisted of a large, rectangular pit, like a swimming pool, dug out six feet below ground level. Its floor, about 40 feet long by 30 feet wide, was composed of hard, flat gravel. Its strong vertical walls were formed from precisely dressed ashlar blocks of varying sizes laid closely against one another without mortar in the joints and interspersed with taller, rough-hewn stelae. A set of steps was let into the southern wall and it was down these I had come when I had entered the structure.

I walked several times around the figure of Viracocha, resting my fingers on the sun-warmed stone pillar, trying to guess its purpose. It was perhaps seven feet tall and it faced south, with its back to the old shoreline of Lake Titicaca (originally less than six hundred feet away).[4] Ranged out behind this central obelisk, furthermore, there were two others, of smaller stature, possibly intended to represent Viracocha's legendary companions. All three figures, being severely, functionally vertical, cast clean-edged shadows as I gazed at them, for the sun was past its zenith.

I sat down on the ground again and looked slowly all around the temple. Viracocha dominated it, like the conductor of an orchestra, and yet its most striking feature undoubtedly lay elsewhere: lining the walls, at various points and heights, were dozens and dozens of human heads sculpted in stone. These were complete heads, protruding three dimensionally out of the walls. There were several different (and contradictory) scholarly opinions as to their function.

Pyramid

From the floor of the sunken temple, looking west, I could see an immense wall into which was set an impressive geometrical gateway made of large stone slabs. Silhouetted in this gateway by the afternoon sun was the figure of a giant. The wall, I knew, enclosed a parade-ground-sized area called the Kalasasaya (a word in the local Aymara language meaning simply 'Place of the Upright Standing Stones'[5]). And the giant was one of the huge time-worn pieces of sculpture referred to by Garcilaso de la Vega.

I was eager to take a look at it, but for the moment my attention was diverted southwards towards an artificial hill, 50 feet high, which lay almost directly ahead of me as I climbed the steps out of the sunken temple. The hill, which had also been mentioned by Garcilaso, was known as the Akapana Pyramid. Like the pyramids at Giza in Egypt, it was oriented with surprising precision towards the cardinal points. Unlike those pyramids its ground-plan was somewhat irregular. Nonetheless, it measured roughly 690 feet on each side which meant that it was a hulking piece of architecture and the dominant edifice of Tiahuanaco.

I walked towards it now, and spent some time strolling around it and clambering over it. Originally it had been a clean-sided step-pyramid of earth faced with large andesite blocks. In the centuries since the conquest, however, it had been used as a quarry by builders from as far away as La Paz, with the result that only about ten per cent of its superb facing blocks now remained.

What clues, what evidence, had those nameless thieves carried off with them? As I climbed up the broken sides and around the deep grassy troughs in the top of the Akapana, I realized that the true function of the pyramid was probably never going to be understood. All that was certain was that it had not been merely decorative or ceremonial. On the contrary, it seemed almost as though it might have functioned as some kind of arcane 'device' or machine. Deep within its bowels, archaeologists had discovered a complex network of zig-zagging stone channels, lined with fine ashlars. These had been meticulously angled and jointed (to a tolerance of one-fiftieth of an inch), and had served to sluice water down from a large reservoir at the top of the structure, through a series of descending levels, to a moat that encircled the entire site, washing against the pyramid's base on its southern side.[6]

So much care and attention had been lavished on all this plumbing, so many man-hours of highly skilled and patient labour, that the Akapana made no sense unless it had been endowed with a significant purpose. A number of archaeologists, I knew, had speculated that this purpose might have been connected with a rain or river cult involving a primitive veneration of the powers and attributes of fast-flowing water.

One sinister suggestion, which implied that the unknown 'technology' of the pyramid might have had a lethal purpose, was derived from the meaning of the words *Hake* and *Apana* in the ancient Aymara language still spoken hereabouts: '*Hake* means "people" or "men"; *Apana* means "to perish" (probably by water). Thus *Akapana* is a place where people perish . . ."[7]

Another commentator, however, after making a careful assessment of all the characteristics of the hydraulic system, proposed a different solution, namely that the sluices had most probably been part of 'a processing technique – the use of flowing water for washing ores, perhaps?'[8]

Gateway of the Sun

Leaving the western side of the enigmatic pyramid, I made my way towards the south-west corner of the enclosure known as the Kalassaya. I could now see why it had been called the Place of the Upright Standing Stones for this was precisely what it was. At regular intervals in a wall composed of bulky trapezoidal blocks, huge dagger-like monoliths more than twelve feet high had been sunk hilt-first into the red earth of the Altiplano. The effect was of a giant stockade, almost 500 feet square, rising about twice as far above the ground as the sunken temple had been interred beneath it.

Had the Kalasasaya been a fortress then? Apparently not. Scholars now generally accept that it functioned as a sophisticated celestial observatory. Rather than keeping enemies at bay, its purpose had been to fix the equinoxes and the solstices and to predict, with mathematical precision, the various seasons of the year. Certain structures within its walls, (and, indeed, the walls themselves), appeared to have been lined up to particular star groups and designed to facilitate measurement of the amplitude of the sun in summer, winter, autumn and spring.[9] In addition, the famous 'Gateway of the Sun', which stood in the north-west corner of the enclosure, was not only a world-class work of art but was thought by those who had studied it to be a complex and accurate calendar carved in stone:

> The more one gets acquainted with the sculpture the greater becomes one's conviction that the peculiar lay-out and pictorialism of this Calendar cannot possibly have been the result merely of the ultimately unfathomable whim of an *artist*, but that its glyphs, deeply senseful, constitute the eloquent record of the observations and calculations of a

scientist . . . The Calendar could not have been drawn up and laid out in any other way than this.[10]

My background research had made me especially curious about the Gateway of the Sun and, indeed, about the Kalasasaya as a whole. This was so because certain astronomical and solar alignments which we review in the next chapter had made it possible to calculate the approximate period when the Kalasasaya must originally have been laid out. These alignments suggested the controversial date of 15,000 BC – about seventeen thousand years ago.

Chapter 11

Intimations of Antiquity

In his voluminous work *Tiahuanacu: the Cradle of American Man*, the late Professor Arthur Posnansky (a formidable German–Bolivian scholar whose investigations at the ruins lasted for almost fifty years) explains the archaeo-astronomical calculations which led to his controversial re-dating of Tiahuanaco. These, he says, were based 'solely and exclusively on the difference in the obliquity of the ecliptic of the period in which the Kalasasaya was built and that which it is today'.[1]

What exactly is 'the obliquity of the ecliptic', and why does it make Tiahuanaco 17,000 years old?

According to the dictionary definition it is 'the angle between the plane of the earth's orbit and that of the celestial equator, equal to approximately 23° 27' at present'.[2]

To clarify this obscure astronomical notion, it helps to picture the earth as a ship, sailing on the vast ocean of the heavens. Like all such vessels (be they planets or schooners), it *rolls* slightly with the swell that flows beneath it. Picture yourself on board that ship as it rolls, standing on the deck, gazing out to sea. You rise up on the crest of a wave and your visible horizon increases; you fall back into a trough and it decreases. The process is regular, mathematical, like the tick-tock of a great metronome: a constant, almost imperceptible, nodding, perpetually changing the angle between yourself and the horizon.

Now picture the earth again. Floating in space, as every schoolchild

1 The Nazca spider, southern Peru. Recent research by Dr Phillis Pitluga, a senior astronomer with Chicago's Adler Planetarium, has demonstrated that the spider, like the Great Pyramids at Giza in Egypt (see Parts VI and VII), was designed as a terrestrial image of the constellation of Orion. Is it possible that the incorporation of a 'celestial plan' in ancient and mysterious monuments from many different parts of the world, and a particular focus on the three stars of Orion's Belt (represented at Nazca by the narrow waist of the spider), could be parts of a global scientific legacy passed on by a lost civilization of very remote times?

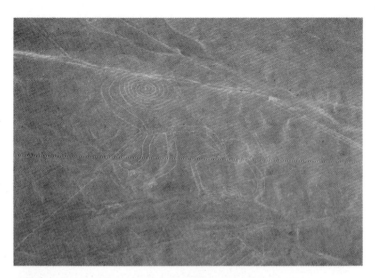

2 The Nazca monkey; 3 The hummingbird. All these figures are marked out on the landscape in a single continuous line, and are so immense that they can only be viewed from the air.

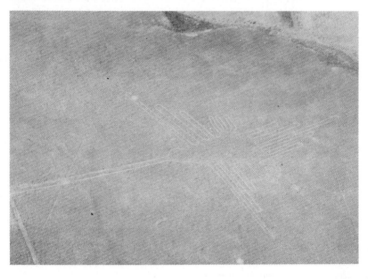

Above: **4** A view of Machu Picchu. This remote site features astronomical alignments which indicate that it may be many thousands of years older than the Inca civilization that is supposed to have built it. Is it possible that it was not a work of the Incas at all and that it was merely occupied and used by them at a much later date? *Below*: **5** and **6** Characteristic 'jigsaw puzzle' masonry of the Cuzco–Machu Picchu area. Again archaeologists unhesitatingly attribute this style to the Incas, but compare pictures 66, 67 and 68 in Part VII below.

Above: **7** The *Intihuatana* ('hitching post of the sun') at Machu Picchu. *Below*: **8** and **9** The author dwarfed by the giant blocks of Sacsayhuaman, which routinely weigh as much as 500 family-sized automobiles. There are indications that these massive fortifications, like Machu Picchu, were not built by the Incas but by unknown hands thousands of years earlier. Compare picture 9 with picture 65 in Part VII below.

Above: **10** and **11** Tiahuanaco, Bolivia. The two principal 'idols' in the Kalasasaya both carry unidentifiable implements in their hands. *Below*: **12** A view of the Kalasasaya from the north. Astronomical calculations indicate that this huge structure may originally have been set out and aligned to the equinoctial sunrise as early as 15,000 BC.

Above: **13** Tiahuanaco's Gateway of the Sun, viewed from the west. It is carved out of a single piece of solid andesite and weighs more than 10 tons. *Below*: **14** Several researchers believe that the 'Calendar frieze' on the east side of the Gateway incorporates advanced scientific information.

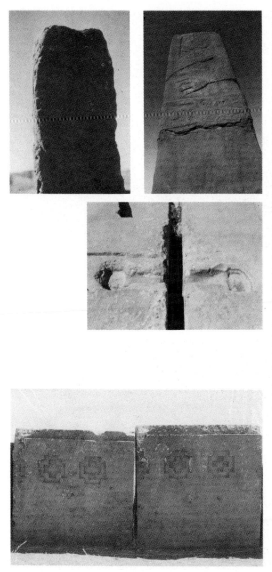

Top left: **15** This idol, depicting a bearded figure, stands in the Subterranean Temple at Tiahuanaco, and is presumed to represent Viracocha, the civilizing hero of Andean mythology. *Top right*: **16** A stele at Tiahuanaco carved with bearded heads (above the figure's right arm and, sideways, on its belt). The physical types depicted on this and on the Viracocha pillar are not indigenous to the South American region. *Left*: **17** The characteristic indentation marks which indicate that these blocks were joined together by an I-shaped metal clamp. This masonary technique is not known to have been employed anywhere else in South America but was used in ancient Egypt more than 4000 years ago. *Below*: **18** The symbolism of the cross was present at Tiahuanaco thousands of years before the coming of Christianity.

Above: **19** Building a traditional reed boat on the island of Suriqui, Lake Titicaca. Boats of a near-identical design, though on a much larger scale, were used on the Nile in Egypt in the Pyramid Age (see Part VI, pictures 53, 54 and 55). *Below*: **20** Navigating the waters of Lake Titicaca. Tiahuanaco was originally built to serve as a port on the shores of this vast inland sea. Since then, however, the lake's level has fallen by more than 100 feet and its shores have receded some 12 miles to the north – a process which geologists estimate could not have been completed in less than 10,000 years.

knows, the axis of daily rotation of our beautiful blue planet lies slightly tilted away from the vertical in its orbit around the sun. From this it follows that the terrestrial equator, and hence the 'celestial equator' (which is merely an imaginary extension of the earth's equator into the celestial sphere) must also lie at an angle to the orbital plane. That angle, at any one time, *is* the obliquity of the ecliptic. But because the earth is a ship that rolls, its obliquity *changes* in a cyclical manner over very long periods. During each cycle of 41,000 years the obliquity varies, with the precision and predictability of a Swiss chronograph, between 22.1° and 24.5°.[3] The sequence in which one angle will follow another, as well as the sequence of all previous angles (at any period of history) can be calculated by means of a few straightforward equations. These have been expressed as a curve on a graph (originally plotted out in Paris in 1911 by the International Conference of Ephemerids) and from this graph it is possible to match angles and precise historical dates with confidence and accuracy.

Posnansky was able to date the Kalasasaya because the obliquity cycle gradually alters the azimuth position of sunrise and sunset from century to century.[4] By establishing the solar alignments of certain key structures that now looked 'out of true', he convincingly demonstrated that the obliquity of the ecliptic at the time of the building of the Kalasasaya had been 23° 8' 48". When that angle was plotted on the graph drawn up by the International Conference of Ephemerids it was found to correspond to a date of 15,000 BC.[5]

Of course, not a single orthodox historian or archaeologist was prepared to accept such an early origin for Tiahuanaco preferring, as noted in Chapter Eight, to agree on the safe estimate of AD 500. During the years 1927–30, however, several scientists from other disciplines checked carefully Posnansky's 'astronomic-archaeological investigations'. These scientists, members of a high-powered team which also studied many other archaeological sites in the Andes, were Dr Hans Ludendorff (then director of the Astronomical Observatory of Potsdam), Dr Friedrich Becker of the Specula Vaticanica, and two other astronomers: Professor Dr Arnold Kohlschutter of the University of Bonn and Dr Rolf Muller of the Astrophysical Institute of Potsdam.[6]

At the end of their three years of work the scientists concluded that

Posnansky was basically right. They didn't concern themselves with the implications of their findings for the prevailing paradigm of history; they simply stated the observable facts about the astronomical alignments of various structures at Tiahuanaco. Of these, the most important by far was that the Kalasasaya had been laid out to conform with observations of the heavens made a very long time ago – much, much further back than AD 500. Posnansky's figure of 15,000 BC was pronounced to be well within the bounds of possibility.[7]

If Tiahuanaco had indeed flourished so long before the dawn of history, what sort of people had built it, and for what purpose?

Fish-garbed figures

There were two massive pieces of statuary inside the Kalasasaya. One, a figure nicknamed *El Fraile* (The Friar) stood in the south-west corner; the other, towards the centre of the eastern end of the enclosure, was the giant that I had observed from the sunken temple.

Carved in red sandstone, worn and ancient beyond reckoning, El Fraile stood about six feet high, and portrayed a humanoid, androgenous being with massive eyes and lips. In its right hand it clutched something resembling a knife with a wavy blade like an Indonesian kris. In its left hand was an object like a hinged and case-bound book. From the top of this 'book', however, protruded a device which had been inserted into it as though into a sheath.

From the waist down the figure appeared to be clad in a garment of fish scales, and, as though to confirm this perception, the sculptor had formed the individual scales out of rows and rows of small, highly-stylized fish-heads. This sign had been persuasively interpreted by Posnansky as meaning fish in general.[8] It seemed, therefore, that El Fraile was a portrayal of an imaginary or symbolic 'fish man'. The figure was also equipped with a belt sculpted with the images of several large crustaceans, so this notion seemed all the more probable. What had been intended?

I had learned of one local tradition I thought might shed light on the matter. It was very ancient and spoke of 'gods of the lake, with fish tails, called Chullua and Umantua'.[9] In this, and in the fish-garbed figures, it seemed that there was a curious out-of-place echo of

Mesopotamian myths, which spoke strangely, and at length, about amphibious beings, 'endowed with reason' who had visited the land of Sumer in remote prehistory. The leader of these beings was named Oannes (or *Uan*).[10] According to the Chaldean scribe, Berossus:

> The whole body of [Oannes] was like that of a fish; and had under a fish's head another head, and also feet below, similar to those of a man, subjoined to the fish's tail. His voice too, and language, was articulate and human; and a representation of him is preserved even to this day . . . When the sun set, it was the custom of this Being to plunge again into the sea, and abide all night in the deep; for he was amphibious.[11]

According to the traditions reported by Berossus, Oannes was, above all, a civilizer:

> In the day-time he used to converse with men; but took no food at that season; and he gave them an insight into letters and sciences, and every kind of art. He taught them to construct houses, to found temples, to compile laws, and explained to them the principles of geometrical knowledge. He made them distinguish the seeds of the earth, and showed them how to collect fruits; in short, he instructed them in every thing which could tend to soften manners and to humanise mankind. From that time, so universal were his instructions, nothing has been added materially by way of improvement . . .[12]

Surviving images of the Oannes creatures I had seen on Babylonian and Assyrian reliefs clearly portrayed *fish-garbed men*. Fish-scales formed the dominant motif on their garments, just as they did on those worn by El Fraile. Another similarity was that the Babylonian figures held unidentified objects in both their hands. If my memory served me right (and I later confirmed that it did) these objects were by no means identical to those carried by El Fraile. They were, however, similar enough to be worthy of note.[13]

The other great 'idol' of the Kalasasaya was positioned towards the eastern end of the platform, facing the main gateway, and was an imposing monolith of grey andesite, hugely thick and standing about nine feet tall. Its broad head rose straight up out of its hulking shoulders and its slablike face stared expressionlessly into the distance. It was wearing a crown, or head-band of some kind, and its

Assyrian relief of fish-garbed figure.

hair was braided into orderly rows of long vertical ringlets which were most clearly visible at the back.

The figure was also intricately carved and decorated across much of its surface almost as though it were tattooed. Like El Fraile, it was clad below the waist in a garment composed of fish-scales and fish symbols. And, also like El Fraile, it held two unidentifiable objects in its hands. This time the left-hand object looked more like a sheath than a case-bound book, and from it protruded a forked handle. The right-hand object was roughly cylindrical, narrow in the centre where it was held, wider at the shoulders and at the base, and then narrowing again towards the top. It appeared to have several different sections, or parts, fitted over and into one another, but it was impossible to guess what it might represent.

Images of extinct species

Leaving the fish-garbed figures, I came at last to the Gateway of the Sun, located in the north-west corner of the Kalasasaya.

It proved to be a freestanding monolith of grey-green andesite about $12\frac{1}{2}$ feet wide, 10 feet high and 18 inches thick, weighing an estimated 10 tons.[14] Perhaps best envisaged as a sort of Arc de Triomphe, though on a much smaller scale, it looked in this setting like a door connecting two invisible dimensions – a door between nowhere and nothing. The stonework was of exceptionally high quality and authorities agreed that it was 'one of the archaeological wonders of the Americas'.[15] Its most enigmatic feature was the so-called 'calendar frieze' carved into its eastern façade along the top of the portal.

At its centre, in an elevated position, this frieze was dominated by what scholars took to be another representation of Viracocha,[16] but this time in his more terrifying aspect as the god-king who could call down fire from heaven. His gentle, fatherly side was still expressed: tears of compassion were running down his cheeks. But his face was set stern and hard, his tiara was regal and imposing, and in either hand he grasped a thunderbolt.[17] In the interpretation given by Joseph Campbell, one of the twentieth century's best-known students of myth, 'The meaning is that the grace that pours into the universe through the sun door is the same as the energy of the bolt that annihilates and is itself indestructible . . .'[18]

I turned my head to right and left, slowly studying the remainder of the frieze. It was a beautifully balanced piece of sculpture with three rows of eight figures, twenty-four in all, lined up on either side of the elevated central image. Many attempts, none of them particularly convincing, have been made to explain the assumed calendrical function of these figures.[19] All that could really be said for sure was that they had a peculiar, bloodless, cartoonlike quality, and that there was something coldly mathematical, almost machinelike, about the way they seemed to march in regimented lines towards Viracocha. Some apparently wore bird masks, others had sharply pointed noses, and each had in his hand an implement of the type the high god was himself carrying.

The base of the frieze was filled with a design known as the 'Meander' – a geometrical series of step-pyramid forms set in a continuous line, and arranged alternately upside down and right side up, which was also thought to have had a calendrical function. On the third column from the right-hand side (and, more faintly, on the third column from the left-hand side too) I could make out a clear carving of an elephant's head, ears, tusks and trunk. This was unexpected since there are no elephants anywhere in the New World. There had been, however, in prehistoric times, as I was able to confirm much later. Particularly numerous in the southern Andes, until their sudden extinction around 10,000 BC,[20] had been the members of a species called *Cuvieronius*, an elephantlike proboscid complete with tusks and a trunk, uncannily similar in appearance to the 'elephants' of the Gateway of the Sun.[21]

I stepped forward a few paces to take a closer look at these elephants. Each turned out to be composed of the heads of two crested condors, placed throat to throat (the crests constituting the 'ears' and the upper part of the necks the 'tusks'). The creatures thus formed still looked like elephants to me, perhaps because a characteristic visual trick the sculptors of Tiahuanaco had employed again and again in their subtle and otherworldly art had been to use one thing to depict another. Thus an apparently human ear on an apparently human face might turn out to be a bird's wing. Likewise an ornate crown might be composed of alternate fishes' and condors' heads, an eyebrow a bird's neck and head, the toe of a slipper an animal's head, and so on. Members of the elephant family formed out of condors' heads, therefore, need not necessarily be optical illusions; on the contrary, such inventive composites would be perfectly in keeping with the overall artistic character of the frieze.

Among the riot of stylized animal figures carved into the Gateway of the Sun were a number of other extinct species as well. I knew from my research that one of these had been convincingly identified by several observers as Toxodon[22] – a three-toed amphibious mammal about nine feet long and five feet high at the shoulder, resembling a short, stubby cross between a rhino and a hippo.[23] Like *Cuvieronius*, Toxodon had flourished in South America in the late Pliocene (1.6 million years ago) and had died out at the end of the Pleistocene, about 12,000 years ago.[24]

To my eye this looked like striking corroboration for the astro-archaeological evidence that dated Tiahuanaco to the end of the Pleistocene, and further undermined the orthodox historical chronology which made the city only 1500 years old, since Toxodon, presumably, could only have been modelled from life. It was therefore obviously a matter of some importance that *no fewer that forty-six Toxodon heads* had been carved into the frieze of the Gateway of the Sun.[25] Nor was this creature's ugly caricature confined only to the Gateway. On the contrary, Toxodon had been identified on numerous fragments of Tiahuanacan pottery. Even more convincingly, he had been portrayed in several pieces of sculpture which showed him in full three-dimensional glory.[26] Moreover representations of other extinct species had been found: the species included *Shelidoterium*, a diurnal quadruped, and *Macrauchenia*, an animal somewhat larger than the modern horse, with distinctive three-toed feet.[27]

Such images meant that Tiahuanaco was a kind of picture-book from the past, a record of bizarre animals, now deader than the dodo, expressed in everlasting stone.

But the record-taking had come to an abrupt halt one day and darkness had descended. This, too, was recorded in stone – the Gateway of the Sun, that surpassing work of art, had never been

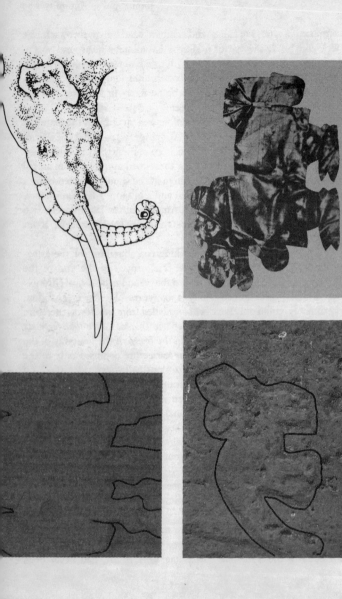

Top left: Detail from Tiahuanaco's Gateway of the Sun showing proboscid, tusked elephant-like figure.
Top right: Biological reconstruction-drawing of *Cuverionius*, a South American proboscid, once common in the Tiahuanaco area but extinct since approximately 10,000 BC. *Above left*: Unidentified animal, possibly *Toxodon*, carved on the side of the Viracocha figure in the Subterranean Temple. *Above right*: Another possible representation of *Toxodon* from Tiahuanaco. The raised nostrils are indicative of a semi-aquatic animal, somewhat like a modern hippopotamus in its habits, which is what *Toxodon* is known to have been.

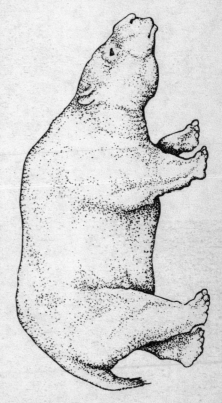

Left: Reconstruction-drawing of *Toxodon*, a South American species that became extinct in the eleventh millennium BC.

completed. Certain unfinished aspects of the frieze made it seem probable that something sudden and dreadful had happened which had caused the sculptor, in the words of Posnansky, 'to drop his chisel for ever' at the moment when he was 'putting the final touches to his work'.[28]

Chapter 12

The End of the Viracochas

We saw in Chapter Ten that Tiahuanaco was originally built as a port on the shores of Lake Titicaca, when that lake was far wider *and more than 100 feet deeper* than it is today. Vast harbour constructions, piers and dykes (and even dumped cargoes of quarried stone at points beneath the old waterline), leave no doubt that this must have been the case.[1] Indeed, according to the unorthodox estimates of Professor Posnansky, Tiahuanaco had been in active use as a port as early as 15,000 BC, the date he proposed for the construction of the Kalasasaya, and had continued to serve as such for approximately another five thousand years, during which great expanse of time its position in relation to the shore of Lake Titicaca hardly changed.[2]

Throughout this epoch the principal harbour of the port city was located several hundred metres south-west of the Kalasasaya at a site now known as *Puma Punku* (literally, the Puma Gate). Here Posnansky's excavations revealed two artificially dredged docks on either side of: 'a true and magnificent pier or wharf ... where hundreds of ships could at the same time take on and unload their heavy burdens'.[3]

One of the construction blocks from which the pier had been fashioned still lay on site and weighed an estimated *440 tons*.[4] Numerous others weighed between 100 and 150 tons.[5] Furthermore, many of the biggest monoliths had clearly been joined to each other by I-shaped metal clamps. In the whole of South America, I knew, this

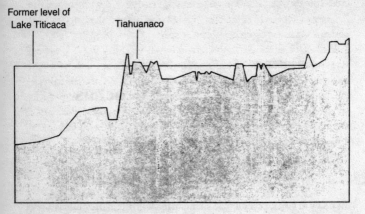

Former level of
Lake Titicaca

Tiahuanaco

12,000 years ago, when Lake Titicaca was more than 100 feet deeper than it is today, Tiahuanaco would have been an island, as shown above.

masonry technique had been found only on Tiahuanacan structures.[6] The last time I had seen the characteristic notched depressions which proved its use had been on ruins on the island of Elephantine in the Nile in Upper Egypt.[7]

Equally thought-provoking was the appearance of the symbol of the cross on many of these ancient blocks. Recurring again and again, particularly at the northern approach to Puma Punku, this symbol always took the same form: a double crucifix with pure clean lines, perfectly balanced and harmonious, deeply recessed into the hard grey stone. Even according to orthodox historical chronology these crosses were not less than 1500 years old. In other words, they had been carved here, by a people with absolutely no knowledge of Christianity, a full millennium before the arrival of the first Spanish missionaries on the Altiplano.

Where, come to that, had the Christians obtained their crosses? Not only from the shape of the structure to which Jesus Christ was nailed, I thought, but from some much older source as well. Hadn't the Ancient Egyptians, for example, used a hieroglyph very like a

cross (the *ankh*, or *crux ansata*) to symbolize life . . . the breath of life
. . . eternal life itself?[8] Had that symbol originated in Egypt, or had it
perhaps occurred elsewhere, earlier still?

With such ideas chasing one another around my head, I walked
slowly around Puma Punku. The extensive perimeter, which formed
a rectangle several hundred feet long, outlined a low pyramidal hill,
much overgrown with tall grass. Dozens and dozens of hulking blocks
lay scattered in all directions, tossed like matchsticks, Posnansky
argued, in the terrible natural disaster that had overtaken Tiahuanaco
during the eleventh millennium BC:

> This catastrophe was caused by seismic movements which resulted in
> an overflow of the waters of Lake Titicaca and in volcanic eruptions
> . . . It is also possible that the temporary increase in the level of the lake
> may have been caused in part by the breaking of the bulwarks on some
> of the lakes further to the north and situated at a greater altitude . . .
> thus releasing the waters which descended toward Lake Titicaca in
> onrushing and unrestrainable torrents.[9]

Posnansky's evidence that a flood had been the agent of the
destruction of Tiahuanaco included

> The discovery of lacustrine flora, *Paludestrina culminea*, and *Paludes-*
> *trina andecola*, *Ancylus titicacensis*, *Planorbis titicacensis*, etc., mixed in
> the alluvia with the skeletons of human beings who perished in the
> cataclysm . . . and the discovery of various skeletons of *Orestias*, fish of
> the family of the present *bogas*, in the same alluvia which contain the
> human remains . . .[10]

In addition, fragments of human and animal skeletons had been found
lying

> in chaotic disorder among wrought stones, utensils, tools and an
> endless variety of other things. All of this has been moved, broken and
> accumulated in a confused heap. Anyone who would dig a trench here
> two metres deep could not deny that the destructive force of water, in
> combination with brusque movements of the earth, must have
> accumulated those different kinds of bones, mixing them with
> pottery, jewels, tools and utensils . . . Layers of alluvium cover the

whole field of the ruins and lacustrine sand mixed with shells from
Titicaca, decomposed feldspar and volcanic ashes have accumulated
in the places surrounded by walls . . .'[11]

It had been a terrible catastrophe indeed that had overwhelmed
Tiahuanaco. And if Posnansky was right, it took place more than
12,000 years ago. Thereafter, though the flood waters subsided, 'the
culture of the Altiplano did not again attain a high point of
development but fell rather into a total and definitive decadence'.[12]

Struggle and abandonment

This process was hastened by the fact that the earthquakes which had
caused Lake Titicaca to engulf Tiahuanaco were only the first of many
upheavals in the area. These initially resulted in the lake swelling and
overflowing its banks but they soon began to have the opposite effect,
slowly reducing Titicaca's depth and surface area. As the years
passed, the lake continued to drain inch by inch, marooning the great
city, remorselessly separating it from the waters which had previously
played such a vital role in its economic life.

At the same time, there was evidence that the climate of the
Tihuanaco area had become colder and much less favourable for the
growing of crops than had previously been the case,[13] so much less
favourable that today staples such as maize cannot ripen properly and
even potatoes come out of the ground stunted.[14]

Although it was difficult to piece together all the different elements
of the complex chain of events that had occurred, it seemed that 'a
period of calm had followed the critical moment of seismic
disturbance' which had temporarily flooded Tiahuanaco.[15] Then,
slowly but surely, 'the climate worsened and became inclement.
Finally there ensued mass emigrations of the Andean peoples towards
locations where the struggle for life would not be so arduous.'[16]

It seems that the highly civilized inhabitants of Tiahuanaco,
remembered in local traditions as 'the Viracocha people', had not
gone without a struggle. There was puzzling evidence from all over
the Altiplano that agricultural experiments of an advanced and

scientific nature had been carried out, with great ingenuity and dedication, to try to compensate for the deterioration of the climate. For example, recent research has demonstrated that astonishingly sophisticated analyses of the chemical compositions of many poisonous high-altitude plants and tubers had been undertaken by *somebody* in this region in the furthest antiquity. Such analyses, furthermore, had been coupled with the invention of detoxification techniques which had rendered these otherwise nutritious vegetables harmless and edible.[17] There was as yet 'no satisfactory explanation for the development of these detoxification processes', admitted David Browman, associate professor of Anthropology at Washington University.[18]

Likewise, in the same ancient period, *somebody* as yet unidentified by scholarship went to great lengths to build raised fields on the newly exposed lands that had so recently been under the waters of the lake – a procedure which created characteristic corrugated strips of alternately high and low ground. It was not until the 1960s that the original function of these undulating patterns of earthen platforms and shallow canals was correctly worked out. Still visible today, and known as *waru waaru* by the local Indians, they proved to be part of a complex agricultural design, perfected in prehistoric times, which had the ability 'to out-perform modern farming techniques'.[19]

In recent years some of the raised fields were reconstructed by archaeologists and agronomists. These experimental plots consistently yielded three times more potatoes than even the most productive conventional plots. Likewise, during one particularly cold spell, a severe frost 'did little damage to the experimental fields'. The following year the crops on the elevated platforms survived an equally ruinous drought: 'then later rode high and dry through a flood that swamped surrounding farmlands'. Indeed this simple but effective agricultural technique, invented by a culture so ancient that no one today could even remember its name, had proved such a success in rural Bolivia that it had attracted the attention of governmental and international development agencies and was now under test in several other parts of the world as well.[20]

An artificial language

Another possible legacy of Tiahuanaco, and of the Viracochas, lay embedded in the language spoken by the local Aymara Indians – a language regarded by some specialists as the oldest in the world.[21]

In the 1980s Ivan Guzman de Rojas, a Bolivian computer scientist, accidentally demonstrated that Aymara might be not only very ancient but, significantly, that it might be a 'made-up' language – something deliberately and skilfully *designed*. Of particular note was the seemingly artificial character of its syntax, which was rigidly structured and unambiguous to an extent thought inconceivable in normal 'organic' speech.[22] This synthetic and highly organized structure meant that Aymara could easily be transformed into a computer algorithm to be used to translate one language into another: 'The Aymara Algorithm is used as a bridge language. The language of an original document is translated into Aymara and then into any number of other languages.'[23]

Was it just coincidence that an apparently artificial language governed by a computer-friendly syntax should be spoken today in the environs of Tiahuanaco? Or could Aymara be a legacy of the high learning that legend attributed to the Viracochas? If so, what other legacies might there be? What other incomplete fragments of an old and forgotten wisdom might be lying scattered around – fragments which had perhaps contributed to the richness and diversity of many of the cultures that had evolved in this region during the 10,000 years before the conquest? Perhaps it was the possession of fragments like these that had made possible the drawing of the Nazca lines and enabled the predecessors of the Incas to build the 'impossible' stone walls at Machu Picchu and Sacsayhuaman?

Mexico

The image I could not get out of my mind was of the Viracocha people leaving, 'walking on the waters' of the Pacific Ocean, or 'going miraculously' by sea as so many of the legends told.

Where had these seafarers been going? What had their objective been? And why, come to think of it, had they made such dogged efforts to stay in Tiahuanaco for so long before admitting defeat and moving on? What had they been trying to achieve there that had been so important to them?

After several weeks work on the Altiplano, travelling back and forth between La Paz and Tiahuanaco, it became clear that neither the otherworldly ruins nor the libraries of the capital were going to provide me with any further answers. Indeed, in Bolivia at least, the trail seemed to have gone cold.

It was not until I reached Mexico, 2000 miles north, that I picked up its traces again.

Part III

Plumed Serpent:
Central America

'If the victim's heart was to be taken out,' reported one Spanish observer in the sixteenth century,

> they conducted him with great display . . . and placed him on the sacrificial stone. Four of them took hold of his arms and legs, spreading them out. Then the executioner came, with a flint knife in his hand, and with great skill made an incision between the ribs on the left side, below the nipple; then he plunged in his hand and like a ravenous tiger tore out the living heart, which he laid on the plate . . . [3]

What kind of culture could have nourished and celebrated such demonic behaviour? Here, in Chichen Itza, amid ruins dating back more than 1200 years, a hybrid society had formed out of inter-mingled Maya and Toltec elements. This society was by no means exceptional in its addiction to cruel and barbaric ceremonies. On the contrary, *all* the great indigenous civilizations known to have flourished in Mexico had indulged in the ritualized slaughter of human beings.

Slaughterhouses

Villahermosa, Tabasco Province

I stood looking at the Altar of Infant Sacrifice. It was the creation of the Olmecs, the so-called 'mother-culture' of Central America, and it was more than 3000 years old. A block of solid granite about four feet thick, its sides bore reliefs of four men wearing curious head-dresses. Each man carried a healthy, chubby, struggling infant, whose desperate fear was clearly visible. The back of the altar was undecorated; at the front another figure was portrayed, holding in his arms, as though it were an offering, the slumped body of a dead child.

The Olmecs are the earliest recognized high civilization of Ancient Mexico, and human sacrifice was well established with them. Two and a half thousand years later, at the time of the Spanish conquest, the Aztecs were the last (but by no means the least) of the peoples of this region to continue an extremely old and deeply ingrained tradition.

They did so with fanatical zeal.

It is recorded, for example, that Ahuitzotl, the eighth and most powerful emperor of the Aztec royal dynasty, 'celebrated the dedication of the temple of Huitzilopochtli in Tenochitlan by marshalling four lines of prisoners past teams of priests who worked four days to dispatch them. On this occasion as many as 80,000 were slain during a single ceremonial rite.'[4]

The Aztecs liked to dress up in the flayed skins of sacrificial victims. Bernardino de Sahagun, a Spanish missionary, attended one such ceremony soon after the conquest:

> The celebrants flayed and dismembered the captives; they then lubricated their own naked bodies with grease and slipped into the skin . . . Trailing blood and grease, the gruesomely clad men ran through the city, thus terrifying those they followed . . . The second-day's rite also included a cannibal feast for each warrior's family.[5]

Another mass sacrifice was witnessed by the Spanish chronicler Diego de Duran. In this instance the victims were so numerous that when the streams of blood running down the temple steps 'reached bottom and cooled they formed fat clots, enough to terrify anyone'.[6] All in all, it has been estimated that the number of sacrificial victims in the Aztec empire as a whole had risen to around 250,000 a year by the beginning of the sixteenth century.[7]

What was this manic destruction of human life for? According to the Aztecs themselves, it was done to delay the coming of the end of the world.[8]

Children of the Fifth Sun

Like the many different peoples and cultures that had preceded them in Mexico, the Aztecs believed that the universe operated in great cycles. The priests stated as a matter of simple fact that there had been four such cycles, or 'Suns', since the creation of the human race. At the time of the conquest, it was the Fifth Sun that prevailed. And it is within that same Fifth Sun, or epoch, that humankind still lives today. This account is taken from a rare collection of Aztec documents known as the *Vaticano–Latin Codex*:

> First Sun, *Matlactli Atl*: duration 4008 years. Those who lived then ate water maize called *atzitzintli*. In this age lived the giants . . . The

First Sun was destroyed by water in the sign *Matlactli Atl* (Ten Water). It was called *Apachiohualiztli* (flood, deluge), the art of sorcery of the permanent rain. Men were turned into fish. Some say that only one couple escaped, protected by an old tree living near the water. Others say that there were seven couples who hid in a cave until the flood was over and the waters had gone down. They repopulated the earth and were worshipped as gods in their nations . . .

Second Sun, *Ehecoatl*: duration 4010 years. Those who lived then ate wild fruit known as *acotzintli*. This Sun was destroyed by *Ehecoatl* (Wind Serpent) and men were turned into monkeys . . . One man and one woman, standing on a rock, were saved from destruction . . .

Third Sun, *Tleyquiyahuillo*: duration 4,081 years. Men, the descendants of the couple who were saved from the Second Sun, ate a fruit called *tzincoacoc*. This Third Sun was destroyed by fire . . .

Fourth Sun, *Tzontlilic*: duration 5,026 years . . . Men died of starvation after a deluge of blood and fire . . . [9]

Another 'cultural document' of the Aztecs that has survived the ravages of the conquest is the 'Sun Stone' of Axayacatl, the sixth emperor of the royal dynasty. This huge monolith was hewn out of solid basalt in AD 1479. It weighs 24.5 tons and consists of a series of concentrically inscribed circles, each bearing intricate symbolic statements. As in the codex, these statements focus attention on the belief that the world has already passed through four epochs, or Suns. The first and most remote of these is represented by *Ocelotonatiuh*, the jaguar god: 'During that Sun lived the giants that had been created by the gods but were finally attacked and devoured by jaguars.' The Second Sun is represented by the serpent head of *Ehecoatl*, the god of the air: 'During that period the human race was destroyed by high winds and hurricanes and men were converted into monkeys.' The symbol of the Third Sun is a head of rain and celestial fire: 'In this epoch everything was destroyed by a rain of fire from the sky and the forming of lava. All the houses were burnt. Men were converted into birds to survive the catastrophe.' The Fourth Sun is represented by the head of the water-goddess *Chalchiuhtlicue*: 'Destruction came in the form of torrential rains and floods. The mountains disappeared and men were transformed into fish.' [10]

The symbol of the Fifth Sun, our current epoch, is the face of *Tonatiuh*, the sun god himself. His tongue, fittingly depicted as an obsidian knife, juts out hungrily, signalling his need for the nourishment of human blood and hearts. His features are wrinkled to indicate his advanced age and he appears within the symbol *Ollin* which signifies Movement.[11]

Why is the Fifth Sun known as 'The Sun of Movement'? Because, 'the elders say: in it there will be a movement of the earth and from this we shall all perish.'[12]

And when will this catastrophe strike? Soon, according to the Aztec priests. They believed that the Fifth Sun was already very old and approaching the end of its cycle (hence the wrinkles on the face of Tonatiuh). Ancient meso-American traditions dated the birth of this epoch to a remote period corresponding to the fourth millennium BC of the Christian calendar.[13] The method of calculating its end, however, had been forgotten by the time of Aztecs.[14] In the absence of this essential information, human sacrifices were apparently carried out in the hope that the impending catastrophe might be postponed. Indeed, the Aztecs came to regard themselves as a chosen people; they were convinced that they had been charged with a divine mission to wage war and offer the blood of their captives to feed Tonatiuh, thereby preserving the life of the Fifth Sun.[15]

Stuart Fiedel, an authority on the prehistory of the Americas, summed up the whole issue in these words: 'The Aztecs believed that to prevent the destruction of the universe, which had already occurred four times in the past, the gods must be supplied with a steady diet of human hearts and blood.'[16] This same belief, with remarkably few variations, was shared by all the great civilizations of Central America. Unlike the Aztecs, however, some of the earlier peoples had calculated *exactly* when a great movement of the earth could be expected to bring the Fifth Sun to an end.

Lightbringer

No documents, only dark and menacing sculptures, have come down to us from the Olmec era. But the Mayas, justifiably regarded as the greatest ancient civilization to have arisen in the New World, left behind a wealth of calendrical records. Expressed in terms of the modern dating system, these enigmatic inscriptions convey a rather curious message: the Fifth Sun, it seems, is going to come to an end on 23 December, AD 2012.[17]

In the rational intellectual climate of the late twentieth century it is unfashionable to take doomsday prophecies seriously. The general consensus is that they are the products of superstitious minds and can safely be ignored. As I travelled around Mexico, however, I was from time to time bothered by a nagging intuition that the voices of the ancient sages might deserve a hearing after all. I mean, suppose by some crazy offchance they weren't the superstitious savages we'd always believed them to be? Suppose they knew something we didn't? Most pertinent of all, suppose that their projected date for the end of the Fifth Sun turned out to be correct? Suppose, in other words, that some truly awful geological catastrophe is already unfolding, deep in the bowels of the earth, as the wise men of the Maya predicted?

In Peru and Bolivia I had become aware of the obsessive concern with the calculation of time shown by the Incas and their predecessors. Now, in Mexico, I discovered that the Maya, who believed that they had worked out the date of the end of the world, had been possessed by the same compulsion. Indeed, for these people, just about everything boiled down to numbers, the passage of the years and the manifestations of events. The belief was that if the numbers which lay beneath the manifestations could be properly understood, it would be possible to predict successfully the timing of the events themselves.[18] I felt disinclined to ignore the obvious implications of the recurrent destructions of humanity depicted so vividly in the Central American traditions. Coming complete with giants and floods, these traditions were eerily similar to those of the far-off Andean region.

Meanwhile, however, I was keen to pursue another, related line of inquiry. This concerned the bearded white-skinned deity named Quetzalcoatl, who was believed to have sailed to Mexico from across the seas in remote antiquity. Quetzalcoatl was credited with the invention of the advanced mathematical and calendrical formulae that the Maya were later to use to calculate the date of doomsday.[19] He also bore a striking resemblance to Viracocha, the pale god of the Andes, who came to Tiahuanaco 'in the time of darkness' bearing the gifts of light and civilization.

Chapter 14

People of the Serpent

After spending so long immersed in the traditions of Viracocha, the bearded god of the distant Andes, I was intrigued to discover that Quetzalcoatl, the principal deity of the ancient Mexican pantheon, was described in terms that were extremely familiar.

For example, one pre-Colombian myth collected in Mexico by the sixteenth-century Spanish chronicler Juan de Torquemada asserted that Quetzalcoatl was 'a fair and ruddy complexioned man with a long beard'. Another spoke of him as, '*era Hombre blanco*; a large man, broad browed, with huge eyes, long hair, and a great, rounded beard – *la barba grande y redonda*'[1] Another still described him as

> a mysterious person . . . a white man with strong formation of body, broad forehead, large eyes, and a flowing beard. He was dressed in a long, white robe reaching to his feet. He condemned sacrifices, except of fruits and flowers, and was known as the god of peace . . . When addressed on the subject of war he is reported to have stopped up his ears with his fingers.[2]

According to a particularly striking Central American tradition, this 'wise instructor . . . '

> came from across the sea in a boat that moved by itself without paddles. He was a tall, bearded white man who taught people to use fire for cooking. He also built houses and showed couples that they

could live together as husband and wife; and since people often quarreled in those days, he taught them to live in peace.[3]

Viracocha's Mexican twin

The reader will recall that Viracocha, in his journeys through the Andes, went by several different aliases. Quetzalcoatl did this too. In some parts of Central America (notably among the Quiche Maya) he was called Gucumatz. Elsewhere, at Chichen Itza for example, he was known as Kukulkan. When both these words were translated into English, they turned out to mean exactly the same thing: Plumed (or Feathered) Serpent. This, also, was the meaning of Quetzalcoatl.[4]

There were other deities, among the Maya in particular, whose identities seemed to merge closely with those of Quetzalcoatl. One was Votan, a great civilizer, who was also described as pale-skinned, bearded and wearing a long robe. Scholars could offer no translation for his name but his principal symbol, like that of Quetzalcoatl, was a serpent.[5] Another closely related figure was Izamana, the Mayan god of healing, who was a robed and bearded individual; his symbol, too, was the rattlesnake.[6]

What emerged from all this, as the leading authorities agreed, was that the Mexican legends collected and passed on by Spanish chroniclers at the time of the conquest were often the confused and conflated products of extremely long oral traditions. Behind them all, however, it seemed that there must lie some solid historical reality. In the judgement of Sylvanus Griswold Morley, the doyen of Maya studies:

> The great god Kukulkan, or Feathered Serpent, was the Mayan counterpart of the Aztec Quetzalcoatl, the Mexican god of light, learning and culture. In the Maya pantheon he was regarded as having been the great organizer, the founder of cities, the former of laws and the teacher of the calendar. Indeed his attributes and life history are so human that it is not improbable that he may have been an actual historical character, some great lawgiver and organizer, the memory of whose benefactions lingered long after death, and whose personality was eventually deified.[7]

All the legends stated unambiguously that Quetzalcoatl/Kukulkan/

Gucumatz/Votan/Izamana had arrived in Central America from somewhere very far away (across the 'Eastern Sea') and that amid great sadness he had eventually sailed off again in the direction whence he had come.[8] The legends added that he had promised solemnly that he would return one day[9] – a clear echo of Viracocha it would be almost perverse to ascribe to coincidence. In addition, it will be recalled that Viracocha's departure across the waves of the Pacific Ocean had been portrayed in the Andean traditions as a miraculous event. Quetzalcoatl's departure from Mexico also had a strange feel about it: he was said to have sailed away 'on a raft of serpents'.[10]

All in all, I felt Morley was right in looking for a factual historical background behind the Mayan and Mexican myths. What the traditions seemed to indicate was that the bearded pale-skinned foreigner called Quetzalcoatl (or Kukulkan or whatever) had been not just one person but probably several people who had come from the same place and had belonged to the same distinctively non-Indian ethnic type (bearded, white-skinned, etc.). This wasn't only suggested by the existence of a 'family' of obviously related[11] but slightly different gods sharing the symbol of the snake. Quetzalcoatl/Kukulkan/Izamana was quite explicitly portrayed in many of the Mexican and Mayan accounts as having been accompanied by 'attendants' or 'assistants'.

Certain myths set out in the Ancient Mayan religious texts known as the Books of Chilam Balam, for instance, reported that 'the first inhabitants of Yucatan were the "People of the Serpent". They came from the east in boats across the water with their leader Itzamana, "Serpent of the East", a healer who could cure by laying on hands, and who revived the dead.'[12]

'Kukulkan,' stated another tradition, 'came with nineteen companions, two of whom were gods of fish, two others gods of agriculture, and a god of thunder . . . They stayed ten years in Yucatan. Kukulkan made wise laws and then set sail and disappeared in the direction of the rising sun . . . [13]

According to the Spanish chronicler Las Casas: 'The natives affirmed that in ancient times there came to Mexico twenty men, the chief of whom was called Kukulkan . . . They wore flowing robes and sandals on their feet, they had long beards and their heads were bare . . . Kukulkan instructed the people in the arts of peace, and caused various important edifices to be built . . .'[14]

Meanwhile Juan de Torquemada recorded this very specific pre-conquest tradition concerning the imposing strangers who had entered Mexico with Quetzalcoatl:

> They were men of good carriage, well-dressed, in long robes of black linen, open in front, and without capes, cut low at the neck, with short sleeves that did not come to the elbow . . . These followers of Quetzalcoatl were men of great knowledge and cunning artists in all kinds of fine work.[15]

Like some long-lost twin of Viracocha, the white and bearded Andean deity, Quetzalcoatl was depicted as having brought to Mexico all the skills and sciences necessary to create a civilized life, thus ushering in a golden age.[16] He was believed, for example, to have introduced the knowledge of writing to Central America, to have invented the calendar, and to have been a master builder who taught the people the secrets of masonry and architecture. He was the father of mathematics, metallurgy, and astronomy and was said to have 'measured the earth'. He also founded productive agriculture, and was reported to have discovered and introduced corn – literally the staff of life in these ancient lands. A great doctor and master of medicines, he was the patron of healers and diviners 'and disclosed to the people the mysteries of the properties of plants'. In addition, he was revered as a lawgiver, as a protector of craftsmen, and as a patron of all the arts.

As might be expected of such a refined and cultured individual he forbade the grisly practice of human sacrifice during the period of his ascendancy in Mexico. After his departure the bloodspattered rituals were reintroduced with a vengeance. Nevertheless, even the Aztecs, the most vehement sacrificers ever to have existed in the long history of Central America, remembered 'the time of Quetzalcoatl' with a kind of nostalgia. 'He was a teacher,' recalled one legend, 'who taught that no living thing was to be harmed and that sacrifices were to be made not of human beings but of birds and butterflies.'[17]

Cosmic struggle

Why did Quetzalcoatl go away? What went wrong?

Mexican legends provided answers to these questions. They said that the enlightened and benevolent rule of the Plumed Serpent had been brought to an end by Tezcatilpoca, a malevolent god whose name meant 'Smoking Mirror' and whose cult demanded human sacrifice. It seemed that a near-cosmic struggle between the forces of light and darkness had taken place in Ancient Mexico, and that the forces of darkness had triumphed . . .

The supposed stage for these events, now known as Tula, was not believed to be particularly old – not much more than 1000 years anyway – but the legends surrounding it linked it to an infinitely more distant epoch. In those times, outside history, it had been known as Tollan. All the traditions agreed that it had been at Tollan that Tezcatilpoca had vanquished Quetzalcoatl and forced him to quit Mexico.

Fire serpents

Tula, Hidalgo Province
I was sitting on the flat square summit of the unimaginatively named Pyramid B. The late-afternoon sun was beating down out of a clear blue sky, and I was facing south, looking around.

At the base of the pyramid, to the north and east, were murals depicting jaguars and eagles feasting on human hearts. Immediately behind me were ranged four pillars and four fearsome granite idols each nine feet tall. Ahead and, to my left lay the partially unexcavated Pyramid C, a cactus-covered mound about 40 feet high, and farther away were more mounds not yet investigated by archaeologists. To my right was a ball court. In that long, I-shaped arena, terrible gladitorial games had been staged in ancient times. Teams, or sometimes just two individuals pitted against each other, would compete for possession of a rubber ball; the losers were decapitated.

The idols on the platform behind me had a solemn and intimidating aura. I stood up to look at them more closely. Their sculptor had given them hard, implacable faces, hooked noses and

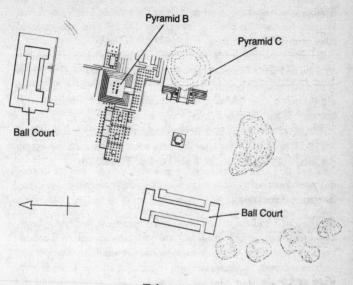

Tula.

hollow eyes and they seemed without sympathy or emotion. What interested me most, however, was not so much their ferocious appearance as the objects that they clutched in their hands. Archaeologists admitted that they didn't really know what these objects were but had tentatively identified them anyway. This identification had stuck and it was now received wisdom that spearthrowers called *atl-atls* were held in the right hands of the idols and 'spears or arrows and incense bags' in the left hands.[18] It didn't seem to matter that the objects did not in any way resemble *atl-atls*, spears, arrows, or incense bags.

Santha Faiia's photographs will help the reader to form his or her own impression of these peculiar objects. As I studied the objects themselves I had the distinct sense that they were meant to represent devices which had originally been made out of metal. The right-hand device, which seemed to emerge from a sheath or hand-guard, was lozenge-shaped with a curved lower edge. The left-hand device could have been an instrument or weapon of some kind.

I remembered legends which related that the gods of ancient Mexico had armed themselves with *xiuhcoatl*, 'fire serpents'.[19] These apparently emitted burning rays capable of piercing and dismembering human bodies.[20] Was it 'fire serpents' that the Tula idols were holding? What, for that matter, were fire serpents?

Whatever they were, both devices looked like pieces of technology. And both in certain ways resembled the equally mysterious objects in the hands of the idols in the Kalasasaya at Tiahuanaco.

Serpent Sanctuary

Santha and I had come to Tula/Tollan because it had been closely associated both with Quetzalcoatl and with his arch-enemy Tezcatilpoca, the Smoking Mirror.[21] Ever-young, omnipotent, omnipresent and omniscient, Tezcatilpoca was associated in the legends with night, darkness and the sacred jaguar.[22] He was 'invisible and implacable, appearing to men sometimes as a flying shadow, sometimes as a dreadful monster'.[23] Often depicted as a glaring skull, he was said to have been the owner of a mysterious object, the Smoking Mirror after which he was named, which he made use of to observe from afar the activities of men and gods. Scholars quite reasonably suppose that it must have been a primitive obsidian scrying stone: 'Obsidian had an especial sanctity for the Mexicans, as it provided the sacrificial knives employed by the priests . . . Bernal Diaz [Spanish chronicler] states that they called this stone "Tezcat". From it mirrors were also manufactured as divinatory media to be used by wizards.'[24]

Representing the forces of darkness and rapacious evil, Tezcatilpoca was said in the legends to have been locked in a conflict with Quetzalcoatl that had continued over an immense span of years.[25] At certain times one seemed to be gaining the upper hand, at certain times the other. Finally the cosmic struggle came to an end when good was vanquished by evil and Quetzalcoatl driven out from Tollan.[26]

Thereafter, under the influence of Tezcatilpoca's nightmarish cult, human sacrifice was reintroduced throughout Central America.

As we have seen, Quetzalcoatl was believed to have fled to the coast and to have been carried away on a raft of serpents. One legend says, 'He burned his houses, built of silver and shells, buried his treasure, and set sail on the Eastern Sea preceded by his attendants who had been changed into bright birds.'[27]

This poignant moment of departure was supposedly staged at a place called Coatzacoalos, meaning 'Serpent Sanctuary'.[28] There, before taking his leave, Quetzalcoatl promised his followers he would return one day to overthrow the cult of Tezcatilpoca and to inaugurate an era when the gods would again 'accept sacrifices of flowers' and cease their clamour for human blood.[29]

Chapter 15

Mexican Babel

We drove south-east from Tula, by-passing Mexico City on an anarchic series of fast freeways that dragged us through the creeping edge of the capital's eye-watering, lung-searing pollution. Our route then took us up over pine-covered mountains, past the snowy peak of Popocatepetl and thence along tree-lined lanes amid fields and farmsteads.

In the late afternoon we arrived at Cholula, a sleepy town with 11,000 inhabitants and a spacious main square. After turning east through the narrow streets, we crossed a railway line and pulled to a halt in the shadow of *tlahchiualtepetl*, the 'man-made mountain' we had come here to see.

Once sacred to the peaceful cult of Quetzalcoatl, but now surmounted by an ornate Catholic church, this immense edifice was ranked among the most extensive and ambitious engineering projects ever undertaken anywhere in the ancient world. Indeed, with a base area of 45 acres and a height of 210 feet, it was three times more massive than the Great Pyramid of Egypt.[1] Though its contours were now blurred by age and its sides overgrown with grass, it was still possible to recognize that it had once been an imposing ziggurat which had risen up towards the heavens in four clean-angled 'steps'. Measuring almost half a kilometre along each side at its base, it had also succeeded in preserving a dignified but violated beauty.

The past, though often dry and dusty, is rarely dumb. Sometimes it can speak with passion. It seemed to me that it did so here, bearing witness to the physical and psychological degradation visited upon the native peoples of Mexico when the Spanish *conquistador* Hernan Cortez almost casually 'beheaded a culture as a passer-by might sweep off the head of a sunflower'.[2] In Cholula, a great centre of pilgrimage with a population of around 100,000 at the time of the conquest, this decapitation of ancient traditions and ways of life required that something particularly humiliating be done to the man-made mountain of Quetzalcoatl. The solution was to smash and desecrate the temple which had once stood on the summit of the ziggurat and replace it with a church.

Cortez and his men were few, the Cholulans were many. When they marched into town, however, the Spaniards had one major advantage: bearded and pale-skinned, dressed in shining armour, they looked like the fulfilment of a prophecy – had it not always been promised that Quetzalcoatl, the Plumed Serpent, would return 'from across the Eastern Sea' with his band of followers?[3]

Because of this expectation, the naive and trusting Cholulans permitted the *conquistadores* to climb the steps of the ziggurat and enter the great courtyard of the temple. There troupes of gaily bedecked dancing girls greeted them, singing and playing on instruments, while stewards moved back and forth with heaped platters of bread and delicate cooked meats.

One of the Spanish chroniclers, an eyewitness to the events that followed, reported that adoring townsfolk of all ranks 'unarmed, with eager and happy faces, crowded in to hear what the white men would say'. Realizing from this incredible reception that their intentions were not suspected, the Spaniards closed and guarded all the entrances, drew their weapons of steel and murdered their hosts.[4] Six thousand died in this horrible massacre[5] which matched, in its savagery, the most bloodstained rituals of the Aztecs: 'Those of Cholula were caught unawares. With neither arrows nor shields did they meet the Spaniards. Just so they were slain without warning. They were killed by pure treachery.'[6]

It was ironic, I thought, that the *conquistadores* in both Peru and Mexico should have benefited in the same way from local legends that prophesied the return of a pale, bearded god. If that god was indeed a deified human, as seemed likely, he must have been a person of high civilization and exemplary character – or more probably two different people from the same background, one working in Mexico and providing the model for Quetzalcoatl, the other in Peru being the model for Viracocha. The superficial resemblance that the Spanish bore to those earlier fair-skinned foreigners opened many doors that would otherwise certainly have been closed. Unlike their wise and benevolent predecessors, however, Pizarro in the Andes and Cortez in Central America were ravening wolves. They ate up the lands and the peoples and the cultures they had seized upon. They destroyed almost everything . . .

Tears for the past

Their eyes scaled with ignorance, bigotry and greed, the Spanish erased a precious heritage of mankind when they arrived in Mexico. In so doing they deprived the future of any detailed knowledge concerning the brilliant and remarkable civilizations which once flourished in Central America.

What, for example, was the true history of the glowing 'idol' that rested in a sacred sanctuary in the Mixtec capital Achiotlan? We know of this curious object through the writings of a sixteenth-century eyewitness, Father Burgoa:

> The material was of marvellous value, for it was an emerald of the size of a thick pepper-pod [capsicum], upon which a small bird was engraved with the greatest skill, and, with the same skill, a small serpent coiled ready to strike. The stone was so transparent that it shone from its interior with the brightness of a candle flame. It was a very old jewel, and there is no tradition extant concerning the origin of its veneration and worship.[7]

What might we learn if we could examine this 'very old' jewel today? And how *old* was it really? We shall never find out because Fr Benito, the first missionary of Achiotlan, seized the stone from the Indians: 'He had it ground up, although a Spaniard offered three thousand ducats for it, stirred the powder in water, poured it upon the earth and trod upon it . . .'[8]

Equally typical of the profligate squandering of the intellectual riches concealed in the Mexican past was the shared fate of two gifts given to Cortez by the Aztec emperor Montezuma. These were circular calendars, as big as cartwheels, one of solid silver, and the other of solid gold. Both were elaborately engraved with beautiful hieroglyphs which may have contained material of great interest. Cortez had them melted down for ingots on the spot.[9]

More systematically, all over Central America, vast repositories of knowledge accumulated since ancient times were painstakingly gathered, heaped up and burned by zealous friars. In July 1562, for example, in the main square of Mani (just south of modern Merida in Yucatan Province) Fr Diego de Landa burned thousands of Maya codices, story paintings and hieroglyphs inscribed on rolled-up deer skins. He also destroyed countless 'idols' and 'altars', all of which he described as 'works of the devil, designed by the evil one to delude the Indians and to prevent them from accepting Christianity . . .'[10] Elsewhere he elaborated on the same theme:

> We found great numbers of books [written in the characters of the Indians] but as they contained nothing but superstitions and falsehoods of the devil we burned them all, which the natives took most grievously, and which gave them great pain.[11]

Not only the 'natives' should have felt this pain but anyone and everyone – then and now – who would like to know the truth about the past.

Many other 'men of God', some even more ruthlessly efficient than Diego de Landa, participated in Spain's satanic mission to wipe clear the memory banks of Central America. Notable among these was Juan de Zumarraga, Bishop of Mexico, who boasted of having destroyed 20,000 idols and 500 Indian temples. In November 1530 he burned a Christianized Aztec aristocrat at the stake for having allegedly reverted to worship of the 'rain-god' and later, in the market-place at Texcoco, built a vast bonfire of astronomical documents, paintings, manuscripts and hieroglyphic texts which the *conquistadores* had forcibly extracted from the Aztecs during the previous eleven years.[12] As this irreplaceable storehouse of knowledge and history went up in flames, a chance to shake off at least some of the collective amnesia that clouds our understanding was lost to mankind for ever.

What remains to us of the written records of the ancient peoples of Central America? The answer, thanks to the Spanish, is less than twenty original codices and scrolls. [13]

We know from hearsay that many of the documents which the friars reduced to ashes contained 'records of ages past'.[14]

What did those lost records say? what secrets did they hold?

Gigantic men of deformed stature

Even while the the orgy of book-burning was still going on, some Spaniards began to realize that 'a truly great civilization had once existed in Mexico prior to the Aztecs'.[15] Oddly enough, one of the first to act on this realization was Diego de Landa. He appears to have undergone 'Damascus-road experience' after staging his *auto-da-fé* at Mani. In later years, determined to save what he could of the ancient wisdom he had once played such a large part in destroying, he became an assiduous gatherer of the traditions and oral histories of the native peoples of the Yucatan.[16]

Bernardino de Sahagun, a Franciscan friar, was a chronicler to whom we owe much. A great linguist, he is reported to have 'sought out the most learned and often the oldest natives, and asked each to paint in his Aztec picture writing as much as he could clearly remember of Aztec history, religion and legend'.[17] In this way Sahagun was able to accumulate detailed information on the anthropology, mythology and social history of ancient Mexico, which he later set down in a learned twelve-volume work. This was suppressed by the Spanish authorities. Fortunately one copy has survived, though it is incomplete.

Diego de Duran, a conscientious and courageous collector of indigenous traditions, was yet another Franciscan who fought to recover the lost knowledge of the past. He visited Cholula in AD 1585, a time of rapid and catastrophic change. There he interviewed a venerated elder of the town, said to have been more than one hundred years old, who told him this story about the making of the great ziggurat:

> In the beginning, before the light of the sun had been created, this place, Cholula, was in obscurity and darkness; all was a plain, without

hill or elevation, encircled in every part by water, without tree or created thing. Immediately after the light and the sun arose in the east there appeared gigantic men of deformed stature who possessed the land. Enamoured of the light and beauty of the sun they determined to build a tower so high that its summit should reach the sky. Having collected materials for the purpose they found a very adhesive clay and bitumen with which they speedily commenced to build the tower . . .
And having reared it to the greatest possible altitude, so that it reached the sky, the Lord of the Heavens, enraged, said to the inhabitants of the sky, 'Have you observed how they of the earth have built a high and haughty tower to mount hither, being enamoured of the light of the sun and his beauty? Come and confound them, because it is not right that they of the earth, living in the flesh, should mingle with us.' Immediately the inhabitants of the sky sallied forth like flashes of lightning; they destroyed the edifice and divided and scattered its builders to all parts of the earth.[18]

It was this story, almost but not quite the biblical account of the Tower of Babel (which was itself a reworking of a far older Mesopotamian tradition), that had brought me to Cholula.

The Central American and Middle Eastern tales were obviously closely related. Indeed, the similarities were unmissable, but there were also differences far too significant to be ignored. Of course, the similarities could be due to unrecorded pre-Colombian contacts between the cultures of the Middle East and the New World, but there was one way to explain the similarities *and* the differences in a single theory. Suppose that the two versions of the legend had evolved separately for several thousands of years, but prior to that both had descended from the same remotely ancient ancestor?

Remnants

Here's what the *Book of Genesis* says about the 'tower that reached to heaven':

Throughout the earth men spoke the same language, with the same vocabulary. Now as they moved eastwards they found a plain in the land of Shinar, where they settled. There they said to one another, 'Come, let us make bricks and bake them in the fire.' For stone they used bricks and for mortar they used bitumen. 'Come,' they said, 'let us build ourselves a town and a tower with its top reaching heaven. Let us make a name for ourselves, so that we may not be scattered about the entire earth.'

Now Yahewh [the Hebrew God] came down to see the town and the tower that the sons of man had built. 'So they are all a single people with a single language!' said Yahweh. 'This is but the start of their undertakings! There will be nothing too hard for them to do. Come, let us go down and confuse their language on the spot so that they can no longer understand one another.'

Yahweh scattered them thence over the whole face of the earth, and they stopped building the tower. It was named Babel, therefore, because there Yahweh confused the language of the whole earth. It was from there that Yahweh scattered them over the whole face of the earth.[19]

The verse which most interested me suggested very clearly that the ancient builders of the Tower of Babel had set out to create a lasting monument to themselves so that their name would not be forgotten – even if their civilization and language were. Was it possible that the same considerations could have applied at Cholula?

Only a handful of monuments in Mexico were thought by archaeologists to be more than 2000 years old. Cholula was definitely one of them. Indeed no one could say for sure in what distant age its ramparts had first begun to be heaped up. For thousands of years before development and extension of the site began in earnest around 300 BC, it looked as though some other, older structure might have been positioned at the spot over which the great ziggurat of Quetzalcoatl now rose.

There was a precedent for this which further strengthened the intriguing possibility that the remnants of a truly ancient civilization might still be lying around in Central America waiting to be recognized. For example, just south of the university campus of Mexico City, off the main road connecting the capital to Cuernavaca, stands a circular step pyramid of great complexity (with four galleries and a central staircase). It was partially excavated in the 1920s from beneath a mantle of lava. Geologists were called to the site to help date the lava, and carried out a detailed examination. To everyone's surprise, they concluded that the volcanic eruption which had completely buried three sides of this pyramid (and had then gone on to cover about sixty square miles of the surrounding territory) must have taken place *at least seven thousand years ago*.[20]

This geological evidence seems to have been ignored by historians and archaeologists, who do not believe that any civilization capable of building a pyramid could have existed in Mexico at such an early date. It is worth noting, however, that Byron Cummings, the American archaeologist who originally excavated the site for the National Geographical Society, was convinced by clearly demarcated stratification layers above and below the pyramid (laid down both before and after the volcanic eruption) that it was 'the oldest temple yet uncovered on the American continent'. He went further than the geologists and stated categorically that this temple 'fell into ruins some 8500 years ago'.[21]

Pyramids upon pyramids

Going inside the Cholula pyramid really did feel like entering a man-made mountain. The tunnels (and there were more than six miles of them) were not old: they had been left behind by the teams of archaeologists who had burrowed here diligently from 1931 until funds ran out in 1966. Somehow, these narrow, low-ceilinged corridors had borrowed an atmosphere of antiquity from the vast structure all around them. Moist and cool, they offered an inviting and secretive darkness.

Following a ribbon of torchlight we walked deeper inside the pyramid. The archaeological excavations had revealed that it was not the product of one dynasty (as was thought to have been the case with the pyramids at Giza in Egypt), but that it had been built up over a very long period period of time – two thousand years or so, at a conservative estimate. In other words it was a collective project, created by an inter-generational labour force drawn from the many different cultures, Olmec, Teotihuacan, Toltec, Zapotec, Mixtec, Cholulan and Aztec, that had passed through Cholula since the dawn of civilization in Mexico.[22]

Though it was not known who had been the first builders here, as far as it had been possible to establish the earliest major edifice on the site consisted of a tall conical pyramid, shaped like an upturned bucket, flattened at the summit where a temple had stood. Much later a second, similar structure was imposed on top of this primordial mound, i.e. a second inverted bucket of clay, and compacted stone was placed directly over the first, raising the temple platform to more than 200 feet above the surrounding plain. Thereafter, during the next fifteen hundred years or so, an estimated four or five other cultures contributed to the final appearance of the monument. This they did by extending its base in several stages, but never again by increasing its maximum height. In this way, almost as though a master plan were being implemented, the man-made mountain of Cholula gradually attained its characteristic, four-tier ziggurat shape. Today, its sides at the base are each almost 1500 feet long – about twice the length of the sides of the Great Pyramid at Giza – and its total volume has been estimated at a staggering three million cubic metres.[23] This makes it, as one authority succinctly states, 'the largest building ever erected on earth.'[24]

Why?

Why go to all that trouble?

What sort of name for themselves were the peoples of Central America trying to make?

Walking through the network of corridors and passageways, inhaling the cool, loamy air, I was uncomfortably conscious of the great weight and mass of the pyramid pressing down upon me. It was *the largest building in the world* and it had been placed here in honour of a Central American deity of whom almost nothing was known.

We had the *conquistadores* and the Catholic Church to thank for leaving us so deeply in the dark about the true story of Quetzalcoatl and his followers. The smashing and desecration of his ancient temple at Cholula, the destruction of idols, altars and calendars, and the great bonfires made out of codices, paintings and hieroglyphic scrolls, had succeeded almost completely in silencing the voices of the past. But the legends did offer us one graphic and powerful piece of imagery: a memory of the 'gigantic men of deformed stature' who were said to have been the original builders.

Chapter 16

Serpent Sanctuary

From Cholula we drove east, past the prosperous cities of Puebla, Orizaba and Cordoba, towards Veracruz and the Gulf of Mexico. We crossed the mist-enshrouded peaks of the Sierra Madre Oriental, where the air was thin and cold, and then descended towards sea level on to tropical plains overgrown with lush plantations of palms and bananas. We were heading into the heartlands of Mexico's oldest and most mysterious civilization: that of the so-called Olmecs, whose name meant 'rubber people'.

Dating back to the second millennium BC, the Olmecs had ceased to exist fifteen hundred years before the rise of the Aztec empire. The Aztecs, however, had preserved haunting traditions concerning them and were even responsible for naming them after the rubber-producing area of Mexico's gulf coast where they were believed to have lived.[1] This area lies between modern Veracruz in the west and Ciudad del Carmen in the east. In it the Aztecs found a number of ancient ritual objects produced by the Olmecs. and for reasons unknown they collected these objects and placed them in positions of importance in their own temples.[2]

Looking at my map, I could see the blue line of the Coatzecoalcos River running into the Gulf of Mexico more or less at the midpoint of the legendary Olmec homeland. The oil industry proliferates here now, where rubber trees once flourished, transforming a tropical paradise into something resembling the lowest circle of Dante's

Inferno. Since the oil boom of 1973 the town of Coatzecoalcos, once easy-going but not very prosperous, had mushroomed into a transport and refining centre with air-conditioned hotels and a population of half a million. It lay close to the black heart of an industrial wasteland in which virtually everything of archaeological interest that had escaped the depredations of the Spanish at the time of the conquest had been destroyed by the voracious expansion of the oil business. It was therefore no longer possible, on the basis of hard evidence, to confirm or deny the intriguing suggestion that the legends seemed to make: that something of great importance must once have occurred here.

I remembered that Coatzecoalcos meant 'Serpent Sanctuary'. It was here, in remote antiquity, that Quetzalcoatl and his companions were said to have landed when they first reached Mexico, arriving from across the sea in vessels 'with sides that shone like the scales of serpents' skins'.[3] And it was from here too that Quetzalcoatl was believed to have sailed (on his raft of serpents) when he left Central America. Serpent Sanctuary, moreover, was beginning to look like the *name* for the Olmec homeland, which had included not only Coatzecoalcos but several other sites in areas less blighted by development.

First at Tres Zapotes, west of Coatzecoalcos, and then at San Lorenzo and La Venta, south and east of it, numerous pieces of characteristically Olmec sculpture had been unearthed. All were monoliths carved out of basalt and similarly durable materials. Some took the form of gigantic heads weighing up to thirty tons. Others were massive stelae engraved with encounter scenes apparently involving two distinct races of mankind, neither of them American–Indian.

Whoever had produced these outstanding works of art had obviously belonged to a refined, well organized, prosperous and technologically advanced civilization. The problem was that absolutely nothing remained, except the works of art, from which anything could be deduced about the character and origins of that civilization. All that seemed clear was that 'the Olmecs' (the archaeologists were happy to accept the Aztec designation) had

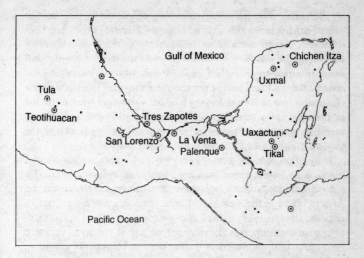

The Olmec sites of Tres Zapotes, San Lorenzo and La Venta along the
Gulf of Mexico, with other Central American archaeological sites.

materialized in Central America around 1500 BC with their sophisticated culture fully evolved.

Santiago Tuxtla

We passed the night at the fishing port of Alvarado and continued our
journey east the next day. The road we were following wound in and
out of fertile hills and valleys, giving us occasional views of the Gulf of
Mexico before turning inland. We passed green meadows filled with
flame trees, and little villages nestled in grassy hollows. Here and
there we saw private gardens where hulking pigs grubbed amongst
piles of domestic refuse. Then we crested the brow of a hill and looked
out across a giant vista of fields and forests bound only by the morning
haze and the faint outlines of distant mountains.

Some miles farther on we dropped into a hollow; at its bottom lay
the old colonial town of Santiago Tuxtla. The place was a riot of

colour: garish shop-fronts, red-tile roofs, yellow straw hats, coconut palms, banana trees, kids in bright clothes. Several of the shops and cafés were playing music from loudspeakers. In the Zocalo, the main square, the air was thick with humidity and the fluttering wings and songs of bright-eyed tropical birds. A leafy little park occupied the centre of this square, and in the centre of the park, like some magic talisman, stood an enormous grey boulder, almost ten feet tall, carved in the shape of a helmeted African head. Full-lipped and strong-nosed, its eyes serenely closed and its lower jaw resting squarely on the ground, this head had a sombre and patient gravity.

Here, then, was the first mystery of the Olmecs: a monumental piece of sculpture, more than 2000 years old, which portrayed a subject with unmistakable negroid features. There were, of course, no African blacks in the New World 2000 years ago, nor did any arrive until the slave trade began, well after the conquest. There is, however, firm palaeoanthropological evidence that one of the many different migrations into the Americas during the last Ice Age *did* consist of peoples of negroid stock. This migration occurred around 15,000 BC.[4]

Known as the 'Cobata' head after the estate on which it was found, the huge monolith in the Zocalo was the largest of sixteen similar Olmec sculptures so far excavated in Mexico. It was thought to have been carved not long before the time of Christ and weighed more than thirty tons.

Tres Zapotes

From Santiago Tuxtla we drove twenty-five kilometres south-west through wild and lush countryside to Tres Zapotes, a substantial late Olmec centre believed to have flourished between 500 BC and AD 100. Now reduced to a series of mounds scattered across maize fields, the site had been extensively excavated in 1939-40 by the American archaeologist Matthew Stirling.

Historical dogmatists of that period, I remembered, had held tenaciously to the view that the civilization of the Mayas was the oldest in Central America. One could be precise about this, they argued, because the Mayan dot-and-bar calendrical system (which had recently been decoded) made possible accurate dating of huge

numbers of ceremonial inscriptions. The earliest date ever found on a
Mayan site corresponded to AD 228 of the Christian calendar.[5] It
therefore came as quite a jolt to the academic status quo when Stirling
unearthed a stela at Tres Zapotes which bore an earlier date. Written
in the familiar bar-and-dot calendrical code used by the Maya, it
corresponded to 3 September 32 BC.[6]

What was shocking about this was that Tres Zapotes was not a
Maya site – not in any way at all. It was entirely, exclusively,
unambiguously Olmec. This suggested that the Olmecs, not the
Maya, must have been the inventors of the calendar, and that the
Olmecs, not the Maya, ought to be recognized as 'the mother culture'
of Central America. Despite determined opposition from gangs of
furious Mayanists the truth which Stirling's spade had unearthed at
Tres Zapotes gradually came out. The Olmecs were much, *much* older
than the Maya. They'd been a smart, civilized, technologically
advanced people and they did, indeed, appear to have invented the
bar-and-dot system of calendrical notation, with the enigmatic
starting date of 13 August 3114 BC, which predicted the end of the
world in AD 2012.

Lying close to the calendar stela at Tres Zapotes, Stirling also
unearthed a giant head. I sat in front of that head now. Dated to
around 100 BC,[7] it was approximately six feet high, 18 feet in
circumference and weighed over 10 tons. Like its counterpart in
Santiago Tuxtla, it was unmistakably the head of an African man
wearing a close-fitting helmet with long chin-straps. The lobes of the
ears were pierced by plugs; the pronounced negroid features were
furrowed by deep frown lines on either side of the nose, and the entire
face was concentrated forwards above thick, down-curving lips. The
eyes were open and watchful, almond-shaped and cold. Beneath the
curious helmet, the heavy brows appeared beetling and angry.

Stirling was amazed by this discovery and reported,

> The head was a head only, carved from a single massive block of basalt,
> and it rested on a prepared foundation of unworked slabs of
> stone ... Cleared of the surrounding earth it presented an awe-
> inspiring spectacle. Despite its great size the workmanship is delicate
> and sure, the proportions perfect. Unique in character among
> aboriginal American sculptures, it is remarkable for its realistic

treatment. The features are bold and amazingly negroid in character . . . [8]

Soon afterwards the American archaeologist made a second unsettling
discovery at Tres Zapotes: children's toys in the form of little wheeled
dogs.[9] These cute artefacts conflicted head-on with prevailing
archaeological opinion, which held that the wheel had remained
undiscovered in Central America until the time of the conquest. The
'dogmobiles' proved, at the very least, that the *principle* of the wheel
had been known to the Olmecs, Central America's earliest civilization. And if a people as resourceful as the Olmecs had worked out the
principle of the wheel, it seemed highly unlikely that they would have
used it just for children's toys.

Chapter 17

The Olmec Enigma

After Tres Zapotes our next stop was San Lorenzo, an Olmec site lying south-west of Coatzecoalcos in the heart of the 'Serpent Sanctuary' the legends of Quetzalcoatl made reference to. It was at San Lorenzo that the earliest carbon-dates for an Olmec site (around 1500 BC) had been recorded by archaeologists.[1] However, Olmec culture appeared to have been fully evolved by that epoch and there was no evidence that the evolution had taken place in the vicinity of San Lorenzo.[2]

In this there lay a mystery.

The Olmecs, after all, had built a significant civilization which had carried out prodigious engineering works and had developed the capacity to carve and manipulate vast blocks of stone (several of the huge monolithic heads, weighing twenty tons or more, had been moved as far as 60 miles overland after being quarried in the Tuxtla mountains).[3] So where, if not at ancient San Lorenzo, had their technological expertise and sophisticated organization been experimented with, evolved and refined?

Strangely, despite the best efforts of archaeologists, not a single, solitary sign of anything that could be described as the 'developmental phase' of Olmec society had been unearthed anywhere in Mexico (or, for that matter, anywhere in the New World). These people, whose characteristic form of artistic expression was the carving of huge negroid heads, appeared to have come from nowhere.[4]

San Lorenzo

We reached San Lorenzo late in the afternoon. Here, at the dawn of history in Central America, the Olmecs had heaped up an artificial mound more than 100 feet high as part of an immense structure some 4000 feet in length and 2000 feet in width. We climbed the dominant mound, now heavily overgrown with thick tropical vegetation, and from the summit we could see for miles across the surrounding countryside. A great many lesser mounds were also visible and around about were several of the deep trenches the archaeologist Michael Coe had dug when he had excavated the site in 1966.

Coe's team made a number of finds here, which included more than twenty artificial reservoirs, linked by a highly sophisticated network of basalt-lined troughs. Part of this system was built into a ridge; when it was rediscovered water still gushed forth from it during heavy rains, as it had done for more than 3000 years. The main line of the drainage ran from east to west. Into it, linked by joints made to an advanced design, three subsidiary lines were channelled.[5] After surveying the site thoroughly, the archaeologists admitted that they could not understand the purpose of this elaborate system of sluices and water-works.[6]

Nor were they able to come up with an explanation for another enigma. This was the deliberate burial, along specific alignments, of five of the massive pieces of sculpture, showing negroid features, now widely identified as 'Olmec heads'. These peculiar and apparently ritualistic graves also yielded more than sixty precious objects and artefacts, including beautiful instruments made of jade and exquisitely carved statuettes. Some of the statuettes had been systematically mutilated before burial.

The way the San Lorenzo sculptures had been interred made it extremely difficult to fix their true age, even though fragments of charcoal were found in the same strata as some of the buried objects. Unlike the sculptures, these charcoal pieces could be carbon-dated. They were, and produced readings in the range of 1200 BC.[7] This did not mean, however, that the sculptures had been carved in 1200 BC. They could have been. But they could have originated in a period hundreds or even thousands of years earlier than that. It was by no means impossible that these great works of art, with their intrinsic beauty and an indefinable numinous power, could have been preserved and venerated by many different cultures before being buried at San Lorenzo. The charcoal associated with them proved only that the sculptures were *at least as old* as 1200 BC; it did not set any upper limit on their antiquity.

La Venta

We left San Lorenzo as the sun was going down, heading for the city of Villahermosa, more than 150 kilometres to the east in the province of Tabasco. To get there we rejoined the main road running from Acayucan to Villahermosa and by-passed the port of Coatzecoalcos in a zone of oil refineries, towering pylons and ultra-modern suspension bridges. The change of pace between the sleepy rural backwater where San Lorenzo was located and the pockmarked industrial landscape around Coatzecoalcos was almost shocking. Moreover, the only reason that the timeworn outlines of the Olmec site could still be seen at San Lorenzo was that oil had not yet been found there.

It had, however, been found at La Venta – to the eternal loss of archaeology . . .

We were now passing La Venta.

Due north, off a slip-road from the freeway, this sodium-lit petroleum city glowed in the dark like a vision of nuclear disaster. Since the 1940s it had been extensively 'developed' by the oil industry: an airstrip now bisected the site where a most unusual pyramid had once stood, and flaring smokestacks darkened the sky which Olmec star-gazers must once have searched for the rising of the planets. Lamentably, the bulldozers of the developers had flattened virtually everything of interest before proper excavations could be conducted, with the result that many of the ancient structures had not been explored at all.[8] We will never know what they could have said about the people who built and used them.

Matthew Stirling, who excavated Tres Zapotes, carried out the bulk of the archaeological work done at La Venta before progress and oil money erased it. Carbon-dating suggested that the Olmecs had established themselves here between 1500 and 1100 BC and had continued to occupy the site – which consisted of an island lying in marshes to the east of the Tonala river – until about 400 BC.[9] Then construction was suddenly abandoned, all existing buildings were ceremonially defaced or demolished, and several huge stone heads and other smaller pieces of sculpture were ritually buried in peculiar graves, just as had happened at San Lorenzo. The La Venta graves were elaborate and carefully prepared, lined with thousands of tiny blue tiles and filled up with layers of multicoloured clay.[10] At one spot some 15,000 cubic feet of earth had been dug out of the ground to make a deep pit; its floor had been carefully covered with serpentine blocks, and all the earth put back. Three mosaic pavements were also found, intentionally buried beneath several alternating layers of clay and adobe.[11]

La Venta's principal pyramid stood at the southern end of the site. Roughly circular at ground level, it took the form of a fluted cone, the rounded sides consisting of ten vertical ridges with gullies between. The pyramid was 100 feet tall, almost 200 feet in diameter and had an overall mass in the region of 300,000 cubic feet – an impressive monument by any standards. The remainder of the site stretched for almost half a kilometre along an axis that pointed precisely 8° west of north. Centred on this axis, with every structure in flawless alignment, were several smaller pyramids and plazas, platforms and mounds, covering a total area of more than three square miles.

There was something detached and odd about La Venta, a sense that its original function had not been properly understood. Archaeologists referred to it as a 'ceremonial centre', and very probably that is what it was. If one were honest, however, one would admit that it could also have been several other things. The truth is that nothing is known about the social organization, ceremonies and belief systems of the Olmecs. We do not know what language they spoke, or what traditions they passed to their children. We don't even know what ethnic group they belonged to. The exceptionally humid conditions of the Gulf of Mexico mean that not a single Olmec skeleton has survived.[12] In reality, despite the names we have given them and the views we've formed about them, these people are completely obscure to us.

It is even possible that the enigmatic sculptures 'they' left behind, which we presume depicted them, were not 'their' work at all, but the

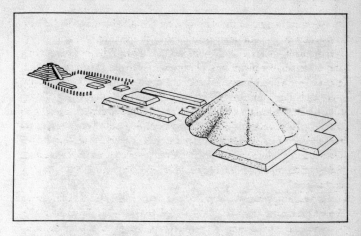

Reconstruction of La Venta. Note the unusual fluted-cone pyramid that dominates the site.

work of a far earlier and forgotten people. Not for the first time I found myself wondering whether some of the great heads and other remarkable artefacts attributed to the Olmecs might not have been handed down like heirlooms, perhaps over many millennia, to the cultures which eventually began to build the mounds and pyramids at San Lorenzo and La Venta.

If so, then who are we speaking of when we use the label 'Olmec'? The mound-builders? Or the powerful and imposing men with negroid features who provided the models for the monolithic heads?

Fortunately some fifty pieces of 'Olmec' monumental sculpture, including three of the giant heads, were rescued from La Venta by Carlos Pellicer Camara, a local poet and historian who intervened forcefully when he discovered that oil-drilling by the PEMEX company jeopardized the ruins. By determined lobbying of the politicians of Tabasco (within which La Venta lies), he arranged to have the significant finds moved to a park on the outskirts of the regional capital Villahermosa.

Taken together these finds constitute a precious and irreplaceable

Profile view of the head of the Great Sphinx at Giza, Egypt.

Profile view of Olmec Head from La Venta, Mexico.

Front view of the head of the Sphinx.

Front view of Olmec Head.

Double-puma statue at Uxmal, Mexico.

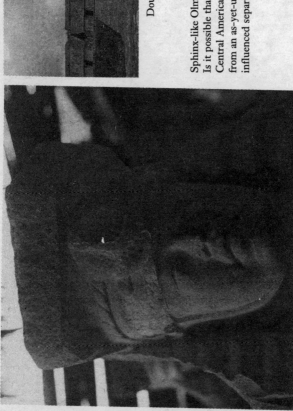
Sphinx-like Olmec sculpture from San Lorenzo, Mexico.
Is it possible that the many cultures of pre-Columbian
Central America and Ancient Egypt could have stemmed
from an as-yet-unidentified 'third-party' civilization that
influenced separated regions at a remote and early date?

Double-lion symbolism from Ancient Egypt, depicting the *Akeru*, lion gods of yesterday and today (*Akeru* was written in hieroglyphs as ⌒⌒). The religions of both regions share many other common images and ideas. Also noteworthy is the fact that *p'achi*, the Central American word for 'human sacrifice', means, literally 'to open the mouth' – which calls to mind a strange Ancient Egyptian funerary ritual known as 'the opening of the mouth'. Likewise it was believed in both regions that the souls of dead kings were reborn as stars.

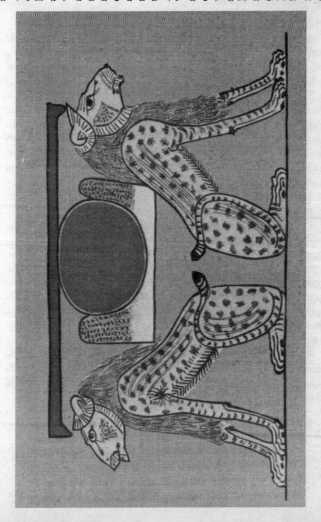

cultural record – or rather a whole library of cultural records – left behind by a vanished civilization. But nobody knows how to read the language of these records.

Deus ex machina

Villahermosa, Tabasco province

I was looking at an elaborate relief that had been dubbed 'Man in Serpent' by the archaeologists who found it at La Venta. According to expert opinion it showed 'an Olmec, wearing a head-dress and holding an incense bag, enveloped by a feathered serpent'.[13]

The relief was carved into a slab of solid granite measuring about four feet wide by five feet high and showed a man sitting with his legs stretched out in front him as though he were reaching for pedals with his feet. He held a small, bucket-shaped object in his right hand. With his left he appeared to be raising or lowering a lever. The 'head-dress' he wore was an odd and complicated garment. To my eye it seemed more functional than ceremonial, although I could not imagine what its function might have been. On it, or perhaps on a console above it, were two x-shaped crosses.

I turned my attention to the other principal element of the sculpture, the 'feathered serpent'. On one level it did, indeed, depict exactly that: a plumed or feathered serpent, the age-old symbol of Quetzalcoatl, whom the Olmecs, therefore, must have worshipped (or at the very least recognized). Scholars do not dispute this interpretation.[14] It is generally accepted that Quetzalcoatl's cult was immensely ancient, originating in prehistoric times in Central America and thereafter receiving the devotion of many cultures during the historic period.

The feathered serpent in this particular sculpture, however, had certain characteristics that set it apart. It seemed to be more than just a religious symbol; indeed, there was something rigid and structured about it that made it look almost like a piece of machinery.

Whispers of ancient secrets

Later that day I took shelter in the giant shadow cast by one of the

Olmec heads Carlos Pellicer Camara had rescued from La Venta. It was the head of an old man with a broad flat nose and thick lips. The lips were slightly parted, exposing strong, square teeth. The expression on the face suggested an ancient, patient wisdom, and the eyes seemed to gaze unafraid into eternity, like those of the Great Sphinx at Giza in lower Egypt.

It would probably be impossible, I thought, for a sculptor to *invent* all the different combined characteristics of an authentic racial type. The portrayal of an authentic combination of racial characteristics therefore implied strongly that a human model had been used.

I walked around the great head a couple of times. It was 22 feet in circumference, weighed 19.8 tons, stood almost 8 feet high, had been carved out of solid basalt, and displayed clearly 'an authentic combination of racial characteristics'. Indeed, like the other pieces I had seen at Santiago Tuxtla and at Tres Zapotes, it unmistakably and unambiguously showed a negro.

The reader can form his or her own opinion after examining the relevant photographs in this book. My own view is that the Olmec heads present us with physiologically accurate images of *real* individuals of negroid stock – charismatic and powerful African men whose presence in Central America 3000 years ago has not yet been explained by scholars. Nor is there any certainty that the heads were actually carved in that epoch. Carbon-dating of fragments of charcoal found in the same pits tells us only the age of the charcoal. Calculating the true antiquity of the heads themselves is a much more complex matter.

It was with such thoughts that I continued my slow walk among the strange and wonderful monuments of La Venta. They whispered of ancient secrets – the secret of the man in the machine . . . the secret of the negro heads . . . and, last but not least, the secret of a legend brought to life. For it seemed that flesh might indeed have been put on the mythical bones of Quetzalcoatl when I found that several of the La Venta sculptures contained realistic likenesses not only of negroes but of tall, thin-featured, long-nosed, apparently Caucasian men with straight hair and full beards, wearing flowing robes . . .

Chapter 18

Conspicuous Strangers

Matthew Stirling, the American archaeologist who excavated La Venta in the 1940s, made a number of spectacular discoveries there. The most spectacular of all was the Stele of the Bearded Man.

The plan of the ancient Olmec site, as I have said, lay along an axis pointing 8° west of north. At the southern end of this axis, 100 feet tall, loomed the fluted cone of the great pyramid. Next to it, at ground level, was what looked like a curb about a foot high enclosing a spacious rectangular area one-quarter the size of an average city block. When the archaeologists began to uncover this curb they found, to their surprise, that it consisted of the upper parts of a wall of columns. Further excavation through the undisturbed layers of stratification that had accumulated revealed that the columns were ten feet tall. There were more than 600 of them and they had been set together so closely that they formed a near-impregnable stockade. Hewn out of solid basalt and transported to La Venta from quarries more than sixty miles distant, the columns weighed approximately two tons each.

Why all this trouble? What had the stockade been built to contain?

Even before excavation began, the tip of a massive chunk of rock had been visible jutting out of the ground in the centre of the enclosed area, about four feet higher than the illusory 'curb' and leaning steeply forward. It was covered with carvings. These extended down, out of sight, beneath the layers of soil that filled the ancient stockade to a height of about nine feet.

Stirling and his team worked for two days to free the great rock. When exposed it proved to be an imposing stele fourteen feet high, seven feet wide and almost three feet thick. The carvings showed an encounter between two tall men, both dressed in elaborate robes and wearing elegant shoes with turned-up toes. Either erosion or deliberate mutilation (quite commonly practised on Olmec monuments) had resulted in the complete defacement of one of the figures. The other was intact. It so obviously depicted a Caucasian male with a high-bridged nose and a long, flowing beard that the bemused archaeologists promptly christened it 'Uncle Sam'.[1]

I walked slowly around the twenty-ton stele, remembering as I did so that it had lain buried in the earth for more than 3000 years. Only in the brief half century or so since Stirling's excavations had it seen the light of day again. What would its fate be now? Would it stand here for another thirty centuries as an object of awe and splendour for future generations to gawp at and revere? Or, in such a great expanse of time, was it possible that circumstances might change so much that it would once again be buried and concealed?

Perhaps neither would happen. I remembered the ancient calendrical system of Central America, which the Olmecs had initiated. According to them, and to their more famous successors the Mayas, there just weren't any great expanses of time left, let alone three millennia. The Fifth Sun was all used up and a tremendous earthquake was building to destroy humanity two days before Christmas in AD 2012.

I turned my attention back to the stele. Two things seemed to be clear: the encounter scene it portrayed must, for some reason, have been of immense importance to the Olmecs, hence the grandeur of the stele itself, and the construction of the remarkable stockade of columns built to contain it. And, as was the case with the negro heads, it was obvious that the face of the bearded Caucasian man could only have been sculpted from a human model. The racial verisimilitude was too good for an artist to have invented it.

The same went for two other Caucasian figures I was able to identify among the surviving monuments from La Venta. One was carved in low relief on a heavy and roughly circular slab of stone about three feet in diameter. Dressed in what looked like tight-fitting leggings, his features were those of an Anglo-Saxon. He had a full pointed beard and wore a curious floppy cap on his head. In his left hand he extended a flag, or perhaps a weapon of some kind. His right hand, which he held across the middle of his chest, appeared to be empty. Around his slim waist was tied a flamboyant sash. The other Caucasian figure, this time carved on the side of a narrow pillar, was similarly bearded and attired.

Who were these conspicuous strangers? What were they doing in Central America? When did they come? And what relationship did they have with those other strangers who had settled in this steamy rubber jungle – the ones who had provided the models for the great negro heads?

Some radical researchers, who rejected the dogma concerning the isolation of the New World prior to 1492, had proposed what looked like a viable solution to the problem: the bearded, thin-featured individuals could have been Phoenicians from the Mediterranean who had sailed through the Pillars of Hercules and across the Atlantic Ocean as early as the second millennium BC. Advocates of this theory went on to suggest that the negroes shown at the same sites were the 'slaves' of the Phoenicians, picked up on the coast of West Africa prior to the trans-Atlantic run.[2]

The more consideration I gave to the strange character of the La Venta sculptures, the more dissatisfied I became with these ideas. Probably the Phoenicians and other Old World peoples *had* crossed the Atlantic ages before Columbus. There was compelling evidence for that, although it is outside the scope of this book.[3] The problem was that the Phoenicians, who had left unmistakable examples of their distinctive handiwork in many parts of the ancient world,[4] had *not* done so at the Olmec sites in Central America. Neither the negro heads, nor the reliefs portraying bearded Caucasian men showed any signs of anything remotely Phoenician in their style, handiwork or character.[5] Indeed, from a stylistic point of view, these powerful works of art seemed to belong to no known culture, tradition or genre. They seemed to be without antecedents either in the New World or in the Old.

They seemed rootless . . . and that, of course, was impossible, because all forms of artistic expression have roots somewhere.

Hypothetical third party

It occurred to me that one plausible explanation might lie in a variant of the 'hypothetical third party' theory originally put forward by a number of leading Egyptologists to explain one of the great puzzles of Egyptian history and chronology.

The archaeological evidence suggested that rather than developing slowly and painfully, as is normal with human societies, the civilization of Ancient Egypt, like that of the Olmecs, emerged *all at once and fully formed*. Indeed, the period of transition from primitive to advanced society appears to have been so short that it makes no kind of historical sense. Technological skills that should have taken hundreds or even thousands of years to evolve were brought into use almost overnight – and with no apparently antecedents whatever.

For example, remains from the pre-dynastic period around 3500 BC show no trace of writing. Soon after that date, quite suddenly and inexplicably, the hieroglyphs familiar from so many of the ruins of Ancient Egypt begin to appear in a complete and perfect state. Far from being mere pictures of objects or actions, this written language was complex and structured at the outset, with signs that represented sounds only and a detailed system of numerical symbols. Even the very earliest hieroglyphs were stylized and conventionalized; and it is clear that an advanced cursive script was in common usage by the dawn of the First Dynasty.[6]

What is remarkable is that there are no traces of evolution from simple to sophisticated, and the same is true of mathematics, medicine, astronomy and architecture and of Egypt's amazingly rich and convoluted religio–mythological system (even the central content of such refined works as the *Book of the Dead* existed *right at the start* of the dynastic period).[7]

The majority of Egyptologists will not consider the implications of Egypt's early sophistication. These implications are startling, according to a number of more daring thinkers. John Anthony West, an expert on the early dynastic period, asks:

> How does a complex civilization spring full-blown into being? Look at
> a 1905 automobile and compare it to a modern one. There is no

mistaking the process of 'development'. But in Egypt there are no parallels. Everything is right there at the start.

The answer to the mystery is of course obvious but, because it is repellent to the prevailing cast of modern thinking, it is seldom considered. *Egyptian civilization was not a 'development', it was a legacy.*[8]

West has been a thorn in the flesh of the Egyptological establishment for many years. But other more mainstream figures have also confessed puzzlement at the suddenness with which Egyptian civilization appeared. Walter Emery, late Edwards Professor of Egyptology at the University of London, summed up the problem:

> At a period approximately 3400 years before Christ, a great change took place in Egypt, and the country passed rapidly from a state of neolithic culture with a complex tribal character to one of well-organized monarchy . . .
>
> At the same time the art of writing appears, monumental architecture and the arts and crafts develop to an astonishing degree, and all the evidence points to the existence of a luxurious civilization. All this was achieved within a comparatively short period of time, *for there appears to be little or no background to these fundamental developments in writing and architecture.*[9]

One explanation could simply be that Egypt received its sudden and decisive cultural boost from some other known civilization of the ancient world. Sumer, on the Lower Euphrates in Mesopotamia, is the most likely contender. Despite many basic differences, a variety of shared building techniques and architectural styles[10] do suggest a link between the two regions. But none of these similarities is strong enough to infer that the connection could have been in any way causal, with one society directly influencing the other. On the contrary, as Professor Emery writes:

> The impression we get is of an *indirect* connection, and perhaps the existence of a third party, whose influence spread to both the Euphrates and the Nile . . . Modern scholars have tended to ignore the possibility of immigration to both regions from some hypothetical and as yet undiscovered area. [However] a third party whose cultural

achievements were passed on independently to Egypt and Mesopotamia would best explain the common features and fundamental differences between the two civilizations.[11]

Among other things, this theory sheds light on the mysterious fact that the Egyptians and Sumerian people of Mesopotamia appear to have worshipped virtually identical lunar deities, who were among the oldest in their respective pantheons (*Thoth* in the case of the Egyptians, *Sin* in the case of the Sumerians).[12] According to the eminent Egyptologist Sir E.A. Wallis Budge, 'The similarity between the two gods is too close to be accidental . . . It would be wrong to say that the Egyptians borrowed from the Sumerians or the Sumerians from the Egyptians, but it may be submitted that the literati of both peoples borrowed their theological systems from some common but exceedingly ancient source.'[13]

The question, therefore, is this: what was that 'common but exceedingly ancient source', that 'hypothetical and as yet undiscovered area', that advanced 'third party' to which both Budge and Emery refer? And if it left a legacy of high culture in Egypt and in Mesopotamia, why shouldn't it have done so in Central America?

It's not good enough to argue that civilization 'took off' much later in Mexico than it had in the Middle East. It is possible that the initial impulse could have been felt at the same time in both places but that the subsequent outcome could have been completely different.

On this scenario, the civilizers would have succeeded brilliantly in Egypt and in Sumer, creating lasting and remarkable cultures there. In Mexico, on the other hand (as also seems to have been the case in Peru), they suffered some serious setback – perhaps getting off to a good start, when the gigantic stone heads and reliefs of bearded men were made, but going rapidly downhill. The light of civilization would never quite have been lost, but perhaps things didn't pick up again until around 1500 BC, the so-called 'Olmec horizon'. By then the great sculptures would have been hoary with age, ancient relics of immense spiritual power, their all-but-forgotten origins wrapped in myths of giants and bearded civilizers.

If so, we may be gazing at faces from a much more remote past than we imagine when we stare into the almond eyes of one of the negro heads or into the angular, chiselled Caucasian features of 'Uncle

Sam'. It is by no means impossible that these great works preserve the images of peoples from a vanished civilization which embraced several different ethnic groups.

That, in a nutshell, is the 'hypothetical third party' theory as applied to Central America: the civilization of Ancient Mexico did not emerge without external influence, and it did not emerge as a result of influence from the Old World; instead certain cultures in the Old World and in the New World may both have received a legacy of influence and ideas from a third party at some exceedingly remote date.

Villahermosa to Oaxaca

Before leaving Villahermosa I visited CICOM, the Centre for Investigation of the Cultures of the Olmecs and Maya. I wanted to find out from the scholars there whether there were any other significant Olmec sites in the region. To my surprise, they suggested that I should look farther afield. At Monte Alban, in Oaxaca province hundreds of kilometres to the south-west, archaeologists had apparently unearthed 'Olmecoid' artefacts and a number of reliefs thought to represent the Olmecs themselves.

Santha and I had intended to drive straight on from Villahermosa into the Yucatan Peninsula, which lay north-east. The journey to Monte Alban would involve a huge detour, but we decided to make it, in the hope that it might shed further light on the Olmecs. Besides, it promised to be a spectacular drive over immense mountains and into the heart of the hidden valley where the city of Oaxaca lies.

We drove almost due west past the lost site of La Venta, past Coatzecoalcos once again, and on past Sayula and Loma Bonita to the road-junction town of Tuxtepec. In so doing, by degrees we left behind countryside scarred and blackened by the oil industry, crossed long gentle hillsides carpeted in lush green grass, and ran between fields ripe with crops.

At Tuxtepec, where the sierras really began, we turned sharply south following Highway 175 to Oaxaca. On the map it looked barely half the distance that we had driven from Villahermosa. The road, however, proved to be a complicated, nerve-racking, muscle-wrenching, apparently endless zig-zag of hairpin bends – narrow, winding and precipitous – which went up into the clouds like a stairway to heaven. It took us through many different layers of alpine vegetation, each occupying a specialized climatological niche, until it brought us out above the clouds in a place where familiar plants flourished in giant forms, like John Wyndham's triffids, creating a surreal and alien landscape. It took twelve hours to drive the 700 kilometres from Villahermosa to Oaxaca. By the time the journey was over, my hands were blistered from gripping the steering-wheel too tight for too long around too many hairpin bends. My eyes were blurred and I kept having mental retrospectives of the vertiginous chasms we had skirted on Highway 175, in the mountains, where the triffids grew.

The city of Oaxaca is famous for magic mushrooms, marijuana and D. H. Lawrence (who wrote and set part of his novel *The Plumed Serpent* here in the 1920s). There is still a bohemian feel about the place and until late at night a current of excitement seems to ripple among the crowds filling its bars and cafés, narrow cobbled streets, old buildings and spacious plazas.

We checked into a room overlooking one of the three open courtyards in the Hotel Las Golondrinas. The bed was comfortable. There were starry skies overhead. But, tired as I was, I couldn't sleep.

What kept me awake was the idea of the civilizers . . . the bearded gods and their companions. In Mexico, as in Peru, they seemed to have confronted failure. That was what the legends implied, and not only the legends, as I discovered when we reached Monte Alban the next morning.

Chapter 19

Adventures in the Underworld, Journeys to the Stars

The 'hypothetical third party' theory explains the similarities and fundamental differences between Ancient Egypt and Ancient Meso-potamia by proposing that both received a common legacy of civilization from the same remote ancestor. No serious suggestions have been made as to where that ancestral civilization might have been located, its nature, or when it flourished. Like a black hole in space, it cannot be seen. Yet its presence can be deduced from its effects on things that can be seen – in this case the civilizations of Sumer and Egypt.

Is it possible that the same mysterious ancestor, the same invisible source of influence, could also have left its mark in Mexico? If so, we would expect to find certain cultural similarities between Mexico's ancient civilizations and those of Sumer and Egypt. We would also expect to be confronted by immense differences resulting from the long period of divergent evolution which separated all these areas in historical times. We would, however, expect the differences to be less between Sumer and Egypt, which were in regular contact with each other during the historical period, than between the two Middle Eastern cultures and the cultures of far-off Central America, which enjoyed at most only haphazard, slight and intermittent contacts prior to the 'discovery' of the New World by Columbus in AD 1492.

Eaters of the dead, earth monsters, star kings, dwarves and other relatives

For some curious reason that has not been explained, the Ancient Egyptians had a special liking and reverence for dwarves.[1] So, too, did the civilized peoples of ancient Central America, right back to Olmec times.[2] In both cases it was believed that dwarves were directly connected to the gods.[3] And in both cases dwarves were favoured as dancers and were shown as such in works of art.[4]

In Egypt's early dynastic period, more than 4500 years ago, an 'Ennead' of nine omnipotent deities was particularly adored by the priesthood at Heliopolis.[5] Likewise, in Central America, both the Aztecs and the Mayas believed in an all-powerful system of nine deities.[6]

The *Popol Vuh*, the sacred book of the ancient Quiche Maya of Mexico and Guatemala, contains several passages which clearly indicate a belief in 'stellar rebirth' – the reincarnation of the dead as stars. After they had been killed, for example, the Hero Twins named Hunahpu and Xbalanque 'rose up in the midst of the light, and instantly they were lifted into the sky . . . Then the arch of heaven and the face of the earth were lighted. And they dwelt in heaven.'[7] At the same time ascended the Twins' 400 companions who had also been killed, 'and so they again became the companions of Hunahpu and Xbalanque and were changed into stars in the sky.'[8]

The majority of the traditions of the God–King Quetzalcoatl, as we have seen, focus on his deeds and teachings as a civilizer. His followers in ancient Mexico, however, also believed that his human manifestation had experienced death and that *afterwards he was reborn as a star*.[9]

It is therefore curious, at the very least, to discover that in Egypt, in the Pyramid Age, more than 4000 years ago, the state religion revolved around the belief that the deceased pharaoh was reborn as a star.[10] Ritual incantations were chanted, the purpose of which was to facilitate the dead monarch's rapid rebirth in the heavens: 'Oh king, you are this Great Star, the Companion of Orion, who traverses the sky with Orion . . . you ascend from the east of the sky, being renewed in your due season, and rejuvenated in your due time . . .'[11] We have encountered the Orion constellation before, on the plains of Nazca, and we shall encounter it again . . .

Meanwhile, let us consider the *Ancient Egyptian Book of the Dead*. Parts of its contents are as old as the civilization of Egypt itself and it serves as a sort of Baedeker for the transmigration of the soul. It instructs the deceased on how to overcome the dangers of the afterlife, enables him to assume the form of several mythical creatures, and equips him with the passwords necessary for admission to the various stages, or levels, of the underworld.[12]

Is it a coincidence that the peoples of Ancient Central America preserved a parallel vision of the perils of the afterlife? There it was widely believed that the underworld consisted of nine strata through which the deceased would journey for four years, overcoming obstacles and dangers on the way.[13] The strata had self-explanatory names like 'place where the mountains crash together', 'place where the arrows are fired', 'mountain of knives', and so on. In both Ancient Central America and Ancient Egypt, it was believed that the deceased's voyage through the underworld was made in a boat, accompanied by 'paddler gods' who ferried him from stage to stage.[14] The tomb of 'Double Comb', an eighth-century ruler of the Mayan city of Tikal, was found to contain a representation of this scene.[15] Similar images appear throughout the Valley of the Kings in Upper Egypt, notably in the tomb of Thutmosis III, an Eighteenth Dynasty pharaoh.[16] Is it a coincidence that the passengers in the barque of the dead pharaoh, and in the canoe in which Double Comb makes his final journey, include (in both cases) a dog or dog-headed deity, a bird or bird-headed deity, and an ape or ape-headed deity?[17]

The seventh stratum of the Ancient Mexican underworld was called *Teocoyolcualloya*: 'place where beasts devour hearts'.[18]

Is it a coincidence that one of the stages of the Ancient Egyptian underworld, 'the Hall of Judgement', involved an almost identical series of symbols? At this crucial juncture the deceased's heart was weighed against a feather. If the heart was heavy with sin it would tip the balance. The god Thoth would note the judgement on his palette and the heart would immediately be devoured by a fearsome beast, part crocodile, part hippopotamus, part lion, that was called 'the Eater of the Dead'.[19]

Finally, let us turn again to Egypt of the Pyramid Age and the privileged status of the pharaoh, which enabled him to circumvent the trials of the underworld and to be reborn as a star. Ritual incantations were part of the process. Equally important was a mysterious ceremony known as 'the opening of the mouth', always conducted after the death of the pharaoh and believed by archaeologists to date back to pre-dynastic times.[20] The high priest and four assistants participated, wielding the *peshenkhef*, a ceremonial cutting instrument. This was used 'to open the mouth' of the deceased God-King, an action thought necessary to ensure his resurrection in the heavens. Surviving reliefs and vignettes showing this ceremony leave no doubt that the mummified corpse was struck a hard physical blow with the *peshenkhef*.[21] In addition, evidence has recently emerged which indicates that one of the chambers within the Great Pyramid at Giza may have served as the location for the ceremony.[22]

All this finds a strange, distorted twin in Mexico. We have seen the prevalence of human sacrifice there in pre-conquest times. Is it coincidental that the sacrificial venue was a pyramid, that the ceremony was conducted by a high priest and four assistants, that a cutting instrument, the sacrificial knife, was used to strike a hard physical blow to the body of the victim, and that the victim's soul was believed to ascend directly to the heavens, sidestepping the perils of the underworld?[23]

As such 'coincidences' continue to multiply, it is reasonable to wonder whether there may not be some underlying connection. This is certainly the case when we learn that the general term for 'sacrifice' throughout Ancient Central America was *p'achi*, meaning 'to open the mouth'.[24]

Could it be, therefore, that what confronts us here, in widely separated geographical areas, and at different periods of history, is not just a series of startling coincidences but some faint and garbled common memory originating in the most distant antiquity? It doesn't seem that the Egyptian ceremony of the opening of the mouth influenced directly the Mexican ceremony of the same name (or vice versa, for that matter). The fundamental differences between the two cases rule that out. What does seem possible, however, is that their similarities may be the remnants of a shared legacy received from a common ancestor. The peoples of Central America did one thing with that legacy and the Egyptians another, but some common symbolism and nomenclature was retained by both.

This is not the place to expand on the sense of an ancient and elusive connectedness that emerges from the Egyptian and Central American evidence. Before moving on, however, it is worth noting that a similar 'connectedness' links the belief systems of pre-Colombian Mexico with those of Sumer in Mesopotamia. Again the evidence is more suggestive of an ancient common ancestor than of any direct influence.

Take the case of Oannes, for example.

'Oannes' is the Greek rendering of the Sumerian Uan, the name of the amphibious being, described in Part II, believed to have brought the arts and skills of civilization to Mesopotamia.[25] Legends dating back at least 5000 years relate that Uan lived under the sea, emerging from the waters of the Persian Gulf every morning to civilize and tutor mankind.[26] Is it a coincidence that *uaana*, in the Mayan language, means 'he who has his residence in water'?[27]

Let us also consider Tiamat, the Sumerian goddess of the oceans and of the forces of primitive chaos, always shown as a ravening monster. In Mesopotamian tradition, Tiamat turned against the other deities and unleashed a holocaust of destruction before she was eventually destroyed by the celestial hero Marduk:

> She opened her mouth, Tiamat, to swallow him.
> He drove in the evil wind so that she could not close her lips.
> The terrible winds filled her belly. Her heart was seized,
> She held her mouth wide open,
> He let fly an arrow, it pierced her belly,
> Her inner parts he clove, he split her heart,
> He rendered her powerless and destroyed her life,
> He felled her body and stood upright on it.[28]

How do you follow an act like that?

Marduk could. Contemplating his adversary's monstrous corpse, 'he conceived works of art',[29] and a great plan of world creation began to take shape in his mind. His first move was to split Tiamat's skull and cut her arteries. Then he broke her into two parts 'like a dried fish', using one half to roof the heavens and the other to surface the earth. From her breasts he made mountains, from her spittle, clouds, and he directed the rivers Tigris and Euphrates to flow from her eyes.[30]

A strange and violent legend, and a very old one.

The ancient civilizations of Central America had their own version of this story. Here Quetzalcoatl, in his incarnation as the creator deity, took the role of Marduk while the part of Tiamat was played by Cipactli, the 'Great Earth Monster'. Quetzalcoatl seized Cipactli's limbs 'as she swam in the primeval waters and wrenched her body in half, one part forming the sky and the other the earth'. From her hair and skin he created grass, flowers and herbs; 'from her eyes, wells and springs; from her shoulders, mountains'.[31]

Are the peculiar parallels between the Sumerian and Mexican myths pure coincidence or could both have been marked by the cultural fingerprints of a lost civilization? If so, the faces of the heroes of that ancestral culture may indeed have been carved in stone and passed down as heirlooms through thousands of years, sometimes in full view, sometimes buried, until they were dug up for the last time by archaeologists in our era and given labels like 'Olmec Head' and 'Uncle Sam'.

The faces of those heroes also appear at Monte Alban, where they seem to tell a sad story.

Monte Alban: the downfall of masterful men

A site thought to be about 3000 years old,[32] Monte Alban stands on a vast artifically flattened hilltop overlooking Oaxaca. It consists of a huge rectangular area, the Grand Plaza, which is enclosed by groups of pyramids and other buildings laid out in precise geometrical relationships to one another. The overall feel of the place is one of harmony and proportion emerging from a well-ordered and symmetrical plan.

Following the advice of CICOM, whom I had spoken to before leaving Villahermosa, I made my way first to the extreme south-west corner of the Monte Alban site. There, stacked loosely against the side of a low pyramid, were the objects I had come all this way to see: several dozen engraved stelae depicting negroes and Caucasians . . . equal in life . . . equal in death.

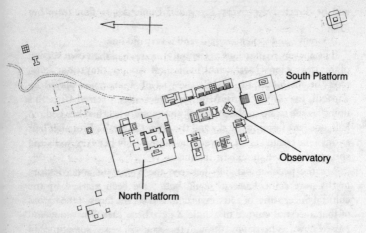

Monte Alban.

If a great civilization had indeed been lost to history, and if these sculptures told part of its story, the message conveyed was one of racial equality. No one who has seen the pride, or felt the charisma, of the great negro heads from La Venta could seriously imagine that the original subjects of these magisterial sculptures could have been slaves. Neither did the lean-faced, bearded men look as if they would have bent their knees to anyone. They, too, had an aristocratic demeanour.

At Monte Alban, however, there seemed to be carved in stone a record of the downfall of these masterful men. It did not look as if this could have been the work of the same people who made the La Venta sculptures. The standard of craftsmanship was far too low for that. But what was certain – whoever they were, and however inferior their work – was that these artists had attempted to portray the same negroid subjects and the same goatee-bearded Caucasians as I had seen at La Venta. There the sculptures had reflected strength, power and vitality. Here at Monte Alban the remarkable strangers were corpses. All were naked, most were castrated, some were curled up in foetal positions as though to avoid showers of blows, others lay sprawled slackly.

Archaeologists said the sculptures showed 'the corpses of prisoners captured in battle'.[33]

What prisoners? From where?

The location, after all, was Central America, the New World, thousands of years before Columbus, so wasn't it odd that these images of battlefield casualties showed not a single native American but only and exclusively Old World racial types?

For some reason, orthodox academics did not find this puzzling, even though, by their reckoning, the carvings were extremely old (dating to somewhere between 1000 and 600 BC[34]). As at other sites, this time-frame had been derived from tests on associated organic matter, not on the carvings themselves, which were incised on granite stele and therefore hard to date objectively.

Legacy

An as yet undeciphered but fully elaborated hieroglyphic script had been found at Monte Alban,[35] much of it carved on to the same stele as the crude Caucasian and negro figures. Experts accepted that it was 'the earliest-known writing in Mexico'.[36] It was also clear that the people who had lived here had been accomplished builders and more than usually preoccupied with astronomy. An observatory, consisting of a strange arrowhead-shaped structure, lay at an angle of 45° to the main axis (which was deliberately tilted several degrees from north-south).[37] Crawling into this observatory, I found it to be a warren of tiny, narrow tunnels and steep internal stairways, giving sightlines to different regions of the sky.[38]

The people of Monte Alban, like the people of Tres Zapotes, left definite evidence of their knowledge of mathematics, in the form of bar-and-dot computations.[39] They had also used the remarkable calendar,[40] introduced by the Olmecs and much associated with the later Maya,[41] which predicted the end of the world on 23 December AD 2012.

If the calendar, and the preoccupation with time, had been part of the legacy of an ancient and forgotten civilization, the Maya must be ranked as the most faithful and inspired inheritors of that legacy. 'Time' as the archaeologist Eric Thompson put it in 1950, 'was the supreme mystery of Maya religion, a subject which pervaded Maya thought to an extent without parallel in the history of mankind.'[42]

As I continued my journey through Central America I felt myself drawn ever more deeply into the labyrinths of that strange and awesome riddle.

Chapter 20

Children of the First Men

Palenque, Chiapas Province

Evening was settling in. I sat just beneath the north-east corner of the Mayan Temple of the Inscriptions and gazed north over the darkening jungle where the land dropped away towards the flood plain of the Usumacinta.

The Temple consisted of three chambers and rested on top of a nine-stage pyramid almost 100 feet tall. The clean and harmonious lines of this structure gave it a sense of delicacy, but not of weakness. It felt strong, rooted into the earth, enduring – a creature of pure geometry and imagination.

Looking to my right I could see the Palace, a spacious rectangular complex on a pyramidal base, dominated by a narrow, four-storeyed tower, thought to have been used as an observatory by Maya priests.

Around about me, where bright-feathered parrots and macaws skimmed the treetops, a number of other spectacular buildings lay half swallowed by the encroaching forest. These were the Temple of the Foliated Cross, the Temple of the Sun, the Temple of the Count, and the Temple of the Lion – all names made up by archaeologists. So much of what the Maya had stood for, cared about, believed in and remembered from earlier times was irretrievably lost. Though we'd long ago learned to read their dates, we were only just beginning to make headway with the deciphering of their intricate hieroglyphs.

I stood and climbed the last few steps into the central chamber of

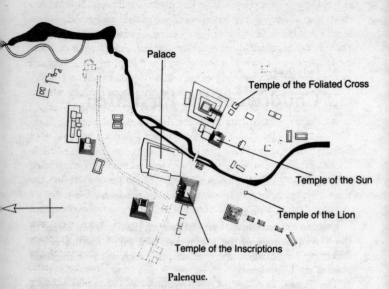

Palace

Temple of the Foliated Cross

Temple of the Sun

Temple of the Lion

Temple of the Inscriptions

Palenque.

the Temple. Set into the rear wall were two great grey slabs, and inscribed on them, in regimented rows like pieces on a chequerboard, were 620 separate Mayan glyphs. These took the form of faces, monstrous and human, together with a writhing bestiary of mythical creatures.

What was being said here? No one knew for sure because the inscriptions, a mixture of word pictures and phonetic symbols, had not yet been fully decoded. It was evident, however, that a number of the glyphs referred to epochs thousands of years in the past, and spoke of people and gods who had played their parts in prehistoric events.[1]

Pacal's tomb

To the left of the hieroglyphs, let into the huge flagstones of the temple floor, was a steep descending internal stairway. This led to a room buried deep in the bowels of the pyramid, where the tomb of Lord Pacal lay. The stairs, of highly polished limestone blocks, were narrow and surprisingly slippery and moist. Adopting a crabbed, sideways stance, I switched on my torch and stepped gingerly down into the gloom, steadying myself against the southern wall as I did so.

This damp stairway had been a secret place from the date when it was originally sealed, in AD 683, until June 1952 when the Mexican archaeologist Alberto Ruz lifted the flagstones in the temple floor. Although a second such tomb was found at Palenque in 1994,[2] Ruz had the honour of being the first man to discover such a feature inside a New World pyramid. The stairway had been intentionally filled with rubble by its builders, and it took four more years before the archaeologists cleared it out completely and reached the bottom.

When they had done so they entered a narrow corbel-vaulted chamber. Spread out on the floor in front of them were the mouldering skeletons of five or possibly six young victims of sacrifice. A huge triangular slab of stone was visible at the far end of the chamber. When it was removed, Ruz was confronted by a remarkable tomb. He described it as 'an enormous room that appeared to be graven in ice, a kind of grotto whose walls and roof seemed to have been planed in perfect surfaces, or an abandoned chapel whose cupola was draped with curtains of stalactites, and from whose floor arose thick stalagmites like the dripping of a candle.'[3]

The room, also roofed with a corbel vault, was 30 feet long and 23 feet high. Around the walls, in stucco relief, could be seen the striding figures of the Lords of the Night – the 'Ennead' of nine deities who ruled over the hours of darkness. Centre-stage, and overlooked by these figures, was a huge monolithic sarcophagus lidded with a five-ton slab of richly carved stone. Inside the sarcophagus was a tall skeleton draped with a treasure trove of jade ornaments. A mosaic death mask of 200 fragments of jade was affixed to the front of the skull. These, supposedly, were the remains of Pacal, a ruler of Palenque in the seventh century AD. The inscriptions stated that this monarch had been eighty years old at the time of his death, but the jade-draped skeleton the archaeologists found in the sarcophagus appeared to belong to a man half that age.[4]

Having reached the bottom of the stairway, some eighty-five feet below the floor of the temple, I crossed the chamber where the sacrificial victims had lain and gazed directly into Pacal's tomb. The air was dank, full of mildew and damp-rot, and surprisingly cold. The sarcophagus, set into the floor of the tomb, had a curious shape, flared strikingly at the feet like an Ancient Egyptian mummy case. These were made of wood and were equipped with wide bases since they were frequently stood upright. But Pacal's coffin was made of solid stone and was uncompromisingly horizontal. Why, then, had the Mayan artificers gone to so much trouble to widen its base when they must have known that it served no useful purpose? Could they have been slavishly copying a design-feature from some ancient model long after the *raison d'être* for the design had been forgotten?[5] Like the beliefs concerning the perils of the afterlife, might Pacal's sarcophagus not be an expression of a common legacy linking Ancient Egypt with the ancient cultures of Central America?

Rectangular in shape, the heavy stone lid of the sarcophagus was ten inches thick, three feet wide and twelve and a half feet long. It, too, seemed to have been modelled on the same original as the magnificent engraved blocks the Ancient Egyptians had used for this exact purpose. Indeed, it would not have looked out of place in the Valley of the Kings. But there was one major difference. The scene carved on top of the sarcophagus lid was unlike anything that ever came out of Egypt. Lit in my torch beam, it showed a clean-shaven man dressed in what looked like a tight-fitting body-suit, the sleeves and leggings of which were gathered into elaborate cuffs at the wrists and ankles. The man lay semi-reclined in a bucket seat which supported his lower back and thighs, the nape of his neck resting comfortably against some kind of headrest, and he was peering forward intently. His hands seemed to be in motion, as though they were operating levers and controls, and his feet were bare, tucked up loosely in front of him.

Was this supposed to be Pacal, the Maya king?

If so, why was he shown operating some kind of machine? The Maya weren't supposed to have had machines. They weren't even supposed to have discovered the wheel. Yet with its side panels, rivets, tubes and other gadgets, the structure Pacal reclined in resembled a technological device much more strongly than it did 'the transition of one man's living soul to the realms of the dead',[6] as one authority claimed, or the king 'falling back into the fleshless jaws of the earth monster',[7] as another argued.

I remembered 'Man in Snake', the Olmec relief described in Chapter Seventeen. It, too, had looked like a naïve depiction of a piece of technology. Furthermore, 'Man in Snake' had come from La Venta, where it had been associated with several bearded figures, apparently Caucasians. Pacal's tomb was at least a thousand years younger than any of the La Venta treasures. Nevertheless, a tiny jade statuette was found lying close to the skeleton inside the sarcophagus, and it appeared to be much older than the other grave-goods also placed there. It depicted an elderly Caucasian, dressed in long robes, with a goatee beard.[8]

Pyramid of the Magician

Uxmal, Yucatan

On a stormy afternoon, 700 kilometres north of Palenque, I began to climb the steps of yet another pyramid. It was a steep building, oval rather than square in plan, 240 feet long at the base and 120 feet wide. It was, moreover, very high, rising 120 feet above the surrounding plain.

Since time out of mind this edifice, which did look like the castle of a necromancer, had been known as the 'Pyramid of the Magician' and also as the 'House of the Dwarf'. These names were derived from a Maya legend which asserted that a dwarf with supernatural powers had raised the entire building in just one night.[9]

The steps, as I climbed them, seemed more and more perversely narrow. My instinct was to lean forward, flatten myself against the side of the pyramid, and cling on for dear life. Instead I looked up at the angry, overcast sky above me. Flocks of birds circled, screeching wildly as though seeking refuge from some impending disaster, and the thick mass of low-lying cloud that had blotted out the sun a few hours earlier was now so agitated by high winds that it seemed to boil.

The Pyramid of the Magician was by no means unique in being associated with the supernatural powers of dwarves, whose architectural and masonry skills were widely renowned in Central America.

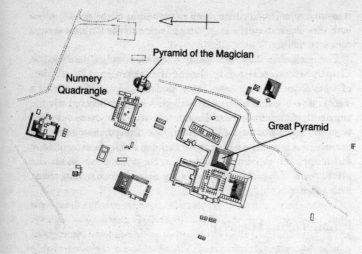

Uxmal.

'Construction work was easy for them,' asserted one typical Maya legend, 'all they had to do was whistle and heavy rocks would move into place.'[10]

A very similar tradition, as the reader may recall, claimed that the gigantic stone blocks of the mysterious Andean city of Tiahuanaco had been 'carried through the air to the sound of a trumpet'.[11]

In both Central America and in the far-off regions of the Andes, therefore, strange sounds had been associated with the miraculous levitation of massive rocks.

What was I to make of this? Maybe, through some fluke, two almost identical 'fantasies' could have been independently invented in both these geographically remote areas. But that didn't seem very likely. Equally worthy of consideration was the possibility that common recollections of an ancient building technology could have been preserved in stories such as these, a technology capable of lifting huge blocks of stone off the ground with 'miraculous' ease. Could it be relevant that memories of almost identical miracles were preserved in

Ancient Egypt? There, in one typical tradition, a magician was said to have raised into the air 'a huge vault of stone 200 cubits long and 50 cubits broad'?[12]

The sides of the stairway I was climbing were richly decorated with what the nineteenth-century American explorer John Lloyd Stephens described as 'a species of sculptured mosaic'.[13] Oddly, although the Pyramid of the Magician had been built long centuries before the Conquest, the symbol most frequently featured in these mosaics was a close approximation of the Christian cross. Indeed there were two distinct kinds of 'Christian' crosses: one the wide-pawed *croix-patte* favoured by the Knights Templar and other crusading orders in the twelfth and thirteenth centuries; the other the x-shaped Saint Andrew's cross.

After climbing a further shorter flight of steps I reached the temple at the very top of the Magician's pyramid. It consisted of a single corbel-vaulted chamber from the ceiling of which large numbers of bats hung suspended. Like the birds and the clouds, they were visibly distressed by the sense of a huge storm brewing. In a furry mass they shuffled restlessly upside down, folding and unfolding their small leathery wings.

I took a rest on the high platform that surrounded the chamber. From here, looking down, I could see many more crosses. They were everywhere, literally all over this bizarre and ancient structure. I remembered the Andean city of Tiahuanaco and the crosses that had been carved there, in distant pre-Colombian times, on some of the great blocks of stone lying scattered around the building known as Puma Punku.[14] 'Man in Snake', the Olmec sculpture from La Venta, had also been engraved with two Saint Andrew's crosses long before the birth of Christ. And now, here at the Pyramid of the Magician in the Mayan site of Uxmal, I was confronted by crosses yet again.

Bearded men . . .

Serpents . . .

Crosses . . .

How likely was it to be an accident that symbols as distinctive as these should repeat themselves in widely separated cultures and at different periods of history? Why were they so often built into the fabric of sophisticated works of art and architecture?

A science of prophecy

Not for the first time I suspected that I might be looking at signs and icons left behind by some cult or secret society which had sought to keep the light of civilization burning in Central America (and perhaps elsewhere) through long ages of darkness. I thought it notable that the motifs of the bearded man, the Plumed Serpent, and the cross all tended to crop up whenever and wherever there were hints that a technologically advanced and as yet unidentified civilization might once have been in contact with the native cultures. And there was a sense of great age about this contact, as though it took place at such an early date that it had been almost forgotten.

I thought again about the sudden way the Olmecs had emerged, around the middle of the second millennium BC, out of the swirling mists of opaque prehistory. All the archaeological evidence indicated that from the beginning they had venerated huge stone heads and stele showing bearded men. I found myself increasingly drawn to the possibility that some of those remarkable pieces of sculpture could have been part of a vast inheritance of civilization handed down to the peoples of Central America many thousands of years *before* the second millenium BC, and thereafter entrusted to the safekeeping of a secret wisdom cult, perhaps the cult of Quetzalcoatl.

Much had been lost. Nevertheless the tribes of this region – in particular the Maya, the builders of Palenque and Uxmal – had preserved something even more mysterious and wonderful than the enigmatic monoliths, something which declared itself even more persistently to be the legacy of an older and a higher civilization. We see in the next chapter that it was the mystical science of an ancient star-gazing folk, a science of time and measurement and prediction – a science of prophecy even – that the Maya had preserved most perfectly from the past. With it they inherited memories of a terrible, earth-destroying flood and an idiosyncratic legacy of empirical knowledge, knowledge of a high order which they shouldn't really have possessed, knowledge that we have only reacquired very recently . . .

Chapter 21

A Computer for Calculating the End of the World

The Maya knew where their advanced learning originated. It was handed down to them, they said, from the First Men, the creatures of Quetzalcoatl, whose names had been Balam-Quitze (Jaguar with the Sweet Smile), Balam-Acab (Jaguar of the Night), Mahucutah (The Distinguished Name) and Iqui-Balam (Jaguar of the Moon).[1] According to the *Popol Vuh*, these forefathers:

> were endowed with intelligence; they saw and instantly they could see far; they succeeded in seeing; they succeeded in knowing all that there is in the world. The things hidden in the distance they saw without first having to move . . . Great was their wisdom; their sight reached to the forests, the rocks, the lakes, the seas, the mountains, and the valleys. In truth, they were admirable men . . . They were able to know all, and they examined the four corners, the four points of the arch of the sky, and the round face of the earth.[2]

The achievements of this race aroused the envy of several of the most powerful deities. 'It is not well that our creatures should know all,' opined these gods, 'Must they perchance be the equals of ourselves, their Makers, who can see afar, who know all and see all? . . . Must they also be gods?'[3]

Obviously such a state of affairs could not be allowed to continue. After some deliberation an order was given and appropriate action taken:

Let their sight reach only to that which is near; let them see only a little
of the face of the earth . . . Then the Heart of Heaven blew mist into
their eyes which clouded their sight as when a mirror is breathed
upon. Their eyes were covered and they could only see what was close,
only that was clear to them . . . In this way the wisdom and all the
knowledge of the First Men were destroyed.[4]

Anyone familiar with the Old Testament will remember that the
reason for the expulsion of Adam and Eve from the Garden of Eden
had to do with similar divine concerns. After the First Man had eaten
of the fruit of the tree of the knowledge of good and evil,

The Lord God said, 'Behold, the man has become as one of us, to
know good and evil. Now, lest he put forth his hand and take also of
the tree of life and eat and live for ever, [let us] send him forth from the
Garden of Eden . . .'[5]

The *Popol Vuh* is accepted by scholars as a great reservoir of
uncontaminated, pre-Colombian tradition.[6] It is therefore puzzling to
find such similarities between these traditions and those recorded in
the *Genesis* story. Moreover, like so many of the other Old World/
New World links we have identified, the character of the similarities is
not suggestive of any kind of direct influence of one region on the
other but of two different interpretations of the same set of events.
Thus, for example:

• The biblical Garden of Eden looks like a metaphor for the state of
  blissful, almost 'godlike', knowledge that the 'First Men' of the
  Popol Vuh enjoyed.
• The essence of this knowledge was the ability to 'see all' and to
  'know all'. Was this not precisely the ability Adam and Eve acquired
  after eating the forbidden fruit, which grew on the branches of 'the
  tree of the knowledge of good and evil'?
• Finally, just as Adam and Eve were driven out of the Garden, so
  were the four First Men of the *Popol Vuh* deprived of their ability to
  'see far'. Thereafter 'their eyes were covered and they could only see
  what was close . . .'

Both the *Popol Vuh* and *Genesis* therefore tell the story of mankind's
fall from grace. In both cases, this state of grace was closely associated
with *knowledge*, and the reader is left in no doubt that the knowledge

in question was so remarkable that it conferred godlike powers on those who possessed it.

The Bible, adopting a dark and muttering tone of voice, calls it 'the knowledge of good and evil' and has nothing further to add. The *Popol Vuh* is much more informative. It tells us that the knowledge of the First Men consisted of the ability to see 'things hidden in the distance', that they were astronomers who 'examined the four corners, the four points of the arch of the sky', and that they were geographers who succeeded in measuring 'the round face of the earth'.[7]

Geography is about maps. In Part I we saw evidence suggesting that the cartographers of an as yet unidentified civilization might have mapped the planet with great thoroughness at an early date. Could the *Popol Vuh* be transmitting some garbled memory of that same civilization when it speaks nostalgically of the First Men and of the miraculous geographical knowledge they possessed?

Geography is about maps and astronomy is about stars. Very often the two disciplines go hand in hand because stars are essential for navigation on long sea-going voyages of discovery (and long sea-going voyages of discovery are essential for the production of accurate maps).

Is it accidental that the First Men of the *Popol Vuh* were remembered not only for studying 'the round face of the earth' but for their contemplation of 'the arch of heaven'?[8] And is it a coincidence that the outstanding achievement of Mayan society was its observational astronomy, upon which, through the medium of advanced mathematical calculations, was based a clever, complex, sophisticated and very accurate calendar?

Knowledge out of place

In 1954 J. Eric Thompson, a leading authority on the archaeology of Central America, confessed to a deep sense of puzzlement at a number of glaring disparities he had identified between the generally unremarkable achievements of the Mayas, as a whole and the advanced state of their astro-calendrical knowledge, 'What mental quirks,' he asked, 'led the Maya intelligentsia to chart the heavens, yet fail to grasp the principle of the wheel; to visualize eternity, as no other semi-civilized people has ever done, yet ignore the short step from corbelled to true arch; to count in millions, yet never to learn to weigh a sack of corn?"[9]

Perhaps the answer to these questions is much simpler than Thompson realized. Perhaps the astronomy, the deep understanding of time, and the long-term mathematical calculations, were not 'quirks' at all. Perhaps they were the constituent parts of a coherent *but very specific body of knowledge* that the Maya had inherited, more or less intact, from an older and wiser civilization. Such an inheritance would explain the contradictions observed by Thompson, and there is no need for any dispute on the point. We already know that the Maya received their calendar as a legacy from the Olmecs (a thousand years earlier, the Olmecs were using exactly the same system). The real question, should be, where did the Olmecs get it? What kind of level of technological and scientific development was required for a civilization to devise a calendar as good as this?

Take the case of the solar year. In modern Western society we still make use of a solar calendar which was introduced in Europe in 1582 and is based on the best scientific knowledge then available: the famous Gregorian calendar. The Julian calendar, which it replaced, computed the period of the earth's orbit around the sun at 365.25 days. Pope Gregory XIII's reform substituted a finer and more accurate calculation: 365.2425 days. Thanks to scientific advances since 1582 we now know that the *exact* length of the solar year is 365.2422 days. The Gregorian calendar therefore incorporates a very small plus error, just 0.0003 of a day – pretty impressive accuracy for the sixteenth century.

Strangely enough, though its origins are wrapped in the mists of antiquity far deeper than the sixteenth century, the Mayan calendar achieved even greater accuracy. It calculated the solar year at 365.2420 days, a minus error of only 0.0002 of a day.[10]

Similarly, the Maya knew the time taken by the moon to orbit the earth. Their estimate of this period was 29.528395 days – extremely close to the true figure of 29.530588 days computed by the finest modern methods.[11] The Mayan priests also had in their possession very accurate tables for the prediction of solar and lunar eclipses and were aware that these could occur only within plus or minus eighteen days of the node (when the moon's path crosses the apparent path of the sun).[12] Finally, the Maya were remarkably accomplished mathematicians. They possessed an advanced technique of metrical calculation by means of a chequerboard device we ourselves have only discovered (or rediscovered?) in the last century.[13] They also understood perfectly and used the abstract concept of zero[14] and were acquainted with place numerations.

These are esoteric fields. As Thompson observed,

> The cipher (nought) and place numerations are so much parts of our cultural heritage and seem such obvious conveniences that it is difficult to comprehend how their invention could have been long delayed. Yet neither ancient Greece with its great mathematicians, nor ancient Rome, had any inkling of either nought or place numeration. To write 1848 in Roman numerals requires eleven letters: MDCCCXLVIII. Yet the Maya had a system of place-value notation very much like our own at a time when the Romans were still using their clumsy method.[15]

Isn't it a bit odd that this otherwise unremarkable Central American tribe should, at such an early date, have stumbled upon an innovation which Otto Neugebauer, the historian of science, has described as 'one of the most fertile inventions of humanity'[16]

Someone else's science?

Let us now consider the question of Venus, a planet that was of immense symbolic importance to all the ancient peoples of Central America, who identified it strongly with Quetzalcoatl (or Gucumatz or Kukulkan, as the Plumed Serpent was known in the Maya dialects).[17]

Unlike the Ancient Greeks, but like the Ancient Egyptians, the Maya understood that Venus was both 'the morning star' and 'the evening star'.[18] They understood other things about it as well. The 'synodical revolution' of a planet is the period of time it takes to return to any given point in the sky – as viewed from earth. Venus revolves around the sun every 224.7 days, while the earth follows its own slightly wider orbit. The composite result of these two motions is that

Venus rises in exactly the same place in the earth's sky approximately every 584 days.

Whoever invented the sophisticated calendrical system inherited by the Maya had been aware of this and had found ingenious ways to integrate it with other interlocking cycles. Moreover, it is clear from the mathematics which brought these cycles together that the ancient calendar masters had understood that 584 days was only an *approximation* and that the movements of Venus are by no means regular. They had therefore worked out the exact figure established by today's science for the *average* synodical revolution of Venus over very long periods of time.[19] That figure is 583.92 days and it was knitted into the fabric of the Mayan calendar in numerous intricate and complex ways.[20] For example, to reconcile it with the so-called 'sacred year' (the *tzolkin* of 260 days, which was divided into 13 months of 20 days each) the calendar called for a correction of four days to be made every 61 Venus years. In addition, during every fifth cycle, a correction of eight days was made at the end of the 57th revolution. Once these steps were taken, the *tzolkin* and the synodical revolution of Venus were intermeshed so tightly that the degree of error to which the equation was subject was staggeringly small – one day in 6000 years.[21] And what made this all the more remarkable was that a further series of precisely calculated adjustments kept the Venus cycle and the *tzolkin* not only in harmony with each other but in exact relationship with the solar year. Again this was achieved in a manner which ensured that the calendar was capable of doing its job, virtually error-free, over vast expanses of time.[22]

Why did the 'semi-civilized' Maya *need* this kind of high-tech precision? Or did they inherit, in good working order, a calendar engineered to fit the needs of a much earlier and far more advanced civilization?

Consider the crowning jewel of Maya calendrics, the so-called 'Long Count'. This system of calculating dates also expressed beliefs about the past – notably, the widely held belief that time operated in Great Cycles which witnessed recurrent creations and destructions of the world. According to the Maya, the current Great Cycle began in darkness on 4 *Ahau* 8 *Cumku*, a date corresponding to 13 August 3114 BC in our own calendar.[23] As we have seen, it was also believed that the cycle will come to an end, amid global destruction, on 4 *Ahau* 3 *Kankin*: 23 December AD 2012 in our calendar. The function of the Long Count was to record the elapse of time since the beginning of the current Great Cycle, literally to count off, one by one, the 5125 years allotted to our present creation.[24]

The Long Count is perhaps best envisaged as a sort of celestial adding machine, constantly calculating and recalculating the scale of our growing debt to the universe. Every last penny of that debt is going to be called in when the figure on the meter reads 5125.

So, at any rate, thought the Maya.

Calculations on the Long Count computer were not, of course, done in our numbers. The Maya used their own notation, which they had derived from the Olmecs, who had derived it from . . . nobody knows. This notation was a combination of dots (signifying ones or units or multiples of twenty), bars (signifying fives or multiples of five times twenty), and a shell glyph signifying zero. Spans of time were counted by days (*kin*), periods of twenty days (*uinal*), 'computing years' of 360 days (*tun*), periods of 20 *tuns* (known as *katun*), and periods of 20 *katuns* (known as *bactun*). There were also 8000-*tun* periods (*pictun*) and 160,000-*tun* periods (*calabtun*) to mop up even larger calculations.[25]

All this should make clear that although the Maya believed themselves to be living in one Great Cycle that would surely come to a violent end they also knew that time was infinite and that it proceeded with its mysterious revolutions regardless of individual lives or civilizations. As Thompson summed up in his great study on the subject:

> In the Maya scheme the road over which time had marched stretched into a past so distant that the mind of man cannot comprehend its remoteness. Yet the Maya undauntedly retrod that road seeking its starting point. A fresh view, leading further backward, unfolded at every stage; the mellowed centuries blended into millennia, and they into tens of thousands of years, as those tireless inquirers explored deeper and still deeper into the eternity of the past. On a stela at Quiriga in Guatemala a date over 90 million years ago is computed; on another a date over 300 million years before that is given. These are actual computations, stating correctly day and month positions, and are comparable to calculations in our calendar giving the month

positions on which Easter would have fallen at equivalent distances in the past. The brain reels at such astronomical figures . . .[26]

Isn't all this a bit *avant-garde* for a civilization that didn't otherwise distinguish itself in many ways? It's true that Mayan architecture was good within its limits. But there was precious little else that these jungle-dwelling Indians did which suggested they might have had the capacity (or the need) to conceive of really *long* periods of time.

It's been a good deal less than two centuries since the majority of Western intellectuals abandoned Bishop Usher's opinion that the world was created in 4004 BC and accepted that it must be infinitely older that that.[27] In plain English this means that the ancient Maya had a far more accurate understanding of the true immensity of geological time, and of the vast antiquity of our planet, than did anyone in Britain, Europe or North America until Darwin propounded the theory of evolution.

So how come the Maya got handy with big periods like hundreds of millions of years? Was it a freak of cultural development? Or did they inherit the calendrical and mathematical tools which facilitated, and enabled them to develop, this sophisticated understanding? If an inheritance was involved, it is legimate to ask what the original inventors of the Mayan calendar's computerlike circuitry had intended it to do. What had they designed it for? Had they simply conceived of all its complexities to concoct 'a challenge to the intellect, a sort of tremendous anagram', as one authority claimed?[28] Or could they have had a more pragmatic and important objective in mind?

We have seen that the obsessive concern of Mayan society, and indeed of all the ancient cultures of Central America, was with calculating – and if possible postponing – the end of the world. Could this be the purpose the mysterious calendar was designed to fulfil? Could it have been a mechanism for predicting some terrible cosmic or geological catastrophe?

Chapter 22

City of the Gods

The overwhelming message of a large number of Central American legends is that the Fourth Age of the world ended very badly. A catastrophic deluge was followed by a long period during which the light of the sun vanished from the sky and the air was filled with a tenebrous darkness. Then:

> The gods gathered together at Teotihuacan ['the place of the gods'] and wondered anxiously who was to be the next Sun. Only the sacred fire [the material representation of Huehueteotl, the god who gave life its beginning] could be seen in the darkness, still quaking following the recent chaos. 'Someone will have to sacrifice himself, throw himself into the fire,' they cried, 'only then will there be a Sun.'[1]

A drama ensued in which two deities (Nanahuatzin and Tecciztecatl) immolated themselves for the common good. One burned quickly in the centre of the sacred fire; the other roasted slowly on the embers at its edge 'The gods waited for a long time until eventually the sky started to glow red as at dawn. In the east appeared the great sphere of the sun, life-giving and incandescent . . .'[2]

It was at this moment of cosmic rebirth that Quetzalcoatl manifested himself. His mission was with humanity of the Fifth Age. He therefore took the form of a human being – a bearded white man, just like Viracocha.

In the Andes, Viracocha's capital was Tiahuanaco. In Central

America, Quetzalcoatl's was the supposed birth-place of the Fifth Sun, Teotihuacan, the city of the gods.[3]

The Citadel, the Temple and the Map of Heaven

Teotihuacan, 50 kilometres north-east of Mexico City

I stood in the airy enclosure of the Citadel and looked north across the morning haze towards the Pyramids of the Sun and the Moon. Set amid grey-green scrub country, and ringed by distant mountains, these two great monuments played their parts in a symphony of ruins strung out along the axis of the so-called 'Street of the Dead'. The Citadel lay at the approximate mid point of this wide avenue which ran perfectly straight for more than four kilometres. The Pyramid of the Moon was at its northern extreme, the Pyramid of the Sun offset somewhat to its east.

In the context of such a geometric site, an exact north-south or east-west orientation might have been expected. It was therefore surprising that the architects who had planned Teotihuacan had deliberately chosen to incline the Street of the Dead 15° 30′ east of north. There were several theories as to why this eccentric orientation had been selected, but none was especially convincing. Growing numbers of scholars, however, were beginning to wonder whether astronomical alignments might have been involved. One, for example, had proposed that the Street of the Dead might have been 'built to face the setting of the Pleiades at the time when it was constructed'.[4] Another, Professor Gerald Hawkins, had suggested that a 'Sirius–Pleiades axis' could also have played a part.[5] And Stansbury Hagar (secretary of the Department of Ethnology at the Brooklyn Institute of the Arts and Sciences), had suggested that the street might represent the Milky Way.[6]

Indeed Hagar went further than this, seeing the portrayal of specific planets and stars in many of the pyramids, mounds and other structures that hovered like fixed satellites around the axis of the Street of the Dead. His complete thesis was that Teotihuacan had been designed as a kind of 'map of heaven': 'It reproduced on earth a supposed celestial plan of the sky-world where dwelt the deities and spirits of the dead.'[7]

21 Temple of the Warriors at Chichen Itza, Yucatan, Mexico. In the foreground is a *Chacmool* idol, gazing westwards, the direction traditionally associated with death. In the background, at the rear of the Temple behind the idol, can be seen a sacrificial altar supported on low pillars. The plate that the idol holds across its belly was used to hold the freshly-extracted hearts of victims sacrificed in the belief that their deaths might delay the coming of the end of the world.

Above: **22** Temple of Kukulcan/Quetzalcoatl at Chichen Itza. An advanced geodetic science was used to position this striking ziggurat so that special light and shadow effects would occur with clockwork precision on the vernal and autumnal equinoxes. On both days, these effects continue to create the illusion of a giant serpent undulating on the northern staircase. *Below*: **23** and **24** Side and front views of the Altar of Infant Sacrifice found at La Venta and associated with the Olmecs – the so-called 'mother culture' of Central America because it is the oldest so far identified. *Facing page*: **25, 26, 27, 28** Various 'Olmec Heads', weighing as much as 60 tons each, which depict a racial type that is alien to the Americas.

29, 30, 31, 32 Found in the same ancient archaeological strata with the strongly negroid Olmec heads, are images like these (from La Venta and Monte Alban) that appear to depict bearded Caucasian figures. The Central American deity Quetzalcoatl (like Viracocha in the Andes) was reported to have been tall, pale-skinned and bearded.

Above: **33** 'Man in Serpent' sculpture from the Olmec site of La Venta. Note the X-shaped crosses on the head-dress and compare with pre-Christian crucifix and serpent symbology found elsewhere – for example at Tiahuanaco in the Andes and in ancient Egypt. Note also the curiously mechanical appearance of the 'feathered serpent' device inside which the man is seated. *Below*: **34** The Temple of the Inscriptions, an elegant step-pyramid, at the Classical Mayan site of Palenque.

Previous page, top left: **35** Tomb-chamber within the Temple of the Inscriptions, supposed burial place of Lord Pacal, ruler of Palenque. *Top right*: **36** A rubbing from the sarcophagus lid reveals another curiously mechanical design involving a man who appears to be seated inside some kind of device. *Bottom left*: **37** Group of idols on the pyramid platform at Tula, Mexico. *Bottom right*: **38** Detail of weapon held by one of the idols. Central American legends speak of weapons known as *xiuhcoatl*, 'fire-serpents' which emitted burning rays capable of piercing and dismembering human bodies. *This page, above*: **39** Pyramid of the Magician at Uxmal. Maya traditions assert that a dwarf, with supernatural powers, raised up the entire 120-foot-high building in just one night.

Above: **40** Day-trippers from Mexico City gather near the apex of the Pyramid of the Moon at Teotihuacan to gaze down the immense astronomically-aligned axis known as the Way of the Dead, which is flanked, to the east, by the huge bulk of the Pyramid of the Sun. The culture that founded Teotihuacan has been lost to history. *Below*: **41** The Pyramid of the Sun (foreground) and the Pyramid of the Moon viewed from the Temple of Quetzalcoatl.

Pyramid of the Moon

Pyramid of the Sun

Pyramid of the Quezalcoatl

The Citadel

Teotihuacan.

During the 1960s and 1970s Hagar's intuitions were tested in the field by Hugh Harleston Jr, an American engineer resident in Mexico, who carried out a comprehensive mathematical survey at Teotihuacan. Harleston reported his findings in October 1974 at the International Congress of Americanists.[8] His paper, which was full of daring and innovative ideas, contained some particularly curious information about the Citadel and about the Temple of Quetzalcoatl located at the eastern extreme of this great square compound.

The Temple was regarded by scholars as one of the best-preserved archaeological monuments in Central America.[9] This was because the original, prehistoric structure had been partially buried beneath another much later mound imediately in front of it to the west. Excavation of that mound had revealed the elegant six-stage pyramid that now confronted me. It stood 72 feet high and its base covered an area of 82,000 square feet.

Still bearing traces of the original multicoloured paints which had coated it in antiquity, the exposed Temple was a beautiful and strange sight. The predominant sculptural motif was a series of huge serpent heads protruding three-dimensionally out of the facing blocks and lining the sides of the massive central stairway. The elongated jaws of these oddly humanoid reptiles were heavily endowed with fangs, and the upper lips with a sort of handlebar moustache. Each serpent's thick neck was ringed by an elaborate plume of feathers – the unmistakable symbol of Quetzalcoatl.[10]

What Harleston's investigations had shown was that a complex mathematical relationship appeared to exist among the principal structures lined up along the Street of the Dead (and indeed beyond it). This relationship suggested something extraordinary, namely that Teotihuacan might originally have been designed as a precise scale-model of the solar system. At any rate, if the centre line of the Temple of Quetzalcoatl were taken as denoting the position of the sun, markers laid out northwards from it along the axis of the Street of the Dead seemed to indicate the correct orbital distances of the inner planets, the asteroid belt, Jupiter, Saturn (represented by the so-called 'Sun' Pyramid), Uranus (by the 'Moon' Pyramid), and Neptune and Pluto, by as yet unexcavated mounds some kilometres farther north.[11]

If these correlations were more than coincidental, then, at the very least, they indicated the presence at Teotihuacan of an advanced observational astronomy, one not surpassed by modern science until a relatively late date. Uranus remained unknown to our own astronomers until 1787, Neptune until 1846 and Pluto until 1930. Even the most conservative estimate of Teotihuacan's antiquity, by contrast, suggested that the principal ingredients of the site-plan (including the Citadel, the Street of the Dead and the Pyramids of the Sun and the Moon) must date back *at least* to the time of Christ.[12] No known civilization of that epoch, either in the Old World or in the New, is supposed to have had any knowledge at all of the outer planets – let alone to have possessed accurate information concerning their orbital distances from each other and from the sun.

Egypt and Mexico – more coincidences?

After completing his studies of the pyramids and avenues of Teotihuacan, Stansbury Hagar concluded: 'We have not yet realized either the importance or the refinement, or the widespread distribution throughout ancient America, of the astronomical cult of which the celestial plan was a feature, and of which Teotihuacan was one of the principal centres.'[13]

But was this just an astronomical 'cult'? Or was it something approximating more closely to what we might call a science? And whether cult or science, was it realistic to suppose that it had enjoyed 'widespread distribution' only in the Americas when there was so much evidence linking it to other parts of the ancient world?

For example, archaeo-astronomers making use of the latest star-mapping computer programmes had recently demonstrated that the three world-famous pyramids on Egypt's Giza plateau formed an exact terrestrial diagram of the three belt stars in the constellation of Orion.[14] Nor was this the limit of the celestial map the Ancient Egyptian priests had created in the sands on the west bank of the Nile. Included in their overall vision, as we shall see in Parts VI and VII, there was a natural feature – the river Nile – which was exactly where it should be had it been designed to represent the Milky Way.[15]

The incorporation of a 'celestial plan' into key sites in Egypt and

Mexico did not by any means exclude religious functions. On the contrary, whatever else they may have been intended for it is certain that the monuments of Teotihuacan, like those of the Giza plateau, played important religious roles in the lives of the communities they served.

Thus Central American traditions collected in the sixteenth century by Father Bernardino de Sahagun gave eloquent expression to a widespread belief that Teotihuacan had fulfilled at least one specific and important religious function in ancient times. According to these legends the City of the Gods was so known because 'the Lords therein buried, after their deaths, did not perish but turned into gods . . .'[16] In other words, it was 'the place where men became gods'.[17] It was additionally known as 'the place of those who had the road of the gods',[18] and 'the place where gods were made'.[19]

Was it a coincidence, I wondered, that this seemed to have been the religious purpose of the three pyramids at Giza? The archaic hieroglyphs of the Pyramid Texts, the oldest coherent body of writing in the world, left little room for doubt that the ultimate objective of the rituals carried out within those colossal structures was to bring about the deceased pharaoh's transfiguration – to 'throw open the doors of the firmament and to make a road' so that he might 'ascend into the company of the gods'.[20]

The notion of pyramids as devices designed (presumably in some metaphysical sense) 'to turn men into gods' was, it seemed to me, too idiosyncratic and peculiar to have been arrived at independently in both Ancient Egypt and Mexico. So, too, was the idea of using the layout of sacred sites to incorporate a celestial plan.

Moreover, there were other strange similarities that deserved to be considered.

Just as at Giza, three principal pyramids had been built at Teotihuacan: the Pyramid/Temple of Quetzalcoatl, the Pyramid of the Sun and the Pyramid of the Moon. Just as at Giza, the site plan was not symmetrical, as one might have expected, but involved two structures in direct alignment with each other while the third appeared to have been deliberately offset to one side. Finally, at Giza, the summits of the Great Pyramid and the Pyramid of Cephren were level, even though the former was a taller building than the latter.

Likewise, at Teotihuacan, the summits of the Pyramids of the Sun and the Moon were level even though the former was taller. The reason was the same in both cases: the Great Pyramid was built on lower ground than the Pyramid of Cephren, and the Pyramid of the Sun on lower ground than the Pyramid of the Moon.[21]

Could all this be coincidence? Was it not more logical to conclude that there was an ancient connection between Mexico and Egypt?

For reasons I have outlined in Chapters Eighteen and Nineteen I doubted whether any direct, causal link was involved – at any rate within historic times. Once again, however, as with the Mayan calendar, and as with the early maps of Antarctica, was it not worth keeping an open mind to the possibility that we might be dealing with a legacy: that the pyramids of Egypt and the ruins of Teotihuacan might express the technology, the geographical knowledge, the observational astronomy (and perhaps also the religion) of a forgotten civilization of the past which had once, as the *Popul Vuh* claimed, 'examined the four corners, the four points of the arch of the sky, and the round face of the earth'?

There was widespread agreement among academics concerning the antiquity of the Giza pyramids, thought to be about 4500 years old.[22] No such unanimity existed with regard to Teotihuacan. Neither the Street of the Dead, nor the Temple of Quetzalcoatl, nor the Pyramids of the Sun and the Moon had ever been definitively dated.[23] The majority of scholars believed that the city had flourished between between 100 BC and AD 600, but others argued strongly that it must have risen to prominence much earlier, between 1500 and 1000 BC. There were others still who sought, largely on geological grounds, to push the foundation date back to 4000 BC before the eruption of the nearby volcano Xitli.[24]

Amid all this uncertainty about the age of Teotihuacan, I had not been surprised to discover that no one had the faintest idea of the identity of those who had actually built the largest and most remarkable metropolis ever to have existed in the pre-Colombian New World.[25] All that could be said for sure was this: when the Aztecs, on their march to imperial power, first stumbled upon the mysterious city in the twelfth century AD, its colossal edifices and avenues were already old beyond imagining and so densely overgrown that they seemed more like natural features than works of man.[26] Attached to them, however, was a thread of local legend, passed down from generation to generation, which asserted that they had been built by giants[27] and that their purpose had been to transform men into gods.

Hints of forgotten wisdom

Leaving the Temple of Quetzalcoatl behind me, I recrossed the Citadel in a westerly direction.

There was no archaeological evidence that this enormous enclosure had ever served as a citadel – or, for that matter, that it had any kind of military or defensive function at all. Like so much else about Teotihuacan it had clearly been planned with painstaking care, and executed with enormous effort, but its true purpose remained unidentified by modern scholarship.[28] Even the Aztecs, who had been responsible for naming the Pyramids of the Sun and the Moon (an attribution which had stuck though no one had any idea what the original builders had called them) had failed to invent a name for the Citadel. It had been left to the Spaniards to label it as they did – an understandable conceit since the 36-acre central patio of La Ciuda-dela was surrounded by massively thick embankments more than 23 feet high and some 1500 feet long on each side.[29]

My walk had now brought me to the western extreme of the patio. I climbed a steep set of stairs that led to the top of the embankment and turned north on to the Street of the Dead. Once again I had to remind myself that this was almost certainly not what the Teotihuacanos (whoever they were) had called the immense and impressive avenue. The Spanish name Calle de los Muertos was of Aztec origin, apparently based on speculation that the numerous mounds on either side of the Street were graves (which, as it happened, they were not).[30]

We have already considered the possibility that the Way of the Dead may have served as a terrestrial counterpart of the Milky Way. Of interest in this regard is the work of another American, Alfred E. Schlemmer, who – like Hugh Harleston Jr – was an engineer. Schlemmer's field was technological forecasting, with specific refer-ence to the prediction of earthquakes,[31] on which he presented a paper at the Eleventh National Convention of Chemical Engineers (in Mexico City in October 1971).

Schlemmer's argument was that the Street of the Dead might never have been a street at all. Instead, it might originally have been laid out as a row of linked reflecting pools, filled with water which had descended through a series of locks from the Pyramid of the Moon, at the northern extreme, to the Citadel in the south.

As I walked steadily northward towards the still-distant Moon Pyramid, it seemed to me that this theory had several points in its favour. For a start the 'Street' was blocked at regular intervals by high partition walls, at the foot of which the remains of well-made sluices could clearly be seen. Moreover, the lie of the land would have facilitated a north-south hydraulic flow since the base of the Moon Pyramid stood on ground that was approximately 100 feet higher than the area in front of the Citadel. The partitioned sections could easily have been filled with water and might indeed have served as reflecting pools, creating a spectacle far more dramatic than those offered by the Taj Mahal or the fabled Shalimar Gardens. Finally, the Teotihuacan Mapping Project (financed by the National Science Foundation in Washington DC and led by Professor Rene Millon of the University of Rochester) had demonstrated conclusively that the ancient city had possessed 'many carefully laid-out canals and systems of branching waterways, artificially dredged into straightened portions of a river, which formed a network within Teotihuacan and ran all the way to [Lake Texcoco], now ten miles distant but perhaps closer in antiquity'.[32]

There was much argument about what this vast hydraulic system had been designed to do. Schlemmer's contention was that the particular waterway he had identified had been built to serve a pragmatic purpose as 'a long-range seismic monitor' – part of 'an ancient science, no longer understood'.[33] He pointed out that remote earthquakes 'can cause standing waves to form on a liquid surface right across the planet' and suggested that the carefully graded and spaced reflecting pools of the Street of the Dead might have been designed 'to enable Teotihuacanos to read from the standing waves formed there the location and strength of earthquakes around the

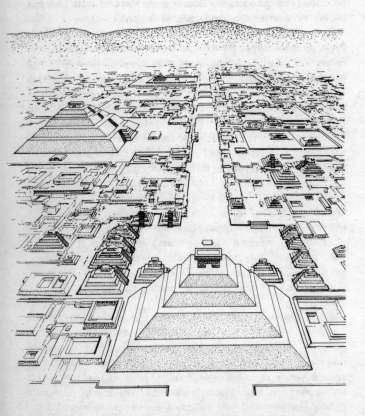

Reconstruction of Teotihuacan, looking down the Way of the Dead from behind the Pyramid of the Moon. The Pyramid of the Sun lies to the left of the Way of the Dead. Visible in the distance beyond it is the pyramid-temple of Quetzalcoatl inside the large compound of the citadel.

globe, thus allowing them to predict such an occurrence in their own area'.[34]

There was, of course, no proof of Schlemmer's theory. However, when I remembered the fixation with earthquakes and floods apparent everywhere in Mexican mythology, and the equally obsessive concern with forecasting future events evident in the Maya calendar, I felt less inclined to dismiss the apparently far-fetched conclusions of the American engineer. If Schlemmer were right, if the ancient Teotihuacanos had indeed understood the principles of resonant vibration and had put them into practice in seismic forecasting, the implication was that they were the possessors of an advanced science. And if people like Hagar and Harleston were right – if, for example, a scale-model of the solar system had also been built into the basic geometry of Teotihuacan – this too suggested that the city was founded by a scientifically evolved civilization not yet identified.

I continued to walk northwards along the Street of the Dead and turned east towards the Pyramid of the Sun. Before reaching this great monument, however, I paused to examine a ruined patio, the principal feature of which was an ancient 'temple' which concealed a perplexing mystery beneath its rock floor.

Chapter 23

The Sun and the Moon
and the Way of the Dead

Some archaeological discoveries are heralded with much fanfare; others, for various reasons, are not. Among this latter category must be included the thick and extensive layer of sheet mica found sandwiched between two of the upper levels of the Teotihuacan Pyramid of the Sun when it was being probed for restoration in 1906. The lack of interest which greeted this discovery, and the absence of any follow-up studies to determine its possible function is quite understandable because the mica, which had a considerable commercial value, was removed and sold as soon as it had been excavated. The culprit was apparently Leopoldo Bartres, who had been commissioned to restore the time-worn pyramid by the Mexican government.[1]

There has also been a much more recent discovery of mica at Teotihuacan (in the 'Mica Temple') and this too has passed almost without notice. Here the reason is harder to explain because there has been no looting and the mica remains on site.[2]

One of a group of buildings, the Mica Temple is situated around a patio about 1000 feet south of the west face of the Pyramid of the Sun. Directly under a floor paved with heavy rock slabs, archaeologists financed by the Viking Foundation excavated two massive sheets of mica which had been carefully and purposively installed at some extremely remote date by a people who must have been skilled in cutting and handling this material. The sheets are ninety feet square and form two layers, one laid directly on top of the other.[3]

Mica is a not a uniform substance but contains trace elements of different metals depending on the kind of rock formation in which it is found. Typically these metals include potassium and aluminium and also, in varying quantities, ferrous and ferric iron, magnesium, lithium, manganese and titanium. The trace elements in Teotihuacan's Mica Temple indicate that the underfloor sheets belong to a type which occurs only in Brazil, some 2000 miles away.[4] Clearly, therefore, the builders of the Temple must have had a specific need for this particular kind of mica and were prepared to go to considerable lengths to obtain it, otherwise they could have used the locally available variety more cheaply and simply.

Mica does not leap to mind as an obvious general-purpose flooring material. Its use to form layers *underneath* a floor, and thus completely out of sight, seems especially bizarre when we remember that no other ancient structure in the Americas, or anywhere else in the world, has been found to contain a feature like this.[5]

It is frustrating that we will never be able to establish the exact position, let alone the purpose, of the large sheet that Bartres excavated and removed from the Pyramid of the Sun in 1906. The two intact layers in the Mica Temple, on the other hand, resting as they do in a place where they had no decorative function, look as though they were designed to do a particular job. Let us note in passing that mica possesses characteristics which suit it especially well for a range of technological applications. In modern industry, it is used in the construction of capacitors and is valued as a thermal and electric insulator. It is also opaque to fast neutrons and can act as a moderator in nuclear reactions.

Erasing messages from the past

Pyramid of the Sun, Teotihuacan
Having climbed more than 200 feet up a series of flights of stone stairs I reached the summit and looked towards the zenith. It was midday 19 May, and the sun was directly overhead, as it would be again on 25

July. On these two dates, and not by accident, the west face of the pyramid was oriented precisely to the position of the setting sun.[6]

A more curious but equally deliberate effect could be observed on the equinoxes, 20 March and 22 September. Then the passage of the sun's rays from south to north resulted at noon in the progressive obliteration of a perfectly straight shadow that ran along one of the lower stages of the western façade. The whole process, from complete shadow to complete illumination, took exactly 66.6 seconds. It had done so without fail, year-in year-out, ever since the pyramid had been built and would continue to do so until the giant edifice crumbled into dust.[7]

What this meant, of course, was that at least one of the many functions of the pyramid had been to serve as a 'perennial clock', precisely signalling the equinoxes and thus facilitating calendar corrections as and when necessary for a people apparently obsessed, like the Maya, with the elapse and measuring of time. Another implication was that the master-builders of Teotihuacan must have possessed an enormous body of astronomic and geodetic data and referred to this data to set the Sun Pyramid at the precise orientation necessary to achieve the desired equinoctial effects.

This was planning and architecture of a high order. It had survived the passage of the millennia and it had survived the wholesale remodelling of much of the pyramid's outer shell conducted in the first decade of the twentieth century by the self-styled restorer, Leopoldo Bartres. In addition to plundering precious evidence that might have helped us towards a better understanding of the purposes for which the enigmatic structure had been built, this repulsive lackey of Mexico's corrupt dictator Porfirio Diaz had removed the outer layer of stone, mortar and plaster *to a depth of more than twenty feet* from the entire northern, eastern and southern faces. The result was catastrophic: the underlying adobe surface began to dissolve in heavy rains and to exhibit plastic flow which threatened to destroy the whole edifice. Although the slippage was halted with hasty remedial measures, nothing could change the fact that the Sun Pyramid had been deprived of almost all its original surface features.

By modern archaeological standards this was, of course, an unforgivable act of desecration. Because of it, we will never learn the significance of the many sculptures, inscriptions, reliefs and artefacts that had almost certainly been removed with those twenty feet of the outer shell. Nor was this the only or even the most regrettable consequence of Bartres's grotesque vandalism. There was startling evidence which suggested that the unknown architects of the Pyramid of the Sun might have intentionally incorporated scientific data into many of the key dimensions of the great structure. This evidence had been gathered and extrapolated from the intact west face (which, not accidentally, was also the face where the intended equinoctial effects could still be seen), but thanks to Bartres, no similar information was likely to be forthcoming from the other three faces because of the arbitrary alterations imposed upon them. Indeed, by drastically distorting the original shape and size of so much of the pyramid, the Mexican 'restorer' had possibly deprived posterity of some of the most important lessons Teotihuacan had to teach.

Eternal numbers

The transcendental number known as *pi* is fundamental to advanced mathematics. With a value slightly in excess of 3.14 it is the ratio of the diameter of a circle to its circumference. In other words if the diameter of a circle is 12 inches, the circumference of that circle will be 12 inches x 3.14 = 37.68 inches. Likewise, since the diameter of a circle is exactly double the radius, we can use *pi* to calculate the circumference of any circle from its radius. In this case, however, the formula is the length of the radius multiplied by 2*pi*. As an illustration let us take again a circle of 12 inches diameter. Its radius will be 6 inches and its circumference can be obtained as follows: 6 inches x 2 x 3.14 = 37.68 inches. Similarly a circle with a radius of 10 inches will have a circumference of 67.8 inches (10 inches x 2 x 3.14) and a circle with a radius of 7 inches will have a circumference of 43.96 inches (7 inches x 2 x 3.14).

These formulae using the value of *pi* for calculating circumference from either diameter or radius apply to all circles, no matter how large or how small, and also, of course, to all spheres and hemispheres. They seem relatively simple – with hindsight. Yet their discovery, which represented a revolutionary breakthrough in mathematics, is thought to have been made late in human history. The orthodox view is that Archimedes in the third century BC was the first man to calculate *pi* correctly at 3.14.[8] Scholars do not accept that any of the mathematicians of the New World ever got anywhere near *pi* before the arrival of the Europeans in the sixteenth century. It is therefore disorienting to discover that the Great Pyramid at Giza (built more than 2000 years before the birth of Archimedes) and the Pyramid of the Sun at Teotihuacan, which vastly predates the conquest, both incorporate the value of *pi*. They do so, moreover, in much the same way, and in a manner which leaves no doubt that the ancient builders on both sides of the Atlantic were thoroughly conversant with this transcendental number.

The principal factors involved in the geometry of any pyramid are (1) the height of the summit above the ground, and (2) the perimeter of the monument at ground level. Where the Great Pyramid is concerned, the ratio between the original height (481.3949 feet[9]) and the perimeter (3023.16 feet[10]) turns out to be the same as the ratio between the radius and the circumference of a circle, i. e. 2*pi*.[11] Thus, if we take the pyramid's height and multiply it by 2*pi* (as we would with a circle's radius to calculate its circumference) we get an accurate read-out of the monument's perimeter (481.3949 feet 2 x 3.14 = 3023.16 feet). Alternatively, if we turn the equation around and start with the circumference at ground level, we get an equally accurate read-out of the height of the summit (3023.16 feet divided by 2 divided by 3.14 = 481.3949 feet).

Since it is almost inconceivable that such a precise mathematical correlation could have come about by chance, we are obliged to conclude that the builders of the Great Pyramid were indeed conversant with *pi* and that they deliberately incorporated its value into the dimensions of their monument.

Now let us consider the Pyramid of the Sun at Teotihuacan. The angle of its sides is 43.5°[12] (as opposed to 52° in the case of the Great Pyramid[13]). The Mexican monument has the gentler slope because the perimeter of its base, at 2932.8 feet,[14] is not much smaller than that of its Egyptian counterpart while its summit is considerably lower (approximately 233.5 feet prior to Bartres's 'restoration'[15]).

The 2*pi* formula that worked at the Great Pyramid does not work

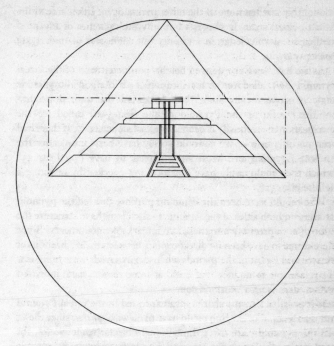

The height of the Pyramid of the Sun × 4*pi* = the perimeter of its base.
The height of the Great Pyramid at Giza × 2*pi* = the perimeter of its base.

with these measurements. A 4*pi* formula does. Thus if we take the height of the Pyramid of the Sun (233.5 feet) and multiply it by 4*pi* we once again obtain a very accurate read-out of the perimeter: 233.5 feet x 4 x 3.14 = 2932.76 feet (a discrepancy of less than half an inch from the true figure of 2932.8 feet).

This, surely, can no more be a coincidence than the *pi* relationship extrapolated from the dimensions of the Egyptian monument. Moreover, the very fact that both structures incorporate *pi* relationships (when none of the other pyramids on either side of the Atlantic does) strongly suggests not only the existence of advanced mathematical knowledge in antiquity but some sort of underlying *common purpose*.

As we have seen the desired height/perimeter ratio of the Great Pyramid ($2pi$) called for the specification of a tricky and idiosyncratic angle of slope for its sides: 52°. Likewise, the desired height/ perimeter ratio of the Pyramid of the Sun ($4pi$) called for the specification of an equally eccentric angle of slope: 43.5°. If there had been no ulterior motive, it would surely have been simpler for the Ancient Egyptian and Mexican architects to have opted for 45° (which they could easily have obtained and checked by bisecting a right angle).

What could have been the common purpose that led the pyramid builders on both sides of the Atlantic to such lengths to structure the value of *pi* so precisely into these two remarkable monuments? Since there seems to have been no direct contact between the civilizations of Mexico and Egypt in the periods when the pyramids were built, is it not reasonable to deduce that both, at some remote date, inherited certain ideas from a common source?

Is it possible that the shared idea expressed in the Great Pyramid and the Pyramid of the Sun could have to do with *spheres*, since these, like the pyramids, are three-dimensional objects (while circles, for example, have only two dimensions)? The desire to symbolize spheres in three-dimensional monuments with flat surfaces would explain why so much trouble was taken to ensure that both incorporated unmistakable *pi* relationships. Furthermore it seems likely that the intention of the builders of both of these monuments was not to symbolize spheres in general but to focus attention on one sphere in particular: the planet earth.

It will be a long while before orthodox archaeologists are prepared to accept that some peoples of the ancient world were advanced enough in science to have possessed good information about the shape and size of the earth. However, according to the calculations of Livio Catullo Stecchini, an American professor of the History of Science and an acknowledged expert on ancient measurement, the evidence for the existence of such anomalous knowledge in antiquity is irrefutable.[16] Stecchini's conclusions, which relate mainly to Egypt, are particularly impressive because they are drawn from mathematical and astronomical data which, by common consent, are beyond serious dispute.[17] A fuller examination of these conclusions, and of the nature of the data on which they rest, is presented in Part VII. At this point, however, a few words from Stecchini may shed further light on the mystery that confronts us:

> The basic idea of the Great Pyramid was that it should be a representation of the northern hemisphere of the earth, a hemisphere projected on flat-surfaces as is done in map-making . . . The Great Pyramid was a projection on four triangular surfaces. The apex represented the pole and the perimeter represented the equator. This is the reason why the perimeter is in relation 2pi to the height. The Great Pyramid represents the northern hemisphere in a scale of 1:43,200.[18]

In Part VII we shall see why this scale was chosen.

Mathematical city

Rising up ahead of me as I walked towards the northern end of the Street of the Dead, the Pyramid of the Moon, mercifully undamaged by restorers, had kept its original form as a four-stage ziggurat. The Pyramid of the Sun, too, had consisted of four stages but Bartres had whimsically sculpted in a fifth stage between the original third and fourth levels.

There was, however, one original feature of the Pyramid of the Sun that Bartres had been unable to despoil: a subterranean passageway leading from a natural cave under the west face. After its accidental discovery in 1971 this passageway was thoroughly explored. Seven feet high, it was found to run eastwards for more than 300 feet until it reached a point close to the pyramid's geometrical centre.[19] Here it debouched into a second cave, of spacious dimensions, which had been artificially enlarged into a shape very similar to that of a four-leaf clover. The 'leaves' were chambers, each about sixty feet in circumference, containing a variety of artefacts such as beautifully engraved slate discs and highly polished mirrors. There was also a complex drainage system of interlocking segments of carved rock pipes.[20]

This last feature was particularly puzzling because there was no known source of water within the pyramid.[21] The sluices, however, left little doubt that water must have been present in antiquity, most probably in large quantities. This brought to mind the evidence for water having once run in the Street of the Dead, the sluices and partition walls I had seen earlier to the north of the Citadel, and Schlemmer's theory of reflecting pools and seismic forecasting.

Indeed, the more I thought about it the more it seemed that water had been the dominant motif at Teotihuacan. Though I had hardly registered it that morning, the Temple of Quetzalcoatl had been decorated not only with effigies of the Plumed Serpent but with unmistakable aquatic symbolism, notably an undulating design suggestive of waves and large numbers of beautiful carvings of seashells. With these images in my mind, I reached the wide plaza at the base of the Pyramid of the Moon and imagined it filled with water, as it might have been, to a depth of about ten feet. It would have looked magnificent: majestic, powerful and serene.

The Akapana Pyramid in far-off Tiahuanaco had also been surrounded by water, which had been the dominant motif there – just as I now found it to be at Teotihuacan.

I began to climb the Pyramid of the Moon. It was smaller than the Pyramid of the Sun, indeed less than half the size, and was estimated to be made up of about one million tons of stone and earth, as against two and a half million tons in the case of the Pyramid of the Sun. The two monuments, in other words, had a combined weight of three and a half million tons. It was thought unlikely that this quantity of material could have been manipulated by fewer than 15,000 men and it was calculated that such a workforce would have taken at least thirty years to complete such an enormous task.[22]

Sufficient labourers would certainly have been available in the vicinity: the Teotihuacan Mapping Project had demonstrated that the population of the city in its heyday could have been as large as 200,000, making it a bigger metropolis than Imperial Rome of the Caesars. The Project had also established that the main monuments visible today covered just a small part of the overall area of ancient

Teotihuacan. At its peak the city had extended across more than twelve square miles and had incorporated some 50,000 individual dwellings in 2000 apartment compounds, 600 subsidiary pyramids and temples, and 500 'factory' areas specializing in ceramic, figurine, lapidary, shell, basalt, slate and ground-stone work.[23]

At the top level of the Pyramid of the Moon I paused and turned slowly around. Across the valley floor, which sloped gently downhill to the south, the whole of Teotihuacan now stretched before me – a geometrical city, designed and built by unknown architects in the time before history began. In the east, overlooking the arrow-straight Street of the Dead, loomed the Pyramid of the Sun, eternally 'printing out' the mathematical message it had been programmed with long ages ago, a message which seemed to direct our attention to the shape of the earth. It almost looked as though the civilization that had built Teotihuacan had made a deliberate choice to encode complex information in enduring monuments and to do it using a mathematical language.

Why a mathematical language?

Perhaps because, no matter what extreme changes and transformations human civilization might go through, the radius of a circle multiplied by $2pi$ (or half the radius multiplied by $4pi$) would always give the correct figure for that circle's circumference. In other words, a mathematical language could have been chosen for practical reasons: unlike any verbal tongue, such a code could always be deciphered, even by people from unrelated cultures living thousands of years in the future.

Not for the first time I felt myself confronted by the dizzying possibility that an entire episode in the story of mankind might have been forgotten. Indeed it seemed to me then, as I overlooked the mathematical city of the gods from the summit of the Pyramid of the Moon, that our species could have been afflicted with some terrible amnesia and that the dark period so blithely and dismissively referred to as 'prehistory' might turn out to conceal unimagined truths about our own past.

What is prehistory, after all, if not a time forgotten – a time for which we have no records? What is prehistory if not an epoch of impenetrable obscurity through which our ancestors passed but about which we have no conscious remembrance? It was out of this epoch of obscurity, configured in mathematical code along astronomical and geodetic lines, that Teotihuacan with all its riddles was sent down to us. And out of that same epoch came the great Olmec sculptures, the inexplicably precise and accurate calendar the Mayans inherited from their predecessors, the inscrutable geoglyphs of Nazca, the mysterious Andean city of Tiahuanaco . . . and so many other marvels of which we do not know the provenance.

It is almost as though we have awakened into the daylight of history from a long and troubled sleep, and yet continue to be disturbed by the faint but haunting echoes of our dreams . . .

Part IV

The Mystery of the Myths

1 A Species with Amnesia

Chapter 24

Echoes of Our Dreams

In some of the most powerful and enduring myths that we have inherited from ancient times, our species seems to have retained a confused but resonant memory of a terrifying global catastrophe.

Where do these myths come from?

Why, though they derive from unrelated cultures, are their storylines so similar? why are they laden with common symbolism? and why do they so often share the same stock characters and plots? If they are indeed *memories*, why are there no historical records of the planetary disaster they seem to refer to?

Could it be that *the myths themselves* are historical records? Could it be that these cunning and immortal stories, composed by anonymous geniuses, were the medium used to record such information and pass it on in the time before history began?

And the ark went upon the face of the waters

There was a king, in ancient Sumer, who sought eternal life. His name was Gilgamesh. We know of his exploits because the myths and traditions of Mesopotamia, inscribed in cuneiform script upon tablets of baked clay, have survived. Many thousands of these tablets, some dating back to the beginning of the third millennium BC, have been excavated from the sands of modern Iraq. They transmit a unique picture of a vanished culture and remind us that even in those days of lofty antiquity human beings preserved memories of times still more remote – times from which they were separated by the interval of a great and terrible deluge:

> I will proclaim to the world the deeds of Gilgamesh. This was the man to whom all things were known; this was the king who knew the countries of the world. He was wise, he saw mysteries and knew secret things, he brought us a tale of the days before the flood. He went on a long journey, was weary, worn-out with labour, returning he rested, he engraved on a stone the whole story.[1]

The story that Gilgamesh brought back had been told to him by a certain Utnapishtim, a king who had ruled thousands of years earlier, who had survived the great flood, and who had been rewarded with the gift of immortality because he had preserved the seeds of humanity and of all living things.

It was long, long ago, said Utnapishtim, when the gods dwelt on earth: Anu, lord of the firmament, Enlil, the enforcer of divine decisions, Ishtar, goddess of war and sexual love and Ea, lord of the waters, man's natural friend and protector.

> In those days the world teemed, the people multiplied, the world bellowed like a wild bull, and the great god was aroused by the clamour. Enlil heard the clamour and he said to the gods in council, 'The uproar of mankind is intolerable and sleep is no longer possible by reason of the babel.' So the gods agreed to exterminate mankind.[2]

Ea, however, took pity on Utnapishtim. Speaking through the reed wall of the king's house he told him of the imminent catastrophe and instructed him to build a boat in which he and his family could survive:

> Tear down your house and build a boat, abandon possessions and look for life, despise worldly goods and save your soul . . . Tear down your house, I say, and build a boat with her dimensions in proportion – her width and length in harmony. Put aboard the seed of all living things, into the boat.[3]

In the nick of time Utnapishtim built the boat as ordered. 'I loaded into her all that I had,' he said, 'loaded her with the seed of all living things':

I put on board all my kith and kin, put on board cattle, wild beasts from open country, all kinds of craftsmen . . . The time was fulfilled. When the first light of dawn appeared a black cloud came up from the base of the sky; it thundered within where Adad, lord of the storm was riding . . . A stupor of despair went up to heaven when the god of the storm turned daylight to darkness, when he smashed the land like a cup . . .

On the first day the tempest blew swiftly and brought the flood . . . No man could see his fellow. Nor could the people be distinguished from the sky. Even the gods were afraid of the flood. They withdrew; they went up to the heaven of Anu and crouched in the outskirts. The gods cowered like curs while Ishtar cried, shrieking aloud, 'Have I given birth unto these mine own people only to glut with their bodies the sea as though they were fish?'⁴

Meanwhile, continued Utnapishtim:

For six days and nights the wind blew, torrent and tempest and flood overwhelmed the world, tempest and flood raged together like warring hosts. When the seventh day dawned the storm from the south subsided, the sea grew calm, the flood was stilled. I looked at the face of the world and there was silence. The surface of the sea stretched as flat as a roof-top. All mankind had returned to clay . . . I opened a hatch and light fell on my face. Then I bowed low, I sat down and I wept, the tears streamed down my face, for on every side was the waste of water . . . Fourteen leagues distant there appeared a mountain, and there the boat grounded; on the mountain of Nisir the boat held fast, she held fast and did not budge . . . When the seventh day dawned I loosed a dove and let her go. She flew away, but finding no resting place she returned. Then I loosed a swallow, and she flew away but finding no resting place she returned. I loosed a raven, she saw that the waters had retreated, she ate, she flew around, she cawed, and she did not come back.'⁵

Utnapishtim knew that it was now safe to disembark:

I poured out a libation on the mountain top . . . I heaped up wood and cane and cedar and myrtle . . . When the gods smelled the sweet savour they gathered like flies over the sacrifice . . .'⁶

These texts are not by any means the only ones to come down to us from the ancient land of Sumer. In other tablets – some almost 5000 years old, others less than 3000 years old – the 'Noah figure' of Utnapishtim is known variously as Zisudra, Xisuthros or Atrahasis. Even so, he is always instantly recognizable as the same patriarchal character, forewarned by the same merciful god, who rides out the same universal flood in the same storm-tossed ark and whose descendants repopulate the world.

There are many obvious resemblances between the Mesopotamian flood myth and the famous biblical story of Noah and the deluge[7] (see note). Scholars argue endlessly about the nature of these resemblances. What really matters, however, is that in each sphere of influence the same solemn tradition has been preserved for posterity – a tradition which tells, in graphic language, of a global catastrophe and of the near-total annihilation of mankind.

Central America

The identical message was preserved in the Valley of Mexico, far away across the world from Mounts Ararat and Nisir. There, culturally and geographically isolated from Judaeo-Christian influences, long ages before the arrival of the Spaniards, stories were told of a great deluge. As the reader will recall from Part III, it was believed that this deluge had swept over the entire earth at the end of the Fourth Sun: 'Destruction came in the form of torrential rain and floods. The mountains disappeared and men were transformed into fish . . .'[8]

According to Aztec mythology only two human beings survived: a man, Coxcoxtli, and his wife, Xochiquetzal, who had been forewarned of the cataclysm by a god. They escaped in a huge boat they had been instructed to build and came to ground on the peak of a tall mountain. There they descended and afterwards had many children who were dumb until the time when a dove on top of a tree gave them the gift of languages. These languages differed so much that the children could not understand one another.[9]

A related Central American tradition, that of the Mechoacanesecs, is in even more striking conformity with the story as we have it in *Genesis* and in the Mesopotamian sources. According to this tradition, the god Tezcatilpoca determined to destroy all mankind with a flood, saving only a certain Tezpi who embarked in a spacious vessel with his wife, his children and large numbers of animals and birds, as well as supplies of grains and seeds, the preservation of which were essential to the future subsistence of the human race. The vessel came to rest on an exposed mountain top after Tezcatilpoca had decreed that the waters of the flood should retire. Wishing to find out whether it was now safe for him to disembark, Tezpi sent out a vulture which, feeding on the carcases with which the earth was now strewn, did not return. The man then sent out other birds, of which only the hummingbird came back, with a leafy branch in its beak. With this sign that the land had begun to renew itself, Tezpi and his family went forth from their ark, multiplied and repopulated the earth.[10]

Memories of a terrible flood resulting from divine displeasure are also preserved in the *Popal Vuh*. According to this archaic text, the Great God decided to create humanity soon after the beginning of time. It was an experiment and he began it with 'figures made of wood that looked like men and talked like men'. These creatures fell out of favour because 'they did not remember their Creator':

> And so a flood was brought about by the Heart of Heaven; a great flood was formed which fell on the heads of the wooden creatures . . . A heavy resin fell from the sky . . . the face of the earth was darkened and a black rain began to fall by day and by night . . . The wooden figures were annihilated, destroyed, broken up and killed.'[11]

Not everyone perished, however. Like the Aztecs and the Mechoaca-nesecs, the Maya of the Yucatan and Guatemala believed that a Noah figure and his wife, 'the Great Father and the Great Mother', had survived the flood to populate the land anew, thus becoming the ancestors of all subsequent generations of humanity.[12]

South America

Moving to South America, we encounter the Chibcas of central Colombia. According to their myths, they had originally lived as savages, without laws, agriculture or religion. Then one day there appeared among them an old man of a different race. He wore a thick long beard and his name was Bochica. He taught the Chibcas how to build huts and live together in society.

His wife, who was very beautiful and named Chia, appeared after him, but she was wicked and enjoyed thwarting her husband's altruistic efforts. Since she could not overcome his power directly, she used magical means to cause a great flood in which the majority of the population died. Bochica was very angry and exiled Chia from the earth to the sky, where she became the moon given the task of lighting the nights. He also caused the waters of the flood to dissipate and brought down the few survivors from the mountains where they had taken refuge. Thereafter he gave them laws, taught them to cultivate the land and instituted the worship of the sun with periodic festivals, sacrifices and pilgrimages. He then divided the power to govern among two chiefs and spent the remainder of his days on earth living in quiet contemplation as an ascetic. When he ascended to heaven he became a god.[13]

Farther south still, the Canarians, an Indian tribe of Ecuador, relate an ancient story of a flood from which two brothers escaped by going to the top of a high mountain. As the water rose the mountain grew higher, so that the two brothers survived the disaster.[14]

When they were discovered, the Tupinamba Indians of Brazil venerated a series of civilizing or creator heroes. The first of these heroes was Monan (ancient, old) who was said to have been the creator of mankind but who then destroyed the world with flood and fire . . .[15]

Peru, as we saw in Part II, is particularly rich in flood legends. A typical story tells of an Indian who was warned by a llama of a deluge. Together man and llama fled to a high mountain called Vilca-Coto:

> When they reached the top of the mountain they saw that all kinds of birds and animals had already taken refuge there. The sea began to rise, and covered all the plains and mountains except the top of Vilca-Coto; and even there the waves dashed up so high that the animals were forced to crowd into a narrow area . . . Five days later the water ebbed, and the sea returned to its bed. But all human beings except one were drowned, and from him are descended all the nations on earth.[16]

The Araucnaians of pre-Colombian Chile preserved a tradition that there was once a flood which very few Indians escaped. The survivors took refuge on a high mountain called Thegtheg ('the thundering' or 'the glittering') which had three peaks and the ability to float on water.[17]

In the far south of the continent a Yamana legend from Tierra del Fuego states: 'The moon woman caused the flood. This was at the time of the great upheaval . . . Moon was filled with hatred towards human beings . . . At that time everybody drowned with the exception of those few who were able to escape to the five mountain peaks that the water did not cover.'[18]

Another Tierra del Fuegan tribe, the Pehuenche, associate the flood with a prolonged period of darkness: 'The sun and the moon fell from the sky and the world stayed that way, without light, until finally two giant condors carried both the sun and the moon back up to the sky.'[19]

North America

Meanwhile, at the other end of the Americas, among the Inuit of Alaska, there existed the tradition of a terrible flood, accompanied by an earthquake, which swept so rapidly over the face of the earth that only a few people managed to escape in their canoes or take refuge on the tops of the highest mountains, petrified with terror.[20]

The Luiseno of lower California had a legend that a flood covered the mountains and destroyed most of mankind. Only a few were saved because they fled to the highest peaks which were spared when all the rest of the world was inundated. The survivors remained there until the flood ended.[21] Farther north similar flood myths were recorded amongst the Hurons.[22] And a legend of the Montagnais, belonging to the Algonquin family, related how Michabo, or the Great Hare, re-established the world after the flood with the help of a raven, an otter and a muskrat.[23]

Lynd's *History of the Dakotas*, an authoritative work of the nineteenth century which preserved many indigenous traditions that would otherwise have been lost, reports an Iroquois myth that 'the sea and waters had at one time infringed upon the land, so that all human life was destroyed'. The Chickasaws asserted that the world had been destroyed by water 'but that one family was saved and two animals of every kind'. The Sioux also spoke of a time when there was no dry land and when all men disappeared from existence.[24]

Water water everywhere

How far and how widely across the myth memories of mankind do the ripples of the great flood spread?

Very widely indeed. More than 500 deluge legends are known around the world and, in a survey of 86 of these (20 Asiatic, 3 European, 7 African, 46 American and 10 from Australia and the Pacific), the specialist researcher Dr Richard Andree concluded that 62 were entirely independent of the Mesopotamian and Hebrew accounts.[25]

For example, early Jesuit scholars who were among the first Europeans to visit China had the opportunity in the Imperial Library to study a vast work, consisting of 4320 volumes, said to have been handed down from ancient times and to contain 'all knowledge'. This great book included a number of traditions which told of the consequences that followed when mankind rebelled against the high gods and the system of the universe fell into disorder': 'The planets altered their courses. The sky sank lower towards the north. The sun, moon and stars changed their motions. The earth fell to pieces and the waters in its bosom rushed upwards with violence and overflowed the earth.'[26]

In the Malaysian tropical forest the Chewong people believe that every so often their own world, which they call Earth Seven, turns upside down so that everything is flooded and destroyed. However, through the agency of the Creator God Tohan, the flat new surface of what had previously been the underside of Earth Seven is moulded into mountains, valleys and plains. New trees are planted, and new humans born.[27]

A flood myth of Laos and northern Thailand has it that beings called the Thens lived in the upper kingdom long ages ago, while the masters of the lower world were three great men, Pu Leng Seung, Khun K'an and Khun K'et. One day the Thens announced that before eating any meal people should give them a part of their food as a sign of respect. The people refused and in a rage the Thens created a flood which devastated the whole earth. The three great men built a raft, on top of which they made a small house, and embarked with a number of women and children. In this way they and their descendants survived the deluge.[28]

In similar fashion the Karens of Burma have traditions of a global deluge from which two brothers were saved on a raft.[29] Such a deluge is also part of the mythology of Viet Nam, where a brother and a sister are said to have survived in a great wooden chest which also contained two of every kind of animal.[30]

Several aboriginal Australian peoples, especially those whose traditional homelands are along the tropical northern coast, ascribe their origins to a great flood which swept away the previous landscape and society. Meanwhile, in the origin myths of a number of other tribes, the cosmic serpent Yurlunggur (associated with the rainbow) is held responsible for the deluge.[31]

There are Japanese traditions according to which the Pacific islands of Oceania were formed after the waters of a great deluge had receded.[32] In Oceania itself a myth of the native inhabitants of Hawaii tells how the world was destroyed by a flood and later recreated by a god named Tangaloa. The Samoans believe that there was once an inundation that wiped out almost all mankind. It was survived only by two human beings who put to sea in a boat while eventually came to rest in the Samoan archipelago.[33]

Greece, India and Egypt

On the other side of the world, Greek mythology too is haunted by memories of a deluge. Here, however (as in Central America) the inundation is not viewed as an isolated event but as one of a series of destructions and remakings of the world. The Aztecs and the Maya spoke in terms of successive 'Suns' or epochs (of which our own was thought to be the Fifth and last). In similar fashion the oral traditions of Ancient Greece, collected and set down in writing by Hesiod in the eighth century BC, related that prior to the present creation there had been four earlier races of men on earth. Each of these was thought more advanced than the one that followed it. And each, at the appointed hour, had been 'swallowed up' in a geological cataclysm.

The first and most ancient creation had been mankind's 'golden race' who had 'lived like the gods, free from care, without trouble or woe . . . With ageless limbs they revelled at their banquets . . . When they died it was as men overcome by sleep.' With the passing of time, and at the command of Zeus, this golden race eventually 'sank into the depths of the earth'. It was succeeded by the 'silver race' which was supplanted by the 'bronze race', which was replaced by the race of 'heroes', which was followed by the 'iron' race – our own – the fifth and most recent creation.[34]

It is the fate of the bronze race that is of particular interest to us here. Described in the myths as having 'the strength of giants, and mighty hands on their mighty limbs',[35] these formidable men were exterminated by Zeus, king of the gods, as a punishment for the misdeeds of Prometheus, the rebellious Titan who had presented humanity with the gift of fire.[36] The mechanism the vengeful deity used to sweep the earth clean was an overwhelming flood.

In the most widespread version of the story Prometheus impregnated a human female. She bore him a son named Deucalion, who ruled over the country of Phthia, in Thessaly, and took to wife Pyrrha, 'the red-blonde', daughter of Epimetheus and Pandora. When Zeus reached his fateful decision to destroy the bronze race, Deucalion, forewarned by Prometheus, made a wooden box, stored in it 'all that was necessary', and climbed into it with Pyrrha. The king of the gods caused mighty rains to pour from heaven, flooding the greater part of the earth. All mankind perished in this deluge, save a few who had fled to the highest mountains. 'It also happened at this time that the mountains of Thessaly were split asunder, and the whole country as far as the Isthmus and the Peloponnese became a single sheet of water.'

Deucalion and Pyrrha floated over this sea in their box for nine days and nights, finally landing on Mount Parnassus. There, after the rains had ceased, they disembarked and sacrificed to the gods. In response Zeus sent Hermes to Deucalion with permission to ask for whatever he wished. He wished for human beings. Zeus then bade him take stones and throw them over his shoulder. The stones Deucalion threw became men, and those that Pyrrha threw became women.[37]

As the Hebrews looked back on Noah, so the Greeks of ancient historical times looked back upon Deucalion – as the ancestor of their nation and as the founder of numerous towns and temples.[38]

A similar figure was revered in Vedic India more than 3000 years ago. One day (the story goes)

> when a certain wise man named Manu was making his ablutions, he found in the hollow of his hand a tiny little fish which begged him to allow it to live. Taking pity on it he put it in a jar. The next day, however, it had grown so much bigger that he had to carry it to a lake. Soon the lake was too small. 'Throw me into the sea,' said the fish [which was in reality a manifestation of the god Vishnu] 'and I shall be more comfortable.' Then he warned Manu of a coming deluge. He sent him a large ship, with orders to load it with two of every living species and the seeds of every plant, and then to go on board himself.'[39]

Manu had only just carried out these orders when the ocean rose and submerged everything, and nothing was to be seen but Vishnu in his fish form – now a huge, one-horned creature with golden scales. Manu moored his ark to the horn of the fish and Vishnu towed it across the brimming waters until it came to rest on the exposed peak of 'the Mountain of the North':[40]

> The fish said, 'I have saved thee; fasten the vessel to a tree, that the water may not sweep it away while thou art on the mountain; and in proportion as the waters decrease thou shalt descend.' Manu descended with the waters. The Deluge had carried away all creatures and Manu remained alone.[41]

With him, and with the animals and plants he had saved from destruction, began a new age of the world. After a year there emerged from the waters a woman who announced herself as 'the daughter of Manu'. The couple married and produced children, thus becoming the ancestors of the present race of mankind.[42]

Last but by no means least, Ancient Egyptian traditions also refer to a great flood. A funerary text discovered in the tomb of Pharaoh Seti I, for example, tells of the destruction of sinful humanity by a deluge.[43] The reasons for this catastrophe are set out in Chapter CLXXV of the *Book of the Dead*, which attributes the following speech to the Moon God Thoth:

> They have fought fights, they have upheld strifes, they have done evil,

they have created hostilities, they have made slaughter, they have caused trouble and oppression . . . [Therefore] I am going to blot out everything which I have made. This earth shall enter into the watery abyss by means of a raging flood, and will become even as it was in primeval time.[44]

On the trail of a mystery

With the words of Thoth we have come full circle to the Sumerian and biblical floods. 'The earth was filled with violence', says *Genesis*:

And God looked upon the earth, and, behold, it was corrupt; for all flesh had corrupted his way upon the earth. And God said unto Noah, 'The end of all flesh is come before me; for the earth is filled with violence through them; and behold I will destroy them with the earth.'[45]

Like the flood of Deucalion, the flood of Manu, and the flood that destroyed the Aztecs' 'Fourth Sun', the biblical deluge was the end of a world age. A new age succeeded it: our own, populated by the descendants of Noah. From the very beginning, however, it was understood that this age too would in due course come to a catastrophic end. As the old song puts it, 'God gave Noah the rainbow sign; no more water, the fire next time.'

The Scriptural source for this prophecy of world destruction is to be found in 2 Peter 3:

We must be careful to remember that during the last days there are bound to be people who will be scornful and [who will say], 'Everything goes on as it has since it began at the creation'. They are choosing to forget that there were heavens at the beginning, and that the earth was formed by the word of God out of water and between the waters, so that the world of that time was destroyed by being flooded by water. But by the same word, the present sky and earth are destined for fire, and are only being reserved until Judgement Day so that all sinners may be destroyed . . . The Day of the Lord will come as a thief in the night, and then with a roar the sky will vanish, the elements will catch fire and fall apart, and the earth and all that it contains will be burnt up.[46]

The Bible, therefore, envisages two ages of the world, our own being the second and last. Elsewhere, in other cultures, different numbers of creations and destructions are recorded. In China, for instance, the perished ages are called *kis*, ten of which are said to have elapsed from the beginning of time until Confucius. At the end of each *kis*, 'in a general convulsion of nature, the sea is carried out of its bed, mountains spring up out of the ground, rivers change their course, human beings and everything are ruined, and the ancient traces effaced . . .'[47]

Buddhist scriptures speak of 'Seven Suns', each brought to an end by water, fire or wind.[48] At the end of the Seventh Sun, the current 'world cycle', it is expected that the 'earth will break into flames'.[49] Aboriginal traditions of Sarawak and Sabah recall that the sky was once 'low' and tell us that 'six Suns perished . . . at present the world is illuminated by the seventh Sun'.[50] Similarly, the Sibylline Books speak of 'nine Suns that are nine ages' and prophesy two ages yet to come – those of the eighth and the ninth Sun.'[51]

On the other side of the Atlantic Ocean, the Hopi Indians of Arizona (who are distant relatives of the Aztecs[52]) record three previous Suns, each culminating in a great annihilation followed by the gradual re-emergence of mankind. In Aztec cosmology, of course, there were four Suns prior to our own. Such minor differences concerning the precise number of destructions and creations envisaged in this or that mythology should not distract us from the remarkable convergence of ancient traditions evident here. All over the world these traditions appear to commemmorate a widespread series of catastrophes. In many cases the character of each successive cataclysm is obscured by the use of poetic language and the piling up of metaphor and symbols. Quite frequently, also, at least two different kinds of disaster may be portrayed as having occurred simultaneously (most frequently floods and earthquakes, but sometimes fire and a terrifying darkness).

All this contributes to the creation of a confused and jumbled picture. The myths of the Hopi, however, stand out for their straightforwardness and simplicity. What they tell us is this:

The first world was destroyed, as a punishment for human misdemeanours, by an all-consuming *fire* that came from above and below. The second world ended when the terrestrial globe toppled from its axis and everything was covered with *ice*. The third world ended in a universal *flood*. The present world is the fourth. Its fate will depend on whether or not its inhabitants behave in accordance with the Creator's plans.[53]

We are on the trail of a mystery here. And while we may never hope to fathom the plans of the Creator we should be able to reach a judgement concerning the riddle of our converging myths of global destruction.

Through these myths the voices of the ancients speak to us directly. What are they trying to say?

Chapter 25

The Many Masks
of the Apocalypse

Like the Hopi Indians of North America, the Avestic Aryans of pre-Islamic Iran believed that there were three epochs of creation prior to our own. In the first epoch men were pure and sinless, tall and long lived, but at its close the Evil One declared war against Ahura Mazda, the holy god, and a tumultuous cataclysm ensued. During the second epoch the Evil One was unsuccessful. In the third good and evil were exactly balanced. In the fourth epoch (the present age of the world), evil triumphed at the outset and has maintained its supremacy ever since.[1]

The end of the fourth epoch is predicted soon, but it is the cataclysm at the end of the first epoch that interests us here. It is not a flood, and yet it converges in so many ways with many global flood traditions that some connection is strongly suggested.

The Avestic scriptures take us back to a time of paradise on earth, when the remote ancestors of the ancient Iranian people lived in the fabled Airyana Vaejo, the first good and happy creation of Ahura Mazda that flourished in the first age of the world: the mythical birthplace and original home of the Aryan race.

In those days Airyana Vaejo enjoyed a mild and productive climate with seven months of summer and five of winter. Rich in wildlife and in crops, its meadows flowing with streams, this garden of delights was converted into an uninhabitable wasteland of ten months' winter and only two months summer as a result of the onslaught of Angra Mainyu, the Evil One:

> The first of the good lands and countries which I, Ahura Mazda, created was the Airyana Vaejo . . . Then Angra Mainyu, who is full of death, created an opposition to the same, a mighty serpent and snow. Ten months of winter are there now, two months of summer, and these are cold as to the water, cold as to the earth, cold as to the trees . . . There all around falls deep snow; that is the direst of plagues . . .'[2]

The reader will agree that a sudden and drastic change in the climate of Airyana Vaejo is indicated. The Avestic scriptures leave us in no doubt about this. Earlier they describe a meeting of the celestial gods called by Ahura Mazda, and tell us that 'the fair Yima, the good shepherd of high renown in the Airyana Vaejo', attended this meeting with all his excellent mortals.

It is at this point that the strange parallels with the traditions of the biblical flood begin to crop up, for Ahura Mazda takes advantage of the meeting to warn Yima of what is about to happen as a result of the powers of the Evil One:

> And Ahura Mazda spake unto Yima saying: 'Yima the fair . . . Upon the material world a fatal winter is about to descend, that shall bring a vehement, destroying frost. Upon the corporeal world will the evil of winter come, wherefore snow will fall in great abundance. . . .
>
> 'And all three sorts of beasts shall perish, those that live in the wilderness, and those that live on the tops of the mountains, and those that live in the depths of the valleys under the shelter of stables.
>
> 'Therefore make thee a var [a hypogeum or underground enclosure] the length of a riding ground to all four corners. Thither bring thou the representatives of every kind of beast, great and small, of the cattle, of the beasts of burden, and of men, of dogs, of birds, and of the red burning fires.[3]
>
> 'There shalt thou make water flow. Thou shalt put birds in the trees along the water's edge, in verdure which is everlasting. There put specimens of all plants, the loveliest and most fragrant, and of all fruits the most succulent. All these kinds of things and creatures shall not perish as long as they are in the var. But put there no deformed creature, nor impotent, nor mad, neither wicked, nor deceitful, nor rancorous, nor jealous; nor a man with irregular teeth, nor a leper . . .'[4]

Apart from the scale of the enterprise there is only one real difference between Yima's divinely inspired *var* and Noah's divinely inspired ark: the ark is a means of surviving a terrible and devastating flood which will destroy every living creature by drowning the world in water; the *var* is a means of surviving a terrible and devastating 'winter' which will destroy every living creature by covering the earth with a freezing blanket of ice and snow.

In the *Bundahish*, another of the Zoroastrian scriptures (believed to incorporate ancient material from a lost part of the original *Avesta*), more information is provided on the cataclysm of glaciation that overwhelmed Airyana Vaejo. When Angra Mainyu sent the 'vehement destroying frost', he also 'assaulted and deranged the sky'.[5] The *Bundahish* tells us that this assault enabled the Evil One to master 'one third of the sky and overspread it with darkness' as the encroaching ice sheets tightened their grip.[6]

Indescribable cold, fire, earthquakes and derangement of the skies

The Avestic Aryans of Iran, who are known to have migrated to western Asia from some other, distant homeland,[7] are not the only possessors of archaic traditions which echo the basic setting of the great flood in ways unlikely to be coincidental. Indeed, though these are most commonly associated with the deluge, the familiar themes of the divine warning, and of the salvation of a remnant of mankind from a universal disaster, are also found in many different parts of the world in connection with the sudden onset of glacial conditions.

In South America, for example, Toba Indians of the Gran Chaco region that sprawls across the modern borders of Paraguay, Argentina and Chile, still repeat an ancient myth concerning the advent of what they call 'the Great Cold'. Forewarning comes from a semi-divine hero figure named Asin:

> Asin told a man to gather as much wood as he could and to cover his hut with a thick layer of thatch, because a time of great cold was coming. As soon as the hut had been prepared Asin and the man shut themselves inside and waited. When the great cold set in, shivering people arrived to beg a firebrand from them. Asin was hard and gave

embers only to those who had been his friends. The people were freezing, and they cried the whole night. At midnight they were all dead, young and old, men and women . . . this period of ice and sleet lasted for a long time and all the fires were put out. Frost was as thick as leather.[8]

As in the Avestic traditions it seems that the great cold was accompanied by great darkness. In the words of one Toba elder, these afflictions were sent 'because when the earth is full of people it has to change. The population has to be thinned out to save the world . . . In the case of the long darkness the sun simply disappeared and the people starved. As they ran out of food, they began eating their children. Eventually they all died . . .'[9]

The Mayan *Popol Vuh* associates the flood, with 'much hail, black rain and mist, and indescrible cold'.[10] It also says that this was a period when 'it was cloudy and twilight all over the world . . . the faces of the sun and the moon were covered.'[11] Other Maya sources confirm that these strange and terrible phenomena were experienced by mankind, 'in the time of the ancients. The earth darkened . . . It happened that the sun was still bright and clear. Then, at midday, it got dark . . .'[12] Sunlight did not return till the twenty-sixth year after the flood.'[13]

The reader may recall that many deluge and catastrophe myths contain references not only to the onset of a great darkness but to other changes in the appearance of the heavens. In Tierra del Fuego, for instance, it was said that the sun and the moon 'fell from the sky'[14] and in China that 'the planets altered their courses. The sun, moon and stars changed their motions.'[15] The Incas believed that 'in ancient times the Andes were split apart when the sky made war on the earth.'[16] The Tarahumara of northern Mexico have preserved world destruction legends based on a change in the sun's path.[17] An African myth from the lower Congo states that 'long ago the sun met the moon and threw mud at it, which made it less bright. When this meeting happened there was a great flood . . .'[18] The Cahto Indians of California say simply that 'the sky fell'.[19] And ancient Graeco-Roman myths tell that the flood of Deucalion was immediately preceded by awesome celestial events.[20] These events are graphically symbolized in the story of how Phaeton, child of the sun, harnessed his father's chariot but was unable to guide it along his father's course:

Soon the fiery horses felt how their reins were in an unpractised hand. Rearing and swerving aside, they left their wonted way; then all the earth was amazed to see that the glorious Sun, instead of holding his stately, beneficent course across the sky, seemed to speed crookedly overhead and to rush down in wrath like a meteor.'[21]

This is not the place to speculate on what may have caused the alarming disturbances in the patterns of the heavens that are linked with cataclysm legends from all over the world. For our purposes at present, it is sufficient to note that such traditions seem to refer to the same 'derangement of the sky' that accompanied the fatal winter and spreading ice sheets described in the Iranian *Avesta*.[22] Other linkages occur. Fire, for example, often follows or precedes the flood. In the case of Phaeton's adventure with the Sun, 'the grass withered; the crops were scorched; the woods went up in fire and smoke; then beneath them the bare earth cracked and crumbled and the blackened rocks burst asunder under the heat.'[23]

Volcanism and earthquakes are also mentioned frequently in association with the flood, particularly in the Americas. The Auracanians of Chile say quite explicitly that 'the flood was the result of volcanic eruptions accompanied by violent earthquakes.'[24] The Mam Maya of Santiago Chimaltenango in the western highlands of Guatemala retain memories of 'a flood of burning pitch' which, they say, was one of the instruments of world destruction.[25] And in the Gran Chaco of Argentina, the Mataco Indians tell of 'a black cloud that came from the south at the time of the flood and covered the whole sky. Lightning struck and thunder was heard. Yet the drops that fell were not like rain. They were like fire . . .'[26]

A monster chased the sun

There is one ancient culture that perhaps preserves more vivid memories in its myths than any other; that of the so-called Teutonic tribes of Germany and Scandinavia, a culture best remembered through the songs of the Norse scalds and sages. The stories those songs retell have their roots in a past which may be much older than scholars imagine and which combine familiar images with strange symbolic devices and allegorical language to recall a cataclysm of awesome magnitude:

> In a distant forest in the east an aged giantess brought into the world a whole brood of young wolves whose father was Fenrir. One of these monsters chased the sun to take possession of it. The chase was for long in vain, but each season the wolf grew in strength, and at last he reached the sun. Its bright rays were one by one extinguished. It took on a blood red hue, then entirely disappeared.
>
> Thereafter the world was enveloped in hideous winter. Snowstorms descended from all points of the horizon. War broke out all over the earth. Brother slew brother, children no longer respected the ties of blood. It was a time when men were no better than wolves, eager to destroy each other. Soon the world was going to sink into the abyss of nothingness.
>
> Meanwhile the wolf Fenrir, whom the gods had long ago so carefully chained up, broke his bonds at last and escaped. He shook himself and the world trembled. The ash tree Yggdrasil [envisaged as the axis of the earth] was shaken from its roots to its topmost branches. Mountains crumbled or split from top to bottom, and the dwarfs who had their subterranean dwellings in them sought desperately and in vain for entrances so long familiar but now disappeared.
>
> Abandoned by the gods, men were driven from their hearths and the human race was swept from the surface of the earth. The earth itself was beginning to lose its shape. Already the stars were coming adrift from the sky and falling into the gaping void. They were like swallows, weary from too long a voyage, who drop and sink into the waves.
>
> The giant Surt set the entire earth on fire; the universe was no longer more than an immense furnace. Flames spurted from fissures in the rocks; everywhere there was the hissing of steam. All living things, all plant life, were blotted out. Only the naked soil remained, but like the sky itself the earth was no more than cracks and crevasses.
>
> And now all the rivers, all the seas, rose and overflowed. From every side waves lashed against waves. They swelled and boiled slowly over all things. The earth sank beneath the sea . . .
>
> Yet not all men perished in the great catastrophe. Enclosed in the wood itself of the ash tree Yggdrasil – which the devouring flames of the universal conflagration had been unable to consume – the ancestors of a future race of men had escaped death. In this asylum

they had found that their only nourishment had been the morning dew.

Thus it was that from the wreckage of the ancient world a new world was born. Slowly the earth emerged from the waves. Mountains rose again and from them streamed cataracts of singing waters.[27]

The new world this Teutonic myth announces is our own. Needless to say, like the Fifth Sun of the Aztecs and the Maya, it was created long ago and is new no longer. Can it be a coincidence that one of the many Central American flood myths about the 'fourth epoch, 4 *Atl* ('water')', does not install the Noah couple in an ark but places them instead in a great tree just like Yggdrasil? '4 *Atl* was ended by floods. The mountains disappeared . . . Two persons survived because they were ordered by one of the gods to bore a hole in the trunk of a very large tree and to crawl inside when the skies fell. The pair entered and survived. Their offspring repopulated the world.'[28]

Isn't it odd that the same symbolic language keeps cropping up in ancient traditions from so many widely scattered regions of the world? How can this be explained? Are we talking about some vast, subconscious wave of intercultural telepathy, or could elements of these remarkable universal myths have been engineered, long ages ago, by clever and purposeful people? Which of these improbable propositions is the more likely to be true? Or are there other possible explanations for the enigma of the myths?

We shall return to these questions in due course. Meanwhile, what are we to conclude about the apocalyptic visions of fire and ice, floods, volcanism and earthquakes, which the myths contain? They have about them a haunting and familiar realism. Could this be because they speak to us of a past we suspect to be our own but can neither remember clearly nor forget completely?

Chapter 26

A Species Born in
the Earth's Long Winter

In all that we call 'history' – everything we clearly remember about ourselves as a species – humanity has not once come close to total annihilation. In various regions at various times there have been terrible natural disasters. But there has not been a single occasion in the past 5000 years when mankind as a whole can be said to have faced extinction.

Has this always been so? Or is it possible, if we go back far enough, that we might discover an epoch when our ancestors were nearly wiped out? It is just such an epoch that seems to be the focus of in the great myths of cataclysm. Scholars normally attribute these myths to the fantasies of ancient poets. But what if the scholars are wrong? What if some terrible series of natural catastrophes did reduce our prehistoric ancestors to a handful of individuals scattered here and there across the face of the earth, far apart, and out of touch with one another?

We are looking for an epoch that will fit the myths as snugly as the slipper on Cinderella's foot. In this search, however, there is obviously no point in investigating any period prior to the emergence on the planet of recognizably modern human beings. We're not interested here in *Homo habilis* or *Homo erectus* or even *Homo sapiens neanderthalensis*. We're interested only in *Homo sapiens sapiens*, our own species, and we haven't been around very long.

Students of early Man disagree to some extent over how long we have been around. Some researchers, as we shall see, claim that partial human remains in excess of 100,000 years old may be 'fully modern'. Others argue for a reduced antiquity in the range of 35–40,000 years, and yet others propose a compromise of 50,000 years. But no one knows for sure. 'The origin of fully modern humans denoted by the subspecies name *Homo sapiens sapiens* remains one of the great puzzles of palaeoanthropology,' admits one authority.[1]

About three and a half million years of more or less relevant evolution are indicated in the fossil record. For all practical purposes, that record starts with a small, bipedal hominid (nicknamed Lucy) whose remains were discovered in 1974 in the Ethiopian section of East Africa's Great Rift Valley. With a brain capacity of 400cc (less than a third of the modern average) Lucy definitely wasn't human. But she wasn't an ape either and she had some remarkably 'human-like' features, notably her upright gait, and the shape of her pelvis and back teeth. For these and other reasons, her species – classified as *Australopithecus afarensis* – has been accepted by the majority of palaeoanthropologists as our earliest direct ancestor.[2]

About two million years ago representatives of *Homo habilis*, the founder members of the *Homo* line to which we ourselves belong, began to leave their fossilized skulls and skeletons behind. As time went by this species showed clear signs of evolution towards an ever more 'gracile' and refined form, and towards a larger and more versatile brain. *Homo erectus*, who overlapped with and then succeeded *Homo habilis*, appeared about 1.6 million years ago with a brain capacity in the region of 900cc (as against 700cc in the case of *habilis*).[3] The million or so years after that, down to about 400,000 years ago, saw no significant evolutionary changes – or none attested to by surviving fossils. Then *Homo erectus* passed through the gates of extinction into hominid heaven and slowly – very, very slowly – what the palaeoanthropologists call 'the sapient grade' began to appear:

> Exactly when the transition to a more sapient form began is difficult to establish. Some believe the transition, which involved an increase in brain size and a decrease in the robustness of the skull bones, began as early as 400,000 years ago. Unfortunately, there are simply not enough

fossils from this important period to be sure about what was happening.'⁴

What was definitely *not* happening 400,000 years ago was the emergence of anything identifiable as our own story-telling, myth-making subspecies *Homo sapiens sapiens*. The consensus is that 'sapient humans must have evolved from *Homo erectus*',⁵ and it is true that a number of 'archaic sapient' populations did come into existence between 400,000 and 100,000 years ago. Unfortunately, the relationship of these transitional species to ourselves is far from clear. As noted, the first contenders for membership of the exclusive club of *Homo sapiens sapiens* have been dated by some researchers to the latter part of this period. But these remains are all partial and their identification is by no means universally accepted. The oldest, part of a skullcap, is a putative modern human specimen from about 113,000 BC.⁶ Around this date, too, *Homo sapiens neanderthalensis* first appears, a quite distinct subspecies which most of us know as 'Neanderthal Man'.

Tall, heavily muscled, with prominent brow ridges and a protruding face, Neanderthal Man had a bigger average brain size than modern humans (1400cc as against our 1360cc).⁷ The possession of such a big brain was no doubt an asset to these 'intelligent, spiritually sensitive, resourceful creatures'⁸ and the fossil record suggests that they were the dominant species on the planet from about 100,000 years ago until 40,000 years ago. At some point during this lengthy and poorly understood period, *Homo sapiens sapiens* established itself, leaving behind fossil remains from about 40,000 years ago that are undisputably those of modern humans, and supplanting the Neanderthals completely by about 35,000 years ago.⁹

In summary, human beings like ourselves, whom we could pass in the street without blinking an eyelid if they were shaved and dressed in modern clothes, are creatures of the last 115,000 years at the very most – and more probably of only the last 50,000 years. It follows that if the myths of cataclysm we have reviewed do reflect an epoch of geological upheaval experienced by humanity, these upheavals took place within the last 115,000 years, and more probably within the last 50,000 years.

Cinderella's slipper

It is a curious coincidence of geology and palaeoanthropology that the onset and progress of the last Ice Age, and the emergence and proliferation of modern Man, more or less shadow each other. Curious too is the fact that so little is known about either.

In North America the last Ice Age is called the Wisconsin Glaciation (named for rock deposits studied in the state of Wisconsin) and its early phase has been dated by geologists to 115,000 years ago.[10] There were various advances and retreats of the ice-cap after that, with the fastest rate of accumulation taking place between 60,000 years ago and 17,000 years ago – a process culminating in the Tazewell Advance, which saw the glaciation reach its maximum extent around 15,000 BC.[11] By 13,000 BC, however, millions of square miles of ice had melted, for reasons that have never properly been explained, and by 8000 BC the Wisconsin had withdrawn completely.[12]

The Ice Age was a global phenomenon, affecting both the northern and the southern hemispheres; similar climatic and geological conditions therefore prevailed in many other parts of the world as well (notably in eastern Asia, Australia, New Zealand, and South America). There was massive glaciation in Europe, where the ice reached outward from Scandinavia and Scotland to cover most of Great Britain, Denmark, Poland, Russia, large parts of Germany, all of Switzerland, and big chunks of Austria, Italy and France.[13] (Known technically as the Wurm Glaciation, this European Ice Age started about 70,000 years ago, a little later than its American counterpart, but attained its maximum extent at the same time, 17,000 years ago, and then experienced the same rapid withdrawal, and shared the same terminal date).[14]

The crucial stages of Ice Age chronology thus appear to be:
1 around 60,000 years ago, when the Wurm, the Wisconsin and other glaciations were well under way;
2 around 17,000 years ago, when the ice sheets had reached their maximum extent in both the Old World and the New;
3 the 7000 years of deglaciation that followed.

The emergence of *Homo sapiens sapiens* thus coincided with a lengthy period of geological and climatic turbulence, a period marked, above all else, by ferocious freezing and flooding. The many millennia during which the ice was remorselessly expanding must have been terrifying and awful for our ancestors. But those final 7000 years of *de*glaciation, particularly the episodes of very rapid and extensive melting, must have been worse.

Let us not jump to conclusions about the state of social, or religious, or scientific, or intellectual development of the human beings who lived through the sustained collapse of that tumultuous epoch. The popular stereotype may be wrong in assuming that they were all primitive cave dwellers. In reality little is known about them and almost the only thing that can be said is that they were men and women *exactly like ourselves* physiologically and psychologically.

It is possible that they came close to total extinction on several occasions during the upheavals they experienced; it is also possible that the great myths of cataclysm, to which scholars attribute no historical value, may contain accurate records and eyewitness accounts of real events. As we see in the next chapter, if we are looking for an epoch that fits those myths as snugly as the slipper on Cinderella's foot, it would seem that the last Ice Age is it.

Chapter 27

The Face of the Earth was Darkened and a Black Rain Began to Fall

Terrible forces were unleashed on all living creatures during the last Ice Age. We may deduce how these afflicted humanity from the firm evidence of their consequences for other large species. Often this evidence looks puzzling. As Charles Darwin observed after visiting South America:

> No one I think can have marvelled more at the extinction of species than I have done. When I found in La Plata [Argentina] the tooth of a horse embedded with the remains of Mastodon, Megatherium, Toxodon, and other extinct monsters, which all co-existed at a very late geological period, I was filled with astonishment; for seeing that the horse, since its introduction by the Spaniards in South America, has run wild over the whole country and has increased its numbers at an unparalleled rate, I asked myself what could have so recently exterminated the former horse under conditions of life apparently so favourable?[1]

The answer, of course, was the Ice Age. That was what exterminated the former horses of the Americas, and a number of other previously successful mammals. Nor were extinctions limited to the New World. On the contrary, in different parts of the earth (for different reasons and at different times) the long epoch of glaciation witnessed several quite distinct *episodes* of extinction. In all areas, the vast majority of the many destroyed species were lost in the final seven thousand years from about 15,000 BC down to 8000 BC.[2]

At this stage of our investigation is it not necessary to establish the specific nature of the climatic, seismic and geological events linked to the various advances and retreats of the ice sheets which killed off the animals. We might reasonably guess that tidal waves, earthquakes, gigantic windstorms and the sudden onset and remission of glacial conditions played their parts. But more important – whatever the actual agencies involved – is the stark empirical reality that mass extinctions of animals *did* take place as a result of the turmoil of the last Ice Age.

This turmoil, as Darwin concluded in his *Journal*, must have shaken 'the entire framework of the globe'.[3] In the New World, for example, more than seventy genera of large mammals became extinct between 15,000 BC and 8000 BC, including all North American members of seven families, and one complete order, the Proboscidea.[4] These staggering losses, involving the violent obliteration of more than forty million animals, were not spread out evenly over the whole period; on the contrary, the vast majority of the extinctions occurred in just two thousand years, between 11,000 BC and 9000 BC.[5] To put this in perspective, during the previous 300,000 years only about twenty genera had disappeared.[6]

The same pattern of late and massive extinctions was repeated across Europe and Asia. Even far-off Australia was not exempt, losing perhaps nineteen genera of large vertebrates, not all of them mammals, in a relatively short period of time.[7]

Alaska and Siberia: the sudden freeze

The northern regions of Alaska and Siberia appear to have been the worst hit by the murderous upheavals between 13,000 and 11,000 years ago. In a great swathe of death around the edge of the Arctic Circle the remains of uncountable numbers of large animals have been found – including many carcasses with the flesh still intact, and astonishing quantities of perfectly preserved mammoth tusks. Indeed, in both regions, mammoth carcasses have been thawed to feed to sled dogs and mammoth steaks have featured on restaurant menus in Fairbanks.[8] One authority has commented, 'Hundreds of thousands of individuals must have been frozen immediately after death and remained frozen, otherwise the meat and ivory would have spoiled . . . Some powerful general force was certainly at work to bring this catastrophe about.'[9]

Dr Dale Guthrie of the Institute of Arctic Biology has made an interesting point about the sheer *variety* of animals that flourished in Alaska before the eleventh millennium BC:

> When learning of this exotic mixture of sabertooth cats, camels, horses, rhinos, asses, deer with gigantic antlers, lions, ferrets, and saiga, one cannot help wondering about the world in which they lived. This great diversity of species, so different from that encountered today, raises the most obvious question: is it not likely that the rest of the environment was also different?[10]

The Alaskan muck in which the remains are embedded is like a fine, dark-grey sand. Frozen solid within this mass, in the words of Professor Hibben of the University of New Mexico:

> lie the twisted parts of animals and trees intermingled with lenses of ice and layers of peat and mosses . . . Bison, horses, wolves, bears, lions . . . Whole herds of animals were apparently killed together, overcome by some common power . . . Such piles of bodies of animals or men simply do not occur by any ordinary natural means . . .'[11]

At various levels stone artefacts have been found 'frozen in situ at great depths, and in association with Ice Age fauna, which confirms that men were contemporary with extinct animals in Alaska'.[12]

Throughout the Alaskan mucks, also there is:

> evidence of atmospheric disturbances of unparalleled violence. Mammoth and bison alike were torn and twisted as though by a cosmic hand in Godly rage. In one place we can find the foreleg and shoulder of a mammoth with portions of the flesh and toenails and hair still clinging to the blackened bones. Close by is the neck and skull of a bison with the vertebrae clinging together with tendons and ligaments and the chitinous covering of the horns intact. There is no mark of knife or cutting instrument [as there would be if human hunters, for example, had been involved]. The animals were simply torn apart and scattered over the landscape like things of straw and string, even though some of them weighed several tons. Mixed with piles of bones

are trees, also twisted and torn and piled in tangled groups; and the whole is covered with a fine sifting muck, then frozen solid.[13]

Much the same picture emerges in Siberia where catastrophic climatic changes and geological upheavals occurred at around the same time. Here the frozen mammoth graveyards, 'mined' for their ivory since the Roman era, were still yielding an estimated 20,000 pairs of tusks every decade at the beginning of the twentieth century.[14]

Once again, some mysterious factor appears to have been at work in bringing about these mass extinctions. With their woolly coats and thick skins, mammoths are generally considered adapted to cold weather, and we are not surprised to come across their remains in Siberia. Harder to explain is the fact that human beings perished alongside them,[15] as well as many other animals that in no sense can be described as cold-adapted species:

The northern Siberian plains supported vast numbers of rhinoceroses, antelope, horses, bison, and other herbivorous creatures, while a variety of carnivores, including the sabertooth cat, preyed upon them . . . . Like the mammoths, these other animals ranged to the extreme north of Siberia, to the shores of the Arctic Ocean, and yet further north to the Lyakhov and New Siberian Islands, only a very short distance from the North Pole.[16]

Researchers have confirmed that of the thirty-four animal species living in Siberia prior to the catastrophes of the eleventh millennium BC – including Ossip's mammoth, giant deer, cave hyena and cave lions – no less than twenty-eight were adapted *only to temperate conditions*.[17] In this context, one of the most puzzling aspects of the extinctions, which runs quite contrary to what today's geographical and climatic conditions lead us to expect, is that the farther north one goes, the more the mammoth and other remains *increase* in number.[18] Indeed some of the New Siberian Islands, well within the Arctic Circle, were described by the explorers who first discovered them as being made up almost entirely of mammoth bones and tusks.[19] The only logical conclusion, as the nineteenth-century French zoologist Georges Cuvier put it, is that 'this eternal frost did not previously exist in those parts in which the animals were frozen, for they could not have survived in such a temperature. The same instant that these creatures were bereft of life, the country which they inhabited became frozen.'[20]

There is a great deal of other evidence which suggests that a sudden freeze took place in Siberia during the eleventh millennium BC. In his survey of the New Siberian Islands, the Arctic explorer Baron Eduard von Toll found the remains 'of a sabretooth tiger, and a fruit tree that had been 90 feet tall when it was standing. The tree was well preserved in the permafrost, with its roots and seeds. Green leaves and ripe fruit still clung to its branches ... At the present time the only representative of tree vegetation on the islands is a willow that grows one inch high'.[21]

Equally indicative of the cataclysmic change that took place at the onset of the great cold in Siberia is the food the extinct animals were eating when they perished: 'The mammoths died suddenly, in intense cold, and in great numbers. Death came so quickly that the swallowed vegetation is yet undigested ... Grasses, bluebells, buttercups, tender sedges, and wild beans have been found, yet identifiable and undeteriorated, in their mouths and stomachs.'[22]

Needless to say, such flora does not grow anywhere in Siberia today. Its presence there in the eleventh millennium BC compels us to accept that the region had a pleasant and productive climate – one that was temperate or even warm.[23] Why the *end* of the last Ice Age in other parts of the world should have been the *beginning* of fatal winter in this former paradise is a question we shall postpone until Part VIII. What is certain, however, is that at some point between 12–13,000 years ago a destroying frost descended with horrifying speed upon Siberia and has never relaxed its grip. In an eerie echo of the Avestic traditions, a land which had previously enjoyed seven months of summer was converted almost overnight into a land of ice and snow with ten months of harsh and frozen winter.[24]

A thousand Krakatoas, all at once

Many of the myths of cataclysm speak of times of terrible cold, of darkened skies, of black, burning, bituminous rain. For centuries it must have been like that all the way across the arc of death incorporating immense tracts of Siberia, the Yukon and Alaska. Here,

'Interspersed in the muck depths, and sometimes through the very piles of bones and tusks themselves, are layers of volcanic ash. There is no doubt that coincidental with the [extinctions] there were volcanic eruptions of tremendous proportions.'[25]

There is a remarkable amount of evidence of excessive volcanism during the decline of the Wisconsin ice cap.[26] Far to the south of the frozen Alaskan mucks, thousands of prehistoric animals and plants were mired, all at once, in the famous La Brea tar pits of Los Angeles. Among the creatures unearthed were bison, horses, camels, sloths, mammoths, mastodons and at least *seven hundred* sabre-toothed tigers.[27] A disarticulated human skeleton was also found, completely enveloped in bitumen, mingled with the bones of an extinct species of vulture. In general, the La Brea remains ('broken, mashed, contorted, and mixed in a most heterogeneous mass'[28]) speak eloquently of a sudden and dreadful volcanic cataclysm.[29]

Similar finds of typical late Ice Age birds and mammals have been unearthed from asphalt at two other locations in California (Carpinteria and McKittrick). In the San Pedro Valley, mastodon skeletons were discovered still standing upright, engulfed in great heaps of volcanic ash and sand. Fossils from the glacial Lake Floristan in Colorado, and from Oregon's John Day Basin, were also excavated from tombs of volcanic ash.[30]

Although the tremendous eruptions that created such mass graves may have been at their most intense during the last days of the Wisconsin, they appear to have been recurrent throughout much of the Ice Age, not only in North America but in Central and South America, in the North Atlantic, in continental Asia, and in Japan.[31]

It is difficult to imagine what this widespread volcanism might have meant for people living in those strange and terrible times. But those who recall the cauliflower-shaped clouds of dust, smoke and ash ejected into the upper atmosphere by the eruption of Mount Saint Helens in 1980 will appreciate that a large number of such explosions (occurring sequentially over a sustained period at different points around the globe) would not only have had devastating local effects but would have caused a severe deterioration in the world's climate.

Mount Saint Helens spat out an estimated one cubic kilometre of rock and was small-scale by comparison with the typical volcanism of the Ice Age.[32] A more representative impression would be the Indonesian volcano Krakatoa, which erupted in 1883 with such violence that more than 36,000 people were killed and the explosion was heard 3000 miles away. From the epicentre in the Sunda Strait, *tsunamis* 100 feet high roared across the Java Sea and the Indian Ocean, carrying steamships miles inland and causing flooding as far away as East Africa and the western coasts of the Americas. Eighteen cubic kilometres of rock and vast quantities of ash and dust were pumped into the upper atmosphere; skies all over the world were noticeably darker for more than two years and sunsets notably redder. Average global temperatures fell measurably during this period because volcanic dust-particles reflect the sun's rays back into space.[33]

During the episodes of intense volcanism which characterized the Ice Age, we must envisage not one but many Krakatoas. The combined effect would at first have been a great intensification of glacial conditions, as the light of the sun was cut by the boiling dust clouds, and as already low temperatures plummeted even further. Volcanoes also inject enormous volumes of carbon dioxide into the atmosphere, and carbon dioxide is a 'greenhouse gas', so it is reasonable to suppose, as the dust began to settle during periods of relative calm, that a degree of global warming would have occurred. A number of authorities attribute the repeated advances and retreats of the great ice sheets to precisely this see-saw interaction between volcanism and climate.[34]

Global flooding

Geologists agree that by 8000 BC the great Wisconsin and Wurm ice-caps had retreated. The Ice Age was over. However, the seven thousand years *prior* to that date had witnessed climatic and geological turbulence on a scale that was almost unimaginable. Lurching from cataclysm to disaster and from misfortune to calamity, the few scattered tribes of surviving humans must have led lives of constant terror and confusion: there would have been periods of quiescence, when they might have hoped that the worst was over. While the melting of the giant glaciers continued, however, these episodes of tranquillity would have been punctuated again and again by violent floods. Moreover, sections of the earth's crust hitherto pressed down into the asthenosphere by billions of tons of ice would have been liberated by the thaw and begun to rise again, sometimes rapidly, causing devastating earthquakes and filling the air with terrible noise.

Some times were much worse than others. The bulk of the animal extinctions took place between 11,000 BC and 9000 BC when there were violent and unexplained fluctuations of climate.[35] (In the words of geologist John Imbrie, 'a climatic revolution took place around 11,000 years ago.'[36]) There were also greatly increased rates of sedimentation[37] and an abrupt temperature increase of 6–10 degrees Centigrade in the surface waters of the Atlantic Ocean.[38]

Another turbulent episode, again accompanied by mass extinctions, took place between 15,000 BC and 13,000 BC. We saw in the previous chapter that the Tazewell Advance brought the ice sheets to their maximum extent around 17,000 years ago and that a dramatic and prolonged thaw then ensued, completely deglaciating millions of square miles of North America and Europe in less than two thousand years.

There were some anomalies: all of western Alaska, the Yukon territory in Canada, and most of Siberia including the New Siberian Islands (now among the coldest parts of the world), remained unglaciated until the Ice Age was near its end. They acquired their present climate only about 12,000 ago, apparently very abruptly, when the mammoths and other large mammals were frozen in their tracks.[39]

Elsewhere the picture was different. Most of Europe was buried under ice two miles thick.[40] So too was most of North America where the ice-cap had spread from centres near Hudson Bay to enshroud all of eastern Canada, New England and much of the Midwest down to the 37th parallel – well to the south of Cincinnati in the Mississippi Valley and more than halfway to the equator.[41]

At its peak 17,000 years ago, it is calculated that the total ice volume covering the northern hemisphere was in the region of six million cubic miles, and of course there were extensive glaciations in the southern hemisphere too as we noted. The surplus water flow from which these numerous ice-caps were formed had been provided by the world's seas and oceans which were then about 400 feet lower than they are today.[42]

It was at this moment that the pendulum of climate swung violently in the opposite direction. The great meltdown began so suddenly and over such vast areas that it has been described 'as a sort of miracle'.[43] Geologists refer to it as the Bolling phase of warm climate in Europe and as the Brady interstadial in North America. In both regions:

An ice-cap that may have taken 40,000 years to develop disappeared for the most part, in 2000. It must be obvious that this could not have been the result of gradually acting climatic factors usually called upon to explain ice ages . . . The rapidity of the deglaciation suggests that some extraordinary factor was affecting the climate. The dates suggest that this factor first made itself felt about 16,500 years ago, that it had destroyed most, perhaps three-quarters of the glaciers by 2000 years later, and that [the vast bulk of these dramatic developments took place] in a millennium or less.'[44]

Inevitably the first consequence was a precipitous rise in sea levels, perhaps as much as 350 feet.[45] Islands and land bridges disappeared and vast sections of low-lying continental coastline were submerged. From time to time great tidal waves rose up to engulf higher land as well. They ebbed away, but in the process left unmistakable traces of their presence.

In the United States, 'Ice Age marine features are present along the Gulf coast east of the Mississippi River, in some places at altitudes that may exceed 200 feet.'[46] In bogs covering glacial deposits in Michigan, skeletons of two whales were discovered. In Georgia marine deposits occur at altitudes of 160 feet, and in northern Florida at altitudes of at least 240 feet. In Texas, well to the south of the farthest extent of the Wisconsin Glaciation, the remains of Ice Age land mammals are found in marine deposits. Another marine deposit, containing walrus, seals and at least five genera of whales, overlies the seaboard of the north-eastern states and the Arctic coast of Canada. In many areas along the Pacific coast of North America Ice Age marine deposits extend 'more than 200 miles inland.'[47] The bones of a whale have been found north of Lake Ontario, about 440 feet above sea level, a skeleton of another whale in Vermont, more than 500 feet above sea level, and another in the Montreal-Quebec area about 600 feet above sea level.[48]

Flood myths from all over the world characteristically and recurrently describe scenes when humans and animals flee the rising tides and take refuge on mountain tops. The fossil record confirms that this did indeed happen during the melting of the ice sheets and that the mountains were not always high enough to save the refugees from disaster. For example, fissures in the rocks on the tops of isolated hills in central France are filled with what is known as 'osseous breccia', consisting of the splintered bones of mammoths, woolly rhinoceroses and other animals. The 1430 feet peak of Mount Genay in Burgundy 'is capped by a breccia containing remains of mammoth, reindeer, horse and other animals'.[49] Much farther south, so too is the Rock of Gibraltar where 'a human molar and some flints worked by Paleolithic man were discovered among the animal bones.'[50]

Hippo remains, together with mammoth, rhinoceros, horse, bear, bison, wolf and lion, have been found in England, in the neighbourhood of Plymouth on the Channel.[51] The hills around Palermo in Sicily disclosed an 'extraordinary quantity of bones of hippopotami – in complete hecatombs'.[52] On the basis of this and other evidence, Joseph Prestwich, formerly professor of Geology at Oxford University, concluded that Central Europe, England, and the Mediterranean islands of Corsica, Sardinia and Sicily were all completely submerged on several occasions during the rapid melting of the ice sheets:

> The animals naturally retreated, as the waters advanced, deeper into the hills until they found themselves embayed . . . They thronged together in vast multitudes, crushing into the more accessible caves, until overtaken by the waters and destroyed . . . Rocky debris and large blocks from the sides of the hills were hurled down by the currents of water, crushing and smashing the bones . . . Certain communities of early man must have suffered in this general catastrophe.[53]

It is probable that similar flood disasters occurred in China at much the same time. In caves near Peking, bones of mammoths and buffaloes have been found in association with human skeletal remains.[54] A number of authorities attribute the violent intermingling of mammoth carcases with splintered and broken trees in Siberia 'to a great tidal wave that uprooted forests and buried the tangled carnage in a flood of mud. In the polar region this froze solid and has preserved the evidence in permafrost to the present.'[55]

All over South America, too, Ice-Age fossils have been unearthed, 'in which incongruous animal types (carnivores and herbivores) are mixed promiscuously with human bones. No less significant is the association, over truly widespread areas, of fossilized land and sea creatures mingled in no order and yet entombed in the same geological horizon.'[56]

North America was also badly affected by flooding. As the great Wisconsin ice sheets melted they created huge but temporary lakes which filled up with incredible speed, drowning everything in their paths, then drained away in a few hundred years. Lake Agassiz, for example, the largest glacial lake in the New World, once occupied an area of 110,000 square miles, covering large parts of what are now Manitoba, Ontario and Saskatchewan in Canada, and North Dakota and Minnesota in the United States.[57] Remarkably, it endured for less than a millennium, indicating a catastrophically sudden episode of melting and flooding followed by a period of quiescence.[58]

A token of good faith

It was long believed that human beings did not reach the New World until around 11,000 years ago, but recent finds have steadily pushed that horizon back. Stone implements dating to 25,000 BC have been identified by Canadian researchers in the Old Crow Basin in the Yukon Territory of Alaska.[59] In South America (as far south as Peru and Tierra del Fuego) human remains and artefacts have been found which have been reliably dated to 12,000 BC – with another group between 19,000 BC and 23,000 BC.[60] With this and other evidence taken into account, 'a very reasonable conclusion on the peopling of the Americas is that it began at least 35,000 years ago, but may well have included waves of immigrants at later dates too.'[61]

Those newly arriving Ice Age Americans, trekking in from Siberia across the Bering land bridge, would have faced the most appalling conditions between 17,000 and 10,000 years ago. It was then that the Wisconsin glaciers, all at once, went into their ferocious meltdown, forcing a 350-foot rise in global sea levels amid scenes of unprecedented climatic and geological turmoil. For *seven thousand years of human experience*, earthquakes, volcanic eruptions and immense floods, interspersed with eerie periods of peace, must have dominated the day-to-day lives of the New World peoples. Perhaps this is why so many of their myths speak with such conviction of fire and floods and times of darkness and of the creation and destruction of Suns.

Moreover, as we have seen, the myths of the New World are not in this respect isolated from those of the Old. All around the globe, a remarkable uniformity reveals itself over issues such as 'the great flood' and 'the great cold' and 'the time of the great upheaval'. It is not just that the same experiences are being recounted again and again; that, on its own, would be quite understandable since the Ice Age and its aftereffects were global phenomena. More curious by far is the way in which the same symbolic motifs keep recurring: the one good man and his family, the warning given by a god, the seeds of all living things saved, the survival ship, the enclosure against the cold, the trunk of a tree in which the pregenitors of future humanity hide themselves, the birds and other creatures released after the flood to find land . . . and so on.

Isn't it also odd that so many of the myths turn out to contain descriptions of figures like Quetzalcoatl and Viracocha, said to have come in the time of darkness, after the flood, to teach architecture, astronomy, science and the rule of law to the scattered and devastated tribes of survivors.

Who were these civilizing heroes? Were they figments of the primitive imagination? Or gods? Or men? If they were men, could they have tampered with the myths in some way, turning them into vehicles for transporting knowledge through time?

Such notions seem fanciful. But, as we shall see in Part V, astronomical data of a disturbingly accurate and scientific nature turns up repeatedly in certain myths, as time-worn and as universal in their distribution as those of the great flood.

Where did their scientific content come from?

Part V

The Mystery of the Myths

2 The Precessional Code

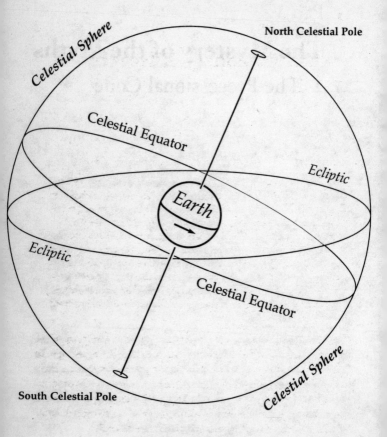

The Celestial Sphere.

Chapter 28

The Machinery of Heaven

Although a modern reader does not expect a text on celestial mechanics to read like a lullaby, he insists on his capacity to understand mythical 'images' instantly, because he can respect as 'scientific' only page-long approximation formulas, and the like.

He does not think of the possibility that equally relevant knowledge might once have been expressed in everyday language. He never suspects such a possibility, although the visible accomplishments of ancient cultures – to mention only the pyramids or metallurgy – should be a cogent reason for concluding that serious and intelligent men were at work behind the stage, men who were bound to have used a technical language . . .[1]

The quotation is from the late Giorgio de Santillana, professor of the History of Science at the Massachusetts Institute of Technology. In the chapters that follow, we shall be learning about his revolutionary investigations into ancient mythology. In brief, however, his proposition is this: long ages ago, serious and intelligent people devised a system for veiling the technical terminology of an advanced astronomical science behind the everyday language of myth.

Is Santillana right? And if he is right, who were these serious and intelligent people – these astronomers, these ancient scientists – who worked behind the stage of prehistory?

Let us start with some basics.

The wild celestial dance

The earth makes a complete circuit around its own axis once every twenty-four hours and has an equatorial circumference of 24,902.45 miles. It follows, therefore, that a man standing still on the equator is in fact in motion, revolving with the planet at just over 1,000 miles per hour.[2] Viewed from outer space, looking down on the North Pole, the direction of rotation is anti-clockwise.

While spinning daily on its own axis, the earth also orbits the sun (again in an anti-clockwise direction) on a path which is slightly elliptical rather than completely circular. It pursues this orbit at truly breakneck speed, travelling as far along it in an hour – 66,600 miles – as the average motorist will drive in six years. To bring the calculations down in scale, this means that we are hurtling through space much faster than any bullet, at the rate of 18.5 miles *every second*. In the time that it has taken you to read this paragraph, we have voyaged about 550 miles farther along earth's path around the sun.[3]

With a year required to complete a full circuit, the only evidence we have of the tremendous orbital race we are participating in is the slow march of the seasons. And in the operations of the seasons themselves it is possible to see a wondrous and impartial mechanism at work distributing spring, summer, autumn and winter fairly around the globe, across the northern and southern hemispheres, year in and year out, with absolute regularity.

The earth's axis of rotation is tilted in relation to the plane of its orbit (at about 23.5° to the vertical). This tilt, which causes the seasons, 'points' the North Pole, and the entire northern hemisphere away from the sun for six months a year (while the southern hemisphere enjoys its summer) and points the South Pole and the southern hemisphere away from the sun for the remaining six months (while the northern hemisphere enjoys its summer). The seasons result from the annual variation in the angle at which the sun's rays reach any particular point on the earth's surface and from the annual variation in the number of hours of sunlight received there at different times of the year.

The earth's tilt is referred to in technical language as its 'obliquity', and the plane of its orbit, extended outwards to form a great circle in the celestial sphere, is known as the 'ecliptic'. Astronomers also speak of the 'celestial equator', which is an extension of the earth's equator into the celestial sphere. The celestial equator is today inclined at about 23.5° to the ecliptic, because the earth's axis is inclined at 23.5° to the vertical. This angle, termed the 'obliquity of the ecliptic', is not fixed and immutable for all time. On the contrary (as we saw in Chapter Eleven in relation to the dating of the Andean city of Tiahuanaco) it is subject to constant, though very slow, oscillations. These occur across a range of slightly less than 3°, rising closest to the vertical at 22.1° and falling farthest away at 24.5°. A full cycle, from 24.5° to 22.1°, and back again to 24.5°, takes approximately 41,000 years to complete.[4]

So our fragile planet nods and spins while soaring along its orbital path. The orbit takes a year and the spin takes a day and the nod has a cycle of 41,000 years. A wild celestial dance seems to be going on as we skip and skim and dive through eternity, and we feel the tug of contradictory urges: to fall into the sun on the one hand; to make a break for the outer darkness on the other.

Recondite influences

The sun's gravitational domain, in the inner circles of which the earth is held captive, is now known to extend more than fifteen *trillion* miles into space, almost halfway to the nearest star.[5] Its pull upon our planet is therefore immense. Also affecting us is the gravity of the other planets with which we share the solar system. Each of these exerts an attraction which tends to draw the earth out of its regular orbit around the sun. The planets are of different sizes, however, and revolve around the sun at different speeds. The combined gravitational influence they are able to exert thus changes over time in complex but predictable ways, and the orbit changes its shape constantly in response. Since the orbit is an ellipse these changes affect its degree of elongation, known technically as its 'eccentricity'. This varies from a low value close to zero (when the orbit approaches the form of a perfect circle) to a high value of about six per cent when it is at its most elongated and elliptical.[6]

There are other forms of planetary influence too. Thus, though no explanation has yet been forthcoming, it is known that shortwave

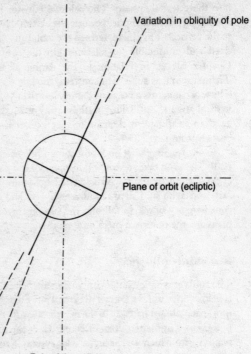

Variation in obliquity of pole

Plane of orbit (ecliptic)

Pole of the ecliptic

The obliquity of the ecliptic varies from 22.1° to 24.5° over a cycle of 41,000 years.

radio frequencies are disturbed when Jupiter, Saturn and Mars line up.[7] And in this connection evidence has also emerged

of a strange and unexpected correlation between the positions of Jupiter, Saturn and Mars, in their orbits around the sun, and violent electrical disturbances in the earth's upper atmosphere. This would seem to indicate that the planets and the sun share in a cosmic-

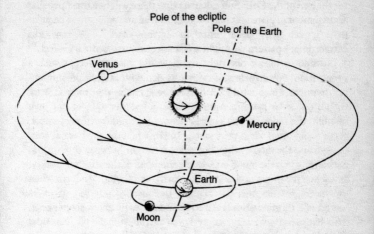

Inner planets of the solar system.

electrical balance mechanism that extends a billion miles from the centre of our solar system. Such an electrical balance is not accounted for in current astrophysical theories.'[8]

The *New York Times*, from which the above report is taken, does not attempt to clarify matters further. Its writers are probably unaware of just how much they sound like Berosus, the Chaldean historian, astronomer and seer of the third century BC, who made a deep study of the omens he believed would presage the final destruction of the world. He concluded, 'I Berosus, interpreter of Bellus, affirm that all the earth inherits will be consigned to flame when the five planets assemble in Cancer, so arranged in one row that a straight line may pass through their spheres.'[9]

A conjunction of five planets that can be expected to have profound gravitional effects will take place on 5 May in the year 2000 when Neptune, Uranus, Venus, Mercury and Mars will align with earth on the other side of the sun, setting up a sort of cosmic tug-of-war.[10] Let us also note that modern astrologers who have charted the Mayan date for the end of the Fifth Sun calculate that there will be a most peculiar arrangement of planets at that time, indeed an arrangement *so* peculiar that 'it can only occur once in 45,200 years ... From this extraordinary pattern we might well expect an extraordinary effect.'[11]

No one in his or her right mind would rush to accept such a proposition. Nevertheless, it cannot be denied that multiple influences, many of which we do not fully understand, appear to be at work within our solar system. Among these influences, that of our own satellite, the moon, is particularly strong. Earthquakes, for example, occur more often when the moon is full or when the earth is between the sun and the moon; when the moon is new or between the sun and the earth; when the moon crosses the meridian of the affected locality; and when the moon is closest to the earth on its orbit.[12] Indeed, when the moon reaches this latter point (technically referred to as its 'perigree'), its gravitational attraction increases by about six per cent. This happens once every twenty-seven and one-third days. The tidal pull that it exerts on these occasions affects not only the great movements of our oceans but those of the reservoirs of hot magma penned within the earth's thin crust (which has been described as resembling 'a paper bag filled with honey or molasses swinging along at a rate of more than 1000 miles an hour in equatorial rotation, and more than 66,000 miles an hour in orbit'[13]).

The wobble of a deformed planet

All this circular motion, of course, generates immense centrifugal forces and these, as Sir Isaac Newton demonstrated in the seventeenth century, cause the earth's 'paper bag' to bulge outwards at the equator. The corollary is a flattening at the poles. In consequence, our planet deviates slightly from the form of a perfect sphere and is more accurately described as an 'oblate spheroid'. Its radius at the equator (3,963.374 miles) is about fourteen miles longer than its polar radius (3,949.921 miles).[14]

For billions of years the flattened poles and the bulging equator have been engaged in a covert mathematical interaction with the recondite influence of gravity. 'Because the Earth is flattened,' explains one authority, 'the Moon's gravity tends to tilt the Earth's axis so that it becomes perpendicular to the Moon's orbit, and to a lesser extent the same is true for the Sun.'[15]

At the same time the equatorial bulge – the extra mass distributed around the equator – acts like the rim of a gyroscope to keep the earth steady on its axis.[16]

Year in, year out, on a planetary scale, it is this gyroscopic effect that prevents the tug of the sun and the moon from radically altering the earth's axis of rotation. The pull these two bodies jointly exert is, however, sufficiently strong to force the axis to 'precess', which means that it wobbles slowly in a clockwise direction opposite to that of the earth's spin.

This important motion is our planet's characteristic signature within the solar system. Anyone who has ever set a top spinning should be able to understand it without much difficulty; a top, after all, is simply another type of gyroscope. In full uninterrupted spin it stands upright. But the moment its axis is deflected from the vertical it begins to exhibit a second behaviour: a slow and obstinate reverse wobble around a great circle. This wobble, which *is* precession, changes the direction in which the axis points while keeping constant its newly tilted angle.

A second analogy, somewhat different in approach, may help to clarify matters a little further:

1 Envisage the earth, floating in space, inclined at approximately 23.5° to the vertical and spinning around on its axis once every 24 hours.

2 Envisage this axis as a massively strong pivot, or *axle*, passing through the centre of the earth, exiting via the North and South Poles and extending outwards from there in both directions.

3 Imagine that you are a giant, striding through the solar system, with orders to carry out a specific task.

4 Imagine approaching the tilted earth (which, because of your great size, now looks no bigger to you than a millwheel).

5 Imagine reaching out and grasping the two ends of the extended axis.

6 And imagine yourself slowly beginning to inter-rotate them, pushing one end, pulling the other.

7 The earth was already spinning when you arrived.

The northern sky as seen from Earth

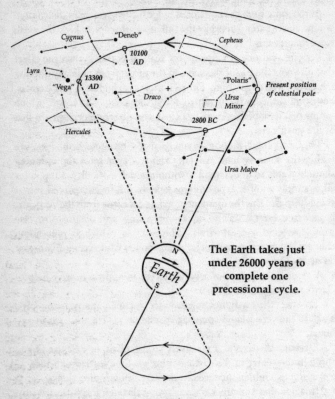

The Earth takes just
under 26000 years to
complete one
precessional cycle.

Precession.

8 Your orders, therefore, are not to get involved in its axial
rotation, but rather to impart to it its *other* motion: that slow
clockwise wobble called precession.

9 To fulfil this commission you will have to push the northern
tip of the extended axis up and around a great circle in the

northern celestial hemisphere while at the same time pulling the southern tip around an equally large circle in the southern celestial hemisphere. This will involve a slow swivelling pedalling motion with your hands and shoulders.

10 Be warned, however. The 'millwheel' of the earth is heavier than it looks, so much heavier, in fact, that it's going to take you 25,776 years[17] to turn the two tips of its axis through one full precessional cycle (at the end of which they will be aiming at the same points in the celestial sphere as when you arrived).

11 Oh, and by the way, now that you've started the job we may as well tell you that you're never going to be allowed to leave. As soon as one precessional cycle is over another must begin. And another . . . and another . . . and another . . . and so on, endlessly, for ever and ever and ever.

12 You can think of this, if you like, as one of the basic mechanisms of the solar system, or, if you prefer, as one of the fundamental commandments of the divine will.

In the process, little by little, as you slowly sweep the extended axis around the heavens, its two tips will point to one star after another in the polar latitudes of the southern celestial hemisphere (and sometimes, of course, to empty space), and to one star after another in the polar latitudes of the northern celestial hemisphere. We are talking here, about a kind of musical chairs among the circumpolar stars. And what keeps everything in motion is the earth's axial precession – a motion driven by giant gravitational and gyroscopic forces, that is regular, predictable and relatively easy to work out with the aid of modern equipment. Thus, for example, the northern pole star is presently alpha Ursae Minoris (which we know as Polaris). But computer calculations enable us to state with certainty that in 3000 BC alpha Draconis occupied the pole position; at the time of the Greeks the northern pole star was beta Ursae Minoris; and in AD 14,000 it will be Vega.[18]

A great secret of the past

It will not hurt to remind ourselves of some of the fundamental data concerning the movements of the earth and its orientation in space:

• It tilts at about 23.5° to the vertical, an angle from which it can

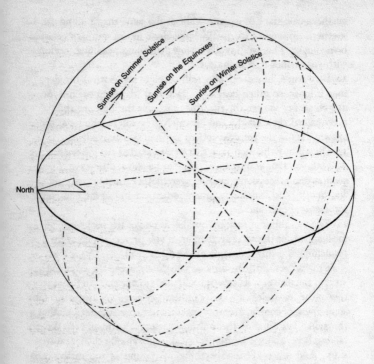

Equinoxes and solstices.

vary by as much as 1.5° on either side over periods of 41,000 years.

- It completes a full precessional cycle once every 25,776 years.[19]
- It spins on its own axis once every twenty-four hours.
- It orbits the sun once every 365 days (actually 365.2422 days).
- The most important influence on its seasons is the angle at which the rays of the sun strike it at various points on its orbital path.

Let us also note that there are four crucial astronomical moments in the year, marking the official beginning of each of the four seasons.

These moments (or cardinal points), which were of immense importance to the ancients, are the winter and the summer solstices and the spring and autumn equinoxes. In the northern hemisphere the winter solstice, the shortest day, falls on 21 December, and the summer solstice, the longest day, on 21 June. In the southern hemisphere, on the other hand, everything is literally upside down: there winter begins on 21 June and summer on 21 December.

The equinoxes, by contrast, are the two points in the year on which night and day are of equal length all over the planet. Once again, however, as with the solstices, the date that marks the onset of spring in the northern hemisphere (20 March) marks that of autumn in the southern hemisphere, and the date for the onset of autumn in the northern hemisphere (22 September) marks the onset of spring in the southern hemisphere.

Like the subtler variations of the seasons, all this is brought about by the benevolent obliquity of the planet. The northern hemisphere's summer solstice falls at that point in the orbit when the North Pole is aimed most directly *towards* the sun; six months later the winter solstice marks that point when the North Pole is aimed most directly *away* from the sun. And, logically enough, the reason that day and night are of exactly equal length all over the planet on the spring and autumn equinoxes is that these mark the two points when the earth's axis of rotation lies broadside-on to the sun.

Let us now take a look at a strange and beautiful phenomenon of celestial mechanics.

This phenomenon is known as 'the precession of the equinoxes'. It has rigid and repetitive mathematical qualities that can be analysed and predicted precisely. It is, however, extremely difficult to observe, and even harder to measure accurately, without sophisticated instrumentation.

In this, there may lie a clue to one of the great mysteries of the past.

Chapter 29

The First Crack
in an Ancient Code

The plane of the earth's orbit, projected outwards to form a great circle in the celestial sphere, is known as the ecliptic. Ringed around the ecliptic, in a starry belt that extends approximately 7° north and south, are the twelve constellations of the zodiac: Aries, Taurus, Gemini, Cancer, Leo, Virgo, Libra, Scorpius, Sagittarius, Capricornus, Aquarius and Pisces. These constellations are irregular in size, shape and distribution. Nevertheless (and one assumes by chance!) their spacing around the rim of the ecliptic is sufficiently even to bestow a sense of cosmic order upon the diurnal risings and settings of the sun.

To picture what is involved here, do the following: (1) mark a dot in the centre of a blank sheet of paper; (2) draw a circle around the dot, about half an inch away from it; (3) enclose that circle in a second, larger, circle.

The dot represents the sun. The smaller of the two concentric circles represents the earth's orbit. The larger circle represents the rim of the ecliptic. Around the perimeter of this larger circle, therefore, you should now draw twelve boxes, spacing them evenly, to represent the constellations of the zodiac. Since there are 360° in a circle, each constellation can be considered to occupy a space of 30° along the ecliptic. The dot is the sun. The inner of the two concentric circles is the earth's orbit. We know that the earth travels on this orbit in an anti-clockwise direction, from the west towards the east, and that every twenty-four hours it also makes one complete rotation around its own axis (again from the west towards the east).

From these two movements two illusions result:

1 Each day as the planet turns from west to east, the sun (which is of course a fixed point) appears to 'move' across the sky from east to west.

2 Roughly every thirty days, as the spinning earth journeys along its orbital path around the sun, the sun itself slowly appears to 'pass' through one after another of the twelve zodiacal constellations (which are also fixed points), and again it appears to be 'moving' in an east–west direction.

On any particular day of the year, in other words, (corresponding on our diagram to any point we care to choose around the inner concentric circle marking the earth's orbit), it is obvious that the sun will lie *between* an observer on the earth and one of the twelve zodiacal constellations. On that day what the observer will see, so long as he or she is up and about well before dawn, is the sun rising in the east in the portion of the sky occupied by that particular constellation.

Beneath the clear and unpolluted heavens of the ancient world, it is easy to understand how human beings might have felt reassured by regular celestial motions such as these. It is equally easy to understand why the four cardinal points of the year – the spring and autumn equinoxes, the winter and summer solstices – should everywhere have been accorded immense significance. Even greater significance was accorded to the conjunction of these cardinal points with the zodiacal constellations. But most significant of all was the constellation in which the sun was observed to rise on the morning of the spring (or vernal) equinox. Because of the earth's axial precession, the ancients discovered that this constellation was *not* fixed or permanent for all time but that the honour of 'housing' or 'carrying' the sun on the day of the vernal equinox circulated – *very, very slowly* – among all the constellations of the zodiac.

In the words of Giorgio de Santillana: 'The sun's position amongst the constellations at the vernal equinox was the pointer that indicated the "hours" of the precessional cycle – very long hours indeed, the equinoctial sun occupying each zodiacal constellation for almost 2200 years.'[1]

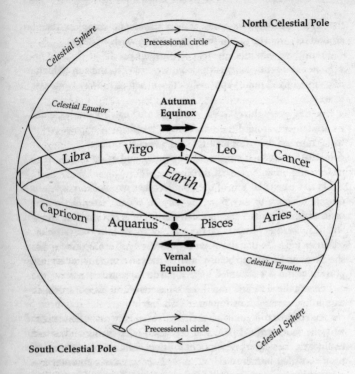

During the course of each year the earth's movement along its orbit causes the stellar background against which the sun is seen to rise to change from month to month: Aquarius —→ Pisces —→ Aries —→ Taurus —→ Gemini —→ Cancer —→ Leo, etc, etc. At present, on the vernal equinox, the sun rises due east between Pisces and Aquarius. The effect of precession is to cause the 'vernal point' to be reached fractionally earlier in the orbit each year with the result that it very gradually shifts through all 12 houses of the zodiac, spending 2160 years 'in' each sign and making a complete circuit in 25,920 years. The direction of this 'precessional drift', in opposition to the annual 'path of the sun', is: Leo —→ Cancer —→ Gemini —→ Taurus —→ Aries —→ Pisces —→ Aquarius. To give one example, the 'Age of Leo', i.e. the 2160 years during which the sun on the vernal equinox rose against the stellar background of the constellation of Leo, lasted from 10,970 until 8810 BC. We live today in the astrological no man's land at the end of the 'Age of Pisces', on the threshold of the 'New Age' of Aquarius. Traditionally these times of transition between one age and the next have been regarded as ill-omened.

The *direction* of the earth's slow axial precession is clockwise (i. e., east to west) and thus in opposition to the direction of the planet's annual path around the sun. In relation to the constellations of the zodiac, lying fixed in space, this causes the point at which the spring equinox occurs 'to move stubbornly along the ecliptic in the opposite direction to the yearly course of the sun, that is, against the "right" sequence of the zodiacal signs (Taurus —> Aries —> Pisces —> Aquarius, instead of Aquarius —> Pisces —> Aries —> Taurus).'[2]

That, in a nutshell, is the meaning of 'precession of the equinoxes'. And that is exactly what is involved in the notion of the 'dawning of the Age of Aquarius'. The famous line from the musical *Hair* refers to the fact that every year, for the last 2000 years or so, the sun has risen in Pisces on the vernal equinox. The *age* of Pisces, however, is now approaching its end and the vernal sun will soon pass out of the sector of the Fish and begin to rise against the new background of Aquarius.

The 25,776-year cycle of precession is the engine that drives this majestic celestial juggernaut along its never-ending tour of the heavens. But the details of exactly *how* precession moves the equinoctial points from Pisces into Aquarius – and thence onwards around the zodiac – are also worth knowing.

Remember that the equinoxes occur on the only two occasions in the year when the earth's tilted axis lies broadside-on to the sun. These are when the sun rises due east all over the world and day and night are of equal length. Because the earth's axis is slowly but surely *precessing* in a direction opposite to that of its own orbit, the points at which it lies broadside-on to the sun must occur fractionally earlier in the orbit each year. These annual changes are so small as to be almost imperceptible (a one degree shift along the ecliptic – equivalent to the width of your little finger held up to the horizon – requires approximately seventy-two years to complete). However, as de Santillana points out, such minute changes add up in just under 2200 years to a 30° passage through a complete house of the zodiac, and in just under 26,000 years to a 360° passage through a complete cycle of precession.

When did the ancients first work out precession?

In the answer to this question lies a great secret, and mystery, of the past. Before we try to penetrate the mystery and to learn the secret, we should acquaint ourselves with the 'official' line. The *Encyclopaedia Britannica* is as good a repository as any of conventional historical wisdom, and this is what it tells us about a scholar named Hipparchus, the supposed discoverer of precession:

> **Hipparchus**, also spelled HIPPARCHOS (b. Nicaea, Bithynia; d. after 127 BC, Rhodes), Greek astronomer and mathematician who discovered the precession of the equinoxes . . . This notable discovery was the result of painstaking observations, worked upon by an acute mind. Hipparchus observed the positions of the stars, and then compared his results with those of Timocharis of Alexandria about 150 years earlier and with even earlier observations made in Babylonia. He discovered that the celestial longitudes were different and that this difference was of a magnitude exceeding that attributable to errors of observation. He therefore proposed precession to account for the size of the difference and he gave a value of 45' or 46' (seconds of arc) for annual changes. This is very close to the figure of 50.274 seconds of arc accepted today . . .'[3]

First, a point of terminology. Seconds of arc are the smallest subdivisions of a degree of arc. There are 60 of these arc seconds in one arc minute, 60 minutes in one degree, and 360 degrees in the full circle of earth's path around the sun. An annual change of 50.274 seconds of arc represents a distance somewhat under one-sixtieth of one degree so that it takes roughly 72 years (an entire human lifetime) for the equinoctial sun to migrate just one degree along the ecliptic. It is because of the observational difficulties entailed in detecting this snails' pace rate of change that the value worked out by Hipparchus in the second century BC is hailed in the *Britannica* as a 'notable discovery'.

Would this discovery seem so notable if it turned out to be a rediscovery? Would the mathematical and astronomical achievements of the Greeks shine so brightly if we could prove that the difficult challenge of measuring precession had been taken up thousands of years *before* Hipparchus? What if this heavenly cycle, almost 26,000 years long, had been made the object of precise scientific investigations long epochs before the supposed dawn of scientific thought?

In seeking answers to such questions there is much that may be relevant which would never be accepted by any court of law as concrete proof. Let us not accept it either. We have seen that Hipparchus proposed a value of 45 or 46 seconds of arc for one year of precessional motion. Let us therefore not attempt to dislodge the Greek astronomer from his pedestal as the discoverer of precession unless we can find a significantly more accurate value recorded in a significantly more ancient source.

Of course, there are many potential sources. At this point, however, in the interests of succinctness, we shall limit our inquiry to universal myths. We have already examined one group of myths in detail (the traditions of flood and cataclysm set out in Part IV) and we have seen that they possess a range of intriguing characteristics:

1 There is no doubt that they are immensely old. Take the Mesopotamian flood story, versions of which have been found inscribed on tablets from the earliest strata of Sumerian history, around 3000 BC. These tablets, handed down from the dawn of the recorded past, leave no room for doubt that the tradition of a world-destroying flood was ancient even then, and therefore originated long before the dawn. We cannot say how long. The fact remains that no scholar has ever been able to establish a date for the creation of any myth, let alone for these venerable and widespread traditions. In a very real sense they seem always to have been around – part of the permanent baggage of human culture.

2 The possibility cannot be ruled out that this aura of vast antiquity is not an illusion. On the contrary, we have seen that many of the great myths of cataclysm seem to contain accurate eye-witness accounts of real conditions experienced by humanity during the last Ice Age. In theory, therefore, these stories could have been constructed at almost the same time as the emergence of our subspecies *Homo sapiens sapiens*, perhaps as long 50,000 years ago. The geological evidence, however, suggests a more recent provenance, and we have identified the epoch 15,000–8000 BC as the most likely. Only then, in the whole of human experience, were there rapid climatic changes on the convulsive scale the myths so eloquently describe.

3 The Ice Age and its tumultuous demise were global phenomena.

It is therefore perhaps not surprising that the cataclysm traditions of many different cultures, widely scattered around the globe, should be characterized by a high degree of uniformity and convergence.

4 What is surprising, however, is that the myths not only describe shared experiences but that they do so in what appears to be a shared symbolic language. The same 'literary motifs' keep cropping up again and again, the same stylistic 'props', the same recognizable characters, and the same plots.

According to Professor de Santillana, this type of uniformity suggests a guiding hand at work. In *Hamlet's Mill*, a seminal and original thesis on ancient myth written in collaboration with Hertha von Dechend (professor of the History of Science at Frankfurt University) he argues that:

> universality is in itself a test when coupled with a firm design. When something found, say, in China, turns up also in Babylonian astrological texts, then it must be assumed to be relevant if it reveals a complex of uncommon images which nobody could claim had risen independently by spontaneous generation. Take the origin of music. Orpheus and his harrowing death may be a poetic creation born in more than one instance in diverse places. But when characters who do not play the lyre but blow pipes get themselves flayed alive for various absurd reasons, and their identical end is rehearsed on several continents, then we feel we have got hold of something, for such stories cannot be linked by internal sequence. And when the Pied Piper turns up both in the German myth of Hamelin and in Mexico long before Columbus, and is linked in both places to certain attributes like the colour red, it can hardly be a coincidence ... Likewise, when one finds numbers like 108, or 9 × 13 reappearing under several multiples in the *Vedas*, in the temples of Angkor, in Babylon, in Heraclitus' dark utterances, and also in the Norse Valhalla, it is not accident ...[4]

Connecting the great universal myths of cataclysm, is it possible that such coincidences that cannot be coincidences, and accidents that cannot be accidents, could denote the global influence of an ancient, though as yet unidentified, guiding hand? If so, could it be that same hand, during and after the last Ice Age, which drew the series of highly accurate and technically advanced world maps reviewed in Part I? And might not that same hand have left its ghostly fingerprints on another body of universal myths? those concerning the death and resurrection of gods, and great trees around which the earth and heavens turn, and whirlpools, and churns, and drills, and other similar revolving, grinding contrivances?

According to Santillana and von Dechend, all such images refer to celestial events[5] and do so, furthermore, in the refined technical language of an archaic but 'immensely sophisticated' astronomical and mathematical science:[6] 'This language ignores local beliefs and cults. It concentrates on numbers, motions, measures, overall frames, schemas – on the structure of numbers, on geometry.'[7]

Where could such a language have come from? *Hamlet's Mill* is a labyrinth of brilliant but deliberately evasive scholarship, and offers us no straightforward answer to this question. Here and there, however, almost with embarrassment, inconclusive hints are dropped. For example, at one point the authors say that the scientific language or 'code' they believe they have identified is of 'awe-inspiring antiquity'.[8] On another occasion they pin down the depth of this antiquity more precisely to a period at least '6,000 years before Virgil'[9] – in other words 8000 years ago or more.

What civilization *known to history* could have developed and made use of a sophisticated technical language more than 8000 years ago? The honest answer to this question is 'none', followed by a frank admission that what is being conjectured is nothing less than a forgotten episode of high technological culture in prehistoric times. Once again, Santillana and von Dechend are elusive when it comes to the crunch, speaking only of the legacy we all owe to 'some almost unbelievable ancestor civilization' that 'first dared to understand the world as created according to number, measure and weight.'[10]

The legacy, it is clear, has to do with scientific thinking and complex information of a mathematical nature. Because it is so extremely old, however, the passage of time has dissipated it:

When the Greeks came upon the scene the dust of centuries had already settled upon the remains of this great world-wide archaic construction. Yet something of it survived in traditional rites, in myths and fairy-tales no longer understood . . . These are tantalising fragments of a lost whole. They make one think of those 'mist landscapes' of which Chinese painters are masters, which show here a rock, here a gable, there the tip of a tree, and leave the rest to imagination. Even when the code shall have yielded, when the techniques shall be known, we cannot expect to gauge the thought of these remote ancestors of ours, wrapped as it is in its symbols, since the creating, ordering minds that devised the symbols have vanished forever.'[11]

What we have here, therefore, are two distinguished professors of the History of Science, from esteemed universities on both sides of the Atlantic, claiming to have discovered the remnants of a coded scientific language *many thousands of years older* than the oldest human civilizations identified by scholarship. Moreover, though generally cautious, Santillana and von Dechend also claim to have 'broken part of that code'.[12]

This is an extraordinary statement for two serious academics to have made.

Chapter 30

The Cosmic Tree and the Mill of the Gods

In their brilliant and far-reaching study *Hamlet's Mill*, Professors de Santillana and von Dechend present a formidable array of mythical and iconographic evidence to demonstrate the existence of a curious phenomenon. For some inexplicable reason, and at some unknown date, it seems that certain archaic myths from all over the world were 'co-opted' (no other word will really do) to serve as vehicles for a body of complex technical data concerning the precession of the equinoxes. The importance of this astonishing thesis, as one leading authority on ancient measurement has pointed out, is that it has fired the first salvo in what may prove to be 'a Copernican revolution in current conceptions of the development of human culture.'[1]

Hamlet's Mill was published in 1969, more than a quarter of a century ago, so the revolution has been a long time coming. During this period, however, the book has been neither widely distributed among the general public nor widely understood by scholars of the remote past. This state of affairs has not come about because of any inherent problems or weaknesses in the work. Instead, in the words of Martin Bernal, professor of Government Studies at Cornell University, it has happened because 'few archaeologists, Egyptologists and ancient historians have the combination of time, effort and skill necessary to take on the very technical arguments of de Santillana.'[2]

What those arguments predominantly concern is the recurrent and persistent transmission of a 'precessional message' in a wide range of ancient myths. And, strangely enough, many of the key images and symbols that crop up in these myths – notably those that concern a 'derangement of the heavens' – are also to be found embedded in the ancient traditions of worldwide cataclysm reviewed in Chapters Twenty-four and Twenty-five.

In Norse mythology for example, we saw how the wolf Fenrir, whom the gods had so carefully chained up, broke his bonds at last and escaped: 'He shook himself and the world trembled. The ash-tree Yggdrasil was shaken from its roots to its topmost branches. Mountains crumbled or split from top to bottom . . . The earth began to lose its shape. Already the stars were coming adrift in the sky.'

In the opinion of de Santillana and von Dechend, this myth mixes the familiar theme of catastrophe with the quite separate theme of precession. On the one hand we have an earthly disaster on a scale that seems to dwarf even the flood of Noah. On the other we hear that ominous changes are taking place in the heavens and that the stars, which have come adrift in the sky, are 'dropping into the void.'³

Such celestial imagery, repeated again and again with only relatively minor variations in myths from many different parts of the world, belongs to a category earmarked in *Hamlet's Mill* as 'not mere storytelling of the kind that comes naturally'.⁴ Moreover the Norse traditions that speak of the monstrous wolf Fenrir, and of the shaking of Yggdrasil, go on to report the final apocalypse in which the forces of Valhalla issue forth on the side of 'order' to participate in the terrible last battle of the gods – a battle that will end in apocalyptic destruction:

> 500 doors and 40 there are
> I ween, in Valhalla's walls;
> 800 fighters through each door fare,
> When to war with the Wolf they go.'⁵

With a lightness of touch that is almost subliminal, this verse has encouraged us to *count* Valhalla's fighters, thus momentarily obliging us to focus our attention on their total number (540 × 800 = 432,000). This total, as we shall see in Chapter Thirty-one is mathematically linked to the phenomenon of precession. It is, unlikely to have found its way into Norse mythology by accident, especially in a context that has previously specified a 'derangement of the heavens' severe enough to have caused the stars to come adrift from their stations in the sky.

To understand what is going on here it is essential to grasp the basic imagery of the ancient 'message' that Santillana and von Dechend claim to have stumbled upon. This imagery transforms the luminous dome of the celestial sphere into a vast and intricate piece of machinery. And, like a millwheel, like a churn, like a whirlpool, like a quern, this machine turns and turns and turns endlessly (its motions being calibrated all the time by the sun, which rises first in one constellation of the zodiac, then in another, and so on all the year round).

The four key points of the year are the spring and summer equinoxes and the winter and summer solstices. At each point, naturally, the sun is seen to rise in a different constellation (thus if the sun rises in Pisces at the spring equinox, as it does at present, it must rise in Virgo at the autumn equinox, in Gemini at the winter solstice and in Sagittarius at the summer solstice). On each of these four occasions for the last 2000 years or so, this is exactly what the sun has been doing. As we have seen, however, precession of the equinoxes means that the vernal point will change in the not so distant future from Pisces to Aquarius. When that happens, the three other constellations marking the three key points will change as well (from Virgo, Gemini and Sagittarius to Leo, Taurus and Scorpius) – almost as though the giant mechanism of heaven has ponderously switched gears . . .

Like the axle of a mill, Santillana and von Dechend explain, Yggdrasil 'represents the world axis' in the archaic scientific language they have identified: an axis which extends outwards (for a viewer in the northern hemisphere) to the North Pole of the celestial sphere:

> This instinctively suggests a straight, upright post . . . but that would be an oversimplification. In the mythical context it is best not to think of the axis in analytical terms, one line at a time, but to consider it, and the frame to which it is connected, as a whole: . . . As radius automatically calls circle to mind so axis should invoke the two determining great circles on the surface of the sphere, the equinoctial and solstitial colures.[6]

These colures are the imaginary hoops, intersecting at the celestial

North Pole, which connect the two equinoctial points on the earth's path around the sun (i. e. where it stands on 20 March and 22 September) and the two solstitial points (where it stands on 21 June and 21 December). The implication, is that: 'The rotation of the polar axis must not be disjointed from the great circles that shift along with it in heaven. The framework is thought of as all one with the axis.'[7]

Santillana and von Dechend are certain that what confronts us here is *not a belief but an allegory*. They insist that the notion of a spherical frame composed of two intersecting hoops suspended from an axis is not under any circumstances to be understood as the way in which ancient science envisaged the cosmos. Instead it is to be seen as a 'thought tool' designed to focus the minds of people bright enough to crack the code upon the hard-to-detect astronomical fact of precession of the equinoxes.

It is a thought tool that keeps on cropping up, in numerous disguises, all over the myths of the ancient world.

At the mill with slaves

One example, from Central America (which also provides a further illustration of the curious symbolic 'cross-overs' between myths of precession and myths of catastrophe), was summarized by Diego De Landa in the sixteenth century:

> Among the multitude of gods worshipped by these people [the Maya] were four whom they called by the name *Bacab*. These were, they say, four brothers placed by God when he created the world at its four corners to sustain the heavens lest they fall. They also say that these Bacabs escaped when the world was destroyed by a deluge.[8]

It is the opinion of Santillana and von Dechend that the Mayan astronomer-priests did not subscribe for a moment to the simple-minded notion that the earth was flat with four corners. Instead, they say, the image of the four Bacabs is used as a technical allegory intended to shed light on the phenomenon of precession of the equinoxes. The Bacabs stand, in short, for the system of coordinates of an astrological age. They represent the equinoctial and solstitial colures, binding together the four constellations in which the sun continues to rise at the spring and autumn equinoxes and at the winter and summer solstices for epochs of just under 2200 years.

Of course it is understood that when the gears of heaven change, the old age comes crashing down and a new age is born. All this, so far, is routine precessional imagery. What stands out, however, is the explicit linkage to an earthly disaster – in this case a flood – which the Bacabs survive. It may also be relevant that relief carvings at Chichen Itza unmistakably represent the Bacabs as being bearded and of European appearance.[9]

Be that as it may, the Bacab image (linked to a number of badly misunderstood references to 'the four corners of heaven', 'the quadrangular earth', and so on) is only one among many that seem to have been designed to serve as thought tools for precession. Archetypal among these is, of course, the 'Mill' of Santillana's title – Hamlet's Mill.

It turns out that the Shakespearean character, 'whom the poet made one of us, the first unhappy intellectual', conceals a past as a legendary being, his features predetermined, preshaped by long-standing myth.[10] In all his many incarnations, this Hamlet remains strangely himself. The original Amlodhi (or sometimes Amleth) as his name was in Icelandic legend, 'shows the same characteristics of melancholy and high intellect. He, too, is a son dedicated to avenge his father, a speaker of cryptic but inescapable truths, an elusive carrier of Fate who must yield once his mission is accomplished . . .'[11]

In the crude and vivid imagery of the Norse, Amlodhi was identified with the ownership of a fabled mill, or quern, which, in its time, ground out gold and peace and plenty. In many of the traditions, two giant maidens (Fenja and Menja) were indentured to turn this great contraption, which could not be budged by any human strength. Something went wrong, and the two giantesses were forced to work day and night with no rest:

> Forth to the mill bench they were brought,
>   To set the grey stone in motion;
> He gave them no rest nor peace,
>   Attentive to the creak of the mill.
>
> Their song was a howl,
>   Shattering silence;

> 'Lower the bin and lighten the stones!'
> Yet he would have them grind more.[12]

Rebellious and angry, Fenja and Menja waited until everyone was asleep and then began to turn the mill in a mad whirl until its great props, though cased in iron, burst asunder.[13] Immediately afterwards, in a confusing episode, the mill was stolen by a sea king named Mysinger and loaded aboard his ship together with the giantesses. Mysinger ordered the pair to grind again, but this time they ground out salt. At midnight they asked him whether he was not weary of salt; he bade them grind longer. They had ground but a little longer when down sank the ship:

> The huge props flew off the bin,
> The iron rivets burst,
> The shaft tree shivered,
> The bin shot down.[14]

When it reached the bottom of the sea, the mill continued to turn, but it ground out rock and sand, creating a vast whirlpool, the Maelstrom.[15]

Such images, Santillana and von Dechend assert, signify precession of the equinoxes.[16] The axis and 'iron props' of the mill stand for:

a system of coordinates in the celestial sphere and represent the frame of a world age. Actually the frame defines a world age. Because the polar axis and the colures form an invisible whole, the entire frame is thrown out of kilter if one part is moved. When that happens a new Pole star with appropriate colures of its own must replace the obsolete apparatus.[17]

Furthermore, the engulfing whirlpool:

belongs to the stock-in-trade of ancient fable. It appears in the *Odyssey* as Charybdis in the Straits of Messina, and again in other cultures in the Indian Ocean and the Pacific. It is found there, too, curiously enough, with an overhanging fig-tree to whose boughs the hero can cling as the ship goes down, whether it be Satyavrata in India or Kae in Tonga . . . The persistence of detail rules out free invention. Such stories have belonged to the cosmographical literature since antiquity.[18]

The appearance of the whirlpool in Homer's *Odyssey* (which is a compilation of Greek myths more than 3000 years old), should not surprise us, because the great Mill of Icelandic legend appears there also (and does so, moreover, in familiar circumstances). It is the last night before the decisive confrontation. Odysseus, bent on revenge, has landed in Ithaca and is hiding under the magic spell of the goddess Athena, which protects him from recognition. Odysseus prays to Zeus to send him an encouraging sign before the great ordeal:

> Straightaway Zeus thundered from shining Olympus . . . and goodly Odysseus was glad. Moreover, a woman, a grinder at the mill, uttered a voice of omen from within the house hard by, where stood the mills of the shepherd of the people. At these handmills twelve women in all plied their task, making meal of barley and of wheat the marrow of men. Now all the others were asleep, for they had ground out their task of grain, but this one alone rested not yet, being the weakest of all. She now stayed her quern and spake the word . . . 'May the [enemies of Odysseus] on this day, for the last time make their sweet feasting in his halls. They that have loosened my knees with cruel toil to grind their barley meal, may they now sup their last!'[19]

Santillana and von Dechend argue that it is no accident that the allegory of the 'orb of heaven that turns around like a millstone and ever does something bad'[20] also makes an appearance in the biblical tradition of Samson, 'eyeless in Gaza at the mill with slaves'.[21] His merciless captors unbind him so that he can 'make sport' for them in their temple; instead, with his last strength, he takes hold of the middle pillars of that great structure and brings the whole edifice crashing down, killing everybody.[22] Like Fenja and Menja, he gets his revenge.

The theme resurfaces in Japan,[23] in Central America,[24] among the Maoris of New Zealand,[25] and in the myths of Finland. There the Hamlet/Samson figure is known as Kullervo and the mill has a peculiar name: the Sampo. Like Fenja and Menja's mill it is ultimately stolen and loaded on board a ship. And like their mill, it ends up being broken in pieces.[26]

It turns out that the word 'Sampo' has its origins in the Sanskrit *skambha*, meaning 'pillar or pole'.[27] And in the *Atharvaveda*, one of

the most ancient pieces of north Indian literature, we find an entire
hymn dedicated to the Skambha:

> In whom earth, atmosphere, in whom sky is set, where fire, moon, sun,
> wind stand fixed . . . The Skambha sustains both heaven and earth;
> the Skambha sustains the wide atmosphere; the Skambha sustains the
> six wide directions; into the Skambha entered all existence.

Whitney, the translator (*Atharvaveda* 10:7) comments in some
perplexity: 'Skambha, lit, prop, support, pillar, strangely used in this
hymn as frame of the universe'.[28] Yet with an awareness of the
complex of ideas linking cosmic mills, and whirlpools and world trees
and so on, the archaic Vedic usage should not seem so strange. What is
being signalled here, as in all the other allegories, is *the frame of a world
age* – that same heavenly mechanism that turns for more than 2000
years with the sun rising always in the same four cardinal points and
then slowly shifts those celestial coordinates to four new constellations for the next couple of thousand years.

This is why the mill always breaks, why the huge props always fly
off the bin in one way or another, why the iron rivets burst, why the
shaft-tree shivers. Precession of the equinoxes merits such imagery
because, at widely separated intervals of time it does indeed change, or
break, the stabilizing coordinates of the entire celestial sphere.

Openers of the way

What is remarkable about all this is the way that the mill (which
continues to serve as an allegory for cosmic processes) stubbornly
keeps on resurfacing, all over the world, even where the context has
been jumbled or lost. Indeed, in Santillana and von Dechend's
argument, it doesn't really matter if the context is lost. 'The particular
merit of mythical terminology,' they say, 'is that it can be used as a
vehicle for handing down solid knowledge independently from the
degree of insight of the people who do the actual telling of stories,
fables, etc.'[29] What matters, in other words, is that certain central
imagery should survive and continue to be passed on in retellings,
however far these may drift from the original storyline.

An example of such drift (coupled with the retention of essential imagery and information) is found among the Cherokees, whose name for the Milky Way (our own galaxy) is 'Where the Dog Ran'. In ancient times, according to Cherokee tradition, the 'people in the South had a corn mill', from which meal was stolen again and again. In due course the owners discovered the thief, a dog, who 'ran off howling to his home in the North, with the meal dropping from his mouth as he ran, and leaving behind a white trail where now we see the Milky Way, which the Cherokee call to this day . . . "Where the Dog Ran".'[30]

In Central America, one of the many myths concerning Quetzalcoatl depicts him playing a key role in the regeneration of mankind after the all-destroying flood that ended the Fourth Sun. Together with his dog-headed companion Xolotl, he descends into the underworld to retrieve the skeletons of the people killed by the deluge. This he succeeds in doing, after tricking Miclantechuhtli, the god of death, and the bones are brought to a place called Tamoanchan. There, like corn, they are milled into a fine meal on a grindstone. Upon this ground meal the gods then release blood, thus creating the flesh of the current age of men.[31]

Santillana and von Dechend do not think that the presence of a canine character in both the above variants of the myth of the cosmic mill is likely to be accidental. They point out that Kullervo, the Finnish Hamlet, is also accompanied by 'the black dog Musti'.[32] Likewise, after his return to his estates in Ithaca, Odysseus is first recognized by his faithful dog,[33] and as anyone who has been to Sunday school will remember, Samson is associated with foxes (300 of them to be precise[34]), which are members of the dog family. In the Danish version of the Amleth/Hamlet saga, 'Amleth went on and a wolf crossed his path amid the thicket.'[35] Last but not least an alternative recension of the Kullervo story from Finland has the hero (rather weirdly) being 'sent to Esthonia to bark under the fence; he barked one year . . .'[36]

Santillana and von Dechend are confident that all this 'doggishness' is purposive: another piece of the ancient code, as yet unbroken, persistently tapping out its message from place to place. They list these and many other canine symbols among a series of 'morphological markers' which they have identified as likely to suggest the presence, in ancient myths, of scientific information concerning precession of the equinoxes.[37] These markers may have had meanings of their own or been intended simply to alert the target audience that a piece of hard data was coming up in the story being told. Beguilingly, sometimes they may also have been designed to serve as 'openers of the way' – conduits to enable initiates to follow the trail of scientific information from one myth to another.

Thus, even though none of the familiar mills and whirlpools is in sight, we should perhaps sit up and pay attention when we learn that Orion, the great hunter of Greek myth, was the owner of a dog. When Orion tried to ravish the virgin goddess Artemis she produced a scorpion from the earth which killed him and the dog. Orion was transported to the skies where he became the constellation that bears his name today; his dog was transformed into Sirius, the Dog Star.[38]

Precisely the same identification of Sirius was made by the ancient Egyptians,[39] who linked the Orion constellation specifically to their god Osiris.[40] It is in Ancient Egypt too that the character of the faithful celestial dog achieves its fullest and most explicit mythical elaboration in the form of Upuaut, a jackal-headed deity whose name means 'Opener of the Ways'.[41] If we follow this way opener to Egypt, turn our eyes to the constellation of Orion, and enter the potent myth of Osiris, we find ourselves enveloped in a net of familiar symbols.

The reader will recall that the myth presents Osiris as the victim of a plot. The conspirators initially dispose of him by sealing him in a box and casting him adrift on the waters of the Nile. In this respect does he not resemble Utnapishtim, and Noah and Coxcoxtli and all the other deluge heroes in their arks (or boxes, or chests) riding out the waters of the flood?

Another familiar element is the classic precessional image of the world-tree and/or roof-pillar (in this case combined). The myth tells us how Osiris, still sealed inside his coffer, is carried out into the sea and washed up at Byblos. The waves lay him to rest among the branches of a tamarisk tree, which rapidly grows to a magnificent size, enclosing the coffer within its trunk.[42] The king of the country, who much admires the tamarisk tree, cuts it down and fashions the part which contains Osiris into a roof pillar for his palace. Later Isis, the wife of Osiris, removes her husband's body from the pillar and takes it back to Egypt to undergo rebirth.[43]

The Osiris myth also includes certain key numbers. Whether by accident or by design, these numbers give access to a of 'science' of precession, as we shall see in the next chapter.

Chapter 31

The Osiris Numbers

Archaeo-astronomer Jane B. Sellers, who studied Egyptology at the University of Chicago's Oriental Institute, spends her winters in Portland, Maine, and summers at Ripley Neck, a nineteenth-century enclave 'downeast' on Maine's rocky coast. 'There,' she says, 'the night skies can be as clear as the desert, and no one minds if you read the Pyramid Texts out loud to the seagulls . . .'[1]

One of the few serious scholars to have tested the theory advanced by Santillana and von Dechend in *Hamlet's Mill*, Sellers has been hailed for having drawn attention to the need to use astronomy, and more particularly precession, for the proper study of ancient Egypt and its religion.[2] In her words: 'Archaeologists by and large lack an understanding of precession, and this affects their conclusions concerning ancient myths, ancient gods and ancient temple alignments . . . For astronomers precession is a well-established fact; those working in the field of ancient man have a responsibility to attain an understanding of it.'[3]

It is Sellers's contention, eloquently expressed in her recent book, *The Death of Gods in Ancient Egypt*, that the Osiris myth may have been deliberately encoded with a group of key numbers that are 'excess baggage' as far as the narrative is concerned but that offer an eternal calculus by which surprisingly exact values can be derived for the following:

1 The time required for the earth's slow precessional wobble to

cause the position of sunrise on the vernal equinox to complete a shift of **one degree** along the ecliptic (in relation to the stellar background);

2 The time required for the sun to pass through one full zodiacal segment of **thirty degrees**;

3 The time required for the sun to pass through two full zodiacal segments (totalling **sixty degrees**);

4 The time required to bring about the 'Great Return'[4], i. e, for the sun to shift **three hundred and sixty degrees** along the ecliptic, thus fulfilling one complete precessional cycle or 'Great Year'.

Computing the Great Return

The precessional numbers highlighted by Sellers in the Osiris myth are 360, 72, 30 and 12. Most of them are found in a section of the myth which provides us with biographical details of the various characters. These have been conveniently summarized by E. A. Wallis Budge, formerly keeper of Egyptian Antiquities at the British Museum:

> The goddess Nut, wife of the sun god Ra, was beloved by the god Geb. When Ra discovered the intrigue he cursed his wife and declared that she should not be delivered of a child in any month of any year. Then the god Thoth, who also loved Nut, played at tables with the moon and won from her five whole days. These he joined to the 360 days *of which the year then consisted* [emphasis added]. On the first of these five days Osiris was brought forth; and at the moment of his birth a voice was heard to proclaim that the lord of creation was born.[5]

Elsewhere the myth informs us that the 360-day year consists of '12 months of 30 days each'.[6] And in general, as Sellers observes, 'phrases are used which prompt simple mental calculations and an attention to numbers'.[7]

Thus far we have been provided with three of Sellers's precessional numbers: 360, 12 and 30. The fourth number, which occurs later in the text, is by far the most important. As we saw in Chapter Nine, the evil deity known as Set led a group of conspirators in a plot to kill Osiris. The number of these conspirators was 72.

With this last number in hand, suggests Sellers, we are now in a position to boot-up and set running an ancient computer programme:

12 = the number of constellations in the zodiac;

30 = the number of degrees allocated along the ecliptic to each zodiacal constellation;

72 = the number of years required for the equinoctial sun to complete a precessional shift of one degree along the ecliptic;

360 = the total number of degrees in the ecliptic;

72 × 30 = 2160 (the number of years required for the sun to complete a passage of 30 degrees along the ecliptic, i. e., to pass entirely through any one of the 12 zodiacal constellations);

2160 × 12 (or 360 × 72) = 25,920 (the number of years in one complete precessional cycle or 'Great Year', and thus the total number of years required to bring about the 'Great Return').

Other figures and combinations of figures also emerge, for example:

36, the number of years required for the equinoctial sun to complete a precessional shift of half a degree along the ecliptic;

4320, the number of years required for the equinoctial sun to complete a precessional shift of 60 degrees (i. e., two zodiacal constellations).

These, Sellers believes, constitute the basic ingredients of a precessional code which appears again and again, with eerie persistence, in ancient myths and sacred architecture. In common with much esoteric numerology, it is a code in which it is permissible to shift decimal points to left or right at will and to make use of almost any conceivable combinations, permutations, multiplications, divisions and fractions of the *essential* numbers (all of which relate precisely to the rate of precession of the equinoxes).

The pre-eminent number in the code is 72. To this is frequently added 36, making 108, and it is permissible to multiply 108 by 100 to get 10,800 or to divide it by 2 to get 54, which may then be multiplied by 10 and expressed as 540 (or as 54,000. or as 540,000, or as 5,400,000, and so on). Also highly significant is 2160 (the number of years required for the equinoctial point to transit one zodiacal constellation), which is sometimes multiplied by 10 and by factors of ten (to give 216,000, 2,160,000, and so on) and sometimes by 2 to give 4320, or 43,200, or 432,000, or 4,320,000, *ad infinition*.

Better than Hipparchus

If Sellers is correct in her hypothesis that the calculus needed to produce these numbers was deliberately encoded into the Osiris myth to convey precessional information to initiates, we are confronted by an intriguing anomaly. If they are indeed about precession, the numbers are out of place in time. The science they contain is too advanced for them to have been calculated by any known civilization of antiquity.

Let us not forget that they occur in a myth which is present at the very dawn of writing in Egypt (indeed elements of the Osiris story are to be found in the Pyramid Texts dating back to around 2450 BC, in a context which suggests that they were exceedingly old even then[8]). Hipparchus, the so-called discoverer of precession lived in the second century BC. He proposed a value of 45 or 46 seconds of arc for one year of precessional motion. These figures yield a one-degree shift along the ecliptic in 80 years (at 45 arc seconds per annum), and in 78.26 years (at 46 arc seconds per annum). The true figure, as calculated by twentieth century science, is 71.6 years.[9] If Sellers's theory is correct, therefore, the 'Osiris numbers', which give a value of 72 years, are *significantly more accurate* than those of Hipparchus. Indeed, within the obvious confines imposed by narrative structure, it is difficult to see how the number 72 could have been improved upon, even if the more precise figure had been known to the ancient myth-makers. One can hardly insert 71.6 conspirators into a story, but 72 will fit comfortably.

Working from this rounded-up figure, the Osiris myth is capable of yielding a value of 2160 years for a precessional shift through one complete house of the zodiac. The correct figure, according to today's calculations, is 2148 years.[10] The Hipparchus figures are 2400 years and 2347.8 years respectively. Finally, Osiris enables us to calculate 25,920 as the number of years required for the fulfilment of a complete precessional cycle through 12 houses of the zodiac.

Hipparchus gives us either 28,800 or 28,173.6 years. The correct figure, by today's estimates, is 25,776 years.[11] The Hipparchus calculations for the Great Return are therefore around 3000 years out of kilter. The Osiris calculations miss the true figure by only 144 years, and may well do so because the narrative context forced a rounding-up of the base number from the correct value of 71.6 to a more workable figure of 72.

All this, however, assumes that Sellers is right to suppose that the numbers 360, 72, 30 and 12 did not find their way into the Osiris myth by chance but were placed there deliberately by people who understood – and had accurately measured – precession.

Is Sellers right?

Times of decay

The Osiris myth is not the only one to incorporate the calculus for precession. The relevant numbers keep surfacing in various forms, multiples and combinations, all over the ancient world.

An example was given in Chapter Thirty-three – the Norse myth of the 432,000 fighters who sallied forth from Valhalla to do battle with 'the Wolf'. A glance back at that myth shows that it contains several permutations of 'precessional numbers'.

Likewise, as we saw in Chapter Twenty-four, ancient Chinese traditions referring to a universal cataclysm were said to have been written down in a great text consisting of precisely 4320 volumes.

Thousands of miles away, is it a coincidence that the Babylonian historian Berossus (third century BC) ascribed a total reign of 432,000 years to the mythical kings who ruled the land of Sumer before the flood? And is it likewise a coincidence that this same Berossus ascribed 2,160,000 years to the period 'between creation and universal catastrophe'?[12]

Do the myths of ancient Amerindian peoples like the Maya also contain or enable us to compute numbers such as 72, 2160, 4320, etc. We shall probably never know, thanks to the conquistadores and zealous friars who destroyed the traditional heritage of Central America and left us so little to work with. What we can say, however, is that the relevant numbers do turn up, in relative profusion, in the

Mayan Long Count calendar. Details of that calendar were given in Chapter Twenty-one. The numerals necessary for calculating precession are found there in these formulae: 1 *Katun* = 7200 days; 1 *Tun* = 360 days; 2 *Tuns* = 720 days; 5 *Baktuns* = 720,000 days; 5 *Katuns* = 36,000 days; 6 *Katuns* = 43,200 days; 6 *Tuns* = 2160 days; 15 *Katuns* = 2,160,000 days.[13]

Nor does it seem that Sellers's 'code' is confined to mythology. In the jungles of Kampuchea the temple complex of Angkor looks as though it could have been purpose-built as a precessional metaphor. It has, for example, five gates to each of which leads a road bridging the crocodile-infested moat that surrounds the whole site. Each of these roads is bordered by a row of gigantic stone figures, 108 per avenue, 54 on each side (540 statues in all) and each row carries a huge Naga serpent. Furthermore, as Santillana and von Dechend point out in *Hamlet's Mill*, the figures do not 'carry' the serpent but are shown to 'pull' it, which indicates that these 540 statues are 'churning the Milky Ocean'. The whole of Angkor 'thus turns out to be a colossal model set up with true Hindu fantasy and incongruousness' to express the idea of precession.[14]

The same may be true of Java's famous temple of Borobudur, with its 72 bell-shaped stupas, and perhaps also of the megaliths of Baalbeck in the Lebanon – which are thought to be the world's biggest blocks of cut stone. Long predating Roman and Greek structures on the site, the three that make up the so-called 'Trilithion' are as tall as five-storey buildings and weigh over 600 tons each. A fourth megalith is almost 80 feet in length and weighs 1100 tons. Amazingly these giant blocks were cut, perfectly-shaped and somehow transported to Baalbeck from a quarry several miles away. In addition they were skilfully incorporated, at a considerable height above ground-level into the retaining walls of a magnificient temple. This temple was surrounded by 54 columns of immense size and height.[15]

In the subcontinent of India (where the Orion constellation is known as Kal-Purush, meaning Time-Man[16]), we find that Sellers's Osiris numbers are transmitted through a wide range of media in ways increasingly difficult to ascribe to chance. There are, for instance, 10,800 bricks in the Agnicayana, the Indian fire altar. There are 10,800 stanzas in the *Rigveda*, the most ancient of the Vedic texts and

Churning the Milky Ocean, one of the several 'thought tools' for precession encountered in ancient myths.

a rich repository of Indian mythology. Each stanza is made up of 40 syllables with the result that the entire composition consists of 432,000 syllables . . . no more, and no less.[17] And in *Rigveda* I:164 (a typical stanza) we read of 'the 12-spoked wheel in which 720 sons of Agni are established'.[18]

In the Hebrew Cabala there are 72 angels through whom the Sephiroth (divine powers) may be approached, or invoked, by those who know their names and numbers.[19] Rosicrucian tradition speaks of cycles of 108 years (72 plus 36) according to which the secret brotherhood makes its influence felt.[20] Similarly the number 72 and its permutations and subdivisions are of great significance to the Chinese secret societies known as Triads. An ancient ritual requires that each candidate for initiation pay a fee including '360 cash for "making clothes", 108 cash "for the purse", 72 cash for instruction, and 36 cash for decapitating the "traiterous subject".'[21] The 'cash' (the old universal brass coin of China with a square hole in the centre) is of course no longer in circulation but the *numbers* passed down in the ritual since times immemorial have survived. Thus in modern Singapore, candidates for Triad membership pay an entrance fee which is calculated according to their financial circumstances but which must always consist of multiples of $1.80, $3.60, $7.20, $10.80 (and thus, $18, $36, $72, $108.00, or $360, $720, $1,080, and so on.)[22]

Of all the secret societies, the most mysterious and archaic by far is undoubtedly the Hung League, which scholars believe to be 'the depository of the old religion of the Chinese'.[23] In one Hung initiation ritual the neophyte is put through a question and answer session that goes:

Q. What did you see on your walk?
A. I saw two pots with red bamboo.

Q. Do you know how many plants there were?
A. In one pot were 36 and in the other 72 plants, together 108.

Q. Did you take home some of them for your use?
A. Yes, I took home 108 plants . . .

Q.   How can you prove that?
A.   I can prove it by a verse.

Q.   How does this verse run?
A.   The red bamboo from Canton is rare in the world.
     In the groves are 36 and 72.
     Who in the world knows the meaning of this?
     When we have set to work we will know the secret.

The atmosphere of intrigue that such passages generate is accentuated by the reticent behaviour of the Hung League itself, an organization resembling the medieval European Order of the Knights Templar (and the higher degrees of modern Freemasonry) in many ways that are beyond the remit of this book to describe.[24] It is intriguing, too, that the Chinese character *Hung*, composed of *water* and *many*, signifies *inundation*, i. e. the Flood.

   Finally, returning to India, let us note the content of the sacred scriptures known as the *Puranas*. These speak of four 'ages of the earth', called Yugas, which together are said to extend to 12,000 'divine years'. The respective durations of these epochs, in 'divine years', are Krita Yuga = 4800; Treta Yuga = 3600; Davpara Yuga = 2400; Kali Yuga = 1200.[25]

   The *Puranas* also tell us that 'one year of the mortals is equal to one day of the gods'.[26] Furthermore, and exactly as in the Osiris myth, we discover that the number of *days* in the years of both gods and mortals has been artificially set at 360, so one year of the gods is equivalent to 360 mortal years.[27]

   The Kali Yuga, therefore, at 1200 years of the gods, turns out to have a duration of 432,000 mortal years.[28] One Mahayuga, or Great Age (made up of the 12,000 divine years contained in the four lesser Yugas) is equivalent to 4,320,000 years of mortals. A thousand such Mahayugas (which constitute a Kalpa, or Day of Brahma) extend over 4,320,000,000 ordinary years,[29] again supplying the digits for basic precessional calculations. Separately there are Manvantaras (periods of Manu) of which we are told in the scriptures that 'about 71 systems of four Yugas elapse during each Manvantara'.[30] The reader will recall that one degree of precessional motion along the ecliptic requires 71.6 years to complete, a number that can be rounded down to 'about 71' in India just as easily as it was rounded up to 72 in Ancient Egypt.

The Kali Yuga, with a duration of 432,000 mortal years, is, by the way, our own. 'In the Kali Age,' the scriptures say, 'shall decay flourish, until the human race approaches annihilation.'[31]

Dogs, uncles and revenge

It was a dog that brought us to these decaying times.

We came here by way of Sirius, the Dog Star, who stands at the heel of the giant constellation of Orion where it towers in the sky above Egypt. In that land, as we have seen, Orion is Osiris, the god of death and resurrection, whose numbers – perhaps by chance – are 12, 30, 72, and 360. But can chance account for the fact that these and other prime integers of precession keep cropping up in supposedly unrelated mythologies from all over the world, and in such stolid but enduring vehicles as calendar systems and works of architecture?

Santillana and von Dechend, Jane Sellers and a growing body of other scholars rule out chance, arguing that the *persistence of detail* is indicative of a guiding hand.

If they are wrong, we need to find some other explanation for how such specific and inter-related numbers (the only obvious function of which is to calculate precession) could by accident have got themselves so widely imprinted on human culture.

But suppose they are *not* wrong? Suppose that a guiding hand really was at work behind the scenes?

Sometimes, when you slip into Santillana's and von Dechend's world of myth and mystery, you can almost feel the influence of that hand . . . Take the business of the dog . . . or jackal, or wolf, or fox. The subtle way this shadowy canine slinks from myth to myth is peculiar – stimulating, then baffling you, always luring you onwards.

Indeed, it was this lure we followed from the Mill of Amlodhi to the myth of Osiris in Egypt. Along the way, according to the design of the ancient sages (if Sellers, Santillana and von Dechend are right) we were first encouraged to build a clear mental picture of the celestial sphere. Second, we were provided with a mechanistic model so that we could visualize the great changes precession of the equinoxes periodically effects in all the coordinates of the sphere. Finally, after allowing the dog Sirius to open the way for us, we were were given the figures to calculate precession more or less exactly.

Nor is Sirius, in his eternal station at Orion's heel, the only doggish character around Osiris. We saw in Chapter Eleven how Isis (who was both the wife and sister of Osiris[32]) searched for her dead husband's body after he had been murdered by Set (who, incidentally, was also her brother, and the brother of Osiris). In this search, according to ancient tradition, she was assisted by dogs (jackals in some versions).[33] Likewise, mythological and religious texts from all periods of Egyptian history assert that the jackal–god Anubis ministered to the spirit of Osiris after his death and acted as his guide through the underworld.[34] (Surviving vignettes depict Anubis as virtually identical in appearance to Upuaut, the Opener of the Ways.)

Last but not least, Osiris himself was believed to have taken the form of a wolf when he returned from the underworld to assist his son Horus in the final battle against Set.[35]

Investigating this kind of material, one sometimes has the spooky sense of being manipulated by an ancient intelligence which has found a way to reach out to us across vast epochs of time, and for some reason has set us a puzzle to solve in the language of myth.

If it were just dogs that kept cropping up again and again, it would be easy to brush off such weird intuitions. The dog phenomenon seems more likely to be coincidence than anything else. But it isn't just dogs.

The ways between the two very different myths of Osiris and Amlodhi's Mill (which nonetheless both seem to contain accurate scientific data about precession of the equinoxes) are kept open by another strange common factor. Family relationships are involved. Amlodhi/Amleth/Hamlet is always a son who revenges the murder of his father by entrapping and killing the murderer. The murderer, furthermore, is always the father's own brother, i.e., Hamlet's uncle.[36]

This is precisely the scenario of the Osiris myth. Osiris and Seth are brothers.[37] Seth murders Osiris. Horus, the son of Osiris, then takes revenge upon his uncle.[38]

Another twist is that the Hamlet character often has some sort of incestuous relationship with his sister.[39] In the case of Kullervo, the Finnish Hamlet, there is a poignant scene in which the hero, returning home after a long absence, meets a maiden in the woods, gathering berries. They lie together. Only later do they discover that they are brother and sister. The maiden drowns herself at once. Later, with 'the black dog Musti' padding along at his heels, Kullervo wanders into the forest and throws himself upon his sword.[40]

There are no suicides in the Egyptian myth of Osiris, but there is the incest of Osiris and his sister Isis. Out of their union is born Horus the avenger.

So once again it seems reasonable to ask: what is going on? Why are there all these apparent links and connections? Why do we have these 'strings' of myths, ostensibly about different subjects, all of which prove capable in their own ways of shedding light on the phenomenon of precession of the equinoxes? And why do all these myths have dogs running through them, and characters who seem unusually inclined to incest, fratricide and revenge? It surely drives scepticism beyond its limits to suggest that so many identical literary devices could keep on turning up purely by chance in so many different contexts.

If not by chance, however, then who exactly was responsible for creating this intricate and clever connecting pattern? Who were the authors and designers of the puzzle and what motives might they have had?

Scientists with something to say

Whoever it was, they must have been smart – smart enough to have observed the infinitesimal creep of precessional motion along the ecliptic and to have calculated its rate at a value uncannily close to that obtained by today's advanced technology.

It therefore follows that we are talking about highly civilized people. Indeed, we are talking about people who deserve to be called scientists. They must, moreover, have lived in extremely remote antiquity because we can be certain that the creation and dissemination of the common heritage of precessional myths on both sides of the Atlantic did *not* take place in historic times. On the contrary the evidence suggests that all these myths were 'tottering with age' when what we call history began about 5000 years ago.[41]

The great strength of the ancient stories was this: as well as being for ever available for use and adaptation free of copyright, like intellectual chameleons, subtle and ambiguous, they had the capacity to change their colour according to their surroundings. At different times, in different continents, the ancient tales could be retold in a variety of ways, but would always retain their essential symbolism and always continue to transmit the coded precessional data they had been programmed with at the outset.

But to what end?

As we see in the next chapter, the long slow cycles of precession are *not* limited in their consequences to a changing view of the sky. This celestial phenomenon, born of the earth's axial wobble, has direct effects on the earth itself. In fact, it appears to be one of the principal correlates of the sudden onset of ice ages and their equally sudden and catastrophic decay.

Chapter 32

Speaking to the Unborn

It is understandable that a huge range of myths from all over the ancient world should describe geological catastrophes in graphic detail. Mankind survived the horror of the last Ice Age, and the most plausible source for our enduring traditions of flooding and freezing, massive volcanism and devastating earthquakes is in the tumultuous upheavals unleashed during the great meltdown of 15,000 to 8000 BC. The final retreat of the ice sheets, and the consequent 300-400 foot rise in global sea levels, took place only a few thousand years before the beginning of the historical period. It is therefore not surprising that all our early civilizations should have retained vivid memories of the vast cataclysms that had terrified their forefathers.

Much harder to explain is the peculiar but distinctive way the myths of cataclysm seem to bear the intelligent imprint of a guiding hand.[1] Indeed the degree of convergence between such ancient stories is frequently remarkable enough to raise the suspicion that they must all have been 'written' by the same 'author'.

Could that author have had anything to do with the wondrous deity, or superhuman, spoken of in so many of the myths we have reviewed, who appears immediately after the world has been shattered by a horrifying geological catastrophe and brings comfort and the gifts of civilization to the shocked and demoralized survivors?

White and bearded, Osiris is the Egyptian manifestation of this universal figure, and it may not be an accident that one of the first acts he is remembered for in myth is the abolition of cannibalism among the primitive inhabitants of the Nile Valley.[2] Viracocha, in South America, was said to have begun his civilizing mission immediately after a great flood; Quetzalcoatl, the discoverer of maize, brought the benefits of crops, mathematics, astronomy and a refined culture to Mexico after the Fourth Sun had been overwhelmed by a destroying deluge.

Could these strange myths contain a record of encounters between scattered palaeolithic tribes which survived the last Ice Age and an as yet unidentified high civilization which passed through the same epoch?

And could the myths be attempts to communicate?

A message in the bottle of time

'Of all the other stupendous inventions,' Galileo once remarked,

> what sublimity of mind must have been his who conceived how to communicate his most secret thoughts to any other person, though very distant either in time or place, speaking with those who are in the Indies, speaking to those who are not yet born, nor shall be this thousand or ten thousand years? And with no greater difficulty than the various arrangements of two dozen little signs on paper? Let this be the seal of all the admirable inventions of men.[3]

If the 'precessional message' identified by scholars like Santillana, von Dechend and Jane Sellers is indeed a deliberate attempt at communication by some lost civilization of antiquity, how come it wasn't just written down and left for us to find? Wouldn't that have been easier than encoding it in myths? Perhaps.

Nevertheless, suppose that whatever the message was written on got destroyed or worn away after many thousands of years? Or suppose that the language in which it was inscribed was later forgotten utterly (like the enigmatic Indus Valley script, which has been studied closely for more than half a century but has so far resisted all attempts at decoding)? It must be obvious that in such circumstances a written legacy to the future would be of no value at all, because nobody would be able to make sense of it.

What one would look for, therefore, would be a *universal language*, the kind of language that would be comprehensible to any technologically advanced society in any epoch, even a thousand or ten thousand years into the future. Such languages are few and far between, but mathematics is one of them – and the city of Teotihuacan may be the calling-card of a lost civilization written in the eternal language of mathematics.

Geodetic data, related to the exact positioning of fixed geographical points and to the shape and size of the earth, would also remain valid and recognizable for tens of thousands of years, and might be most conveniently expressed by means of cartography (or in the construction of giant geodetic monuments like the Great Pyramid of Egypt, as we shall see).

Another 'constant' in our solar system is the language of time: the great but regular intervals of time calibrated by the inch-worm creep of precessional motion. Now, or ten thousand years in the future, a message that prints out numbers like 72 or 2160 or 4320 or 25,920 should be instantly intelligible to any civilization that has evolved a modest talent for mathematics and the ability to detect and measure the almost imperceptible reverse wobble that the sun appears to make along the ecliptic against the background of the fixed stars (one degree in 71.6 years, 30 degrees in 2148 years, and so on).

The sense that a correlation exists is strengthened by something else. It is neither as firm nor as definite as the number of syllables in the Rigveda; nevertheless, it feels relevant. Through powerful stylistic links and shared symbolism, myths to do with global cataclysms and with precession of the equinoxes quite frequently intermesh. A detailed interconnectedness exists between these two categories of tradition, both of which additionally bear what appear to be the recognizable fingerprints of a conscious design. Quite naturally, therefore, one is prompted to discover whether there might not *be* an important connection between precession of the equinoxes and global catastrophes.

Mill of pain

Although several different mechanisms of an astronomical and geological nature seem to be involved, and although not all of these are fully understood, the fact is that the cycle of precession does correlate very strongly *with the onset and demise of ice ages.*

Several trigger factors must coincide, which is why not every shift from one astronomical age to another is implicated. Nevertheless, it is accepted that precession does have an impact on both glaciation and deglaciation, at widely separated intervals. The knowledge that it does so has only been established by our own science since the late 1970's.[4] Yet the evidence of the myths suggests that the same level of knowledge might have been possessed by an as yet unidentified civilization in the depths of the last Ice Age. The clear suggestion we may be meant to grasp is that the terrible cataclysms of flood and fire and ice which the myths describe were in some way *causally connected* to the ponderous movements of the celestial coordinates through the great cycle of the zodiac. In the words of Santillana and von Dechend, 'It was not a foreign idea to the ancients that the mills of the gods grind slowly and that the result is usually pain.'[5]

Three principal factors, all of which we have met before, are now known to be deeply implicated in the onset and the retreat of ice ages (together, of course, with the diverse cataclysms that ensue from sudden freezes and thaws). These factors all have to do with variations in the earth's orbital geometry. They are:

1 The obliquity of the ecliptic (i. e., the angle of tilt of the planet's axis of rotation, which is also the angle between the celestial equator and the ecliptic). This, as we have seen, varies over immensely long periods of time between 22.1 degrees (the closest point that the axis reaches to vertical) and 24.5 degrees (the furthest it falls away from the vertical);

2 The eccentricity of the orbit (i. e., whether the earth's elliptical path around the sun is more or less elongated in any given epoch);

3 Axial precession, which causes the four cardinal points on the earth's orbit (the two equinoxes and the winter and summer solstices) to creep backwards very, very slowly around the orbital path.

We are dipping our toes into the waters of a technical and

specialized scientific discipline here – one largely outside the scope of this book. Readers seeking detailed information are referred to the multidisciplinary work of the US National Science Foundation's CLIMAP Project, and to a keynote paper by Professors J. D. Hays and John Imbrie entitled 'Variations in the Earth's Orbit: Pacemaker of the Ice Ages' (see Note 4).

Briefly, what Hays, Imbrie and others have proved is that the onset of ice ages can be predicted when the following evil and inauspicious conjunctions of celestial cycles occur: (a) **maximum eccentricity**, which takes the earth millions of miles further away from the sun at 'aphelion' (the extremity of its orbit) than is normal; (b) **minimum obliquity**, which means that the earth's axis, and consequently the North and South poles, stand much closer to the vertical than is normal; and (3) **precession of the equinoxes** which, as the great cycle continues, eventually causes winter in one hemisphere or the other to set in when the earth is at 'perihelion' (its closest point to the the sun); this in turn means that summer occurs at aphelion and is thus relatively cold, so that ice laid down in winter fails to melt during the following summer and a remorseless build-up of glacial conditions occurs.[6]

Levered by the changing geometry of the orbit, 'global insolation' – the differing amounts and intensity of sunlight received at various latitudes in any given epoch – can thus be an important trigger factor for ice ages.

Is it possible that the ancient myth-makers were trying to *warn* us of great danger when they so intricately linked the pain of global cataclysms to the slow grinding of the mill of heaven?

This is a question we will return to in due course, but meanwhile it is enough to observe that by identifying the significant effects of orbital geometry on the planet's climate and wellbeing, and by combining this information with precise measurements of the rate of precessional motion, the unknown scientists of an unrecognized civilization seem to have found a way to catch our attention, to bridge the chasm of the ages, and to communicate with us directly.

Whether or not we listen to what they have to say is, of course, entirely up to us.

Part VI

The Giza Invitation

Egypt 1

Chapter 33

Cardinal Points

Giza, Egypt, 16 March 1993, 3.30 a. m.

We walked through the deserted lobby of our hotel and stepped into the white Fiat waiting for us in the driveway outside. It was driven by a lean, nervous Egyptian named Ali whose job it was to get us past the guards at the Great Pyramid and away again before sunrise. He was nervous because if things went wrong Santha and I would be deported from Egypt and he would go to jail for six months.

Of course, things were not supposed to go wrong. That was why Ali was with us. The day before we'd paid him 150 US dollars which he had changed into Egyptian pounds and spread among the guards concerned. They, in return, had agreed to turn a blind eye to our presence during the next couple of hours.

We drove to within half a mile of the Pyramid, then walked the rest of the way – around the side of the steep embankment that looms above the village of Nazlet-el-Samaan and leads to the monument's north face. None of us said very much as we trudged through the soft sand just out of range of the security lights. We felt excited and apprehensive at the same time. Ali was by no means certain that his bribes were going to work.

For a while we stood still in the shadows, gazing at the monstrous bulk of the Pyramid reaching into the darkness above us and blotting out the southern stars. Then a patrol of three men armed with shotguns and wrapped in blankets against the night chill came into view at the north-eastern corner, about fifty yards away, where they stopped to share a cigarette. Indicating that we should stay put, Ali stepped forward into the light and walked over to the guards. He talked to them for several minutes, apparently arguing heatedly. Finally he beckoned to us, indicating that we should join him.

'There's a problem,' he explained. 'One of them, the captain here, [he indicated a short, unshaven, disgruntled looking fellow] is insisting that we pay an extra thirty dollars otherwise the deal is off. What do you want to do?' I fished around in my wallet, counted out thirty dollars and handed the bills to Ali. He folded them and passed them to the captain. With an air of aggrieved dignity, the captain stuffed the money into his shirt pocket, and finally, we all shook hands.

'OK,' said Ali, 'let's go.'

Inexplicable precision

As the guards continued their patrol in a westerly direction along the northern face of the Great Pyramid, we made our way around the north-eastern corner and along the base of the eastern face.

I had long ago fallen into the habit of orienting myself according to the monument's sides. The northern face was aligned, almost perfectly, to true north, the eastern face almost perfectly to true east, the southern to true south, and the western face to true west. The average error was only around three minutes of arc (down to less than two minutes on the southern face)[1] – incredible accuracy for any building in any epoch, and an inexplicable, almost supernatural feat here in Egypt 4500 years ago when the Great Pyramid was supposed to have been built.

An error of three arc minutes represents an infinitesimal deviation from true of less than 0.015 per cent. In the opinion of structural engineers, with whom I had discussed the Great Pyramid, the need for such precision was impossible to understand. From their point of view as practical builders, the expense, difficulty and time spent achieving it would not have been justified by the apparent results: even if the base of the monument had been as much as two or three

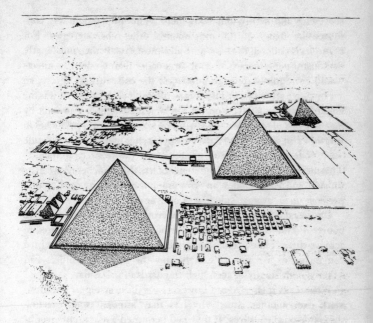

Overview of Giza from the north looking south, with the Great Pyramid in the foreground.

degrees out of true (an error of say 1 per cent) the difference to the naked eye would still have been too small to be noticeable. On the other hand the difference in the magnitude of the tasks required (to achieve accuracy within three minutes as opposed to three degrees) would have been immense.

Obviously, therefore, the ancient master-builders who had raised the Pyramid at the very dawn of human civilization must have had powerful motives for wanting to get the alignments with the cardinal directions just right. Moreover, since they had achieved their objective with uncanny exactness they must have been highly skilled, knowledgeable and competent people with access to excellent surveying and setting-out equipment. This impression was confirmed by many of the monument's other characteristics. For example, its sides at the base were all almost exactly the same length, demonstrating a margin of error far smaller than modern architects would be required to achieve today in the construction of, say, an average-size office block. This was no office block, however. It was the Great Pyramid of Egypt, one of the largest structures ever built by man and one of the oldest. Its north side was 755 feet 4.9818 inches in length; its west side was 755 feet 9.1551 inches in length; its east side was 755 feet 10.4937 inches; its south side 756 feet 0.9739 inches.[2] This meant that there was a difference of less than 8 inches between its shortest and longest sides: an error amounting to a tiny fraction of 1 per cent on an average side length of over 9063 inches.

Once again, I knew from an engineering perspective that the bare figures did not do justice to the enormous care and skill required to achieve them. I knew, too, that scholars had not yet come up with a convincing explanation of exactly how the Pyramid builders had adhered consistently to such high standards of precision.[3]

What really interested me, however, was the even bigger question-mark over another issue: why had they imposed such exacting standards on themselves? If they had permitted a margin of error of 1–2 per cent – instead of less than one-tenth of 1 per cent – they could have simplified their tasks with no apparent loss of quality. Why hadn't they done so? Why had they insisted on making everything so difficult? Why, in short, in a supposedly 'primitive' stone monument built more than 4500 years ago were we seeing this strange, obsessional adherence to machine-age standards of precision?

Black hole in history

Our plan was to climb the Great Pyramid – something that had been strictly illegal since 1983 when the messy falls of several foolhardy tourists had forced the government of Egypt to impose a ban. I realized that we were being foolhardy too (particularly in attempting the climb at night) and I didn't feel good about breaking what was basically a sensible law. By this stage, however, my intense interest in the Pyramid, and my desire to learn everything I could about it, had over-ridden my common sense.

Now, after parting company with the guard patrol at the north-eastern corner of the monument, we continued to make our way surreptitiously along the eastern face towards the south-eastern corner.

There were dense shadows among the twisted and broken paving stones that separated the Great Pyramid from the three much smaller 'subsidiary' pyramids lying immediately to its east. There were also three deep and narrow rock-cut pits which resembled giant graves. These had been found empty by the archaeologists who had excavated them, but were shaped as though they had been intended to enclose the hulls of high-prowed, streamlined boats.

Roughly halfway along the Pyramid's eastern face we encountered another patrol. This time it consisted of two guards, one of whom must have been eighty years old. His companion, a teenager with pustulant acne, informed us that the money Ali had paid was insufficient and that fifty more Egyptian pounds would be required if we were to proceed. I already had the notes in my hand and gave them to the lad without delay. I was past caring how much this was costing; I just wanted to make the climb and get down and away before dawn without being arrested.

We walked on, reaching the south-eastern corner at a little after 4.15 a.m.

Very few modern buildings, even the houses we live in, have corners that consist of perfect ninety degree right angles; it is common for them to be a degree or more out of true. It doesn't make any difference structurally and nobody notices such minute errors. In the case of the Great Pyramid, however, I knew that the ancient master-builders had found a way to narrow the margin of error to almost nothing. Thus, while falling short of the perfect ninety degrees, the south-eastern corner achieved an impressive 89° 56′ 27″. The north-eastern corner measured 90° 3′ 2″; the south-western 90 0′ 33″, and the north-western was just two seconds of a degree out of true at 89 59′ 58″.[4]

This was, of course, extraordinary. And like almost everything else about the Great Pyramid it was also extremely difficult to explain.

Such accurate building techniques – as accurate as the best we have today – could have evolved only after thousands of years of development and experimentation. Yet there was no evidence that any process of this kind had ever taken place in Egypt. The Great Pyramid and its neighbours at Giza had emerged out of a black hole in architectural history so deep and so wide that neither its bottom nor its far side had ever been identified.

Ships in the desert

Guided by the increasingly perspiring Ali, who had not yet explained why it was necessary for us to circumnavigate the Pyramid before climbing it, we now began to make our way in a westerly direction along the monument's southern side. Here there were two further boat-shaped pits, one of which, although still sealed, had been investigated with fibre-optic cameras and was known to contain a high-prowed sea-going vessel more than 100 feet long. The other pit had been excavated in 1950s. Its contents – an even larger seagoing vessel, a full 141 feet in length[5] – had been placed in the so-called Boat Museum, an ugly modern structure that gangled on stilts beneath the south face of the Pyramid.

Made of cedarwood, the beautiful ship in the museum was still in perfect condition 4500 years after it had been built. With a displacement of around 40 tons, its design was particularly thought-provoking, incorporating, in the words of one expert, 'all the sea-going ship's characteristic properties, with prow and stern soaring upward, higher than in a Viking ship, to ride out the breakers and high seas, not to contend with the little ripples of the Nile.'[6]

Another authority felt that the careful and clever design of this strange pyramid boat could potentially have made it 'a far more seaworthy craft than anything available to Columbus'.[7] Moreover, the experts agreed that it had been built to a pattern that could only have been 'created by shipbuilders from a people with a long, solid tradition of sailing on the open sea.'[8]

Present at the very beginning of Egypt's 3000-year history, who had those as yet unidentified shipbuilders been? They had not accumulated their 'long, solid tradition of sailing on the open sea' while ploughing the fields of the landlocked Nile Valley. So where and when had they developed their maritime skills?

There was yet another puzzle. I knew that the Ancient Egyptians had been very good at making scale models and representations of all manner of things for symbolic purposes.[9] I therefore found it hard to understand why they would have gone to the trouble of manufacturing and then burying a boat as big and sophisticated as this if its only function, as the Egyptologists claimed, had been as a token of the spiritual vessel that would carry the soul of the deceased king to heaven.[10] That could have been achieved as effectively with a much smaller craft, and only one would have been needed, not several. Logic therefore suggested that these gigantic vessels might have been intended for some other purpose altogether, or had some quite different and still unsuspected symbolic significance . . .

We had reached the rough midpoint of the southern face of the Great Pyramid when we at last realized why we were being taken on this long walkabout. The objective was for us to be relieved of moderate sums of money at each of the four cardinal points. The tally thus far was 30 US dollars at the northern face and 50 Egyptian pounds at the eastern face. Now I shelled out a further 50 Egyptian pounds to yet another patrol Ali was supposed to have paid off the day before.

'Ali,' I hissed, 'when are we going to climb the Pyramid?'

'Right away, Mr Graham,' our guide replied. He walked confidently forward, gesturing directly ahead, then added, 'We shall ascend at the south-west corner . . .'

Chapter 34

Mansion of Eternity

Have you ever climbed a pyramid, at night, fearful of arrest, with your nerves in shreds?

It's a surprisingly difficult thing to do, especially where the Great Pyramid is concerned. Even though its top 31 feet are no longer intact, its presently exposed summit platform still stands more than 450 feet above ground level.[1] It consists, moreover, of 203 separate courses of masonry, with the average course height being about two and a quarter feet.[2]

Averages do not tell you everything, as I discovered soon after we began the climb. The courses turned out to be of unequal depth, some barely reaching knee level while others came up almost to my chest and created formidable obstacles. At the same time the horizontal ledges between each of the steps were very narrow, often only a little wider than my foot, and many of the big limestone blocks, which had looked so solid from below, proved to be crumbling and broken.

Somewhere around 30 courses up Santha and I began to appreciate what we had let ourselves in for. Our muscles were aching and our knees and fingers stiff and bruised – yet we were barely one-seventh of the way to the summit and there were still more than 170 courses to climb. Another worry was the vertiginous drop steadily opening beneath us. Looking down along the ruptured contours that marked the line of the south-western corner, I was taken aback to see how far we had already climbed and experienced a momentary, giddying presentiment of how easy it would be for us to fall, head over heels like Jack and Jill, bouncing and jolting over the huge layers of stone, breaking our crowns at the bottom.

Ali had permitted a pause of a few moments for us to catch our breaths, but now he signalled that we should press on and began to climb again. Still using the corner as a guideline, he rapidly disappeared into the darkness above.

Somewhat less confidently, Santha and I followed.

Time and motion

The 35th course of masonry was a hard one to clamber over, being made of particularly massive blocks, much larger than any of the others we had so far encountered (except those at the very base) and estimated to weigh between 10 and 15 tons apiece.[3] This contradicted engineering logic and commonsense, both of which called for a progressive decrease in the size and weight of the blocks that had to be transported to the summit as the pyramid rose ever higher. Courses 1–18, which diminished from a height of about 55.5 inches at ground level to just over 23 inches at course 17, did obey this rule. Then suddenly, at course 19, the block height rose again to almost 36 inches. At the same time the other dimensions of the blocks also increased and their weight grew from the relatively manoeuvrable range of 2–6 tons that was common in the first 18 courses to the more ponderous and cumbersome range of 10–15 tons.[4] These, therefore, were really *big* monoliths that had been carved out of solid limestone and raised more than 100 feet into the air before being placed faultlessly in position.

To have worked effectively the pyramid builders must have had nerves of steel, the agility of mountain goats, the strength of lions and the confidence of trained steeplejacks. With the cold morning wind whipping around my ears and threatening to launch me into flight, I tried to imagine what it must have been like for them, poised dangerously at this (and much higher) altitudes, lifting, manoeuvring and positioning exactly an endless production line of chunky limestone monoliths – the smallest of which weighed as much as two modern family cars.

How long had the pyramid taken to complete? How many men had worked on it? The consensus among Egyptologists was two decades and 100,000 men.[5] It was also generally agreed that the construction project had not been a year-round affair but had been confined (through labour force availability) to the annual three-month agricultural lay-off season imposed by the flooding of the Nile.[6]

As I continued to climb, I reminded myself of the implications of all this. It wasn't just the tens of thousands of blocks weighing 15 tons or more that the builders would have had to worry about. Year in, year out, the real crises would have been caused by the *millions* of 'average-sized' blocks, weighing say 2.5 tons, that also had to be brought to the working plane. The Pyramid has been reliably estimated to consist of a total of 2.3 million blocks.[7] Assuming that the masons worked ten hours a day, 365 days a year, the mathematics indicate that they would have needed to place 31 blocks in position every hour (about one block every two minutes) to complete the Pyramid in twenty years. Assuming that construction work had been confined to the annual three-month lay-off, the problems multiplied: four blocks a minute would have had to be delivered, about 240 every hour.

Such scenarios are, of course, the stuff construction managers' nightmares are made of. Imagine, for example, the daunting degree of coordination that must have been maintained between the masons and the quarries to ensure the requisite rate of block flow across the production site. Imagine also the havoc if even a single 2.5 ton block had been dropped from, say, the 175th course.

The physical and managerial obstacles seemed staggering on their own, but beyond these was the geometrical challenge represented by the pyramid itself, which had to end up with its apex positioned exactly over the centre of its base. Even the minutest error in the angle of incline of any one of the sides at the base would have led to a substantial misalignment of the edges at the apex. Incredible accuracy, therefore, had to be maintained throughout, at every course, hundreds of feet above the ground, with great stone blocks of killing weight.

Rampant stupidity

How had the job been done?

At the last count there were more than thirty competing and conflicting theories attempting to answer that question. The majority of academic Egyptologists have argued that ramps of one kind or another must have been used. This was the opinion, for example, of Professor I.E.S Edwards, a former keeper of Egyptian Antiquities at the British Museum who asserted categorically: 'Only one method of lifting heavy weights was open to the ancient Egyptians, namely by means of ramps composed of brick and earth which sloped upwards from the level of the ground to whatever height was desired.'[8]

John Baines, professor of Egyptology at Oxford University, agreed with Edwards's analysis and took it further: 'As the pyramid grew in height, the length of the ramp and the width of its base were increased in order to maintain a constant gradient (about 1 in 10) and to prevent the ramp from collapsing. Several ramps approaching the pyramid from different sides were probably used.'[9]

To carry an inclined plane to the top of the Great Pyramid at a gradient of 1:10 would have required a ramp 4800 feet long and more than three times as massive as the Great Pyramid itself (with an estimated volume of 8 million cubic metres as against the Pyramid's 2.6 million cubic metres).[10] Heavy weights could not have been dragged up any gradient steeper than this by any normal means.[11] If a lesser gradient had been chosen, the ramp would have had to be even more absurdly and disproportionately massive.

The problem was that mile-long ramps reaching a height of 480 feet could not have been made out of 'bricks and earth' as Edwards and other Egyptologists supposed. On the contrary, modern builders and architects had proved that such ramps would have caved in under their own weight if they had consisted of any material less costly and less stable than the limestone ashlars of the Pyramid itself.[12]

Since this obviously made no sense (besides, where had the 8 million cubic metres of surplus blocks been taken after completion of the work?), other Egyptologists had proposed the use of *spiral* ramps made of mud brick and attached to the sides of the Pyramid. These would certainly have required less material to build, but they would also have failed to reach the top.[13] They would have presented deadly and perhaps insurmountable problems to the teams of men attempting to drag the big blocks of stone around their hairpin corners. And they would have crumbled under constant use. Most problematic of all, such ramps would have cloaked the whole pyramid, thus making it impossible for the architects to check the accuracy of the setting-out during building.[14]

But the pyramid builders *had* checked the accuracy of the setting out, and they *had* got it right, because the apex of the pyramid was poised exactly over the centre of the base, its angles and its corners were true, each block was in the correct place, and each course had been laid down level – in near-perfect symmetry and with near-perfect alignment to the cardinal points. Then, as though to demonstrate that such *tours-de-force* of technique were mere trifles, the ancient master-builders had gone on to play some clever mathematical games with the monument's dimensions, presenting us, for example, as we saw in Chapter Twenty-three, with an accurate use of the transcendental number *pi* in the ratio of its height to its base perimeter.[15] For some reason, too, it had taken their fancy to place the Great Pyramid almost exactly on the 30th parallel at latitude 29° 58′ 51″. This, as a former astronomer royal of Scotland once observed, was 'a sensible defalcation from 30°', but not necessarily in error:

> For if the original designer had wished that men should see with their body, rather than their mental eyes, the pole of the sky from the foot of the Great Pyramid, at an altitude before them of 30°, he would have had to take account of the refraction of the atmosphere; and that would have necessitated the building standing not at 30° but at 29° 58′ 22″.[16]

Compared to the true position of 29° 58′ 51″, this was an error of less than half an arc minute, suggesting once again that the surveying and geodetic skills brought to bear here must have been of the highest order.

Feeling somewhat overawed, we climbed on, past the 44th and 45th courses of the hulking and enigmatic structure. At the 46th course an angry voice hailed us in Arabic from the plaza below and we looked down to see a tiny, turbaned man dressed in a billowing kaftan. Despite the range, he had unslung his shotgun and was preparing to take aim at us.

The guardian and the vision

He was, of course, the guardian of the Pyramid's western face, the patrolman of the fourth cardinal point, and he had not received the extra funds dispensed to his colleagues of the north, east and south faces.

I could tell from Ali's perspiration that we were in a potentially tricky situation. The guard was ordering us to come down at once so that he could place us under arrest. 'This, however, could probably be avoided with a further payment,' Ali explained.

I groaned. 'Offer him 100 Egyptian pounds.'

'Too much,' Ali cautioned, 'it will make the others resentful. I shall offer him 50.'

More words were exchanged in Arabic. Indeed, over the next few minutes, Ali and the guard managed to have quite a sustained conversation up and down the south-western corner of the Pyramid at 4.40 in the morning. At one point a whistle was blown. Then the guards of the southern face put in a brief appearance and stood in conference with the guard of the western face, who had now also been joined by the two other members of his patrol.

Just when it seemed that Ali had lost whatever argument he was having on our behalf, he smiled and heaved a sigh of relief. 'You will pay the extra 50 pounds when we have returned to the ground,' he explained. 'They're letting us continue but they say that if any senior officer comes along and sees us they will not be able to help us.'

We struggled upwards in silence for the next ten minutes or so until we had reached the 100th course – roughly the halfway mark and already well over 250 feet above the ground. We gazed over our shoulders to the south-west, where a once-in-a-lifetime vision of staggering beauty and power confronted us. The crescent moon, which hung low in the sky to the south-east, had emerged from behind a scudding cloud bank and projected its ghostly radiance directly at the northern and eastern faces of the neighbouring Second Pyramid, supposedly built by the Fourth Dynasty Pharaoh Khafre (Chephren). This stunning monument, second only in size and majesty to the Great Pyramid itself (being just a few feet shorter and 48 feet narrower at the base) appeared lit up, as though energized from within, by a pale and unearthly fire. Behind it in the distance, slightly offset among the dark desert shadows, was the smaller Pyramid of Menkaure (Mycerinus), measuring 356 feet along each side and some 215 feet in height.[17]

For a moment, against the glittering backdrop of the inky sky, I experienced the illusion of being in motion, of standing at the stern of some great ship of the heavens and looking back at two other vessels which seemed to follow in my wake, strung out in battle order behind me.

So where was this convoy going, this squadron of pyramids? And were the prodigious structures all the work of megalomaniac pharaohs, as the Egyptologists believed? Or had they been designed by mysterious hands to voyage eternally through time and space towards some as yet unidentified objective?

From this altitude, though the southern sky was partially occluded by the vast bulk of the Pyramid of Khafre, I could see all the western sky as it arched down from the celestial north pole towards the distant rim of the revolving planet. Polaris, the Pole Star, was far to my right, in the constellation of the Little Bear. Low on the horizon, about ten degrees north of west, Regulus, the paw-star of the imperial constellation of Leo, was about to set.

Under Egyptian skies

Just above the 150th course, Ali hissed at us to keep our heads down. A police car had come into view around the north-western corner of the Great Pyramid and was now proceeding along the western flank of the monument with its blue light slowly flashing. We stayed motionless in the shadows until the car had passed. Then we began to climb again, with a renewed sense of urgency, heading as fast as we could towards the summit, which we now imagined we could see jutting out above the misty pre-dawn haze.

For what seemed like five minutes we climbed without stopping. When I looked up, however, the top of the Pyramid still seemed as far away as ever. We climbed again, panting and sweating, and once again the summit drew back before us like some legendary Welsh peak. Then, just when we'd resigned ourselves to an endless succession of such disappointments, we found ourselves at the top, under a

breathtaking canopy of stars, more than 450 feet above the surrounding plateau on the most extraordinary viewing platform in the world.
To our north and east, sprawled out across the wide, sloping valley of
the River Nile, lay the city of Cairo, a jumble of skyscrapers and flat
traditional roofs separated by the dark defiles of narrow streets and
interspersed with the needle-point minarets of a thousand and one
mosques. A film of reflected street-lighting shimmered over the
whole scene, closing the eyes of modern Cairenes to the wonder of the
stars but at the same time creating the hallucination of a fairyland
illuminated in greens and reds and blues and sulphurous yellows.

I felt privileged to witness this strange, electronic mirage from such
an incredible vantage point, perched on the summit platform of the
last surviving wonder of the ancient world, hovering in the sky over
Cairo like Aladdin on his magic carpet.

Not that the 203rd course of the Great Pyramid of Egypt could be
described as a carpet! Measuring just under 30 feet on each side (as
against the monument's side length of around 755 feet at the base) it
consisted of several hundred waist-high limestone blocks, each of
which weighed about five tons. The course was not completely level: a
few blocks were missing or broken, and rising towards the southern
end there were the substantial remains of about half an additional step
of masonry. Moreover, at the very centre of the platform, someone
had arranged for a triangular wooden scaffold to be erected, through
the middle of which rose a thick pole, just over 31 feet long, which
marked the monument's original true height of 481.3949 feet.[18]
Beneath this a scrawl of grafitti had been carved into the limestone by
generations of tourists.[19]

The complete ascent of the Pyramid had taken us about half an
hour and it was now just after 5 a. m., the time of morning worship.
Almost in unison, the voices of a thousand and one muezzins rang out
from the balconies of the minarets of Cairo, calling the faithful to
prayer and reaffirming the greatness, the indivisibility, the mercy and
the compassion of God. Behind me, to the south-west, the top 22
courses of Khafre's Pyramid, still clad with their original facing
stones, seemed to float like an iceberg on the ocean of moonlight.

Knowing that we could not stay long in this bewitching place, I sat
down and gazed around at the heavens. Over to the west, across

limitless desert sands, Regulus had now set beneath the horizon, and the rest of the lion's body was poised to follow. The constellations of Virgo and Libra were also dropping lower in the sky and, much farther to the north, I could see the Great and Little Bears slowly pacing out their eternal cycle around the celestial pole.

I looked south-east across the Nile Valley and there was the crescent moon still spreading its spectral radiance from the bank of the Milky Way. Following the course of the celestial river, I looked due south: there, crossing the meridian, was the resplendent constellation of Scorpius dominated by the first-magnitude star Antares – a red supergiant 300 times the diameter of the sun. North-east, above Cairo, sailed Cygnus the swan, his tail feathers marked by Deneb, a blue-white supergiant visible to us across more than 1800 light years of interstellar space. Last but not least, in the northern sky, the dragon Draco coiled sinuously among the circumpolar stars. Indeed, 4500 years ago, when the Great Pyramid was supposedly being built for the Fourth Dynasty Pharaoh Khufu (Cheops), one of the stars of Draco had stood close to the celestial north pole and had served as the Pole Star. This had been alpha Draconis, also known as Thuban. With the passing of the millennia, however, it had gradually been displaced from its position by the remorseless celestial mill of the earth's axial precession so that the Pole Star today is Polaris in the Little Bear.[20]

I lay back, cushioned my head in my hands and gazed directly up towards the zenith of heaven. Through the smooth cold stones I rested on, I thought I could sense beneath me, like a living force, the stupendous gravity and mass of the pyramid.

Thinking like giants

Covering a full 13.1 acres at the base, it weighed about six million tons – more than all the buildings in the Square Mile of the City of London added together,[21] and consisted, as we have seen, of roughly 2.3 million individual blocks of limestone and granite. To these had once been added a 22-acre, mirrorlike cladding consisting of an estimated 115,000 highly polished casing stones, each weighing 10 tons, which had originally covered all four of its faces.[22]

After being shaken loose by a massive earthquake in AD 1301, the majority of the facing blocks had subsequently been removed for the construction of Cairo.[23] Here and there around the base, however, I knew that enough had remained in position to permit the great nineteenth century archaeologist, W.M. Flinders Petrie, to carry out a detailed study of them. He had been stunned to encounter tolerances of less than one-hundredth of an inch and cemented joints so precise and so carefully aligned that it was impossible to slip even the fine blade of a pocket knife between them. 'Merely to place such stones in exact contact would be careful work', he admitted, 'but to do so with cement in the joint seems almost impossible; it is to be compared to the finest opticians' work on a scale of acres.'[24]

Of course, the jointing of the casing stones was by no means the only 'almost impossible' feature of the Great Pyramid. The alignments to true north, south, east and west were 'almost impossible', so too were the near-perfect ninety-degree corners, and the incredible symmetry of the four enormous sides. And so were the engineering logistics of raising millions of huge stones hundreds of feet in the air . . .

Whoever they had been, therefore, the architects, engineers and stonemasons who had designed and successfully built this stupendous monument must indeed have 'thought like men 100 feet tall', as Jean-François Champollion, the founder of modern Egyptology, had once observed. He had seen clearly what generations of his successors were to close their eyes to: that the pyramid builders could only have been men of giant intellectual stature. Beside the Egyptians of old, he had added, 'we in Europe are but Lilliputians.'[25]

Chapter 35

Tombs and Tombs Only?

Climbing down the Great Pyramid was more nerve wracking than climbing up. We were no longer struggling against the force of gravity, so the physical effort was less. But the possibilities of a fatal fall seemed greatly magnified now that our attention was directed exclusively towards the ground rather than the heavens. We picked our way with exaggerated care towards the base of the enormous mountain of stone, sliding and slithering among the treacherous masonry blocks, feeling as though we had been reduced to ants.

By the time we had completed the descent the night was over and the first wash of pale sunlight was filtering into the sky. We paid the 50 Egyptian pounds promised to the guard of the pyramid's western face and then, with a tremendous sense of release and exultation, we walked jauntily away from the monument in the direction of the Pyramid of Khafre, a few hundred metres to the south-west.

Khufu, Khafre, Menkaure . . . Cheops, Chephren, Mycerinus. Whether they were referred to by their Egyptian or their Greek names, the fact remained that these three pharaohs of the Fourth Dynasty (2575–2467 BC) were universally acclaimed as the builders of the Giza pyramids. This had been the case at least since Ancient Egyptian tour guides had told the Greek historian Herodotus that the Great Pyramid had been built by Khufu. Herodotus had incorporated this information into the oldest surviving written description of the monuments, which continued:

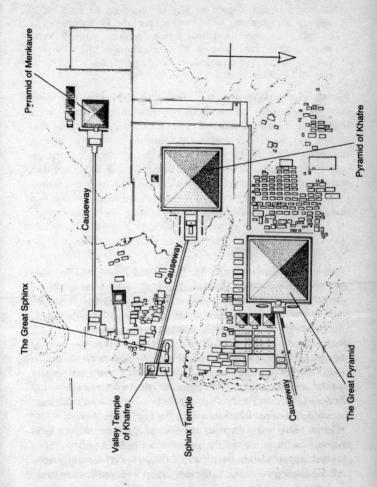

Site plan of the Giza necropolis.

Cheops, they said, reigned for fifty years, and on his death the kingship was taken over by his brother Chephren. He also made a pyramid . . . it is forty feet lower than his brother's pyramid, but otherwise of the same greatness . . . Chephren reigned for fifty-six years . . . then there succeeded Mycerinus, the son of Cheops . . . This man left a pyramid much smaller than his father's.[1]

Herodotus saw the monuments in the fifth century BC, more than 2000 years after they had been built. Nevertheless it was largely on the foundation of his testimony that the entire subsequent judgement of history was based. All other commentators, up to the present, continued uncritically to follow in the Greek historian's footsteps. And down the ages – although it had originally been little more than hearsay – the attribution of the Great Pyramid to Khufu, the Second Pyramid to Khafre and the Third Pyramid to Menkaure had assumed the stature of unassailable fact.

Trivializing the mystery

Having parted company with Ali, Santha and I continued our walk into the desert. Skirting the immense south-western corner of the Second Pyramid, our eyes were drawn towards its summit. There we noted again the intact facing stones that still covered its top 22 courses. We also noticed that the first few courses above its base, each of which had a 'footprint' of about a dozen acres, were composed of truly massive blocks of limestone, almost too high to clamber over, which were about 20 feet long and 6 feet thick. These extraordinary monoliths, as I was later to discover, weighed 200 tons apiece and belonged to a distinct style of masonry to be found at several different and widely scattered locations within the Giza necropolis.

On its north and west sides the Second Pyramid sat on a level platform cut down out of the surrounding bedrock and was thus enclosed within a wide trench more than 15 feet deep in places. Walking due south, parallel to the monument's scarred western flank, we picked our way along the edge of this trench towards the much smaller Third Pyramid, which lay some 400 metres ahead of us in the desert.

Khufu . . . Khafre . . . Menkaure . . . According to all orthodox

Egyptologists the pyramids had been built as tombs – and only as tombs – for these three pharaohs. Yet there were some obvious difficulties with such assertions. For example, the spacious burial chamber of the Khafre Pyramid was empty when it was opened in 1818 by the European explorer Giovanni Belzoni. Indeed, more than empty, the chamber was starkly, austerely bare. The polished granite sarcophagus which lay embedded in its floor had also been found empty, with its lid broken into two pieces nearby.[2] How was this to be explained?

To Egyptologists the answer seemed obvious. At some early date, probably not many hundreds of years after Khafre's death, tomb robbers must have penetrated the chamber and cleared all its contents including the mummified body of the pharaoh.

Much the same thing seemed to have happened at the smaller Third Pyramid, towards which Santha and I were now walking – that attributed to Menkaure. Here the first European to break in had been a British colonel, Howard Vyse, who had entered the burial chamber in 1837. He found an empty basalt sarcophagus, an anthropoid coffin lid made of wood, and some bones. The natural assumption was that these were the remains of Menkaure. Modern science had subsequently proved, however, that the bones and coffin lid dated from the early Christian era, that is, from 2500 years after the Pyramid Age, and thus represented the 'intrusive burial' of a much later individual (quite a common practice throughout Ancient Egyptian history). As to the basalt sarcophagus – well, it could have belonged to Menkaure. Unfortunately, however, nobody had the opportunity to examine it because it had been lost at sea when the ship on which Vyse sent it to England had sunk off the coast of Spain.[3] Since it was a matter of record that the sarcophagus had been found empty by Vyse, it was once again assumed that the body of the pharaoh must have been removed by tomb robbers.

A similar assumption had been made about the body of Khufu, which was also missing. Here the scholarly consensus, expressed as well as anyone by George Hart of the British Museum, was that 'no later than 500 years after Khufu's funeral' robbers had forced their way into the Great Pyramid 'to steal the burial treasure'.[4] The implication is that this incursion must have occurred by or before

2000 BC – since Khufu is believed to have died in 2528 BC.[5] Moreover it was assumed by Professor I.E.S Edwards, a leading authority on these matters, that the burial treasure had been removed from the famous inner sanctum now known as the King's Chamber and that the empty 'granite sarcophagus' which stood at the western end of that sanctum had 'once contained the King's body, probably enclosed within an inner coffin made of wood'.[6]

All this is orthodox, mainstream, modern scholarship, which is unquestioningly accepted as historical fact and taught as such at universities everywhere.[7]

But suppose it isn't fact.

The cupboard was bare

The mystery of the missing mummy of Khufu begins with the records of Caliph Al-Ma'mun, a Muslim governor of Cairo in the ninth century AD. He had engaged a team of quarriers to tunnel their way into the pyramid's northern face, urging them on with promises that they would discover treasure. Through a series of lucky accidents 'Ma'mun's Hole', as archaeologists now refer to it, had joined up with one of the monument's several internal passageways, the 'descending corridor' leading downwards from the original concealed doorway in the northern face (the location of which, though known in classical times, had been forgotten by Ma'mun's day). By a further lucky accident the vibrations that the Arabs had caused with their battering rams and drills dislodged a block of limestone from the ceiling of the descending corridor. When the socket from which it had fallen was examined it was found to conceal the opening to another corridor, this time *ascending* into the bowels of the pyramid.

There was a problem, however. The opening was blocked by a series of enormous plugs of solid granite, clearly contemporaneous with the construction of the monument, which were held in place by a narrowing of the lower end of the corridor.[8] The quarriers were unable either to break or to cut through the plugs. They therefore tunnelled into the slightly softer limestone surrounding them and, after several weeks of backbreaking toil, rejoined the ascending

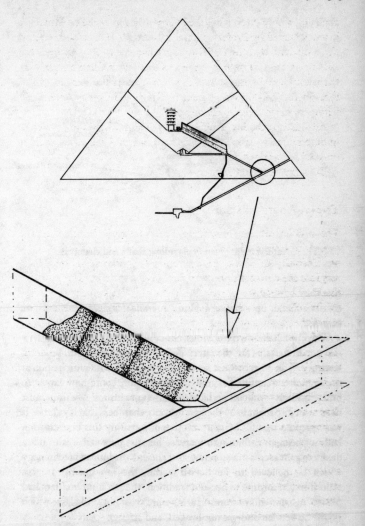

The Great Pyramid: entrance and plugging blocks in the ascending
corridor.

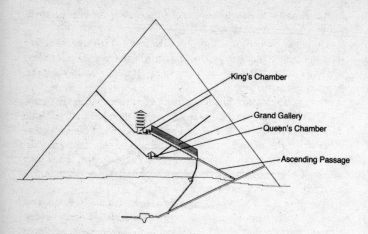

The Great Pyramid: detail of corridors, shafts and chambers.

corridor higher up – *having bypassed a formidable obstacle never before breached.*

The implications were obvious. Since no previous treasure-seekers had penetrated this far, the interior of the pyramid must still be virgin territory. The diggers must have licked their lips with anticipation at the immense quantities of gold and jewels they could now expect to find. Similarly – though perhaps for different reasons, Ma'mun must have been impatient to be the first into any chambers that lay ahead. It was reported that his primary motive in initiating this investigation had not been an ambition to increase his vast personal wealth but a desire to gain access to a storehouse of ancient wisdom and technology which he believed to lie buried within the monument. In this repository, according to age-old tradition, the pyramid builders had placed 'instruments of iron and arms which rust not, and glasse which might be bended and yet not broken, and strange spells . . .'[9]

But Ma'mun and his men found nothing, not even any down-to-earth treasure – and certainly not any high-tech, anachronistic plastic or instruments of iron or rustproof weapons ... or strange spells either.

The erroneously named 'Queen's Chamber' (which lay at the end a long horizontal passageway that branched off from the ascending corridor) turned out to be completely empty – just a severe, geometrical room.[10]

More disappointing still, the King's Chamber (which the Arabs reached after climbing the imposing Grand Gallery) also offered little of interest. Its only furniture was a granite coffer just big enough to contain the body of a man. Later identified, on no very good grounds, as a 'sarcophagus', this undecorated stone box was approached with trepidation by Ma'mun and his team, who found it to be lidless and as empty as everything else in the pyramid.[11]

Why, how and when exactly had the Great Pyramid been emptied of its contents? Had it been 500 years after Khufu's death, as the Egyptologists suggested? Or was it not more likely, as the evidence was beginning to suggest, that the inner chambers of the pyramid had been empty all along, from the very beginning, that is, from the day that the monument had originally been sealed? Nobody, after all, had reached the upper part of the ascending corridor before Ma'mun and his men. And it was certain, too, that nobody had cut through the granite plugs blocking the entrance to that corridor.

Commonsense ruled out the possibility of any earlier incursion – unless there was another way in.

Bottlenecks in the well-shaft

There was another way in.

Farther down the descending corridor, more than 200 feet beyond the point where the plugged end of the ascending corridor had been found, lies the concealed entrance to another secret passageway, deep within the subterranean bedrock of the Giza plateau. If Ma'mun had discovered this passageway, he could have saved himself a great deal of trouble, since it provided a readymade route around the plugs blocking the ascending corridor. His attention, however, had been distracted by the challenge of tunnelling past those plugs, and he made no effort to investigate the lower reaches of the descending corridor (which he ended up using as a dump for the tons of stone his diggers removed from the core of the pyramid).[12]

The full extent of the descending corridor was, however, well-known and explored in classical times. The Graeco–Roman geographer Strabo left quite a clear description of the large subterranean chamber it debouched into (at a depth of almost 600 feet below the apex of the pyramid).[13] Graffitti from the period of the Roman occupation of Egypt was also found inside this underground chamber, confirming that it had once been regularly visited. Yet, because it had been so cunningly hidden in the beginning, the secret doorway leading off to one side about two-thirds of the way down the western wall of the descending corridor, remained sealed and undiscovered until the nineteenth century.[14]

What the doorway led to was a narrow well-shaft, about 160 feet in extent, which rose almost vertically through the bedrock and then through more than twenty complete courses of the Great Pyramid's limestone core blocks, until it joined up with the main internal corridor system at the base of the Grand Gallery. There is no evidence to indicate what the purpose of this strange architectural feature might have been (although several scholars have hazarded guesses).[15] Indeed the only thing is clear is that it was engineered at the time of the construction of the pyramid and was not the result of an intrusion by tunnelling tomb-robbers.[16] The question remains open, however, as to whether tomb-robbers might have *discovered* the hidden entrance to the shaft, and made use of it to siphon off the treasures from the King's and Queen's Chambers.

Such a possibility cannot be ruled out. Nevertheless, a review of the historical record indicates little in its favour.

For example, the upper end of the well-shaft was entered off the Grand Gallery by the Oxford astronomer John Greaves in 1638. He managed to descend to a depth of about sixty feet. In 1765 another Briton, Nathaniel Davison, penetrated to a depth of about 150 feet but found his way blocked by an impenetrable mass of sand and stones. Later, in the 1830, Captain G.B. Caviglia, an Italian adventurer, reached the same depth and encountered the same obstacle. More enterprising than his predecessors, he hired Arab workers to start excavating the rubble in the hope that there might be something of interest beneath it. Several days of digging in claustrophobic conditions followed before the connection with the descending corridor was discovered.[17]

Is it likely that such a cramped, blocked-up shaft could have been a viable conduit for the treasures of Khufu, supposedly the greatest pharaoh of the magnificent Fourth Dynasty?

Even if it hadn't been choked with debris and sealed at the lower end, it could not have been used to bring out more than a tiny fraction of the treasures of a typical royal tomb. This is because the well-shaft is only three feet in diameter and incorporates several tricky vertical sections.

At the very least, therefore, when Ma'mun and his men battered their way into the King's Chamber around the year AD 820, one would have expected some of the bigger and heavier pieces from the original burial to be still in place – like the statues and shrines that bulked so large in Tutankhamen's much later and presumably inferior tomb.[18] But *nothing* was found inside Khufu's Pyramid, making this and the alleged looting of Khafre's monument the only tomb robberies in the history of Egypt which achieved a clean sweep, leaving not a single trace behind – not a torn cloth, not a shard of broken pottery, not an unwanted figurine, not an overlooked piece of jewellery – just the bare floors and walls and the gaping mouths of empty sarcophagi.

Not like other tombs

It was now after six in the morning and the rising sun had bathed the summits of Khufu's and Khafre's Pyramids with a fleeting blush of pastel-pink light. Menkaure's Pyramid, being some 200 feet lower than the other two, was still in shadow as Santha and I skirted its north-western corner and continued our walk into the rolling sand dunes of the surrounding desert.

I still had the tomb robbery theory on my mind. As far as I could see the only real 'evidence' in favour of it was the absence of grave goods and mummies that it had been invented to explain in the first place. All the other facts, particularly where the Great Pyramid was concerned, seemed to speak persuasively against any robbery having occurred. It was not just a matter of the narrowness and unsuitability of the well-shaft as an escape route for bulky treasures. The other remarkable feature of Khufu's Pyramid was the absence of inscriptions or decorations anywhere within its immense network of galleries, corridors, passageways and chambers, and the same was true of Khafre's and Menkaure's Pyramids. In none of these amazing monuments had a single word been written in praise of the pharaohs whose bodies they were supposed to house.

This was exceptional. No other proven burial place of any Egyptian monarch had ever been found undecorated. The fashion throughout Egyptian history had been for the tombs of the pharaohs to be *extensively* decorated, beautifully painted from top to bottom (as in the Valley of the Kings at Luxor, for example) and densely inscribed with the ritual spells and invocations required to assist the deceased on his journey towards eternal life (as in the Fifth Dynasty pyramids at Saqqara, just twenty miles to the south of Giza.)[19]

Why had Khufu, Khafre and Menkaure done things so differently? Had they not built their monuments to serve as tombs at all, but for another and more subtle purpose? Or was it possible, as certain Arab and esoteric traditions maintained, that the Giza pyramids had been erected long before the Fourth Dynasty by the architects of some earlier and more advanced civilization?

Neither hypothesis was popular with Egyptologists for reasons that were easy to understand. Moreover, while conceding that the Second and Third Pyramids were completely devoid of internal inscriptions, lacking even the *names* of Khafre and Menkaure, the scholars were able to cite certain hieroglyphic 'quarry marks' (graffitti daubed on stone blocks before they left the quarry) found inside the Great Pyramid, which did seem to bear the name of Khufu.

A certain smell . . .

The discoverer of the quarry marks was Colonel Howard Vyse, during the destructive excavations he undertook at Giza in 1837. Extending an existing crawlway, he cut a tunnel into the series of narrow cavities, called 'relieving chambers', which lay directly above the King's Chamber. The quarry marks were found on the walls and ceilings of the top four of these cavities and said things like this:

THE CRAFTSMEN–GANG, HOW POWERFUL IS THE WHITE CROWN OF
KHNUM–KHUFU
KHUFU
KHNUM–KHUFU
YEAR SEVENTEEN[20]

It was all very convenient. Right at the end of a costly and otherwise fruitless digging season, just when a major archaeological discovery was needed to legitimize the expenses he had run up, Vyse had stumbled upon the find of the decade – the first incontrovertible proof that Khufu had indeed been the builder of the hitherto anonymous Great Pyramid.

One would have thought that a discovery of this nature would have settled conclusively any lingering doubts over the ownership and purpose of that enigmatic monument. But the doubts remained, largely because, from the beginning, 'a certain smell' hung over Vyse's evidence:

1 It was odd that the marks were the only signs of the name Khufu ever found anywhere inside the Great Pyramid.[21]
2 It was odd that they had been found in such an obscure, out-of-the-way corner of that immense building.
3 It was odd that they had been found *at all* in a monument otherwise devoid of inscriptions of any kind.
4 And it was extremely odd that they had been found only in the top four of the five relieving chambers. Inevitably, suspicious minds began to wonder whether 'quarry marks' might also have appeared in the lowest of these five chambers had that chamber, too, been discovered by Vyse (rather than by Nathaniel Davison seventy years earlier).[22]
5 Last but not least it was odd that several of the hieroglyphs in the 'quarry marks' had been painted upside down, and that some were unrecognizable while others had been misspelt or used ungrammatically.[23]

Was Vyse a forger?

I know of one plausible case made to suggest he was exactly that,[24] and although final proof will probably always be lacking, it seemed to me incautious of academic Egyptology to have accepted the authenticity of the quarry marks without question. Besides, there was alternative hieroglyphic evidence, arguably of purer provenance, which appeared to indicate that Khufu could not have built the Great Pyramid. Strangely, the same Egyptologists who readily ascribed immense importance to Vyse's quarry marks were quick to downplay the significance of these other, contradictory, hieroglyphs, which appeared on a rectangular limestone stela which now stood in the Cairo Museum.[25]

The Inventory Stela, as it was called, had been discovered at Giza in the nineteenth century by the French archaeologist Auguste Mariette. It was something of a bombshell because its text clearly indicated that both the Great Sphinx and the Great Pyramid (as well as several other structures on the plateau) were *already in existence* long before Khufu came to the throne. The inscription also referred to Isis as the 'Mistress of the Pyramid', implying that the monument had been dedicated to the goddess of magic and not to Khufu at all. Finally, there was a strong suggestion that Khufu's pyramid might have been one of the three subsidiary structures alongside the Great Pyramid's eastern flank.[26]

All this looked like damaging evidence against the orthodox chronology of Ancient Egypt. It also challenged the consensus view that the Giza pyramids had been built as tombs and only as tombs. However, rather than investigating the anachronistic statements in the Inventory Stela, Egyptologists chose to devalue them. In the words of the influential American scholar James Henry Breasted, 'These references would be of the highest importance if the stela were contemporaneous with Khufu; but the orthographic evidences of its late date are entirely conclusive . . .'[27]

Breasted meant that the nature of the hieroglyphic writing system used in the inscription was not consistent with that used in the Fourth Dynasty but belonged to a more recent epoch. All Egyptologists concurred with this analysis and the final judgement, still accepted today, was that the stela had been carved in the Twenty-First Dynasty, about 1500 years after Khufu's reign, and was therefore to be regarded as a work of historical fiction.[28]

Thus, citing orthographic evidence, an entire academic discipline found reason to ignore the boat-rocking implications of the Inventory Stela and at no time gave proper consideration to the possibility that it could have been based upon a genuine Fourth Dynasty inscription (just as the New English Bible, for example, is based on a much older original). Exactly the same scholars, however, had accepted the authenticity of a set of dubious 'quarry marks' without demur, turning a blind eye to their othographic and other peculiarities.

Why the double standard? Could it have been because the information contained in the 'quarry marks' conformed strictly to orthodox opinion that the Great Pyramid had been built as a tomb for Khufu? whereas the information in the Inventory Stela contradicted that opinion?

Overview

By seven in the morning Santha and I had walked far out into the desert to the south-west of the Giza pyramids and had made ourselves comfortable in the lee of a huge dune that offered an unobstructed panorama over the entire site.

The date, 16 March, was just a few days away from the Spring Equinox, one of the two occasions in the year when the sun rose precisely due east of wherever you stood in the world. Ticking out the days like the pointer of a giant metronome, it had bisected the horizon this morning at a point a hair's breadth south of due east and had already climbed high enough to shrug off the Nile mists which clung like a shroud to much of the city of Cairo.

Khufu, Khafre, Menkaure . . . Cheops, Chephren, Mycerinus. Whether you called them by their Egyptian or their Greek names, there was no doubt that the three famous pharaohs of the Fourth Dynasty had been commemorated by the most splendid, the most honourable, the most beautiful and the most enormous monuments ever seen anywhere in the world. Moreover, it was clear that these pharaohs must indeed have been closely associated with the monuments, not only because of the folklore passed on by Herodotus (which surely had some basis in fact) but because inscriptions and references to Khufu, Khafre and Menkaure had been found in moderate quantities, *outside* the three major pyramids, at several different parts of the Giza necropolis. Such finds had been made consistently in and around the six subsidiary pyramids, three of which lay to the east of the Great Pyramid and the other three to the south of the Menkaure Pyramid.

Since much of this external evidence was ambiguous and uncertain, I found it difficult to understand why the Egyptologists were happy to go on citing it as confirmation of the 'tombs and tombs only' theory.

The problem was that this same evidence was capable of supporting – as equally valid – a number of different and mutually contradictory interpretations. To give just one example, the 'close association' observed between the three great pyramids and the three Fourth Dynasty pharaohs could indeed have come about because these pharaohs had built the pyramids as their tombs. But it could also have come about if the gigantic monuments of the Giza plateau had been standing long before the dawn of the historical civilization known as Dynastic Egypt. In that case, it was only necessary to assume that in due course Khufu, Khafre and Menkaure had come along and built a number of the subsidiary structures around the three older pyramids – something that they would have had every reason to do because in this way they could have appropriated the high prestige of the original anonymous monuments (and would, almost certainly, be viewed by posterity as their builders).

There were other possibilities too. The point was, however, that the evidence for exactly who had built which great pyramid, when and for what purpose was far too thin on the ground to justify the dogmatism of the orthodox 'tombs and tombs only' theory. In all honesty, it was *not clear* who built the pyramids. It was *not* clear in what epoch they had been built. And it was *not at all clear* what their function had been.

For all these reasons they were surrounded by a wonderful, impenetrable air of mystery and as I gazed down at them out of the desert they seemed to march towards me across the dunes . . .

Chapter 36

Anomalies

Viewed from our vantage point in the desert south west of the Giza necropolis, the site plan of the three great pyramids seemed majestic but bizarre.

Menkaure's pyramid was closest to us, with Khafre's and Khufu's monuments behind it to the north-east. These two were situated along a near perfect diagonal – a straight line connecting the south-western and north-eastern corners of the pyramid of Khafre would, if extended to the north-east, also pass through the south-western and north-eastern corners of the Great Pyramid. This, presumably, was not an accident. From where we sat, however, it was easy to see that if the same imaginary straight line was extended to the south-west it would completely miss the Third Pyramid, the entire body of which was offset to the east of the principal diagonal.

Egyptologists refused to recognize any anomaly in this. Why should they? As far as they were concerned there was *no* site plan at Giza. The pyramids were tombs and tombs only, built for three different pharaohs over a period of about seventy-five years.[1] It made sense to assume that each ruler would have sought to express his own personality and idiosyncrasies through his monument, and this was probably why Menkaure had 'stepped out of line'.

The Egyptologists were wrong. Though I was unaware of it that March morning in 1993, a breakthrough had been made proving beyond doubt that the necropolis did have an overall site plan, which dictated the exact positioning of the three pyramids not only in relation to one another but in relation to the River Nile a few kilometres east of the Giza plateau. With eerie fidelity, this immense and ambitious layout modelled a *celestial* phenomenon[2] – which was perhaps why Egyptologists (who pride themselves on looking exclusively at the ground beneath their feet) had failed to spot it. On a truly giant scale, as we see in later chapters, it also reflected the same obsessive concern with orientations and dimensions demonstrated in each of the monuments.

A singular oppression

Giza, Egypt, 16 March 1993, 8 a.m.

At a little over 200 feet tall (and with a side length at the base of 356 feet) the Third Pyramid was less than half the height and well under half the mass of the Great Pyramid. Nevertheless, it possessed a stunning and imposing majesty of its own. As we stepped out of the desert sunlight and into its huge geometrical shadow, I remembered what the Iraqi writer Abdul Latif had said about it when he had visited it in the twelfth century: 'It appears small compared with the other two; but viewed at a short distance and to the exclusion of these, it excites in the imagination a singular oppression and cannot be contemplated without painfully affecting the sight . . .'[3]

The lower sixteen courses of the monument were still cased, as they had been since the beginning, with facing blocks quarried out of red granite ('so extremely hard', in Abdul Latif's words, 'that iron takes a long time, with difficulty, to make an impression on it').[4] Some of the blocks were very large; they were also closely and cunningly fitted together in a complex interlocking jigsaw-puzzle pattern strongly reminiscent of the cyclopean masonry at Cuzco, Macchu Pichu and other locations in far-off Peru.

As was normal, the entrance to the Third Pyramid was situated in its northern face well above the ground. From here, at an angle of 26° 2′, a descending corridor lanced arrow-straight down into the darkness.[5] Oriented exactly north to south, this corridor was rectangular in section and so cramped that we had to bend almost double to fit into it. Where it passed through the masonry of the monument its ceiling and walls consisted of well-fitted granite blocks. More surprisingly, these continued for some distance below ground level.

At about seventy feet from the entrance, the corridor levelled off and opened out into a passageway where we could stand up. This led into a small ante-chamber with carved panelling and grooves cut into its walls, apparently to take portcullis slabs. Reaching the end of the chamber, we had to crouch again to enter another corridor. Bent double, we proceeded south for about forty feet before reaching the first of the three main burial chambers – if burial chambers they were.

These sombre, soundless rooms were all hewn out of solid bedrock. The one that we stood in was rectangular in plan and oriented east to west. Measuring about 30 feet long × 15 wide × 15 high, it had a flat ceiling and a complex internal structure with a large, irregular hole in its western wall leading into a dark, cavelike space beyond. There was also an opening near the centre of the floor which gave access to a ramp, sloping westwards, leading down to even deeper levels. We descended the ramp. It terminated in a short, horizontal passage to the right of which, entered through a narrow doorway, lay a small empty chamber. Six cells, like the sleeping quarters of medieval monks, had been hewn out of its walls: four on the eastern side and two to the north. These were presumed by Egyptologists to have functioned as 'magazines . . . for storing objects which the dead king wished to have close to his body.'[6]

Coming out of this chamber, we turned right again, back into the horizontal passage. At its end lay another empty chamber,[7] the design of which is unique among the pyramids of Egypt. Some twelve feet long by eight wide, and oriented north to south, its walls and extensively broken and damaged floor were fashioned out of a peculiarly dense, chocolate-coloured granite which seemed to absorb light and sound waves. Its ceiling consisted of eighteen huge slabs of the same material, nine on each side, laid in facing gables. Because they had had been hollowed from below to form a markedly concave surface, the effect of these great monoliths was of a perfect barrel vault, much as one might expect to find in the crypt of a Romanesque cathedral.

Retracing our steps, we left the lower chambers and walked back up the ramp to the large, flat-roofed, rock-hewn room above. Passing through the ragged aperture in its western wall, we found ourselves looking directly at the upper sides of the eighteen slabs which formed the ceiling of the chamber below. From this perspective their true form as a pointed gable was immediately apparent. What was less clear was how they had been brought in here in the first place, let alone laid so perfectly in position. Each one must have weighed many tons, heavy enough to have made them extremely difficult to handle under any circumstances. And these were no ordinary circumstances. As though they had set out deliberately to make things more complicated for themselves (or perhaps because they found such tasks simple?) the pyramid builders had disdained to provide an adequate working area between the slabs and the bedrock above them. By crawling into the cavity, I was able to establish that the clearance varied from approximately two feet at the southern end to just a few inches at the northern end. In such a restricted space there was no possibility that the monoliths could have been lowered into position. Logically, therefore, they must have been raised from the chamber floor, but how had that been done? The chamber was so small that only a few men could have worked inside it at any one time – too few to have had the muscle-power to lift the slabs by brute force. Pulleys were not supposed to have existed in the Pyramid Age[8] (even if they had, there would have been insufficient room to set up block-and-tackle). Had some unknown system of levers been used? Or might there be more substance than scholars realized to the Ancient Egyptian legends that spoke of huge stones being effortlessly levitated by priests or magicians through the utterance of 'words of power'?[9]

Not for the first time when confronted by the mysteries of the pyramids I knew that I was looking at an *impossible* engineering feat which had nevertheless been carried out to astonishingly high and precise standards. Moreover, if Egyptologists were to be believed, the construction work had supposedly been undertaken at the dawn of human civilization by a people who had not accumulated any experience of massive construction projects.

This was, of course, a startling cultural paradox, and one for to which no adequate explanation had ever been offered by an orthodox academic.

The moving finger writes and having writ it moves on

Leaving the underground chambers, which seemed to vibrate at the core of the Third Pyramid like the convoluted, multi-valved heart of some slumbering Leviathan, we made our way along the narrow entrance corridor and into the open air.

Our objective now was the Second Pyramid. We walked along its western flank (just under 708 feet in length), turned right and eventually came to the point on its north side, about 40 feet east of the main north-south axis, where the principal entrances were located. One of these was carved directly into the bedrock at ground level about 30 feet in front of the monument; the other was cut into the northern face at a height of just under 50 feet. From the latter a corridor sloped downwards at an angle of 25° 55'.[10] From the former, by which we now entered the pyramid, another descending corridor led deeply underground then levelled off for a short distance, giving access to a subterranean chamber, then ascended steeply and finally levelled off again into a long horizontal passageway, heading due south (into which also fed the upper corridor that sloped down from the entrance in the north face).

High enough to stand up in, and lined at first with granite and then with smoothly polished limestone, the horizontal passageway was almost at ground level, that is, it lay directly beneath the pyramid's lowest course of masonry. It was also extremely long, running dead straight for a further 200 feet until it debouched in the single 'burial chamber' at the heart of the monument.

As we have already noted, no mummy had ever been found in this latter chamber, nor any inscriptions, with the result that the so-called Pyramid of Khafre was wholly anonymous. Latter-day adventurers had, however, carved *their* names on to its walls – notably the former circus strongman Giovanni Battista Belzoni (1778–1823) who had forced his way into the monument in 1818. His huge and flamboyant graffito, daubed in black paint high on the south side of the chamber, was a reminder of basic human nature: the desire that all of us feel to be recognized and remembered. It was clear that Khafre himself had been far from immune from this ambition, since repeated references to him (as well as a number of flattering statues) appeared in the surrounding funerary complex.[11] If he had indeed built the pyramid

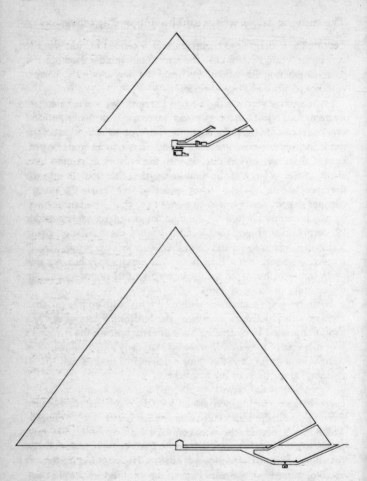

Above Chamber and passageway system of the Pyramid of Menkaure.
Below Chamber and passageway system of the Pyramid of Khafre.

as his tomb, it seemed inconceivable that such a man would have failed to stamp his name and identity *somewhere* within its interior. I found myself wondering yet again why Egyptologists were so unwilling to consider the possibility that the funerary complex might have been Khafre's work and the pyramid someone else's?

But *who* else's?

In many ways this – rather than the absence of identifying marks – was the central problem. Prior to the reigns of Khufu, Khafre and Menkaure there was not a single pharaoh whose name could be put forward as a candidate. Khufu's father Snefru, the first king of the Fourth Dynasty was believed to have built the so-called 'Bent' and 'Red' Pyramids at Dhashur, about thirty miles south of Giza – an attribution that was itself mysterious (if pyramids were indeed tombs) since it seemed strange that one pharaoh required two pyramids to be buried in. Snefru was also credited by some Egyptologists with the construction of the 'Collapsed' Pyramid at Meidum (although a number of authorities insisted that this was the tomb of Huni, the last king of the Third Dynasty).[12] The only other builders in the Archaic Period had been Zoser, the second pharaoh of the Third Dynasty, to whom was attributed the construction of the 'Step Pyramid' at Saqqara,[13] and Zoser's successor, Sekhemkhet, whose pyramid also stood at Saqqara. Therefore, despite the lack of inscriptions, it was now assumed as obvious that the three pyramids at Giza *must* have been built by Khufu, Khafre and Menkaure and *must* have been intended to serve as their tombs.

We need not reiterate here the many shortcomings of the 'tombs and tombs only' theory. However, these shortcomings were not limited to the Giza pyramids but applied to *all the other* Third and Fourth Dynasty Pyramids listed above. Not a single one of these monuments had ever been found to contain the body of a pharaoh, or any signs whatsoever of a royal burial.[14] Some of them were not even equipped with sarcophagi, for example the Collapsed Pyramid at Meidum. The Pyramid of Sekhemkhet at Saqqara (first entered in 1954 by the Egyptian Antiquities Organization) did contain a sarcophagus – one, which had certainly remained sealed and undisturbed since its installation in the 'tomb'.[15] Grave robbers had never succeeded in finding their way to it, but when it was opened, it was empty.[16]

So what was going on? How come more than twenty-five million tons of stone had been piled up to form pyramids at Giza, Dhashur, Meidum and Saqqara if the only point of the exercise had been to install empty sarcophagi in empty chambers? Even admitting the hypothetical excesses of one or two megalomaniacs, it seemed unlikely that a whole succession of pharaohs would have sanctioned such wastefulness.

Pandora's Box

Buried beneath the five million tons of the Second Pyramid at Giza, Santha and I now stepped into the monument's spacious inner chamber, which might have been a tomb but might equally have served some other as yet unidentified purpose. Measuring 46.5 feet in length from east to west, and 16.5 in breadth from north to south, this naked and sterile apartment was topped off with an immensely strong gabled ceiling reaching a height of 22.5 feet at its apex. The gable slabs, each a massive 20-ton limestone monolith, had been laid in position at an angle of $53° 7' 28''$ (which exactly matched the angle of slope of the pyramid's sides).[17] Here there were no relieving chambers (as there were above the King's Chamber in the Great Pyramid). Instead, for more than 4000 years – perhaps far more – the gabled ceiling had taken the immense weight of the second largest stone building in the world.

I looked slowly around the room, which reflected a yellowish-white radiance back at me. Quarried directly out of the living bedrock, its walls were not at all smoothly finished, as one might have expected, but were noticeably rough and irregular. The floor too was peculiar: of split-level design with a step about a foot deep separating its eastern and western halves. The supposed sarcophagus of Khafre lay near the western wall, embedded in the floor. Measuring just over six feet in length, quite shallow, and somewhat narrow to have contained the wrapped and embalmed mummy of a noble pharaoh, its smooth red granite sides reached to about knee height.

As I gazed into its dark interior, it seemed to gape like the doorway to another dimension.

Chapter 37

Made by Some God

I had climbed the Great Pyramid the night before, but as I approached it in the full glare of midday, I experienced no sense of triumph. On the contrary, standing at its base on the north side, I felt fly-sized and puny – an impermanent creature of flesh and blood confronted with the awe-inspiring splendour of eternity. I had the impression that it might have been here for ever, 'made by some god and set down bodily in the surrounding sand', as the Greek historian Diodorus Siculus commented in the first century BC.[1] But which god had made it, if not the God–King Khufu whose name generations of Egyptians had associated with it?

For the second time in twelve hours, I began to climb the monument. Up close in this light, indifferent to human chronologies and subject only to the slow erosive forces of geological time, it reared above me like a frowning, terrifying crag. Fortunately, I only had six courses to clamber over, assisted in places by modern steps, before reaching Ma'mun's Hole, which now served as the pyramid's principal entrance.

The *original* entrance, still well-hidden in the ninth century when Ma'mun began tunnelling, was some ten courses higher, 55 feet above ground level and 24 feet east of the main north–south axis. Protected by giant limestone gables, it contained the mouth of the descending corridor, which led downwards at an angle of 26° 31′ 23″. Strangely, although itself measuring only some 3 feet 5 inches × 3 feet 11 inches, this corridor was sandwiched between roofing blocks 8 feet 6 inches thick and 12 feet wide and a flooring slab (known as the 'Basement Sheet') 2 feet 6 inches thick and 33 feet wide.[2]

Hidden structural features like these abounded in the Great Pyramid, manifesting both incredible complexity and apparent pointlessness. Nobody knew how blocks of this size had been successfully installed, neither did anybody know how they had been set so carefully in alignment with other blocks, or at such precise angles (because, as the reader may have realized, the 26° slope of the descending corridor was part of a deliberate and regular pattern). Nobody knew either *why* these things had been done.

The Beacon

Entering the pyramid through Ma'mun's Hole did not feel right. It was like entering a cave or grotto cut into the side of a mountain; it lacked the sense of deliberate and geometrical purposefulness that would have been conveyed by the original descending corridor. Worse still, the dark and inauspicious horizontal tunnel leading inwards looked like an ugly, deformed thing and still bore the marks of violence where the Arab workmen had alternately heated and chilled the stones with fierce fires and cold vinegar before attacking them with hammers and chisels, battering rams and borers.

On the one hand, such vandalism seemed gross and irresponsible. On the other, a startling possibility had to be considered: was there not a sense in which the pyramid seemed to have been designed to *invite* human beings of intelligence and curiosity to penetrate its mysteries? After all, if you were a pharaoh who wanted to ensure that his deceased body remained inviolate for eternity, would it make better sense (a) to advertise to your own and all subsequent generations the whereabouts of your burial place, or (b) to choose some secret and unknown location, of which you would never speak and where you might never be found?

The answer was obvious: you would go for secrecy and seclusion, as the vast majority of the pharaohs of Ancient Egypt had done.[3]

Why, then, if it was indeed a royal tomb, was the Great Pyramid so conspicuous? Why did it occupy a ground area of more than thirteen acres? Why was it almost 500 feet high? Why, in other words, if its purpose was to conceal and protect the body of Khufu, had it been designed so that it could not fail to attract the attention – in all epochs and under all imaginable circumstances – of treasure-crazed adventurers and of prying and imaginative intellectuals?

It was simply not credible that the brilliant architects, stonemasons, surveyors and engineers who had created the Great Pyramid could have been ignorant of basic human psychology. The vast ambition and the transcendent beauty, power and artistry of their handiwork spoke of refined skills, deep insight, and a complete understanding of the symbols and primordial patterns by which the minds of men could be manipulated. Logic therefore suggested that the pyramid builders must also have understood exactly what kind of beacon they were piling up (with such incredible precision) on this windswept plateau, on the west bank of the Nile, in those high and far away times.

They must, in short, have wanted this remarkable structure to exert a perennial fascination: to be violated by intruders, to be measured with increasing degrees of exactitude, and to haunt the collective imagination of mankind like a persistent ghost summoning intimations of a profound and long-forgotten secret.

Mind games of the pyramid builders

The point where Ma'mun's Hole intersected with the 26° descending corridor was closed off by a modern steel door. Beyond it, to the north, that corridor sloped up until it reached the gables of the monument's original entrance. To the south, as we have seen, the corridor sloped down for almost another 350 feet into the bedrock, before opening out into a huge subterranean chamber 600 feet beneath the apex of the pyramid. The accuracy of this corridor was astonishing. From top to bottom the average deviation from straight amounted to less than $\frac{1}{4}$-inch in the sides and $\frac{3}{10}$-inch on the roof.[4]

Passing the steel door, I continued through Ma'mun's tunnel, breathing in its ancient air and adjusting my eyes to the gloom of the low-wattage bulbs that lit it. Then ducking my head I began to climb through the steep and narrow section hacked upwards by the Arab diggers in their feverish thrust to by-pass the series of granite plugs blocking the lower part of the ascending corridor. At the top of the tunnel two of the original plugs could be seen, still *in situ* but partially exposed by quarrying. Egyptologists assumed that they had been slid into their present position from above[5] – all the way down the 129-foot length of the ascending corridor from the foot of the Grand Gallery.[6] Builders and engineers, however, whose trend of thought was perhaps more practical, had pointed out that it was physically impossible for the plugs to have been installed in this way. Because of the leaf-thin clearance that separated them from the walls, floor and ceiling of the corridor, friction would have foiled any 'sliding' operation in a matter of inches, let alone 100 feet.[7]

The puzzling implication was therefore that the ascending corridor must have been plugged while the pyramid was still being built. But why would anyone have wished to block the main entrance to the monument at such an early stage in its construction (even while continuing to enlarge and elaborate its inner chambers)? Moreover, if the objective had been to deny intruders admission, wouldn't it have been much easier and more efficient to have plugged the *descending* corridor from its entrance in the north face to a point below its junction with the ascending corridor? That would have been the most logical way to seal the pyramid and would have made plugs unnecessary in the ascending corridor.

There was only one certainty: since the beginning of history, the single known effect of the granite plugs had not been to prevent an intruder from gaining access; instead, like Bluebeard's locked door, the barrier had magnetized Ma'mun's attention and inflamed his curiosity so that he had felt compelled to tunnel his way past them, convinced that something of inestimable value must lie beyond them.

Might this not have been what the pyramid builders had *intended* the first intruder who reached this far to feel? It would be premature to rule out such a strange and unsettling possibility. At any rate, thanks to Ma'mun (and to the predictable constants of human nature) I was now able to insert myself into the unblocked upper section of the original ascending corridor. A smoothly cut aperture measuring 3 feet 5 inches wide × 3 feet 11 inches high (exactly the same dimensions as the descending corridor), it sloped up into the darkness at an angle of 26° 2′ 30″[8] (as against 26° 31′ 23″ in the descending corridor).[9]

What was this meticulous interest in the angle of 26°, and was it a coincidence that it amounted to half of the angle of inclination of the pyramid's sides – 52°.[10]

The reader may recall the significance of this angle. It was a key ingredient of the sophisticated and advanced formula by which the design of the Great Pyramid had been made to correspond precisely to the dynamics of spherical geometry. Thus the original height of the monument (481.3949 feet), and the perimeter of its base (3023.16 feet), stood in the same ratio to each other as did the radius of a sphere to its circumference. This ratio was $2pi$ (2×3.14) and to express it the builders had been obliged to specify the tricky and idiosyncratic angle of 52° for the pyramid's sides (since any greater or lesser slope would have meant a different height-to-perimeter ratio).

In Chapter Twenty-three we saw that the so-called Pyramid of the Sun at Teotihuacan in Mexico also expressed a knowledge and deliberate use of the transcendental number pi; in its case the height (233.5 feet) stood in a relationship of $4pi$ to the perimeter of its base (2932.76 feet).[11]

The crux, therefore, was that the most remarkable monument of Ancient Egypt and the most remarkable monument of Ancient Mexico both incorporated pi relationships long before and far away from the official 'discovery' of this transcendental number by the Greeks.[12] Moreover, the evidence invited the conclusion that something was being signalled by the use of pi – almost certainly the *same* thing in both cases.

Not for the first time, and not for the last, I was overwhelmed by a sense of contact with an ancient intelligence, not necessarily Egyptian or Mexican, which had found a way to reach out across the ages and draw people towards it like a beacon. Some might look for treasure; others, captivated by the deceptively simple manner in which the builders had used pi to demonstrate their mastery of the secrets of transcendental numbers, might be inspired to search for further mathematical epiphanies.

Bent almost double, my back brushing against the polished limestone ceiling, it was with such thoughts in my mind that I began to scramble up the 26° slope of the ascending corridor, which seemed to penetrate the vast bulk of the six million ton building like a trigonometrical device. After I had banged my head on its ceiling a couple of times, however, I began to wonder why the ingenious people who'd designed it hadn't made it two or three feet higher. If they could erect a monument like this in the first place (which they obviously could) and equip it with corridors, surely it would not have been beyond their capabilities to make those corridors roomy enough to stand up in? Once again I was tempted to conclude that it was the result of a deliberate decision by the pyramid builders: they had made the ascending corridor this way because they had wanted it this way (rather than because such a design had been forced upon them.)

Was there motive in the apparent madness of these archaic mind games?

Unknown dark distance

At the top of the ascending corridor I emerged into yet another inexplicable feature of the pyramid, 'the most celebrated architectural work to have survived from the Old Kingdom'[13] – the Grand Gallery. Soaring upwards at the continuing majestic angle of 26°, and almost entirely vanishing into the airy gloom above, its spacious corbelled vault made a stunning impression.

It was not my intention to climb the Grand Gallery yet. Branching off due south at its base was a long horizontal passageway, 3 feet 9 inches high and 127 feet in length, that led to the Queen's Chamber.[14] I wanted to revisit this room, which I had admired for its stark beauty since becoming acquainted with the Great Pyramid several years previously. Today, however, to my considerable irritation, the passageway was barred within a few feet of its entrance.

The reason, though I was unaware of it at the time, was that a German robotics engineer named Rudolf Gantenbrink was at work within, slowly and painstakingly manoeuvring a $250,000 robot up the narrow southern shaft of the Queen's Chamber. Hired by the Egyptian Antiquities Organization to improve the ventilation of the Great Pyramid, he had already used his high-tech equipment to clear debris from the King's Chamber's narrow 'southern shaft' (believed by Egyptologists to have been designed as a ventilation shaft in the first place) and had installed an electric fan at its mouth. At the

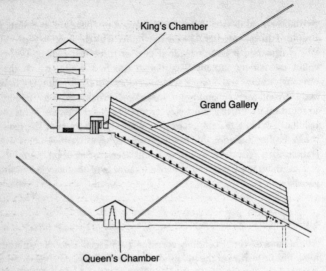

King's Chamber

Grand Gallery

Queen's Chamber

The Grand Gallery and the King's and Queen's Chambers with their northern and southern shafts.

beginning of March 1993 he transferred his attentions to the Queen's Chamber, deploying *Upuaut*, a miniaturized remote-controlled robot camera to explore *its* southern shaft. On 22 March, some 200 feet along the steeply sloping shaft (which rose at an angle of 39.5° and was only about 8 inches high × 9 inches wide),[15] the floor and walls suddenly became very smooth as *Upuaut* crawled into a section made of fine Tura limestone, the type normally used for lining sacred areas such as chapels or tombs. That, in itself, was intriguing enough, but at the end of this corridor, apparently leading to a sealed chamber deep within the pyramid's masonry, was a solid limestone door complete with metal fittings . . .

It had long been known that neither this southern shaft nor its counterpart in the Chamber's northern wall had any exit on the outside of the Great Pyramid. In addition, and equally inexplicably, neither had originally been fully cut through. For some reason the builders had left the last five inches of stone intact in the last block over the mouth of each of the shafts, thus rendering them invisible and inaccessible to any casual intruder.

Why? To make sure they would never be found? Or to make sure that they *would* be found, some day, under the right circumstances?

After all, there had from the beginning been two conspicuous shafts in the King's Chamber, penetrating the north and south walls. It should not have been beyond the mental powers of the pyramid builders to predict that sooner or later some inquiring person would be tempted to look for shafts in the Queen's Chamber as well. In the event nobody did look for more than a thousand years after Caliph Ma'mun had opened the monument to the world in AD 820. Then in 1872 an English engineer named Waynman Dixon, a Freemason who 'had been led to suspect the existence of the shafts by their presence in the King's Chamber above',[16] went tapping around the Queen's Chamber's walls and located them. He opened the southern shaft first, setting his 'carpenter and man-of-all-work, Bill Grundy, to jump a hole with a hammer and steel chisel at that place. So to work the faithful fellow went, and with a will which soon began to make a way into the soft stone [limestone] at this point, when lo! after a comparatively very few strokes, flop went the chisel right through into something or other.'[17]

The 'something or other' Bill Grundy's chisel had reached turned out to be 'a rectangular, horizontal, tubular channel, about 9 inches by 8 inches in transverse breadth and height, going back 7 feet into the wall, and then rising at an angle into an unknown, dark distance . . .'[18]

It was up that angle, and into that 'unknown dark distance', 121 years later, that Rudolf Gantenbrink sent his robot – the technology of our species having finally caught up with our powerful instincts to pry. Those instincts were clearly no weaker in 1872 than in 1993; among the many interesting things the remote-controlled camera succeeded in filming in the Queen's Chamber shafts was the far end of a long, sectioned metal rod of nineteenth century design which Waynman Dixon and the faithful Bill Grundy had secretly stuffed up the intriguing channel.[19] Predictably, they had assumed that if the pyramid builders had gone to the trouble of constructing and then concealing the shafts, then they must have hidden something worth looking for inside them.

The notion that there might have been an *intention* from the outset to stimulate such investigations would seem quite implausible if the final upshot of the discovery and exploration of the shafts had been a dead-end. Instead, as we have seen, a door was found – a sliding, portcullis door with curious metal fittings and an enticing gap at its base beneath which the laser-spot projected by Gantenbrink's robot was seen to disappear entirely . . .

Once again there seemed to be a clear invitation to proceed further, the latest in a long line of invitations which had encouraged Caliph Ma'mun and his diggers to break into the central passageways and chambers of the monument, which had waited for Waynman Dixon to test the hypothesis that the walls of the Queen's Chamber might contain concealed shafts, and which had then waited again until arousing the curiosity of Rudolf Gantenbrink, whose high-tech robot revealed the existence of the hidden door and brought within reach whatever secrets – or disappointments, or further invitations – might lie behind it.

The Queen's Chamber

We shall hear more of Rudolf Gantenbrink and *Upuaut* in later chapters. On 16 March 1993, however, knowing nothing of this, I was frustrated to find the Queen's Chamber closed, and glared resentfully through the metal grille that barred its entrance corridor.

I remembered that the height of that corridor, 3 feet 9 inches, was not constant. Approximately 110 feet due south from where I stood, and only about 15 feet from the entrance to the Chamber, a sudden downward step in the floor increased the standing-room to 5 feet 8 inches.[20] Nobody had come up with a convincing explanation for this peculiar feature.

The Queen's Chamber itself – apparently empty since the day it was built – measured 17 feet 2 inches from north to south and 18 feet 10 inches from east to west. It was equipped with an elegant gabled ceiling, 20 feet 5 inches in height, which lay exactly along the east–west axis of the pyramid.[21] Its floor, however, was the opposite of elegant and looked unfinished. There was a constant salty emanation through its pale, rough-hewn limestone walls, giving rise to much fruitless speculation.

In the north and south walls, still bearing the incised legend OPENED 1872, were the rectangular apertures discovered by Waynman Dixon which led into the dark distance of the mysterious shafts. The western wall was quite bare. Offset a little over two feet to the south of its centre line, the eastern wall was dominated by a niche in the form of a corbel vault 15 feet 4 inches high and 5 feet 2 inches wide at the base. Originally 3 feet 5 inches deep, a further cavity had been cut in the back of this niche in medieval times by Arab treasure-seekers looking for hidden chambers.[22] They had found nothing.

Egyptologists had also been unable to come to any persuasive conclusions about the original function of the niche, or, for that matter, of the Queen's Chamber as a whole.

All was confusion. All was paradox. All was mystery.

Instrument

The Grand Gallery had its mysteries too. Indeed it was among the most mysterious of all the internal features of the Great Pyramid. Measuring 6 feet 9 inches wide at the floor, its walls rose vertically to a height of 7 feet 6 inches; above that level seven further courses of masonry (each one projecting inwards some 3 inches beyond the course immediately below it) carried the vault to its full height of 28 feet and its culminating width of 3 feet 5 inches.[23]

Remember that structurally the Gallery was required to support, *for ever*, the multi-million ton weight of the upper three-quarters of the largest and heaviest stone monument ever built on planet earth. Was it not quite remarkable that a group of supposed 'technological primitives' had not only envisaged and designed such a feature but had completed it successfully, more than 4500 years before our time?

Even if they had made the Gallery only 20 feet long, and had sought to erect it on a level plane, the task would have been difficult enough – indeed extraordinarily difficult. But they had opted to erect this astonishing corbel vault at a slope of 26°, and to extend its length to a staggering 153 feet.[24] Moreover, they had made it with perfectly dressed limestone megaliths throughout – huge, smoothly polished blocks carved into sloping parallelograms and laid together so closely and with such rigorous precision that the joints were almost invisible to the naked eye.

The pyramid builders had also included some interesting symmetries in their work. For example, the culminating width of the Gallery at its apex was 3 feet 5 inches while its width at the floor was 6 feet 9 inches. At the exact centre of the floor, running the entire length of the Gallery – and sandwiched between flat-topped masonry ramps each 1 foot 8 inches wide – there was a sunken channel 2 feet deep and 3 feet 5 inches wide. What could have been the purpose of this slot? And why had it been necessary for it to mirror so precisely the width and form of the ceiling, which also looked like a 'slot' sandwiched between the two upper courses of masonry?

I knew that I was not the first person to have stood at the foot of the Grand Gallery and to have been overtaken by the disorienting sense of being 'in the inside of some enormous instrument of some sort.'[25] Who was to say that such intuitions were completely wrong? Or, for that matter, that they were right? No record as to function remained, other than in mystical and symbolic references in certain ancient Egyptian liturgical texts. These appeared to indicate that the pyramids had been seen as devices designed to turn dead men into immortal beings: to 'throw open the doors of the firmament and make a road', so that the deceased pharaoh might 'ascend into the company of the gods'.[26]

I had no difficulty accepting that such a belief system might have been at work here, and obviously it could have provided a motive for the whole enterprise. Nevertheless, I was still puzzled why more than six million tons of *physical* apparatus, intricately interlaced with channels and tubes, corridors and chambers, had been deemed necessary to achieve a mystical, spiritual and symbolic objective.

Being inside the Grand Gallery did feel like being inside a enormous instrument. It had an undeniable aesthetic impact upon me (admittedly a heavy and domineering one), but it was also completely devoid of decorative features and of anything (figures of deities, reliefs of liturgical texts, and so on) which might be suggestive of worship or religion. The primary impression it conveyed was one of strict functionalism and purposefulness – as though it had been built to do a job. At the same time I was aware of its focused solemnity of style and gravity of manner, which seemed to demand nothing less than serious and complete attention.

By now I had climbed steadily through about half the length of the Gallery. Ahead of me, and behind, shadows and light played tricks amid the looming stone walls. Pausing, I turned my head, looking upwards through the gloom towards the vaulted ceiling which supported the crushing weight of the Great Pyramid of Egypt.

It suddenly hit me how dauntingly and disturbingly *old* it was, and how completely my life at this moment depended on the skills of the ancient builders. The hefty blocks that spanned the distant ceiling were examples of those skills – every one of them laid at a slightly steeper gradient than that of the Gallery. As the great archaeologist and surveyor Flinders Petrie had observed, this had been done

> in order that the lower edge of each stone should hitch like a pawl into a ratchet cut into the top of the walls; hence no stone can press on the one below it, so as to cause a cumulative pressure all down the roof; and each stone is separately upheld by the side walls which it lies across.[27]

And this was the work of a people whose civilization had only recently emerged from neolithic hunter-gathering?

I began to walk up the Gallery again, using the 2-foot-deep central flooring slot. A modern wooden covering fitted with helpful slats and side railings made the ascent relatively easy. In antiquity, however, the floor had been smoothly polished limestone, which, at a gradient of 26°, must have been almost impossible to climb.

How had it been done? Had it been done at all?

Looming ahead at the end of the Grand Gallery was the dark opening to the King's Chamber beckoning each and every inquiring pilgrim into the heart of the enigma.

Chapter 38

Interactive Three-Dimensional Game

Reaching the top of the Grand Gallery, I clambered over a chunky granite step about three feet high. I remembered that it lay, like the roof of the Queen's Chamber, exactly along the east–west axis of the Great Pyramid, And therefore marked the point of transition between the northern and southern halves of the monument.[1] Somewhat like an altar in appearance, the step also provided a solid horizontal platform immediately in front of the low square tunnel that served as the entrance to the King's Chamber.

Pausing for a moment, I looked back down the Gallery, taking in once again its lack of decoration, its lack of religious iconography, and its absolute lack of any of the recognizable symbolism normally associated with the archaic belief system of the Ancient Egyptians. All that registered upon the eye, along the entire 153-foot length of this magnificent geometrical cavity, was its disinterested regularity and its stark machinelike simplicity.

Looking up, I could just make out the opening of a dark aperture, chiselled into the top of the eastern wall above my head. Nobody knew when or by whom this foreboding hole had been cut, or how deep it had originally penetrated. It led to the first of the five relieving chambers above the King's Chamber and had been extended in 1837 when Howard Vyse had used it to break through to the remaining four. Looking down again, I could just make out the point at the bottom of the Gallery's western wall where the near-vertical well-shaft began its precipitous 160 foot descent through the core of the pyramid to join the descending corridor far below ground-level.

Why would such a complicated apparatus of pipes and passageways have been required? At first sight it didn't make sense. But then nothing about the Great Pyramid did make much sense, unless you were prepared to devote a great deal of attention to it. In unpredictable ways, when you did that, it would from time to time reward you.

If you were sufficiently numerate, for example, as we have seen, it would respond to your basic inquiries into its height and base perimeter by 'printing out' the value of *pi*. And if you were prepared to investigate further, as we shall see, it would download other useful mathematical tit-bits, each a little more complex and abstruse that its predecessor.

There was a programmed feel about this whole process, as though it had been carefully prearranged. Not for the first time, I found myself willing to consider the possibility that the pyramid might have been designed as a gigantic challenge or learning machine – or, better still, as an interactive three-dimensional puzzle set down in the desert for humanity to solve.

Antechamber

Just over 3 feet 6 inches high, the entry passage to the King's Chamber required all humans of normal stature to stoop. About four feet farther on, however, I reached the 'Antechamber', where the roof level rose suddenly to 12 feet above the floor. The east and west walls of the Antechamber were composed of red granite, into which were cut four opposing pairs of wide parallel slots, assumed by Egyptologists to have held thick portcullis slabs.[2] Three of these pairs of slots extended all the way to the floor, and were empty. The fourth (the northernmost) had been cut down only as far as the roof level of the entry passage (that is, 3 feet 6 inches *above* floor level) and still contained a hulking sheet of granite, perhaps nine inches thick and six feet high. There was a horizontal space of only 21 inches between this suspended stone portcullis and the northern end of the entry passage from which I had just emerged. There was also a gap of a little over 2 feet deep between the top of the portcullis and the ceiling. Whatever

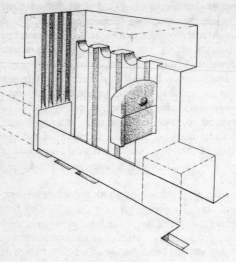

The antechamber.

function it was designed to serve it was hard to agree with the Egyptologists that this peculiar structure could have been intended to deny access to tomb robbers.

Genuinely puzzled, I ducked under it and then stood up again in the southern portion of the Antechamber, which was some 10 feet long and maintained the same roof height of 12 feet. Though much worn, the grooves for the three further 'portcullis' slabs were still visible in the eastern and western walls. There was no sign of the slabs themselves and, indeed, it was difficult to see how such cumbersone pieces of stone could have been installed in so severely constricted a working space.

I remembered that Flinders Petrie, who had systematically surveyed the entire Giza necropolis in the late nineteenth century, had commented on a similar puzzle in the Second Pyramid: 'The granite portcullis in the lower passage shows great skill in moving masses, as it would need 40 or 60 men to lift it; yet it has been moved, and raised into place, in a narrow passage, where only a few men could possibly reach it.'³ Exactly the same observations applied to the portcullis slabs of the Great Pyramid. If they were portcullis slabs – gateways capable of being raised and lowered.

The problem was that the physics of raising and lowering them required they be shorter than the full height of the Antechamber, so that they could be drawn into the roof space to allow the entry and exit of legitimate individuals prior to the closure of the tomb. This meant, of course, that when the bottom edges of the slabs were lowered to the floor to block the Antechamber at that level, an equal and opposite space would have opened up between the top edges of the slabs and the ceiling, through which any enterprising tomb-robber would certainly have been able to climb.

The Antechamber clearly qualified as another of the pyramid's many thought-provoking paradoxes, in which complexity of structure was combined with apparent pointlessness of function.

An exit tunnel, the same height and width as the entrance tunnel and lined with solid red granite, led off from the Antechamber's southern wall (also made of granite but incorporating a 12-inch thick limestone layer at its very top). After about a further 9 feet the tunnel debouched into the King's Chamber, a massive sombre red room made entirely of granite, which radiated an atmosphere of prodigious energy and power.

Stone enigmas

I moved into the centre of the King's Chamber, the long axis of which was perfectly oriented east to west while the short axis was equally perfectly oriented north to south. The room was exactly 19 feet 1 inch in height and formed a precise two-by-one rectangle measuring 34 feet 4 inches long by 17 feet 2 inches wide. With a floor consisting of 15 massive granite paving stones, and walls composed of 100 gigantic granite blocks, each weighing 70 tons or more and laid in five courses, and with a ceiling spanned by nine further granite blocks each weighing aproximately 50 tons,⁴ the effect was of intense and overwhelming *compression*.

At the Chamber's western end was the object which, if the

Egyptologists were to be believed, the entire Great Pyramid, had been built to house. That object, carved out of one piece of dark chocolate-coloured granite containing peculiarly hard granules of feldspar, quartz and mica, was the lidless coffer presumed to have been the sarcophagus of Khufu.[5] Its interior measurements were 6 feet 6.6 inches in length, 2 feet 10.42 inches in depth, and 2 feet 2.81 inches in width. Its exterior measurements were 7 feet 5.62 inches in length, 3 feet 5.31 inches in depth, and 3 feet 2.5 inches in width[6] an inch too wide, incidentally, for it to have been carried up through the lower (and now plugged) entrance to the ascending corridor.[7]

Some routine mathematical games were built into the dimensions of the sarcophagus. For example, it had an internal volume of 1166.4 litres and an external volume of exactly twice that 2332.8 litres.[8] Such a precise coincidence could not have been arrived at accidentally: the walls of the coffer had been cut to machine-age tolerances by craftsmen of enormous skill and experience. It seemed, moreover, as Flinders Petrie admitted with some puzzlement after completing his painstaking survey of the Great Pyramid, that these craftsmen had access to tools 'such as we ourselves have only now reinvented . . .'[9]

Petrie examined the sarcophagus particularly closely and reported that it must have been cut out of its surrounding granite block with straight saws '8 feet or more in length'. Since the granite was extremely hard, he could only assume that these saws must have had bronze blades (the hardest metal then supposedly available) inset with 'cutting points' made of even harder jewels: 'The character of the work would certainly seem to point to diamond as being the cutting jewel; and only the considerations of its rarity in general, and its absence from Egypt, interfere with this conclusion . . .'[10]

An even bigger mystery surrounded the hollowing out of the sarcophagus, obviously a far more difficult enterprise than separating it from a block of bedrock. Here Petrie concluded that the Egyptians must have:

> adapted their sawing principle into a circular instead of a rectilinear form, curving the blade round into a tube, which drilled out a circular groove by its rotation; thus by breaking away the cores left in such grooves, they were able to hollow out large holes with a minimum of

labour. These tubular drills varied from 1/4 inch to 5 inches diameter, and from 1/30 to 1/5 inch thick . . .[11]

Of course, as Petrie admitted, no actual jewelled drills or saws had ever been found by Egyptologists.[12] The visible evidence of the kinds of drilling and sawing that had been done, however, compelled him to infer that such instruments must have existed. He became especially interested in this and extended his study to include not only the King's Chamber sarcophagus but many other granite artefacts and granite 'drill cores' which he collected at Giza. The deeper his research, however, the more puzzling the stone-cutting technology of the Ancient Egyptians became:

> The amount of pressure, shown by the rapidity with which the drills and saws pierced through the hard stones, is very surprising; probably a load of at least a ton or two was placed on the 4-inch drills cutting in granite. On the granite core No 7 the spiral of the cut sinks 1 inch in the circumference of 6 inches, a rate of ploughing out which is astonishing . . . These rapid spiral grooves cannot be ascribed to anything but the descent of the drill into the granite under enormous pressure . . .[13]

Wasn't it peculiar that at the supposed dawn of human civilization, more than 4500 years ago, the Ancient Egyptians had acquired what sounded like industrial-age drills packing a ton or more of punch and capable of slicing through hard stones like hot knives through butter?

Petrie could come up with no explanation for this conundrum. Nor was he able to explain the kind of instrument used to cut hieroglyphs into a number of diorite bowls with Fourth Dynasty inscriptions which he found at Giza: 'The hieroglyphs are incised with a very free-cutting point; they are not scraped or ground out, but are ploughed through the diorite, with rough edges to the line . . .'[14]

This bothered the logical Petrie because he knew that diorite was one of the hardest stones on earth, far harder even than iron.[15] Yet here it was in Ancient Egypt being cut with incredible power and precision by some as yet unidentified graving tool:

> As the lines are only 1/150 inch wide it is evident that the cutting point must have been much harder than quartz; and tough enough not to splinter when so fine an edge was being employed, probably only 1/200

inch wide. Parallel lines are graved only 1/30 inch apart from centre to centre.[16]

In other words, he was envisaging an instrument with a needle-sharp point of exceptional, unprecedented hardness capable of penetrating and furrowing diorite with ease, and capable also of withstanding the enormous pressures required throughout the operation. What sort of instrument was that? By what means would the pressure have been applied? How could sufficient accuracy have been maintained to scour parallel lines at intervals of just 1/30-inch?

At least it was possible to conjure a mental picture of the circular drills with jewelled teeth which Petrie supposed must have been used to hollow out the King's Chamber sarcophagus. I found, however, that it was not so easy to do the same for the unknown instrument capable of incising hieroglyphs into diorite at 2500 BC, at any rate not without assuming the existence of a far higher level of technology than Egyptologists were prepared to consider.

Nor was it just a few hieroglyphs or a few diorite bowls. During my travels in Egypt I had examined many stone vessels – dating back in some cases to pre-dynastic times – that had been mysteriously hollowed out of a range of materials such as diorite, basalt, quartz crystal and metamorphic schist.[17]

For example, more than 30,000 such vessels had been found in the chambers beneath the Third Dynasty Step Pyramid of Zoser at Saqqara.[18] That meant that they were at least as old as Zoser himself (i.e. around 2650 BC[19]). Theoretically, they could have been even older than that, because identical vessels had been found in pre-dynastic strata dated to 4000 BC and earlier,[20] and because the practice of handing down treasured heirlooms from generation to generation had been deeply ingrained in Egypt since time immemorial.

Whether they were made in 2500 BC or in 4000 BC or even earlier, the stone vessels from the Step Pyramid were remarkable for their workmanship, which once again seemed to have been accomplished by some as yet unimagined (and, indeed, almost unimaginable) tool.

Why unimaginable? Because many of the vessels were tall vases with long, thin, elegant necks and widely flared interiors, often incorporating fully hollowed-out shoulders. No instrument yet invented was capable of carving vases into shapes like these, because such an instrument would have had to have been narrow enough to have passed through the necks and strong enough (and of the right shape) to have scoured out the shoulders and the rounded interiors. And how could sufficient upward and outward pressure have been generated and applied within the vases to achieve these effects?

The tall vases were by no means the only enigmatic vessels unearthed from the Pyramid of Zoser, and from a number of other archaic sites. There were monolithic urns with delicate ornamental handles left attached to their exteriors by the carvers. There were bowls, again with extremely narrow necks like the vases, and with widely flared, pot-bellied interiors. There were also open bowls, and almost microscopic vials, and occasional strange wheel-shaped objects cut out of metamorphic schist with inwardly curled edges planed down so fine that they were almost translucent.[21] In all cases what was really perplexing was the precision with which the interiors and exteriors of these vessels had been made to correspond – curve matching curve – over absolutely smooth, polished surfaces with no tool marks visible.

There was no technology known to have been available to the Ancient Egyptians capable of achieving such results. Nor, for that matter, would any stone-carver today be able to match them, even if he were working with the best tungsten-carbide tools. The implication, therefore, is that an unknown or secret technology had been put to use in Ancient Egypt.

Ceremony of the sarcophagus

Standing in the King's Chamber, facing west – the direction of death amongst both the Ancient Egyptians and the Maya – I rested my hands lightly on the gnarled granite edge of the sarcophagus which Egyptologists insist had been built to house the body of Khufu. I gazed into its murky depths where the dim electric lighting of the chamber seemed hardly to penetrate and saw specks of dust swirling in a golden cloud.

It was just a trick of light and shadow, of course, but the King's Chamber was full of such illusions. I remembered that Napoleon Bonaparte had paused to spend a night alone here during his conquest of Egypt in the late eighteenth century. The next morning he had emerged pale and shaken, having experienced something which had profoundly disturbed him but about which he never afterwards spoke.[22]

Had he tried to sleep in the sarcophagus?

Acting on impulse, I climbed into the granite coffer and lay down, face upwards, my feet pointed towards the south and my head to the north.

Napoleon was a little guy, so he must have fitted comfortably. There was plenty of room for me too. But had Khufu been here as well?

I relaxed and tried not to worry about the possibility of one of the pyramid guards coming in and finding me in this embarrassing and probably illegal position. Hoping that I would remain undisturbed for a few minutes, I folded my hands across my chest and gave voice to a sustained low-pitched tone – something I had tried out several times before at other points in the King's Chamber. On those occasions, in the centre of the floor, I had noticed that the walls and ceiling seemed to collect the sound, to gather and to amplify it and project it back at me so that I could sense the returning vibrations through my feet and scalp and skin.

Now in the sarcophagus I was aware of very much the same effect, although seemingly amplified and concentrated many times over. It was like being in the sound-box of some giant, resonant musical instrument designed to emit for ever just one reverberating note. The sound was intense and quite disturbing. I imagined it rising out of the coffer and bouncing off the red granite walls and ceiling of the King's Chamber, shooting up through the northern and southern 'ventila-tion' shafts and spreading across the Giza plateau like a sonic mushroom cloud.

With this ambitious vision in my mind, and with the sound of my low-pitched note echoing in my ears and causing the sarcophagus to vibrate around me, I closed my eyes. When I opened them a few minutes later it was to behold a distressing sight: six Japanese tourists of mixed ages and sexes had congregated around the sarcophagus – two of them standing to the east, two to the west and one each to the north and south.

They all looked ... amazed. And I was amazed to see them. Because of recent attacks by armed Islamic extremists there were now almost no tourists at Giza and I had expected to have the King's Chamber to myself.

What does one do in a situation like this?

Gathering as much dignity as I could muster, I stood upright, smiling and dusting myself off. The Japanese stepped back and I climbed out of the sarcophagus. Cultivating a businesslike manner, as though I did things like this all the time, I strolled to the point two-thirds of the way along the northern wall of the King's Chamber where the entrance to what Egyptologists refer to as the 'northern ventilation shaft' is located, and began to examine it minutely.

Some 8 inches wide by 9 inches high, it was, I knew, more than 200 feet in length and emerged into open air at the pyramid's 103rd course of masonry. Presumably by design rather than by accident, it pointed to the circumpolar regions of the northern heavens at an angle of 32° 30'. This, in the Pyramid Age around 2500 BC, would have meant that it was directed on the upper culmination of Alpha Draconis, a prominent star in the constellation of Draco.[23]

Much to my relief the Japanese rapidly completed their tour of the King's Chamber and left, stooping, without a backward glance. As soon as they had gone I crossed over to the other side of the room to take a look at the southern shaft. Since I had last been here some months before, its appearance had changed horribly. Its mouth now contained a massive electrical air-conditioning unit installed by Rudolf Gantenbrink, who even now was turning his attentions to the neglected shafts of the Queen's Chamber.

Since Egyptologists were satisfied that the King's Chamber shafts had been built for ventilation purposes, they saw nothing untoward in using modern technology to improve the efficiency of this task. Yet wouldn't *horizontal* shafts have been more effective than sloping ones if their primary purpose had been ventilation, and easier to build?[24] It was therefore unlikely to be an accident that the southern shaft of the King's Chamber targeted the southern heavens at 45°. During the Pyramid Age this was the location for the meridian transit of Zeta Orionis, the lowest of the three stars of Orion's Belt[25] – an alignment, I was to discover in due course, that would turn out to be of the utmost significance for future pyramid research.

The game-master

Now that I had the Chamber to myself again, I walked over to the western wall, on the far side of the sarcophagus, and turned to face east.

The huge room had an endless capacity to generate indications of mathematical game-playing. For example, its height (19 feet 1 inch) was exactly half of the length of its floor diagonal (38 feet 2 inches).[26] Moreover, since the King's Chamber formed a perfect 1 × 2 rectangle was it conceivable that the pyramid builders were unaware that they had also made it express and exemplify the 'golden section'?

Known as *phi*, the golden section was another irrational number like *pi* that could not be worked out arithmetically. Its value was the square root of 5 plus 1 divided by 2, equivalent to 1.61803.[27] This proved to be the 'limiting value of the ratio between successive numbers in the Fibonacci series – the series of numbers beginning 0, 1, 1, 2, 3, 5, 8, 13 – in which each term is the sum of the two previous terms.'[28]

Phi could also be obtained schematically by dividing a line A–B at a point C in such a way that the whole line A–B was longer than the first part, A–C, in the same proportion as the first part, A–C, was longer than the remainder, C–B.[29] This proportion, which had been proven particularly harmonious and agreeable to the eye, had supposedly been first discovered by the Pythagorean Greeks, who incorporated it into the Parthenon at Athens. There is absolutely no doubt, however, that *phi* was illustrated and obtained at least 2000 years previously in the King's Chamber of the Great Pyramid at Giza.

To understand how it is necessary to envisage the rectangular floor of the chamber as being divided into two imaginary squares of equal size, with the side length of each square being given a value of 1. If either of these two squares were then split in half, thus forming two new rectangles, and if the diagonal of the rectangle nearest to the centreline of the King's Chamber were swung down to the base, the point where its tip touched the base would be *phi*, or 1.618, in relation to the side length (i.e., 1) of the original square.[30] (An alternative way

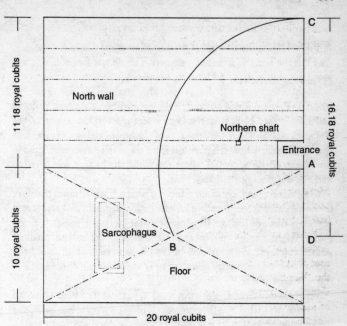

At the very beginning of its Dynastic history, Egypt inherited a system of measures from unknown predecessors. Expressed in these ancient measures, the floor dimensions of the King's Chamber (34 ft 4″ × 17 ft 2″) work out at exactly 20 × 10 'royal cubits', while the height of the side walls to the ceiling is exactly 11.18 royal cubits. The semi-diagonal of the floor (A–B) is also exactly 11.18 royal cubits and can be 'swung up' to C to confirm the height of the chamber. *Phi* is defined mathematically as the square root of 5 + 1 ÷ 2, i.e. 1.618. Is it a coincidence that the distance C–D (i.e. the wall height of the King's Chamber plus half the width of its floor) equals 16.18 royal cubits, thus incorporating the essential digits of *phi*?

of obtaining *phi*, also built into the king's chamber's dimensions, is illustrated above.)

The Egyptologists considered all this was pure chance. Yet the pyramid builders had done *nothing* by chance. Whoever they had been, I found it hard to imagine more systematic and mathematically minded people.

I'd had had quite enough of their mathematical games for one day. As I left the King's Chamber, however, I could not forget that it was located in line with the 50th course of the Great Pyramid's masonry at a height of almost 150 feet above the ground.[31] This meant, as Flinders Petrie pointed out with some astonishment, that the builders had managed to place it 'at the level where the vertical section of the Pyramid was halved, where the area of the horizontal section was half that of the base, where the diagonal from corner to corner was equal to the length of the base, and where the width of the face was equal to half the diagonal of the base'.[32]

Confidently and efficiently fooling around with more than six million tons of stone, creating galleries and chambers and shafts and corridors more or less at will, achieving near-perfect symmetry, near-perfect right angles, and near-perfect alignments to the cardinal points, the mysterious builders of the Great Pyramid had found the time to play a great many other tricks as well with the dimensions of the vast monument.

Why did their minds work this way? What had they been trying to say or do? And why, so many thousands of years after it was built, did the monument still exert a magnetic influence upon so many people, from so many different walks of life, who came into contact with it?

There was a Sphinx in the neighbourhood, so I decided that I would put these riddles to it . . .

Chapter 39

Place of the Beginning

Giza, Egypt, 16 March 1993, 3.30 p. m..

It was mid afternoon by the time I left the Great Pyramid. Retracing the route that Santha and I had followed the night before when we had climbed the monument, I walked eastwards along the northern face, southwards along the flank of the eastern face, clambered over mounds of rubble and ancient tombs that clustered closely in this part of the necropolis, and came out on to the sand-covered limestone bedrock of the Giza plateau, which sloped down towards the south and east.

At the bottom of this long gentle slope, about half a kilometre from the south-eastern corner of the Great Pyramid, the Sphinx crouched in his rock-hewn pit. Sixty-six feet high and more than 240 feet long, with a head measuring 13 feet 8 inches wide,[1] he was, by a considerable margin, the largest single piece of sculpture in the world – and the most renowned:

'A shape with lion body and the head of a man
A gaze blank and pitiless as the sun.[2]

Approaching the monument from the north-west I crossed the ancient causeway that connected the Second Pyramid with the so-called Valley Temple of Khafre, a most unusual structure located just

50 feet south of the Sphinx itself on the eastern edge of the Giza necropolis.

This Temple had long been believed to be far older than the time of Khafre. Indeed throughout much of the nineteenth century the consensus among scholars was that it had been built in remote prehistory, and had nothing to do with the architecture of dynastic Egypt.[3] What changed all that was the discovery, buried within the Temple precincts, of a number of inscribed statues of Khafre. Most were pretty badly smashed, but one, found upside down in a deep pit in an antechamber, was almost intact. Life-sized, and exquisitely carved out of black, jewel-hard diorite, it showed the Fourth Dynasty pharaoh seated on his throne and gazing with serene indifference towards infinity.

At this point the razor-sharp reasoning of Egyptology was brought to bear, and a solution of almost awe-inspiring brilliance was worked out: statues of Khafre had been found in the Valley Temple therefore the Valley Temple had been built by Khafre. The normally sensible Flinders Petrie summed up: 'The fact that the only dateable remains found in the Temple were statues of Khafre shows that it is of his period; since the idea of his appropriating an earlier building is very unlikely.'[4]

But why was the idea so unlikely?

Throughout the history of Dynastic Egypt many pharaohs appropriated the buildings of their predecessors, sometimes deliberately striking out the cartouches of the original builders and replacing them with their own.[5] There was no good reason to assume that Khafre would have been deterred from linking himself to the Valley Temple, particularly if it had not been associated in his mind with any previous historical ruler but with the great 'gods' said by the Ancient Egyptians to have brought civilization to the Nile Valley in the distant and mythical epoch they spoke of as the First Time.[6] In such a place of archaic and mysterious power, *which he does not appear to have interfered with in any other way*, Khafre might have thought that the setting up of beautiful and lifelike statues of himself could bring eternal benefits. And if, among the gods, the Valley Temple had been associated with Osiris (whom it was every pharaoh's objective to join in the afterlife),[7] Khafre's use of statues to forge a strong symbolic link would be even more understandable.

Temple of the giants

After crossing the causeway, the route I had chosen to reach the Valley Temple took me through the rubble of a 'mastaba' field, where lesser notables of the Fourth Dynasty had been buried in subterranean tombs under bench-shaped platforms of stone (*mastaba* is a modern Arabic word meaning bench, hence the name given to these tombs). I walked along the southern wall of the Temple itself, recalling that this ancient building was almost as perfectly oriented north to south as was the Great Pyramid (with an error of just 12 arc minutes).[8]

The Temple was square in plan, 147 feet along each side. It was built in to the slope of the plateau, which was higher in the west than in the east. In consequence, while its western wall stood only a little over 20 feet tall, its eastern wall exceeded 40 feet.[9]

Viewed from the south, the impression was of a wedge-shaped structure, squat and powerful, resting firmly on bedrock. A closer examination revealed that it incorporated several characteristics quite alien and inexplicable to the modern eye, which that must have seemed almost as alien and inexplicable to the Ancient Egyptians. For a start, there was the stark absence, both inside and out, of inscriptions and other identifying marks. In this respect, as the reader will appreciate, the Valley Temple could be compared with a few of the other anonymous and frankly undatable monuments on the Giza plateau, including the great pyramids (and also with a mysterious structure at Abydos known as the Osireion, which we consider in detail in a later chapter) but otherwise bore no resemblance to the typical and well-known products of Ancient Egyptian art and architecture – all copiously decorated, embellished and inscribed.[10]

Another important and unusual feature of the Valley Temple was that its core structure was built entirely, *entirely*, of gigantic limestone megaliths. The majority of these measured about 18 feet long × 10 feet wide × 8 feet high and some were as large as 30 feet long × 12 feet wide × 10 feet high.[11] Routinely exceeding 200 tons in weight, each was heavier than a modern diesel locomotive – and there were hundreds of blocks.[12]

Was this in any way mysterious?

Egyptologists did not seem to think so; indeed few of them had bothered to comment, except in the most superficial manner – either on the staggering size of these blocks or the mind-bending logistics of how they might have been put in place. As we have seen, monoliths of up to 70 tons, each about as heavy as 100 family-sized cars, had been lifted to the level of the King's Chamber in the Great Pyramid – again without provoking much comment from the Egyptological fraternity – so the lack of curiosity about the Valley Temple was perhaps no surprise. Nevertheless, the block size was truly extraordinary, seeming to belong not just to another epoch but to another *ethic* altogether – one that reflected incomprehensible aesthetic and structural concerns and suggested a scale of priorities utterly different from our own. Why, for example, insist on using these cumbersome 200-ton monoliths when you could simply slice each of them up into 10 or 20 or 40 or 80 smaller and more manoeuvrable blocks? Why make things so difficult for yourself when you could achieve much the same visual effect with much less effort?

And how had the builders of the Valley Temple lifted these colossal megaliths to heights of more than 40 feet?

At present there are only two land-based cranes in the world that could lift weights of this magnitude. At the very frontiers of construction technology, these are both vast, industrialized machines, with booms reaching more than 220 feet into the air, which require on-board counterweights of 160 tons to prevent them from tipping over. The preparation-time for a single lift is around six weeks and calls for the skills of specialized teams of up to 20 men.[13]

In other words, modern builders with all the advantages of high-tech engineering at their disposal, can barely hoist weights of 200 tons. Was it not, therefore, somewhat surprising that the builders at Giza had hoisted such weights on an almost routine basis?

Moving closer to the Temple's looming southern wall I observed something else about the huge limestone blocks: not only were they ridiculously large but, as though to complicate still further an almost impossible task, they had been cut and fitted into multi-angled jigsaw-

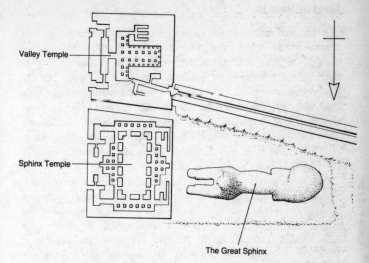

Valley Temple

Sphinx Temple

The Great Sphinx

The Sphinx and the Sphinx Temple with the Valley Temple of Khafre.

puzzle patterns similar to those employed in the cyclopean stone structures at Sacsayhuaman and Machu Picchu in Peru (see Part II).

Another point I noticed was that the Temple walls appeared to have been constructed in two stages. The first stage, most of which was intact (though deeply eroded), consisted of the strong and heavy core of 200-ton limestone blocks. On to both sides of these had been grafted a façade of dressed granite which (as we shall see) was largely intact in the interior of the building but had mainly fallen away on the outside. A closer look at some of the remaining exterior facing blocks where they had become detached from the core revealed a curious fact. When they had been placed here in antiquity the backs of these blocks had been cut to fit into and around the deep coves and scallops of *existing weathering patterns* on the limestone core. The presence of those patterns seemed to imply that the core blocks must have stood here, exposed to the elements, for an immense span of time before they had been faced with granite.

Lord of Rostau

I now moved around to the entrance of the Valley Temple, located near the northern end of the 43-foot high eastern wall. Here I saw that the granite facing was still in perfect condition, consisting of huge slabs weighing between 70 and 80 tons apiece which protected the underlying limestone core blocks like a suit of armour. Incorporating a tall, narrow, roofless corridor, this dark and imposing portal ran east to west at first, then made a right-angle turn to the south, leading me into a spacious antechamber. It was here that the lifesize diorite statue of Khafre had been found, upside down and apparently ritually buried, at the bottom of a deep pit.

Lining the entire interior of the antechamber was a majestic jigsaw puzzle of smoothly polished granite facing blocks (which continued through the whole building). Exactly like the blocks on some of the bigger and more bizarre pre-Inca monuments in Peru, these incorporated multiple, finely chiselled angles in the joints and presented a complex overall pattern. Of particular note was the way certain blocks wrapped around corners and were received by re-entering angles cut into other blocks.

From the antechamber I passed through an elegant corridor which led west into a spacious T-shaped hall. I found myself standing at the head of the T looking further westwards along an imposing avenue of monolithic columns. Reaching almost 15 feet in height and measuring 41 inches on each side, all these columns supported granite beams, which were again 41 inches square. A row of six further columns, also supporting beams, ran along the north–south axis of the T; the overall effect was of massive but refined simplicity.

What was this building for? According to the Egyptologists who attributed it to Khafre its purpose was obvious. It had been designed, they said, as a venue for certain of the purification and rebirth rituals required for the funeral of the pharaoh. The Ancient Egyptians themselves, however, had left no inscriptions confirming this. On the contrary, the only written evidence that has come down to us indicated that the Valley Temple could *not* (originally at any rate) have had anything to do with Khafre, for the simple reason that it was built before his reign. This written evidence is the Inventory Stela, (referred to in Chapter Thirty-five), which also indicated a much greater age for the Great Pyramid and the Sphinx.

What the Inventory Stela had to say about the Valley Temple was that it had been standing during the reign of Khafre's predecessor Khufu, when it had been regarded not as a recent but as a remotely ancient building. Moreover, it was clear from the context that it was not thought to have been the work of any earlier pharaoh. Instead, it was believed to have come down from the 'First Time' and to have been built by the 'gods' who had settled in the Nile Valley in that remote epoch. It was referred to quite explicitly as the 'House of Osiris, Lord of Rostau'[14] (Rostau being an archaic name for the Giza necropolis).[15]

As we shall see in Part VII, Osiris was in many respects the Egyptian counterpart of Viracocha and Quetzalcoatl, the civilizing deities of the Andes and of Central America. With them he shared not only a common mission but a vast heritage of common symbolism. It seemed appropriate, therefore, that the 'House' (or sanctuary, or temple) of such a wise teacher and lawgiver should have been established at Giza within sight of the Great Pyramid and in the immediate vicinity of the Great Sphinx.

Vastly, remotely, fabulously ancient

Following the directions given in the Inventory Stela – which stated that the Sphinx lay 'on the north-west of the House of Osiris'[16] – I made my way to the north end of the western wall that enclosed the Valley Temple's T-shaped hall. I passed through a monolithic doorway and entered a long, sloping, alabaster floored corridor (also oriented north-west) which eventually opened out on to the lower end of the causeway that led up to the Second Pyramid.

From the edge of the causeway I had an unimpeded view of the Sphinx immediately to my north. As long as a city block, as high as a six-storey building it was *perfectly* oriented due east and thus faced the rising sun on the two equinoctial days of the year. Man-headed, lion-bodied, crouched as though ready at last to move its slow thighs after millennia of stony sleep, it had been carved in one piece out of a single ridge of limestone on a site that must have been meticulously preselected. The exceptional characteristic of this site, as well as overlooking the Valley of the Nile, was that its geological make-up incorporated a knoll of hard rock jutting at least 30 feet above the general level of the limestone ridge. From this knoll the head and neck of the Sphinx had been carved, while beneath it the vast rectangle of limestone that would be shaped into the body had been isolated from the surrounding bedrock. The builders had done this by excavating an 18-foot wide, 25-foot deep trench all around it, creating a free-standing monolith.

The first and lasting impression of the Sphinx, and of its enclosure, is that it is very, very old – not a mere handful of thousands of years, like the Fourth Dynasty of Egyptian pharaohs, but vastly, remotely, fabulously old. This was how the Ancient Egyptians in all periods of their history regarded the monument, which they believed guarded the 'Splendid Place of The Beginning of all Time' and which they revered as the focus of 'a great magical power extending over the whole region'.[17]

This, as we have already seen, is the general message of the Inventory Stela. More specifically, it is also the message of the 'Sphinx Stela' erected here in around 1400 BC by Thutmosis IV, an Eighteenth Dynasty pharaoh. Still standing between the paws of the Sphinx, this granite tablet records that prior to Thutmosis's rule the monument had been covered up to its neck in sand. Thutmosis liberated it by clearing all the sand, and erected the stela to commemorate his work.[18]

There have been no significant changes in the climate of the Giza plateau over the last 5000 years.[19] It therefore follows that throughout this entire period the Sphinx enclosure must have been as susceptible to sand encroachment as when Thutmosis cleared it – and, indeed, as it still is today. Recent history proves that the enclosure can fill up rapidly if left unattended. In 1818 Captain Caviglia had it cleared of sand for the purposes of his excavations, and in 1886, when Gaston Maspero came to re-excavate the site, he was obliged to have it cleared of sand once again. Thirty-nine years later, in 1925, the sands had returned in full force and the Sphinx was buried to its neck when the Egyptian Service des Antiquités undertook its clearance and restoration once more.[20]

Does this not suggest that the climate could have been very different when the Sphinx enclosure was carved out? What would have been the sense of creating this immense statue if its destiny were merely to be engulfed by the shifting sands of the eastern Sahara? However, since the Sahara is a young desert, and since the Giza area in particular was wet and relatively fertile 11,000–15,000 years ago, is it not worth considering another scenario altogether? Is it not possible that the Sphinx enclosure was carved out during those distant green millennia when topsoil was still anchored to the surface of the plateau by the roots of grasses and shrubs and when what is now a desert of wind-blown sand more closely resembled the rolling savannahs of modern Kenya and Tanzania?

Under such congenial climatic conditions, the creation of a semi-subterranean monument like the Sphinx would not have outraged common sense. The builders would have had no reason to anticipate the slow desiccation and desertification of the plateau that would ultimately follow.

Yet, is it feasible to imagine that the Sphinx could have been built when Giza was still green – long, long ago?

As we shall see, such ideas are anathema to modern Egyptologists, who are nevertheless obliged to admit (to quote Dr Mark Lehner, director of the Giza Mapping Project) that 'there is no direct way to date the Sphinx itself, because the Sphinx is carved right out of natural rock.'[21] In the absence of more objective tests, Lehner went on to point out, archaeologists had 'to date things *by context*'. And the context of the Sphinx, that is, the Giza necropolis – a well-known Fourth Dynasty site – made it obvious that the Sphinx belonged to the Fourth Dynasty as well.[22]

Such reasoning was not regarded as axiomatic by Lehner's distinguished predecessors in the nineteenth century, who were at one time convinced that the Sphinx long predated the Fourth Dynasty.

Whose Sphinx is it anyway?

In his *Passing of Empires*, published in 1900, the distinguished French Egyptologist Gaston Maspero, who made a special study of the content of the Sphinx Stela erected by Thutmosis IV, wrote:

> The stela of the Sphinx bears, on line 13, the cartouche of Khafre in the middle of a gap ... There, I believe, is an indication of [a renovation and clearance] of the Sphinx carried out under this prince, and consequently the more or less certain proof that the Sphinx was *already covered with sand* during the time of Khufu and his predecessors ...[23]

The equally distinguished Auguste Mariette agreed – naturally enough since he had been the finder of the Inventory Stela (which, as we have seen, asserted matter-of-factly that the Sphinx was standing on the Giza plateau long before the time of Khufu).[24] Also generally concurring were Brugsch (*Egypt under the Pharaohs*, London, 1891), Petrie, Sayce and many other eminent scholars of the period.[25] Travel writers such as John Ward affirmed that 'the Great Sphinx must be numberless years older even than the Pyramids'. And as late as 1904 Wallis Budge, the respected keeper of Egyptian Antiquities at the British Museum, had no hesitation in making this unequivocal assertion:

> The oldest and finest human-headed lion statue is the famous 'Sphinx' at Giza. This marvellous object was in existence in the days of Khafre, the builder of the Second Pyramid, and was, most probably, very old even at that early period ... The Sphinx was thought to be connected in some way with foreigners or with a foreign religion which dated from predynastic times.[26]

Between the beginning and the end of the twentieth century, however, Egyptologists' views about the antiquity of the Sphinx changed dramatically. Today there is not a single orthodox Egyptologist who would even discuss, let alone consider seriously, the wild and irresponsible suggestion, once a commonplace, that the Sphinx might have been built thousands of years before Khafre's reign.

According to Dr Zahi Hawass, for example, director of Giza and Saqqara for the Egyptian Antiquities Organization, many such theories have been put forward but have 'gone with the wind' because 'we Egyptologists have solid evidence to state that the Sphinx is dated to the time of Khafre.'[27]

Likewise, Carol Redmont, an archaeologist at the University of California's Berkeley campus, was incredulous when it was suggested to her that the Sphinx might be thousands of years older than Khafre: 'There's just no way that could be true. The people of that region would not have had the technology, the governing institutions or even the will to build such a structure thousands of years before Khafre's reign.'[28]

When I first started to research this issue, I had assumed, as Hawass appeared to claim, that some incontrovertible new evidence must have been found which had settled the identity of the monument's builder. This was not the case. Indeed there are only *three* 'contextual' reasons why the construction of the anonymous, uninscribed and enigmatic Sphinx is now so confidently attributed to Khafre:

1 **Because of the cartouche of Khafre on line 13 of the Sphinx Stela erected by Thutmosis IV:** Maspero gave a perfectly reasonable explanation for the presence of this cartouche: Thutmosis had been a restorer of the Sphinx and had paid due tribute to an earlier restoration of the monument – one undertaken during the Fourth Dynasty by Khafre. This explanation, which bears the obvious implication that the Sphinx must *already* have been old in Khafre's time, is rejected by modern Egyptologists. With their usual telepathic likemindedness they now agree that Thutmosis put the cartouche on to the stela to recognize that Khafra had been the original builder (and *not* a mere restorer).

Since there had only ever been this single cartouche – and since the texts on either side of it were missing when the stela was excavated, is it not a little premature to come to such hard-and-fast conclusions? What sort of 'science' is it that allows the mere presence of the cartouche of a Fourth Dynasty pharaoh (on a stele erected by an Eighteenth Dynasty pharaoh) to determine the entire identification of an otherwise anonymous monument? Besides, even that cartouche has now flaked off and cannot be examined . . .

2 **Because the Valley Temple next door is also attributed to Khafre:** That attribution (based on statues which may well have

been intrusive) is shaky to say the least. It has nevertheless received the wholehearted endorsement of the Egyptologists, who in the process decided to attribute the Sphinx to Khafre too (since the Sphinx and the Valley Temple are so obviously connected).

3 Because the face of the Sphinx is thought to resemble the intact statue of Khafre found in the pit in the Valley Temple: This, of course, is a matter of opinion. I have never seen the slightest resemblance between the two faces. Nor for that matter had forensic artists from the New York Police Department who had recently been brought in to do an Identikit comparison between the Sphinx and the statue[29] (as we shall see in Part VII).

All in all, therefore, as I stood overlooking the Sphinx in the late afternoon of 16 March 1993, I considered that the jury was still very much out on the correct attribution of this monument – either to Khafre on the one hand or to the architects of an as yet unidentified high civilization of prehistoric antiquity on the other.[30] No matter what the current flavour of the month (or century) happened to be with the Egyptologists, the fact was that *both* scenarios were plausible. What was needed, therefore, was some completely hard and unambiguous evidence which would settle the matter one way or the other.

Part VII

Lord of Eternity

Egypt 2

Chapter 40

Are There Any Secrets Left in Egypt?

During the early evening of 26 November 1922 the British archaeologist Howard Carter, together with his sponsor Lord Carnarvon, entered the tomb of a youthful pharaoh of the Eighteenth Dynasty who had ruled Egypt from 1352–43 BC. The name of that pharaoh, which has since resounded around the world, was Tutankhamun.

Two nights later, on 28 November, the tomb's 'Treasury' was breached. It was filled with a huge golden shrine and gave access to another chamber beyond. Rather unusually, this chamber, although heaped with a dazzling array of precious and beautiful artefacts, had no door: its entrance was watched over by an extraordinarily lifelike effigy of the jackal-headed mortuary god Anubis. With ears erect, the god crouched doglike, forepaws stretched out, on the lid of a gilded wooden casket perhaps four feet long, three feet high and two feet wide.

The Egyptian Museum, Cairo, December 1993
Still perched astride his casket, but now locked away in a dusty glass display case, Anubis held my attention for a long, quiet moment. His effigy had been carved out of stuccoed wood, entirely covered with black resin, then painstakingly inlaid with gold, alabaster, calcite, obsidian and silver – materials used to particular effect in the eyes, which glittered watchfully with an unsettling sense of fierce and

focused intelligence. At the same time his finely etched ribs and lithe musculature gave off an aura of understated strength, energy and grace.

Captured by the force field of this occult and powerful presence, I was vividly reminded of the universal myths of precession I had been studying during the past year. Canine figures moved back and forth among these myths in a manner which at times had seemed almost plotted in the literary sense. I had begun to wonder whether the symbolism of dogs, wolves, jackals, and so on, might have been *deliberately* employed by the long-dead myth-makers to guide initiates through a maze of clues to secret reservoirs of lost scientific knowledge.

Among these reservoirs, I suspected, was the myth of Osiris. Much more than a myth, it had been dramatized and performed each year in Ancient Egypt in the form of a mystery play – a 'plotted' literary artefact, passed down as a treasured tradition since prehistoric times.[1] This tradition, as we saw in Part V, contained values for the rate of precessional motion that were so accurate and so consistent it was extremely difficult to attribute them to chance. Nor did it seem likely to be an accident that the jackal god had been assigned a role centre-stage in the drama, serving as the spirit guide of Osiris on his journey through the underworld.[2] It was tempting, too, to wonder whether there was any significance in the fact that in ancient times Anubis had been referred to by Egyptian priests as the 'guardian of the secret and sacred writings'.[3]) Under the grooved edge of the gilded casket on which his effigy now crouched was found an inscription: 'initiated into the secrets'.[4] Alternative translations of the same hieroglyphic text rendered it variously as 'he who is upon the secrets', and as 'guardian of the secrets'.[5]

But were there any secrets left in Egypt?

After more than a century of intensive archaeological investigations, could the sands of this antique land yield any further surprises?

Bauval's Stars and West's Stones

In 1993 there was an astonishing new discovery which suggested that there was much still to learn about Ancient Egypt. The discoverer, moreover, was not some astigmatic archaeologist sieving his way through the dust of ages but an outsider to the field: Robert Bauval, a Belgian construction engineer with a flair for astronomy who observed a correlation in the sky that the experts had missed in their fixation with the ground at their feet.

What Bauval saw was this: as the three belt stars of the Orion constellation crossed the meridian at Giza they lay in a not quite straight line high in the southern heavens. The lower two stars, *Al Nitak* and *Al Nilam*, formed a perfect diagonal but the third star, *Mintaka*, appeared to be offset to the observer's left, that is, towards the east.

Curiously enough (as we saw in Chapter Thirty-six), this was exactly the site-plan of the three enigmatic pyramids of the Giza plateau. Bauval realized that an aerial view of the Giza necropolis would show the Great Pyramid of Khufu occupying the position of *Al Nitak*, and the Second Pyramid of Khafre occupying the position of *Al Nilam*, while the Third Pyramid of Menkaure was offset to the east of the diagonal formed by the other two – thus completing what seemed at first to be a vast diagram of the stars.

Was this indeed what the Giza pyramids represented? I knew that Bauval's later work, which had been wholeheartedly endorsed by mathematicians and astronomers, had borne out his inspired hunch. His evidence (reviewed fully in Chapter Forty-nine) showed that the three pyramids were an unbelievably precise terrestrial map of the three stars of Orion's belt, accurately reflecting the angles between each of them and even (by means of their respective sizes) providing some indication of their individual magnitudes.[6] Moreover, this map extended outwards to the north and south to encompass several other structures on the Giza plateau – once again with faultless precision.[7] However, the real surprise revealed by Bauval's astronomical calculations was this: despite the fact that some aspects of the Great Pyramid did relate astronomically to the Pyramid Age, the Giza monuments as a whole were so arranged as to provide a picture of the skies (which alter their appearance down the ages as a result of precession of the equinoxes) not as they had looked in the Fourth Dynasty around 2500 BC, but as they had looked – and *only* as they had looked – around the year 10,450 BC.[8]

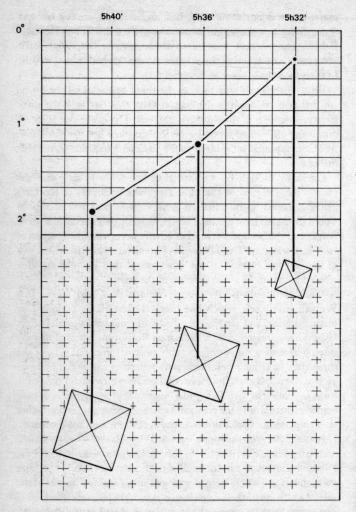

The three pyramids of Giza plotted against the three belt stars of the Orion constellation.

I had come to Egypt to go over the Giza site with Robert Bauval and to question him about his star-correlation theory. In addition I wanted to canvass his views on what sort of human society, if any, could have had the technological knowhow, such a very long while ago, to measure accurately the altitudes of the stars and to devise a plan as mathematical and ambitious as that of the Giza necropolis.

I had also come to meet another researcher who had challenged the orthodox chronology of Ancient Egypt with a well-founded claim to have found hard evidence of a high civilization in the Nile Valley in 10,000 BC or earlier. Like Bauval's astronomical data, the evidence had always been available but had failed to attract the attention of established Egyptologists. The man responsible for bringing it before the public now was the American scholar, John Anthony West, who argued that the specialists had missed it – not because they had failed to find it, but because they had found it and had failed to interpret it properly.[9]

West's evidence focused on certain key structures, notably the Great Sphinx and the Valley Temple at Giza and, much farther south, the mysterious Osireion at Abydos. He argued that these desert monuments showed many scientifically unmistakable signs of having been weathered by *water*, an erosive agent they could only have been exposed to in sufficient quantities during the damp 'pluvial' period that accompanied the end of the last Ice Age around the eleventh millennium BC.[10] The implication of this peculiar and extremely distinctive pattern of 'precipitation induced' weathering, was that the Osireion, the Sphinx, and other associated structures were built before 10,000 BC.[11]

A British investigative journalist summed up the effect:

> West is really an academic's worst nightmare, because here comes somebody way out of left-field with a thoroughly well thought out, well presented, coherently described theory, full of data they can't refute, and it pulls the rug out from beneath their feet. So how do they deal with it? They ignore it. They hope it'll go away . . . and it won't go away.[12]

The reason the new theory would not, under any circumstances, go away, despite its refection by droves of 'competent Egyptologists', was that it had won widespread support from another scientific branch of scholarship – geology. Dr Robert Schoch, a professor of Geology at Boston University, had played a prominent role in validating West's estimates concerning the true age of the Sphinx, and his views had been endorsed by almost 300 of his peers at the 1992 annual convention of the Geological Society of America.[13]

Since then, most often out of the public eye, an acrimonious dispute had begun to smoulder between the geologists and the Egyptologists.[14] And though very few people other than John West were prepared to say as much, what was at stake in this dispute was a complete upheaval in accepted views about the evolution of human civilization.

According to West:

> We are told that the evolution of human civilization is a linear process – that it goes from stupid cavemen to smart old us with our hydrogen bombs and striped toothpaste. But the proof that the Sphinx is many, many thousands of years older than the archaeologists think it is, that it preceded by many thousands of years even dynastic Egypt, means that there must have been, at some distant point in history, a high and sophisticated civilization – just as all the legends affirm.[15]

My own travels and research during the preceeding four years had opened my eyes to the electrifying possibility that those legends could be true, and this was why I had come back to Egypt to meet West and Bauval. I was struck by the way in which their hitherto disparate lines of enquiry[16] had converged so convincingly on what appeared to be the astronomical and geological fingerprints of a lost civilization, one that might or might not have originated in the Nile Valley but that seemed to have had a presence here as far back as the eleventh millennium BC.

The way of the jackal

Anubis, guardian of the secrets, god of the funerary chamber, jackal-headed opener of the ways of the dead, guide and companion of Osiris . . .

It was around five o'clock in the afternoon, closing-time at the Cairo Museum, when Santha pronounced herself satisfied with her photographs of the sinister black effigy. Down below us guards were whistling and clapping their hands as they sought to herd the last few sightseers out of the halls, but up on the second floor of the hundred-year-old building, where ancient Anubis crouched in his millennial watchfulness, all was quiet, all was still.

We left the sombre museum and walked down into the sunlight still bathing Cairo's bustling Tahrir Square.

Anubis, I reflected, had shared his duties as spirit guide and guardian of the secret writings with another god whose type and symbol had also been the jackal and whose name, Upuaut, literally meant Opener of the Ways.[17] Both these canine deities had been linked since time immemorial with the ancient town of Abydos in upper Egypt, the original god of which, Khenti-Amentiu (the strangely named 'Foremost of the Westerners') had also been represented as a member of the dog family, usually lying recumbent on a black standard.[18]

Was there any significance in the repeated recurrence at Abydos of all this mythical and symbolic doggishness, with its promise of high secrets waiting to unfold? It seemed worthwhile trying to find out since the extensive ruins there included the structure known as the Osireion, which West's geological research had indicated might be far older than the archaeologists thought. Besides, I had already arranged to meet West in a few days in the upper Egyptian town of Luxor, less than 200 kilometres south of Abydos. Rather than flying directly to Luxor from Cairo, as I had originally planned, I now realized that it would be perfectly feasible to go by road and to visit Abydos and a number of other sites along the way.

Our driver, Mohamed Walili, was waiting for us in an underground car-park just off Tahrir Square. A large genial, elderly man, he owned a battered white Peugeot taxi normally to be found standing in the rank outside the Mena House hotel at Giza. Over the last few years, on our frequent research trips to Cairo, we had struck up a friendship with him and he now worked with us whenever we were in Egypt. We haggled for some time about the appropriate daily rate for the long return journey to Abydos and Luxor. Many matters had to be taken into account, including the fact that some of the areas we would be passing through had recently been targets of terrorist attacks by Islamic militants. Eventually we agreed on a price and arranged to set off early the following morning.

Chapter 41

City of the Sun, Chamber of the Jackal

Mohamed picked us up at our hotel in Heliopolis at 6 a. m. when it was still half dark.

We drank small cups of thick black coffee at a roadside stall and then drove west, along dusty streets still almost deserted, towards the River Nile. I had asked Mohamed to take us through Maydan al-Massallah Square, which was dominated by one of the world's oldest intact Egyptian obelisks.[1] Weighing an estimated 350 tons, this was a pink granite monolith, 170 feet high, erected by Pharaoh Senuseret I (1971–1928 BC). It had originally been one of a pair at the gateway of the great Heliopolitan Temple of the Sun. In the 4000 years since then the temple itself had entirely vanished, as had the second obelisk. Indeed, almost all of ancient Heliopolis had now been obliterated, cannibalized for its handsome dressed stones and ready-made building materials by countless generations of the citizens of Cairo.[2]

Heliopolis (City of the Sun) was referred to in the Bible as On but was originally known in the Egyptian language as Innu, or Innu Mehret – meaning 'the pillar' or 'the northern pillar'.[3] It was a district of immense sanctity, associated with a strange group of nine solar and stellar deities, and was old beyond reckoning when Senuseret chose it as the site for his obelisk. Indeed, together with Giza (and the distant southern city of Abydos) Innu/Heliopolis was believed to have been part of the first land that emerged from the primeval waters at the moment of creation, the land of the 'First Time', where the gods had commenced their rule on earth.[4]

Heliopolitan theology rested on a creation-myth distinguished by a number of unique and curious features. It taught that in the beginning the universe had been filled with a dark, watery nothingness, called the Nun. Out of this inert cosmic ocean (described as 'shapeless, black with the blackness of the blackest night') rose a mound of dry land on which Ra, the Sun God, materialized in his self-created form as Atum (sometimes depicted as an old bearded man leaning on a staff):[5]

> The sky had not been created, the earth had not been created, the children of the earth and the reptiles had not been fashioned in that place . . . I, Atum, was one by myself . . . There existed no other who worked with me . . .[6]

Conscious of being alone, this blessed and immortal being contrived to create two divine offspring, Shu, god of the air and dryness, and Tefnut the goddess of moisture: 'I thrust my phallus into my closed hand. I made my seed to enter my hand. I poured it into my own mouth. I evacuated under the form of Shu, I passed water under the form of Tefnut.'[7]

Despite such apparently inauspicious beginnings, Shu and Tefnut (who were always described as 'Twins' and frequently depicted as lions) grew to maturity, copulated and produced offspring of their own: Geb the god of the earth and Nut, the goddess of the sky. These two also mated, creating Osiris and Isis, Set and Nepthys, and so completed the Ennead, the full company of the Nine Gods of Heliopolis. Of the nine, Ra, Shu, Geb and Osiris were said to have ruled in Egypt as kings, followed by Horus, and lastly – for 3226 years – by the Ibis-headed wisdom god Thoth.[8]

Who were these people – or creatures, or beings, or gods? Were they figments of the priestly imagination, or symbols, or ciphers? Were the stories told about them vivid myth memories of real events which had taken place thousands of years previously? Or were they, perhaps, part of a coded message from the ancients that had been transmitting itself over and over again down the epochs – a message only now beginning to be unravelled and understood?

Such notions seemed fanciful. Nevertheless I could hardly forget that out of this very same Heliopolitan tradition the great myth of Isis and Osiris had flowed, covertly transmitting an accurate calculus for the rate of precessional motion. Moreover the priests of Innu, whose responsibility it had been to guard and nurture such traditions, had been renowned throughout Egypt for their high wisdom and their proficiency in prophecy, astronomy, mathematics, architecture and the magic arts. They were also famous for their possession of a powerful and sacred object known as the Benben.[9]

The Egyptians called Heliopolis Innu, the pillar, because tradition had it that the Benben had been kept here in remote pre-dynastic times, when it had balanced on top of a pillar of rough-hewn stone.

The Benben was believed to have fallen from the skies. Unfortunately, it had been lost so long before that its appearance was no longer remembered by the time Senuseret took the throne in 1971 BC. In that period (the Twelfth Dynasty) all that was clearly recalled was that the Benben had been pyramidal in form, thus providing (together with the pillar on which it stood) a prototype for the shape of all future obelisks. The name Benben was likewise applied to the pyramidion, or apex stone, usually placed on top of pyramids.[10] In a symbolic sense, it was also associated closely and directly with Ra–Atum, of whom the ancient texts said, 'You became high on the height; you rose up as the Benben stone in the Mansion of the Phoenix . . .'[11]

Mansion of the Phoenix described the original temple at Heliopolis where the Benben had been housed. It reflected the fact that the mysterious object had also served as an enduring symbol for the mythical Phoenix, the divine Bennu bird whose appearances and disappearances were believed to be linked to violent cosmic cycles and to the destruction and rebirth of world ages.[12]

Conections and similarities

Driving through the suburbs of Heliopolis at around 6.30 in the morning I closed my eyes and tried to summon up a picture of the landscape as it might have looked in the mythical First Time after the Island of Creation[13] – the primordial mound of Ra–Atum – had risen out of the flood waters of the Nun. It was tempting to see a connection between this imagery and the Andean traditions that spoke of the emergence of the civilizer god Viracocha from the waters of Lake Titicaca after an earth-destroying flood. Moreover there was the figure of Osiris to consider – a conspicuously *bearded* figure, like Viracocha, and like Quetzalcoatl as well – remembered for having abolished cannibalism among the Egyptians, for having taught them agriculture and animal husbandry, and for introducing them to such arts as writing, architecture, and music.[14]

The similarities between the Old and New World traditions were hard to miss but even harder to interpret. It was possible they were just a series of beguiling coincidences. On the other hand, it was possible that they might reveal the fingerprints of an ancient and unidentified global civilization – fingerprints that were essentially the same whether they appeared in the myths of Central America, or of the high Andes, or of Egypt. The priests of Heliopolis, after all, had taught of the creation, but who had taught *them*? Had they sprung out of nowhere, or was it more likely that their doctrine, with all its complex symbolism, was the product of a long refinement of religious ideas?

If so, when and where had these ideas developed?

I looked up to discover that we had left Heliopolis behind and were winding our way through the noisy and crowded streets of downtown Cairo. We crossed over to the west bank of the Nile by way of the 6 October Bridge and soon afterwards entered Giza. Fifteen minutes later, passing the massive bulk of the Great Pyramid on our right, we turned south on the road to upper Egypt, a road which followed the meridional course of the world's longest river through a landscape of palms and green fields fringed by the encroaching red wastes of pitiless deserts.

The ideas of the Heliopolitan priesthood had influenced every aspect of secular and religious life in Ancient Egypt, but had those ideas developed locally, or had they been introduced to the Nile Valley from elsewhere? The traditions of the Egyptians provided an unambiguous answer to questions such as these. All the wisdom of Heliopolis was a legacy, they said, and this legacy had been passed to humankind by the gods.

Gift of the Gods?

About ten miles south of the Great Pyramid we pulled off the main road to visit the necropolis of Saqqara. Rearing up on the desert's edge, the site was dominated by a six-tier ziggurat, the step-pyramid of the Third Dynasty Pharaoh Zoser. This imposing monument, almost 200 feet tall, was dated to approximately 2650 BC. It stood within its own compound, surrounded by an elegant enclosure wall, and was reckoned by archaeologists to be the earliest massive construction of stone ever attempted by humanity.[15] Tradition had it that its architect was the legendary Imhotep, 'Great of Magic', a high priest of Heliopolis, whose other titles were Sage, Sorcerer, Astronomer and Doctor.[16]

We shall have more to say about the step-pyramid and its builder in a later chapter, but on this occasion I had not come to Saqqara to see it. My sole objective was to spend a few moments in the burial chamber of the nearby pyramid of Unas, a Fifth Dynasty pharaoh who had reigned from 2356 to 2323 BC.[17] The walls of this chamber, which I had visited several times before, were inscribed from floor to ceiling with the most ancient of the Pyramid Texts, an extravaganza of hieroglyphic inscriptions giving voice to a range of remarkable ideas – in acute contrast to the mute and unadorned interiors of the Fourth Dynasty pyramids at Giza.

A phenomenon exclusively of the Fifth and Sixth Dynasties (2465–2152 BC), the Pyramid Texts were sacred writings, parts of which were thought to have been composed by the Heliopolitan priesthood in the late third millennium BC, and parts of which had been received and handed down by them from pre-dynastic times.[18] It was the latter parts of these Texts, dating to a remote and impenetrable antiquity, which had particularly aroused my curiosity when I had begun to research them a few months previously. I had also been amused – and a little intrigued – by the strange way that nineteenth century French archaeologists appeared almost to have been directed to the hidden chamber of the Pyramid Texts by a mythological 'opener of the ways.' According to reasonably well-documented reports, an Egyptian foreman of the excavations at Saqqara had been up and about at dawn one morning and had found

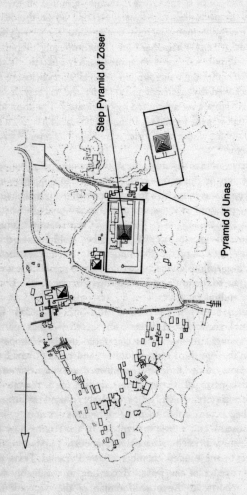

Step Pyramid of Zoser

Pyramid of Unas

Saqqara.

himself by the side of a ruined pyramid looking into the bright amber eyes of a lone desert jackal:

> It was as if the animal were taunting his human observer . . . and inviting the puzzled man to chase him. Slowly the jackal sauntered towards the north face of the pyramid, stopping for a moment before disappearing into a hole. The bemused Arab decided to follow his lead. After slipping through the narrow hole, he found himself crawling into the dark bowels of the pyramid. Soon he emerged into a chamber and, lifting his light, saw that the walls were covered from top to bottom with hieroglyphic inscriptions. These were carved with exquisite craftsmanship into the solid limestone and painted over with turquoise and gold.'[19]

Today the hieroglyph-lined chamber beneath the ruined pyramid of Unas is still reached through the north face by the long descending passage the French archaeological team excavated soon after the foreman's astonishing discovery. The chamber consists of two rectangular rooms separated by a partition wall, into which is let a low doorway. Both rooms are covered by a gabled ceiling painted with myriads of stars. Emerging stooped from the cramped passage, Santha and I entered the first of the two rooms and passed through the connecting doorway into the second. This was the tomb chamber proper, with the massive black granite sarcophagus of Unas at its western end and the strange utterances of the Pyramid Texts proclaiming themselves from every wall.

Speaking to us directly (rather than through riddles and mathematical legerdemain like the unadorned walls of the Great Pyramid), what were the hieroglyphs saying? I knew that the answer depended to some extent on which translation you were using, largely because the language of the Pyramid Texts contained so many archaic forms and so many unfamiliar mythological allusions that scholars were obliged to fill in the gaps in their knowledge with guesswork.[20] Nevertheless it was generally agreed that the late R. O. Faulkner, a professor of the Ancient Egyptian Language at University College London, had produced the most authoritative version.[21]

Faulkner, whose translation I had studied line by line, described the Texts as constituting 'the oldest corpus of Egyptian religious and funerary literature now extant' and added, 'they are the least corrupt of all such collections and are of fundamental importance to the student of Egyptian religion . . . '[22] The reason *why* the Texts were so important (as many scholars agreed), was that they were the last completely open channel connecting the relatively short period of the past that humanity remembers to the far longer period that has been forgotten: 'They vaguely disclose to us a vanished world of thought and speech, the last of the unnumbered aeons through which prehistoric man has passed, till finally he . . . enters the historic age.'[23]

It was hard to disagree with sentiments like these: the Texts did disclose a vanished world. But what intrigued me most about this world was the possibility that it might have been inhabited not only by primitive savages (as one would have expected in remote prehistory) but, paradoxically, by men and women whose minds had been enlightened by a scientific understanding of the cosmos. The overall picture was equivocal: there were genuinely primitive elements locked into the Pyramid Texts alongside the loftier sequences of ideas. Nevertheless, every time I immersed myself in what Egyptologists call 'these ancient spells', I was impressed by the strange glimpses they seemed to afford of a high intelligence at work, darting from behind layers of incomprehension, reporting on experiences that 'prehistoric man' should never have had and expressing notions he should never have been able to formulate. In short, the effect the Texts achieved through the medium of hieroglyphs was akin to the effect the Great Pyramid achieved through the medium of architecture. In both cases the dominant impression was of *anachronism* – of advanced technological processes used or described at a period in human history when there was supposed to have been no technology at all . . .

Chapter 42

Anachronisms and Enigmas

I looked around the grey-walled chamber of Unas, up and down the long registers of hieroglyphs in which the Pyramid Texts were inscribed. They were written in a dead language. Nevertheless, the constant affirmation, repeated over and over again in these ancient compositions, was that of *life* – eternal life – which was to be achieved through the pharaoh's rebirth as a star in the constellation of Orion. As the reader will recall from Chapter Nineteen, (where we compared Egyptian beliefs with those of Ancient Mexico), there were several utterances which voiced this aspiration explicitly:

> Oh King, you are this Great Star, the Companion of Orion, who traverses the sky with Orion . . . you ascend from the east of the sky being renewed in your due season, and rejuvenated in your due time . . . '[1]

Though undeniably beautiful there was nothing inherently extraordinary about these sentiments, and it was by no means impossible to attribute them to a people assessed by the French archaeologist Gaston Maspero as having 'always remained half savage'.[2] Furthermore, since Maspero had been the first Egyptologist to enter the pyramid of Unas,[3] and was considered a great authority on the Texts, it was hardly surprising that his opinions should have shaped all academic responses to this literature since he began to publish translations from it in the 1880s.[4] Maspero (with a little help from a jackal) had brought the Pyramid Texts to the world. Thereafter, the dominance of his particular prejudices about the past had functioned as a filter on knowledge, inhibiting variant interpretations of the more opaque or puzzling utterances. This seemed to me to be unfortunate to say the least. What it meant was that, despite the technical and scientific puzzles raised by monuments like the Great Pyramid at Giza, scholars had ignored the implications of some striking passages in the Texts.

These passages sounded suspiciously like attempts to express complex technical and scientific imagery *in an entirely inappropriate idiom*. Maybe it was coincidence, but the result resembled the outcome that we might expect today if we were to try to translate Einstein's Theory of Relativity into Chaucerian English or to describe a supersonic aircraft in vocabulary derived from Middle High German.

Broken images of a lost technology?

Take for example some of the peculiar equipment and accessories designated for the pharaoh's use as he journeyed to his eternal resting place among the stars:

> The gods who are in the sky are brought to you, the gods who are on earth assemble for you, they place their hands under you, they make a *ladder* for you that you may ascend on it into the sky, the doors of the sky are thrown open to you, the doors of the starry firmament are thrown open for you.[5]

The ascending pharaoh was identified with, and frequently referred to, as 'an Osiris'. Osiris himself, as we have seen, was frequently linked to and associated with the constellation of Orion. Osiris-Orion was said to have been the first to have climbed the great ladder the gods had made. And several utterances left no doubt that this ladder had not extended upwards from earth to heaven but downwards from heaven to earth. It was described as a *rope-ladder*[6] and the belief was that it had hung from an 'iron plate' suspended in the sky.[7]

Were we dealing here, I wondered simply with the bizarre

imaginings of half-savage priests? Or might there be some other explanation for allusions such as these?

In Utterance 261, 'The King is a flame, moving before the wind to the end of the sky and to the end of the earth . . . the King travels the air and traverses the earth . . . there is brought to him a way of ascent to the sky . . .'[8]

Switching to dialogue, Utterance 310 proclaimed,

' O you whose vision is in his face and whose vision is in the back of his head, bring this to me!'

'What ferry-boat shall be brought to you?'

'Bring me: "It-flies-and-alights".'[9]

Utterance 332, supposedly spoken by the King himself, confided, 'I am this one who has escaped from the coiled serpent, I have ascended in a blast of fire having turned myself about. The two skies go to me.[10]

And in Utterance 669 it was asked, 'Wherewith can the King be made to fly-up?'

The reply was given: 'There shall be brought to you the *Hnw*-bark [italicized word unstranslatable] and the . . . [text missing] of the *hn*-bird [italicized word untranslatable]. You shall fly up therewith . . . You shall fly up and alight.'[11]

Other passages also seemed to me worthy of more thorough investigation than they have received from scholars. Here are a few examples:

O my father, great King, the aperture of the sky-window is opened for you.[12]

'The door of the sky at the horizon opens to you, the gods are glad at meeting you . . . May you sit on this iron throne of yours, as the Great One who is in Heliopolis.[13]

O King, may you ascend . . . The sky reels at you, the earth quakes at you, the Imperishable Stars are afraid of you. I have come to you, O you whose seats are hidden, that I may embrace you in the sky . . . [14]

The earth speaks, the gate of the earth god is open, the doors of Geb are opened for you . . . May you remove yourself to the sky upon your iron throne.[15]

> O my father the King, such is your going when you have gone as a god, your travelling as a celestial being . . . you stand in the Conclaves of the horizon . . . and sit on this throne of iron at which the gods marvel . . . [16]

The constant references to iron, though easy to overlook, were puzzling. Iron, I knew, had been a rare metal in Ancient Egypt, particularly in the Pyramid Age when it had supposedly only been available in meteoritic form.[17] Yet here, in the Pyramid Texts, there seemed to be an embarrassment of iron riches: iron plates in the sky, iron thrones, and elsewhere an iron sceptre (Utterance 665C) and even iron bones for the King (Utterances 325, 684 and 723).[18]

In the Ancient Egyptian language the name for iron had been *bja*, a word that meant literally 'metal of heaven' or 'divine metal'.[19] The knowledge of iron was thus regarded as yet another gift from the gods . . .

Repositories of a lost science?

What other fingerprints might these gods have left behind in the Pyramid Texts?[20]

In my readings – here and there among the most archaic of the Utterances – I had come across several metaphors that seemed to refer to the passage of *epochs of precessional time*. These metaphors stood out from the surrounding material because they were expressed in what had become a clear and familiar terminology to me: that of the archaic scientific language identified by Santillana and von Dechend in *Hamlet's Mill*.[21]

The reader may recall that a cosmic 'diagram' of the four props of the sky was one of the standard thought tools employed in that ancient language. Its purpose was to assist visualisation of the four imaginary bands conceived as framing, supporting and defining a precessional world age. These were what astronomers call the 'equinoctial and solstitial colures' and were seen as hooping down from the celestial north pole and marking the four constellations against the background of which, for periods of 2160 years at a time, the sun would consistently rise on the spring and autumn equinoxes and on the winter and summer solstices.[22]

The Pyramid Texts appear to contain several versions of this diagram. Moreover, as is so often the case with prehistoric myths which transmit hard astronomical data, the precessional symbolism is interwoven tightly with violent images of terrestrial destruction – as though to suggest that the 'breaking of the mill of heaven', that is the transition every 2160 years from one zodiacal age to another, could under ill-omened circumstances bring catastrophic influences to bear on terrestrial events.

Thus it was said that

> Ra–Atum, the god who created himself, was originally king over gods and men together but mankind schemed against his sovereignty, for he began to grow old, his bones became silver, his flesh gold and his hair [as] lapis lazuli.[23]

When he realized what was happening, the ageing Sun God (so reminiscent of Tonatiuh, the bloodthirsty Fifth Sun of the Aztecs) determined that he would punish this insurrection by killing off most of the human race. The instrument of the havoc he unleashed was symbolized at times as a raging lioness wading in blood and at times as the fearsome lion-headed goddess Sekhmet who 'poured fire out of herself' and savaged mankind in an ecstasy of slaughter.[24]

The terrible destruction continued unabated for a long period. Then at last Ra intervened to save the lives of a 'remnant', the ancestors of present humanity. This intervention took the form of a flood which the lioness thirstily lapped up and then fell asleep. When she awoke, she was no longer interested in pursuing the destruction, and peace descended upon the devastated world.[25]

Meanwhile Ra had resolved to 'draw away' from what was left of his creation: 'As I live my heart is weary of staying with Mankind. I have gone on killing them [almost] to the very last one, so the [insignificant] remnant is not my affair . . .'[26]

The Sun God then rose into the sky on the back of the sky-goddess Nut who (for the purposes of the precessional metaphor about to be delivered) had transformed herself into a cow. Before very long – in a close analogy to the 'shaft-tree' that 'shivered' on Amlodhi's wildly gyrating mill – the cow grew 'dizzy and began to shake and to tremble because she was so high above the earth.'[27] When she complained to

Ra about this precarious state of affairs he commanded, 'Let my son Shu be put beneath Nut to keep guard for me over the heavenly supports – which exist in the twilight. Put her above your head and keep her there.'[28] As soon as Shu had taken his place beneath the cow and had stabilized her body, 'the heavens above and the earth beneath came into being'. At the same moment, 'the four legs of the cow', as Egyptologist Wallis Budge commented in his classic study *The Gods of the Egyptians*, 'became the four props of heaven at the four cardinal points'.[29]

Like most scholars, Budge understandably assumed that the 'cardinal points' referred to in this Ancient Egyptian tradition had strictly terrestrial connotations and that 'heaven' represented nothing more than the sky above our heads. He took it for granted that the point of the metaphor was for us to envisage the cow's four legs as positioned at the four points of the compass – north, south, east and west. He also thought – and even today few Egyptologists would disagree with him – that the simple-minded priests of Heliopolis had actually *believed* that the sky had four corners which were supported on four legs and that Shu, 'the skybearer *par excellence*', had stood immobile like a pillar at the centre of the whole edifice.[30]

Reinterpreted in the light of Santillana's and von Dechend's findings, however, Shu and the four legs of the celestial cow look much more like the components of an archaic scientific symbol depicting the frame of a precessional world age – the polar axis (Shu) and the colures (the four legs or 'props' marking the equinoctial and solstitial cardinal points in the annual round of the sun).

Moreover, it is tempting to speculate *which* world age was being signalled here . . .

With a cow involved it could have been the Age of Taurus, although the Egyptians knew the difference between bulls and cows as well as anyone. But a much more likely contender – at any rate on purely symbolic grounds – the age of Leo, from approximately 10,970 to 8810 BC.[31] The reason is that Sekhmet, the agent of the destruction of Mankind referred to in the myth, was *leonine* in form. What better way to symbolize the troubled birth of the new world age of Leo than to depict its harbinger as a rampaging lion, particularly since the Age of Leo coincided with the final ferocious meltdown of the last Ice Age, during which huge numbers of animal species all over the earth were suddenly and violently rendered extinct.'[32] Mankind survived the immense floods and earthquakes and rapid changes of climate that took place, but very probably in much reduced numbers and much reduced circumstances.

The train of the Sun and the dweller in Sirius

Of course the ability to recognize and define precessional world ages in myth implies that the Ancient Egyptians posessed better observational astronomy and a more sophisticated understanding of the mechanics of the solar system than any ancient people have hitherto been credited with.[33] There is no doubt that knowledge of this calibre, if it existed at all, would have been highly regarded by the Ancient Egyptians, who would have transmitted it from generation to generation in a secretive manner. Indeed, it would have ranked among the highest arcana entrusted to the keeping of the priestly elite at Heliopolis and would have been passed on, in the main, through an oral and initiatory tradition.[34] If, by chance it had found its way into the Pyramid Texts, is it not likely that its form would have been veiled by metaphors and allegories?

I walked slowly across the dusty floor of the tomb chamber of Unas, noting the heavy stillness in the air, casting my eyes over the faded blue and gold inscriptions. Expressed in coded language several millennia before Copernicus and Galileo, some of the passages inscribed on these walls seemed to offer clues to the true heliocentric nature of the solar system.

In one, for example, Ra, the Sun God, was depicted as seated upon an iron throne encircled by lesser gods who moved around him constantly and who were said to be 'in his train'.[35] Likewise, in another passage, the deceased Pharaoh was urged to 'stand at the head of the two halves of the sky and weigh the words of the gods, the aged ones, who revolve around Ra.'[36]

If the 'aged ones' and the 'encircling gods' revolving around Ra should prove to be parts of a terminology referring to the planets of our solar system, the original authors of the Pyramid Texts must have enjoyed access to some remarkably advanced astronomical data. They must have known that the earth and the planets revolved around the sun rather than vice versa.[37] The problem this raises is that neither the Ancient Egyptians at any stage in their history, nor even their successors the Greeks, or for that matter the Europeans until the Renaissance, are supposed to have possessed cosmological data of anything approaching this quality. How, therefore, can its presence be explained in compositions which date back to the dawn of Egyptian civilization?

Another (and perhaps related) mystery concerns the star Sirius, which the Egyptians identified with Isis, the sister and consort of Osiris and the mother of Horus. In a passage addressed to Osiris himself, the Pyramid Texts state:

> Thy sister Isis cometh unto thee rejoicing in her love for thee. Thou settest her upon thee, thy issue entereth into her, and she becometh great with child like the star Sept [Sirius, the Dog Star]. Horus–Sept cometh forth from thee in the form of Horus, dweller in Sept.[38]

Many interpretations of this passage are, of course, possible. What intrigued me, however, was the clear implication that Sirius was to be regarded as a *dual entity* in some way comparable to a woman 'great with child'. Moreover, after the birth (or coming forth) of that child, the text makes a special point of reminding us that Horus remained a 'dweller in Sept', presumably suggesting that he stayed close to his mother.

Sirius is an unusual star. A sparkling point of light particularly prominent in the winter months in the night skies of the northern hemisphere, it consists of a *binary* star system, i. e. it is in fact, as the Pyramid Texts suggest, a 'dual entity'. The major component, Sirius-A, is what we see. Sirius-B, on the other hand – the dwarf-star which revolves around Sirius A – is absolutely invisible to the naked eye. Its existence did not become known to Western science until 1862, when US astronomer Alvin Clark spotted it through one of the largest and most advanced telescopes of the day.[39] How could the scribes who wrote the Pyramid Texts possibly have obtained the information that Sirius was two stars in one?

In *The Sirius Mystery*, an important book published in 1976, I knew that the American author Robert Temple had offered some extraordinary answers to this question.[40] His study focused on the traditional beliefs of the Dogon tribe of West Africa – beliefs in which the binary character of Sirius was explicitly described and in which the correct figure of fifty years was given for the period of the orbit of Sirius-B around Sirius-A.[41] Temple argued cogently that this high quality technical information had been passed down to the Dogon from the *Ancient Egyptians* through a process of cultural diffusion, and that it was to the Ancient Egyptians that we should look for an answer to the Sirius mystery. He also concluded that the ancient Egyptians must have received the information from intelligent beings from the region of Sirius'.[42]

Like Temple, I had begun to suspect that the more advanced and sophisticated elements of Egyptian science made sense only if they were understood as parts of an inheritance. Unlike Temple, I saw no urgent reason to attribute that inheritance to extra-terrestrials. To my mind the anomalous star knowledge the Heliopolitan priests had apparently possessed was more plausibly explained as the legacy of a lost human civilization which, against the current of history, had achieved a high level of technological advancement in remote antiquity. It seemed to me that the building of an instrument capable of detecting Sirius-B might not have been beyond the ingenuity of the unknown explorers and scientists who originated the remarkable maps of the prehistoric world discussed in Part I. Nor would it have daunted the unknown astronomers and measurers of time who bequeathed to the Ancient Maya a calendar of amazing complexity, a data-base about the movements of the heavenly bodies which could only have been the product of thousands of years of accurately recorded observations, and a facility with very large numbers that seemed more appropriate to the needs of a complex technological society than to those of a 'primitive' Central American kingdom.[43]

Millions of years and the movements of the stars

Very large numbers also appeared in the Pyramid Texts, in the symbolic 'boat of millions of years', for example, in which the Sun God was said to navigate the dark and airless wastes of interstellar space.[44] Thoth, the god of wisdom ('he who reckons in heaven, the counter of the stars, the measurer of the earth') was specifically empowered to grant a life of millions of years to the deceased pharaoh.[45] Osiris, 'king of eternity, lord of everlasting', was described as traversing millions of years in his life.'[46] And figures like 'tens of millions of years' (as well as the more mind-boggling 'one million of millions of years')[47] occurred often enough to suggest that some elements at least of Ancient Egyptian culture must have evolved for the convenience of scientifically minded people with more than passing insight into the immensity of time.

Such a people would, of course, have required an excellent calendar – one that would have facilitated complex and accurate calculations. It was therefore not surprising to learn that the Ancient Egyptians, like the Maya, had possessed such a calendar and that their understanding of its workings seemed to have declined, rather than improved, as the ages went by.[48] It was tempting to see this as the gradual erosion of a corpus of knowledge inherited an extremely long time ago, an impression supported by the Ancient Egyptians themselves, who made no secret of their belief that their calendar was a legacy which they had received 'from the gods'.

We consider the possible identity of these gods in more detail in the following chapters. Whoever they were, they must have spent a great deal of their time observing the stars, and they had accumulated a fund of advanced and specialized knowledge concerning the star Sirius in particular. Further evidence for this came in the form of the most useful calendrical gift which the gods supposedly gave to the Egyptians: the *Sothic* (or Sirian) cycle.[49]

The Sothic cycle was based on what is referred to in technical jargon as 'the periodic return of the heliacal rising of Sirius', which is the first appearance of this star after a seasonal absence, rising at dawn just ahead of the sun in the eastern portion of the sky.[50] In the case of Sirius the interval between one such rising and the next amounts to *exactly* 365.25 days – a mathematically harmonious figure, uncomplicated by further decimal points, which is just twelve minutes longer than the duration of the solar year.[51]

The curious thing about Sirius is that out of an estimated 2000 stars in the heavens visible to the naked eye it is the only one to rise heliacally at this precise and nicely rounded interval of 365 and a quarter days – a unique product of its 'proper motion' (the speed of its own movement through space) combined with the effects of precession of the equinoxes.[52] Moreover, it is known that the day of the heliacal rising of Sirius – New Year's Day in the Ancient Egyptian calendar – was traditionally calculated at Heliopolis, where the Pyramid Texts were compiled, and announced ahead of time to all the other major temples up and down the Nile.[53]

I remembered that Sirius was referred to directly in the Pyramid Texts by 'her name of the New Year'.[54] Together with other relevant utterances (e.g., 669[55]), this confirmed that the Sothic calendar was *at least* as old as the Texts themselves,[56] and their origins stretched back into the mists of distant antiquity. The great enigma, therefore, is this: in such an early period, who could have possessed the necessary knowhow to observe and take note of the coincidence of the period of 365.25 days with the heliacal rising of Sirius – a coincidence described by the French mathematician R.A. Schwaller de Lubicz as 'an entirely exceptional celestial phenomenon'?[57]

> We cannot but admire the greatness of a science capable of discovering such a coincidence. The double star of Sirius was chosen because it was the only star that moves the needed distance and in the right direction against the background of the other stars. This fact, known four thousand years before our time and forgotten until our day, obviously demands an extraordinary and prolonged observation of the sky.[58]

It was such a legacy – built out of long centuries of precise observational astronomy and scientific record-keeping – that Egypt seems to have benefited from at the beginning of the historical period and that was expressed in the Pyramid Texts.

In this, too, there lies a mystery . . .

Copies, or translations?

Writing in 1934, the year of his death, Wallis Budge, former Keeper of Egyptian Antiquities at the British Museum and the author of an authoritative hieroglyphic dictionary,[59] made this frank admission:

The Pyramid Texts are full of difficulties of every kind. The exact meanings of a large number of words found in them are unknown . . . The construction of the sentence often baffles all attempts to translate it, and when it contains wholly unknown words it becomes an unsolved riddle. It is only reasonable to suppose that these texts were often used for funerary purposes, but it is quite clear that their period of use in Egypt was little more than one hundred years. Why they were suddenly brought into use at the end of the Fifth Dynasty and ceased to be used at the end of the Sixth Dynasty is inexplicable.'[60]

Could the answer be that they were copies of an earlier literature which Unas, the last pharaoh of the Fifth Dynasty, together with several of his successors in the Sixth Dynasty, had attempted to fix for ever in stone in the tomb chambers of their own pyramids? Budge thought so, and felt the evidence suggested that some at least of the source documents must have been exceedingly old:

Several passages bear evidence that the scribes who drafted the copies from which the cutters of the inscriptions worked did not understand what they were writing . . . The general impression is that the priests who drafted the copies made extracts from several compositions of different ages and having different contents . . . '[61]

All this assumed that the source documents, whatever they were, must have been written in an archaic form of the Ancient Egyptian language. There was, however, an alternative possibility which Budge failed to consider. Suppose that the task of the priests had been not only to *copy* material but to *translate* into hieroglyphs texts originally composed in another language altogether? If that language had included a technical terminology and references to artefacts and ideas for which no equivalent terms existed in Ancient Egyptian, this would provide an explanation for the strange impression given by certain of the utterances. Moreover, if the copying and translating of the original source documents had been completed by the end of the Sixth Dynasty, it was easy to understand why no more 'Pyramid Texts' had ever been carved: the project would have come to a halt when it had fulfilled its objective – which would have been to create a permanent hieroglyphic record of a sacred literature that had already been tottering with age when Unas had taken the throne of Egypt in 2356 BC.

Last records of the First Time?

Because we wanted to cover as much of the distance to Abydos as was possible before nightfall, Santha and I reluctantly decided that it was time to get back on the road. Although we had originally intended to spend only a few minutes, the sombre gloom and ancient voices of the Unas tomb chamber had lulled our senses and almost two hours had passed since our arrival. Stooping, we left the tomb and climbed the steeply angled passageway to the exit, where we paused to allow our eyes to adjust to the harsh mid-morning sunlight. As we did so, I took the opportunity to look over the pyramid itself, which had fallen into such a crumbling and thoroughly dilapidated state that its original form was barely recognizable. The core masonry, reduced to little more than a nondescript heap of rubble, was evidently of poor quality, and even the facing blocks – some of which were still intact – lacked the finesse and careful workmanship demonstrated by the older pyramids at Giza.

This was hard to explain in conventional historical terms. If the normal evolutionary processes that govern the development of architectural skills and ideas had been at work in Egypt, one would have expected to find the opposite to be true: the design, engineering and masonry of the Unas Pyramid should have been superior to these of the Giza group, which, according to orthodox chronology, had been built about two centuries previously.[62]

The uncomfortable fact that this was not the case (i. e., Giza was 'better' than Unas and not vice versa) created knotty challenges for Egyptologists and raised questions to which no satisfactory answers had been supplied. To reiterate the central problem: everything about the three stunning and superb pyramids of Khufu, Khafre and Menkaure proclaimed that they were the end products of hundreds, perhaps even thousands of years of accumulated architectural and engineering experience. This was not supported by the archaeological evidence which left no doubt that they were among the earliest pyramids ever built in Egypt – in other words, they were not the products of the mature phase of that country's pyramid-building experiment but, anomalously, were the creations of its infancy.

A further mystery also cried out for a solution. In the three great pyramids at Giza, Egypt's Fourth Dynasty had reared up mansions of eternity – unprecedented and unsurpassed masterpieces of stone, hundreds of feet high, weighing millions of tons apiece, which incorporated many extremely advanced features. No pyramids of comparable quality were ever built again. But only a little later, beneath the smaller, shabbier superstructures of the Fifth and Sixth Dynasty pyramids, a sort of Hall of Records seemed to have been deliberately created: a permanent exhibition of copies or translations of archaic documents which was, at the same time, an unprecedented and unsurpassed masterpiece of scribal and hieroglyphic art.

In short, like the pyramids at Giza, it seemed that the Pyramid Texts had burst upon the scene with no apparent antecedents, and had occupied centre-stage for approximately a hundred years before 'ceasing operations', never to be bettered.

Presumably the ancient kings and sages who had arranged these things had known what they were doing? If so, their minds must have contained a plan, and they must have intended a strong connection to be seen between the completely uninscribed (but technically brilliant) – pyramids at Giza, and the brilliantly inscribed (but technically slipshod) pyramids of the Fifth and Sixth Dynasties.

I suspected, too, that at least part of the answer to the problem might lie in the pyramid-field of Dahshur, which we passed fifteen minutes after leaving Saqqara. It was here that the so-called 'Bent' and 'Red' Pyramids were located. Attributed to Sneferu, Khufu's father, these two monuments (by all accounts very well preserved) had been closed to the public many years ago. A military base had been built around them and they had for a long while been impossible to visit – under any circumstances, ever . . .

As we continued our journey south, through the bright colours of that December day, I was overtaken by a compelling sense that the Nile Valley had been the scene of momentous events for humanity long before the recorded history of mankind began. All the most ancient records and traditions of Egypt spoke of such events and associated them with the epoch during which the gods had ruled on earth: the fabled First Time, which was called Zep Tepi.[63] We shall delve into these records in the next two chapters.

Chapter 43

Looking for the First Time

Here is what the Ancient Egyptians said about the First Time, Zep Tepi, when the gods ruled in their country: they said it was a golden age[1] during which the waters of the abyss receded, the primordial darkness was banished, and humanity, emerging into the light, was offered the gifts of civilization.[2] They spoke also of intermediaries between gods and men – the Urshu, a category of lesser divinities whose title meant 'the Watchers'.[3] And they preserved particularly vivid recollections of the gods themselves, puissant and beautiful beings called the Neteru who lived on earth with humankind and exercised their sovereignty from Heliopolis and other sanctuaries up and down the Nile. Some of these Neteru were male and some female but all possessed a range of supernatural powers which included the ability to appear, at will, as men or women, or as animals, birds, reptiles, trees or plants. Paradoxically, their words and deeds seem to have reflected human passions and preoccupations. Likewise, although they were portrayed as stronger and more intelligent than humans, it was believed that they could grow sick – or even die, or be killed – under certain circumstances.[4]

Records of prehistory

Archaeologists are adamant that the epoch of the gods, which the Ancient Egyptians, called the First Time, is nothing more than a myth. The Ancient Egyptians, however, who may have been better informed about their past than we are, did not share this view. The historical records they kept in their most venerable temples included comprehensive lists of all the kings of Egypt: lists naming every pharaoh of every dynasty recognized by scholars today.[5] Some of these lists went even further, reaching back beyond the historical horizon of the First Dynasty into the uncharted depths of a remote and profound antiquity.

Two lists of kings in this category have survived the ravages of the ages and, having been exported from Egypt, are now preserved in European museums. We shall consider these lists in more detail later in this chapter. They are known respectively as the Palermo Stone (dating from the Fifth Dynasty – around the twenty-fifth century BC), and the Turin Papyrus, a nineteenth Dynasty temple document inscribed in a cursive form of hieroglyphs known as hieratic and dated to the thirteenth century BC.[6]

In addition, we have the testimony of a Heliopolitan priest named Manetho. In the third century BC he compiled a comprehensive and widely respected history of Egypt which provided extensive king lists for the entire dynastic period. Like the Turin Papyrus and the Palermo Stone, Manetho's history also reached much further back into the past to speak of a distant epoch when gods had ruled in the Nile Valley.

Manetho's complete text has not come down to us, although copies of it seem to have been in circulation as late as the ninth century AD.[7] Fortuitously, however, fragments of it were preserved in the writings of the Jewish chronicler Josephus (AD 60) and of Christian writers such as Africanus (AD 300), Eusebius (AD 340) and George Syncellus (AD 800).[8] These fragments, in the words of the late Professor Michael Hoffman of the University of South Carolina, provide the 'framework for modern approaches to the study of Egypt's past'.[9]

This is quite true.[10] Nevertheless, Egyptologists are prepared to use Manetho only as a source for the historical (dynastic) period and repudiate the strange insights he provides into prehistory when he speaks of the remote golden age of the First Time. Why should we be so selective in our reliance on Manetho? What is the logic of accepting thirty 'historical' dynasties from him and rejecting all that he has to say about earlier epochs? Moreover, since we know that his chronology for the historical period has been vindicated by archaeology,[11] isn't it a bit premature for us to assume that his pre-dynastic chronology is wrong because excavations have not yet turned up evidence confirming it?[12]

Gods, Demigods and Spirits of the Dead

If we are to allow Manetho to speak for himself, we have no choice but to turn to the texts in which the fragments of his work are preserved. One of the most important of these is the Armenian version of the *Chronica* of Eusebius. It begins by informing us that it is extracted 'from the *Egyptian History* of Manetho, who composed his account in three books. These deal with the Gods, the Demigods, the Spirits of the Dead and the mortal kings who ruled Egypt . . . '[13] Citing Manetho directly, Eusebius begins by reeling of a list of the gods which consists, essentially, of the familiar Ennead of Heliopolis – Ra, Osiris, Isis, Horus, Set, and so on:[14]

> These were the first to hold sway in Egypt. Thereafter, the kingship passed from one to another in unbroken succession . . . through 13,900 years . . . After the Gods, Demigods reigned for 1255 years; and again another line of kings held sway for 1817 years; then came thirty more kings, reigning for 1790 years; and then again ten kings ruling for 350 years. There followed the rule of the Spirits of the Dead . . . for 5813 years . . . '[15]

The total of all these periods adds up to 24,925 years and takes us far beyond the biblical date for the creation of the world (some time in the fifth millennium BC[16]). Because it suggested that biblical chronology was wrong, this created difficulties for Eusebius, a staunchly Christian commentator. But, after a moment's thought, he overcame the problem in an inspired way: 'The year I take to be a lunar one, consisting, that is, of 30 days: what we now call a month the Egyptians used formerly to style a year . . . '[17]

Of course they did no such thing.[18] By means of this sleight of hand, however, Eusebius and others succeeded in boiling down Manetho's grand pre-dynastic span of almost 25,000 years into a sanitized dollop a bit over 2000 years which fits comfortably into the 2242 years orthodox biblical chronology allows between Adam and the Flood.[19]

A different technique for downplaying the disturbing chronological implications of Manetho's evidence is employed by the monk George Syncellus (*c.* AD 800). This commentator, who relies entirely on invective, writes, 'Manetho, chief priest of the accursed temples of Egypt [tells us] of gods who never existed. These, he says, reigned for 11,895 years . . .'[20]

Several other curious and contradictory numbers crop up in the fragments. In particular, Manetho is repeatedly said to have given the enormous figure of 36,525 years for the *entire* duration of the civilization of Egypt from the time of the gods down to the end of the thirtieth (and last) dynasty of mortal kings.[21] This figure of course, incorporates the 365.25 *days* of the Sothic year (the interval between two consecutive heliacal risings of Sirius, as described in the last chapter). More likely by design than by accident, it also represents 25 cycles of 1,460 Sothic years, and 25 cycles of 1,461 *calendar* years (since the ancient Egyptian civil calendar was constructed around a 'vague year' of 365 days exactly).[22]

What, if anything, does all this mean? It's hard to be sure. Out of the welter of numbers and interpretations, however, there is one aspect of Manetho's original message that comes through loud and clear. Irrespective of everything we have been taught about the orderly progress of history, what he seems to be telling us is that civilized beings (either gods or men) were present in Egypt for an immensely long period *before* the advent of the First Dynasty around 3100 BC.

Diodorus Siculus and Herodotus

In this assertion, Manetho finds much support among classical writers.

In the first century BC, for example, the Greek historian Diodorus Siculus visited Egypt. He is rightly described by C.H. Oldfather, his most recent translator, as 'an uncritical compiler who used good sources and reproduced them faithfully'.[23] In plain English, what this means is that Diodorus did not try to impose his prejudices and preconceptions on the material he collected. He is therefore particularly valuable to us because his informants included Egyptian priests whom he questioned about the mysterious past of their country. This is what they told him:

> 'At first gods and heroes ruled Egypt for a little less than 18,000 years, the last of the gods to rule being Horus, the son of Isis ... Mortals have been kings of their country, they say, for a little less than 5000 years ...'[24]

Let us review these figures 'uncritically' and see what they add up to. Diodorus was writing in the first century BC. If we journey back from there for the 5000 years during which the 'mortal kings' supposedly ruled, we get to around 5100 BC. If we go even further back to the beginning of the age of 'gods and heroes', we find that we have arrived at 23,100 BC, when the world was still firmly in the grip of the last Ice Age.

Long before Diodorus, Egypt was visited by another and more illustrious Greek historian: the great Herodotus, who lived in the fifth century BC. He too, it seems, consorted with priests and he too managed to tune in to traditions that spoke of the presence of a high civilization in the Nile Valley at some unspecified date in remote antiquity. Herodotus outlines these traditions of an immense prehistoric period of Egyptian civilization in Book II of his *History*. In the same document he also hands on to us, without comment, a peculiar nugget of information which had originated with the priests of Heliopolis:

> During this time, they said, there were four occasions when the sun rose out of his wonted place – twice rising where he now sets, and twice setting where he now rises.[25]

What is this all about?

According to the French mathematician Schwaller de Lubicz, what Herodotus is transmitting to us (perhaps unwittingly) is a veiled and garbled reference to a *period of time* – that is, to the time that it takes for sunrise on the vernal equinox to precess against the stellar background through one and a half complete cycles of the zodiac.[26]

As we have seen, the equinoctial sun spends roughly 2160 years in each of the twelve zodiacal constellations. A full cycle of precession of the equinoxes therefore takes almost 26,000 years to complete (12 × 2160 years). It follows that one and a half cycles takes nearly 39,000 years (18 × 2160 years).

In the time of Herodotus the sun on the vernal equinox rose due east at dawn against the stellar background of Aries – at which moment the constellation of Libra was 'in opposition', lying due west where the sun would set twelve hours later. If we wind the clock of precession back half a cycle, however – six houses of the zodiac or approximately 13,000 years – we find that the reverse configuration prevails: the vernal sun now rises due east in Libra while Aries lies due west in opposition. A further 13,000 years back, the situation reverses itself once more, with the vernal sun rising again in Aries and with Libra in opposition.

This takes us to 26,000 years before Herodotus.

If we then step back another 13,000 years, another half precessional cycle, to 39,000 years before Herodotus, the vernal sunrise returns to Libra, and Aries is again in opposition.

The point is this: with 39,000 years we have an expanse of time during which the sun can be described as 'twice rising where he now sets', i.e. in Libra in the time of Herodotus (and again at 13,000 and at 39,000 years earlier), and as 'twice setting where he now rises', i.e. in Aries in the time of Herodotus (and again at 13,000 and 39,000 years earlier).[27] If Schwaller's interpretation is correct – and there is every reason to suppose it is – it suggests that the Greek historian's priestly informants must have had access to accurate records of the precessional motion of the sun going back *at least* 39,000 years before their own era.

The Turin Papyrus and the Palermo Stone

The figure of 39,000 years accords surprisingly closely with the testimony of the Turin Papyrus (one of the two surviving Ancient Egyptian king lists that extends back into prehistoric times before the First Dynasty).

Originally in the collection of the king of Sardinia, the brittle and crumbling 3000-year-old papyrus was sent in a box, without packing, to its present home in the Museum of Turin. As any schoolchild could have predicted, it arrived broken into countless fragments. Scholars were obliged to work for years to piece together and make sense of what remained, and they did a superb job.[28] Nevertheless, more than half the contents of this precious record proved impossible to reconstruct.[29]

What might we have learned about the First Time if the Turin Papyrus had remained intact?

The surviving fragments are tantalizing. In one register, for example, we read the names of ten Neteru with each name inscribed in a cartouche (oblong enclosure) in much the same style adopted in later periods for the historical kings of Egypt. The number of years that each Neter was believed to have reigned was also given, but most of these numbers are missing from the damaged document.[30]

In another column there appears a list of the mortal kings who ruled in upper and lower Egypt after the gods but prior to the supposed unification of the kingdom under Menes, the first pharaoh of the First Dynasty, in 3100 BC. From the surviving fragments it is possible to establish that nine 'dynasties' of these pre-dynastic pharaohs were mentioned, among which were 'the Venerables of Memphis', 'the Venerables of the North' and, lastly, the Shemsu Hor (the Companions, or Followers, of Horus) who ruled until the time of Menes. The final two lines of the column, which seem to represent a summing up or inventory, are particularly provocative. They read; ' . . . Venerables Shemsu-Hor, 13,420 years; Reigns before the Shemsu-Hor, 23,200 years; Total 36,620 years'.[31]

The other king list that deals with prehistoric times is the Palermo Stone, which does not take us as far back into the past as the Turin Papyrus. The earliest of its surviving registers record the reigns of 120 kings who ruled in upper and lower Egypt in the late pre-dynastic period: the centuries immediately prior to the country's unification in 3100 BC.[32] Once again, however, we really have no idea how much *other* information, perhaps relating to far earlier periods, might originally have been inscribed on this enigmatic slab of black basalt, because it, too, has not come down to us intact. Since 1887 the largest single part has been preserved in the Museum of Palermo in Sicily; a second piece is on display in Egypt in the Cairo Museum; and a third much smaller fragment is in the Petrie Collection at the University of

London.[33] These are reckoned by archaeologists to have been broken out of the centre of a monolith which would originally have measured about seven feet long by two feet high (stood on its long side).[34] Furthermore, as one authority has observed:

> It is quite possible – even probable – that many more pieces of this invaluable monument remain, if we only knew where to look. As it is we are faced with the tantalising knowledge that a record of the name of every king of the Archaic Period existed, together with the number of years of his reign and the chief events which occurred during his occupation of the throne. And these events were compiled in the Fifth Dynasty, only about 700 years after the Unification, so that the margin of error would in all probability have been very small . . . [35]

The late Professor Walter Emery, whose words these are, was naturally concerned about the absence of much-needed details concerning the Archaic Period, 3200 BC to 2900 BC,[36] the focus of his own specialist interests. We should also spare a thought, however, for what an intact Palermo Stone might have told us about even earlier epochs, notably Zep Tepi – the golden age of the gods.

The deeper we penetrate into the myths and memories of Egypt's long past, and the closer we approach to the fabled First Time, the stranger the landscapes that surround us become . . . as we shall see.

Chapter 44

Gods of the First Time

According to Heliopolitan theology, the nine original gods who appeared in Egypt in the First Time were Ra, Shu, Tefnut, Geb, Nut, Osiris, Isis, Nepthys and Set. The offspring of these deities included well-known figures such as Horus and Anubis. In addition, other companies of gods were recognized, notably at Memphis and Hermopolis, where there were important and very ancient cults dedicated to Ptah and to Thoth.[1] These First Time deities were all in one sense or another gods of creation who had given shape to chaos through their divine will. Out of that chaos they formed and populated the sacred land of Egypt,[2] wherein, for many thousands of years, they ruled among men as divine pharaohs.[3]

What was 'chaos'?

The Heliopolitan priests who spoke to the Greek historian Diodorus Siculus in the first century BC put forward the thought-provoking suggestion that 'chaos' was a flood – identified by Diodorus with the earth-destroying flood of Deucalion, the Greek Noah figure:[4]

> In general, they say that if in the flood which occurred in the time of Deucalion most living things were destroyed, it is probable that the inhabitants of southern Egypt survived rather than any others . . . Or if, as some maintain, the destruction of living things was complete and the earth then brought forth again new forms of animals, nevertheless, even on such a supposition, the first genesis of living things fittingly attaches to this country . . . [5]

Why should Egypt have been so blessed? Diodorus was told that it had something to do with its geographical situation, with the great exposure of its southern regions to the heat of the sun, and with the vastly increased rainfall which the myths said the world had experienced in the aftermath of the universal deluge: 'For when the moisture from the abundant rains which fell among other peoples was mingled with the intense heat which prevails in Egypt itself . . . the air became very well tempered for the first generation of all living things . . .'[6]

Curiously enough, Egypt does enjoy a special geographical situation: as is well known, the latitude and longitude lines which intersect just beside the Great Pyramid (30° north and 31° east) cross more dry land than any others.[7] Curiously, too, at the end of the last Ice Age, when millions of square miles of glaciation were melting in northern Europe, when rising sea levels were flooding coastal areas all around the globe, and when the huge volume of extra moisture released into the atmosphere through the evaporation of the ice fields was being dumped as rain, Egypt benefited for several thousands of years from an exceptionally humid and fertile climate.[8] It is not difficult to see how such a climate might indeed have been remembered as 'well tempered for the first generation of all living things'.

The question therefore has to be asked: whose information about the past are we receiving from Diodorus, and is the apparently accurate description of Egypt's lush climate at the end of the last Ice Age a coincidence, or is an extremely ancient tradition being transmitted to us here – a memory, perhaps, of the First Time?

Breath of the divine serpent

Ra was believed to have been the first king of the First Time and ancient myths say that as long as he remained young and vigorous he reigned peacefully. The passing years took their toll on him, however, and he is depicted at the end of his rule as an old, wrinkled, stumbling man with a trembling mouth from which saliva ceaselessly dribbles.[9]

Shu followed Ra as king on earth, but his reign was troubled by plots and conflicts. Although he vanquished his enemies he was in the end so ravaged by disease that even his most faithful followers revolted against him: 'Weary of reigning, Shu abdicated in favour of his son Geb and took refuge in the skies after a terrifying tempest which lasted nine days . . . '[10]

Geb, the third divine pharaoh, duly succeeded Shu to the throne. His reign was also troubled and some of the myths describing what took place reflect the odd idiom of the Pyramid Texts in which a non technical vocabulary seems to wrestle with complex technical and scientific imagery. For example, one particularly striking tradition speaks of a 'golden box' in which Ra had deposited a number of objects – described, respectively, as his 'rod' (or cane), a lock of his hair, and his *uraeus* (a rearing cobra with its hood extended, fashioned out of gold, which was worn on the royal head-dress).[11]

A powerful and dangerous talisman, this box, together with its bizarre contents, remained enclosed in a fortress on the 'eastern frontier' of Egypt until a great many years after Ra's ascent to heaven. When Geb came to power he ordered that it should be brought to him and unsealed in his presence. In the instant that the box was opened a bolt of fire (described as the 'breath of the divine serpent') ushered from it, struck dead all Geb's companions and gravely burned the god-king himself.[12]

It is tempting to wonder whether what we are confronted by here might not be a garbled account of a malfunctioning man-made device: a confused, awe-stricken recollection of a monstrous instrument devised by the scientists of a lost civilization. Weight is added to such extreme speculations when we remember that this is by no means the only golden box in the ancient world that functioned like a deadly and unpredictable machine. It has a number of quite unmissable similarities to the Hebrews' enigmatic Ark of the Covenant (which also struck innocent people dead with bolts of fiery energy, which also was 'overlaid round about with gold', and which was said to have contained not only the two tablets of the Ten Commandments but 'the golden pot that had manna, and Aaron's rod.')[13]

A proper look at the implications of all these weird and wonderful boxes (and of other 'technological' artefacts referred to in ancient traditions) is beyond the scope of this book. For our purposes here it is sufficient to note that a peculiar atmosphere of dangerous and quasi-technological wizardry seems to surround many of the gods of the Heliopolitan Ennead.

Isis, for example (wife and sister of Osiris and mother of Horus) carries a strong whiff of the science lab. According to the Chester Beatty Papyrus in the British Museum she was 'a clever woman . . . more intelligent than countless gods . . . She was ignorant of nothing in heaven and earth.'[14] Renowned for her skilful use of witchcraft and magic, Isis was particularly remembered by the Ancient Egyptians as 'strong of tongue', that is being in command of words of power 'which she knew with correct pronunciation, and halted not in her speech, and was perfect both in giving the command and in saying the word'.[15] In short, she was believed, by means of her voice alone, to be capable of bending reality and overriding the laws of physics.

These same powers, though perhaps in greater degree, were attributed to the wisdom god Thoth who although not a member of the Heliopolitan Ennead is recognized in the Turin Papyrus and other ancient records as the sixth (or sometimes as the seventh) divine pharaoh of Egypt.[16] Frequently represented on temple and tomb walls as an ibis, or an ibis-headed man, Thoth was venerated as the regulative force responsible for all heavenly calculations and annotations, as the lord and multiplier of time, the inventor of the alphabet and the patron of magic. He was particularly associated with astronomy, mathematics, surveying and geometry, and was described as 'he who reckons in heaven, the counter of the stars and the measurer of the earth'.[17] He was also regarded as a deity who understood the mysteries of 'all that is hidden under the heavenly vault', and who had the ability to bestow wisdom on selected individuals. It was said that he had inscribed his knowledge in secret books and hidden these about the earth, intending that they should be sought for by future generations but found 'only by the worthy' – who were to use their discoveries for the benefit of mankind.[18]

What stands out most clearly about Thoth, therefore, in addition to his credentials as an ancient scientist, is his role as a benefactor and civilizer.[19] In this respect he closely resembles his predecessor Osiris, the high god of the Pyramid Texts and the fourth divine pharaoh of Egypt, 'whose name becometh *Sah* [Orion], whose leg is long, and his stride extended, the President of the Land of the South . . . '[20]

Osiris and the Lords of Eternity

Occasionally referred to in the texts as a *neb tem*, or 'universal master',[21] Osiris is depicted as human but also superhuman, suffering but at the same time commanding. Moreover, he expresses his essential dualism by ruling in heaven (as the constellation of Orion) and on earth as a king among men. Like Viracocha in the Andes and Quetzalcoatl in Central America, his ways are subtle and mysterious. Like them, he is exceptionally tall and always depicted wearing the curved beard of divinity.[22] And like them too, although he has supernatural powers at his disposal, he avoids the use of force wherever possible.[23]

We saw in Chapter Sixteen that Quetzalcoatl, the god-king of the Mexicans, was believed to have departed from Central America by sea, sailing away on a raft of serpents. It is therefore hard to avoid a sense of *déjà vu* when we read in the *Egyptian Book of the Dead* that the abode of Osiris also 'rested on water' and had walls made of 'living serpents'.[24] At the very least, the convergence of symbolism linking these two gods and two far-flung regions is striking.

There are other obvious parallels as well.

The central details of the story of Osiris have been recounted in earlier chapters and we need not go over them again. The reader will not have forgotten that this god – once again like Quetzalcoatl and Viracocha – was remembered principally as a benefactor of mankind, as a bringer of enlightenment and as a great civilizing leader.[25] He was credited, for example, with having abolished cannibalism and was said to have introduced the Egyptians to agriculture – in particular to the cultivation of wheat and barley – and to have taught them the art of fashioning agricultural implements. Since he had an especial liking for fine wines (the myths do not say where he acquired this taste), he made a point of 'teaching mankind the culture of the vine, as well as the way to harvest the grape and to store the wine . . . '[26] In addition to the gifts of good living he brought to his subjects, Osiris helped to wean them 'from their miserable and barbarous manners' by providing them with a code of laws and inaugurating the cult of the gods in Egypt.[27]

When he had set everything in order, he handed over the control of the kingdom to Isis, quit Egypt for many years, and roamed about the world with the sole intention, Diodorus Siculus was told,

> of visiting all the inhabited earth and teaching the race of men how to cultivate the vine and sow wheat and barley; for he supposed that if he made men give up their savagery and adopt a gentle manner of life he would receive immortal honours because of the magnitude of his benefactions . . . [28]

Osiris travelled first to Ethiopia, where he taught tillage and husbandry to the primitive hunter-gatherers he encountered. He also undertook a number of large-scale engineering and hydraulics works: 'He built canals, with flood gates and regulators . . . he raised the river banks and took precautions to prevent the Nile from over-flowing . . . '[29] Later he made his way to Arabia and thence to India, where he established many cities. Moving on to Thrace he killed a barbarian king for refusing to adopt his system of government. This was out of character; in general, Osiris was remembered by the Egyptians for having

> forced no man to carry out his instructions, but by means of gentle persuasion and an appeal to their reason he succeeded in inducing them to practise what he preached. Many of his wise counsels were imparted to his listeners in hymns and songs, which were sung to the accompaniment of instruments of music.'[30]

Once again the parallels with Quetzalcoatl and Viracocha are hard to avoid. During a time of darkness and chaos – quite possibly linked to a flood – a bearded god, or man, materializes in Egypt (or Bolivia, or Mexico). He is equipped with a wealth of practical and scientific skills, of the kind associated with mature and highly developed civilizations, which he uses unselfishly for the benefit of humanity. He is instinctively gentle but capable of great firmness when necessary. He is motivated by a strong sense of purpose and, after establishing his headquarters at Heliopolis (or Tiahuanaco, or Teotihuacan), he sets forth with a select band of companions to impose order and to reinstate the lost balance of the world.[31]

Leaving aside for the present the issue of whether we are dealing here with gods or men, with figments of the primitive imagination or with flesh-and-blood beings, the fact remains that the myths *always* speak of a *company* of civilizers: Viracocha has his 'companions', as have both Quetzalcoatl and Osiris. Sometimes there are fierce internal conflicts within these groups, and perhaps struggles for power: the battles between Seth and Horus, and between Tezcatilpoca and Quetzalcoatl are obvious examples. Moreover, whether the mythical events unfold in Central America, or in the Andes, or in Egypt, the upshot is also always pretty much the same: the civilizer is eventually plotted against and either driven out or killed.

The myths say that Quetzalcoatl and Viracocha never came back (although, as we have seen, their return to the Americas was expected at the time of the Spanish conquest). Osiris, on the other hand, did come back. Although he was murdered by Set soon after the completion of his worldwide mission to make men 'give up their savagery', he won eternal life through his resurrection in the constellation of Orion as the all-powerful god of the dead. Thereafter, judging souls and providing an immortal example of responsible and benevolent kingship, he dominated the religion (and the culture) of Ancient Egypt for the entire span of its known history.

Serene stability

Who can guess what the civilizations of the Andes and of Mexico might have achieved if they too had benefited from such powerful symbolic continuity. In this respect, however, Egypt is unique. Indeed, although the Pyramid Texts and other archaic sources recognize a period of disruption and attempted usurpation by Set (and his seventy-two 'precessional' conspirators), they also depict the transition to the reigns of Horus, Thoth and the later divine pharaohs as being relatively smooth and inevitable.

This transition was mimicked, through thousands of years, by the mortal kings of Egypt. From the beginning to the end, they saw themselves as the lineal descendants and living representatives of Horus, son of Osiris. As generation succeeded generation, it was supposed that each deceased pharaoh was reborn in the sky as 'an Osiris' and that each successor to the throne became a 'Horus'.[32]

This simple, refined, and stable scheme *was already fully evolved and in place at the beginning of the First Dynasty* – around 3100 BC.[33]

Scholars accept this; the majority also accept that what we are dealing with here is a highly developed and sophisticated religion.[34] Strangely, very few Egyptologists or archaeologists have questioned where and when this religion took shape.

Is it not to defy logic to suppose that well-rounded social and metaphysical ideas like those of the Osiris cult sprung up fully formed in 3100 BC, or that they could have taken such perfect shape in the 300 years which Egyptologists sometimes grudgingly allow for them to have done so?[35] There must have been a far longer period of development than that, spread over several thousands rather than several hundreds of years. Moreover, as we have seen every surviving record in which the Ancient Egyptians speak directly about their past asserts that their civilization was a legacy of 'the gods' who were 'the first to hold sway in Egypt'.[36]

The records are not internally consistent: some attribute much greater antiquity to the civilization of Egypt than others. All, however, clearly and firmly direct our attention to an epoch far, far in the past – anything from 8000 to almost 40,000 years before the foundation of the First Dynasty.

Archaeologists insist that no material artefacts have ever been found in Egypt to suggest that an evolved civilization existed at such early dates, but this is not strictly true. As we saw in Part VI, a handful of objects and structures exist which have not yet been conclusively dated by any scientific means.

The ancient city of Abydos conceals one of the most extraordinary of these undatable enigmas . . .

Above: **42** Egypt's Giza necropolis, viewed from the south-west. In the foreground (flanked by three 'satellite' pyramids) we see the Pyramid of Menkaure, the third and smallest of the great Pyramids at Giza. Behind it, still capped by several courses of its original facing-stones, towers the Pyramid of Khafre. Behind that, in the background, can be seen the truncated apex of the Pyramid of Khufu, the Great Pyramid, Seventh Wonder of the Ancient World. The attribution of the three Pyramids to the three Fourth Dynasty Pharaohs is conventional but unsupported by any convincing evidence.
Below: **43** The Great Sphinx at Giza, gazing due east towards the equinoctial sunrise. New geological and archaeo-astronomical evidence indicates that this immense monolithic sculpture may be many thousands of years older than archaeologists currently assume.

Above: **44** The author in the King's Chamber in the heart of the Great Pyramid. The walls are composed of 100 separate blocks weighing around 70 tons each, and the ceiling is spanned by 9 further blocks each weighing 50 tons. The engineering logistics involved in creating such a chamber at a height of 150 feet above the ground are stupefying. *Below*: **45** The author in the King's Chamber sarcophagus. Cut from one piece of solid granite, its interior was hollowed out, more than 4500 years ago, by tubular drills (no examples of which have ever been found) which removed material 500 times faster than the rate that can be achieved by modern diamond-headed power-drills. *Facing page*: **46** The Grand Gallery. Are we looking down? Or up? Measuring 153 feet in length, and 28 feet high, this awe-inspiring corbel vault has an angle of slope of 26° and represents a near-impossible engineering and architectural feat.

Previous page, top left: **47** A view of the Queen's Chamber showing the corbelled niche in the eastern wall and the entrance to the shaft in the southern wall. Some 200 feet long this steeply sloping shaft a concealed portcullis door was discovered by the German robot-camera *Upuaut* in March 1993. *Top right:* **48** The lowest of the three chambers in the Menkaure Pyramid. Its ceiling, defaced with graffiti in modern times, consists of 18 huge granite slabs laid in facing gables, hollowed out from beneath to give the effect of a concave barrel vault. *Bottom:* **49** The author above the latter chamber, crouched on top of the granite gables that form its distinctive ceiling. There is no known mechanism that could have manœuvred such immense blocks into position in the limited space available. *This page, above:* **50** The only surviving statue of Khufu, the supposed builder of the Great Pyramid. *Right:* **51** The beautiful diorite statue of Khafre, the supposed builder of the Second Pyramid. *Below:* **52** The principal chamber in the Khafre Pyramid, with graffiti by Belzoni.

Previous page: **53** The streamlined 4500-year-old boat, built to an advanced ocean-going design, that was found buried beside the Great Pyramid. Other such boats, known to be much older, have recently been found buried in the desert at Abydos in Upper Egypt (see Part VII). *This page, above:* **54** The earliest known piece of graphic art from pre-dynastic Egypt, now in the Cairo Museum, crudely depicts a similar style of boat. *Below:* **55** Such boats were invariably associated with the *Neteru*, the Gods, said to have brought civilization to Egypt in the remote 'First Time'. Compare also pictures 19 and 20 in Part I.

Above: **56** The geometric perfection of the Great Pyramid of Egypt, almost 500 feet high and supposedly built by the Fourth Dynasty Pharaoh Khufu around 2550 BC. Amongst other functions the Great Pyramid was designed to serve as a mathematical model of the northern hemisphere of the earth on a scale of 1:43,200. *Below*: **57** The crumbling dilapidated ruin of the nearby Pyramid of Sahure, a Fifth Dynasty Pharaoh who reigned around 2450 BC. How is it possible to account for such a spectacular decline in building standards and engineering expertise in a period of barely a century?

Chapter 45

The Works of Men and Gods

Among the numberless ruined temples of Ancient Egypt, there is one that is unique not only for its marvellous state of preservation, which (rare indeed!) includes an intact roof, but for the fine quality of the many acres of beautiful reliefs that decorate its towering walls. Located at Abydos, eight miles west of the present course of the Nile, this is the Temple of Seti I, a monarch of the illustrious nineteenth Dynasty, who ruled from 1306–1290 BC.[1]

Seti is known primarily as the father of a famous son: Ramesses II (1290–1224 BC), the pharaoh of the biblical Exodus.[2] In his own right, however, he was a major historical figure who conducted extensive military campaigns outside Egypt's borders, who was responsible for the construction of several fine buildings and who carefully and conscientiously refurbished and restored many older ones.[3] His temple at Abydos, which was known evocatively as 'The House of Millions of Years', was dedicated to Osiris,[4] the 'Lord of Eternity', of whom it was said in the Pyramid Texts:

> You have gone, but you will return, you have slept, but you will awake, you have died, but you will live . . . Betake yourself to the waterway, fare upstream . . . travel about Abydos in this spirit-form of yours which the gods commanded to belong to you.[5]

Atef Crown

It was eight in the morning, a bright, fresh hour in these latitudes, when I entered the hushed gloom of the Temple of Seti I. Sections of its walls were floor-lit by low-wattage electric bulbs; otherwise the only illumination was that which the pharaoh's architects had originally planned: a few isolated shafts of sunlight that penetrated through slits in the outer masonry like beams of divine radiance. Hovering among the motes of dust dancing in those beams, and infiltrating the heavy stillness of the air amid the great columns that held up the roof of the Hypostyle Hall, it was easy to imagine that the spirit-form of Osiris could still be present. Indeed, this was more than just imagination because Osiris was physically present in the astonishing symphony of reliefs that adorned the walls – reliefs that depicted the once and future civilizer-king in his role as god of the dead, enthroned and attended by Isis, his beautiful and mysterious sister.

In these scenes Osiris wore a variety of different and elaborate crowns which I studied closely as I walked from relief to relief. Crowns similar to these in many respects had been important parts of the wardrobe of all the pharaohs of Ancient Egypt, at least on the evidence of reliefs depicting them. Strangely, however, in all the years of intensive excavations, archaeologists had not found a single example of a royal crown, or a small part of one, let alone a specimen of the convoluted ceremonial head-dresses associated with the gods of the First Time.[6]

Of particular interest was the Atef crown. Incorporating the *uraeus*, the royal serpent symbol (which in Mexico was a rattlesnake but in Egypt was a hooded cobra poised to strike), the central core of this strange contraption was recognizable as an example of the *hedjet*, the white skittle-shaped war helmet of upper Egypt (again known only from reliefs). Rearing up on either side of this core were what seemed to be two thin leaves of metal, and at the front was an attached device, consisting of two wavy blades, which scholars normally describe as a pair of rams' horns.[7]

In several reliefs of the Seti I Temple Osiris was depicted wearing the Atef crown, which seemed to stand about two feet high. According to the *Ancient Egyptian Book of the Dead*, it had been given

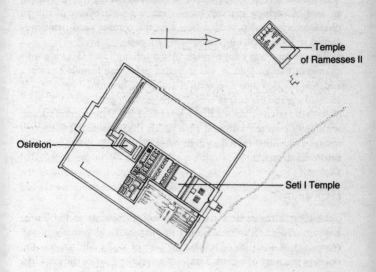

Abydos.

to him by Ra: 'But on the very first day that he wore it Osiris had much suffering in his head, and when Ra returned in the evening he found Osiris with his head angry and swollen from the heat of the Atef crown. Then Ra proceeded to let out the pus and the blood.'[8]

All this was stated in a matter-of-fact way, but – when you stopped to think about it – what kind of crown was it that radiated heat and caused the skin to haemorrhage and break out in pustulant sores?

Seventeen centuries of kings

I walked on into the deeper darkness, eventually finding my way to the Gallery of the Kings. It led off from the eastern edge of the inner Hypostyle Hall about 200 feet from the entrance to the temple.

To pass through the Gallery was to pass through time itself. On the wall to my left was a list of 120 of the gods of Ancient Egypt, together with the names of their principal sanctuaries. On my right, covering an area of perhaps ten feet by six feet, were the names of the 76 pharaohs who had preceded Seti I to the throne; each name was carved in hieroglyphs inside an oval cartouche.

This tableau was known as the 'Abydos King List'. Glowing with colours of molten gold, it was designed to be read from left to right and was divided into five vertical and three horizontal registers. It covered a grand expanse of almost 1700 years, beginning around 3000 BC with the reign of Menes, first king of the First Dynasty, and ending with Seti's own reign around 1300 BC. At the extreme left stood two figures exquisitely carved in high relief: Seti and his young son, the future Ramesses II.

Hypogeum

Belonging to the same class of historical documents as the Turin Papyrus and the Palermo Stone, the list spoke eloquently of the continuity of tradition. An inherent part of that tradition, was the belief or memory of a First Time, long, long ago, when the gods had ruled in Egypt. Principal among those gods was Osiris, and it was therefore appropriate that the Gallery of the Kings should provide access to a second corridor, leading to the rear of the temple where a marvellous building was located – one associated with Osiris from the beginning of written records in Egypt[9] and described by the Greek geographer Strabo (who visited Abydos in the first century BC) as 'a remarkable structure built of solid stone . . . [containing] a spring which lies at a great depth, so that one descends to it down vaulted galleries made of monoliths of surpassing size and workmanship. There is a canal leading to the place from the great river . . . ' [10]

A few hundred years after Strabo's visit, when the religion of Ancient Egypt had been supplanted by the new cult of Christianity, the silt of the river and the sands of the desert began to drift into the Osirieon, filling it foot by foot, century by century, until its upright monoliths and huge lintels were buried and forgotten. And so it remained, out of sight and out of mind, until the beginning of the twentieth century, when the archaeologists Flinders Petrie and Margaret Murray began excavations. In their 1903 season of digging they uncovered parts of a hall and passageway, lying in the desert about 200 feet south-west of the Seti I Temple and built in the recognizable architectural style of the Nineteenth Dynasty. However, sandwiched between these remains and the rear of the Temple, they also found unmistakable signs that 'a large underground building' lay concealed.[11] 'This hypogeum', wrote Margaret Murray, 'appears to Professor Petrie to be the place that Strabo mentions, usually called Strabo's Well.'[12] This was good guesswork on the part of Petrie and Murray. Shortage of cash, however, meant that their theory of a buried building was not tested until the digging season of 1912–13. Then, under the direction of Professor Naville of the Egypt Exploration Fund, a long transverse chamber was cleared, at the end of which, to the north-east, was found a massive stone gateway made up of cyclopean blocks of granite and sandstone.

The next season, 1913–14, Naville and his team returned with 600 local helpers and diligently cleared the whole of the huge underground building:

> What we discovered [Naville wrote] is a gigantic construction of about 100 feet in length and 60 in width, built with the most enormous stones that may be seen in Egypt. In the four sides of the enclosure walls are cells, 17 in number, of the height of a man and without ornamentation of any kind. The building itself is divided into three naves, the middle one being wider than those of the sides; the division is produced by two colonnades made of huge granite monoliths supporting architraves of equal size.[13]

Naville commented with some astonishment on one block he measured in the corner of the building's northern nave, a block more than twenty-five feet long.[14] Equally surprising was the fact that the cells cut into the enclosure walls had no floors, but turned out, as the excavations went deeper, to be filled with increasingly moist sand and earth:

> The cells are connected by a narrow ledge between two and three feet wide; there is a ledge also on the opposite side of the nave, but no floor at all, and in digging to a depth of 12 feet we reached infiltrated water. Even below the great gateway there is no floor, and when there was water in front of it the cells were probably reached with a small boat.[15]

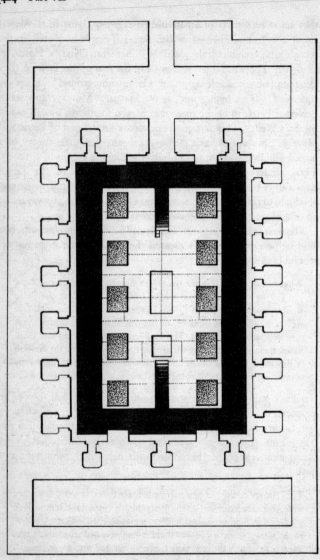

Plan of the Osireion.

The most ancient stone building in Egypt

Water, water, everywhere – this seemed to be the theme of the Osireion, which lay at the bottom of the huge crater Naville and his men had excavated in 1914. It was positioned some 50 feet below the level of the floor of the Seti I Temple, almost flush with the water-table, and was approached by a modern stairway curving down to the south-east. Having descended this stairway, I passed under the hulking lintel slabs of the great gateway Naville (and Strabo) had described and crossed a narrow wooden footbridge – again modern – which brought me to a large sandstone plinth.

Measuring about 80 feet in length by 40 in width, this plinth was composed of enormous paving blocks and was entirely surrounded by water. Two pools, one rectangular and the other square, had been cut into the plinth along the centre of its long axis and at either end stairways led down to a depth of about 12 feet below the water level. The plinth also supported the two massive colonnades Naville mentioned in his report, each of which consisted of five chunky rose-coloured granite monoliths about eight feet square by 12 feet high and weighing, on average, around 100 tons.[16] The tops of these huge columns were spanned by granite lintels and there was evidence that the whole building had once been roofed over with a series of even larger monolithic slabs.[17]

To get a proper understanding of the structure of the Osireion, I found it helpful to raise myself directly above it in my mind's eye, so that I could look down on it. This exercise was assisted by the absence of the original roof which made it easier to envisage the whole edifice in plan. Also helpful was the fact that water had now seeped up to fill all of the building's pools, cells and channels to a depth of a few inches below the lip of the central plinth, as the original designers had apparently intended it should.[18]

Looking down in this manner, it was immediately apparent that the plinth formed a rectangular island, surrounded on all four sides by a water-filled moat about 10 feet wide. The moat was contained by an immense, rectangular enclosure wall, no less than *20 feet thick*,[19] made of very large blocks of red sandstone disposed in polygonal jigsaw-puzzle patterns. Into the huge thickness of this wall were set the 17 cells mentioned in Naville's report. Six lay to the east, six to the west, two to the south and three to the north. Off the central of the three northern cells lay a long transverse chamber, roofed with and composed of limestone. A similar transverse chamber, also of limestone but no longer with an intact roof, lay immediately south of the great gateway. Finally, the whole structure was enclosed within an outer wall of limestone, thus completing a sequence of inter-nested rectangles, i. e., from the outside in, wall, wall, moat, plinth.

Another notable and outstandingly unusual feature of the Osireion was that it was not even approximately aligned to the cardinal points. Instead, like the Way of the Dead at Teotihuacan in Mexico, it was oriented to the east of due north. Since Ancient Egypt had been a civilization that could and normally did achieve precise alignments for its buildings, it seemed to me improbable that this apparently skewed orientation was accidental. Moreover, although 50 feet higher, the Seti I Temple was oriented along exactly the same axis – and again not by accident. The question was: *which was the older building?* Had the axis of the Osireion been predetermined by the axis of the Temple or vice versa? This, it turned out, was an issue over which considerable controversy, now long forgotten, had once raged. In a debate which had many connections with that surrounding the Sphinx and the Valley Temple at Giza, eminent archaeologists had initially argued that the Osireion was a building of truly immense antiquity, a view expressed by Professor Naville in the London *Times* of 17 March 1914:

> This monument raises several important questions. As to its date, its great similarity with the Temple of the Sphinx [as the Valley Temple was then known] shows it to be of the same epoch when building was made with enormous stones without any ornament. This is character-istic of the oldest architecture in Egypt. I should even say that we may call it the most ancient stone building in Egypt.[20]

Describing himself as overawed by the 'grandeur and stern simplicity' of the monument's central hall, with its remarkable granite monoliths, and by 'the power of those ancients who could bring from a distance and move such gigantic blocks', Naville made a suggestion concerning the function the Osireion might originally have been intended to serve: 'Evidently this huge construction was a large reservoir where water was stored during the high Nile . . . It is curious that what we

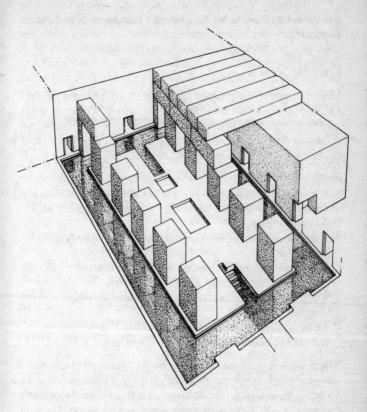

Reconstruction of the Osireion.

may consider as a beginning in architecture is neither a temple nor a tomb, but a gigantic pool, a waterwork . . . [21]

Curious indeed, and well worth investigating further; something Naville hoped to do the following season. Unfortunately, the First World War intervened and no archaeology could be undertaken in Egypt for several years. As a result, it was not until 1925 that the Egypt Exploration Fund was able to send out another mission, which

was led not by Naville but by a young Egyptologist named Henry
Frankfort.

Frankfort's facts

Later to enjoy great prestige and influence as professor of Pre-
Classical Antiquity at the University of London, Frankfort spent
several consecutive digging seasons re-clearing and thoroughly
excavating the Osireion between 1925 and 1930. During the course of
this work he made discoveries which, so far as he was concerned,
'settled the date of the building':

1 A granite dovetail in position at the top of the southern side of
   the main entrance to the central hall, which was inscribed with
   the cartouche of Seti I.
2 A similar dovetail in position inside the eastern wall of the
   central hall.
3 Astronomical scenes and inscriptions by Seti I carved in relief on
   the ceiling of the northern transverse chamber.
4 The remains of similar scenes in the southern transverse
   chamber.
5 An ostracon (piece of broken potsherd) found in the entrance
   passage and bearing the legend 'Seti is serviceable to Osiris'.[22]

The reader will recall the lemming behaviour which led to a dramatic
change of scholarly opinion about the antiquity of the Sphinx and the
Valley Temple (due to the discovery of a few statues and a single
cartouche which seemed to imply some sort of connection with
Khafre). Frankfort's finds at Abydos caused a similar *volte-face* over
the antiquity of the Osireion. In 1914 it was 'the most ancient stone
building in Egypt'. By 1933, it had been beamed forward in time to
the reign of Seti I – around 1300 BC – whose cenotaph it was now
believed to be.[23]

   Within a decade, the standard Egyptological texts began to print
the attribution to Seti I as though it were a fact, verifiable by
experience or observation. It is not a fact, however, merely
Frankfort's interpretation of the evidence he had found.

The only facts are that certain inscriptions and decorations left by Seti appear in an otherwise completely anonymous structure. One plausible explanation is that the structure must have been built by Seti, as Frankfort proposed. The other possibility is that the half-hearted and scanty decorations, cartouches and inscriptions found by Frankfort could have been placed in the Osireion as part of a renovation and repair operation undertaken in Seti's time (implying that the structure was by then ancient, as Naville and others had proposed).

What are the merits of these mutually contradictory propositions which identify the Osireion as (a) the oldest building in Egypt, and (b) a relatively late New Kingdom structure?

Proposition (b) – that it is the cenotaph of Seti I – is the only attribution accepted by Egyptologists. On close inspection, however, it rests on the circumstantial evidence of the cartouches and inscriptions which prove nothing. Indeed part of this evidence appears to contradict Frankfort's case. The ostracon bearing the legend 'Seti is serviceable to Osiris' sounds less like praise for the works of an original builder than praise for a restorer who had renovated, and perhaps added to, an ancient structure identified with the First Time god Osiris. And another awkward little matter has also been overlooked. The south and north 'transverse chambers', which contain Seti I's detailed decorations and inscriptions, lie *outside* the twenty-foot-thick enclosure wall which so adamantly defines the huge, undecorated megalithic core of the building. This had raised the reasonable suspicion in Naville's mind (though Frankfort chose to ignore it) that the two chambers concerned were 'not contemporaneous with the rest of the building' but had been added much later during the reign of Seti I, 'probably when he built his own temple'.[24]

To cut a long story short, therefore, everything about proposition (b) is based in one way or another on Frankfort's not necessarily infallible interpretation of various bits and pieces of possibly intrusive evidence.

Proposition (a) – that the core edifice of the Osireion had been built millennia before Seti's time – rests on the nature of the architecture itself. As Naville observed, the Osireion's similarity to the Valley Temple at Giza 'showed it to be of the same epoch when building was made with enormous stones'. Likewise, until the end of her life, Margaret Murray remained convinced that the Osireion was not a cenotaph at all (least of all Seti's). She said,

> It was made for the celebration of the mysteries of Osiris, and so far is unique among all the surviving buildings of Egypt. It is clearly early, for the great blocks of which it is built are of the style of the Old Kingdom; the simplicity of the actual building also points to it being of that early date. The decoration was added by Seti I, who in that way laid claim to the building, but seeing how often a Pharaoh claimed the work of his predecessors by putting his name on it, this fact does not carry much weight. It is the style of the building, the type of the masonry, the tooling of the stone, and not the name of a king, which date a building in Egypt.[25]

This was an admonition Frankfort might well have paid more attention to, for as he bemusedly observed of his 'cenotaph', 'It has to be admitted that no similar building is known from the Nineteenth Dynasty.'[26]

Indeed it is not just a matter of the Nineteenth Dynasty. Apart from the Valley Temple and other cyclopean edifices on the Giza plateau, no other building remotely resembling the Osireion is known from *any* other epoch of Egypt's long history. This handful of supposedly Old Kingdom structures, built out of giant megaliths, seems to belong in a unique category. They resemble one another much more than they resemble any other known style of architecture and in all cases there are question-marks over their identity.

Isn't this precisely what one would expect of buildings not erected by any historical pharaoh but dating back to prehistoric times? Doesn't it make sense of the mysterious way in which the Sphinx and the Valley Temple, and now the Osireion as well, seem to have become vaguely connected with the names of particular pharaohs (Khafre and Seti I), without ever yielding a single piece of evidence that clearly and unequivocally *proves* those pharaohs built the structures concerned? Aren't the tenuous links much more indicative of the work of restorers seeking to attach themselves to ancient and venerable monuments than of the original architects of those monuments – whoever they might have been and in whatever epoch they might have lived?

Setting sail across seas of sand and time

Before leaving Abydos, there was one other puzzle that I wanted to remind myself of. It lay buried in the desert, about a kilometre north-west of the Osireion, across sands littered with the rolling, cluttered tumuli of ancient graveyards.

Out among these cemeteries, many of which dated back to early dynastic and pre-dynastic times, the jackal gods Anubis and Upuaut had traditionally reigned supreme. Openers of the way, guardians of the spirits of the dead, I knew that they had played a central role in the mysteries of Osiris that had been enacted each year at Abydos – apparently throughout the span of Ancient Egyptian history.

It seemed to me that there was a sense in which they guarded the mysteries still. For what was the Osireion if was not a huge, unsolved mystery that deserved closer scrutiny than it has received from the scholars whose job it is to look into these matters? And what was the burial in the desert of twelve high-prowed, seagoing ships if not also a mystery that cried out, loudly, for solution?

It was the burial place of those ships I was now crossing the cemeteries of the jackal gods to see:

> *The Guardian, London, 21 December 1991*: A fleet of 5000-year-old royal ships has been found buried eight miles from the Nile. American and Egyptian archaeologists discovered the 12 large wooden boats at Abydos . . . Experts said the boats – which are 50 to 60 feet long – are about 5000 years old, making them Egypt's earliest royal ships and among the earliest boats found anywhere . . . The experts say the ships, discovered in September, were probably meant for burial so the souls of the pharaohs could be transported on them. 'We never expected to find such a fleet, especially so far from the Nile,' said David O'Connor, the expedition leader and curator of the Egyptian Section of the University Museum of the University of Pennsylvania . . . [27]

The boats were buried in the shadow of a gigantic mud-brick enclosure, thought to have been the mortuary temple of a Second Dynasty pharaoh named Khasekhemwy, who had ruled Egypt in the twenty-seventh century BC.[28] O'Connor, however, was certain that they were not associated directly with Khasekhemwy but rather with the nearby (and largely ruined) 'funerary-cult enclosure built for

Pharaoh Djer early in Dynasty I. The boat graves are not likely to be earlier than this and may in fact have been built for Djer, but this remains to be proven.'[29]

A sudden strong gust of wind blew across the desert, scattering sheets of sand. I took refuge for a while in the lee of the looming walls of the Khasekhemwy enclosure, close to the point where the University of Pennsylvania archaeologists had, for legitimate security reasons, reburied the twelve mysterious boats they had stumbled on in 1991. They had hoped to return in 1992 to continue the excavations, but there had been various hitches and, in 1993, the dig was still being postponed.

In the course of my research O'Connor had sent me the official report of the 1991 season,[30] mentioning in passing that some of the boats might have been as much as 72 feet in length.[31] He also noted that the boat-shaped brick graves in which they were enclosed, which would have risen well above the level of the surrounding desert in early dynastic times, must have produced quite an extraordinary effect when they were new:

> Each grave had originally been thickly coated with mud plaster and whitewash so the impression would have been of twelve (or more) huge 'boats' moored out in the desert, gleaming brilliantly in the Egyptian sun. The notion of their being moored was taken so seriously that an irregularly shaped small boulder was found placed near the 'prow' or 'stern' of several boat graves. These boulders could not have been there naturally or by accident; their placement seems deliberate, not random. We can think of them as 'anchors' intended to help 'moor' the boats.[32]

Like the 140-foot ocean-going vessel found buried beside the Great Pyramid at Giza (see Chapter Thirty-three), one thing was immediately clear about the Abydos boats – they were of an advanced design capable of riding out the most powerful waves and the worst weather of the open seas. According to Cheryl Haldane, a nautical archaeologist at Texas A-and-M University, they showed 'a high degree of technology combined with grace'.[33] Exactly as was the case with the Pyramid boat, therefore (but at least 500 years earlier) the Abydos fleet seemed to indicate that a people able to draw upon the accumulated experiences of a long tradition of seafaring had been present in Egypt from the very beginning of its 3000 year history. Moreover I knew that the earliest wall paintings found in Nile Valley, dating back perhaps as much as 1500 years before the burial of the Abydos fleet (to around 4500 BC) showed the same long, sleek, high-prowed vessels in action.[34]

Could an experienced race of ancient seafarers have become involved with the indigenous inhabitants of the Nile Valley at some indeterminate period before the official beginning of history at around 3000 BC? Wouldn't this explain Egypt's curious and paradoxical – but nonetheless enduring – obsession with ships in the desert (and references to what sounded like sophisticated ships in the Pyramid Texts, including one said to have been more than 2000 feet long)?[35]

In raising these conjectures, I did not doubt that religious symbolism had existed in Ancient Egypt in which, as scholars endlessly pointed out, ships had been designated as vessels for the pharaoh's soul. Nevertheless that symbolism did not solve the problem posed by the high level of technological achievement of the buried ships; such evolved and sophisticated designs called for a long period of development. Wasn't it worth looking into the possibility – even if only to rule it out – that the Giza and Abydos vessels could have been parts of a cultural legacy, not of a land-loving, riverside-dwelling, agricultural people like the indigenous Ancient Egyptians but of an advanced seafaring nation?

Such seafarers could have been expected to be navigators who would have known how set a course by the stars and who would perhaps also have developed the skills necessary to draw up accurate maps and charts of the oceans they had traversed.

Might they also have been architects and stonemasons whose characteristic medium had been polygonal, megalithic blocks like those of the Valley Temple and the Osireion?

And might they have been associated in some way with the legendary gods of the First Time, said to have brought to Egypt not only civilization and astronomy and architecture, and the knowledge of mathematics and writing, but a host of other useful skills and gifts, by far the most notable and the most significant of which had been the gift of agriculture?

There is evidence of an astonishingly early period of agricultural advance and experimentation in the Nile Valley at about the end of the last Ice Age in the northern hemisphere. The characteristics of this great Egyptian 'leap forward' suggest that it could only have resulted from an influx of new ideas from some as yet unidentified source.

Chapter 46

The Eleventh Millennium BC

If it were not for the powerful mythology of Osiris, and if this civilizing, scientific, law-making deity was not remembered in particular for having introduced domesticated crops into the Nile Valley in the remote and fabled epoch known as the First Time, it would probably not be a matter of any great interest that at some point between 13,000 BC and 10,000 BC Egypt enjoyed a period of what has been described as 'precocious agricultural development' – possibly the earliest agricultural revolution anywhere in the world identified with certainty by historians.[1]

As we saw in recent chapters, sources such as the Palermo Stone, Manetho and the Turin Papyrus contain several different and at times contradictory chronologies. All these chronologies nevertheless agree on a very ancient date for the First Time of Osiris: the golden age when the gods were believed to have ruled in Egypt. In addition, the sources demonstrate a striking convergence over the importance they accord to the *eleventh millennium BC* in particular,[2] the precessional Age of Leo when the great ice sheets of the northern hemisphere were undergoing their final, ferocious meltdown.

Perhaps coincidentally, evidence unearthed since the 1970s by geologists, archaeologists and prehistorians like Michael Hoffman, Fekri Hassan and Professor Fred Wendorff has confirmed that the eleventh millennium BC was indeed an important period in Egyptian prehistory, during which immense and devastating floods swept repeatedly down the Nile Valley.[3] Fekri Hassan has speculated that this prolonged series of natural disasters, which reached a crescendo around or just after 10,500 BC (and continued to recur periodically until about 9000 BC) might have been responsible for snuffing out the early agricultural experiment.[4]

At any rate, that experiment *did* come to an end (for whatever reason), and appears not to have been attempted again for at least another 5000 years.[5]

Kick-start

There is something mysterious about Egypt's so-called 'palaeolithic agricultural revolution'. Here, quoted from the standard texts (Hoffman's *Egypt before The Pharaohs* and Wendorff and Schild's *Prehistory of the Nile Valley*) are some key facts from the little that is known about this great leap forward that occurred so inexplicably towards the end of the last Ice Age:

1 'Shortly after 13,000 BC, grinding stones and sickle blades with a glossy sheen on their bits (the result of silica from cut stems adhering to a sickle's cutting edge) appear in late Palaeolithic tool kits . . . It is clear that the grinding stones were used in preparing plant food.'[6]

2 At many riverside sites, at exactly this time, fish stopped being a significant food source and became a negligible one, as evidenced by the absence of fish remains: 'The decline in fishing as a source of food is related to the appearance of a new food resource represented by ground grain. The associated pollen strongly suggests that this grain was barley, and significantly, this large grass-pollen, tentatively identified as barley, makes a sudden appearance in the pollen profile just before the time when the first settlements were established in this area . . .'[7]

3 'As apparently spectacular as the rise of protoagriculture in the late Palaeolithic Nile Valley was its precipitous decline. No one knows exactly why, but after about 10,500 BC the early sickle blades and grinding disappear to be replaced throughout Egypt by Epipalaeolithic hunting, fishing and gathering peoples who

use stone tools.'[8]

Scanty though the evidence may be, it is clear in its general implications: Egypt enjoyed a golden age of agricultural plenty which began around 13,000 BC and was brought to an abrupt halt around the middle of the eleventh millennium BC. A kick-start to the process appears to have been given by the introduction of already domesticated barley into the Nile Valley, immediately followed by the establishment of a number of farming settlements which exploited the new resource. The settlements were equipped with simple but extremely effective agricultural tools and accessories. After the eleventh millennium BC, however, there was a prolonged relapse to more primitive ways of life.

The imagination is inclined to roam freely over such data in search of an explanation – and all such explanations can only be guesswork. What is certain is that the none of the evidence suggests that palaeolithic Egypt's 'agricultural revolution' could have been a local initiative. On the contrary it feels in every way like a transplant. A transplant appears suddenly, after all, and can be rejected equally fast if conditions change, just as settled agriculture seems to have been rejected in ancient Egypt after the great Nile floods of the eleventh millennium BC.

Climate Change

What was the weather like then?

We've noted in earlier chapters that the Sahara, a relatively young desert, was green savannah until about the tenth millennium BC; this savannah, brightened by lakes, boiling with game, extended across much of upper Egypt. Farther north, the Delta area was marshy but dotted with many large and fertile islands. Overall the climate was significantly cooler, cloudier and *rainier* than it is today.[9] Indeed, for two or three thousand years before and about a thousand years after 10,500 BC it rained and rained and rained. Then, as though marking an ecological turning-point, the floods came. When they were over, increasingly arid conditions set in.[10] This period of desiccation lasted until approximately 7000 BC when the 'Neolithic Subpluvial' began with a thousand years of heavy rains, followed by 3000 years of moderate rainfall which once again proved ideal for agriculture: 'For a time the deserts bloomed and human societies colonized areas that have been unable to support such dense populations since.'[11]

By the birth of dynastic Egypt around 3000 BC, however, the climate had turned around again and a new period of desiccation had begun – one that has continued until the present day.

This, then, in broad outline, is the environmental stage upon which the mysteries of Egyptian civilization have been played out: rain and floods between 13,000 BC and 9500 BC; a dry period until 7000 BC; rain again (though increasingly less frequent) until about 3000 BC; thereafter a renewed and enduring dry period.

The expanse of years is great, but if one is looking for a First Time within it which might accord with the golden age of the gods, one's thoughts turn naturally to the mysterious epoch of early agricultural experimentation that shadowed the great rains and floods between 13,000 BC and 10,500 BC.

Unseen connections?

This epoch was crucial not only for the Ancient Egyptians but for many peoples in other areas. Indeed, as we saw in Part IV, it was the epoch of dramatic climate shifts, rapidly rising sea levels, earth movements, floods, volcanic eruptions, bituminous rains and darkened skies that was the most probable source of many of the great worldwide myths of universal cataclysm.

Could it also have been an epoch in which 'gods' really did walk among men, as the legends said?

On the Bolivian Altiplano those gods were known as the Viracochas and were linked to the astonishing megalithic city of Tiahuanaco, which may have pre-existed the immense floods in the Andes in the eleventh millennium BC. Thereafter, according to Professor Arthur Posnansky, though the flood-waters subsided, 'the culture of the Altiplano did not again attain a high point of development but rather fell into a total and definitive decadence.'[12]

Of course, Posnansky's conclusions are controversial and must be evaluated on their own merits. Nevertheless, it is interesting that both the Bolivian Altiplano and Egypt should have been scoured by immense floods in the eleventh millennium BC. In both areas too, there are signs that extraordinarily early agricultural experiments – apparently based on introduced techniques – were attempted and then abandoned.[13] And in both areas important question-marks have been raised over the dating of monuments: the Puma Punku and the Kalasasaya in Tiahuanaco, for example, which Posnansky argued might have been built as early as 15,000 BC,[14] and, in Egypt, megalithic structures like the Osireion, the Great Sphinx and the Valley Temple of Khafre at Giza, which John West and the Boston University geologist Robert Schoch have dated on geological grounds to earlier than 10,000 BC.

Could there be an unseen connection linking all these beautiful, enigmatic monuments, the anomalous agricultural experiments of 13,000–10,000 BC, and the legends of civilizer gods like Osiris and Viracocha?

'Where is the rest of this civilization?'

As we set out on the road from Abydos to Luxor, where we were to meet John West, I realized that there was a sense in which all the connections would look after themselves if the central issue of the antiquity of the monuments could be settled. In other words, if West's geological evidence proved that the Sphinx was more than 12,000 years old, the history of human civilization was going to have to be rewritten. As part of that exciting process, all the other strange, anachronistic 'fingerprints of the gods' that kept appearing around the world, and the sense of an undercurrent of ancient connections linking apparently unrelated civilizations, would begin to make sense . . .

When West's evidence was presented in 1992 at the annual meeting of the American Association for the Advancement of Science it had been taken seriously enough to be publicly debated by the Chicago University Egyptologist Mark Lehner, director of the Giza Mapping Project, who – to the astonishment of almost everybody present – had been unable to come up with a convincing refutation. 'When you say

something as complex as the Sphinx dates to 9000 or 10,000 BC,'
Lehner had concluded:

> it implies, of course, that there was a very high civilization that was
> capable of producing the Sphinx at that period. The question an
> archaeologist has to ask, therefore, is this: if the Sphinx was made at
> that time then where is the rest of this civilization, where is the rest of
> this culture?'[15]

Lehner, however, was missing the point.

If the Sphinx did date to 9000 or 10,000 BC, the onus was not on
West to produce other evidence for the existence of the civilization
which produced it, but on Egyptologists and archaeologists to explain
how they had got things so wrong, so consistently, for so long.

So could West prove the antiquity of the Sphinx?

Chapter 47

Sphinx

'Egyptologists,' said John West, 'are the last people in the world to address any anomaly.'

Of course, there are many anomalies in Egypt. The one West was referring to at that moment, however, was the anomaly of the Fourth Dynasty pyramids: an anomaly because of what had happened during the Third, Fifth and Sixth Dynasties. Zoser's Step Pyramid at Saqqara (Third Dynasty) was an imposing edifice, but it was built with relatively small, manageable blocks that five or six men working together could carry, and its internal chambers were structurally unsound. The pyramids of the Fifth and Sixth Dynasties (although adorned inside with the beautiful Pyramid Texts) were so poorly built and had collapsed so completely that today most of them amount to little more than mounds of rubble. The Fourth Dynasty pyramids at Giza, however, were wonderfully well made and had endured the passage of thousands of years more or less intact.

It was this sequence of events, or rather its implications, that West felt Egyptologists should have paid more attention to: 'There's a discrepancy in the scenario that reads "building kind of rubbishy pyramids that are structurally unsound, suddenly building absolutely unbelievable pyramids that are structurally the most incredible things ever conceived of, and then immediately afterwards going back to structurally unsound pyramids." It doesn't make sense . . . The parallel scenario in, say, the auto-industry would be inventing and building the Model-T Ford, then suddenly inventing and building the '93 Porsche and making a few of those, then forgetting how to do that and going back to building Model-T Fords again . . . Civilizations don't work this way.'

'So what are you saying?' I asked. 'Are you saying that the Fourth Dynasty pyramids weren't built by the Fourth Dynasty at all?'

'My gut feeling is that they weren't. They don't look like the mastabas in front of them. They don't look like any other Fourth Dynasty stuff either . . . They don't seem to fit in . . .'

'And nor does the Sphinx?'

'And nor does the Sphinx. But the big difference is that we don't have to rely on gut feelings where the Sphinx is concerned. We can prove that it was built long before the Fourth Dynasty . . .'

John West

Santha and I had been fans of John Anthony West ever since we had first started travelling in Egypt. His guide-book, *The Traveller's Key* had been a brilliant and indispensable introduction to the mysteries of this ancient land, and we still carried it with us. At the same time his scholarly works, notably *Serpent in the Sky*, had opened our eyes to the revolutionary possibility that Egyptian civilization – with its manifold glimpses of high science apparently out of place in time – might *not* have developed entirely within the confines of the Nile Valley but might have been a legacy of some earlier, greater and as yet unidentified civilization 'antedating dynastic Egypt, and all other known civilizations, by millennia'.[1]

Tall and strongly built, West was in his early sixties. He had cultivated a neatly trimmed white beard, was dressed in a khaki safari-suit and wore an eccentric nineteenth-century pith helmet. His manner was youthful and energetic and there was a roguish sparkle in his eyes.

The three of us were sitting on the open upper deck of a Nile cruiser, moored off the corniche in Luxor just a few yards downstream from the Winter Palace Hotel. To our west, across the river, a big red sun, distorted by atmospheric refraction, was setting behind the cliffs of the Valley of the Kings. To our east lay the battered but noble ruins of the Luxor and Karnak temples. Beneath us, transmitted through the hull of the boat, we could feel the lap and flow of the water as it rolled by on its meridional course towards the far-off Delta.

West had first presented his thesis for an older Sphinx in *Serpent in the Sky*, a comprehensive exposition of the work of the French mathematician R.A. Schwaller de Lubicz. Schwaller's research at the Luxor Temple between 1937 and 1952 had unearthed mathematical evidence which suggested that Egyptian science and culture had been far more advanced and sophisticated than modern scholars had appreciated. However, as West put it, this evidence had been set out in 'abstruse, complex and uncompromising language . . . Few readers seem comfortable with raw Schwaller. It's a bit like trying to wade directly into high energy physics without extensive prior training.'

Schwaller's principal publications, both originally in French, were the massive three-volume *Temple de l'Homme*, which focused on Luxor, and the more general *Roi de la théocratie Pharaonique*. In this latter work, subsequently translated into English as *Sacred Science*, Schwaller made a passing reference to the tremendous floods and rains which devastated Egypt in the eleventh millennium BC. Almost as an afterthought, he added:

> A great civilization must have preceded the vast movements of water that passed over Egypt, which leads us to assume that the Sphinx already existed, sculptured in the rock of the west cliff at Giza – that Sphinx whose leonine body, except for the head, shows indisputable signs of water erosion.'[2]

While working on *Serpent*, West was struck by the possible significance of this remark and decided to follow it up: 'I realized that if I could prove Schwaller's offhand observation empirically, this would be ironclad evidence for the existence of a previously unidentified high civilization of distant antiquity.'

'Why?'

'Once you've established that water was the agent that eroded the Sphinx the answer is almost childishly simple. It can be explained to anybody who reads the *National Enquirer* or the *News of the World*. It's almost moronically simple . . . The Sphinx is supposed to have been built by Khafre around 2500 BC, but since the beginning of dynastic times – say 3000 BC onwards – there just hasn't been enough rain on the Giza plateau to have caused the very extensive erosion that we see all over the Sphinx's body. You really have to go back to before 10,000 BC to find a wet enough climate in Egypt to account for weathering of this type and on this scale. It therefore follows that the Sphinx must have been built before 10,000 BC and since it's a massive, sophisticated work of art it also follows that it must have been built by a high civilization.'

'But John,' Santha asked, 'how can you be so sure that the weathering *was* caused by rain water? Couldn't the desert winds have done the job just as well? After all even orthodox Egyptologists admit that the Sphinx has existed for nearly 5000 years. Isn't that long enough for these effects to have been caused by wind erosion?'

'Naturally that was one of the first possibilities that I had to exclude. Only if I could show that wind-borne abrasive sand couldn't possibly have brought the Sphinx to its present condition would there be any point in looking further into the implications of water erosion.'

Robert Schoch's geology: Unriddling the Sphinx

A key issue turned out to be the deep trench that the monument was surrounded by on all sides: 'Because the Sphinx is set in a hollow,' West explained, 'sand piles up to its neck within a few decades if it's left untended . . . It has been left untended often during historical times. In fact through a combination of textual references and historical extrapolations it's possible to prove that during the 4500 years that have elapsed since it was ostensibly built by Khafre it's been buried to its neck for as much as 3300 years.[3] That means that in all this time there has only been a cumulative total of just over 1000 years in which its body has been susceptible to wind-erosion; all the rest of the time it's been protected from the desert winds by an enormous blanket of sand. The point is that if the Sphinx was really built by Khafre in the Old Kingdom, and if wind erosion was capable of inflicting such damage on it in so short a time-span, then other Old Kingdom structures in the area, built out of the same limestone, ought to show similar weathering. But none do – you know, absolutely unmistakable Old Kingdom tombs, full of hieroglyphs and inscriptions – none of them show the same type of weathering as the Sphinx.'

Indeed, none did. Professor Robert Schoch, a Boston University geologist and specialist in rock erosion who had played a key role in validating West's evidence, was satisfied as to the reason for this. The weathering of the Sphinx – and of the walls of its surrounding rock-hewn enclosure – had not been caused by wind-scouring at all but by thousands of years of heavy rainfall long ages before the Old Kingdom came into being.

Having won over his professional peers at the 1992 Convention of the Geological Society of America,[4] Schoch went on to explain his findings to a much wider and more eclectic audience (including Egyptologists) at the 1992 Annual Meeting of the American Association for the Advancement of Science (AAAS). He began by pointing out to delegates that 'the body of the Sphinx and the walls of the Sphinx ditch are deeply weathered and eroded . . . This erosion is a couple of metres thick in places, at least on the walls. It's very deep, it's very old in my opinion, and it gives a rolling and undulating profile . . .'[5]

Such undulations are easily recognizable to stratigraphers and palaeontologists as having been caused by 'precipitation-induced weathering'. As Santha Faiia's photographs of the Sphinx and the Sphinx enclosure indicate, this weathering takes the distinctive form of a combination of deep vertical fissures and undulating, horizontal coves – 'a classic textbook example,' in Schoch's words, 'of what happens to a limestone structure when you have rain beating down on it for thousands of years . . . It's clearly rain precipitation that produced these erosional features.'[6]

Wind/sand erosion presents a very different profile of sharp-edged horizontal channels selectively scoured out from the softer layers of the affected rock. Under no circumstances can it cause the vertical fissures particularly visible in the wall of the Sphinx enclosure. These could only have been 'formed by water running down the wall',[7] the result of rain falling in enormous quantities, cascading over the slope of the Giza plateau and down into the Sphinx enclosure below. 'It picked out the weak spots in the rock,' Schoch elaborated, 'and opened them up into these fissures – clear evidence to me as a geologist that this erosional feature was caused by rainfall.'[8]

Although in some places obscured by repair blocks put in place by numerous restorers over the passing millennia, the same observation holds true for the scooped-out, undulating, scalloped coves that run the entire length of the Sphinx's body. Again, these are characteristic of precipitation-induced weathering because only long periods of heavy rainfall beating down on the upper parts of the immense structure (and cascading over its sides) could have produced such effects. Confirmation of this comes from the fact that the limestone out of which the Sphinx was carved is not uniform in its composition, but consists of a series of hard and soft layers in which some of the more durable rocks recede farther than some of the less durable rocks.[9] Such a profile simply could not have been produced by wind erosion (which would have selectively chiselled out the softer layers of rock) but 'is entirely 'consistent with precipitation-induced weathering where you have water, rain water beating down from above. The rocks higher up are the more durable ones but they recede back farther than some of the less durable rocks lower in the section which are more protected.'[10]

In his summing up at the AAAS meeting, Schoch concluded:

> It's well known that the Sphinx enclosure fills with sand very quickly, in just a matter of decades, under the desert conditions of the Sahara. And it has to be dug out periodically. And this has been the case since ancient times. Yet you still get this dramatic rolling, erosional profile in the Sphinx enclosure ... Simply put, therefore, what I'm suggesting is that this rolling profile, these features seen on the body and in the Sphinx ditch, hark back to a much earlier period when there was more precipitation in the area, and more moisture, more rain on the Giza plateau.'[11]

As Schoch admitted, he was not the first geologist to have noticed the 'anomalous precipitation-induced weathering features on the core body of the Sphinx'.[12] He was, however, the first to have become involved in public debates over the immense *historical* implications of this weathering. His attitude was that he preferred to stick to his geology:

I've been told over and over again that the peoples of Egypt, as far as we know, did not have either the technology or the social organization to cut out the core body of the Sphinx in pre-dynastic times . . . However, I don't see it as being my problem as a geologist. I'm not seeking to shift the burden, but its really up to the Egyptologists and archaeologists to figure out who carved it. If my *findings* are in conflict with their *theory* about the rise of civilization then maybe its time for them to re-evaluate that theory. I'm not saying that the Sphinx was built by Atlanteans, or people from Mars, or extra-terrestrials. I'm just following the science where it leads me, and it leads me to conclude that the Sphinx was built much earlier than previously thought . . .'[13]

Legendary civilizations

How much earlier?

John West told us that he and Schoch had 'a friendly debate going' about the age of the Sphinx: 'Schoch puts the date somewhere between 5000 BC and 7000 BC *minimum* [the epoch of the Neolithic Subpluvial] mainly by taking the most cautious view allowed by the data to hand. As a professor of Geology at a big university, he's almost constrained to take a conservative view – and it's true that there were rains between 7000 BC and 5000 BC. However, for a variety of both intuitive and scholarly reasons, I think that the date is much, much older and that most of the weathering of the Sphinx took place in the earlier rainy period before 10,000 BC . . . Frankly, if it was as relatively recent as 5000 to 7000 BC, I think we'd probably have found other evidence of the civilization that carved it. A lot of evidence from that period *has* been found in Egypt. There are some strange anomalies within it, I'll admit,[14] but most of it – the vast bulk – is really quite rudimentary.'

'So who built the Sphinx if it wasn't the pre-dynastic Egyptians?'

'My conjecture is that the whole riddle is linked in some way to those legendary civilizations spoken of in all the mythologies of the world. You know – that there were great catastrophes, that a few people survived and went wandering around the earth and that a bit of knowledge was preserved here, a bit there . . . My hunch is that the Sphinx is linked to all that. If I were asked to place a bet I'd say that it predates the break-up of the last Ice Age and is probably older than 10,000 BC, perhaps even older than 15,000 BC. My conviction – actually it's more than a conviction – is that it's *vastly old*.'

This was a conviction I increasingly shared – and, I reminded myself, that most nineteenth-century Egyptologists had shared it too. Nevertheless the Sphinx's appearance argued against such intuitions since there was no doubt that its head *looked* conventionally pharaonic. 'If it's as old as you think it is,' I now asked John, 'then how do you explain that the sculptors depicted it wearing the characteristic *nemes* head-dress and *uraeus* of dynastic times?'

'I'm not bothered about that. In fact, as you know, Egyptologists contend that the face of the Sphinx resembles the face of Khafre – its one of the reasons why they claim it must have been built by him. Schoch and I have looked into this very carefully. We think, from the proportions of the head relative to the rest of the body, that it's been *recarved* during dynastic times – and that's why it looks very dynastic. But we don't think it was ever meant to represent Khafre. As part of our ongoing research into these issues we had Lieutenant Frank Domingo, a forensic artist with the New York Police Department, come over and do point by point comparisons between the face of the Sphinx and the face of Cephren's statue in the Cairo Museum. His conclusion was that in no way was the Sphinx ever intended to represent Khafre. It's not just a matter of it being a different face – it's probably a different race.[15] So this is a very ancient monument that was recarved at a much later date. Originally it may not even have had a human face. Maybe it started out with a lion's *face* as well as a lion's body.'

Magellan and the first dinosaur bone

After my own explorations at Giza I was interested to know whether West's research had cast doubt on the orthodox dating of any of the other monuments on the plateau – particularly the so-called valley Temple of Khafre.

'We think there's quite a lot of stuff that may be older,' he told me. 'Not just the Valley Temple but also the Mortuary Temple up the hill, probably something to do with the Menkaure complex, maybe even the Pyramid of Khafre . . .'

'What in the Menkaure complex?'

'Well, the Mortuary Temple. And actually I'm only using the conventional atribution of the Pyramids for convenience here . . .'

'OK. So do you think it's possible that the pyramids are as old as the Sphinx too?'

'It's hard to say. I think something was there where those pyramids now are – because of the geometry. The Sphinx was part of a master-plan. And the Khafre Pyramid is maybe the most interesting in that respect because it was definitely built in two stages. If you look at it – maybe you've noticed – you'll see that its base consists of several courses of *gigantic* blocks similar in style to the blocks of the core masonry of the Valley Temple. Superimposed above the base, the rest of the pyramid is composed of smaller, less precisely engineered stuff. But when you look at it, knowing what you're looking for, you see instantly that it's built in two separate bits. I mean I can't help but feel that the vast blocks on the bottom date from the earlier period – from the time the Sphinx was built – and that the second part was added later – but even then not necessarily by Khafre. As you go into this you begin to realize that the more you learn the more complex everything becomes. For example, there may even have been an intermediate civilization, which actually would correspond to the Egyptian texts. They talk themselves about two long prior periods. In the first of these Egypt was supposedly ruled by the gods – the Neteru – and in the second it was ruled by the Shemsu Hor, the "Companions of Horus". So, as I say, the problems just get more and more complicated. Fortunately, however, the bottom line stays simple. The bottom line is the Sphinx wasn't built by Khafre. The geology proves that it's a hell of a lot older . . .'

'Nevertheless the Egyptologists won't accept that it is. One of the arguments they've used against you – Mark Lehner did so – goes something like this: "If the Sphinx was made before 10,000 BC then why can't you show us the rest of the civilization that built it?" In other words, why don't you have any other evidence to put forward for the presence of your legendary lost civilization apart from a few structures on the Giza plateau? What do you say to that?'

'First off, there *are* structures outside Giza – for example the Osireion in Abydos, where you've just come from. We think that amazing edifice may relate to our work on the Sphinx. Even if the Osireion didn't exist, however, the absence of other evidence wouldn't worry me. I mean, to make a big deal out of the fact that further confirmatory evidence *hasn't been found yet* and to use this to try to scuttle the arguments for an older Sphinx is completely illogical. Analogously it's like saying to Magellan . . . "Where are the other guys who've sailed round the world? Of course it's still flat." Or in 1838 when the first dinosaur bone was found they would have said, "Of course there's no such thing as a giant extinct animal. Where's the rest of the skeletons? They've only found one bone." But once a few people began to realize that this bone could only be from an extinct animal, within twenty years the museums of the world were filled up with complete dinosaur skeletons. So it's sort of like that. Nobody's thought to look in the right places. I'm absolutely certain that other evidence will be found once a few people start looking in the right places – along the banks of the ancient Nile, for example, which is miles from the present Nile, or even at the bottom of the Mediterranean, which was dry during the last Ice Age.'

The problem of transmission

I asked John West why he thought that Egyptologists and archaeologists were so unwilling to consider that the Sphinx might be a clue to the existence of a forgotten episode in human history.

'The reason, I think, is that they're quite fixed in their ideas about the linear evolution of civilization. They find it hard to come to terms with the notion that there might have been people, more than 12,000 years ago, who were more sophisticated than we are today . . . The Sphinx, and the geology which proves its antiquity, and the fact that the technology that was involved in making it is in many ways almost beyond our own capacities, contradicts the belief that civilization and technology have evolved in a straightforward, linear way . . . Because even with the best modern technology we almost couldn't carry out the various tasks that were involved in the project. The Sphinx itself, that's not such a staggering feat. I mean if you get enough sculptors to cut the stone away they could carve a statue a mile long. The *technology* was involved in taking the stones, quarrying the stones, to free the Sphinx from its bedrock and then in moving those stones and using them to build the Valley Temple a couple of hundred feet away . . .'

This was news to me: 'You mean that the 200-ton blocks in the Valley Temple walls were quarried right out of the Sphinx enclosure?'

'Yes, no doubt about it. Geologically they're from the identical member of rock. They were quarried out, moved over to the site of the Temple – God knows how – and erected into forty-foot-high walls – again God knows how. I'm talking about the huge limestone core blocks, not the granite facing. I think that the granite was added much later, quite possibly by Khafre. But if you look at the limestone core blocks you'll see that they bear the marks of exactly the same kind of precipitation-induced weathering that are found on the Sphinx. So the Sphinx and the core structure of the Valley Temple were made at the same time by the same people – whoever they may have been.'

'And do you think that those people and the later dynastic Egyptians were connected to each other in some way? In *Serpent in the Sky* you suggested that a legacy must have been passed on.'

'It's still just a suggestion. All that I know for sure on the basis of our work on the Sphinx is that a very, very high, sophisticated civilization capable of undertaking construction projects on a grand scale was present in Egypt in the very distant past. Then there was a lot of rain. Then, thousands of years later, in the same place, pharaonic civilization popped up already fully formed, apparently out of nowhere, with all its knowledge complete. That much we can be certain of. But whether or not the knowledge that Ancient Egypt possessed was the same as the knowledge that produced the Sphinx I really can't say.'

'How about this,' I speculated: 'The civilization that produced the Sphinx wasn't based here, at least not originally . . . It wasn't in Egypt. It put the Sphinx here as some sort of a marker or outpost . . .'

'Perfectly possible. Could be that the Sphinx for that civilization was like, let's say, what Abu Simbel [in Nubia] was for dynastic Egypt.'

'Then that civilization came to an end, was extinguished by some sort of massive catastrophe, and that's when the legacy of high knowledge was handed on . . . Because they had the Sphinx here they knew about Egypt, they knew this place, they knew this country, they had a connection here. Maybe people survived the ending of that civilization. Maybe they came here. . . . Does that work for you?'

'Well, it's a possibility. Again, going back into the mythologies and legends of the world, many of them tell of such a catastrophe and of the few people – the Noah story that's prevalent through endless civilizations – who somehow or other retained and passed on knowledge. The big problem with all this, from my point of view, is the transmission process: how exactly the knowledge does get handed on during the thousands and thousands of years between the construction of the Sphinx and the flowering of dynastic Egypt. Theoretically you're sort of stuck – aren't you? – with this vast period in which the knowledge has to be transmitted. This is not easy to slough off. On the other hand we do know that those legends we're referring to were passed on word for word over countless generations. And in fact oral transmission is a much surer means of transmission than written transmission, because the language may change but as long as whoever's telling the story tells it true in whatever the language of the time is . . . it surfaces some 5000 years later in its original form. So maybe there are ways – in secret societies and religious cults, or through mythology, for example – that the knowledge could have been preserved and passed on before flowering again. The point, I think, with problems as complex and important as these, is simply not to dismiss any possibilities, no matter how outrageous they may at first seem, without investigating them very, very thoroughly . . .'

Second opinion

John West was in Luxor, leading a study group on Egypt's sacred sites. Early the next day he and his students went south to Aswan and Abu Simbel. Santha and I journeyed north again, back towards Giza and the mysteries of the Sphinx and the pyramids. We were to meet there with the archaeo-astronomer Robert Bauval. As we shall see, his stellar correlations provided startling independent corroboration for the geological evidence of Giza's vast antiquity.

Chapter 48

Earth Measurers

Follow these instructions carefully:

Draw two parallel straight lines vertically down a sheet of paper, about seven inches long and a bit under three inches apart. Draw a third line, also vertical, also parallel and of equal length, exactly midway between the first two. Write the letter 'S' – for 'South' – at the top end of your diagram (the end farthest away from you), and the letter 'N' for 'North' at the bottom end. Add the letters 'E' for 'East' and 'W' for 'West' in their appropriate positions at either side of the diagram, to your left for East and to your right for West.

What you are looking at are the outlines of a geometrical map of Egypt incorporating a perspective very different from our own (where 'North' is always equated with 'Up'). This map where 'Up' is 'South' seems to have been worked out an enormously long time ago by cartographers with a scientific understanding of the shape and size of our planet.

To complete the map you should now mark a dot on the central of the three parallel lines about an inch to the south of ('up' from) the northern end of the diagram. Then draw two more lines diagonally down from this point, respectively to the north-east and north-west, until they reach the northern ends of the two outermost parallel lines. Finally link those parallel lines directly with horizontal lines running east to west at the northern and southern ends of the diagram.

The shape produced is a meridional rectangle (oriented north-

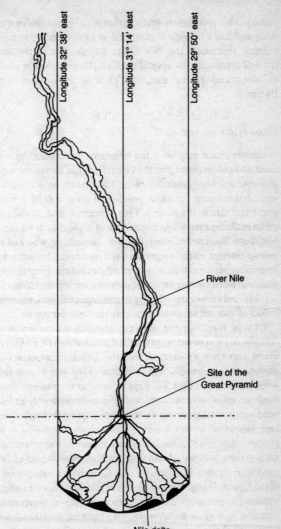

Map showing the geometric conception of Egypt, with the Great Pyramid at the apex of the Nile delta. The Egyptians traditionally thought of south as 'up'.

south). This rectangle is seven inches long by just under three inches wide and has a triangle demarcated at its northern (lower) end. The triangle represents the Nile Delta and the dot at the apex of the triangle represents the apex of the Delta – a point on the ground at 30° 06′ north and 31° 14′ east, very close to the location of the Great Pyramid.

Geodetic marker

Whatever else it may be, it has long been understood by mathematicians and geographers that the Great Pyramid serves the function of a geodetic marker (geodetics being the branch of science concerned with determining the exact position of geographical points and the shape and size of the earth[1]). This realization first dawned in the late eighteenth century when the armies of revolutionary France, led by Napoleon Bonaparte, invaded Egypt. Bonaparte, who had cultivated a deep interest in the enigmas of the pyramids, brought with him a large number of scholars, 175 in all, including several 'greybeards' gathered from various universities who were reputed to have acquired 'a profound knowledge of Egyptian antiquities', and, more usefully, a group of mathematicians, cartographers and surveyors.[2]

One of the tasks the savants were set, after the conquest was completed, was to draw up detailed maps of Egypt. In the process of doing this they discovered that the Great Pyramid was perfectly aligned to true north – and of course to the south, east and west as well, as we saw in Part VI. This meant that the mysterious structure made an excellent reference and triangulation point, and a decision was therefore taken to use the meridian passing through its apex as the base-line for all other measurements and orientations. The team then proceeded to produce the first accurate maps of Egypt drawn up in the modern age. When they had finished, they were intrigued to note that the Great Pyramid's meridian sliced the Nile Delta region into two equal halves. They also found that if the diagonals running from the pyramid's apex to its north-eastern and north-western corners were extended (forming lines on the map running north-east and north-west until they reached the Mediterranean), the triangle thus formed would neatly encapsulate the entire Delta area.[3]

Let us now return to our map, which also incorporates a triangle representing the Delta. Its other main components are the three parallel meridians. The eastern meridian is at longitude 32° 38′ east – the official eastern border of Ancient Egypt from the beginning of dynastic times. The western meridian is at longitude 29° 50′ east, the official western border of ancient Egypt. The central meridian is at longitude 31° 14′ east, exactly midway between the other two (1° 24′ away from each).[4]

What we now have is a representation of a strip on the surface of planet earth that is exactly 2° 48′ wide. How long is this strip? Ancient Egypt's 'official' northern and southern borders (which bore no more relationship to settlement patterns than the official eastern and western boundaries) are marked by the horizontal lines at the top and bottom of the map and are located respectively at 31° 06′ north and 24° 06′ north.[5] The northern border, 31° 06′ north, joins the two outer ends of the estuary of the Nile. The southern border, 24° 06′N, marks the precise latitude of the island of Elephantine at Aswan (Seyne) where an important astronomical and solar observatory was located throughout known Egyptian history.[6] It seems, that this archaic land, sacred since time began – the creation and habitation of the gods – was originally conceived of as a *geometric construct* exactly seven terrestrial degrees in length.

Within this construct, the Great Pyramid appears to have been carefully sited as a goedetic marker for the apex of the Delta. The latter, which we have indicated on our map, is located at 30° 06′N 31 14′E – a point in the middle of the Nile at the northern edge of modern Cairo. Meanwhile the pyramid stands at latitude of 30°N (corrected for atmospheric refraction) and at longitude 31° 09′E, an error of just a few minutes of terrestrial arc to the south and west. This 'error', however, does not appear to have resulted from sloppiness or inaccuracy on the part of the pyramid builders. On the contrary, a close look at the topography of the area suggests that the explanation should be sought in the need to find a site suitable for all the astronomical observations, that had to be taken for accurate setting-out, and with a sufficiently stable geological structure on which to park, for ever, a six-million-ton monument almost 500 feet high with a footprint of over thirteen acres.

The Giza plateau fills the bill on all counts: close to the apex of the Delta, elevated above the Valley of the Nile, and equipped with an excellent foundation of solid limestone bedrock.

Doing things by degrees

We were driving north from Luxor to Giza in the back of Mohamed Walilli's Peugeot 504 – a journey of just over 4 degrees of longitude, i.e., from 25° 42′N, to the 30th parallel. Between Asiut and El Minya, a corridor of conflict in recent months between Islamic extremists and Egyptian government forces, we were provided with an armed escort of soldiers, one of whom wore plain clothes and sat in the passenger seat beside Mohamed fondling an automatic pistol. The others, about a dozen men armed with AK47 assault rifles, were distributed equally between two pick-up trucks which sandwiched us front and rear.

'Dangerous people live here,' Mohamed had confided out of the corner of his mouth when we had been stopped at a road-block in Asiut and ordered to wait for our escort. Now, although obviously rattled at being obliged to match the high speed of the escorting vehicles, he seemed to relish the kudos of being part of an impressive convoy, lights flashing and sirens wailing, weaving in and out of the slower traffic on the main highway from upper to lower Egypt.

I looked out of the car window for a while at the unchanging spectacle of the Nile, at its fertile green banks and the red haze of the deserts a few miles away to east and west. This was Egypt, the real organic Egypt of today and yesterday, which overlapped (but spread out far beyond) the strange 'official' Egypt of the map described, a rectangular fiction exactly seven terrestial degrees in length.

In the nineteenth century the renowned Egyptologist Ludwig Borchardt expressed what is still the conventional wisdom of his colleagues when he remarked, 'One must absolutely exclude the possibility that the ancients may have measured by degrees.'[7] This was a judgement that seemed increasingly unlikely to be tenable. Whoever they may have been, it was obvious that the original planners and architects of the Giza necropolis had belonged to a civilization which knew the earth to be a sphere, knew its dimensions almost as well as we do ourselves, and had divided it into 360 degrees, just as we do today.

The proof of this lay in the creation of a symbolic official 'country' exactly seven terrestrial degrees in length, and in the admirably geodetic location and orientation to the cardinal points of the Great Pyramid. Equally persuasive was the fact, already touched on in Chapter Twenty-three, that the perimeter of the pyramid's base stood in the relationship $2pi$ to its height and that the entire monument seemed to have been designed to serve as a *map-projection* – on a scale of 1:43,200 – of the northern hemisphere of our planet:

> The Great Pyramid was a projection on four triangular surfaces. The apex represented the pole and the perimeter represented the equator. This is the reason why the perimeter is in relation $2pi$ to the height.[8]

The Pyramid/Earth ratio

We have demonstrated the use of pi in the Pyramid[9] and need not go into this matter again; besides, the existence of the pi relationship, though interpreted as *accidental* by orthodox scholars, is not contested by them.[10] But are we seriously supposed to accept that the monument could also be a representation of the northern hemisphere of the earth projected on flat surfaces at a scale of 1:43,200? Let us remind ourselves of the figures.

According to the best modern estimates, based on satellite observations, the equatorial circumference of the earth is 24,902.45 miles and its polar radius is 3949.921 miles.[11] The perimeter of the Great Pyramid's base is 3023.16 feet and its height is 481.3949 feet.[12] The scaling-down, as it turns out, is not *absolutely* exact, but it is very near. Moreover, when we remember the bulge at the earth's equator (our planet being an oblate spheroid rather than a perfect sphere), the results achieved by the pyramid builders seem even closer to 1:43,200.

How close?

If we take the earth's equatorial circumference, 24,902.45 miles, and scale it down (divide it) by 43,200 we get a result of 0.5764 of a mile. There are 5280 feet in a mile. The next step, therefore, is to multiply 0.5764 by 5280, which produces a figure of 3043.39 feet. The earth's equatorial circumference scaled down 43,200 times is therefore 3,043.39 feet. By comparison, as we have seen, the perimeter of the Great Pyramid's base is 3,023.16 feet. This represents an 'error' of only 20 feet – or about three-quarters of 1 per cent. Given the razor-sharp accuracy of the pyramid builders, however (who normally worked to even finer tolerances), the error is less likely to have resulted from mistakes in the construction of the giant monument than in an underestimation of our planet's true circumference *by just 163 miles*, probably caused in part by failure to take account of the equatorial bulge.

Let us now consider the earth's polar radius of 3,949.921 miles. If we scale it down 43,200 times we get 0.0914 of a mile: 482.59 feet. The earth's polar radius scaled down 43,200 times is therefore 482.59 feet. By comparison the Great Pyramid's height is 481.3949 feet – just a foot less than the ideal figure, an error of barely one-fifth of one per cent.

As near as makes no difference, therefore, the perimeter of the Great Pyramid's base is indeed 1:43,200 of the equatorial circumference of the earth. And as near as makes no difference, the height of the Great Pyramid above that base is indeed 1:43,200 of the polar radius of the earth. In other words, during all the centuries of darkness experienced by Western civilization when knowledge of our planet's dimensions was lost to us, all we ever needed to do to rediscover that knowledge was to measure the height and base perimeter of the Great Pyramid and multiply by 43,200!

How likely is this to be an 'accident'?

The commonsense answer is 'not very likely at all,' since it should be obvious to any reasonable person that what we are looking at could only be the result of a deliberate and carefully calculated planning decision. Commonsense, however, has never been a faculty held in high esteem by Egyptologists, and it is therefore necessary to ask whether there is anything else in the data which might confirm that the ratio of 1:43,200 is a purposeful expression of intelligence and knowledge, rather than some numerical fluke.

The ratio itself seems to provide that confirmation, for the simple reason that 43,200 is *not* a random number (like, say, 45,000 or 47,000, or 50,500, or 38,800). On the contrary it is one of a series of numbers, and multiples of those numbers, which relate to the phenomenon of precession of the equinoxes, and which have become embedded in archaic myths all around the world. As the reader can confirm by glancing back at Part V the basic numerals of the Pyramid/Earth ratio crop up again and again in those myths, sometimes directly as 43,200 sometimes as 432, as 4,320, as 432,000, as 4,320,000, and so on.

What we appear to be confronted by are two remarkable propositions, back-to-back, as though designed to reinforce one another. It is surely remarkable enough that the Great Pyramid should be able to function as an accurate scale-model of the northern hemisphere of planet earth. But it is even more remarkable that the *scale involved* should incorporate numbers relating precisely to one of the key planetary mechanisms of the earth. This is the fixed and apparently eternal precession of its axis of rotation around the pole of the ecliptic, a phenomenon which causes the vernal point to migrate around the band of the zodiac at the rate of one degree every 72 years, and 30 degrees (one complete zodiacal constellation) every 2,160 years. Precession through two zodiacal constellations, or 60 degrees along the ecliptic, takes 4320 years [13]

The constant repetition of these precessional numbers in ancient myths could, perhaps, be a coincidence. Viewed in isolation, the appearance of the precessional number 43,200 in the pyramid/earth ratio might also be a coincidence (although the odds against this must be astronomical). But when we find precessional numbers in *both* these very different media – the ancient myths and the ancient monument – it really does strain credulity to suppose that coincidence is all that is involved here. Moreover, just as the Teutonic myth of Valhalla's walls leads us to the precessional number 432,000 by inviting us to *calculate* the warriors who 'go to war with the Wolf' (500 plus 40 multiplied by 800, as saw in Chapter Thirty-three), so the Great Pyramid leads us to the precessional number 43,200 by demonstrating through the *pi* relationship that it might be a scale-model part of the earth and then by inviting us to *calculate* that scale.

Matching fingerprints?

At El Minya our escort vehicles left us, though the plain-clothes soldier in the front seat stayed with us until Cairo. We paused for a late lunch of bread and felafel in a boisterous, noisy village, then mortored north again.

Throughout all this, my thoughts remained focused on the Great Pyramid. Obviously it was not an accident that so immense and conspicuous a structure should occupy a key geographic and geodetic location in a part of the world that appeared, bizarrely, to have been conceived of and 'geometrized' as a rectangular, symbolic construct exactly seven terrestrial degrees in length. But it was the pyramid's other function as a three-dimensional map projection of the northern hemisphere that particularly interested me because it suggested a 'match' with the ancient but advanced maps of the world described in Part I. Those maps, which made use of spherical trigonometry and a range of sophisticated projections, had been claimed by Professor Charles Hapgood to provide tangible, documentary evidence that an advanced civilization with a comprehensive knowledge of the globe must have flourished during the last Ice Age. Now here was the Great Pyramid proving to have a cartographic function *vis-à-vis* the northern hemisphere and also incorporating a sophisticated projection. As one expert explained:

> Each flat face of the Pyramid was designed to represent one curved quarter of the northern hemisphere, or spherical quadrant of 90 degrees. To project a spherical quadrant on to a flat triangle correctly, the arc, or base, of the quadrant must be the same length as the base of the triangle, and both must have the same height. This happens to be the case *only* with a cross-section or meridian bisection of the Great Pyramid, whose slope angle gives the *pi* relation between height and base . . .[14]

Was it possible that surviving copies and compilations of ancient maps – like the Piri Reis Map, for example – might in some cases go back to source documents produced by the same culture that skilfully incorporated its knowledge of the globe into the dimensions of the Great Pyramid (and indeed into the carefully geometrized dimensions of Ancient Egypt itself)?

I could hardly forget that Charles Hapgood and his team had spent months trying to work out where the original projection of the Piri Reis Map had been centred. The answer they finally obtained was Egypt and specifically Seyne (Aswan) in upper Egypt[15] – where, as we have seen, an important astronomical observatory was situated at latitude 24° 06'N, the official southern border.

Needless to say, precise astronomical observations would have been essential for calculations of the circumference of the earth and of latitude positions.[16] But for how long *before* the historical period had the Ancient Egyptians and their ancestors been making such observations? And had they indeed learned this skill, as they stated forthrightly in their traditions, from the gods who had once walked among them?

Navigators in the Boat of Millions of Years

The god believed by the Ancient Egyptians to have taught the principles of astronomy to their ancestors was Thoth: 'He who reckons in heaven, the counter of the stars, the enumerator of the earth and of what is therein, and the measurer of the earth.'[17]

Normally depicted as a man wearing an ibis mask, Thoth was a leading member of the elite company of First Time deities who dominated religious life in Ancient Egypt from the beginning to the end of its civilization. These were the great gods, the Neteru. Although they were believed in one sense to be self-created, it was also openly acknowledged and understood that they had a special connection of some kind with another land – a fabulous and far-off country referred to in the ancient texts as Ta–Neteru, the 'land of the gods'.[18]

Ta–Neteru was thought to have had a definite earthly location a very long way south of Ancient Egypt – seas and oceans away – farther even than the spice country of Punt (which probably lay along East Africa's Somali coast).[19] To confuse matters, however, Punt was also spoken of sometimes as the 'Divine Land', or 'God's Land', and was the source of the sweet-smelling frankincense and myrrh especially favoured by the gods.[20]

Another mythical paradise was also linked to the Neteru – an 'abode of the blessed', where the best of humans were sometimes taken – which was believed to be 'situated away beyond a large expanse of water'. As Wallis Budge observed in his important study, *Osiris and the Egyptian Resurrection*, 'the Egyptians believed that this land could only be reached by means of a boat, or by the personal help of the gods who were thought to transport their favourites thither . . .'[21] Those lucky enough to gain entry would find themselves in a magical garden consisting of 'islands, interconnected by canals filled with running water which caused them to be always green and fertile'.[22] On the islands in this garden, 'the wheat grew to a height of five cubits, the ears being two cubits long and the stalks three, and the barely grew to a height of seven cubits, the ears being three cubits long and the stalks four.'[23]

Was it from a land such as this, superbly irrigated and scientifically farmed, that the agriculture bringer Osiris, whose title was 'President of the Land of the South',[24] had voyaged to Egypt at the dawn of the First Time? And was it from a land such as this, accessible only by boat, that ibis-masked Thoth had also made his way, crossing seas and oceans to deliver the priceless gifts of astronomy and earth-measurement to the primitive inhabitants of the prehistoric Nile Valley?

Whatever the truth behind the tradition, Thoth was remembered and revered by the Ancient Egyptians as the inventor of mathematics, astronomy an engineering.[25] 'It was his will and power', according to Wallis Budge, 'that were believed to keep the forces of heaven and earth in equilibrium. It was his great skill in celestial mathematics which made proper use of the laws upon which the foundation and maintenance of the universe rested.'[26] Thoth was also credited with teaching the ancestral Egyptians the skills of geometry and land-surveying, medicine and botany. He was believed to have been the inventor 'of figures, of the letters of the alphabet, and of the arts of reading and writing'.[27] He was the 'Great Lord of Magic'[28] who could move objects with the power of his voice, 'the author of every work on every branch of knowledge, both human and divine'.[29]

It was to the teachings of Thoth – which they guarded jealously in their temples and claimed to have handed down from generation to generation in the form of forty-two books of instruction[30] – that the Ancient Egyptians ascribed their world-renowned wisdom and knowledge of the skies. This knowledge was spoken of almost in awe, by the classical commentators who visited Egypt from the fifth century BC onwards.

Herodotus, the earliest of these travellers, noted:

> The Egyptians were the first to discover the solar year, and to portion out its course into twelve parts . . . It was observation of the course of the stars which led them to adopt this division . . .[31]

Plato (fourth century BC) reported that the Egyptians had observed the stars 'for ten thousand years'.[32] And later, in the first century BC, Diodorus Siculus left this more detailed account:

> The positions and arrangements of the stars as well as their motions have always been the subject of careful observation among the Egyptians . . . From ancient times to this day they have preserved the records concerning each of these stars over an incredible number of years . . .[33]

Why should the Ancient Egyptians have cultivated an almost obsessional interest in the long-term observation of the stars, and why in particular should they have kept records of their movements 'over an incredible number of years'? Such detailed observations would not have been necessary if their only interest, as a number of scholars have seriously suggested, had been agricultural (the need to predict the seasons, which any country-born person can do). There must have been some other purpose.

Moreover, how did the Ancient Egyptians get started on astronomy in the first place? It is not an obvious hobby for a valley-dwelling landlocked people to develop on their own initiative. Perhaps we should take more seriously the explanation they themselves offer: that their ancestors were taught the study of the stars by a god. We might also pay closer attention to the many unmistakably maritime references in the Pyramid Texts.[34] And there could be important new inferences to draw from ancient Egyptian religious art in which the gods are shown travelling in beautiful, high-prowed, streamlined boats, built to the same advanced ocean-going specifications as the pyramid boats at Giza and the mysterious fleet moored in the desert sands at Abydos.

Landlocked people do not as rule become astronomers; seafaring people do. Is it not possible that the maritime iconography of the Ancient Egyptians, the design of their ships, and also their splendid obsession with observing the stars, could have been part of an inheritance passed on to their ancestors by an unidentified seafaring, *navigating* race, in remote prehistory? It is really only such an archaic race, such a forgotten maritime civilization, that could have left its fingerprints behind in the form of maps which accurately depict the world as it looked before the end of the last Ice Age. It is really only such a civilization, steering its course by the stars 'for ten thousand years' that could have observed and accurately timed the phenomenon of equinoctial precession with the exactitude attested in the ancient myths. And, although hypothetical, it is only such a civilization that could have measured the earth with sufficient precision to have arrived at the dimensions scaled down in the Great Pyramid.

The signature of a distant date

It was almost midnight by the time that we reached Giza. We checked into the Siag, a hotel with an excellent pyramid view, and sat out on our balcony as the three stars of Orion's belt tracked slowly across the southern heavens.

It was the disposition of these three stars, as archaeo-astronomer Robert Bauval had recently demonstrated, that served as the celestial template for the site-plan of the three Giza pyramids. This, in itself, was a remarkable discovery, suggesting a far higher level of observational astronomy, and of surveying and setting-out skills, than scholars had attributed to the Ancient Egyptians. Even more remarkable, however – and the reason that I had arranged to meet him at Giza the next morning – was Bauval's contention that the pattern traced out on the ground (in almost fifteen million tons of perfectly dressed stone) matched exactly the pattern in the sky during the epoch of 10,450 BC.

If Bauval was correct, the pyramids had been devised, using the changes precession effects in the positions of the stars, as the permanent architectural signature of the eleventh millennium BC.

Chapter 49

The Power of the Thing

On a scale of 1:43,200 the Great Pyramid serves as a model, and map-projection, of the northern hemisphere of the earth. What absolutely excludes the possibility that this could be a coincidence is the fact that the scale involved is keyed in numerically to the rate of precession of the equinoxes – one of earth's most characteristic planetary mechanisms. It is therefore clear that we are confronted here by the manifestation of a deliberate planning decision: one intended to be recognizable as such by any culture which had acquired (a) an accurate knowledge of the dimensions of the earth and (b) an accurate knowledge of the rate of precessional motion.

Thanks to the work of Robert Bauval, we can now be certain that another deliberate planning decision was implemented in the Great Pyramid (which – it is increasingly apparent – must be understood as a device designed to fulfil many different functions). In this case the plan was a truly ambitious one involving the Second and Third Pyramids as well, but it bears the fingerprints of the same ancient architects and builders who conceived of the Great Pyramid as a scale model of the earth. Their hallmark seems to have been precession – perhaps because they liked its mathematical regularity and predictability – and they used precession to devise a plan which could be understood properly only by a scientifically advanced culture.

Ours is such a culture, and Robert Bauval is the first to have worked out the basic parameters of the plan – a discovery for which he has received public acclaim and will in due course, get the scientific recognition he deserves.[1] Belgian by nationality, born and brought up in Alexandria, he is tall, lean, clean-shaven, forty-something, and going a little thin on top. His most notable feature is a stubborn lower jaw which characterizes his tenacious, inquiring personality; he speaks with a hybrid French-Egyptian-English accent and is decidedly oriental in manner. He has a first-class mind and is always restlessly accumulating and analysing new data relevant to his interests, finding new ways to look at old problems. In the process, entirely by accident, he has succeeded in transforming himself into a kind of magician of esoteric knowledge.

The Orion Mystery

The roots of Bauval's discoveries at Giza go back to the 1960s when the Egyptologist and architect Dr Alexander Badawy and the American astronomer Virginia Trimble demonstrated that the southern shaft of the King's Chamber in the Great Pyramid was targeted like a gun-barrel on the Belt of Orion during the Pyramid Age – around 2600 to 2400 BC.[2]

Bauval decided to test the southern shaft of the Queen's Chamber, which Badaway and Trimble had not investigated, and established that it had been sighted on the star Sirius during the Pyramid Age. The evidence that proved this was provided by the German engineer Rudolf Gantenbrink as a result of measurements taken by his robot *Upuaut* in March 1993. This was the robot that had made the startling discovery of a closed portcullis door blocking the shaft at a distance of about 200 feet from the Queen's Chamber. Equipped with a high-tech on-board clinometer, the little machine had also provided the first-ever completely accurate reading of the shaft's angle of inclination: 39° 30′.[3]

As Bauval explains:

> I did the calculations and these established that the shaft had been targeted on the meridian transit of Sirius around the epoch 2400 BC. There couldn't be any doubt about it at all. I also recalculated the Orion's Belt alignment worked out by Badawy and Trimble with new data that Gantenbrink gave me on the inclination of the southern shaft

of the King's Chamber. He'd measured that at 45 degrees exactly, whereas Badawy and Trimble had worked with Flinders Petrie's slightly less accurate measurement of 44° 30'. The new data enabled me to refine Badawy's and Trimble's date for the alignment. What I found was that the shaft had been precisely targeted on Al Nitak, the lowest of the three belt stars, which crossed the meridian at altitude 45 degrees around the year 2475 BC.[4]

Up to this point Bauval's conclusions had been well within the chronological bounds set by orthodox Egyptologists, who normally dated the construction of the Great Pyramid to around 2520 BC.[5] If anything, the alignments the archaeo-astronomer had come up with suggested that the shafts had been built a little *later*, rather than earlier, than conventional wisdom allowed.

As the reader is aware, however, Bauval had also made another discovery of an altogether more unsettling nature. Once again it involved the stars of Orion's Belt:

They're slanted along a diagonal in a south-westerly direction relative to the axis of the Milky Way and the pyramids are slanted along a diagonal in a south-westerly direction relative to the axis of the Nile. If you look carefully on a clear night you'll also see that the smallest of the three stars, the one at the top which the Arabs call Mintaka, is slightly offset to the east of the principal diagonal formed by the other two. This pattern is mimicked on the ground where we see that the Pyramid of Menkaure is offset by exactly the right amount to the east of the principal diagonal formed by the Pyramid of Khafre (which represents the middle star, Al Nilam) and the Great Pyramid, which represents Al Nitak. It's really quite obvious that all these monuments were laid out according to a unified site plan that was modelled with extraordinary precision on those three stars. . . . What they did at Giza was to build Orion's Belt on the ground.'[6]

There was more to come. Using a sophisticated computer programme[7] capable of plotting the precessionally induced changes in the declinations of all the stars visible in the sky over any part of the world in any epoch, Bauval found that the Pyramids/Orion's Belt correlation was general and obvious in all epochs, but specific and exact in only one:

At 10450 BC – and at that date only – we find that the pattern of the

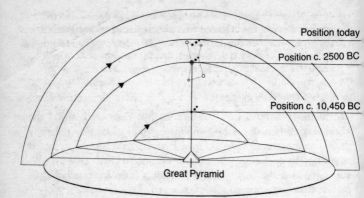

Precession and the stars of Orion's belt.

pyramids on the ground provides a perfect reflection of the pattern of the stars in the sky. I mean it's a *perfect* match – faultless – and it cannot be an accident because the entire arrangement correctly depicts two very unusual celestial events that occurred only at that time. First, and purely by chance, the Milky Way, as visible from Giza in 10450 BC, exactly duplicated the meridional course of the Nile Valley; secondly, to the west of the Milky Way, the three stars of Orion's Belt were at the lowest altitude in their precessional cycle, with Al Nitak, the star represented by the Great Pyramid, crossing the meridien at 11° 08'.[8]

The reader is already familiar with the way the earth's axial precession causes sunrise on the vernal equinox to migrate along the band of the zodiac over a cycle of about 26,000 years. The same phenomenon also affects the declination of all visible stars, producing, in the case of the Orion constellation, very gradual but significant changes in altitude. Thus from its highest point at meridian transit (58° 11' above the southern horizon as viewed from Giza) it takes Al Nitak about 13,000 years to descend to the low point, last registered in 10450 BC, that is immortalized in stone on the Giza plateau – i.e. 11° 08′. As another 13,000 years pass, the belt stars very slowly rise again until Al Nitak is back at 58° 11′; then during the next 13,000 years they gradually fall once more to 11° 08′. This cycle is eternal: 13,000 years up, 13,000 years down, 13,000 years up, 13,000 years down, for ever.[9]

> It's the precise configuration for 10450 BC that we see on the Giza plateau – as though a master-architect came here in that epoch and decided to lay out a huge map on the ground using a mixture of natural and artificial features. He used the meridional course of the Nile Valley to depict the Milky Way, as it looked then. He built the three pyramids to represent the three stars, exactly as they looked then. And he put the three pyramids in exactly the same relationship to the Nile Valley as the three stars then had to the Milky Way. It was a very clever, very ambitious, very exact way to mark an epoch – to freeze a particular date into architecture if you like . . . [10]

The First Time

I found the implications of the Orion correlation complicated and eerie.

On the one hand, the Great Pyramid's southern shafts 'precessionally anchored' the monument to Al Nitak and Sirius in 2475–2400 BC, dates which coincided comfortably with the epoch when Egyptologists said the monument had been built.

On the other hand the disposition of all three of the pyramids in relation to the Nile Valley eloquently signalled the much earlier date of 10450 BC. This coincided with the controversial geological findings John West and Robert Schoch had made at Giza, which suggested the presence of a high civilization in Egypt in the eleventh millennium BC. Moreover, the disposition of the pyramids had not been arrived at by any random or accidental process but seemed to have been deliberately chosen because it marked a precessionally significant event: the lowest point, the beginning, the First Time in Orion's 13,000-year 'up' cycle.

I knew that Bauval believed this astronomical event to have been linked symbolically to the mythical First Time of Osiris – the time of the gods, when civilization had supposedly been brought into the Nile

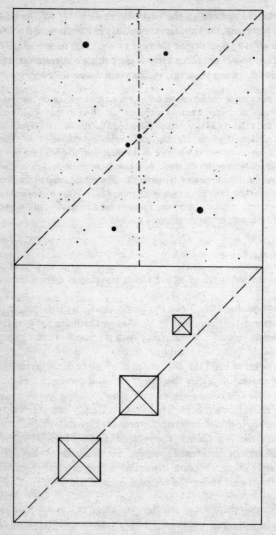

The pyramids and the belt stars of Orion at 10,450 BC, meridian view.

Valley – and that his reasoning for this derived from the mythology of Ancient Egypt which directly associated Osiris with the Orion constellation (and Isis with Sirius).[11]

Had the historical archetypes for Osiris and Isis actually come here in the First Time, twelve and a half thousand years ago?[12] My research into Ice Age mythologies had persuaded me that certain ideas and memories could linger in the human psyche for many millennia, transmitted from generation to generation by oral tradition. I could therefore see no prima facie reasons why the Osirian mythology, with its strange and anomalous characteristics, should not have originated as far back as 10450 BC.

However, it was the civilization of dynastic Egypt that had elevated Osiris to the status of the high god of resurrection. That civilization was one that had few known antecedents, and none at all recognizable in the remote epoch of the eleventh millennium BC. If the Osirian mythology had been transmitted across 8000 years, therefore, then what culture had transmitted it? And had this culture also been responsible for *both* the astronomical alignments proven to have been manifested by the pyramids: 10450 BC and 2450 BC?

These were among the questions I planned to put to Robert Bauval in the shadow of the pyramids. Santha and I had arranged to meet him at dawn, at the Mortuary Temple of Khafre, so that the three of us could watch the sun come up over the Sphinx.

The platform

Positioned beside the eastern face of the Second Pyramid, the largely ruined Mortuary Temple was a spooky, grey, cold place to be at this hour. And as John West had indicated during our conversation at Luxor, there could be little doubt that it belonged to the same severe, imposing and unadorned style of architecture as the better-known Valley Temple. Here, at any rate, were the same enormous blocks, weighing 200 tons or more each.[13] And here too was the same intangible atmosphere of vast antiquity and awakening intelligence, as though some epiphany might be at hand. Even in its present, much despoiled state, this anonymous structure, which Egyptologists had called a Mortuary Temple, was still a place of power that seemed to draw its energy from an epoch far in the past.

I looked up at the huge mass of the Second Pyramid's eastern face just behind us in the pearl-grey dawn light. Again, as John West had pointed out, there was much to suggest that it might have been built in two different stages. The lower courses, up to a height of perhaps forty feet, consisted largely of cyclopean limestone megaliths like those in the temples. Above this height, however, the remainder of the pyramid's gigantic core had been formed out of much smaller blocks weighing around two to three tons each (like the majority of the blocks in the Great Pyramid).

Had there been a time when a twelve-acre, forty-foot-high megalithic *platform* had stood here on the 'hill of Giza', west of the Sphinx, surrounded only by nameless square and rectangular structures such as the Valley and Mortuary Temples? In other words, was it possible that the Second Pyramid's lower courses might have been built *first*, before the other pyramids – perhaps long before, in a much earlier age?

The cult

That question was still on my mind when Robert Bauval arrived. After exchanging a few chilly pleasantries about the weather – a cold desert wind was blowing across the plateau – I asked him, 'How do you account for the 8000-year gap in your correlations?'

'Gap?'

'Yes; shafts that seem to have been aligned in 2450 BC and a site-plan that maps star positions in 10450 BC.'

'Actually, I see two explanations that both make some kind of sense,' said Bauval, 'and I think the answer has to be one or the other of these . . . Either the pyramids were designed as a sort of "star-clock" to mark two particular epochs, 2450 and 10450 BC, in which case we actually can't say *when* they were built. Or they were built up over . . .'

'Hang on with that first point,' I interrupted. 'How do you mean "star-clock"? How do you mean we can't say when they were built?'

'Well, let's assume for a moment that the pyramid builders knew precession. Let's assume they were able to calculate the declination of particular star-groups backwards and forwards in time, just as we can today with computers ... Assuming they could do that then, no matter which epoch they lived in, they'd have been able to make a model of what the skies over Giza looked like in 10450 BC or 2450 BC as required, just as we could. In other words, if they'd built the pyramids in 10450 BC they would have had no difficulty in calculating the correct angles of inclination for the southern shafts so that they would be sighted on Al Nitak and Sirius around 2450 BC. Likewise, if they'd lived in 2450 BC they'd have had no difficulty in calculating the correct site-plan to reflect the position of Orion's Belt in 10450 BC. Agreed?'

'Agreed.'

'OK. That's one explanation. But the second explanation, which I personally favour – and which I think the geological evidence also supports – is that the whole Giza necropolis was developed and built up over an enormously long period of time. I think it's more than possible that the site was originally planned and laid out at around 10450 BC, so that its geometry would reflect the skies as they looked then, but that the work was completed, and the shafts of the Great Pyramid aligned, around 2450 BC.'

'So you're saying that the *ground-plan* of the Pyramids could date back to 10450 BC?

'I think it does. And I think that the geometrical centre of that plan was located more or less where we're standing now, right in front of the Second Pyramid ...'

I pointed out the large blocks in the lower courses of the huge edifice: 'It even *looks* like it was built in two stages, by two completely different cultures ...'

Bauval shrugged. 'Let's speculate ... Maybe it wasn't two different cultures, Maybe it was one culture, or *cult* – the cult of Osiris, perhaps. Maybe it was a very long-lived, very ancient cult dedicated to Osiris that was here in 10450 BC and was still here in 2450 BC. Maybe what happened was that some of the ways that this cult did things changed over time. Maybe they used huge blocks in 10450 BC and smaller blocks in 2450 BC ... It seems to me there's a lot here that supports this notion, a lot that says "very ancient cult", a lot of evidence that has just never been investigated ...'

'For example?'

'Well, obviously the astronomical alignments of the site. I've been among the first to start looking into those properly. And the geology: the work that John West and Robert Schoch have been involved in at the Sphinx. Here are two sciences – both hard, empirical, evidence-driven sciences – that have never been applied to these problems before. But now that we have started to apply them, we're beginning to get a whole new reading on the antiquity of the necropolis. And I honestly think we've just scratched the surface and that much more will emerge from the geology and the astronomy in the future. In addition, nobody's yet made a really detailed study of the Pyramid Texts from anything other than the so-called "anthropological" perspective, which means a preconceived notion that the priests of Heliopolis were a bunch of half-civilized witch-doctors who wanted to live for ever ... Actually they *did* want to live for ever but they certainly weren't witch-doctors ... They were highly civilized, highly *initiated* men and they were, in their own fashion, scientists, as we can judge from their works. Therefore I suggest that it's as scientific or at least quasi-scientific documents that the Pyramid Texts need to be read, not as mumbo-jumbo. I'm already satisfied that they respond to precessional astronomy. There may be other keys too: mathematics, geometry – particularly geometry ... Symbolism ... What's needed is a multi-disciplinary approach to understanding the Pyramid Texts ... and to understanding the pyramids themselves. Astronomers, mathematicians, geologists, engineers, architects, even philosophers to deal with the symbolism – everybody who can bring a fresh eye and fresh skills to bear on these very important problems should be encouraged to do so.'

'Why do you feel the problems are so important?'

'Because they have a colossal bearing on our understanding of the past of our own species. The very careful, very precise site-planning and setting-out that appears to have been done here in 10450 BC could only have been the work of a highly-evolved, probably technological civilization . . . .'

'Whereas no such civilization is supposed to have existed anywhere on earth in that epoch . . .'

'Exactly. It was the Stone Age. Human society was supposed to have been at a very primitive level, with our ancestors wearing skins, sheltering in caves, following a hunting-gathering way of life and so on and so forth. So its rather unsettling to discover that civilized people seem to have been present in Giza in 10450 BC, who understood the obscure science of precession extremely well, who had the technical capacity to work out that they were witnessing the *lowest point in Orion's precessional cycle* – and thus the beginning of the constellation's 13,000 year upwards journey – and who set out to create a permanent memorial of that moment here on the plateau. By putting Orion's Belt on the ground in the way they did they knew that they were freezing a very specific moment in time.'

A perverse thought occurred to me: 'How can we be so sure that the moment that they were freezing was 10450 BC? After all, Orion's Belt takes up that same configuration in the southern sky, west of the Milky Way at 11-plus degrees above the horizon, once every 26,000 years. So why shouldn't they have been immortalizing 36450 BC or even the precessional cycle that began 26,000 years before that?'

Robert was clearly ready for this question. 'Some ancient records do suggest that Egyptian civilization had roots going back almost 40,000 years,' he mused, 'like that strange report in Herodotus that talks about the sun rising where it once set and setting where it once rose . . .'

'Which is also a precessional metaphor . . .'

'Yes. Precession again. Most peculiar the way it always keeps cropping up . . . At any rate, you're right, they could have been marking the beginning of the *previous* precessional cycle . . .'

'But do you think they were?'

'No. I think 10450 BC is the more likely date. It's more within the range of what we know about the evolution of *homo sapiens*. And although its still leaves a lot of years to account for before the sudden emergence of dynastic Egypt around 3000 BC, it isn't *too* long a period . . .'

'Too long a period for what?'

'It's the answer to your question about the 8000-year gap between the alignment of the site and the alignment of the shafts. Eight thousand years is a very long time but it isn't too long for a dedicated highly motivated cult to have preserved and nurtured and faithfully passed on the high-knowledge of the people who invented this place in 10450 BC.'[14]

The machine

How high was the knowledge of those prehistoric inventors?

'They knew their epochs,' said Bauval, 'and the clock that they used was the natural clock of the stars. Their working language was precessional astronomy and these monuments express that language in a very clear, unambiguous, scientific manner. They were also highly skilled surveyors – I mean the people who originally prepared the site and laid out the orientations for the pyramids – because they worked to an exacting geometry and because they knew how to align the base-platforms, or whatever it was they built, perfectly to the cardinal points.'

'Do you think they also knew that they were marking out the site of the Great Pyramid on latitude 30° North?'

Bauval laughed: 'I'm certain they knew. I think they knew everything about the shape of the earth. They knew their astronomy. They had a good understanding of the solar system and of celestial mechanics. They were also incredibly accurate and incredibly precise in everything they did. So, all in all, I don't think anything really happened here by chance – at least not between 10450 and 2450 BC. I get the feeling that everything was planned, intended, carefully worked out . . . Indeed I get the feeling that they were fulfilling a long-term objective – some kind of *purpose*, if you like, and that they brought this to fruition in the third millennium BC . . .'

'In the form of the fully built pyramids which they then precessionally anchored to Al Nitak and to Sirius at the time of completion?'

'Yes. And also, I think, in the form of the Pyramid Texts. My guess is that the Pyramid Texts are part of the puzzle.'

'The software to the Pyramids' hardware?'

'Quite possibly. Why not? At any rate it's certain that there's a connection. I think what it means is that if we're going to decode the pyramids properly then we're going to have to use the Texts . . .'

'What's your guess?' I asked Bauval. 'What do you think the purpose of the pyramid builders really might have been?'

'They *didn't* do it because they wanted an eternal tomb,' he replied firmly. 'In my view, they had no doubts at all that they would eternally live. They did it – whoever did it – they have transmitted the power of their ideas through something that is to all intents and purposes eternal. They succeeded in creating a force that is functional in itself, provided you understand it, and that force is the *questions* it challenges you to ask. My guess is that they knew the human mind to perfection. They knew the game of ritual . . . Right? I'm serious. They knew what they were doing. They knew that they could initiate people far ahead in the future into their way of thinking even though they couldn't be there themselves. They knew that they could do this by creating an eternal machine, the function of which was to generate questions.'

I suppose that I must have looked puzzled.

'The machine is the pyramids!' Bauval exclaimed, 'the whole of the Giza necropolis really. And look at us. What are we doing? We're asking questions. We're standing out here, shivering, at an ungodly hour, watching the sun come up, and we're asking questions, lots and lots of questions just as we've been programmed to do. We're in the hands of real magicians here, and real magicians know that with symbols – with the right symbols, with the right questions – they can lead you into *initiating yourself*. Provided, that is, you are a person who asks questions. And, if you are, then the minute you start asking questions about the pyramids you begin to stumble into a whole series of answers which lead you to other questions, and then more answers until finally you initiate yourself . . .'

'Sow the seed . . .'

'Yes. They were sowing the seed. Believe me, they were magicians, and they knew the power of ideas . . . They knew how to set ideas growing and developing in people's minds. And if you start with such ideas, and follow the process of reasoning like I did, you arrive at things like Orion, and 10450 BC. In short, this is a process that works on its own. When it enters, when it settles into the subconscious, it is a self-willing conversion. Once it's there you can't even resist it . . .'

'You're talking as though this Giza cult, whatever it was – revolving around precession, and geometry, and the pyramids, and the Pyramid Texts – you're talking as though it still exists.'

'In a sense it does still exist,' Robert replied. 'Even if the driver is no longer at the wheel, the Giza necropolis is still a machine that was designed to provoke questions.' He paused and pointed up to the summit of the Great Pyramid where Santha and I had climbed, at dead of night, nine months previously. 'Look at its power,' he continued. 'Five thousand years on it still gets you. It involves you whether you like it or not . . . It forces you into a process of thinking . . . forces you to learn. The minute you ask a question about it you've asked a question about engineering, you've asked a question about geometry, you've asked a question about astronomy. So it forces you to learn about engineering and geometry and astronomy, and gradually you begin to realize how sophisticated it is, how incredibly clever and skilful and knowledgeable its builders must have been, which forces you to ask questions about mankind, about human history, eventually about yourself too. *You want to find out*. This is the power of the thing.'

The second signature

As Robert, Santha and I sat out on the Giza plateau that cold December morning at the end of 1993, we watched the winter sun, now very close to solstice, rising over the right shoulder of the Sphinx, almost as far south of east as it would travel on its yearly journey before turning north again.

The Sphinx was an equinoctial marker, with its gaze directed precisely at the point of sunrise on the vernal equinox. Was it, too, part of the Giza 'grand plan'?

I reminded myself that in any epoch, and at any period of history or prehistory, the Sphinx's due east gaze would *always* have been sighted on the equinoctial rising of the sun, at both the vernal and the autumnal equinoxes. As the reader will recall from Part V, however, it was the vernal equinox that was considered by ancient man to be the marker of the astronomical age. In the words of Santillana and von Dechend:

The constellation that rose in the east, just before the sun, marked the 'place' where the sun rested . . . It was known as the sun's 'carrier' and the vernal equinox was recognised as the fiducial point of the 'system' determining the first degree of the sun's yearly cycle . . .'[15]

Why should an equinoctial marker have been made in the shape of a giant lion?

In our own lifetimes, the epoch of AD 2000, a more suitable shape for such a marker – should anyone wish to build one – would be a representation of a fish. This is because the sun on the vernal equinox rises against the stellar background of Pisces, as it has done for approximately the last 2000 years. The astronomical Age of Pisces began around the time of Christ.[16] Readers must judge for themselves whether it is a coincidence that the principal symbol used for Christ by the very early Christians was not the cross but the fish.[17]

During the preceeding age, which broadly-speaking encompassed the first and second millennia BC, it was the constellation of Aries – the Ram – which had the honour of carrying the sun on the vernal equinox. Again, readers must judge whether it is a coincidence that the religious iconography of that epoch was predominantly ram-oriented.[18] Is it a coincidence, for example, that Yahweh, God of Old Testament Israel, provided a ram as a substitute for Abraham's offered sacrifice of his son Isaac?[19] (Abraham and Isaac are assumed by biblical scholars and archaeologists to have lived during the early second millennium BC[20]). Is it likewise coincidental that rams, in one context or another, are referred to in almost every book of the Old Testament (entirely composed during the Age of Aries) but in not a single book of the New Testament?[21] And is it an accident that the advent of the Age of Aries, shortly before the beginning of the second millennium BC, was accompanied in Ancient Egypt by an upsurge in the worship of the god Amon whose symbol was a ram with curled horns?[22] Work on the principal sanctuary of Amon – the Temple of Karnak at Luxor in upper Egypt – was begun at around 2000 BC[23] and, as those who have visited that temple will recall, its principal icons are rams, long rows of which guard its entrances.

The immediate predecessor to the Age of Aries was the Age of Taurus – the Bull – which spanned the period between 4380 and 2200 BC.[24] It was during this precessional epoch, when the sun on the vernal equinox rose in the constellation of Taurus, that the Bull-cult of Minoan Crete flourished.[25] And during this epoch, too, the civilization of dynastic Egypt burst upon the historical scene, fully formed, apparently without antecedents. Readers must judge whether it is a coincidence that Egyptians at the very beginning of the dynastic period were already venerating the Apis and Mnevis Bulls – the former being considered a theophany of the god Osiris and the latter, the sacred animal of Helipolis, a theophany of the god Ra.[26]

Why should an equinoctial marker have been made in the form of a lion?

I looked down the slope of the Giza plateau towards the great leonine body of the Sphinx.

Khafre, the Fourth Dynasty pharaoh believed by Egyptologists to have carved the monument out of bedrock around 2500 BC, had been a monarch of the Age of Taurus. For almost 1800 years before his reign, and more than 300 years after it, the sun on the vernal equinox rose unfailingly in the constellation of the Bull. It follows that if a monarch at such a time had set out to create an equinoctial marker at Giza, he would have had every reason to have it carved in the form of a bull, and none whatsoever to have it carved in the form of a lion. Indeed, and it was obvious, there was only *one* epoch when the celestial symbolism of a leonine equinoctial marker would have been appropriate. That epoch was, of course, the Age of Leo, from 10970 to 8810 BC.[27]

Why, therefore, should an equinoctial marker have been made in the shape of a lion? Because it was made during the Age of Leo when the sun on the vernal equinox rose against the stellar background of the constellation of the Lion, thus marking the coordinates of a precessional epoch that would not experience its 'Great Return' for another 26,000 years.

Around 10450 BC the three stars of Orion's Belt reached the lowest point in their precessional cycle: west of the Milky Way, 11° 08' above the southern horizon at meridian transit. On the ground west of the Nile, this event was frozen into architecture in the shape of the three pyramids of Giza. Their layout formed the signature of an unmistakable epoch of precessional time.

Around 10450 BC, the sun on the vernal equinox rose in the

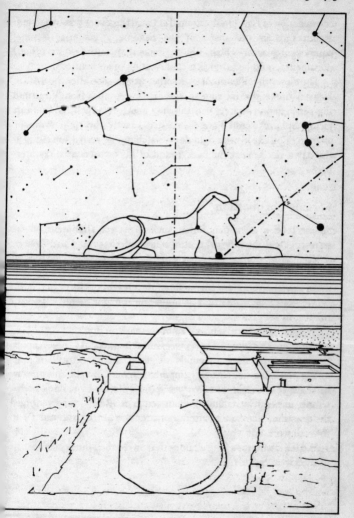

Looking due east at dawn on the vernal equinox in 10,450 BC. The Sphinx and the constellation of Leo.

constellation of Leo. On the ground at Giza, this event was frozen into architecture in the shape of the Sphinx, a gigantic, leonine, equinoctial marker which, like the second signature on an official document, could be taken as a confirmation of authenticity.

The eleventh millennium BC, in other words, soon after the 'Mill of Heaven' broke, shifting sunrise on the spring equinox from Virgo into the constellation of Leo, was the only epoch in which the due east facing Sphinx would have manifested exactly the right symbolic alignment on exactly the right day – watching the vernal sun rising in the dawn sky against the background of his own celestial counterpart . . .

Forcing the question

'It can't be a coincidence that such a perfect alignment of the terrestrial and the celestial occurs at around 10450 BC,' said Robert. 'In fact I don't think coincidence is any longer an issue. To me the real question is *why*? Why was it done? Why did they go to such lengths to make this enormous statement about the eleventh millennium BC?'

'Obviously because it was an important time for them,' suggested Santha.

'It must have been very, *very* important. You don't do something like this, create a series of vast precessional markers like these, carve a Sphinx, put up three pyramids weighing almost 15 million tons, unless you have some hugely important reason. So the question is: *what was that reason*? They've forced this question by making such a strong, imperative statement about 10450 BC. Really, they've forced the question. They want to draw our attention to 10450 BC and it's up to us to work out why.'

We fell silent, for a long while as the sun climbed the sky south-east of the Great Sphinx.

Part VIII

Conclusion

Where's the Body?

Chapter 50

Not a Needle in a Haystack

When I was only a few months into this investigation, my research assistant sent me a fifteen-page letter explaining why he had decided to resign. At that stage I hadn't yet begun to put the pieces of the puzzle together and I was working more on hunches than on hard evidence. I was captivated by all the mysteries, anomalies, anachronisms and puzzles, and wanted to learn as much about them as I could. My researcher, meanwhile, had been looking into the long, slow processes by which some *known* civilizations had come into global history.

It transpired that, in his opinion, certain significant economic, climatic, topographical and geographical preconditions had to be met before a civilization could evolve:

> So if you are looking for a hitherto undiscovered civilization of great originators who made it on their own, separate from any of the ones we already know, *you are not looking for a needle in a haystack*. You are looking for something more like a city in its hinterland. What you are looking for is a vast region which occupied a land area at least a couple of thousand miles across. This is a landmass as big as the Gulf of Mexico, or twice the size of Madagascar. It would have had major mountain ranges, huge river systems and a Mediterranean to subtropical climate which was buffered by its latitude from the adverse effects of short-term climatic cooling. It would have needed this relatively undisturbed climate to last for around ten thousand years . . . Then the population of several hundred thousand sophisticated

people, we are to believe, suddenly vanished, together with their homeland, leaving very little physical trace, with only a few surviving individuals who were shrewd enough to see the end coming, wealthy enough and in the right place, with the resources they needed to be able to do something about escaping the cataclysm.

So there I was without a researcher. My proposition was *a priori* impossible. There could be no lost advanced civilization because a landmass big enough to support such a civilization was too big to lose.

Geophysical impossibilities

The problem was a serious one and it continued to nag at the back of my mind all the way through my own research and travels. It was, indeed, this exact problem, more than any other, which had scuppered Plato's Atlantis as a serious proposition for scholars. As one critic of the lost continent theory put it:

> There never was an Atlantic landbridge since the arrival of man in the world; there is no sunken landmass in the Atlantic: the Atlantic Ocean must have existed in its present form for at least a million years. In fact it is a geophysical impossibility for an Atlantis of Plato's dimensions to have existed in the Atlantic . . .[1]

The adamant and assertive tone, I had long ago learnt, was entirely justified. Modern oceanographers had thoroughly mapped the floor of the Atlantic Ocean and there was definitely no lost continent lurking there.

But if the evidence that I was gathering did represent the fingerprints of a vanished civilization, a continent had to have got lost *somewhere*.

So where? For a while I used the obvious working hypothesis that it might be under some other ocean. The Pacific was very big but the Indian Ocean looked more promising because it was located relatively close to the Middle East's Fertile Crescent, where several of the earliest known historical civilizations had emerged with extreme suddenness at around 3000 BC. I had plans to go chasing rumours of ancient pyramids in the Maldive Islands and along the Somali coast of

East Africa to see if I could pick up any clues of a lost paradise of antiquity. I thought I might even work in a trip to the Seychelles.

The problem was the oceanographers again. The floor of the Indian Ocean, too, had been mapped and it didn't conceal any lost continents. *Ditto* every other ocean and every other sea. There seemed to be nowhere now under water into which a landmass big enough to have nurtured a high civilization could have vanished.

Yet, as my research continued, the evidence kept mounting that precisely such a civilization had once existed. I began to suspect that it must have been a maritime civilization: a nation of navigators. In support of this hypothesis, among other anomalies, were the remarkable ancient maps of the world, the 'Pyramid Boats' of Egypt, the traces of advanced astronomical knowledge in the astonishing calendar system of the Maya, and the legends of seafaring gods like Quetzalcoatl and Viracocha.

A nation of navigators, then. And a nation of builders, too: Tiahuanaco builders, Teotihuacan builders, pyramid builders, Sphinx builders, builders who could lift and position 200-ton blocks of limestone with apparent ease, builders who could align vast monuments to the cardinal points with uncanny accuracy. Whoever they were, these builders appeared to have left their characteristic fingerprints all over the world in the form of cyclopean polygonal masonry, site layouts involving astronomical alignments, mathematical and geodetic puzzles, and myths about gods in human form. But a civilization advanced enough to build like that – rich enough, sufficiently well organized and mature to have explored and mapped the world from pole to pole, a civilization smart enough to have calculated the dimensions of the earth – simply could *not* have evolved on an insignificant landmass. Its homeland, as my researcher had rightly pointed out, must have been blessed with major mountain ranges, huge river systems and a congenial climate, and with many other obvious environmental prerequisites for the development of an advanced and prosperous economy: good agricultural lands, mineral resources, forests, and so on.

So where could such a landmass have been located, if not under any of the world's oceans?

Library angels

Where could it have been located and *when* might it have disappeared? And if it had disappeared (and no other explanation would do) then *how*, *why*, and *under what circumstances*?

Seriously, how do you lose a continent?

Commonsense suggested that the answer had to lie in a cataclysm of some kind, a planetary disaster capable of wiping out almost all physical traces of a large civilization. But if so, why were there no records of such a cataclysm? Or perhaps there were.

As my research progressed I studied many of the great myths of flood, fire, earthquakes and ice handed down from generation to generation around the world. We saw in Part IV that it was difficult to resist the conclusion that the myths were describing real geological and climatic events, quite possibly the different local effects of the *same* events in all cases.

During the short history of mankind's presence on this planet, I found that there was only one known and documented catastrophe that fitted the bill: the dramatic and deadly meltdown of the last Ice Age between 15,000 and 8000 BC. Moreover, as was more obviously the case with architectural relics like Teotihuacan and the Egyptian pyramids, many of the relevant myths appeared to have been designed to serve as vehicles for encrypted scientific information, again an indication of what I was coming to think of as 'the fingerprints of the gods'.

What I had become sensitized to, although I did not properly realize its implications at the time, was the possibility that a strong connection might exist between the collapsing chaos of the Ice Age and the disappearance of an archaic civilization which had been the stuff of legend for millennia.

It was at this moment exactly that the library angels intervened . . .

The missing piece of the puzzle

The novelist Arthur Koestler, who had a great interest in synchronicity, coined the term 'library angel' to describe the unknown agency responsible for the lucky breaks researchers sometimes get which lead to exactly the right information being placed in their hands at exactly the right moment.[2]

At exactly the right moment, one of those lucky breaks came my way. The moment was the summer of 1993. I was at a low ebb physically and spiritually after months of hard travel, and the geophysical impossibility of actually *losing* a continent-sized landmass was beginning to undermine my confidence in the strength of my findings. It was then that I received a letter from the town of Nanaimo in British Columbia, Canada. The letter referred to my previous book *The Sign and the Seal*, in which I had made passing mention of the Atlantis theory and of traditions of civilizing heroes who had been 'saved from water':

19 July 1993
Dear Mr Hancock,
    After 17 years of research into the fate of Atlantis, my wife and I have finished a manuscript entitled *When the Sky Fell*. Our frustration is that despite positive feedback about the book's approach from the few publishers who have seen it, the mere mention of Atlantis closes minds.[3]
    In *The Sign and the Seal* you write of 'a tradition of secret wisdom started by the survivors of a flood . . .' Our work explores sites where some survivors might have relocated. High altitude, fresh-water lakes made ideal post-deluge bases for the survivors of Atlantis. Lake Titicaca and Lake Tana [in Ethiopia, where much of *The Sign and the Seal* was set] fit the climatic criteria. Their stable environment provided the raw materials for restarting agriculture.
    We have taken the liberty of enclosing an outline of *When the Sky Fell*. If you are interested we will be pleased to send you a copy of the manuscript.
    Sincerely,
    Rand Flem-Ath

I turned to the enclosure and there, in the first few paragraphs, found the missing piece of the jigsaw puzzle I had been looking for. It meshed perfectly with the ancient global maps I had studied – maps which accurately depicted the *subglacial topography* of the continent of Antarctica (see Part I). It made perfect sense of all the great worldwide myths of cataclysm and planetary disaster, with their differing climatic effects. It explained the enigma of the huge numbers of apparently 'flash-frozen' mammoths in northern Siberia and Alaska, and the 90-foot tall fruit trees locked in the permafrost deep inside the Arctic Circle at a latitude where nothing now grows. It provided a solution to the problem of the extreme suddenness with which the last Ice Age in the northern hemisphere melted down after 15,000 BC. It also solved the mystery of the exceptional worldwide volcanic activity that accompanied the meltdown. It answered the question, 'How do you lose a continent?' And it was solidly based in Charles Hapgood's theory of 'earth-crust displacement' – a radical geological hypothesis with which I was already familiar:

> Antarctica is our least understood continent [wrote the Flem-Aths in their outline]. Most of us assume that this immense island has been ice-bound for millions of years. But new discoveries prove that parts of Antarctica were free of ice *thousands of years ago*, recent history by the geological clock. The theory of 'earth-crust displacement' explains the mysterious surge and ebb of Antarctica's vast ice sheet.

What the Canadian researchers were referring to was Hapgood's suggestion that until the end of the last Ice Age – say the eleventh millennium BC – the landmass of Antarctica had been positioned some 2000 miles further north (at a congenial and temperate latitude) and that it had been moved to its present position inside the Antarctic Circle as a result of a massive displacement of the earth's crust.[4] This displacement, the Flem-Aths continued, had

> also left other evidence of its deadly visit in a ring of death around the globe. All the continents that experienced rapid and massive extinctions of animal species (notably the Americas and Siberia) underwent a massive change in their latitudes . . .
>
> The consequences of a displacement are monumental. The earth's crust ripples over its interior and the world is shaken by incredible quakes and floods. The sky appears to fall as continents groan and shift position. Deep in the ocean, earthquakes generate massive tidal waves which crash against coastlines, flooding them. Some lands shift to warmer climes, while others, propelled into polar zones, suffer the direst of winters. Melting ice caps raise the ocean's level higher and higher. All living things must adapt, migrate or die . . .
>
> If the horror of an earth-crust displacement were to be visited upon today's interdependent world the progress of thousands of years of

civilization would be torn away from our planet like a fine cobweb. Those who live near high mountains might escape the global tidal waves, but they would be forced to leave behind, in the lowlands, the slowly constructed fruits of civilization. Only among the merchant marine and navies of the world might some evidence of civilization remain. The rusting hulls of ships and submarines would eventually perish but the valuable maps that are housed in them would be saved by survivors, perhaps for hundreds, even thousands of years. Until once again mankind could use them to sail the World Ocean in search of lost lands . . .

As I read these words I remembered Charles Hapgood's account of how the layer of the earth that geologists call the lithosphere – the thin but rigid outer crust of the planet – could at times be displaced, moving in one piece 'over the soft inner body, much as the skin of an orange, if it were loose, might shift over the inner part of the orange all in one piece.'[5]

Thus far, I felt I was on familiar ground. But then the Canadian researchers made two vital connections which I had missed.

Gravitational influences

The first of these was the possibility that *gravitational* influences (as well as the variations in the earth's orbital geometry discussed in Part V) might, through the mechanism of earth-crust displacement, play a role in the onset and decline of Ice Ages:

When the naturalist and geologist Louis Agassiz presented the idea of ice ages to the scientific community in 1837 he was met with great skepticism. However, as evidence slowly gathered in his favour, the skeptics were forced to accept that the earth had indeed been gripped by deadly winters. But the trigger of these paralysing ice ages remained a puzzle. It was not until 1976 that solid evidence existed to establish the timing of ice ages. The explanation was found in various astronomical features of the earth's orbit and the tilt of the axis. Astronomical factors have clearly played a role in the timing of glacial epochs. But this is only part of the problem. Of equal importance is the *geography* of glaciation. It is here that the theory of earth-crust displacement plays its role in unravelling the mystery.

Albert Einstein investigated the possibility that the weight of the

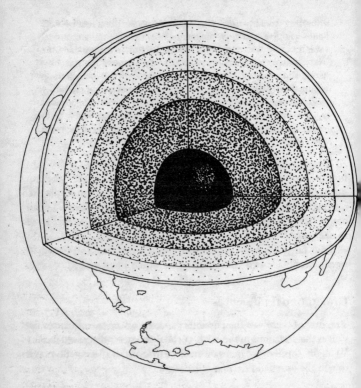

Section through the earth. The crustal displacement theory envisages the possibility of periodic displacements of the entire crust in one piece. Often less than 30 miles thick, the crust rests on a lubricating layer known as the asthenosphere.

ice-caps, which are not symmetrically distributed about the pole, might cause such a displacement. Einstein wrote: 'The earth's rotation acts on these unsymmetrically deposited masses, and produces centrifugal momentum that is transmitted to the rigid crust of the earth. The constantly increasing centrifugal momentum produced this way will, when it reaches a certain point, produce a movement of the earth's crust over the earth's body, and *this will displace the polar regions towards the equator*.

When Einstein wrote these words [1953] the astronomical causes of ice ages were not fully appreciated. When the shape of the earth's orbit deviates from a perfect circle by more than one per cent, the gravitational influence of the sun increases, exercising more pull on the planet and its massive ice sheets. Their ponderous weight pushes against the crust and this immense pressure, combined with the greater incline in the earth's tilt [another changing factor of the orbital geometry] forces the crust to shift . . .

The connection with the onset and decline of ice ages?

Very straightforward.

In a displacement, those parts of the earth's crust which are situated at the North and South Poles (and which are therefore as completely glaciated as Antarctica is today) shift suddenly into warmer latitudes and begin to melt with extraordinary rapidity. Conversely, land that has hitherto been located at warmer latitudes is shifted equally suddenly into the polar zones, suffers a devastating climate change, and begins to vanish under a rapidly expanding ice-cap.

In other words, when huge parts of northern Europe and north America were heavily glaciated in what we think of as the last Ice Age, it was not because of some mysterious slow-acting climatic factor, but rather because those areas of land were then situated much closer to the North Pole than they are today. Similarly, when the Wisconsin and Wurm glaciations described in Part IV began to go into their meltdown at around 15,000 BC the trigger was not global climate change but a shift of the ice-caps into warmer latitudes . . .

In other words: there is an Ice Age going on right now – inside the Arctic Circle and *in Antarctica*.

The lost continent

The second connection the Flem-Aths made followed logically from the first: if there was such a recurrent, cyclical geological phenomenon as earth-crust displacement, and if the last displacement had shifted the enormous landmass we call Antarctica out of temperate latitudes and into the Antarctic Circle, it was possible that the substantial remains of a lost civilization of remote antiquity might today be lying under two miles of ice at the South Pole.

It was suddenly clear to me how a continent-sized landmass, which had been the home of a large and prosperous society for thousands of years, could indeed get lost almost without trace. As the Flem-Aths concluded: 'It is to icy Antarctica that we look to find answers to the very roots of civilization – answers which may yet be preserved in the frozen depths of the forgotten island continent.'

I hauled out my researcher's resignation letter from the files and started to check off his preconditions for the emergence of an advanced civilization. He wanted 'major mountain ranges'. He wanted 'huge river systems'. He wanted 'a vast region which occupied a land area at least a couple of thousand miles across'. He also wanted a stable, congenial climate for ten thousand years, to allow time for a developed culture to evolve.

Antarctica is by no means a needle in a haystack. It's a huge landmass, much, much bigger than the Gulf of Mexico, about seven times larger than Madagascar – indeed roughly the size of the continental USA. Moreover, as seismic surveys have demonstrated, there *are* major mountain ranges in Antarctica. And as several of the ancient maps seem to prove, unknown prehistoric cartographers, who possessed a scientific understanding of latitude and longitude, depicted these mountain ranges *before* they disappeared beneath the ice-cap that covers them today. These same ancient maps also show 'huge river systems' flowing down from the mountains, watering the extensive valleys and plains below and running into the surrounding ocean. And these rivers, as I already knew from the Ross Sea cores,[6] had left physical evidence of their presence in the composition of ocean bottom sediments.

Last but not least, I noted that the earth-crust displacement theory did not conflict with the requirement for 10,000 years of stable climate. Prior to the supposed sudden shift of the crust, at around the end of the last Ice Age in the northern hemisphere, the climate of Antarctica would have been stable, perhaps for a great deal longer than 10,000 years. And if the theory was right in suggesting that Antarctica's latitude in that epoch had been about 2000 miles (30 degrees of arc) further north than it is today, the northernmost parts of it would have been situated in the vicinity of latitude 30° South and would, indeed, have enjoyed a Mediterranean to sub-tropical climate.

Had the earth's crust really shifted? And could the ruins of a lost civilization really lie beneath the ice of the southern continent?

As we see in the following chapters, it might have . . . and they could.

Chapter 51

The Hammer and the Pendulum

Although beyond the scope of this book, a detailed exposition of the earth-crust displacement theory is to be found in Rand and Rose Flem-Ath's *When the Sky Fell* (published by Stoddart, Canada, 1995).

As noted, this geological theory was formulated by Professor Charles Hapgood and supported by Albert Einstein. In brief, what it suggests is a complete slippage of our planet's thirty-mile-thick lithosphere over its nearly 8000-mile-thick central core, forcing large parts of the western hemisphere southward towards the equator and thence towards the Antarctic Circle. This movement is not seen as taking place along a due north-south meridian but on a swivelling course – pivoting, as it were, around the central plains of what is now the United States. The result is that the north-eastern segment of North America (in which the North Pole was formerly located in Hudson's Bay) is dragged southwards out of the Arctic Circle and into more temperate latitudes while at the same time the north-western segment (Alaska and the Yukon) swivels northwards into the Arctic Circle along with large parts of northern Siberia.

In the southern hemisphere, Hapgood's model shows the landmass that we now call Antarctica, much of which was previously at temperate or even warm latitudes, being shifted *in its entirety* inside the Antarctic Circle. The overall movement is seen as having been in the region of 30 degrees (approximately 2000 miles) and as having

According to the earth-crust displacement theory, large parts of Antarctica were positioned outside the Antarctic circle prior to 15,000 BC and thus could have been inhabited, with a climate and resources suitable for the development of civilization. A cataclysmic slippage of the crust then shifted the continent to the position it occupies today – dead centre within the Antarctic circle.

been concentrated, in the main, between the years 14,500 BC and 12,500 BC – but with massive aftershocks on a planetary scale continuing at widely-separated intervals down to about 9500 BC.

Suppose that, before the displacement of the earth's crust, a great civilization had grown up in Antarctica, when much of it was located at green and pleasant latitudes? If so, that civilization might easily have been destroyed by the effects of the displacement: the tidal waves, the hurricane-force winds and electric storms, the volcanic eruptions as seismic faults split open all around the planet, the darkened skies, and the remorselessly expanding ice-cap. Moreover, as the millennia passed, the ruins left behind – the cities, the monuments, the great libraries, and the engineering works of the destroyed civilization – would have been ever more deeply buried beneath the mantle of ice.

Little wonder, if the earth-crust displacement theory is correct, that all that can be found today, scattered around the world, are the tantalizing fingerprints of the gods. These would be the traces, the echoes of the works and deeds, the much misunderstood teachings and the geometrical edifices left behind by the few survivors of Antarctica's former civilization who had made it across the turbulent oceans in great ships and settled themselves in faraway lands: in the Nile Valley, for example (or perhaps, first, around Lake Tana at the headwaters of the Blue Nile), and in the Valley of Mexico, and near Lake Titicaca in the Andes – and no doubt in several other places as well . . .

Here and there around the globe, in other words, the *fingerprints* of a lost civilization remain faintly visible. The *body* is out of sight, buried under two miles of Antarctic ice and almost as inaccessible to archaeologists as if it were located on the dark side of the moon.

Fact?

Or fiction?

Possibility?

Or impossibility?

Is it a geophysical *possibility* or a geophysical *impossibility* that Antarctica, the world's fifth-largest continent (with a surface area of almost six million square miles) could (a) previously have been located in a more temperate zone and (b) have been shifted out of that zone and into the Antarctic Circle within the last 20,000 years?

Is Antarctica movable?

A lifeless polar desert

'Continental drift' and/or 'plate-tectonics' are key terms used to describe an important geological theory that has become increasingly well understood by the general public since the 1950s. It is unnecessary to go into the basic mechanisms here. But most of us are aware that the continents in some way 'float around', relocate and change position on the earth's surface. Common sense confirms this: if you take a look at a map of the west coast of Africa and the east coast of South America it's pretty obvious that these two landmasses were once joined. The time-scale according to which continental drift operates is, however, immense: continents can typically be expected to float apart (or together) at a rate of no more than 2000 miles every 200 million years or so: in other words, very, very slowly.[1]

Plate-tectonics and Charles Hapgood's earth-crust displacement theory are by no means mutually contradictory. Hapgood envisaged that both could occur: that the earth's crust did indeed exhibit continental drift as the geologists claimed – almost imperceptibly, over hundreds of millions of years – but that it also occasionally experienced very rapid one-piece displacements which had no effect on the relationships *between* individual landmasses but which thrust entire continents (or parts of them) into and out of the planet's two fixed polar zones (the perennially cold and icy regions surrounding the North and South Poles of the axis of spin).

Continental drift?

Earth-crust displacement?

Both?

Some other cause?

I honestly don't know. Nevertheless, the simple facts about Antarctica are really strange and difficult to explain without invoking some notion of sudden, catastrophic and geologically recent change.

Before reviewing a few of these facts, let us remind ourselves that we are referring to a landmass today oriented by the curvature of the earth so that the sun never rises on it during the six winter months and never sets during the six summer months (but rather, as viewed from the Pole, remains low above the horizon, appearing to transcribe a circular path around the sky during each twenty-four hours of daylight).

Antarctica is also by far the world's coldest continent, where temperatures on the polar plain can fall as low as minus 89.2 degrees centigrade. Although the coastal areas are slightly warmer (minus 60 degrees centigrade) and shelter huge numbers of seabird rookeries, there are no native land mammals and there is only a small community of cold-tolerant plants capable of surviving lengthy winter periods of total or near-total darkness. The *Encyclopaedia Britannica* lists these plants laconically: 'Lichens, mosses and liverworts, moulds, yeasts, other fungi, algae and bacteria . . .'[2]

In other words, although magnificent to behold in the long-drawn-out antipodean dawn, Antarctica is a freezing, unforgiving, almost lifeless polar desert, as it has been throughout mankind's entire 5000-year 'historical' period.

Was it always so?

Exhibit 1

Discover The World Of Science Magazine, **February 1993, page 17**: Some 260 million years ago, during the Permian period, deciduous trees adapted to a warm climate grew in Antarctica. This is the conclusion palaeo-botanists are drawing from a stand of fossilized tree stumps discovered at an altitude of 7000 feet on Mount Achernar in the Transantarctic mountains. The site is at 84° 22' south, some 500 miles north of the South Pole.

' "The interesting thing about this find is that it's really the only forest, living or fossil, that's been found at 80 or 85 degrees latitude," says Ohio State University palaeobotanist Edith Taylor, who has studied the fossil trees. "The first thing we palaeobotanists do is look for something in the modern records that is comparable, and there are no forests growing at that latitude today. We can go to the tropics and find trees growing in a warm environment, but we can't find trees growing in a warm environment with the light regime these trees had: 24 hours of light in the summer and 24 hours of dark in the winter".'[3]

Exhibit 2

Geologists have found no evidence of *any* glaciation having been present anywhere on the Antarctic continent prior to the Eocene (about 60 million years ago.)[4] And if we go as far back as the Cambrian (*c.* 550 million years ago) we find irrefutable evidence of a warm sea stretching nearly or right across Antarctica, in the form of thick limestones rich in reef-building *Archaeocyathidae*: 'Millions of years later, when these marine formations had appeared above the sea, warm climates brought forth a luxuriant vegetation in Antarctica. Thus Sir Ernest Shackleton found coal beds within 200 miles of the South Pole, and later, during the Byrd expedition of 1935, geologists made a rich discovery of fossils on the lofty sides of Mount Weaver, in latitude 86° 58′ S., about the same distance from the Pole and about two miles above sea level. These included leaf and stem impressions and fossilized wood. In 1952 Dr Lyman H. Dougherty, of the Carnegie Institution of Washington, completing a study of these fossils, identified two species of a tree fern called *Glossopteris*, once common to the other southern continents (Africa, South America, Australia) and a giant fern tree of another species . . . '[5]

Exhibit 3

Admiral Byrd's own comment on the significance of the Mount Weaver finds: 'Here at the southernmost known mountain in the world, scarcely two hundred miles from the South Pole, was found conclusive evidence that the climate of Antarctica was once temperate or even sub-tropical.'[6]

Exhibit 4

'Soviet scientists have reported finding evidence of tropical flora in Graham Land, another part of Antarctica, dating from the early Tertiary Period (perhaps the Paleocene or Eocene) . . . Further evidence is provided by the discovery by British geologists of great fossil forests in Antarctica, of the same type that grew on the Pacific coast of the United States 20 million years ago. This of course shows that after the earliest known Antarctic glaciation in the Eocene [60 million years ago] the continent did not remain glacial but had later episodes of warm climate.'[7]

Exhibit 5

'On 25 December 1990 geologists Barrie McKelvey and David Harwood were working 1830 metres above sea level and 400 kilometres [250 miles] from the South Pole in Antarctica. The geologists discovered fossils from a deciduous southern beech forest dating from between two and three million years ago'.[8]

Exhibit 6

In 1986 the discovery of fossilized wood and plants showed that parts of Antarctica may have been ice free as little as two and a half a million years ago. Further discoveries showed that some places on the continent were ice-free 100,000 years ago.[9]

Exhibit 7

As we saw in Part I, sedimentary cores collected from the bottom of the Ross Sea by one of the Byrd Antarctic Expeditions provide conclusive evidence that 'great rivers, carrying down fine well grained sediments' did flow in this part of Antarctica until perhaps as late as 4000 BC. According to the report of Dr Jack Hough of the University of Illinois: 'The log of core N-5 shows glacial marine sediment from the present to 6000 years ago. From 6000 to 15,000 years ago the sediment is fine-grained with the exception of one granule at about 12,000 years ago. This suggests an absence of ice from the area during that period, except perhaps for a stray iceberg 12,000 years ago.'[10]

Exhibit 8

The Orontaeus Finnaeus World Map reviewed in Part I accurately depicts the Ross Sea as it would look if it were free of ice and, in addition, shows Antarctica's ranges of lofty coastal mountains with great rivers flowing from them where only mile-deep glaciers are to be found today.[11]

Charles Hapgood, *The Path Of The Pole*, 1970, page 111ff: 'It is rare that geological investigations receive important confirmation from archaeology; yet in this case, it seems that the matter of the deglaciation of the Ross Sea can be confirmed by an old map that has somehow survived many thousands of years . . . It was discovered and published in 1531 by the French geographer Oronce Fine [Oronteus Finnaeus] and is part of his Map of the World . . .

It has been possible to establish the authenticity of this map. In several years of research the projection of this ancient map was worked out. It was found to have been drawn on a sophisticated map projection, with the use of spherical trigonometry, and to be so scientific that over 50 locations on the Antarctic continent have been found to be located on it with an accuracy that was not attained by modern cartographic science until the 19th century. And, of course, when this map was first published, in 1531, nothing at all was known of Antarctica. The continent was not discovered in modern times until about 1818 and was not fully mapped until after 1920 . . .'[12]

Exhibit 9

The Buache Map, also reviewed in Part 1, accurately depicts the *subglacial* topography of Antarctica.[13] Does it do so by chance or might the continent indeed have been entirely ice-free recently enough for the cartographers of a lost civilization to have mapped it?

Exhibit 10

The reverse side of the coin. If the lands presently inside the Antarctic Circle were once temperate or tropical, what about lands inside the *Arctic* Circle? Were they affected by the same dramatic climate changes, suggesting that some common factor might have been at work?

• 'On the island of Spitzbergen (Svalbard), palm leaves ten and twelve feet long have been fossilized, along with fossilized marine crustaceans of a type that could only inhabit tropical waters. This suggests that at one time the temperatures of the Arctic Ocean were similar to the contemporary temperatures of the Bay of Bengal or the Caribbean Sea. Spitzbergen is half way between the northern tip of Norway and the North Pole, at a latitude of 80 degrees N. Today, ships can reach Spitzbergen through the ice only about two or at the most three months during the year.[14]

- There is firm fossil evidence that stands of swamp cypress flourished within 500 miles of the North Pole in the Miocene [between 20 million and 6 million years ago], and that water-lillies flourished in Spitzbergen in the same period: 'The Miocene floras of Grinnell Land and Greenland, and Spitzbergen, all required temperate climatic conditions with plentiful moisture. The water lillies of Spitzbergen would have required flowing water for the greater part of the year. In connection with the flora of Spitzbergen it should be realized that the island is in polar darkness for half the year. It lies on the Arctic Circle, as far north of Labrador as Labrador is north of Bermuda.'[15]

- Some of the islands in the Arctic Ocean were never covered by ice during the last Ice Age. On Baffin Island, for example, 900 miles from the North Pole, alder and birch remains found in peat suggest a much warmer climate than today less than 30,000 years ago. These conditions prevailed until 17,000 years ago: 'During the Wisconsin ice age there was a temperate-climate refuge in the middle of the Arctic Ocean for the flora and fauna that could not exist in Canada and the United States.'[16]

- Russian scientists have concluded that the Arctic Ocean was warm during most of the last Ice Age. A report by academicians Saks, Belov and Lapina covering many phases of their oceanographic work highlights the period from about 32,000 to about 18,000 years ago as being one during which particularly warm conditions prevailed.[17]

- As we saw in Part IV, huge numbers of warm-blooded, temperate adapted mammal species were instantly frozen, and their bodies preserved in the permafrost, all across a vast zone of death stretching from the Yukon, through Alaska and deep into northern Siberia. The bulk of this destruction appears to have taken place during the eleventh millennium BC, although there was an earlier episode of large-scale extinctions around 13,500 BC.[18]

- We also saw (Chapter Twenty-seven) that the last Ice Age came to an end between 15,000 and 8000 BC, but principally between 14,500 and 12,500 BC, with a further outburst of extraordinarily intense activity in the eleventh millennium BC. During this geologically brief period of time, glaciation up to two miles deep covering millions of square miles which had taken more than 40,000 years to build-up suddenly and inexplicably melted: 'It must be obvious that this could not have been the result of the gradually acting climatic factors usually called upon to explain ice ages . . . The rapidity of the deglaciation suggests that some extraordinary factor was affecting climate . . . '[19]

The icy executioner

Some extraordinary factor was affecting climate . . .

Was it a 30° one-piece shift of the lithosphere that abruptly terminated the Ice Age in the northern hemisphere (by pushing the most heavily glaciated areas southwards from the northern pole of the spin axis)? If so, why shouldn't the same 30° one-piece shift of the lithosphere have swivelled a largely deglaciated six-million-square-mile *southern hemisphere* continent from temperate latitudes to a position directly over the southern pole of the spin axis?

On the issue of the movability of Antarctica, we now know that it *is* movable and, more to the point, that it has moved, because trees have grown there and trees simply cannot grow at latitudes which suffer six months of continual darkness.

What we do not know (and may never know for certain) is whether this movement was a consequence of earth-crust displacement, or of continental drift, or of some other unguessed-at factor.

Let us consider Antarctica for a moment.

We have already seen that it is big. It has a land area of 5.5 million square miles, and is presently covered by something in excess of seven million *cubic* miles of ice weighing an estimated 19 *quadrillion* tons (19 followed by 15 zeros).[20] What worries the theorists of earth-crust displacement is that this vast ice-cap is remorselessly increasing in size and weight: 'at the rate of 293 cubic miles of ice each year – almost as much as if Lake Ontario were frozen solid annually and added to it.'[21]

The fear is that when it is coupled with the effects of precession, obliquity, orbital eccentricity, the earth's own centrifugal motion, and the gravitational tug of the sun, moon and planets, Antarctica's huge, ever-expanding burden of glaciation could provide the final trigger-factor for a massive displacement of the crust:

> The growing South Pole ice-cap [wrote Hugh Auchincloss Brown, somewhat colourfully, in 1967] has become a stealthy, silent and relentless force of nature – a result of the energy created by its eccentric rotation. The ice-cap is the creeping peril, the deadly menace and the executioner of our civilization.[22]

Did this 'executioner' cause the end of the last Ice Age in the northern hemisphere by setting in motion a 7000-year shift of the crust between 15,000 BC and 8000 BC – a shift that was perhaps at its most rapid, and would have had its most devastating effects, between 14,500 BC and 10,000 BC?[23] Or were the sudden and dramatic climate changes experienced in the northern hemisphere during this period the result of some other catastrophic agency simultaneously capable of melting millions of cubic miles of ice and of sparking off the worldwide increase in volcanism that accompanied the melt-down?[24]

Modern geologists are opposed to catastrophes, or rather to catastrophism, preferring to follow the 'uniformitarian' doctrine: 'that existing processes, *acting as at present*, are sufficient to account for all geological changes'. Catastrophism, on the other hand, holds that 'changes in the earth's crust have generally been effected *suddenly* by physical forces.'[25] Is it possible, however, that the mechanism responsible for the traumatic earth changes which took place at the end of the last Ice Age could have been a geological event both catastrophic and uniform?

The great biologist Sir Thomas Huxley remarked in the nineteenth century:

> To my mind there appears to be no sort of theoretical antagonism between Catastrophism and Uniformitarianism; on the contrary, it is very conceivable that catastrophes may be part and parcel of

uniformity. Let me illustrate my case by analogy. The working of a clock is a model of uniform action. Good timekeeping means uniformity of action. But the striking of a clock is essentially a catastrophe. The hammer might be made to blow up a barrel of gunpowder, or turn on a deluge of water and, by proper arrangement, the clock, instead of marking the hours, might strike at all sorts of irregular intervals, never twice alike in the force or number of its blows. Nevertheless, all these irregular and apparently lawless catastrophes would be the result of an absolutely uniformitarian action, and we might have two schools of clock theorists, one studying the hammer and the other the pendulum.[26]

Could continental drift be the pendulum?

Could earth-crust displacement be the hammer?

Mars and earth

Crustal displacements are thought to have taken place on other planets. In the December 1985 issue of *Scientific American*, Peter H. Schultz drew attention to meteorite impact craters visible on the Martian surface. Craters in polar areas have a distinctive 'signature' because the meteorites land amid the thick deposits of dust and ice that accumulate there. Outside the *present* polar circles of Mars, Schultz found two other such areas: 'These zones are antipodal; they arc on opposite faces of the planet. The deposits show many of the processes and characteristics of today's poles, but they lie near the present-day equator . . .'

What could have caused this effect? Judging from the evidence, Shultz put forward the theory that the mechanism appeared to have been 'the movement of the entire lithosphere, the solid outer portion of the planet as one plate . . . [This movement seems to have taken place] in rapid spurts followed by long pauses.'[27]

If crustal displacements can happen on Mars, why not on earth? And if they *don't* happen on earth, how do we account for the otherwise awkward fact that *not a single one* of the ice-caps built up around the world during previous Ice Ages seems to have occurred at – or even near – either of the present poles.[28] On the contrary, land areas bearing the marks of former glaciation are very widely distributed. If we cannot assume crustal shifts, we must find some other way to explain why the ice-caps appear to have reached sea level within the tropics on three continents: Asia, Africa and Australia.[29]

Charles Hapgood's solution to this problem is simple, extremely elegant and does not affront commonsense:

> The only ice age that is adequately explained is the present ice age in Antarctica. This is excellently explained. It exists, quite obviously, because Antarctica is at the pole, and for no other reason. No variation of the sun's heat, no galactic dust, no volcanism, no subcrustal currents, and no arrangements of land elevations or sea currents account for the fact. We may conclude that the best theory to account for an ice age is that the area concerned was at the pole. We thus account for the Indian and African ice sheets, though the areas once occupied by them are now in the tropics. We account for all ice sheets of continental size in the same way.[30]

The logic is close to inescapable. Either we accept that the Antarctic ice cap is the *first* continent-sized ice sheet *ever* to have been situated at a pole – which seems improbable – or we are obliged to suppose that earth-crust displacement, or a similar mechanism, must have been at work.

Memories of the polar dawn?

Our ancestors may have preserved in their most ancient traditions memories of a displacement. We saw some of these memories in Part IV: cataclysm myths that appear to be eyewitness accounts of the series of geological disasters which accompanied the end of the last Ice-Age in the northern hemisphere.[31] There are other myths too, which may have come down to us from that epoch between 15,000 and 10,000 BC. Among these are several which speak of lands of the gods and of former paradises, all of which are described as being in the south (for example, the Ta Neteru of the Egyptians) and many of which seem to have experienced polar conditions.

The great Indian epic, *Mahabaratha*, speaks of Mount Meru, the land of the gods:

> At Meru the sun and moon go round from left to right every day, and so do all the stars . . . The mountain by its lusture, so overcomes the

darkness of night, that the night can hardly be distinguished from the day. . . . The day and night are together equal to a year to the residents of the place . . . '[32]

Similarly, as the reader will recall from Chapter Twenty-five, Airyana Vaejo, the mythical paradise and former homeland of the Avestic Aryans of Iran, seems to have been rendered uninhabitable by the sudden onset of glaciation. In later years it was spoken of as a place in which: 'the stars, the moon and the sun are only once a year seen to rise and set, and a year seems only as a day.'[33]

In the *Surya Siddhanta*, an ancient Indian text, we read, 'The gods behold the sun, after it has once arisen, for half a year.'[34] The seventh Mandala of the *Rigveda* contains a number of 'Dawn' hymns. One of these (VII, 76) says that the dawn has raised its banner on the horizon with its usual splendour and reports in Verse 3 that a period of *several days* elapsed between the first appearance of the dawn and the rising of the sun that followed it.[35] Another passage states, 'many were the days between the first beams of the dawn and actual sunrise'.[36]

Are these eyewitness accounts of polar conditions?

Although we can never be sure, it may be relevant that in Indian tradition the Vedas are believed to be revealed texts, passed down from the time of the gods.[37] It may also be relevant that in describing the processes of transmission, all the traditions refer to the *pralayas* (cataclysms) which occasionally overtake the world and claim that in each of these the written scriptures are physically destroyed. After each destruction, however, certain *Rishis* or 'wise men' survive who

> repromulgate, at the beginning of the new age, the knowledge inherited by them as a sacred trust from their forefathers in the preceding age . . . Each *manvantara* or age thus has a Veda of its own which differs only in expression and not in sense from the antediluvian Veda.[38]

An epoch of turmoil and darkness

As every schoolboy geographer understands, true north (the North Pole) is not quite the same thing as magnetic north (the direction compass needles point). Indeed the magnetic north pole is presently situated in northern Canada, about 11 degrees from the true North

Pole.[39] Recent advances in the study of palaeomagnetism have proved that the earth's magnetic polarity has *reversed itself more than 170 times* during the past 80 million years . . .[40]

What causes these field reversals?

While he was teaching at the University of Cambridge the geologist S. K. Runcorn published an article in *Scientific American* which made a pertinent point:

> There seems no doubt that the earth's magnetic field is tied up in some way to the rotation of the planet. And this leads to a remarkable finding about the earth's rotation itself . . . [The unavoidable conclusion is that] the earth's axis of rotation has changed also. In other words, the planet has rolled about, changing the location of the geographical poles.[41]

Runcorn appears to be envisaging a complete 180-degree flip of the poles, with the earth literally tumbling – although similar palaeomagnetic readings would result from a slippage of the crust *over* the geographical poles. Either way, the consequences for civilization, and indeed for all life, would be unimaginably dreadful.

Of course, Runcorn may be wrong; perhaps field reversals can occur in the absence of any other upheavals.

But he may also be right.

According to reports published in *Nature* and *New Scientist*, the last geomagnetic reversal was completed just 12,400 years ago – during *the eleventh millennium BC*[42]

This is of course the very millennium in which the ancient Tiahuanacan civilization in the Andes seems to have been destroyed. The same millennium is signalled by the alignments and design of the great astronomical monuments on the Giza plateau, and by the erosion patterns on the Sphinx. And it was in the eleventh millennium BC that Egypt's 'precocious agricultural experiment' suddenly failed. Likewise it was in the eleventh millennium BC that huge numbers of large mammal species all around the world vanished into extinction. The list could continue: abrupt rises in sea level, hurricane-force winds, electrical storms, volcanic disturbances, and so on.

Scientists expect the next reversal of the earth's magnetic poles to occur around AD 2030.[43]

Is this an intimation of planetary disaster? After 12,500 years of the pendulum, is the hammer about to strike?

Exhibit 11

Yves Rocard, Professor of the Faculty of Sciences at Paris: 'Our modern seismographs are sensitive to the 'noise' of limited agitation at every point in the earth, even in the absence of any seismic wave. One may in this noise discern a man-made vibration (for example, a train four kilometres away, or a big city ten kilometres off) and also an atmospheric effect (from changing pressure of the wind on the soil) and sometimes one registers also the effects of great storms at a distance. Yet there remains a continued rolling noise of cracklings in the earth which owes nothing to any [such] cause . . .'[44]

Exhibit 12

'The North Pole moved ten feet in the direction of Greenland along the meridien of 45 degrees west longitude during the period from 1900 to 1960 . . . a rate of six centimetres (about two and a half inches) a year. [Between 1900 and *1968*, however,] the pole moved about twenty feet. [The pole therefore] moved ten feet between 1960 and 1968, at a rate of about ten centimetres (four inches) a year . . . If both these observations were accurate when made, as we have every right to expect in view of the eminence of the scientists involved, then we have here evidence that the lithosphere may be in motion at the present time [and that it is experiencing] a geometrical acceleration of the *rate* of motion . . . [45]

Exhibit 13

USA Today, Wednesday 23 November 1994, page 9D:
    'INTERACTIVE IN ANTARCTICA: Students Link
    With South Pole Scientists
  'A live remote broadcast from the South Pole featuring Elizabeth Felton, a 17-year-old graduate of Chicago public schools, will take place Jan 10. Felton will use US Geological Survey data to reposition

the copper marker designating the Earth's geographic South Pole to compensate for the annual slippage of the ice sheet.'[46]

Is it just the ice sheet that is slipping, or is the entire crust of the earth in motion? And was it just an 'unusual interactive education project' that took place on 10 January 1995, or was Elizabeth Felton unknowingly documenting the continued geometrical acceleration of the rate of motion of the crust?

Scientists do not think so. As we shall see in the final chapter, however, the coming century is signalled in a remarkable convergence of ancient prophecies and traditional beliefs as an epoch of unprecedented turmoil and darkness, in which iniquity will be worked in secret, and the Fifth Sun and the Fourth World will come to an end . . .

Exhibit 14

Kobe, Japan, Tuesday 17 January 1995: 'The suddenness with which the earthquake struck was almost cruel. One moment we were fast asleep, an instant later the floor – the entire building – had turned to jelly. But this is no gently undulating liquid motion. This is jarring, gut-wrenching shuddering of awesome proportions . . .

'You are in bed, the safest place in the world. Your bed is on the floor, what you used to think of as solid ground. And with no warning the world has turned into a sickening roller-coaster ride, and you want to get off.

'Possibly the most frightening part is the sound. This is not the dull rumble of thunder. This is a deafening, roaring sound, coming from everywhere and nowhere, and it sounds like the end of the world.' (Eyewitness report on the Kobe earthquake by Dennis Kessler, *Guardian*, London, 18 January 1995. The tremor lasted 20 seconds, registering 7.2 on the Richter scale, and killed more than 5000 people.)

Above: **58** The pyramid complex of Zoser at Saqqara. Reckoned by archaeologists to be the oldest massive construction in stone ever attempted by humanity, the famous Step Pyramid is 200 feet tall and dates to the Third Dynasty, approximately 2650 BC. *Below*: **59** The hieroglyph-lined tomb chamber of the Fifth Dynasty Pyramid of Unas at Saqqara, principal repository of the mysterious Pyramid Texts. Note that the ceiling is prominently decorated with stars.

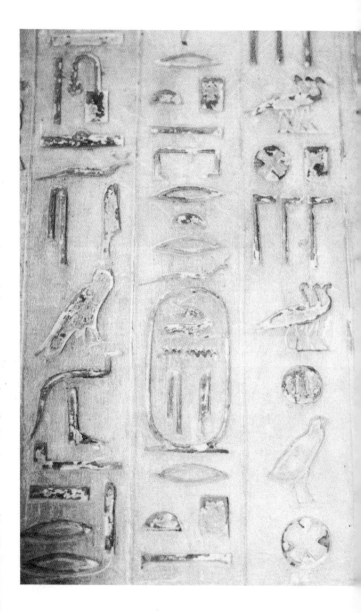

Previous page: **60** Detail of the Pyramid Texts in the Unas tomb chamber at Saqqara, with the name of Unas inscribed in the oval cartouche at the centre of the frame. The Texts speak of the deceased Pharaoh's destiny as a reborn soul in the constellation of Orion and contain a number of bizarre technological references. *This page, above*: **61** The King List in the Seti I Temple at Abydos. At the left of the frame, Pharaoh Seti I (1306–1290 BC) shows his son (the future Rameses II) an inscription of the names of the 76 Pharaohs who had preceded him to the throne of Egypt. *Below*: **62** The Seti I Temple is dedicated to Osiris, 'Lord of Eternity', here shown seated at centre-frame, wearing the Atef Crown and the characteristic beard that links his symbolism to that of Viracocha in the Andes and Quetzalcoatl in Central America.

Above: **63** Overview of the Osireion, the giant subterranean structure excavated from the silt and sand behind the Seti I Temple at Abydos and assumed by Egyptologists also to have been the work of Seti I (early thirteenth millennium BC). Geologists disagree: the Osireion's floor level lies more than 50 feet below that of the Temple, which suggests that it may have been built as much as 10,000 years earlier and then gradually covered by sedimentation. *Below*: **64** The megalithic architectural style of the Osireion, here shown with the author in the foreground for scale, is unlike any of the known buildings of the Seti I period. It closely resembles, however, the austere, gigantic architecture of the Valley and Mortuary Temples at Giza, which themselves bear evidence of a far greater antiquity than archaeologists allow. *Facing page*: **65** The main gateway into the Osireion. Compare with picture 9 in Part I, and with the Valley Temple shown overleaf.

Previous page, top left and right: **66** and **67** Interior views of the so-called Valley Temple of Khafre at Giza. Note the deeply weathered limestone megaliths visible above and behind the granite facing blocks. Could the former have been put in position in a far earlier epoch than the latter? *Bottom left*: **68** Is it a coincidence that patterns of 'jigsaw puzzle' masonry in the Valley Temple so closely resemble those found in Peru? Compare with pictures 5 and 6 in Part I. *Bottom right*: **69** The Great Sphinx, viewed from the south. The distinctive erosion patterns on the body of the Sphinx indicate to geologists that the primary weathering agent was heavy rains – which last fell in this area in the eleventh millennium BC. *This page, above*: **70** The gigantic external walls of the Valley Temple made up of water-eroded blocks that each weigh as much as a modern diesel engine. *Below*: **71** The rear of the pit or trench out of which the body of the Sphinx was carved again shows the characteristic vertical fissures and scalloped coves of precipitation-induced weathering. The rump of the Sphinx, also shown, has been partially covered in repair blocks in modern times.

Above: **72** The Second Pyramid, at dawn, its apex lit up by the first rays of the rising sun. *Below*: **73** Winter solstice sunset over the Third Pyramid at Giza. Recent archaeo-astronomical research has shown that the three Great Pyramids, and the Great Sphinx, are parts of a gigantic map of the skies as they appeared in 10,500 BC.

Chapter 52

Like a Thief in the Night

There are certain structures in the world, certain ideas, certain intellectual treasures, that are truly mysterious. I am beginning to suspect that the human race may have placed itself in grave jeopardy by failing to consider the implications of these mysteries.

We have the ability, unique in the animal kingdom, to learn from the experiences of our predecessors. After Hiroshima and Nagasaki, for example, two generations have grown to adulthood in awareness of the horrific destruction that nuclear weapons unleash. Our children will be aware of this too, without experiencing it directly, and they will pass it on to their children. Theoretically, therefore, the knowledge of what atom bombs do has become part of the permanent historical legacy of mankind. Whether we choose to benefit from that legacy or not is up to us. Nevertheless the knowlege is there, should we wish to use it, because it has been preserved and transmitted in written records, in film archives, in allegorical paintings, in war memorials, and so on.

Not all testimony from the past is accorded the same stature as the records of Hiroshima and Nagasaki. On the contrary, like the Canonical Bible, the body of knowledge that we call 'History' is an edited cultural artefact from which much has been left out. In particular, references to human experiences prior to the invention of writing around 5000 years ago have been omitted *in their entirety* and myth has become a synonym for delusion.

Suppose it is not delusion?

Suppose that a tremendous cataclysm were to overtake the earth today, obliterating the achievements of our civilization and wiping out almost all of us. Suppose, to paraphrase Plato, that we were forced by this cataclysm 'to begin again like children, in complete ignorance of what had happened in early times'.[1] Under such circumstances, ten or twelve thousand years from now (with all written records and film archives long since destroyed) what testimony might our descendants still preserve concerning the events at the Japanese cities of Hiroshima and Nagasaki in August 1945 of the Christian era?

It is easy to imagine how they might speak in mystical terms of explosions that gave off a 'terrible glare of light' and 'immense heat'.[2] Nor would we be too surprised to find that they might have formulated a 'mythical' account something like this:

> The flames of the Brahmastra-charged missiles mingled with each other and surrounded by fiery arrows they covered the earth, heaven and space between and increased the conflagration like the fire and the Sun at the end of the world ... All beings who were scorched by the Brahmastras, and saw the terrible fire of their missiles, felt that it was the fire of *Pralaya* [the cataclysm] that burns down the world.[3]

And what of the *Enola Gay* which carried the Hiroshima bomb? How might our descendants remember that strange aircraft and the squadrons of others like it that swarmed through the skies of planet earth during the twentieth century of the Christian era? Isn't it possible, probable even, that they might preserve traditions of 'celestial cars' and 'heavenly chariots' and 'spacious flying machines', and even of 'aerial cities'.[4] If they did, would they perhaps speak of such wonders in mythical terms a little like these:

- 'Oh you, Uparicara Vasu, the spacious aerial flying machine will come to you – and you alone, of all the mortals, seated on that vehicle will look like a deity.'[5]
- 'Visvakarma, the architect among the Gods, built aerial vehicles for the Gods.'[6]
- 'Oh you descendant of the Kurus, that wicked fellow came on that all-traversing automatic flying vehicle known as Saubhapura and pierced me with weapons.'[7]
- 'He entered into the favourite divine palace of Indra and saw

thousands of flying vehicles intended for the Gods lying at rest.'[8]

- 'The Gods came in their respective flying vehicles to witness the battle between Kripacarya and Arjuna. Even Indra, the Lord of Heaven, came with a special type of flying vehicle which could accommodate 33 divine beings.'[9]

All these quotations have been taken from the *Bhagavata Purana* and from the *Mahabaratha*, two drops in the ocean of the ancient wisdom literature of the Indian subcontinent. And such images are replicated in many other archaic traditions. To give one example (as we saw in Chapter Forty-two), the Pyramid Texts are replete with anachronistic images of flight:

> The King is a flame, moving before the wind to the end of the sky and to the end of the earth . . . the King travels the air and traverses the earth . . . there is brought to him a way of ascent to the sky . . .[10]

Is it possible that the constant references in archaic literatures to something like aviation could be valid historical testimony concerning the achievements of a forgotten and remote technological age?

We will never know unless we try to find out. And so far we haven't tried because our rational, scientific culture regards myths and traditions as 'unhistorical'.

No doubt many are unhistorical, but at the end of the investigation that underlies this book, I am certain that many others are not . . .

For the benefit of future generations of mankind

Here is a scenario:

Suppose that we had calculated, on the basis of sound evidence and beyond any shadow of a doubt, that our civilization was soon to be obliterated by a titanic geological cataclysm – a 30° displacement of the earth's crust, for example, or a head-on collision with a ten-mile-wide nickle-iron asteroid travelling towards us at cosmic speed.

Of course there would at first be much panic and despair. Nevertheless – if there were sufficient advance warning – steps would be taken to ensure that there would be some survivors and that some of what was most valuable in our high scientific knowledge would be preserved for the benefit of future generations.

Strangely enough, the Jewish historian Josephus (who wrote during the first century AD) attributes precisely this behaviour to the clever and prosperous inhabitants of the antediluvian world who lived before the Flood 'in a happy condition without any misfortunes falling upon them':[11]

> They also were the inventors of that peculiar sort of wisdom which is concerned with the heavenly bodies, and their order. And that their inventions might not be lost – upon Adam's prediction that the world was to be destroyed at one time by the force of fire, and at another time by the violence and quantity of water – they made two pillars, one of brick, the other of stone: they inscribed their discoveries upon them both, that in case the pillar of brick should be destroyed by the Flood, the pillar of stone might remain and exhibit these discoveries to mankind; and also inform them that there was another pillar of brick erected by them . . . [12]

Likewise, when the Oxford astronomer John Greaves visited Egypt in the seventeenth century he collected ancient local traditions which attributed the construction of the three Giza pyramids to a mythical antediluvian king:

> The occasion of this was because he saw in his sleep that the whole earth was turned over, with the inhabitants of it lying upon their faces and the stars falling down and striking one another with a terrible noise . . . And he awaked with great feare, and assembled the chief priests of all the provinces of Egypt . . . He related the whole matter to them and they took the altitude of the stars, and made their prognostication, and they foretold of a deluge. The king said, will it come to our country? They answered yes, and will destroy it. And there remained a certain number of years to come, and he commanded in the mean space to build the Pyramids . . . And he engraved in these Pyramids all things that were told by wise men, as also all profound sciences – the science of Astrology, and of Arithmeticke, and of Geometry, and of Physicke. All this may be interpreted by him that knowes their characters and language . . . [13]

Taken at face value, the message of both of these myths seems crystal clear: certain mysterious structures scattered around the world were built to preserve and transmit the knowledge of an advanced civilization of remote antiquity which was destroyed by a terrifying upheaval.

Could this be so? And what are we to make of other strange traditions that have come to us from the dark vault of prehistory?

What are we to make, for example, of the *Popol Vuh*, which speaks in veiled language about a great secret of the human past: a long-forgotten golden age when everything was possible – a magical time of scientific progress and enlightenment when the 'First Men' (who were 'endowed with intelligence') not only 'measured the round face of the earth' but 'examined the four points of the arch of the sky'.

As the reader will recall, the gods became jealous at the rapid progress made by these upstart humans who had 'succeeded in seeing, succeeded in knowing, all that there is in the world.'[14] Divine retribution quickly followed: 'The Heart of Heaven blew mist into their eyes . . . In this way all the wisdom and all the knowledge of the First Men [together with their memory of their] origin and their beginning, were destroyed.'[15]

The secret of what happened was never entirely forgotten because a record of those distant First Times was preserved, until the coming of the Spaniards, in the sacred texts of the original *Popol Vuh*. The abuses of the conquest made it necessary for that primordial document to be concealed from all but the most highly-initiated sages and replaced with a watered-down substitute written 'under the law of Christianity':[16] 'No longer can be seen the book of *Popol Vuh* which the kings had in olden times . . . The original book, written long ago, existed – but now its sight is hidden to the searcher and to the thinker . . .'[17]

On the other side of the world, among the myths and traditions of the Indian subcontinent, there are further tantalizing suggestions of hidden secrets. In the *Puranic* version of the universal flood story, shortly before the deluge was unleashed, the fish god Vishnu warned his human protégé that he 'should conceal the Sacred Scriptures in a safe place' to preserve the knowledge of the antediluvian races from destruction.[18] Likewise, in Mesopotamia, the Noah figure Utnapishtim was instructed by the god Ea 'to take the beginning, the middle and the end of whatever was consigned to writing and then to bury it in the City of the Sun at Sippara'.[19] After the waters of the flood had gone, survivors were instructed to make their way to the site of the City of the Sun 'to search for the writings', which would be found to contain knowledge of benefit to future generations of mankind.[20]

Strangely enough, it was the City of the Sun in Egypt, Innu, known by the Greeks as Heliopolis – which was regarded throughout the dynastic period as the source and centre of the high wisdom handed down to mortal men from the fabled First Time of the gods. It was at Heliopolis that the the Pyramid Texts were collated, and it was the Heliopolitan priesthood – or rather the Heliopolitan cult – that had custody of the monuments of the Giza necropolis.

More than just Kilroy was here

Let us return to our scenario:

1 we know that our late twentieth-century, post-industrial civilization is about to be destroyed by an inescapable cosmic or geological cataclysm;
2 we know – because our science is pretty good – that the destruction is going to be *near-total*;
3 mobilizing massive technological resources, we put our best minds to work to ensure that at least a remnant of our species will survive the catastrophe, and that the core of our scientific, medical, astronomical, geographical, architectural and mathematical knowledge will be preserved;
4 we are of course aware how slim are our chances of succeeding on both counts; nevertheless, galvanized by the prospect of extinction, we make an almighty effort to build the Arks or Vars or strong enclosures in which the chosen survivors can be protected, and we focus our considerable ingenuity on ways to transmit the essence of the knowledge we have accumulated during the 5000 years of our recorded history.

We start by preparing for the worst. We assume that there will be survivors but that they will be blasted back into the Stone Age by the cataclysm. Realizing that it may take ten or twelve thousand years for a civilization as advanced as our own to rise again like a phoenix from the ashes, one of our top priorities is to find a way to communicate with that postulated future civilization. At the least we would want to say to them: KILROY WAS HERE! and to be sure they got the message no matter what language they spoke or what ethical, religious, ideological, metaphysical or philosophical leanings their society might exhibit.

I'm sure we'd want to say more than just 'Kilroy was here'. We'd want, for example, to tell them – those distant grandchildren of ours – *when* we had lived in relation to their time.

How would we do that? How would we express, say, AD 2012 of the Christian era in a language universal enough to be worked out and understood twelve thousand years hence by a civilization that would know nothing of the Christian or of any of the other eras by which we express chronology?

One obvious solution would be to make use of the beautiful predictability of the earth's axial precession, which has the effect of slowly and regularly altering the declination of the entire star-field in relation to a viewer at a fixed point, and which equally slowly and regularly revolves equinoctial point in relation to the twelve zodiacal constellations. From the predictability of this motion it follows that if we can find a way to declare: WE LIVED WHEN THE VERNAL EQUINOX WAS IN THE CONSTELLATION OF PISCES we will provide a means of specifying our epoch to within a single 2160-year period in every grand precessional cycle of 25,920 years.

The only drawback to this scheme would evident if a civilization equivalent to our own failed to arise within 12,000 or even 20,000 years of the cataclysm, but took much longer – perhaps as much as 30,000 years. In that case, a monument or calendrical device declaring 'lived when the vernal equinox was in the constellation of Pisces' would no longer be unambiguous. If discovered by a high culture flourishing at the very beginning of a future Age of Sagittarius for example it could be read as meaning 'we lived 4320 years before your time' – that is, two full precessional 'months' prior to the Sagittarian Age (the 2160-year 'months' of Aquarius and Capricorn). But it could also mean 'We lived 30,240 years before your time', that is those two 'months' plus the full previous precessional cycle of 25,920 years. The Sagittarian archaeologists would not only have to use their wits to work out the meaning of the message (i.e. WE LIVED WHEN THE VERNAL EQUINOX WAS IN PISCES), but would need to decide from other clues *which* Age of Pisces we had lived in: the most recent, or the one in the previous precessional cycle, or perhaps even the cycle before that.

Geology would naturally be of assistance in making such broad judgements . . .

The civilizers

If we could find a way of saying WE LIVED IN THE AGE OF PISCES, and could specify the altitude above the horizon of certain identifiable stars in our own epoch (say, the prominent belt stars of the Orion constellation), we would be able to signal our dates to future generations with greater precision. Alternatively we could do as the builders of the Giza pyramids appear to have done and lay out our monuments in a pattern on the ground reflecting exactly the pattern of the stars in the sky in our time.

There would be several other options and combinations of options open to us, depending on our circumstances, on the level of technology available to us, on the extent of the early warning we were given, and on which chronological facts we wanted to transmit.

Suppose, for example, that there was not time to make proper preparations prior to the catastrophe. Suppose that the disaster, like 'the Day of the Lord' in 2 Peter 3, crept up on us unseen 'as a thief in the night?'[21] What prospects might humanity be faced with?

Whether as the result of an asteroid strike or an earth-crust displacement or some other cosmic or geological cause, let us assume:
1 massive devastation all around the world;
2 the survival of only relatively small numbers of people, the majority of whom rapidly revert to barbarism;
3 the presence, among this remnant, of a minority of well-organized visionaries – including master-builders, scientists, engineers, cartographers, mathematicians, medical doctors and the like – who dedicate themselves to salvaging what they can and finding ways to transmit the knowledge to the future for the benefit of those who might eventually understand it.

Let us call these hypothetical visionaries 'the civilisers'. As they banded together – at first to survive, later to teach and to share ideas –

they might take on something of the manner and belief systems of a religious cult, developing a clear sense of mission and of shared identity. No doubt they would make use of powerful and easily recognizable symbols to strengthen and express this sense of common purpose: the men might wear distinctive beards, for example, or shave their heads, and certain archetypal imagery like the cross and the serpent and the dog might be used to link the members of the cult together as they set out on their civilizing missions to relight the lamps of knowledge around the world.

I suspect, if the situation were bad enough after the cataclysm, that many of the civilizers would fail, or meet with only limited success. But let us suppose that one small group had the skill and dedication sufficient to create a lasting and stable beach-head, perhaps in a region which had suffered relatively little damage in the disaster. Then let us suppose that some other unexpected disaster were to occur – an aftershock or series of aftershocks from the original catastrophe perhaps – and the beach-head was almost totally annihilated.

What might happen next? What might be salvaged from this wreckage of a wisdom cult which had itself been salvaged from a greater wreck?

Transmitting the essence

If the circumstances were right it seems possible that *the essence of the cult* might survive, carried forward by a nucleus of determined men and women. I suspect, too, with the proper motivation and indoctrination techniques, plus a means of recruiting new members from among the half-savage local inhabitants, that such a cult might perpetuate itself *almost indefinitely*. This could happen, however, only if its members (like the Jews awaiting the Messiah) were prepared to bide their time, for thousands and thousands of years, until they felt confident that the moment had come to declare themselves.

If they did that, and if their sacred objective were indeed to preserve and transmit knowledge to some evolved future civilization, it is easy to imagine how the cult members might be described in terms similar to those used for the Egyptian wisdom god Thoth who was said to have

> succeeded in understanding the mysteries of the heavens [and to have]
> revealed them by inscribing them in sacred books which he then hid
> here on earth, intending that they should be searched for by future
> generations but found only by the fully worthy . . .[22]

What might the mysterious 'books of Thoth' have been? Is it
necessary to suppose that all the information they were purported to
contain should have been transmitted in *book* form?

Is it not worth wondering, for example, whether Professors de
Santillana and von Dechend might have earned their place among the
'fully worthy' when they decoded the advanced scientific language
embedded in the great universal myths of precession? In so doing, is it
not possible that they might have stumbled upon one of the
metaphorical 'books' of Thoth and read the ancient science inscribed
upon its pages?

Likewise, what about Posnansky's discoveries at Tiahuanaco, and
Hapgood's maps? What about the new understanding that is dawning
concerning the geological antiquity of the Sphinx at Giza? What
about the questions raised by the gigantic blocks used in the
construction of the Valley and Mortuary Temples? What about the
secrets now being teased, one by one, from the astronomical
alignments and dimensions and concealed chambers of the pyramids?

If these, too, are readings from the metaphorical books of Thoth, it
would seem that the numbers of the 'fully worthy' are increasing, and
that new and even more startling revelations may soon be at hand . . .

To return briefly and for the last time to our evolving scenario:

1 at the begining of the twenty-first century of the Christian era,
near the cusp of the Age of Pisces and the Age of Aquarius,
civilization as we know it is destroyed;

2 among the devastated survivors a few hundred or a few thousand
individuals band together to preserve and transmit the fruits of
their culture's scientific knowledge into a distant and uncertain
future;

3 these civilizers split into small groups and spread across the
globe;

4 by and large they fail, and perish; nevertheless, in certain areas,
some do succeed in making a lasting cultural impression;

5 after thousands of years – and perhaps several false starts – a

branch of the original wisdom cult influences the emergence of a fully fledged civilization . . .

Of course the parallel for this last category is once again to be found in Egypt. I would seriously propose as a hypothesis for further testing that a scientific wisdom cult, made up of the survivors of a great, lost, *maritime* civilization, could perhaps have established itself in the Nile Valley as early as the fourteenth millennium BC. The cult would have been based at Heliopolis, Giza and Abydos, and perhaps at other centres as well, and would have initiated Egypt's early agricultural revolution. Later, however, beaten down by the huge floods and other disturbances of the earth which took place in the eleventh millennium BC, the cult would have been obliged to cut its losses and withdraw until the turmoil of the Ice Age was over – never knowing whether its message would survive the subsequent dark epochs.

Under such circumstances, the hypothesis suggests that a huge and ambitious building project would have been one way cult members could preserve and transmit scientific information into the future independently of their physical survival. In other words, if the buildings were large enough, capable of enduring through immense spans of time and encoded through and through with the cult's message, there would be hope that the message would be *decoded* at some future date even if the cult had by then long since ceased to exist.

The hypothesis proposes that this is what the enigmatic structures on the Giza plateau are all about:

1 that the Great Sphinx is indeed, as we have argued in previous chapters, an equinoctial marker for the Age of Leo, indicating a date in our own chronology of between 10,970 BC and 8810 BC;

2 that the three principal pyramids are indeed laid out in relation to the Nile Valley to mimic the precise dispositions of the three stars of Orion's Belt in relation to the course of the Milky Way in 10,450 BC.

This is a pretty effective means of 'specifying' the epoch of the eleventh millennium BC by using the phenomenon of precession, which has been rightly described as the 'only true clock of our planet'.[23] Confusingly, however, we also know that the Great Pyramid incorporates star shafts 'locked in' to Orion's Belt and Sirius at around 2450 BC.[24] The hypothesis resolves the anomaly of the missing years by supposing the star shafts to be merely the later work of the same long-lived cult that originally laid out the Giza ground-plan in 10,450 BC. Naturally, the hypothesis also suggests that it was this same cult, towards the end of those 8000 missing years, that provided the initiating spark for the sudden and 'fully formed' emergence of the literate historical civilization of dynastic Egypt.

What remains to be guessed at are the *motives* of the pyramid builders, who were presumably the same people as the mysterious cartographers who mapped the globe at the end of the last Ice Age in the northern hemisphere. If so, we might also ask why these highly civilized and technically accomplished architects and navigators were obsessed with charting the gradual glaciation of the enigmatic southern continent of Antarctica from the fourteenth millennium BC – when Hapgood calculates that the source map referred to by Phillipe Buache was drawn up – down to about the end of the fifth millennium BC?

Could they have been making a permanent cartographical record of the slow obliteration of their homeland?

And could their overwhelming desire to transmit a message to the future through a variety of different media – myths, maps, buildings, calendar systems, mathematical harmonies – have been connected to the cataclysms and earth changes that caused this loss?

An urgent mission

The possession of a conscious, articulated history is one of the faculties that distinguishes human beings from animals. Unlike rats, say, or sheep, or cows, or pheasants, we have a past which is separate from ourselves. We therefore have the opportunity, as I have said, to learn from the experiences of our predecessors.

Is it because we are perverse, or misguided, or simply stupid that we refuse to recognize those experiences unless they have come down to us in the form of *bona fide* 'historical records'? And is it arrogance or ignorance which leads us to draw an arbitrary line separating 'history' from 'prehistory' at about 5000 years before the present – defining the records of 'history' as valid testimony and the records of 'prehistory' as primitive delusions?

At this stage in a continuing investigation, my instinct is that we may have put ourselves in danger by closing our ears for so long to the disturbing ancestral voices which reach us in the form of myths. This is more an intuitive than a rational feeling, but it is by no means unreasonable. My research has filled me with respect for the logical thinking, high science, deep psychological insights, and vast cosmographical knowledge of the ancient geniuses who composed those myths, and who, I am now fully persuaded, descended from the same lost civilization that produced the map-makers, pyramid builders, navigators, astronomers and earth-measurers whose fingerprints we have been following across the continents and oceans of the earth.

Since I have learned to respect those long-forgotten and still only hazily identified Newtons and Shakespeares and Einsteins of the last Ice Age, I think it would be foolish to disregard what they seem to be saying. And what they seem to be saying to us is this: that cyclical, recurrent and near-total destructions of mankind are part and parcel of life on this planet, that such destructions have occurred many times before and that they will certainly occur again.

What, after all, is the remarkable calendrical system of the Mayas if it is not a medium for transmitting exactly this message? What, if not vehicles for the same sort of bad news are the traditions of the four previous 'Suns' (or sometimes of the three previous 'Worlds') passed down in the Americas since time immemorial? By the same token, what might be the function of the great myths of precession which speak not just of previous cataclysms but of cataclysms to come and which (through the metaphor of the cosmic mill) link these earthly disasters to 'disturbances in the heavens'? Last but by no means least, what burning motive impelled the pyramid builders to erect, with such care, the powerful and mysterious edifices on the Giza plateau?

Yes, they were saying, 'Kilroy was here'.

And, yes, they found an ingenious way to tell us when they were here.

Of these things I have no doubt.

I am also impressed by the enormous lengths they went to to provide us with convincing proof that theirs was a serious and scientifically advanced civilization. And I am even more impressed by the sense of urgency – of a vitally important mission – that seems to have enlightened all their works and deeds.

I go on intuition again, not on evidence.

It's my guess that their underlying objective could have been to transmit a warning to the future, and that this warning could be to do with a global cataclysm, perhaps even a recurrence of the same cataclysm that so clearly devastated mankind at the end of the last Ice Age when 'Noah saw that the earth had tilted, and that its destruction was near, and cried out in a bitter voice: "Tell me what is being done on the earth that the earth is so afflicted and shaken . . . " '[25] These words are from the Hebrew Book of Enoch, but similar afflictions and shakings have been foretold in all the Central American traditions that speak of the demise of the present epoch of the world – an epoch, as the reader will recall, in which 'the elders say [that] there will be a movement of the earth and from this we shall all perish.'[26]

The reader will also not have forgotten the date calculated by the Ancient Maya calendar for the end of the world:

> The day will be 4 Ahau 3 Kankin [corresponding to 23 December AD 2012], and it will be ruled by the Sun God, the ninth Lord of the Night. The moon will be eight days old, and it will be the third lunation in a series of six . . .[27]

In the Mayan scheme of things we are already living in the last days of the earth.

In the Christian scheme of things too, the last days are understood to be upon us. According to the Watch Tower Bible and Tract Society of Pennsylvania: 'This world will perish just as surely as did the world before the Flood . . . Many things were foretold to occur during the last days, and all of these are being fulfilled. This means that the end of the world is near . . . '[28]

Similarly the Christian psychic Edgar Cayce prophesied in 1934 that around the year 2000: 'There will be a shifting of the poles. There will be upheavals in the Arctic and the Antarctic that will make for the eruption of volcanos in the Torrid areas . . . The upper portion of Europe will be changed in the twinkling of an eye. The earth will be broken up in the western portion of America. The greater portion of Japan must go into the sea.'[29]

Curiously the epoch of the year 2000, which figures in these Christian prophecies, also coincides with the Last Time (or highest point) in the great upwards cycle of the belt stars of the Orion constellation, just as the epoch of the eleventh millennium BC coincided with the First Time (or lowest point) of that cycle.

And curiously, also, as we saw in Chapter Twenty-eight:

> A conjunction of five planets that can be expected to have profound *gravitational* effects will take place on 5 May in the year 2000, when Neptune, Uranus, Venus, Mercury and Mars will align with the Earth on the other side of the sun, setting up a sort of cosmic tug-of-war . . . [30]

Could the recondite influences of gravity, when combined with our planet's precessional wobble, the torsional effects of its axial rotation, and the rapidly growing mass and weight of the Antarctic ice-cap, be enough to spark off a full-scale crustal displacement?

We may never know, one way or another – unless it happens. Meanwhile, I do not think the Egyptian scribe Manetho was being less than literal when he spoke of a harsh and deadly cosmic power at work in the universe:

> Just as iron is likely to be attracted and led after the loadstone, but often turns away and is repelled in the opposite direction, so the salutary, good and rational movement of the world at one time attracts, conciliates and mollifies that harsh power; then again, when the latter has recovered itself, it overthrows the other and reduces it to helplessness . . . [31]

In short, through metaphors and allegories, I suspect the ancients may have tried to find many ways to tell us *exactly* when – and why – the hammer of global destruction is going to strike again. I therefore think, after 12,500 years of the pendulum, that it would only be wise for us to devote more of the resources to studying the signs and messages that have come down to us from that dark and terrifying period of amnesia which our species calls prehistory.

A speeding up of physical research at the Giza plateau would also be highly desirable – not only by Egyptologists determined to resist any threats to the scholarly status quo but by eclectic teams of investigators who could bring some of the newer sciences to bear on the challenges of this most enigmatic and impenetrable of sites. The Chlorine-36 rock-exposure dating technique mentioned in Chapter Six, for example, looks like a particularly promising means of resolving the impasse over the antiquity of the Pyramids and the Sphinx.[32] Likewise, if the will is there, then a way can be found to get through to whatever lies beyond the little door concealed in the Great Pyramid 200 feet up the southern shaft of the Queen's Chamber. At the same time serious efforts should be made to investigate the contents of the large, square-edged and apparently man-made cavity in the bedrock, deep beneath the paws of the Sphinx, that was discovered when a seismic survey was carried out at the site in 1993.[33]

Last but not least, far away from Giza, I suspect that our efforts might also be repaid if we were to undertake a proper investigation of the sub-glacial landscapes of Antarctica – much the most likely continent to hide the complete remains of a lost civilization. If we could establish what destroyed that civilization, then we might be in a better position to save ourselves from a similar cataclysmic fate.

In making these latter suggestions I am, of course, fully aware that there are many who will be scornful and will assert the uniformitarian view that 'all things will continue as they have done since the beginning of creation.'[34] But I am also aware that such 'scoffers in the last days'[35] are those who for one reason or another are deaf to the testimony of our forgotten ancestors. As we have seen, this testimony appears to be trying to tell us that a hideous calamity has indeed descended upon mankind from time to time, that on each occasion it has afflicted us suddenly, without warning and without mercy, like a thief in the night, and that it will certainly recur at some point in the future, obliging us – unless we are well prepared – to begin again like orphaned children in complete ignorance of our true heritage.

Walking in the last days

Hopi Indian Reservation, May 1994: Across the high plains of Arizona, for days and days and days, a desolate wind had been blowing. As we drove across those plains towards the tiny village of Shungopovi, I went over in my mind all I had seen and done in the previous five years: my travels, my research, the false starts and dead-ends I had encountered, the lucky breaks, the moments when everything had come together, the moments when everything seemed about to fall apart.

I had travelled a long road to get here, I realized – far longer than the 300-mile freeway that had whisked us up into these austere badlands from Phoenix, the state capital. Nor did I expect to return with any great degree of enlightenment.

Nevertheless, I had made this journey because the science of prophecy is still believed to be alive among the Hopi: Pueblo Indians, distantly related to the Aztecs of Mexico, whose numbers have been reduced by attrition and misery to barely 10,000.[36] Like the Ancient Maya whose descendants all across the Yucatan are convinced that the end of the world is coming in the year 2000 *y pico* (and a little),[37] the Hopi believe that we are walking in the last days, with a geological sword of Damocles hanging over us.[38] According to their myths, as we saw in Chapter Twenty-four:

> The first world was destroyed, as a punishment for human misde-
> meanours, by an all-consuming fire that came from above and below.
> The second world ended when the terrestrial globe toppled from its
> axis and everything was covered with ice. The third world ended in a
> universal flood. The present world is the fourth. Its fate will depend
> on whether or not its inhabitants behave in accordance with the
> Creator's plans . . .'[39]

I had come to Arizona to see whether the Hopi thought we were behaving in accordance with the Creator's plans . . .

The end of the world

The desolate wind, blowing across the high plains, shook and rattled the sides of the trailer-home we sat in. Beside me was Santha, who'd been everywhere with me, sharing the risks and the adventures, sharing the highs and the lows. Sitting across from us was our friend Ed Ponist, a medical-surgical nurse from Lansing, Michigan. A few years previously Ed had worked on the reservation for a while, and it was thanks to his contacts that we were now here. On my right was Paul Sifki, a ninety-six-year-old Hopi elder of the Spider clan, and a leading spokesman of the traditions of his people. Beside him was his grand-daughter Melza Sifki, a handsome middle-aged woman who had offered to translate.

'I have heard,' I said, 'that the Hopi believe the end of the world is coming. Is this true?'

Paul Sifki was a small, wizened man, nut-brown in colour, dressed in jeans and a cambric shirt. Throughout our conversation he never once looked at me, but gazed intently ahead, as though he were searching for a familiar face in a distant crowd.

Melza put my question to him and a moment later translated her grandfather's reply: 'He says, "why do you want to know"?'

I explained that there were many reasons. The most important was that I felt a sense of urgency: 'My research has convinced me that there was an advanced civilization – long, long ago – that was destroyed in a terrible cataclysm. I fear that our own civilization may be destroyed by a similar cataclysm . . .'

There followed a long exchange in Hopi, then this translation: 'He said that when he was a child, in the 1900s, there was a star that exploded – a star that had been up there in the sky for a long while . . . And he went to his grandfather and asked him to explain the meaning of this sign. His grandfather replied: "This is the way our own world will end – engulfed in flames . . . If people do not change their ways then the spirit that takes care of the world will become so frustrated with us that he will punish the world with flames and it will end just like that star ended." That was what his grandfather said to him – that the earth would explode just like that exploding star . . .'

'So the feeling is that this world will end in fire . . . And having viewed the world for the past ninety years, does he believe that the behaviour of mankind has improved or worsened?'

'He says it has not improved. We're getting worse.'

'So in his opinion, then, the end is coming?'

'He said that the signs are already there to be seen . . . He said that nowadays nothing but the wind blows and that all we do is have a weapon pointed at one another. That shows how far apart we have drifted and how we feel towards each other now. There are no values any more – none at all – and people live any way they want, without morals or laws. These are the signs that the time has come . . .'

Melza paused in her translation, then added on her own account:

'This terrible wind. It dries things out. It brings no moisture. The way we see it, this kind of climate is a consequence of how we're living today – not just us, but your people as well.'

I noticed that her eyes had filled with tears while she was talking. 'I have a cornfield,' she continued, 'that's really dry. And I look up into the sky and try to pray for rain, but there is no rain, no clouds even . . . When we're like this we don't even know who we are.'

There was a long moment of silence and the wind rocked the trailer, blowing hard and steady across the mesa as evening fell around us.

I said quietly, 'Please ask your grandfather if he thinks that anything can now be done for the Hopi and for the rest of mankind?'

'The only thing he knows,' Melza replied when she had heard his answer, 'is that so long as the Hopi do not abandon their traditions they may be able to help themselves and to help others. They have to hold on to what they believed in the past. They have to preserve their memories. These are the most important things . . . But my grandfather wants to tell you also, and for you to understand, that this earth is the work of an intelligent being, a spirit – a creative and intelligent spirit that has designed everything to be the way it is. My grandfather says that nothing is here just by chance, that nothing happens by accident – whether good or bad – and that there is a reason for everything that takes place . . .'

At the millstone grinding

When human beings from around the globe, and from many different cultures, share a powerful and overwhelming intuition that a cataclysm is approaching, we are within our rights to ignore them. And when the voices of our distant ancestors, descending to us through myths and sacred architecture, speak to us of the physical obliteration of a great civilization in remote antiquity (and tell us that our own civilization is in jeopardy), we are entitled, if we wish, to stop our ears . . .

So it was, the Bible says, in the antediluvian world: 'For in those days, before the Flood, people were eating, drinking, taking wives, taking husbands, right up to the moment that Noah went into the Ark, and they suspected nothing till the flood came and swept all away.'[40]

In the same manner it has been prophesied that the next global destruction will fall upon us suddenly 'at an hour we do not suspect, like lightning striking in the east and flashing far into the west . . . The sun will be darkened, the moon will lose its brightness, the stars will fall from the sky and the powers of heaven will be shaken . . . Then of two men in the fields, one is taken, one left; and of two women at the millstone grinding, one is taken, one left . . .'[41]

What has happened before can happen again. What has been done before can be done again.

And perhaps there is, indeed, nothing new under the sun . . .

References

Chapter One

1 Letter reproduced in Charles H. Hapgood FRGS, *Maps of the Ancient Sea Kings*, Chilton Books, Philadelphia and New York, 1966, p. 243.
2 Ibid., pp. 93–98, 235. The period lasted from about 13000 BC to 4000 BC according, for example, to the findings of Dr Jack Hough of Illinois University, supported by experts at the Carnegie Institution, Washington DC. John G. Weiphaupt, a University of Colorado specialist in seismology and gravity and planetary geology, is another who supports the view of a relatively late ice-free period in at least parts of Antarctica. Together with a number of other geologists, he places that period in a narrower band than Hough et al. – from 7000 BC to 4000 BC.
3 Ibid., preface, pp. 1, 209–211.
4 *Encyclopaedia Britannica*, 1991, I:440.
5 *Maps of The Ancient Sea Kings*, p. 235.
6 Ibid.
7 Historians recognize no 'civilizations' as such prior to 4000 BC.
8 *Maps of the Ancient Sea Kings*, pp. 220–4.
9 Ibid., p. 222.
10 Ibid., p. 193
11 *Maps of the Ancient Sea Kings* (revised edition), Turnstone Books, London, 1979, preface.
12 Ibid.
13 Ibid., foreword. See also F. N. Earll, foreword to C. H. Hapgood, *Path of the Pole*, Chilton Books, New York, 1970, p. viii.
14 From Einstein's foreword (written in 1953) to Charles H. Hapgood, *Earth's Shifting Crust: A Key to Some Basic Problems of Earth Science*, Pantheon Books, New York, 1958, pp. 1–2.

15 *Maps of the Ancient Sea Kings*, 1966 edn., p. 189.
16 Ibid., p. 187.
17 Ibid., p. 189.
18 Einstein's foreword to *Earth's Shifting Crust*, p. 1
19 *Maps of the Ancient Sea Kings*, pp. 209–11.
20 Ibid., p. 1.
21 Ibid., pp. 76–7 and 231–2.

Chapter Two

1 *Maps of the Ancient Sea Kings* (henceforth *Maps*), p. 79.
2 Ibid., p. 233.
3 Ibid., p. 89.
4 Ibid., p. 90. These maps were made in 1958, International Geophysical Year, by survey teams from several different nations.
5 Ibid., p. 149.
6 Ibid., p. 93–6.
7 Ibid., p. 97.
8 For a detailed description of the process see *Maps*, P. 96.
9 Ibid., page 98.
10 He left his graffito there. See Peter Tompkins, *Secrets of the Great Pyramid*, Harper & Row Publishers, New York, p. 38, 285.
11 *Maps*, p. 102.
12 Ibid., pp. 103–4.
13 Ibid., p. 93.
14 For a fuller discussion of the evidence behind this theory see Part VIII of this book and Hapgood's *Earth's Shifting Crust*.
15 *Maps*, p. 68.
16 Ibid., p. 222.
17 Ibid., pp. 64–5.
18 Ibid., p. 64.
19 Ibid., p. 65.
20 Ibid., p. 69.
21 Ibid., p. 72.
22 Ibid., p. 65.
23 Ibid., p. 99.
24 Ibid.
25 Ibid., p. 164.
26 Ibid., p. 159.
27 See Luciano Canfora, *The Vanished Library*, Hutchinson Radius, London, 1989
28 *Maps*, p. 159.
29 Ibid., p. 164.
30 Ibid., p. 171
31 Ibid., pp. 171–2.
32 Ibid.

33 Ibid., pp. 176–7.

Chapter Three

1 *Maps*, p. 107.
2 Ibid.
3 Simon Bethon and Andrew Robinson, *The Shape of the World: The Mapping and Discovery of the Earth*, Guild Publishing, London, 1991, p. 117.
4 Ibid., p. 121.
5 Ibid., p. 120.
6 *Encyclopaedia Britannica*, 1991, 3:289.
7 *Shape of the World*, pp. 123–4.
8 Ibid., p. 125.
9 Ibid., p. 131.
10 Ibid.
11 *Maps*, pp. 1, 41.
12 Ibid., p. 116.
13 Ibid.
14 Ibid., pp. 149–58.
15 Ibid, p. 152.
16 Ibid.
17 Ibid., p. 98.
18 Ibid., p. 170.
19 Ibid., p. 173.
20 Ibid., p. 225ff.
21 Ibid., p. 228.
22 Ibid., pp. 244–5.
23 Ibid., p. 135.
24 Ibid., p. 139.
25 Ibid., pp. 139, 145.

Chapter Four

1 Tony Morrison with Professor Gerald S. Hawkins, *Pathways to the Gods*, Book Club Associates, London, 1979, p. 21. See also *The Atlas of Mysterious Places*, (ed. Jennifer Westwood), Guild Publishing, London, 1987, p. 100.
2 *Pathways to the Gods*, p. 21.
3 Personal communications with Dr Pitluga.
4 Firm identification of the Nazca spider with *Ricinulei* was first made by Professor Gerald S. Hawkins. See Gerald S. Hawkins, *Beyond Stonehenge*, Arrow Books, London, 1977, p. 143–4.
5 Ibid.
6 Ibid., p. 144.
7 Maria Reiche, *Mystery on the Desert*, Nazca, Peru, 1989, p. 58.
8 Luis de Monzon was the *corregidor*, or magistrate, of Rucanas and Soras, near Nazca, in 1586. *Pathways to the Gods*, p. 36; *Atlas of Mysterious Places*, p. 100.

Chapter Five

1 See, for example, Father Pablo Joseph, *The Extirpation of Idolatry in Peru* (translated from the Spanish by L. Clark Keating), University of Kentucky Press, 1968.

2 This is the view of Fernando Montesinos, expressed in his *Memorias Antiguas Historiales del Peru* (written in the seventeenth century). English edition translated and edited by P. A. Means, Hakluyt Society, London, 1920.

3 *Encyclopaedia Britannica*, 1991, 6:276–7.

4 Paul Devereux, *Secrets of Ancient and Sacred Places*, Blandford Books, London, 1992, p. 76. See also *Peru*, Lonely Planet Publications, Hawthorne, Australia, 1991, p. 168.

5 *The Facts on File Encyclopaedia of World Mythology and Legend*, London and Oxford 1988, p. 657.

6 Macrobius, cited in Giorgio de Santillana and Hertha von Dechend, *Hamlet's Mill*, David R. Godine, Publisher, Boston, 1992, p. 134. See also A. R. Hope Moncreiff, *The Illustrated Guide to Classical Mythology*, BCA, London, 1992, p. 153.

7 *Peru*, p. 181.

8 *Tan. Terumah*, XI; also, with slight variations, *Yoma* 39b. Cited in *The Jewish Encyclopaedia*, Funk and Wagnell, New York, 1925, vol. II, p. 105.

9 *Peru*, p. 182.

10 *The Facts on File Encyclopaedia* . . ., p. 658.

11 See, for example, H. Osborne, *South American Mythology*, Paul Hamlyn, London, 1968, p. 81.

12 For further evidence and argument in this regard, see Constance Irwin, *Fair Gods and Stone Faces*, W. H. Allen, London, 1964, pp. 31–2.

13 J. Alden Mason, *The Ancient Civilizations of Peru*, Penguin Books, London, 1991, p. 135. See also Garcilaso de la Vega, *The Royal Commentaries of the Incas*, Orion Press, New York, 1961, pp. 132–3, 147–8.

Chapter Six

1 *South American Mythology*, p. 74.

2 Ibid.

3 Arthur Cotterell, *The Illustrated Encyclopaedia of Myths and Legends*, Guild Publishing, London, 1989, p. 174. See also *South American Mythology*, p. 69–88.

4 Francisco de Avila, 'A Narrative of the Errors, False Gods, and Other Superstitions and Diabolical Rites in Which the Indians of the Province of Huarochiri Lived in Ancient Times', in *Narratives of the Rites and Laws of the Yncas* (trans. and ed. Clemens R. Markhem), Hakluyt Society, London, 1873, vol. XLVIII, p. 124.

5 *South American Mythology*, p. 74.

6 Ibid., p. 74–6.

7 Ibid., p. 78.
8 Ibid., p. 81.
9 John Hemming, *The Conquest of the Incas*, Macmillan, London, 1993, p. 97.
10 *South American Mythology*, p. 87.
11 Ibid., p. 72.
12 *Encyclopaedia Britannica*, 1991, 26:42.
13 Ignatius Donnelly, *Atlantis: The Antediluvian World*, Harper & Brothers, New York, 1882, p. 394.
14 From the 'Relacion anonyma de los costumbres antiquos de los naturales del Piru', reported in *The Facts on File Encyclopaedia* . . ., p. 657.
15 *Pears Encyclopaedia of Myths and Legends: Oceania, Australia and the Americas*, (ed. Sheila Savill), Pelham Books, London, 1978, pp. 179–80.
16 *South American Mythology*, p. 76.
17 Ibid.
18 *The Conquest of the Incas*, p. 191.
19 *Royal Commentaries of the Incas*, p. 233.
20 Ibid., p. 237.

Chapter Seven

1 José de Acosta, *The Natural and Moral History of the Indies*, Book I, Chapter four, in *South American Mythology*, p. 61.
2 Ibid., p. 82.
3 D. Gifford and J. Sibbick, *Warriors, Gods and Spirits from South American Mythology*, Eurobook Limited, 1983, p. 54.
4 *Genesis* 6:4.
5 Fr Molina, 'Relacion de las fabulas y ritos de los Yngas', in *South American Mythology*, p. 61.
6 *Royal Commentaries of the Incas*.
7 *The Ancient Civilizations of Peru*, p. 237.
8 Juan de Batanzos, 'Suma y Narracion de los Incas', in *South American Mythology*, p. 79.
9 *The Ancient Civilizations of Peru*, p. 163.
10 Cited in Zecharia Sitchin, *The Lost Realms*, Avon Books, New York, 1990, p. 164.
11 Another scholar, Maria Schulten de D'Ebneth, also worked with mathematical methods (as opposed to historical methods which are heavily speculative and interpretive). Her objective was to rediscover the ancient grid used to determine Machu Picchu's layout in relation to the cardinal points. She did this after first establishing the existence of a central 45° line. In the process she stumbled across something else: 'The sub-angles that she calculated between the central 45° line and sites located away from it . . . indicated to her that the earth's tilt ("obliquity") at the time this grid was laid out was clsoe to 24° 08'. This means that the grid was planned (according to her) 5125 years before her measurements were done in 1953; in other words in 3172 BC.' *The Last Realms*, pp. 204–5.

Chapter Eight

1 Professor Arthur Posnansky, *Tiahuanacu: The Cradle of American Man*, Ministry of Education, La Paz, Bolivia, 1957, volume III p. 192. See also Immanuel Velikovsky, *Earth in Upheaval*, Pocket Books, New York, 1977, pp. 77–8: 'Investigation into the topography of the Andes and the fauna of Lake Titicaca, together with a chemical analysis of this lake and others on the same plateau, has established that the plateau was at one time at sea level, 12,500 feet lower than it is today . . . and that its lakes were originally part of a sea-gulf . . . Sometime in the past the entire Altiplano, with its lakes, rose from the bottom of the ocean . . .'

2 Personal communication with Richard Ellison of the British Geological Survey, 17 September 1993. Ellison is the author of the BGS Overseas Geology and Mineral Resources Paper (No. 65) entitled *The Geology of the Western Corriera and Altiplano*.

3 *Tiahuanacu*, III, p. 192.

4 *Tiahuanacu*, J. J. Augustin, New York, 1945, volume I, p. 28.

5 Ibid.

6 See, for example, H.S. Bellamy, *Built Before the Flood: The Problem of the Tiahuanaco Ruins*, Faber & Faber, London, 1943, p. 57.

7 Ibid., p. 59.

8 *Tiahuanacu*, III, pp. 192–6. See also *Bolivia*, Lonely Planet Publications, Hawthorne, Australia, 1992, p. 156.

9 Ibid. See also Harold Osborne, *Indians of the Andes: Aymaras and Quechuas*, Routledge and Kegan Paul, London, 1952, p. 55.

10 *Earth In Upheaval*, p. 76: 'The conservative view among evolutionists and geologists is that mountain-making is a slow process, observable in minute changes, and that because it is a continuous process there never could have been spontaneous upliftings on a large scale. *In the case of Tiahuanaco, however, the change in altitude apparently occurred after the city was built*, and this could not have been the result of a slow process . . .'

11 See, for example, Ian Cameron, *Kingdom of the Sun God: A History of the Andes and Their People*, Guild Publishing, London, 1990, pp. 48–9.

12 *Tiahuanacu* II, p. 91 and I, p. 39.

Chapter Nine

1 *South American Mythology*, p. 87.

2 Ibid., p. 44.

3 Antonio de la Calancha, *Cronica Moralizada del Orden de San Augustin en el Peru*, 1638, in *South American Mythology*, p. 87.

4 Good summaries of the Plutarch account are given in M. V. Seton-Williams, *Egyptian Legends and Stories*, Rubicon Press, London, 1990, pp. 24–9; and in E. A. Wallis Budge, *From Fetish to God in Ancient Egypt*, Oxford University Press, 1934, pp. 178–83.

5 *From Fetish to God in Ancient Egypt*, p. 180.

6 Thor Heyerdahl, *The Ra Expeditions*, Book Club Associates, London, 1972, pp. 43, 295.
7 Ibid., p. 43.
8 Ibid., p. 295.

Chapter Ten

1 Pedro Cieza de Leon, *Chronicle of Peru*, Hakluyt Society, London, 1864 and 1883, Part I, Chapter 87.
2 *Indians of the Andes: Aymaras and Quechuas*, p. 64. See also *Feats and Wisdom of the Ancients*, Time-Life Books, Alexandria, Virginia, 1990, p. 55.
3 *Royal Commentaries of the Incas*, Book Three, Chapter one. See, for example, version published by Orion Press, New York, 1961 (translated by Maria Jolas from the critical annotated French edition of Alain Gheerbrant), pp. 49–50.
4 *Bolivia*, p. 156 (map).
5 H. S. Bellamy and P. Allan, *The Calendar of Tiahuanaco: The Measuring System of the Oldest Civilization*, Faber & Faber, London, 1956, p. 16.
6 For a detailed discussion of the hydraulic system of the Akapana see *Tiahuanacu:* II, pp. 69–79.
7 Ibid., I, p. 78.
8 *The Lost Realms*, p. 215.
9 *Tiahuanacu*, II, pp. 44–105.
10 *The Calendar of Tiahuanaco*, pp. 17–18.

Chapter Eleven

1 *Tiahuanacu*, II, p. 89.
2 *Collins English Dictionary*, London, 1982, p. 1015. In addition, Dr John Mason of the British Astronomical Association defined obliquity of the ecliptic in a telephone interview on 7 October 1993: 'The earth spins about an axis which goes through its centre and its north and south poles. This axis is inclined to the plane of the earth's orbit around the sun. This tilt is called the obliquity of the ecliptic. The current value for the obliquity of the ecliptic is 23.44 degrees.'
3 J. D. Hays, John Imbrie, N. J. Shackleton, 'Variations in the Earth's Orbit: Pacemaker of the Ice Ages', in *Science*, vol. 194, No. 4270, 10 December 1976, p. 1125.
4 Anthony F. Aveni, *Skywatchers of Ancient Mexico*, University of Texas Press, Iago, p. 103.
5 *Tiahuanacu*, II, p. 90–1.
6 *Tiahuanacu*, II, p. 47.
7 Ibid., p. 91.
8 Ibid., I, p. 119.
9 Ibid., II, p. 183.
10 *Myths from Mesopotamia*, (trans. and ed. Stephanie Dalley), Oxford

University Press, 1990, p. 326.

11 Fragments of Berossus, from Alexander Polyhistor, reprinted as Appendix 2 in Robert K. G. Temple, *The Sirius Mystery*, Destiny Books, Rochester, Vermont, 1987, pp. 250–1.

12 Ibid.

13 Jeremy Black and Anthony Green, *Gods, Demons and Symbols of Ancient Mesopotamia*, British Museum Press, 1992, pp. 46, 82–3.

14 Figures and measurements from *The Ancient Civilizations of Peru*, p. 92.

15 Ibid.

16 Ibid.

17 See Joseph Campbell, *The Hero with a Thousand Faces*, Paladin Books, London, 1988, p. 145.

18 Ibid., p. 146.

19 The calendrical function of the Gateway of the Sun is fully described and analysed by Posnansky in *Tiahuanacu: The Cradle of American Man*, volumes I–IV.

20 *Quaternary Extinctions: A Prehistoric Revolution*, Paul S. Martin, Richard G. Klein, eds. The University of Arizona Press, 1984, p. 85.

21 Ibid.

22 See *The Calendar of Tiahuanaco*, p. 47. Posnansky's work is also replete with references to Toxodon.

23 *Encyclopaedia Britannica*, 1991, 11:878.

24 Ibid., 9:516. See also *Quaternary Extinctions*, pp. 64–5.

25 *The Calendar of Tiahuanaco*, pp. 47–8.

26 *Tiahuanacu*, III, p. 57, 133–4, and plate XCII.

27 Ibid., I, pp. 137–9; *Quaternary Extinctions*, pp. 64–5.

28 *Tiahuanacu*, II, p. 4.

Chapter Twelve

1 *Tiahuanacu*, II, p. 156ff; III, p. 196.

2 Ibid., I, p. 39: 'An extensive series of canals and hydraulic works, dry at present, but which are all in communication with the former lake bed, are just so many more proofs of the extension of the lake as far as Tiahuanacu in this period.'

3 Ibid., II, p. 156.

4 *Bolivia*, p. 158.

5 *The Ancient Civilizations of Peru*, p. 93.

6 Ibid.

7 For example on the paving blocks above the Nilometer at Elepantine Island, Aswan. I am indebted to US film maker Robert Gardner for pointing this similarity out to me.

8 *The Encyclopedia of Ancient Egypt* ed. Margaret Burson), Facts on File, New York and Oxford, 1991, p. 23.

9 *Tiahuanacu*, I, p. 55.

10 Ibid., I, p. 39.

11 Ibid., III, pp. 142–3.
12 Ibid., I, p. 57.
13 Ibid., I, p. 56, and II, p. 96.
14 Quoted in *Earth in Upheaval*, citing Sir Clemens Markham, pp. 75–6.
15 *Tiahuanacu*, III, p. 147.
16 Ibid.
17 David L. Browman, 'New Light on Andean Tiahuanaco', in *American Scientist*, volume 69, 1981, pp. 410–12.
18 Ibid., p. 410. According to Browman: 'Plant domestication in the Altiplano required the simultaneous development of detoxifying techniques. The majority of the plants [which were in regular use in ancient Tiahuanaco] contain significant levels of toxins in an untreated state. For example, the potato species that are most resistant to frost and that grow best at high altitudes also contain the highest levels of glycoalkaloid solanine. In addition, the potato contains an inhibitor for a wide range of digestive enzymes necessary for breaking down proteins – a particularly unfortunate trait at high altitudes where differential partial oxygen pressure already impairs the chemistry of protein breakdown . . .'

The detoxification technique developed at Tiahuanaco to make these potatoes edible also had a preservative effect. Indeed, each of these two important qualities was a by-product of the other. 'Altiplano farmers', explains Browman, 'have, for several thousand years produced the freeze-dried potato, or *ch'uno*, by a process of freezing, leaching, and sun drying. The initial explanation for this process was that it produced a food product that could be stored for long periods of time . . . six years or more . . . But we can now suggest another rationale. Leaching and sun-drying are necessary to remove the majority of the solanine and to lower excessive nitrate levels, and the subsequent cooking of freeze-dried products destroys the inhibitors of digestive enzymes. Rather than arguing that freeze-drying was motivated only by a desire to produce a secure food base, one could hold that this technology was mandatory to make the potato available as a usable nutritive source. Both factors are clearly present.

'The other plants identified as early domesticates at the Titicaca sites have similar levels of toxins, and all require the use of various detoxification techniques to make them suitable for human consumption. *Oca* has significant amounts of oxalates; *quinoa* and *canihua* have high levels of hydrocyanic acid and the alkaloid saponin; *amaranth* is a nitrate accumulator and has high levels of oxalates; *tarwi* contains the poisonous alkaloid lupinine; beans contain varying levels of the cyanogenetic glycoside phaseolunatin; and so on . . . In some cases the detoxifying procedures serendipitously result in an end-product that has excellent storage features, multiplying the beneficial effects of the technology. Where the detoxification technology does not have this added effect – for example, in the case of *quinoa*, *amaranth* and *tarwi* – the plants generally already have excellent natural storage characteristics. There is as yet no satisfactory explanation for the development of these detoxification processes . . .' 'New Light on

Andean Tiahuanaco'.

19 At the heart of the system were 'the earthen platforms about 3 feet high, 30–300 feet long and 10–30 feet wide. These elevated earthworks are separated by canals of similar dimensions and built out of the excavated soil. Over time the platforms were periodically fertilized with organic silt and nitrogen-rich algae scooped from the bottom of the canals during the dry season. Even today . . . the sediment in the old canals is much richer in nutrients than the soil of the surrounding plains.

'But the platform-canal system was not merely a way of enriching infertile ground. It also appears to have created a climate that both extended the high-altitude growing season and helped crops survive hard times. During the area's frequent periods of drought, for example, the canals provided vital moisture, while the higher level of the platforms raised plants above the worst effects of the region's frequent floods. Moreover the canal water may have acted as a kind of thermal storage battery absorbing the sun's heat during the day and radiating it back into the freezing night, to create a blanket of relatively warm air over the growing plants.' *Feats and Wisdom of the Ancients*, pp. 56–7.

20 Ibid.

21 Evan Hadingham, *Lines to the Mountain Gods*, Harrap, London, 1987, p. 34.

22 'Aymara is rigorous and simple – which means that its syntactical rules always apply, and can be written out concisely in the sort of algebraic shorthand that computers understand. Indeed, such is its purity that some historians think it did not just evolve, like other languages, but was actually constructed from scratch.' *Sunday Times*, London, 4 November 1984.

23 M. Betts, 'Ancient Language may Prove Key to Translation System', *Computerworld*, vol IX, No. 8, 25 February 1985, p. 30.

Chapter Thirteen

1 *Mexico*, Lonely Planet Publications, Hawthorne, Australia, 1992, pp. 839.

2 Ronald Wright, *Time Among the Maya*, Futura Publications, London, 1991, pp. 343.

3 Friar Diego de Landa, *Yucatan before and after the Conquest* (trans. with notes by William Gates), Producción Editorial Dante, Merida, Mexico, 1990, p. 71.

4 Joyce Milton, Robert A. Orsi and Norman Harrison, *The Feathered Serpent and the Cross: The Pre-Colombian God-Kings and the Papal States*, Cassell, London, 1980, p. 64.

5 Reported in *Aztecs: Reign of Blood and Splendour*, Time-Life Books, Alexandria, Virginia, 1992, p. 105.

6 Ibid., p. 103.

7 *The Feathered Serpent and the Cross*, p. 55.

8 Mary Miller and Karl Taube, *The Gods and Symbols of Ancient Mexico and the Maya*, Thames & Hudson, London, 1993, pp. 96.

9 From the *Vaticano-Latin Codex 3738*, cited in Adela Fernandez, *Pre-*

Hispanic Gods of Mexico, Panorama Editorial, Mexico City, 1992, pp. 21–2.

10 Eric S. Thompson, *Maya History and Religion*, University of Oklahoma Press, 1990, p. 332. See also *Aztec Calendar: History and Symbolism*, Garcia y Valades Editores, Mexico City, 1992.

11 Ibid.

12 *Pre-Hispanic Gods of Mexico*, p. 24.

13 Peter Tompkins, *Mysteries of the Mexican Pyramids*, Thames & Hudson, London, 1987, p. 286.

14 John Bierhorst, *The Mythology of Mexico and Central America*, William Morrow & Co., New York, 1990, p. 134.

15 *World Mythology*, (ed. Roy Willis, BCA, London, 1993, p. 243.

16 Stuart J. Fiedel, *The Prehistory of the Americas*, (second edition), Cambridge University Press, 1992, pp. 312–13.

17 Professor Michael D. Coe, *Breaking the Maya Code*, Thames & Hudson, London, 1992, pp. 275–6. Herbert Joseph Spinden's correlation gives a slightly earlier date of 24 December, AD 2011. See *Mysteries of the Mexican Pyramids*, p. 286.

18 *Mysteries of the Mexican Pyramids*, p. 286.

19 *World Mythology*, p. 240. See also *Encyclopaedia Britannica*, 1991, 9:855, and Lewis Spence, *The Magic and Mysteries of Mexico*, Rider, London, 1922, pp. 49–50.

Chapter Fourteen

1 Juan de Torquemada, *Monarchichia indiana*, volume I, cited in *Fair Gods and Stone Faces*, pp. 37–8.

2 *North America of Antiquity*, p. 268, cited in *Atlantis: The Antediluvian World*, p. 165.

3 *The Mythology of Mexico and Central America*, p. 161.

4 See Nigel Davis, *The Ancient Kingdoms of Mexico*, Penguin Books, London, 1990, p. 152; *The Gods and Symbols of Ancient Mexico and the Maya*, pp. 141–2.

5 *Fair Gods and Stone Faces*, pp. 98–9.

6 Ibid, p. 100.

7 Sylvanus Griswold Morley, *An Introduction to the Study of Maya Hieroglyphs* (introduction by Eric S. Thompson), Dover Publications Inc., New York, 1975, pp. 16–17.

8 *New Larousse Encyclopaedia of Mythology*, Paul Hamlyn, London, 1989, pp. 437, 439.

9 Ibid., p. 437.

10 *Fair Gods and Stone Faces*, p. 62.

11 Not only obviously related but specifically related. Votan, for example, was often referred to as the grandson of Quetzalcoatl. Itzamana and Kukulkan were sometimes confused by the Indians who transmitted their legends to Spanish chroniclers shortly after the conquest. See *Fair Gods and Stone Faces*, p. 100.

12 *Mysteries of the Mexican Pyramids*, p. 347.

13 *New Larousse Encyclopaedia of Mythology*, p. 439.

14 James Bailey, *The God-Kings and the Titans*, Hodder and Stoughton, London, 1972, p. 206.

15 *Fair Gods and Stone Faces*, pp. 37–8.

16 According to the sixteenth century chronicler Bernardino de Sahagun: 'Quetzalcoatl was a great civilizing agent who entered Mexico at the head of a band of strangers. He imported the arts into the country and especially fostered agriculture. In his time maize was so large in the head that a man might not carry more than one stalk at a time and cotton grew in all colours without having to be dyed. He built spacious and elegant houses, and inculcated a type of religion which fostered peace.'

17 *The God-Kings and the Titans*, p. 57.

18 *Mexico*, pp. 194–5.

19 *The Gods and Symbols of Ancient Mexico and the Maya*, pp. 185, 188–9.

20 Ibid.

21 *New Larousse Encyclopaedia of Mythology*, p. 437.

22 *The Feathered Serpent and the Cross*, pp. 52–3.

23 *New Larousse Encyclopaedia of Mythology*, p. 436.

24 *The Magic and Mysteries of Mexico*, p. 51.

25 *World Mythology*, p. 237.

26 *New Larousse Encyclopaedia of Mythology*, p. 437.

27 Ibid.

28 *Fair Gods and Stone Faces*, pp. 139–40.

29 *The Feathered Serpent and the Cross*, pp. 35, 66.

Chapter Fifteen

1 Figures from *Fair Gods and Stone Faces*, p. 56.

2 Ibid., p. 12.

3 Ibid., pp. 3–4.

4 *Mysteries of the Mexican Pyramids*, p. 6.

5 *Mexico*, p. 224.

6 Contemporary account cited in *Mysteries of the Mexican Pyramids*, p. 6.

7 *The Magic and Mysteries of Mexico*, pp. 228–9.

8 Ibid.

9 *Mysteries of the Mexican Pyramids*, p. 7.

10 *Yucatan before and after the Conquest*, p. 9. See also *Mysteries of the Mexican Pyramids*, p. 20.

11 *Yucatan before and after the Conquest*, p. 104.

12 *Mysteries of the Mexican Pyramids*, p. 21.

13 *Fair Gods and Stone Faces*, p. 34.

14 Ibid.

15 *Mysteries of the Mexican Pyramids*, p. 23.

16 *Yucatan before and after the Conquest*.

17 *Mysteries of the Mexican Pyramids*, p. 24.

18 Diego de Duran, 'Historia antiqua de la Nueve Espana', (1585), in Ignatius Donelly, *Atlantis: The Antediluvian World*, p. 200.
19 *Genesis* 11:1–9.
20 Reported in *Maps of the Ancient Sea Kings*, p. 199. See also *The God-Kings and the Titans*, p. 54, and *Mysteries of the Mexican Pyramids*, p. 207.
21 Byron S. Cummings, 'Cuicuilco and the Archaic Culture of Mexico', *University of Arizona Bulletin*, volume IV:8, 15 November 1933.
22 *Mexico*, p. 223. See also Kurt Mendelssohn, *The Riddle of the Pyramids*, Thames & Hudson, London, 1986, p. 190.
23 *The Riddle of the Pyramids*, p. 190.
24 Ibid.

Chapter Sixteen

1 *The Gods and Symbols of Ancient Mexico and the Maya*, p. 126.
2 *Aztecs: Reign of Blood and Splendour*, p. 50.
3 *Fair Gods and Stone Faces*, pp. 139–40.
4 Ibid., p. 125.
5 *Mexico*, p. 637. See also *The Ancient Kingdoms of Mexico*, p. 24.
6 Ibid.
7 *Mexico*, p. 638.
8 Matthew W. Stirling, 'Discovering the New World's Oldest Dated Work of Man', *National Geographic Magazine*, volume 76, August 1939, pp. 183–218 *passim*
9 Matthew W. Stirling, 'Great Stone Faces of the Mexican Jungle', *National Geographic Magazine*, volume 78, September 1940, pp. 314, 310.

Chapter Seventeen

1 *The Prehistory of the Americas*, pp. 268–71. See also Jeremy A. Sabloff, *The Cities of Ancient Mexico: Reconstructing a Lost World*, Thames and Hudson, London, 1990, p. 35. *Breaking the Maya Code*, p. 61.
2 *The Prehistory of the Americas*, p. 268.
3 *Aztecs: Reign of Blood and Splendour*, p. 158.
4 'Olmec stone sculpture achieved a high, naturalistic plasticity, yet it has no surviving prototypes, as if this powerful ability to represent both nature and abstract concepts was a native invention of this early civilization.' *The Gods and Symbols of Ancient Mexico and the Maya*, p. 15; *The Ancient Kingdoms of Mexico*, p. 55: 'The proto-Olmec phase remains an enigma . . . it is not really known at what time, or in what place, Olmec culture took on its very distinctive form.'
5 *The Ancient Kingdoms of Mexico*, p. 36.
6 *The Prehistory of the Americas*, p. 268.
7 Ibid., pp. 267–8. *The Ancient Kingdoms of Mexico*, p. 55.
8 *The Ancient Kingdoms of Mexico*, p. 30.
9 Ibid., p. 31.

10 *The Prehistory of the Americas*, pp. 268–9.
11 Ibid., p. 269.
12 *The Ancient Kingdoms of Mexico*, p. 28.
13 *The Cities of Ancient Mexico*, p. 37.
14 *The Prehistory of the Americas*, p. 270.

Chapter Eighteen

1 *Fair Gods and Stone Faces*, p. 144.
2 Ibid., p. 141–42.
3 *Fair Gods and Store Faces*, *passim*. See also Cyrus H. Gordon, *Before Columbus: Links Between the Old World and Ancient America*, Crown Publishers Inc, New York, 1971.
4 See, for example, (a) Maria Eugenia Aubet, *The Phoenicians and the West*, Cambridge University Press, 1993; (b) Gerhard Herm, *The Phoenicians*, BCA, London, 1975; (c) Sabatino Moscati, *The World of the Phoenicians*, Cardinal, London, 1973.
5 This can be confirmed in any of the works cited in note 4.
6 W. B. Emery, *Archaic Egypt*, Penguin Books, London, 1987, p. 192.
7 Ibid., p. 38. See also *The Egyptian Book of the Dead* (trans. E.A. Wallis Budge), British Museum, 1895, Introduction, pp. xii, xiii.
8 John Anthony West, *Serpent in the Sky*, Harper and Row, New York, 1979, p. 13.
9 *Archaic Egypt*, p. 38.
10 Ibid., pp. 175–91.
11 Ibid., pp. 31, 177.
12 Ibid., p. 126.
13 E. A. Wallis Budge, *From Fetish to God in Ancient Egypt*, Oxford University Press, 1934, p. 155.

Chapter Nineteen

1 See, for example, *The Encyclopaedia of Ancient Egypt*, pp. 69–70; also Jean-Pierre Hallet, *Pygmy Kitabu*, BCA, London, 1974, pp. 84–106.
2 *The Gods and Symbols of Ancient Mexico and the Maya*, p. 82.
3 Ibid., *The Encyclopaedia of Ancient Egypt*, pp. 69–70, and *Pygmy Kitabu*, pp. 84–106.
4 Ibid.
5 *The Encyclopaedia of Ancient Egypt*, p. 85.
6 *The Mythology of Mexico and Central America*, p. 148.
7 *Popol Vuh: The Sacred Book of the Ancient Quiche Maya*, (English version by Delia Goetz and Sylvanus G. Morley from the translation by Adrian Recinos), University of Oklahoma Press, 1991, p. 163.
8 Ibid., 164.
9 Ibid., p. 181; *The Mythology of Mexico and Central America*, p. 147.
10 *The Ancient Egyptian Pyramid Texts*, (trans. R. O. Faulkner), Oxford

University Press, 1969. Numerous Utterances refer directly to the stellar rebirth of the King, e.g. 248, 264, 265, 268, and 570 ('I am a star which illumines the sky'), etc.

11 Ibid., Utt. 466, p. 155.

12 *The Ancient Egyptian Book of the Dead*, (trans. R. O. Faulkner), British Museum Publications, 1989.

13 *Pre-Hispanic Gods of Mexico*, p. 37.

14 *The Gods and Symbols of Ancient Mexico and the Maya*, pp. 128 9.

15 Reproduced in *National Geographic Magazine*, volume 176, Number 4, Washington DC, October 1989, p. 468: 'Double Comb is being taken to the underworld in a canoe guided by the "paddler twins", gods who appear prominently in Maya mythology. Other figures – an iguana, a monkey, a parrot, and a dog – accompany the dead ruler.' We learn more of the mythological significance of dogs in Part V of this book.

16 Details are reproduced in John Romer, *Valley of the Kings*, Michael O'Mara Books Limited, London, 1988, p. 167, and in J. A. West, *The Traveller's Key to Ancient Egypt*, Harrap Columbus, London, 1989, pp. 282–97.

17 In the case of Ancient Egypt the dog represents *Upuaut*, 'the Opener of the Ways', the bird (a hawk) represents Horus, and the ape, Thoth. See *The Traveller's Key To Ancient Egypt*, p. 284, and *The Ancient Egyptian Book of the Dead*, pp. 116–30. For Ancient Central America see note 15.

18 *Pre-Hispanic Gods of Mexico*, p. 40.

19 *The Egyptian Book of the Dead* (trans. E. A. Wallis Budge), Arkana, London and New York, 1986, p. 21.

20 See, for example, R. T. Rundle-Clark, *Myth and Symbol in Ancient Egypt*, Thames & Hudson, London, 1991, p. 29.

21 Henri Frankfort, *Kingship and the Gods*, University of Chicago Press, 1978, p. 134. *The Ancient Egyptian Pyramid Texts*, e. g. Utts. 20, 21.

22 Robert Bauval and Adrian Gilbert, *The Orion Mystery*, Wm. Heinemann, London, 1994, pp. 208–10, 270.

23 *The Gods and Symbols of Ancient Mexico and the Maya*, pp. 40, 177.

24 *Maya History and Religion*, p. 175.

25 Stephanie Dalley, *Myths from Mesopotamia*, Oxford University Press, 1990, p. 326; Jeremy Black and Anthony Green, *Gods, Demons and Symbols of Ancient Mesopotamia*, British Museum Press, 1992, pp. 163–4.

26 *Gods, Demons and Symbols of Ancient Mesopotamia*, p. 41.

27 *Mysteries of the Mexican Pyramids*, p. 169; *The God-Kings and the Titans*, p. 234.

28 *New Larousse Encyclopaedia of Mythology*, pp. 53–4.

29 Ibid., p. 54.

30 Ibid. See also *Gods, Demons and Symbols of Ancient Mesopotamia*, p. 177.

31 *Pre-Hispanic Gods of Mexico*, p. 59; Inga Glendinnen, *Aztecs*, Cambridge University Press, 1991, p. 177. See also *The Gods and Symbols of Ancient Mexico and the Maya*, p. 144.

32 *Mexico*, p. 669.

33 *The Cities of Ancient Mexico*, p. 53.

34 *The Ancient Kingdoms of Mexico*, p. 53; *Mexico*, p. 671.
35 *The Ancient Kingdoms of Mexico*, pp. 53–4; *The Cities of Ancient Mexico*, p. 50.
36 *The Ancient Kingdoms of Mexico*, pp. 54.
37 *Mexico*, pp. 669–71.
38 For further details, see *The Gods and Symbols of Ancient Mexico and the Maya*, p. 17: 'These buildings probably confirm knowledge of a large body of star lore.'
39 *The Ancient Kingdoms of Mexico*, p. 53.
40 *Mysteries of the Mexican Pyramids*, p. 350.
41 *The Ancient Kingdoms of Mexico*, pp. 44–5.
42 J. Eric Thompson, *Maya Hieroglyphic Writing*, Carnegie Institution, Washington DC, 1950, p. 155.

Chapter Twenty

1 *The Atlas of Mysterious Places* (ed. Jennifer Westwood), Guild Publishing, London, 1987, p. 70.
2 *The Times*, London, 4 June 1994.
3 Quoted in *The Atlas of Mysterious Places*, pp. 68–9.
4 Ibid. Michael D. Coe, *The Maya*, Thames and Hudson, London, 1991, pp. 108–9.
5 *Fair Gods and Stone Faces*, pp. 94–5.
6 *The Atlas of Mysterious Places*, p. 70.
7 *Time Among the Maya*, p. 298.
8 *Fair Gods and Stone Faces*, pp. 95–6.
9 *Mexico: Rough Guide*, Harrap–Columbus, London, 1989, p. 354.
10 *The Mythology of Mexico and Central America*, p. 8. *Maya History and Religion*, p. 340.
11 See Chapter Ten.
12 E. A. Wallis Budge, *Osiris and the Egyptian Resurrection*, The Medici Society Ltd., 1911, volume II, p. 180.
13 John. L. Stephens, *Incidents of Travel in Central America, Chiapas and Yucatan*, Harper and Brothers, New York, 1841, vol II, p. 422.
14 See Chapter Twelve.

Chapter Twenty-One

1 *Popol Vuh*, p. 167.
2 Ibid., pp. 168–9.
3 Ibid., p. 169.
4 Ibid.
5 *Genesis*, 4:22–4
6 *Popol Vuh*, Introduction, p. 16. See also *The Magic and Mysteries of Mexico*, p. 25off.
7 *Popol Vuh*, pp. 168–9.

8 Ibid.

9 J. Eric Thompson, *The Rise and Fall of Maya Civilization*, Pimlico, London, 1993, p. 13.

10 William Gates's notes (p. 81) to Diego de Landa's *Yucatan before and after the Conquest*.

11 This is evident from the Dresden Codex. See, for example, *An Introduction to the Study of Maya Hieroglyphs*, p. 32.

12 *The Maya*, p. 176; *Mysteries of the Mexican Pyramids*, p. 291, *The Rise and Fall of Maya Civilization*, p. 173.

13 *Mysteries of the Mexican Pyramids*, p. 287.

14 *The Maya*, p. 173.

15 *The Rise and Fall of Maya Civilization*, pp. 178–9.

16 Cited in *The Maya*, p. 173.

17 *World Mythology*, p. 241.

18 *The Maya*, p. 176.

19 *The Rise and Fall of Maya Civilization*, p. 170; *Mysteries of the Mexican Pyramids*, p. 290.

20 *The Rise and Fall of Maya Civilization*, p. 170.

21 Ibid., 170–1.

22 Ibid., 169.

23 *Breaking The Maya Code*, p. 275.

24 Ibid., pp. 9, 275.

25 José Arguelles, *The Mayan Factor: Path Beyond Technology*, Bear and Co., Santa Fe, New Mexico, 1987, pp. 26; *The Gods and Symbols of Ancient Mexico and the Maya*, p. 50.

26 *The Rise and Fall of Maya Civilization*, pp. 13–14, 165.

27 *Encyclopaedia Britannica*, 12.214.

28 *The Rise and Fall of Maya Civilization*, p. 168.

Chapter Twenty-Two

1 *Pre-Hispanic Gods of Mexico*, pp. 25–6.

2 Ibid., pp. 26–7.

3 *Ancient America*, Time-Life International, 1970, p. 45; *Aztecs: Reign of Blood and Splendour*, p. 54; *Pre-Hispanic Gods of Mexico*, p. 24.

4 *The Ancient Kingdoms of Mexico*, p. 67.

5 *Beyond Stonehenge*, pp. 187–8.

6 Cited in *Mysteries of the Mexican Pyramids*, pp. 220–1.

7 Ibid.

8 Hugh Harleston Jr, 'A Mathematical Analysis of Teotihuacan', XLI International Congress of Americanists, 3 October 1974.

9 Richard Bloomgarden, *The Pyramids of Teotihuacan*, Editur S. A. Mexico, 1993, p. 14.

10 *Mysteries of the Mexican Pyramids*, p. 215.

11 Ibid., pp. 266–9.

12 *The Ancient Kingdoms of Mexico*, p. 67.

13 *Mysteries of the Mexican Pyramids*, p. 221.
14 *The Orion Mystery*.
15 Ibid.
16 Bernardino de Sahagun, cited in *Mysteries of the Mexican Pyramids*, p. 23.
17 *Mexico: Rough Guide*, p. 216.
18 *The Atlas of Mysterious Places*, p. 158.
19 *Pre-Hispanic Gods of Mexico*, p. 24.
20 *The Ancient Egyptian Pyramid Texts*, Utt. 667A, p. 281.
21 *The Ancient Kingdoms Of Mexico*, p. 74; *The Traveller's Key To Ancient Egypt*, pp. 110–35.
22 See, for example, Ahmed Fakhry, *The Pyramids*, University of Chicago Press, 1969.
23 *Mysteries of the Mexican Pyramids*, pp. 230–3.
24 Ibid.
25 *The Prehistory of the Americas*, p. 282.
26 *Mysteries of the Mexican Pyramids*, pp. 11–12.
27 Ibid.
28 Ibid., p. 213.
29 Ibid.
30 *The Ancient Kingdoms of Mexico*, p. 72.
31 *Mysteries of the Mexican Pyramids*, pp. 271–2.
32 Ibid., p. 232.
33 Ibid., p. 272.
34 Ibid.

Chapter Twenty-Three

1 *Mysteries of the Mexican Pyramids*, p. 202.
2 Ibid. *The Pyramids of Teotihuacan*, p. 16.
3 *The Pyramids of Teotihuacan*, p. 16.
4 *Encyclopaedia Britannica*, 8:90, and *The Lost Realms*, p. 53.
5 *The Pyramids of Teotihuacan*, p. 16.
6 *Mexico: Rough Guide*, p. 217.
7 *Mysteries of the Mexican Pyramids*, p. 252.
8 *Encyclopaedia Britannica*, 9:415.
9 I. E. S. Edwards, *The Pyramids of Egypt*, Penguin, London, 1949, p. 87.
10 Ibid.
11 Ibid., p. 219.
12 *Mysteries of the Mexican Pyramids*, p. 55.
13 *The Pyramids of Egypt*, pp. 87, 219.
14 *The Ancient Kingdoms of Mexico*, p. 74.
15 *Mexico*, p. 201; *The Atlas of Mysterious Places*, p. 156.
16 The most accessible presentation of Stecchini's work is in the appendix he wrote for Peter Tompkins, *Secrets of the Great Pyramid*, pp. 287–382.
17 See *The Traveller's Key to Ancient Egypt*, p. 95.
18 Stecchini, in appendix to *Secrets of the Great Pyramid*, p. 378. The

perimeter of the Great Pyramid equals exactly one-half minute of arc – see *Mysteries of the Mexican Pyramids*, p. 279.

19 *The Pyramids of Teotihuacan*, p. 20.
20 *Mysteries of the Mexican Pyramids*, pp. 335–9.
21 Ibid.
22 *The Riddle of the Pyramids*, pp. 188–93.
23 *The Prehistory of the Americas*, p. 281. See also *The Cities of Ancient Mexico*, p. 178 and *Mysteries of the Mexican Pyramids*, pp. 226–36.

Chapter Twenty-Four

1 *The Epic of Gilgamesh*, Penguin Classics, London, 1988, p. 61.
2 Ibid., p. 108.
3 Ibid., and *Myths from Mesopotamia*, p. 110.
4 *Myths from Mesopotamia*, pp. 112–13; *Gilgamesh*, pp. 109–11; Edmund Sollberger, *The Babylonian Legend of the Flood*, British Museum Publications, 1984, p. 26.
5 *Gilgamesh*, p. 111.
6 Ibid.
7 Extracts from the *Book of Genesis*, Chapters Six, Seven and Eight:

> God saw that the wickedness of man was great in the earth, and that every imagination of the thoughts of his heart was only evil continually. And it repented the Lord that he had made man on the earth, and it grieved him at his heart . . . And God said, The end of all flesh is come before me; for the earth is filled with violence . . . And behold I, even I, do bring a flood of waters upon the earth to destroy all flesh wherein is the breath of life from under heaven; and everything that is in the earth shall die.

Saving only Noah and his family (whom he instructed to build a great survival ship 450 feet long × 75 feet wide × 45 feet high), and ordering the Hebrew patriarch to gather together breeding pairs of every living creature so that they too might be saved, the Lord then sent the flood:

> In the selfsame day entered Noah and Ham and Japheth, the sons of Noah, and Noah's wife, and the wives of his sons with them, into the Ark – they and every beast after his kind, and all the cattle after their kind, and every creeping thing that creepeth upon the earth after his kind, and every fowl after his kind, every bird of every sort. And they went in unto Noah into the Ark, two and two of all flesh wherein is the breath of life. And they that went in, went in male and female of all flesh, as God had commanded, and the Lord shut them in.
>
> And the flood was upon the earth; and the waters increased and bare up the ark, and it was lifted up above the earth. And the waters prevailed, and were increased greatly upon the earth; and the ark went upon the face of the waters. And the high hills that were under the whole heaven were covered . . . And every man was destroyed, all in whose nostrils was the breath of life, and Noah only remained alive, and they that were with him in the ark.

In due course, 'in the seventh month in the seventeenth day of the month, the Ark came to rest upon the mountains of Ararat. And the waters decreased continually until the tenth month':

> And it came to pass at the end of forty days, that Noah opened the window of the ark which he had made: And he sent forth a raven, which went forth to and fro until the waters were dried up from the earth. Also he sent forth a dove from him, to see if the waters were abated from off the face of the ground; but the dove found no rest for the sole of her foot, and she returned unto him into the ark, for the waters were on the face of the whole earth.
>
> And he stayed yet another seven days; and again he sent forth the dove out of the ark. And the dove came in to him in the evening; and, lo, in her mouth was an olive leaf plucked off; so Noah knew that the waters were abated from off the earth . . . And Noah went forth . . . and builded an altar unto the Lord, and offered burnt offerings on the altar. And the Lord smelled the sweet savour . . .

8 *Maya History and Religion*, p. 332.

9 Sir J. G. Frazer, *Folklore in the Old Testament: Studies in Comparative Religion, Legend and Law* (Abridged Edition), Macmillan, London, 1923, p. 107.

10 Lenormant, writing in *Contemporary Review*, cited in *Atlantis: The Antediluvian World*, p. 99.

11 *Popol Vuh*, p. 90.

12 Ibid., p. 93.

13 *New Larousse Encyclopaedia of Mythology*, p. 440; *Atlantis: the Antediluvian World*, p. 105.

14 *Folklore in the Old Testament*, p. 104.

15 *New Larousse Encyclopaedia of Mythology*, p. 445.

16 *Folklore in the Old Testament*, p. 105.

17 Ibid., p. 101.

18 John Bierhorst, *The Mythology of South America*, William Morrow & Co., New York, 1988, p. 165.

19 Ibid., pp. 165–6.

20 *New Larousse Encyclopaedia of Mythology*, p. 426.

21 *Folklore in the Old Testament*, pp. 111–12.

22 *New Larousse Encyclopaedia of Mythology*, p. 431.

23 Ibid., pp. 428–9; *Folklore in the Old Testament*, p. 115. In this version the character of Michabo is called Messou.

24 From Lynd's *History of the Dakotas*, cited in *Atlantis: the Antediluvian World*, p. 117.

25 Frederick A. Filby, *The Flood Reconsidered: A Review of the Evidences of Geology, Archaeology, Ancient Literature and the Bible*, Pickering and Inglis Ltd., London, 1970, p. 58. Andree was an eminent German geographer and anthropologist. His monograph on diluvial traditions is described by J. G. Frazer (in *Folklore in the Old Testament*, pp. 46–7) as 'a model of sound learning and good sense set forth with the utmost clearness and

conciseness . . .'

26 Reported in Charles Berlitz, *The Lost Ship of Noah*, W. H. Allen, London, 1989, p. 126.
27 *World Mythology*, pp. 26–7.
28 Ibid., p. 305.
29 *Folklore in the Old Testament*, p. 81.
30 Ibid.
31 *World Mythology*, p. 280.
32 E. Sykes, *Dictionary Of Non-Classical Mythology*, London, 1961, p. 119.
33 *New Larousse Encyclopaedia of Mythology*, pp. 460, 466.
34 C. Kerenyi, *The Gods of the Greeks*, Thames & Hudson, London, 1974, pp. 226–9.
35 Ibid.
36 *World Mythology*, pp. 130–1.
37 *The Gods of the Greeks*, pp. 226–9.
38 *World Mythology*, pp. 130–1.
39 *New Larousse Encyclopaedia of Mythology*, p. 362.
40 Ibid., *Satapatha Brahmana*, (trans. Max Muller), cited in *Atlantis: the Antediluvian World*, p. 87.
41 Ibid. See also *Folklore in the Old Testament*, pp. 78–9.
42 *Encyclopaedia Britannica*, 1991, 7:798. *The Rig Veda*, Penguin Classics, London, 1981, pp. 100–1.
43 *The Encyclopaedia of Ancient Egypt*, p. 48.
44 From the Theban Recension of *The Egyptian Book of the Dead*, quoted in *From Fetish to God in Ancient Egypt*, p. 198.
45 *Genesis*, 6:11–13.
46 *2 Peter* 3:3–10.
47 See H. Murray, J. Crawford et al., *An Historical and Descriptive Account of China*, 2nd edition, 1836, volume I, p. 40. See also G. Schlegel, *Uranographie chinoise*, 1875, p. 740.
48 Warren, *Buddhism in Translations*, p. 322.
49 Ibid.
50 Dixon, *Oceanic Mythology*, p. 178.
51 *Worlds in Collision*, p. 35.
52 *Encyclopaedia Britannica*, 6:53.
53 *World Mythology*, p. 26. Details of the Hopi world destruction myths are in Frank Waters, *The Book of the Hopi*, Penguin, London, 1977.

Chapter Twenty-Five

1 *The Bundahish* Chapters I, XXXI, XXXIV, cited in William F. Warren, *Paradise Found: The Cradle of the Human Race at the North Pole*, Houghton, Mifflin and Co., Boston, 1885, p. 282.
2 *Vendidad*, Fargard I, cited in Lokamanya Bal Gangadhar Tilak, *The Arctic Home in the Vedas*, Tilak Publishers, Poona, 1956, pp. 340–1.
3 *Vendidad*, Fargard II, cited in *The Arctic Home in the Vedas*, pp. 300, 353–4.

4 *New Larousse Encyclopaedia of Mythology*, p. 320.
5 West, *Pahlavi Texts* Part I, p. 17, London, 1880.
6 Ibid.; Justi, *Der Bundahish*, Leipzig, 1868, p. 5.
7 *The Arctic Home in the Vedas*, p. 390ff.
8 *The Mythology of South America*, pp. 143–4
9 Ibid., p. 144.
10 *Popol Vuh*, p. 178.
11 Ibid., p. 93.
12 *The Mythology of Mexico and Central America*, p. 41.
13 *Maya History and Religion*, p. 333.
14 See Chapter Twenty-four.
15 Ibid.
16 *National Geographic Magazine*, June 1962, p. 87.
17 *The Mythology of Mexico and Central America*, p. 79
18 *New Larousse Encyclopaedia of Mythology*, p. 481.
19 *The Mythology of all Races*, Cooper Square Publishers Inc., New York, 1964, volume X, p. 222.
20 See particularly the writings of Hyginus, cited in *Paradise Found*, p. 195. See also *The Gods of the Greeks*, p. 195.
21 *The Illustrated Guide to Classical Mythology*, p. 15–17.
22 The Iranian *Bundahish* tells us that the planets ran against the sky and created confusion in the entire cosmos.
23 *The Illustrated Guide to Classical Mythology*, p. 17.
24 *Folklore in the Old Testament*, p. 101.
25 *Maya History and Religion*, p. 336.
26 *The Mythology of South America*, pp. 140–2.
27 *New Larousse Encyclopaedia of Mythology*, pp. 275–7.
28 *Maya History and Religion*, p. 332.

Chapter Twenty-Six

1 Roger Lewin, *Human Evolution*, Blackwell Scientific Publications, Oxford, 1984, p. 74.
2 Donald C. Johanson and Maitland C. Eddy, *Lucy: The Beginnings of Humankind*, Paladin, London, 1982, in particular, pp. 28, 259–310.
3 Roger Lewin, *Human Evolution*, pp. 47–49, 53–6; *Encyclopaedia Britannica*, 6:27–8.
4 *Human Evolution*, p. 76.
5 *Encyclopaedia Britannica*, 1991, 18:831.
6 *Human Evolution*, p. 76.
7 Ibid., p. 72.
8 Ibid., p. 73.
9 Ibid., p. 73, 77.
10 *Encyclopaedia Britannica*, 1991, 12:712.
11 *Path of the Pole*, p. 146.
12 Ibid., p. 152; *Encyclopaedia Britannica*, 12:712.

13 John Imbrie and Katherine Palmer Imbrie, *Ice Ages: Solving the Mystery*, Enslow Publishers, New Jersey, 1979, p. 11.
14 Ibid., p. 120; *Encyclopaedia Britannica*, 12:783; *Human Evolution*, p. 73.

Chapter Twenty-Seven

1 Charles Darwin, *The Origin of Species*, Penguin, London, 1985, p. 322.
2 *Quaternary Extinctions*, pp. 360–1, 394.
3 Charles Darwin, *Journal of Researches into the Natural History and Geology of Countries Visited during the Voyage of HMS* Beagle *Round the World*; entry for 9 January 1834.
4 *Quaternary Extinctions*, pp. 360–1, 394.
5 Ibid., pp. 360–1; *The Path of the Pole*, p. 250.
6 *Quaternary Extinctions*, p. 360–1.
7 Ibid., p. 358.
8 Donald W. Patten, *The Biblical Flood and the Ice Epoch: A Study in Scientific History*, Pacific Meridian Publishing Co., Seattle, 1966, p. 194.
9 *The Path of the Pole*, p. 258.
10 David M. Hopkins et al., *The Palaeoecology of Beringia*, Academic Press, New York, 1982, p. 309.
11 Professor Frank C. Hibben, *The Lost Americans*, cited in *The Path of the Pole*, p. 275ff.
12 F. Rainey, 'Archaeological Investigations in Central Alaska', *American Antiquity*, volume V, 1940, page 307.
13 *Path of the Pole*, p. 275ff.
14 *The Biblical Flood and the Ice Epoch*, p. 107–8.
15 A. P. Okladnikov, 'Excavations in the North' in *Vestiges of Ancient Cultures*, Soviet Union, 1951.
16 *The Path of the Pole*, p. 255.
17 A. P. Okladnikov, *Yakutia before its Incorporation into the Russian State*, McGill-Queens University Press, Montreal, 1970.
18 *The Path of the Pole*, p. 250.
19 *The Biblical Flood and the Ice Epoch*, p. 107. Wragnell, the explorer, observed on Bear Island (Medvizhi Ostrova) that the soil consisted of only sand, ice and such a quantity of mammoth bones that they seemed to be the chief substance of the island. On the Siberian mainland he observed that the tundra was dotted with mammoth tusks rather than Arctic shrubbery.
20 Georges Cuvier, *Revolutions and Catastrophes in the History of the Earth*, 1829.
21 Cited in *Path of the Pole*, p. 256.
22 Ivan T. Sanderson, 'Riddle of the Quick-Frozen Giants', *Saturday Evening Post*, 16 January 1960, p. 82.
23 *Path of the Pole*, p. 256.
24 Ibid., p. 256. Winter temperatures fall to 56 degrees below zero.
25 Ibid., p. 277.
26 Ibid., p. 132.

27 R. S. Luss, *Fossils*, 1931, p. 28.
28 G. M. Price, *The New Geology*, 1923, p. 579.
29 Ibid.
30 *Earth In Upheaval*, p. 63
31 *Path of the Pole*, p. 133, 176.
32 *The Evolving Earth*, Guild Publishing, London, 1989, p. 30.
33 *Ice Ages: Solving the Mystery*, p. 64.
34 *Path of the Pole*, pp. 132–5.
35 Ibid., p. 137. A major change from glacial to post-glacial conditions occurred about 11,000 years ago. This temperature change was 'sharp and abrupt' (*Polar Wandering and Continental Drift*, Society of Economic Paleontologists and Mineralogists, Special Publication No. 10, Tulsa, 1953, p. 159). Dramatic climate change around 12,000 years ago is also reported in C.C. Langway and B. Lyle Hansen, *The Frozen Future: A Prophetic Report from Antarctica*, Quadrangle, New York, 1973, p. 202. See also *Ice Ages*, pp. 129, 142; see also *Quaternary Extinctions*, p. 357: 'The last 100,000 years of glacial expansion, as recorded by oxygen–isotope ratios in deep-sea cores from the Atlantic and the Equatorial Pacific, terminated ABRUPTLY around 12,000 years ago. A very rapid ice melt caused a rapid rise in sea level . . . Detailed land fossils show a major movement of plant and animal species at the time, especially into formerly glaciated terrain. American megafaunal extinctions occurred during a time of rapid climatic change as seen in fossil pollen and small animal records.'
36 *Ice Ages*, p. 129.
37 *Path of the Pole*, p. 137.
38 'The relative change is shown by the change in the relative abundance of cold and warm water planktonic foraminifera, and the absolute change is given by oxygen isotope ratio determinations on the fauna.' *Polar Wandering*, p. 96.
39 The reader may recall that inexplicably warm conditions prevailed in the New Siberian Islands until this time, and it is worth noting that many other islands in the Arctic Ocean were also unaffected for a long while by the widespread glaciations elsewhere (e.g. on Baffin Island the remains of alder and birch trees preserved in peat indicate a relatively warm climate extending at least from 30,000 to 17,000 years ago. It is also certain that large parts of Greenland remained enigmatically ice-free during the Ice Age. *Path of the Pole*, p. 93, 96.
40 *The Biblical Flood and the Ice Epoch*, p. 114; *Path of the Pole*, pp. 47–8.
41 *Ice Ages*, p. 11. *Biblical Flood and the Ice Epoch*, p. 117; *Path of the Pole*, p. 47.
42 *Ice Ages*, p. 11; *Biblical Flood and the Ice Epoch*, p. 114.
43 *Path of the Pole*, p. 150.
44 *Path of the Pole*, pp. 148–9, 152, 162–3. In North America, where the ice reached its maximum extent between 17,000 and 16,500 years ago, geologists have made the following discoveries: 'Leaves, needles and fruits' that flourished around 15,300 years ago in Massachusetts; 'A bog which

developed over glacial material in New Jersey at least 16,280 years ago, immediately after the interruption of the ice advance.'; 'In Ohio we have a postglacial sample dated about 14,000 years ago. And that was spruce wood, suggesting a forest that must have taken a few thousand years, by conservative estimate, to get established. What, indeed, does this mean? Does it not clearly suggest that the ice cap, estimated to have been at its maximum at least a mile thick in Ohio, disappeared from Delaware County in that state within only a few centuries?'

Likewise, 'in the Soviet Union, in the Irkutsk area, deglaciation was complete and postglacial life fully established by 14,500 years ago. In Lithuania another bog developed as early as 15,620 years ago. These two dates taken together are rather suggestive. A bog can develop much faster than a forest. First, however, the ice must disappear. And let us not forget that there was a great deal of ice.'

45 *Ice Ages*, p. 11, *Biblical Flood and the Ice Epoch*, p. 117, *Path of the Pole*, p. 47.
46 R. F. Flint, *Glacial Geology and the Pleistocene Epoch*, 1947, pp. 294–5.
47 Ibid., p. 362.
48 *Earth in Upheaval*, p. 43; in general, pp. 42–4.
49 Ibid., p. 47. Joseph Prestwich, *On Certain Phenomena Belonging to the Close of the Last Geological Period and on their Bearing upon the Tradition of the Flood*, Macmillan, London, 1895, p. 36.
50 *On Certain Phenomena*, p. 48.
51 Ibid., p. 25–6.
52 Ibid., p. 50.
53 Ibid., p. 51–2.
54 J. S. Lee, *The Geology of China*, London, 1939, p. 370.
55 *Polar Wandering*, p. 165.
56 J. B. Delair and E.F. Oppe, 'The Evidence of Violent Extinction in South America', in *Path of the Pole* p. 292.
57 *Encyclopaedia Britannica*, 1:141.
58 Warren Upham, *The Glacial Lake Agassiz*, 1895, p. 240.
59 *Human Evolution*, p. 92.
60 Ibid.; see also *Quaternary Extinctions*, p. 375.
61 *Human Evolution*, p. 92.

Chapter Twenty-Eight

1 *Hamlet's Mill*, pp. 57–8.
2 Figures from *Encyclopaedia Britannica*, 1991, 27:530.
3 Ibid.
4 J. D. Hays, John Imbrie, N.J. Shackleton, 'Variations in the Earth's Orbit, Pacemaker of the Ice Ages', *Science*, volume 194, No. 4270, 10 December 1976, p. 1125.
5 *The Biblical Flood and the Ice Epoch*, pp. 288–9. Fifteen trillion miles is equivalent to fifteen thousand billion miles.

6 *Ice Ages*, pp. 80–1.
7 *Earth in Upheaval*, p. 266.
8 *New York Times*, 15 April 1951.
9 Berossus, Fragments.
10 Skyglobe 3.6.
11 Roberta S. Sklower, 'Predicting Planetary Positions', appendix to Frank Waters, *Mexico Mystique*, Sage Books, Chicago, 1975, p. 285ff.
12 *Earth in Upheaval*, p. 138.
13 *Biblical Flood and the Ice Epoch*, p. 49.
14 Figures from *Encyclopaedia Britannica*, 1991, 27:530.
15 Ibid.
16 *Path of the Pole*, p. 3.
17 Jane B. Sellers, *The Death of Gods in Ancient Egypt*, Penguin, London, 1992, p. 205.
18 Skyglobe 3.6.
19 Precise figure from *The Death of Gods in Ancient Egypt*, p. 205.

Chapter Twenty-Nine

1 *Hamlet's Mill*, p. 59.
2 Ibid., p. 58.
3 *Encyclopaedia Britannica*, 1991, 5:937–8. See also *The Death of Gods in Ancient Egypt*, p. 205, where the precise figure of 50.274 is given.
4 *Hamlet's Mill*, p. 7.
5 Ibid.; *Death of Gods in Ancient Egypt*.
6 *Hamlet's Mill*, p. 65.
7 Ibid., p. 345.
8 Ibid., p. 418.
9 Ibid., p. 245.
10 Ibid., p. 132.
11 Ibid., pp. 4–5, 348.
12 Ibid., p. 5.

Chapter Thirty

1 Livio Catullo Stecchini, 'Notes on the Relation of Ancient Measures to the Great Pyramid', in *Secrets of the Great Pyramid*, pp. 381–2.
2 Martin Bernal, *Black Athena: The Afroasiatic Roots of Classical Civilization*, Vintage Books, London, 1991, p. 276.
3 The reader will recall from Chapter Twenty-five how Yggdrasil, the world tree itself, was not destroyed and how the progenitors of future humanity managed to shelter within its trunk until a new earth emerged from the ruins of the old. How likely is it to be pure *coincidence* that exactly the same strategy was adopted by survivors of the universal deluge as described in certain Central American myths? Such links and crossovers in myth between the themes of precession and global catastrophe are extremely

common.

4 *Hamlet's Mill*, p. 7.

5 *Grimnismol* 23, the Poetic *Edda*, p. 93, cied in *Death of Gods in Ancient Egypt*, p. 199; *Hamlet's Mill*, p. 162; Elsa Brita Titchenell, *The Masks of Odin*, Theosophical University Press, Pasadena, 1988, p. 168.

6 *Hamlet's Mill*, p. 232–3.

7 Ibid., p. 231.

8 *Yucatan before and after the Conquest*, p. 82.

9 See, for example, *The God-Kings and the Titans*, p. 64. It may also be relevant that other versions of 'the Bacabs' myth tell us that 'their slightest movement produces an earth tremor or even an earthquake' (*Maya History and Religion*, p. 346).

10 *Hamlet's Mill*, p. 2.

11 Ibid.

12 *Grottasongr*, 'The Song of the Mill', in *The Masks of Odin*, p. 198.

13 Ibid., p. 201.

14 *Grottasongr*, cited in *Hamlet's Mill*, p. 89–90.

15 Ibid., p. 2.

16 Ibid.

17 Ibid., p. 232.

18 Ibid., p. 204.

19 *Odyssey* (Rouse translation), 20:103–19.

20 Trimalcho in Petronius, cited in *Hamlet's Mill*, p. 137.

21 John Milton, *Samson Agonistes*, 1:41.

22 *Judges*, 16:25–30.

23 In Japanese myth the Samson character is named Susanowo. See Post Wheeler, *The Sacred Scriptures of the Japanese*, New York, 1952, p. 44ff.

24 In slightly distorted form in the *Popol Vuh*'s account of the Twins and their 400 companions (see Chapter Nineteen). Zipcana, son of Vucub-Caquix sees the 400 youths dragging a huge log they want as a ridgepole for their house. Zipcana carries the tree without effort to the spot where a hole has been dug for the post to support the ridgepole. The youths try to kill Zipcana by crushing him in the hole, but he escapes and brings down the house on their heads, killing them all. *Popol Vuh*, pp. 99–101.

25 In Maori traditions the Samson character is known as Whakatu. See Sir George Grey, *Polynesian Mythology*, London, 1956 (1st ed. 1858), p. 97ff.

26 Cited in *Hamlet's Mill*, pp. 104–8.

27 Ibid., p. 111.

28 Ibid., 233.

29 Ibid., 312.

30 James Mooney, 'Myths of the Cherokee', Washington, 1900, cited in *Hamlet's Mill*, pp. 249, 389; Jean Guard Monroe and Ray A. Williamson, *They Dance in the Sky: Native American Star Myths*, Houghton Mifflin Co., Boston, 1987, pp. 117–18.

31 *The Gods and Symbols of Ancient Mexico and the Maya*, p. 70.

32 Cited in *Hamlet's Mill*, p. 33.

33 Homer, *The Odyssey*, Book 17.
34 *Judges*, 15:4.
35 Saxo Grammaticus, in *Hamlet's Mill*, p. 13.
36 Ibid., p. 31.
37 Ibid., pp. 7, 31.
38 *World Mythology*, p. 139. It should also be noted that, like Samson, Orion was blind – the only blind figure in constellation mythology. See *Hamlet's Mill*, pp. 177–8.
39 Mercer, *The Religion of Ancient Egypt*, London, 1946, pp. 25, 112.
40 Ibid. *Death of Gods in Ancient Egypt*, p. 39: 'the ancient Egyptians are known to have identified Orion with Osiris'.
41 Also rendered Wapwewet and Ap-uaut. See, for example, E. A. Wallis Budge, *Gods of the Egyptians*, Methuen and Co., London, 1904, vol II, pp. 366–7.
42 *The Egyptian Book of the Dead*, Introduction, p. L.
43 Ibid. Though a mill, as such, is nowhere to be seen, many Ancient Egyptian reliefs depict two of the principal characters in the Osiris myth (Horus and Seth) jointly operating a giant *drill*, again a classic symbol of precession. *Hamlet's Mill*, p. 162: 'This feature is continuously mislabelled the "uniting of the two countries" whether Horus and Seth serve the churn or, as is more often the case, the so-called Nile Gods.'

Chapter Thirty-One

1 *The Death of Gods in Ancient Egypt*, author biography.
2 For example by Robert Bauval in *The Orion Mystery*, pp. 144–5.
3 *The Death of Gods in Ancient Egypt*, p. 174.
4 This phrase was coined by Jane Sellers, whom also detected the precessional calculations embedded in the Osiris myth.
5 *The Egyptian Book of the Dead*, Introduction, page XLIX.
6 Cited in *The Death of Gods in Ancient Egypt*, p. 204.
7 Ibid.
8 Ibid., pp. 125–6ff; see also *The Ancient Egyptian Pyramid Texts*.
9 *Death of Gods in Ancient Egypt*, p. 205.
10 Ibid.
11 Ibid.
12 Ibid., p. 196.
13 *Skywatchers of Ancient Mexico*, p. 143.
14 *Hamlet's Mill*, pp. 162–3; see also *Atlas of Mysterious Places*, pp. 168–70.
15 See, for example, *Feats and Wisdom of the Ancients*, Time-Life Books, 1990, p. 65.
16 Ananda K. Coomaraswamy and Sister Nivedita, *Myths of the Hindus and Buddhists*, George G. Harrap and Company, London, 1913, p. 384.
17 *Hamlet's Mill*, p. 162.
18 *Rig Veda*, I:164, cited in *The Arctic Home in the Vedas*, p. 168.
19 Frances A. Yates, *Girodano Bruno and the Hermetic Tradition*, the University

of Chicago Press, 1991, p. 93.
20 Personal communication from AMORC, San Jose, California, November 1994.
21 Leon Comber, *The Traditional Mysteries of the Chinese Secret Societies in Malaya*, Eastern Universities Press, Singapore, 1961, p. 52.
22 Ibid., p. 53.
23 Gustav Schlegel, *The Hung League*, Tynron Press, Scotland, 1991 (first published 1866), Introduction, p. XXXVII.
24 For fuller details see *The Hung League* and J. S. M. Ward, *The Hung Society*, Baskerville Press, London, 1925 (in three volumes).
25 W. J. Wilkins, *Hindu Mythology: Vedic and Puranic*, Heritage Publishers, New Delhi, 1991, p. 353.
26 Ibid.
27 Ibid.
28 Ibid.
29 Ibid., pp. 353-4.
30 Ibid., p. 354.
31 Ibid., p. 247.
32 For details of these complicated family relationships, see *Egyptian Book of the Dead*, Introduction, p. XLVIIIff.
33 *The Gods of the Egyptians*, volume II, p. 366.
34 *The Traveller's Key to Ancient Egypt*, p. 71.
35 *Gods of the Egyptians*, II, p. 367.
36 *Hamlet's Mill*, p. 2.
37 *Egyptian Book of the Dead*, Introduction, p. XLIX-LI.
38 Ibid.
39 *Hamlet's Mill*, pp. 32-4.
40 Ibid., p. 33.
41 Ibid., p. 119.

Chapter Thirty-Two

See Chapter Twenty-four for details of flood myths. The same kind of convergence among supposedly unconnected myths also occurs with regard to precession of the equinoxes. The mills, the characters who work and own and eventually break them, the brothers and nephews and uncles, the theme of revenge, the theme of incest, the dogs that flit silently from story to story, and the exact *numbers* needed to calculate precessional motion – all crop up everywhere, from culture to culture and from age to age, propagating themselves effortlessly along the jet-stream of time.
Diodorus Siculus, Book I, 14:1-15, translated by C. H. Oldfather, Loeb Classical Library, London, 1989, pp. 47-9.
Galileo, cited in *Hamlet's Mill*, p. 10.
Ice Ages; John Imbrie et al., 'Variations in the Earth's Orbit: Pacemaker of the Ice Ages' in *Science*, volume 194, No. 4270, 10 December 1976.
Hamlet's Mill, pp. 138-9.

6 'Variations in the Earth's Orbit: Pacemaker of the Ice Ages'.

Chapter Thirty-Three

1 *The Pyramids of Egypt*, p. 208.
2 J. H. Cole, *Survey of Egypt*, paper no. 39: 'The Determination of the Exact Size and Orientation of the Great Pyramid of Giza', Cairo, 1925.
3 The conventional explanations, as given in *The Pyramids of Egypt*, for example, are entirely unsatisfactory, as Edwards himself admits; see pp. 85–7, 206–41.
4 Ibid., p. 87.
5 See Lionel Casson, *Ships and Seafaring in Ancient Times*, University of Texas Press, 1994, p. 17; *The Ra Expeditions*, p. 15.
6 *The Ra Expeditions*, p. 17.
7 *Traveller's Key to Ancient Egypt*, pp. 132–3.
8 *The Ra Expeditions*, p. 16.
9 See, for example, Christine Desroches-Noblecourt, *Tutankhamen*, Penguin Books, London, 1989, pages 89, 108, 113, 283.
10 A.J. Spencer, *The Great Pyramid Fact Sheet*, P.J. Publications, 1989.

Chapter Thirty-Four

1 *The Pyramids of Egypt*, p. 8.
2 Peter Lemesurier, *The Great Pyramid: Your Personal Guide*, Element Books, Shaftesbury, 1987, p. 225.
3 Dr Joseph Davidovits and Margie Morris, *The Pyramids: An Enigma Solved*, Dorset Press, New York, 1988, pp. 39–40.
4 Ibid., p. 37.
5 John Baines and Jaromir Malek, *Atlas of Ancient Egypt*, Time-Life Books, Virginia, 1990, p. 160; *The Pyramids of Egypt*, pp. 229–30.
6 *The Pyramids of Egypt*, p. 229.
7 Ibid., p. 85.
8 Ibid., p. 220.
9 *Atlas of Ancient Egypt*, p. 139.
10 Peter Hodges and Julian Keable, *How the Pyramids Were Built*, Element Books, Shaftesbury, 1989, p. 123.
11 Ibid., p. 11.
12 Ibid., p. 13.
13 Ibid., p. 125–6. Failure to reach the top would be because spiral ramps and linked scaffolds overlap and exceed the space available long before arrival at the summit.
14 Ibid., p. 126.
15 See Chapter Twenty-three; *The Pyramids of Egypt*, p. 219; *Atlas of Ancient Egypt*, p. 139.
16 Piazzi Smyth, *The Great Pyramid: Its Secrets and Mysteries Revealed*, Bell Publishing Company, New York, 1990, p. 80.

7 *The Pyramids of Egypt*, p. 125.
8 Ibid., p. 87.
9 'One is irritated by the number of imbeciles' names written everywhere,' Gustave Flaubert commented in his *Letters From Egypt*. 'On the top of the Great Pyramid there is a certain Buffard, 79 rue St Martin, wallpaper manufacturer, in black letters.'
0 Skyglobe 3.6.
1 *How the Pyramids Were Built*, p. 4–5.
2 *Secrets of the Great Pyramid*, pp. 232, 244.
3 Ibid., p. 17.
4 Cited in *Traveller's Key to Ancient Egypt*, p. 90.
5 Ibid., p. 40. Chompollion of course, deciphered the Rosetta Stone.

Chapter Thirty-Five

1 Herodotus, *The History* (translated by David Grene), University of Chicago Press, 1987, pp. 187–9.
2 *The Riddle of the Pyramids*, p. 54.
3 Ibid., p. 55.
4 George Hart, *Pharaohs and Pyramids*, Guild Publishing, London, 1991, p. 91.
5 *Atlas of Ancient Egypt*, p. 36.
6 *The Pyramids of Egypt*, pp. 94–5.
7 *The Pyramids of Egypt* by Professor I. E. S. Edwards is the standard text on the pyramids.
8 W. M. Flinders Petrie, *The Pyramids and Temples of Gizeh* (New and Revised Edition), Histories and Mysteries of Man Ltd., London, 1990, p. 21.
9 John Greaves, *Pyramidographia*, cited in *Serpent in the Sky*, p. 230.
10 *Secrets of the Great Pyramid*, p. 11.
The *Traveller's Key to Ancient Egypt*, p. 120.
Secrets of the Great Pyramid, p. 58.
The Geography of Strabo, (trans. H. L. Jones), Wm. Heinemann, London, 1982, volume VIII, pp. 91–3.
Secrets of the Great Pyramid, p. 58.
In general, it is assumed to have been used as an escape route by workers sealed within the pyramid above the plugging blocks in the ascending passage.
Because, over a distance of several hundred feet through solid masonry, it joins two narrow corridors. This could not have been achieved by accident. *Secrets of the Great Pyramid*, pp. 56–8.
See Nicholas Reeves, *The Complete Tutankhamun*, Thames & Hudson, London, 1990.
See *Valley of the Kings*; for Saqqara (Fifth and Sixth Dynasties) see *Traveller's Key to Ancient Egypt*, pp. 163–7.
The Pyramids of Egypt, p. 211–12; *The Great Pyramid: Your Personal Guide*,

p. 71.

21 *Pyramids of Egypt*, pp. 96.

22 *Secrets of the Great Pyramid*, p. 35–6.

23 Zecharia Sitchin, *The Stairway To Heaven*, Avon Books, New York, 1983, pp. 253–82.

24 Ibid.

25 James Henry Breasted, *Ancient Records of Egypt: Historical Documents from the Earliest Times to the Persian Conquest*, reprinted by Histories and Mysteries of Man Ltd., London, 1988, pp. 83–5.

26 Ibid., p. 85.

27 Ibid., p. 84.

28 Ibid., and *Travellers Key to Ancient Egypt*, p. 139.

Chapter Thirty-Six

1 *Atlas of Ancient Egypt*, p. 36

2 *The Orion Mystery*.

3 Abdul Latif, *The Eastern Key*, cited in *Traveller's Key to Ancient Egypt*, p. 126.

4 Ibid.

5 *Blue Guide*: Egypt, A & C Black, London, 1988, p. 433.

6 *The Pyramids of Egypt*, p. 127.

7 It was in this chamber that Vyse found the intrusive burial (of bones and a wooden coffin lid) referred to in Chapter Thirty-Five. The basalt coffin where he also found (later lost at sea) is believed to have been part of the same intrusive burial and to have not been older than the Twenty-sixth Dynasty. See, for example, *Blue Guide, Egypt*, p. 433.

8 *The Pyramids of Egypt*, p. 220.

9 See, for example, *Osiris and the Egyptian Resurrection*, volume II, p. 180.

10 *The Pyramids of Egypt*, p. 117.

11 *Traveller's Key to Ancient Egypt*, p. 123.

12 *The Riddle of the Pyramids*, p. 49.

13 Ibid., pp. 36–9.

14 Ibid., p. 74.

15 Ibid., p. 42.

16 Ibid.

17 *The Traveller's Key to Ancient Egypt*, p. 123; *The Pyramids Of Egypt*, p. 1

Chapter Thirty-Seven

1 *Diodorus Siculus*, Harvard University Press, 1989, p. 217.

2 *The Pyramids of Egypt*, p. 88; *The Great Pyramid: Your Personal Guide*, pp. 30–1.

3 In the isolated Valley of the Kings in Luxor in upper Egypt, for example.

4 *The Pyramids and Temples of Gizeh*, p. 19.

5 Discussed in *Secrets of the Great Pyramid*, p. 236ff.

6 Dimension from *The Traveller's Key to Ancient Egypt*, p. 114.
7 *Secrets of the Great Pyramid*, p. 236ff.
8 *The Pyramids of Egypt*, p. 91.
9 Ibid., p. 88.
10 Or 51° 50' 35" to be exact, Ibid., page 87; *Traveller's Key to Ancient Egypt*, p. 112.
11 See Chapter Twenty-three.
12 Ibid.
13 *The Pyramids of Egypt*, p. 93.
14 Dimensions from *Traveller's Key to Ancient Egypt*, p. 121, and *The Pyramids of Egypt*, p. 93.
15 *The Pyramids and Temples of Gizeh*, p. 24.
16 *The Pyramids of Egypt*, p. 92.
17 *The Great Pyramid: Its Secrets and Mysteries Revealed*, p. 428.
18 Ibid.
19 Presentation at the British Museum, 22 November 1993, by Rudolf Gantenbrink, of footage shot in the shafts by the robot camera *Upuaut*.
20 *The Pyramids of Egypt*, pp. 92–3.
21 Ibid., p. 92; *The Pyramids and Temples of Gizeh*, p. 23.
22 *The Pyramids of Egypt*, p. 92.
23 Ibid., p. 93; *Traveller's Key to Ancient Egypt*, p. 115.
24 *The Pyramids of Egypt*, p. 93.
25 *Traveller's Key to Ancient Egypt*, p. 115.
26 *The Ancient Egyptian Pyramid Texts*, p. 281, Utt. 667A.
27 *The Pyramids and Temples of Gizeh*, p. 25.

Chapter Thirty-Eight

1 *The Pyramids and Temples of Gizeh*, p. 25.
2 *The Pyramids of Egypt*, p. 94.
3 *The Pyramids and Temples of Gizeh*, p. 36.
4 *The Pyramids of Egypt*, pp. 94–5; *The Great Pyramid: Your Personal Guide*, p. 64.
5 *The Pyramids of Egypt*, pp. 94–5.
6 *The Pyramids and Temples of Gizeh*, p. 30.
7 Ibid., p. 95.
8 Livio Catullo Stecchini in *Secrets of the Great Pyramid*, p. 322. Stecchini gives slightly more accurate measures than those of Petrie (quoted) for the internal and external dimensions of the pyramid.
9 *Secrets of the Great Pyramid*, p. 103.
10 *The Pyramids and Temples of Gizeh*, p. 74.
11 Ibid., p. 76.
12 Ibid., p. 78.
13 Ibid.
14 Ibid., pp. 74–5.
15 *The Pyramids: An Enigma Solved*, p. 8.

16 *The Pyramids and Temples of Gizeh*, p. 75.

17 *The Pyramids: An Enigma Solved*, p. 118.

18 *Egypt: Land of the Pharaohs*, Time–Life Books, 1992, p. 51.

19 *Atlas of Ancient Egypt*, p. 36.

20 For example, see Cyril Aldred, *Egypt to the End of the Old Kingdom*, Thames & Hudson, London, 1988, p. 25.

21 Ibid., p. 57. The relevant artefacts are in the Cairo Museum.

22 Reported in P. W. Roberts, *River in the Desert: Modern Travels in Ancient Egypt*, Random House, New York and Toronto, 1993, p. 115.

23 Robert Bauval, *Discussions in Egyptology* No. 29, 1994.

24 Ibid.

25 Ibid. See also *The Orion Mystery*, p. 172.

26 *Traveller's Key to Ancient Egypt*, p. 117; *The Great Pyramid: Your Personal Guide*, p. 64.

27 John Ivimy, *The Sphinx and the Megaliths*, Abacus, London, 1976, p. 118.

28 Ibid.

29 *Secrets of the Great Pyramid*, p. 191.

30 Ibid. See also *Traveller's Key to Ancient Egypt*, pp. 117–19.

31 *The Great Pyramid: Your Personal Guide*, p. 64.

32 *The Pyramids and Temples of Gizeh*, p. 93.

Chapter Thirty-Nine

1 Measurements from *The Pyramids of Egypt*, p. 106.

2 W. B. Yeats, 'The Second Coming'.

3 *The Pyramids and Temples of Gizeh*, p. 48.

4 Ibid., p. 50.

5 Margaret A. Murray, *The Splendour that was Egypt*, Sidgwick & Jackson, London, 1987, pp. 160–1.

6 See Part VII, for a full discussion of the 'First Time'.

7 Discussed in Part VII; see also Part III for a comparison of the Osirian rebirth cult and of the rebirth beliefs of Ancient Mexico.

8 *The Pyramids and Temples of Gizeh*, p. 47.

9 Measurements from *The Pyramids and Temples of Egypt*, p. 48, and *The Pyramids of Egypt*, p. 108.

10 In addition to the three Giza pyramids, the Mortuary Temples of Khafre and Menkaure can be compared with the Valley Temple in terms of their absence of adornment and use of megaliths weighing 200 tons or more.

11 *Serpent in the Sky*, p. 211; also *Mystery of the Sphinx*, NBC-TV, 1993.

12 For block weights see *The Pyramids of Egypt*, p. 215; *Serpent in the Sky*, p. 242; *The Traveller's Key to Ancient Egypt*, p. 144; *The Pyramids: An Enigma Solved*, p. 51; *Mystery of the Sphinx*, NBC-TV, 1993.

13 Personal communication from John Anthony West. See also *Mystery of the Sphinx*, NBC-TV.

14 *Ancient Records of Egypt*, volume I, p. 85.

15 See, for example, Miriam Lichtheim, *Ancient Egyptian Literature*,

University of California Press, 1976, volume II, pp. 85–6.

16 *Ancient Records of Egypt*, volume I, p. 85.

17 *A History of Egypt*, 1902, volume 4, p. 80ff, 'Stela of the Sphinx'.

18 Ibid.

19 Karl W. Butzer, *Early Hydraulic Civilization in Egypt: A Study in Cultural Ecology*, University of Chicago Press, 1976.

20 *The Pyramids of Egypt*, pp. 106–7.

21 Mark Lehner, 1992 AAAS Annual Meeting, Debate: How Old is the Sphinx?

22 Ibid.

23 Gaston Maspero, *The Passing of Empires*, New York, 1900.

24 See Chapter Thirty-five.

25 For a general summary of these views see John Ward, *Pyramids and Progress*, London, 1900, pp. 38–42.

26 *The Gods of the Egyptians*, volume I, pp. 471–2 and volume II, p. 361.

27 Interview in *Mystery of the Sphinx*, NBC-TV, 1993.

28 Cited in *Serpent In The Sky*, p. 230.

29 Ibid., pp. 230–2; *Mystery of the Sphinx*, NBC-TV.

30 At least one orthodox Egyptologist, Selim Hassan, has admitted that the jury is still out on this issue. After twenty years of excavations at Giza he wrote, 'Except for the mutilated line on the Granite Stela of Thutmosis IV, which proves nothing, there is not one single ancient inscription which connects the Sphinx with Khafre. So, sound as it may appear, we must treat this evidence as circumstantial until such a time as a lucky turn of the spade will reveal to the world definite reference to the erection of this statue.' Cited in *Conde Nast Traveller*, February 1993, pp. 168–9.

Chapter Forty

1 See, for example, Rosalie David, *A Guide to Religious Ritual at Abydos*, Aris and Phillips, Warminster, 1981, in particular p. 121.

2 *The Gods of the Egyptians*, volume II, pp. 262–6.

3 Lucy Lamy, *Egyptian Mysteries*, Thames & Hudson, London, 1986, p. 93.

4 Jean-Pierre Corteggiani, *The Egypt of the Pharaohs at the Cairo Museum*, Scala Publications, London, 1987, p. 118.

5 Ibid.; see also R. A. Schwaller de Lubicz, *Sacred Science: The King of Pharaonic Theocracy*, Inner Traditions International, Rochester, 1988, pp. 182–3.

6 *The Orion Mystery*.

7 Ibid.

8 Ibid.

9 *Serpent in the Sky*, pp. 184–242.

10 Ibid., 186–7.

11 Ibid.

12 *Mystery of the Sphinx*, NBC-TV, 1993.

13 *Conde Nast Traveller*, February 1993, p. 176.

14 E.g, American Association for the Advancement of Science, Chicago, 1992, Debate: How Old is the Sphinx?

15 *Mystery of the Sphinx*.

16 John West and Robert Bauval worked in isolation, unaware of each other's findings, until I introduced them.

17 *The Gods of the Egyptians*, volume II, p. 264.

18 *Blue Guide, Egypt*, p. 509; see also *From Fetish to God in Ancient Egypt*, pp. 211–15; *Osiris and the Egyptian Resurrection*, volume I, p. 31ff; *The Encyclopaedia of Ancient Egypt*, p. 197.

Chapter Forty-One

1 'Saqqara, Egypt: Archaeologists have discovered a green limestone obelisk, the world's oldest-known complete obelisk, dedicated to Inty, a wife of Pharaoh Pepi I, Egypt's ruler almost 4300 years ago, who was regarded as a goddess after her death.' *Times*, London, 9 May 1992; see also *Daily Telegraph*, London, 9 May 1992.

2 *Atlas of Ancient Egypt*, pp. 173–4; Rosalie and Anthony E. David, *A Biographical Dictionary of Ancient Egypt*, Seaby, London, 1992, pp. 133–4; *Blue Guide, Egypt*, p. 413.

3 *The Encyclopaedia of Ancient Egypt*, p. 110.

4 George Hart, *Egyptian Myths*, British Museum Publications, 1990, p. 11.

5 *The Encyclopaedia of Ancient Egypt*, p. 110; *Traveller's Key to Ancient Egypt*, p. 66; *From Fetish to God in Ancient Egypt*, p. 140.

6 Papyrus of Nesiamsu, cited in *Sacred Science: The King of Pharaonic Theocracy*, pp. 188–9; see also *From Fetish to God in Ancient Egypt*, pp. 141–3.

7 *From Fetish to God in Ancient Egypt*, p. 142. In other readings Shu and Tefnut were spat out by Ra-Atum.

8 *New Larousse Encyclopaedia of Mythology*, p. 27. The figure 3126 is given in some accounts.

9 *The Pyramids: An Enigma Solved*, p. 13; C. Jacq, *Egyptian Magic*, Aris and Phillips, Warminster, 1985, p. 8; *The Death of Gods in Ancient Egypt*, p. 36.

10 *Kingship and the Gods*, p. 153.

11 *The Ancient Egyptian Pyramid Texts*, p. 246.

12 For a more detailed discussion see *The Orion Mystery*, p. 17. Bauval suggests that the Benben may have been an oriented meteorite: 'From depictions it would seem that this meteorite was from six to fifteen tons in mass . . . the frightful spectacle of its fiery fall would have been very impressive . . .', p. 204.

13 *The Penguin Dictionary of Religions*, Penguin Books, London, 1988, p. 166.

14 E.g. *The Egyptian Book of the Dead*, Introduction, p. XLIX; *Osiris And The Egyptian Resurrection*, volume II, pp. 1–11.

15 *Traveller's Key to Ancient Egypt*, p. 159.

16 Ibid., p. 158.

17 *Atlas of Ancient Egypt*, p. 36.

8 *From Fetish to God in Ancient Egypt*, p. 147: 'Judging by the Pyramid Texts, the priests of Heliopolis borrowed very largely from the religious beliefs of the predynastic Egyptians . . .' See also *The Ancient Egyptian Book of the Dead*, p. 11.

9 *The Orion Mystery*, pp. 57–8.

10 *Traveller's Key to Ancient Egypt*, pp. 166; *The Ancient Egyptian Pyramid Texts*, p. V: 'The Pyramid Texts . . . include very ancient texts . . . There are many mythological and other allusions of which the purport is obscure to the translator of today . . .'

1 *The Ancient Egyptian Pyramid Texts.*

2 Ibid., p. v.

3 James Henry Breasted, *The Dawn of Conscience*, Charles Scribner's Sons, New York, 1944, p. 69.

Chapter Forty-Two

1 *The Ancient Egyptian Pyramid Texts*, lines 882, 883; see also, *inter alia*, lines 2115 and 2116.

2 *The Gods of the Egyptians*, volume I, p. 117.

3 He did so on 28 February 1881; see *The Orion Mystery*, p. 59.

4 *The Ancient Egyptian Pyramid Texts*, p. v.

5 Ibid., p. 227, Utt. 572.

6 Ibid., p. 297, Utt. 688: 'Atum has done what he said he would do for this King; he ties the rope-ladder for him.'

7 *The Gods of the Egyptians*, volume II, p. 241.

8 *The Ancient Egyptian Pyramid Texts*, p. 70, Utt. 261.

9 Ibid., p. 97.

10 Ibid., p. 107.

11 Ibid., p. 284.

12 Ibid., p. 249, Utt. 604.

13 Ibid., pp. 253–4, Utt. 610.

14 Ibid., p. 280, Utt. 667.

15 Ibid., p. 170, Utt. 483.

16 Ibid., p. 287, Utt. 673.

17 B. Scheel, *Egyptian Metalworking and Tools*, Shire Egyptology, Aylesbury, 1989; G. A. Wainwright, 'Iron in Egypt', *Journal of Egyptian Archaeology*, vol. 18, 1931.

18 *The Ancient Egyptian Pyramid Texts*, pp. 276, 105, 294, 311.

19 *Egyptian Metalworking and Tools*, p. 17; 'Iron in Egypt', p. 6ff.

20 Among the many mysterious aspects of the Pyramid Texts it is perhaps inevitable that a fully qualified Opener of the Ways should put in an appearance. 'The doors of the sky are opened to you, the starry sky is thrown open for you, the jackal of upper Egypt comes down to you as Anubis at your side.' (*The Ancient Egyptian Pyramid Texts*, pp. 288–9, Utt. 675.) Here, as in other contexts, the function of the canine figure seems to be to serve as a *guide* to secret hoards of esoteric information often linked to

mathematics and astronomy.

21 See Part V for full details.
22 Ibid.
23 *Myth and Symbol in Ancient Egypt*, p. 181.
24 The pouring fire allusion is cited in Jean-Pierre Hallet, *Pygmy Kitabu*, p. 185.
25 *Myth and Symbol in Ancient Egypt*, p. 181–5.
26 Ibid., p. 184.
27 Ibid., p. 185.
28 *The Gods of the Egyptians*, volume II, p. 94.
29 Ibid., p. 92–4.
30 Ibid., p. 93.
31 Skyglobe 3.6.
32 See Part IV.
33 For a detailed discussion see *Sacred Science: The King of Pharaonic Theocracy*.
34 The issue of priestly secrecy and the oral tradition is discussed at length in *From Fetish to God in Ancient Egypt*, e.g. p. 43: 'It is impossible to think that the highest order of the priests did not possess esoteric knowledge which they guarded with the greatest care. Each priesthood . . . possessed a "Gnosis", a "superiority of knowledge", which they never put into writing . . . It is therefore absurd to expect to find in Egyptian papyri descriptions of the secrets which formed the esoteric knowledge of the priests.' See also page 27, and *Sacred Science*, pp. 273–4.
35 Pyramid Texts cited in *The Gods of the Egyptians*, volume I, p. 158.
36 *Osiris and the Egyptian Resurrection*, volume I, p. 146.
37 *Sacred Science*, pp. 22–5, 29.
38 *Osiris and the Egyptian Resurrection*, volume I, p. 93.
39 *Encyclopaedia Britannica*, 1991, 10:845.
40 *The Sirius Mystery*.
41 Ibid., p. 3.
42 Ibid., p. 1.
43 See Part III.
44 *The Egyptian Book of the Dead*, p. cxi.
45 Ibid., p. cxviii. See also *The Gods of the Egyptians*, volume I, p. 400.
46 *The Egyptian Book of the Dead*, p. 8.
47 *Osiris and the Egyptian Resurrection*, volume II, p. 248.
48 For a full discussion see *Death of Gods in Ancient Egypt*, particularly pp. 328–30.
49 *Sacred Science*, p. 27.
50 *Death of Gods in Ancient Egypt*, p. 27.
51 *Sacred Science*, p. 172.
52 Ibid., p. 26–7. For numbers of stars visible to the naked eye see Ian Ridpath and Wil Tirion, *Collins Guide to Stars and Planets*, London, 1984, p. 4.
53 *Sacred Science*, p. 173.

54 *The Ancient Egyptian Pyramid Texts*, p. 165, line 964. *Sacred Science*, p. 287.

55 *The Ancient Egyptian Pyramid Texts*, pp. 165, 284; *Sacred Science*, in particular p. 287ff.

56 The established archaeological horizon of the calendar can indeed be pushed back even further because of the recent discovery, in a First Dynasty tomb in upper Egypt, of an inscription reading, 'Sothis, herald of the New Year' (reported in *Death of Gods in Ancient Egypt*, p. 40.)

57 *Sacred Science*, p. 290.

58 Ibid., p. 27.

59 E. A. Wallis Budge, *An Egyptian Hieroglyphic Dictionary*, (2 volumes), John Murray, London, 1920.

60 *From Fetish to God In Ancient Egypt*, pp. 321–2.

61 Ibid., p. 322.

62 *Atlas of Ancient Egypt*, p. 36.

63 *Myth and Symbol in Ancient Egypt*, p. 263.

Chapter Forty-Three

1 *Myth and Symbol in Ancient Egypt*, pp. 263–4; see also Nicolas Grimal, *A History of Ancient Egypt*, Blackwell, Cambridge, 1992, p. 46.

2 *New Larousse Encyclopaedia of Mythology*, p. 16.

3 *The Gods of the Egyptians*, volume I, pp. 84, 161; *The Ancient Egyptian Pyramid Texts*, pp. 124, 308.

4 *Osiris And The Egyptian Resurrection*, volume I, p. 352.

5 Michael Hoffman, *Egypt before the Pharaohs*, Michael O'Mara Books, 1991, pp. 12–13; *Archaic Egypt*, pp. 21–3; *The Encyclopaedia of Ancient Egypt*, pp. 138–9.

6 *Egypt before the Pharaohs*, pp. 12–13; *The Encyclopaedia of Ancient Egypt*, pp. 200, 268.

7 *Egypt before the Pharaohs*, p. 12.

8 *Archaic Egypt*, p. 23; *Manetho*, (trans. W. G. Waddell), William Heinemann, London, 1940, Introduction pp. xvi–xvii.

9 *Egypt before the Pharaohs*, p. 11.

10 Ibid., p. 11–13; *Archaic Egypt*, pp. 5, 23.

11 See, for example, *Egypt before the Pharaohs*, pp. 11–13.

12 This is a particularly important point to remember in a discipline like Egyptology where so much of the record of the past has been lost through looting, the ravages of time, and the activities of archaeologists and treasure hunters. Besides, vast numbers of Ancient Egyptian sites have not been investigated at all, and many more may lie out of our reach beneath the millennial silt of the Nile Delta (or beneath the suburbs of Cairo for that matter), and even at well-studied locations such as the Giza necropolis there are huge areas – the bedrock beneath the Sphinx for example – which still

await the attentions of the excavator.

13 *Manetho*, p. 3.

14 Ibid., pp. 3–5.

15 Ibid., p. 5.

16 *Encyclopaedia Britannica*, 1991, 12:214–15.

17 *Manetho*, p. 5.

18 There is absolutely no evidence that the Ancient Egyptians *ever* confused years and months, or styled one as the other; ibid, p. 4, note 2.

19 Ibid., p. 7.

20 Ibid., p. 15.

21 Ibid., p. 231; see also *The Splendour that was Egypt*, p. 12.

22 Like the Maya, (see Part III), the Ancient Egyptians made use for administrative purposes of a civil calendar year (or vague year) of 365 days exactly. See *Skywatchers of Ancient Mexico*, p. 151, for further details on the Maya vague year. The Ancient Egyptian civil calendar year was geared to the Sothic year so that both would coincide on the same day/month position once every 1461 calendar years.

23 *Diodorus Siculus*, translated by C.H. Oldfather, Harvard University Press, 1989, jacket text.

24 Ibid., volume I, p. 157.

25 *The History*, pp. 193–4. In the first century AD a similar tradition was recorded by the Roman scholar Pomponious Mela: 'The Egyptians pride themselves on being the most ancient people in the world. In their authentic annals one may read that since they have been in existence, the course of the stars has changed direction four times, and that the sun has set twice in the part of the sky where it rises today.' (Pomponious Mela, *De Situ Orbis*.)

26 *Sacred Science*, p. 87

27 As the following table makes clear:

VERNAL EQUINOX	SUNRISE	IN OPPOSITION (DUE WEST) AT SUNRISE
Fifth century BC (time of Herodotus)	Aries	Libra
Approx 13,000 years before Herodotus	Libra	Aries
Approx 26,000 years before Herodotus	Aries	Libra
Approx 39,000 years before Herodotus	Libra	Aries

28 See, for example, Sir A.H. Gardner, *The Royal Cannon of Turin*, Griffith Institute, Oxford.

29 *Archaic Egypt*, p. 4.

30 For further details, *Sacred Science*, p. 86.

31 Ibid., p. 86. See also *Egyptian Mysteries*, p. 68.

32 *Archaic Egypt*, p. 5; *Encyclopaedia of Ancient Egypt*, p. 200.

33 *Archaic Egypt*, p. 5; *Encyclopaedia Britannica*, 1991, 9:81.

34 *Encyclopaedia of Ancient Egypt*, p. 200.

35 *Archaic Egypt*, p. 5.

36 *Egypt to the End of the Old Kingdom*, p. 12.

Chapter Forty-Four

1 *Kingship and the Gods*, pp. 181–2; *The Encyclopaedia of Ancient Egypt*, pp. 209, 264; *Egyptian Myths*, pp. 18–22. See also T. G. H. James, *An Introduction to Ancient Egypt*, British Museum Publications, London, 1979, p. 145ff.

2 Cyril Aldred, *Akhenaton*, Abacus, London, 1968, p. 25: 'It was believed that the gods had ruled in Egypt after first making it perfect.'

3 *Kingship and the Gods*, pp. 153–5; *Egyptian Myths*, pp. 18–22; *Egyptian Mysteries*, pp. 8–11; *New Larousse Encyclopaedia of Mythology*, pp. 10–28.

4 See Part IV.

5 *Diodorus Siculus*, volume I, p. 37.

6 Ibid.

7 *Mystic Places*, Time-Life Books, 1987, p. 62.

8 *Early Hydraulic Civilization in Egypt*, p. 13; *Egypt before the Pharaohs*, pp. 27, 261.

9 *New Larousse Encyclopaedia of Mythology*, p. 11.

10 Ibid., p. 13.

11 Ibid., pp. 14–15.

12 Ibid.

13 *Hebrews* 9:4. For details of the Ark's baleful powers see Graham Hancock, *The Sign and the Seal*, Mandarin, London, 1993, Chapter 12, p. 273ff.

14 Cited in *Egyptian Myths*, p. 44.

15 Sir E. A. Wallis Budge, *Egyptian Magic*, Kegan Paul, Trench, London, 1901, p. 5; *The Gods of the Egyptians*, volume II, p. 214.

16 *New Larousse Encyclopaedia of Mythology*, p. 27. If Set's usurpation is included as a reign, we have seven divine pharoahs up to and including Thoth (i. e., Ra, Shu, Geb, Osiris, Set, Horus, Thoth).

17 *The Gods of the Egyptians*, volume I, p. 400; Garth Fowden, *The Egyptian Hermes*, Cambridge University Press, 1987, pp. 22–3. see also *From Fetish to God in Ancient Egypt*, pp. 121–2; *Egyptian Magic*, pp. 128–9; *New Larousse Encyclopaedia of Mythology*, pp. 27–8.

18 Manetho, quoted by the neo-Platonist Iamblichus. See Peter Lemesurier, *The Great Pyramid Decoded*, Element Books, 1989, p. 15; *The Egyptian Hermes*, p. 33.

19 See, for example, *Diodorus Siculus*, volume I, p. 53, where Thoth (under his Greek name of Hermes) is described as being 'endowed with unusual ingenuity for devising things capable of improving the social life of man'.

20 *Osiris and the Egyptian Resurrection*, volume II, p. 307.

21 *Myth and Symbol in Ancient Egypt*, p. 179; *New Larousse Encyclopaedia of Mythology*, p. 16.

22 *New Larousse Encyclopaedia of Mythology*, pp. 9–10, 16; *Encyclopaedia of Ancient Egypt*, p. 44; *The Gods of the Egyptians*, volume II, pp. 130–1; *From Fetish to God in Ancient Egypt*, p. 190; *Myth and Symbol in Ancient Egypt*, p. 230.

23 *Osiris and the Egyptian Resurrection*, volume I, p. 2.

24 Chapter CXXV, cited in ibid., volume II, p. 81.
25 See Parts II and III for Quetzalcoatl and Viracocha. A good summary of Osiris's civilizing attributes is the *New Larousse Encyclopaedia of Mythology*, p. 16. See also *Diodorus Siculus*, pp. 47–9; *Osiris and the Egyptian Resurrection*, volume I, pp. 1–12.
26 *Diodorus Siculus*, p. 53.
27 Ibid.; *Osiris and the Egyptian Resurrection*, volume I, p. 2.
28 *Diodorus Siculus*, p. 55.
29 *Osiris and the Egyptian Resurrection*, volume I, p. 11.
30 Ibid., p. 2.
31 Ibid., 2–11. For Quetzalcoatl and Viracocha see Parts II and III. Interestingly enough, Osiris was said to have been accompanied on his civilizing mission by two 'openers of the way': (*Diodorus Siculus* page 57), 'Anubis and Macedo, Anubis wearing a dog's skin and Macedo the foreparts of a wolf . . .'
32 *Osiris and the Egyptian Resurrection*, volume II, p. 273. See also in general, *The Ancient Egyptian Pyramid Texts*.
33 *Archaic Egypt*, p. 122; *Myth and Symbol in Ancient Egypt*, p. 98.
34 See, in general, *Kingship and the Gods*; *Osiris and the Egyptian Resurrection*; *The Gods of the Egyptians*.
35 *Archaic Egypt*, p. 38.
36 *Manetho*, p. 5.

Chapter Forty-Five

1 *Atlas of Ancient Egypt*, p. 36.
2 Dates from *Atlas of Ancient Egypt*. For further data on Ramesses II as the pharaoh of the exodus see Profuses K. A. Kitchen, *Pharaoh Triumphant The Life and Times of Ramesses II*, Aris and Phillips, Warminster, 1982, pp 70–1.
3 See, for example, *A Biographical Dictionary of Ancient Egypt*, pp. 135–7.
4 *Traveller's Key to Ancient Egypt*, p. 384.
5 *The Ancient Egyptian Pyramid Texts*, pp. 285, 253.
6 *Traveller's Key to Ancient Egypt*, p. 386.
7 *The Encyclopaedia of Ancient Egypt*, p. 59.
8 Chapter 175 of the *Ancient Egyptian Book of the Dead*, cited in *Myth an Symbol in Ancient Egypt*, p. 137.
9 See Henry Frankfort, *The Cenotaph of Seti I at Abydos*, 39th Memoir of the Egypt Exploration Society, London, 1933, p. 25.
10 *The Geography of Strabo*, volume VIII, pp. 111–13.
11 Margaret A. Murray, *The Osireion at Abydos*, Egyptian Research Accoun ninth year (1903), Bernard Quaritch, London, 1904, p. 2.
12 Ibid.
13 *The Times*, London, 17 March 1914.
14 Ibid.
15 Ibid.

16 *Traveller's Key to Ancient Egypt*, p. 391.
17 *The Cenotaph of Seti I at Abydos*, p. 18.
18 Ibid., p. 28–9.
19 E. Naville, 'Excavations at Abydos: The Great Pool and the Tomb of Osiris', *Journal of Egyptian Archaeology*, volume I, 1914, p. 160.
20 *The Times*, London, 17 March 1914.
21 Ibid.
22 *The Cenotaph of Seti I at Abydos*, pp. 4, 25, 68–80.
23 Ibid., in general.
24 'Excavations at Abydos', pp. 164–5.
25 *The Splendour that was Egypt*, pp. 160–1.
26 *The Cenotaph of Seti I at Abydos*, p. 23.
27 *Guardian*, London, 21 December 1991.
28 David O'Connor, 'Boat Graves and Pyramid Origins', in *Expedition*, volume 33, No. 3, 1991, p. 7ff.
29 Ibid., pp. 9–10.
30 Sent to me by fax 27 January 1993.
31 David O'Connor, 'Boat Graves and Pyramid Origins', p. 12.
32 Ibid., p. 11–12.
33 *Guardian*, 21 December 1991.
34 See Cairo Museum, Gallery 54, wall-painting of ships from Badarian period *c.* 4500 BC.
35 *The Ancient Egyptian Pyramid Texts*, p. 192, Utt. 519: 'O Morning Star, Horus of the Netherworld . . . you having a soul and appearing in front of your boat of 770 cubits . . . Take me with you in the cabin of your boat.'

Chapter Forty-Six

1 *Egypt before the Pharaohs*, pp. 29, 88.
2 To give yet another example, here is Diodorus Siculus (first century BC) passing on what he was told by Egyptian priests: 'The number of years from Osiris and Isis, they say, to the reign of Alexander, who founded the city which bears his name in Egypt [fourth century BC], is over ten thousand . . .' *Diodorus Siculus*, volume I, p. 73.
3 *Egypt before The Pharaohs*, p. 85.
4 Ibid., p. 90.
5 *A History of Ancient Egypt*, p. 21.
6 *Egypt before The Pharaohs*, p. 88.
7 Fred Wendorff and Romuald Schild, *Prehistory of the Nile Valley*, Academic Press, New York, 1976, p. 291.
8 *Egypt before the Pharaohs*, pp. 89–90.
9 Ibid., p. 86.
10 Ibid., pp. 97–8.
11 Ibid., p. 161.
12 See Chapter Twelve.
13 Ibid.

14 Ibid.
15 AAAS Annual Meeting, 1992, Debate: How Old is the Sphinx?

Chapter Forty-Seven

1 *Traveller's Key to Ancient Egypt*; *Serpent in the Sky*, p. 20.
2 *Sacred Science*, p. 96.
3 West's detailed evidence is set out in *Serpent in the Sky*, pp. 184–20.
  Concerning the covering of the Sphinx by sand he arrives at the following
  table:

	Sphinx buried
Chephren–Tuthmosis IV c. 1300 years	1000 years
Thuthmosis IV–Ptolemies c. 1100 years	800 years
Ptolemies–Christianity c. 600 years	0 years
Christianity–Present day c. 1700 years	1500 years
Chephren–present day, c. 4700 years	3300 years

4 'An abstract of our team's work was submitted to the Geological Society of
  America, and we were invited to present our findings at a poster session of
  at the GSA convention in San Diego – the geological Superbowl. Geologists
  from all over the world thronged to our booth, much intrigued. Dozens of
  experts in fields relevant to our research offered help and advice. Shown the
  evidence, some geologists just laughed, astounded [as Schoch had been
  initially] that in two centuries of research, no one, geologist or Egyptologist,
  had noticed that the Sphinx had been weathered by water.' *Serpent in the
  Sky*, p. 229; *Mystery of the Sphinx*. NBC-TV, 1993. 275 geologists endorsed
  Schoch's findings.
5 AAAS, Annual Meeting 1992, Debate: How Old is the Sphinx?
6 *Mystery of the Sphinx*.
7 Ibid.
8 Ibid.
9 Ibid.
10 Ibid.
11 AAAS Annual Meeting 1992.
12 Ibid. The relevant geologists include Farouk El Baz, and Roth and Raffai.
13 Extracts from *Mystery of the Sphinx* and AAAS meeting.
14 Under the category of anomalies, West made specific reference to the bowls
  carved out of diorite and other hard stones described in Part VI.
15 'After reviewing my various drawings, schematics and measurements, my
  final conclusion concurs with my initial reaction: the two works represent
  two separate individuals. The proportions in the frontal view and especially
  the angles and facial protrusion in the lateral views, convinced me that the
  Sphinx is not Khafre. If the ancient Egyptians were skilled technicians and
  capable of duplicating images, then these two works cannot represent the
  same individual.' Frank Domingo, cited in *Serpent in the Sky*, p. 232. See
  also AAAS 1992, for Schoch's views on the recarving of the Sphinx's head.

Chapter Forty-Eight

1 *Collins English Dictionary*, p. 608.
2 *Secrets of the Great Pyramid*, p. 38. Much of the material in this chapter is based directly on the work of Peter Tompkins and of Professor Livio Catullo Stecchini.
3 Ibid., p. 46.
4 Ibid., p. 181.
5 Ibid., p. 299.
6 Ibid., pp. 179–81.
7 Cited in Ibid., p. 333.
8 See Chapter Twenty-three, and Stecchini in *Secrets of the Great Pyramid*, p. 378.
9 See Chapter Twenty-three.
10 Accepted, for example, by Edwards, Petrie, Baines and Malek, and so on.
11 *Encyclopaedia Britannica*, 1991, 27:530.
12 *The Pyramids of Egypt*, p. 87.
13 See Part V.
14 *Secrets of the Great Pyramid*, p. 189.
15 *Maps of the Ancient Sea Kings*, p. 17ff.
16 See, for example, *The Shape of the World*, p. 23.
17 *The Gods of the Egyptians*, volume I, p. 400.
18 Ibid., volume I, p. 443; volume II, pp. 7, 287.
19 Ibid., volume II, p. 7, where the deity Amen–Ra is addressed in a hymn: 'The gods love the smell of thee when thou comest from Punt, thou eldest-born of the dew, who comest from the Divine Land (Ta-Neteru).' See also volume II, p. 287. Punt is thought by many scholars to have been located on the Somali coast of East Africa where the trees that produce frankincense and myrrh ('the food of the gods') are still grown today.
20 Ibid.
21 *Osiris and the Egyptian Resurrection*, volume I, p. 98; Pyramid Texts of Pepi I, Mer-en-Rah and Pepi II, translated in Ibid., volume II, p. 316, where the maritime connections of the land of the blessed are made clear.
22 Ibid., volume I, p. 97.
23 Ibid., pp. 97–8.
24 Ibid., volume II, p. 307.
25 Veronica Ions, *Egyptian Mythology*, Newnes Books, London, 1986, p. 84.
26 *The Gods of the Egyptians*, volume I, pp. 407–8.
27 Ibid., volume I, p. 414.
28 *Egyptian Mythology*, p. 85.
29 *The Gods of the Egyptians*, volume I, p. 414.
30 Ibid., pp 414–15.
31 *The History*, 2:4.
2 Reported in E. M. Antoniadi, *L'Astronomie egyptienne*, Paris, 1934, pp. 3–4; see also Schwaller, p. 279.
3 *Diodorus Siculus*, volume I, pp. 279–80.

34 *The Ancient Egyptian Pyramid Texts*, for example pp. 78, 170, 171, 290.

Chapter Forty-Nine

1 Robert Bauval's *The Orion Mystery* (Heinemann, London; Crown, New York; Doubleday, Canada; List, Germany; Planeta, Spain; Pygmalion, France, etc.) was an international bestseller when it was published in 1994. Egyptologists closed ranks against its implications, which they refused to discuss, but many distinguished astronomers hailed Bauval's findings as a breakthrough.

2 Virginia Trimble, cited in *The Orion Mystery*, p. 241.

3 Ibid., p. 172.

4 Personal communications/interviews, 1993–4.

5 *Atlas of Ancient Egypt*, p. 36.

6 Personal communications/interviews.

7 Skyglobe 3.6.

8 Personal communications/interviews.

9 Skyglobe 3.6

10 Personal communications/interviews.

11 See Chapters Forty-two to Forty-four.

12 'The Egyptians . . . believed that they were a divine nation, and that they were ruled by kings who were themselves gods incarnate; their earliest kings, they asserted, were actually gods, who did not disdain to live on earth, and to go about up and down through it, and to mingle with men.' *The Gods of the Egyptians*, volume I, p. 3.

13 The Mortuary Temple was excavated by von Sieglin in 1910 and was found to consist of blocks of varying sizes weighing 'between 100 and 300 tons'. *Blue Guide: Egypt*, p. 431.

14 Just as any great Christian cathedral, however modern (for example the twentieth-century gothic cathedral on Nob Hill in San Francisco), expresses the thinking, symbolism and iconography of the Judaeo-Christian 'cult' which has roots at least 4000 years old, it should not be impossible to imagine a cult enduring for 8000 years in Ancient Egypt and thus linking the epoch of 10450 BC to 2,450 BC. The completion of the pyramids at that time, like the completion of a cathedral today, would therefore have resulted in structures that expressed extremely old ideas. Plentiful evidence exists within Ancient Egyptian tradition which seems to attest to the existence and preservation of such ancient ideas. For example, 'King Nefer-hetep [XIIIth Dynasty] was a loyal worshipper of Osiris and hearing that his Temple [at Abydos] was in ruins, and that a new statue of the god was required, he went to the temple of Ra–Atum at Heliopolis, and consulted the books in the library there, so that he might learn how to make a statue of Osiris which should be like. that which had existed in the beginning of the world . . .' (*Osiris and the Egyptian Resurrection*, volume II, p. 14). Also *Sacred Science*; pp. 103–4, explains that the construction of temples in the Ptolemaic and late periods of Egyptian history continued to obey very

ancient specifications: 'All the plans always refer to a *divine book*; thus the temple of Edfu was rebuilt under the Ptolemies according to the *book of foundation composed by Imhotep*, a book descended from heaven to the north of Memphis. The temple of Dendera followed *a plan recorded in ancient writings dating from the Companions of Horus.*'

15 *Hamlet's Mill*, p. 59.
16 Ibid.; *Sacred Science*, p. 179.
17 *Oxford Dictionary of the Christian Church*, Oxford University Press, 1988, p. 514.
18 *Sacred Science*, p. 177.
19 *Genesis*: 22:13
20 *Jerusalem Bible*, chronological table, p. 343.
21 *King James Bible*, Franklin, Computerized First Edition.
22 *The Encyclopaedia of Ancient Egypt*, p. 20.
23 Ibid., p. 133.
24 *Sacred Science*, p. 177.
25 As early as 3000 BC. See *Encyclopaedia Britannica*, 1991, 3:731.
26 *Encyclopaedia of Ancient Egypt*, pp. 27, 171.
27 Skyglobe 3.6.

Chapter Fifty

1 Galanopoulos and Bacon, *Lost Atlantis*, p. 75.
2 See, for example, Brian Inglis, *Coincidence*, Hutchinson, London, 1990, p. 48ff.
3 *When the Sky Fell*, with an Introduction by Colin Wilson and Afterword by John Anthony West, is published by Stoddart, Canada, 1995.
4 See Part I.
5 Ibid.
6 Ibid. See Part I and Chapter Fifty-one for details.

Chapter Fifty-One

1 *Encyclopaedia Britannica*, 1991, 3:584.
2 *Encyclopaedia Britannica*, 1991, 1:440.
3 *Discover The World Of Science*, February 1993, p. 17. The fifteen mineralized tree stumps, presumably the remnant of a much larger forest, range from three and a half to seven inches in diameter. They were saplings of a well-known genus of seed fern, *Glossopteris* [found in much of the southern hemisphere's coal]. Unlike true ferns, seed ferns had seeds instead of spores, were often treelike, and are now extinct . . . All around the Mount Achernar tree stumps, Taylor's colleagues found the tongue-shaped imprints of fallen *Glossopteris* leaves.

Deciduous trees are an indicator of a warm climate, and so is the absence of 'frost rings'. When Taylor analysed the growth rings in samples from the stumps she found none of the ice-swollen cells and gaps between cells that arise when the growth of a tree is disrupted by frost. That means there wasn't any frost in the Antarctic at that time.

'In our memory Antarctica has always been cold,' says Taylor. 'It's only by looking at fossil floras that we can see what potential there is for plant communities. This fossil forest, growing at 85 degrees latitude, gives us some idea of what is possible with catastrophic climate change.'

N.B. The trees were killed by a flood or mudflow – another impossibility in Antarctica today.

4 *The Path of the Pole*, p. 61.
5 Ibid., pp. 62–3.
6 In Dolph Earl Hooker, *Those Astounding Ice Ages*, Exposition Press, New York, 1958, page 44, citing *National Geographic Magazine*, October 1935.
7 *Path of the Pole*, p. 62.
8 Rand Flem-Ath, *Does the Earth's Crust Shift?* (MS.).
9 Daniel Grotta, 'Antarctica: Whose Continent Is It Anyway?', *Popular Science*, January 1992, p. 64.
10 *Path of the Pole*, p. 107.
11 See Part I.
12 *Path of the Pole*, p. 111ff.
13 See Part I for details.
14 *The Biblical Flood and the Ice Epoch*, pp. 109–10.
15 *Path of the Pole*, p. 66.
16 Ibid., pp. 93, 96.
17 Ibid., p. 99.
18 See Part IV.
19 Ibid.
20 *Encyclopaedia Britannica*, 1991, I:440; John White, *Pole Shift*, A.R.E. Press, Virginia Beach, 1994, p. 65.
21 *Pole Shift*, p. 77: Twenty billion tons of ice are added each year at Antarctica.
22 H. A. Brown, *Cataclysms of the Earth*, pp. 10–11.
23 See Part IV.
24 Ibid.
25 *Biblical Flood and the Ice Epoch*, p. 228.
26 Thomas Huxley cited in *Path of the Pole*, p. 294.
27 *Scientific American*, December 1985.
28 *Path of the Pole*, pp. 47–9.
29 Ibid., p. 49.
30 Ibid., p. 58.
31 See Part IV.
32 *The Mahabaratha*, cited in *The Arctic Home in the Vedas*, pp. 64–5.
33 Ibid., pp. 66–7.
34 Cited in *Paradise Found: The Cradle of the Human Race at the North Pole*, p. 199.
35 *Arctic Home in the Vedas*, p. 81.
36 Ibid., p. 85.

37 Ibid., pp. 414, 417.
38 Ibid., p. 420.
39 *Pole Shift*, p. 9.
40 Ibid.
41 Ibid., p. 61.
42 *Nature*, volume 234, 27 December 1971, pp. 173–4; *New Scientist*, 6 January 1972, p. 7.
43 J. M. Harwood and S. C. R. Malin writing in *Nature*, 12 February 1976.
44 *The Path of the Pole*, op.cit., Appendix, pp. 325–6.
45 Ibid., p. 44.
46 *USA Today*, 23 November 1994, p. 9D.

Chapter Fifty-Two

1 Plato, *Timaeus and Critias*, Penguin Classics, 1977, p. 36.
2 *The Bhagavata Purana*, Motilal Banardass, Delhi, 1986, Part I, pp. 59, 95.
3 Ibid., p. 60.
4 Dileep Kumar Kanjilal, *Vimana in Ancient India*, Sanskrit Pustak Bhandar, Calcutta, 1985, p. 16.
5 Ibid., p. 17.
6 Ibid., p. 18.
7 Ibid.
8 Ibid.
9 Ibid., p. 19.
10 *The Ancient Egyptian Pyramid Texts*, p. 70, Utt. 261.
11 *The Complete Works Of Josephus*, Kregel Publications, Grand Rapids, Michigan, 1991, p. 27.
12 Ibid.
13 John Greaves, *Pyramidographia*, cited in *Serpent in the Sky*, p. 230.
14 *Popol Vuh*, p. 168.
15 Ibid., p. 169.
16 Ibid., p. 79.
17 Ibid., p. 79–80.
18 *The Bhagavata Purana*, cited in *Atlantis: The Antediluvian World*, p. 88.
19 Berossus Fragments cited in *The Sirius Mystery*, p. 249.
20 Ibid.
21 *2 Peter* 3:10.
22 *The Egyptian Hermes*, p. 33.
23 By Robert Bauval, personal communication.
24 See Part VII.
25 *1 Enoch*, LXV, in *The Apockryphal Old Testament* (ed. H.F.D. Sparks), Clarendon Press, Oxford, 1989, p. 247.
26 *Pre-Hispanic Gods of Mexico*, p. 24.
27 *Breaking the Maya Code*, p. 275.
28 *Will The World Survive?* Watch Tower Bible and Tract Society, 1992.

29 Circulating File, *Earth Changes*, Extracts from the Edgar Cayce Readings, Edgar Cayce Foundation, Virginia Beach, 1994, p. 36.

30 See Part V.

31 *Manetho*, pp. 191–3.

32 The Chlorine-36 rock-exposure dating technique has been developed by Professor David Bowen of the Department of Earth Sciences at the University of Wales. In *The Times* of London, 1 December 1994, Brown observed:

'One way of resolving the controversy of the ages of the Sphinx and the Pyramids may be through the application of Chlorine-36 rock-exposure dating. This provides an estimate of the time that has elapsed since a rock was first exposed to the atmosphere. In the case of the Sphinx and the Pyramids this would be when the rocks were first exposed by quarrying activity . . .'

In 1994 Bowen ran preliminary tests on the famous 'bluestones' of Stonehenge in England, hitherto believed to date to 2250 BC. What the tests showed was that these 123 four-ton monoliths could have been quarried during the the last Ice Age – perhaps as early as 12000 BC. See *The Times*, London, 5 December.

33 *Mystery of the Sphinx*, NBC-TV, 1993.

34 *2 Peter* 3:4.

35 *2 Peter* 3:3.

36 *Community Profile: Hopi Indian Reservation*, Arizona Department of Commerce.

37 *Breaking the Maya Code*, p. 275.

38 *Book of the Hopi*.

39 *World Mythology*, p. 26.

40 *Matthew*, 24: 38–39.

41 *Matthew*, 24: 27–41.

Selected Bibliography

Aldred, Cyril, *Akhenaton*, Abacus, London, 1968.

——*Egypt to the End of the Old Kingdom*, Thames & Hudson, London, 1988.

Ancient America, Time-Life International, 1970.

Ancient Egyptian Book of the Dead (trans. R. O. Faulkner), British Museum Publications, 1989.

Ancient Egyptian Pyramid Texts (trans. R. O. Faulkner), Oxford University Press, 1969.

Antoniadi, E. M., *L'Astronomie egyptienne*, Paris, 1934.

Apocryphal Old Testament (ed. H. F. D. Sparks), Clarendon Press, Oxford, 1989.

Arguelles, José, *The Mayan Factor: Path Beyond Technology*, Bear & Co., Santa Fe, New Mexico, 1987.

Atlas of Mysterious Places (ed. Jennifer Westwood), Guild Publishing, London, 1987.

Aubet, Maria Eugenia, *The Phoenicians and the West*, Cambridge University Press, 1993.

Aveni, Anthony F., *Skywatchers of Ancient Mexico*, University of Texas Press, 1990.

Aztec Calendar: History and Symbolism, Garcia y Valades Editores, Mexico City, 1992.

Aztecs: Reign of Blood and Splendour, Time-Life Books, Virginia, 1992.

Bailey, James, *The God-Kings and the Titans*, Hodder & Stoughton, London, 1972.

Baines, John and Malek, Jaromir, *Atlas of Ancient Egypt*, Time-Life Books, Virginia, 1990.

Bauval, Robert and Gilbert, Adrian, *The Orion Mystery*, Wm. Heinemann, London, 1994.

Bellamy, H. S., *Built Before the Flood: The Problem of the Tiahuanaco Ruins*, Faber & Faber, London, 1943.
——and Allan, P., *The Calendar of Tiahuanaco: The Measuring System of the Oldest Civilization*, Faber & Faber, London, 1956.
Berlitz, Charles, *The Lost Ship of Noah*, W. H. Allen, London, 1989.
Bernal, Martin, *Black Athena: The Afroasiatic Roots of Classical Civilization*, Vintage Books, London, 1991.
Bethon, Simon and Robinson, Andrew, *The Shape of the World: The Mapping and Discovery of the Earth*, Guilt Publishing, London, 1991.
Bhagavata Purana, Motilal Banardess, Delhi, 1986.
Bierhorst, John, *The Mythology of South America*, Wm. Morrow & Co., New York, 1990.
——*The Mythology of Mexico and Central America*, Wm. Morrow & Co., New York, 1990.
Black, Jeremy and Green, Anthony, *Gods, Demons and Symbols of Ancient Mesopotamia*, British Museum Press, 1992.
Bloomgarden, Richard, *The Pyramids of Teotihuacan*, Editur S. A., Mexico, 1993.
Blue Guide: Egypt, A & C Black, London, 1988.
Bolivia, Lonely Planet Publications, Hawthorne, Australia, 1992.
Breasted, J. H., *Ancient Records of Egypt: Historical Documents from the Earliest Times to the Persian Conquest*, Histories and Mysteries of Man, London, 1988.
——*The Dawn of Conscience*, Charles Scribners Sons, New York, 1944.
Butzer, Karl W., *Early Hydraulic Civilization in Egypt: A Study in Cultural Ecology*, University of Chicago Press, 1976.

Cameron, Ian, *Kingdom of the Sun God: A History of the Andes and Their People*, Guild Publishing, London, 1990.
Campbell, Joseph, *The Hero with a Thousand Faces*, Paladin Books, London, 1988.
Canfora, Luciano, *The Vanished Library*, Hutchinson Radius, London, 1989.
Casson, Lionel, *Ships and Seafaring in Ancient Times*, University of Texas Press, 1994.
Cieza de Leon, Pedro, *Chronicle of Peru*, Hakluyt Society, London, 1864 and 1883.
Coe, Michael D., *The Maya*, Thames & Hudson, 1991.
——*Breaking the Maya Code*, Thames & London, 1992.
Cole, J. H., *Survey of Egypt*, Cairo, 1925.
Comber, Leon, *The Traditional Mysteries of the Chinese Secret Societies in Malaya*, Eastern Universities Press, Singapore, 1961.
Community Profile: Hopi Indian Reservation, Arizona Department of Commerce.
Complete Works of Josephus, Kriegel Publications, Grand Rapids, Michigan, 1991.
Cooraswamy, Ananda K. and Sister Nivedita, *Myths of the Hindus and*

Buddhists, George G. Harrap & Co., London, 1913.

Corteggiani, Jean-Pierre, *The Egypt of the Pharoahs at the Cairo Museum*, Scala Publications, London, 1987.

Cotterell, Arthur, *The Illustrated Encyclopaedia of Myths and Legends*, Guild Publishing, London, 1989.

Cuvier, Georges, *Revolutions and Catastrophes in the History of the Earth*, 1829.

Darwin, Charles, *Journal of Researches into the Natural History of Countries Visited during the Voyage of HMS* Beagle *Round the World*.

——*The Origin of Species*, Penguin, London, 1985.

David, Rosalie, *A Guide to Religious Ritual at Abydos*, Aris and Phillips, Warminster, 1981.

——and David, Anthony E., *A Biographical Dictionary of Ancient Egypt*, Seaby, London, 1992.

Davidovits, Joseph and Morris, Margie, *The Pyramids: An Enigma Solved*, Dorset Press, New York, 1988.

Davis, Nigel, *The Ancient Kingdoms of Mexico*, Penguin Books, London, 1990.

Desroches-Noblecourt, Christine, *Tutunkhamen*, Penguin Books, London, 1989.

Devereux, Paul, *Secrets of Ancient and Sacred Places*, Blandford Books, London, 1992.

Diodorus Siculus (trans. C. H. Oldfather), Loeb Classical Library, London, 1989; Harvard University Press, 1989.

Donnelly, Ignatius, *Atlantis: The Antediluvian World*, Harper & Brothers, New York, 1882.

Edwards, I. E. S., *The Pyramids of Egypt*, Penguin, London, 1949.

Egypt: Land of the Pharaohs, Time-Life Books, Virginia, 1992.

Egyptian Book of the Dead (trans. E. A. Wallis Budge), British Museum, 1895; Arkana, London and New York, 1986.

Emery, W. B., *Archaic Egypt*, Penguin Books, London, 1987.

Encyclopaedia of Ancient Egypt (ed. Margaret Bunson), Facts on File, New York and Oxford, 1991.

Encyclopaedia Britannica, 1991 edition.

Epic of Gilgamesh, Penguin Classics, London, 1988.

Evolving Earth, Guild Publishing, London, 1989.

Facts on File Encyclopaedia of World Mythology and Legend, New York and Oxford, 1988.

Fakhry, Ahmed, *The Pyramids*, University of Chicago Press, 1969.

Feats and Wisdom of the Ancients, Time-Life Books, Virginia, 1990.

Fernandez, Adela, *Pre-Hispanic Gods of Mexico*, Panorama Editorial, Mexico City, 1992.

Fiedel, Stuart J., *The Prehistory of the Americas*, Cambridge University Press, 1992.

Filby, Frederick A., *The Flood Reconsidered: A Review of the Evidences of*

    Geology, Archaeology, Ancient Literature and the Bible, Pickering &
        Inglis, London, 1970.
Flem-Ath, Rand and Rose, *When the Sky Fell*, Stoddart, Canada, 1995.
Flint, R. F., *Glacial Geology and the Pleistocene Epoch*, 1947.
Fowden, Garth, *The Egyptian Hermes*, Cambridge Unversity Press, 1978.
Frankfort, Henry, *The Cenotaph of Seti I at Abydos*, 39th memoir of the Egypt
        Exploration Society, London, 1933.
——*Kingship and the Gods*, University of Chicago Press, 1978.
Frazer, J. G., *Folklore in the Old Testament: Studies in Comparative Religion,
        Legend and Law*, Macmillan, London, 1923.

Gardner, A. H., *The Royal Canon of Turin*, Griffith Institute, Oxford.
Geography of Strabo (trans. H. L. Jones), Wm. Heinemann, London, 1982.
Gifford, D. and Sibbick, J., *Warriors, Gods and Spirits from South American
        Mythology*, Eurobook Ltd., 1983.
Gleninnen, Inga, *Aztecs*, Cambridge University Press, 1991.
Gordon, Cyrus H., *Before Columbus: Links between the Old World and Ancient
        America*, Crown Publishers, New York, 1971.
Grey, George, *Polynesian Mythology*, London, 1956.
Grimal, Nicholas, *A History of Ancient Egypt*, Blackwell, Cambridge, 1992.

Hadigham, Evan, *Lines to the Mountain Gods*, Harrap, London, 1987.
Hallet, Jean-Pierre, *Pygmy Kitabu*, BCA, London, 1974.
Hancock, Graham, *The Sign and the Seal*, Mandarin, London, 1993.
Hapgood, Charles H., *Earth's Shifting Crust: A Key to Some Basic Problems of
        Earth Science*, Pantheon Books, New York, 1958.
——*Maps of the Ancient Sea Kings*, Chilton Books, Philadelphia and New
        York, 1966; Turnstone Books, London, 1979.
——*The Path of the Pole*, Chilton Books, New York, 1970.
Hart, George, *Egyptian Myths*, British Museum Publications, 1990.
——*Pharoahs and Pyramids*, Guild Publishing, London, 1991.
Hawkins, Gerald S., *Beyond Stonehenge*, Arrow Books, London, 1977.
Hemming, John, *The Conquest of the Incas*, Macmillan, London, 1993.
Herm, Gerard, *The Phoenicians*, BCA, London, 1975.
Herodotus, *The History* (trans. David Grene), University of Chicago Press,
        1987.
Heyerdahl, Thor, *The Ra Expeditions*, BCA, London, 1972.
Hodges, Peter and Keable, Julian, *How the Pyramids Were Built*, Element
        Books, Shaftesbury, 1989.
Hoffman, Michael, *Egypt before the Pharoahs*, Michael O'Mara Books, London,
        1991.
Homer, *Odyssey* (Rouse translation).
Hooker, Dolph Earl, *Those Astrounding Ice Ages*, Exposition Press, New York,
        1958.
Hopkins, David M. et al., *The Paleoecology of Beringia*, Academic Press, New

York, 1982.

Imbre, John and Imbrie, Katherine Palmer, *Ice Ages: Solving the Mystery*, Enslow Publishers, New Jersey, 1979.

Inglis, Brian, *Coincidence*, Hutchinson, London, 1990.

Ions, Veronica, *Egyptian Mythology*, Newnes Books, London, 1986.

Irwin, Constance, *Fair Gods and Stone Faces*, W. H. Allen, London, 1964.

Ivimy, John, *The Sphinx and the Megaliths*, Abacus, London, 1976.

Jacq, C., *Egyptian Magic*, Aris and Phillips, Warminster, 1985.

Jewish Encyclopaedia, Funk and Wagnell, New York, 1925.

Johanson, Donald C. and Eddy, Maitland C., *Lucy: The Beginnings of Mankind*, Paladin, London, 1982.

Joseph, Pablo, *The Extirpation of Idolatry in Peru* (trans. L. Clark Keating), University of Kentucky Press, 1968.

Kanjilal, Dileep Kumar, *Vimana in Ancient India*, Sanskrit Pustak Bhandar, Calcutta, 1985.

Kerenyi, C., *The Gods of the Greeks*, Thames & Hudson, London, 1974.

Kitchen, K. A., *Pharaoh Triumphant: The Life and Times of Ramesses II*, Aris and Phillips, Warminster, 1982.

Lamy, Lucy, *Egyptian Mysteries*, Thames & Hudson, London, 1986.

Landa, Diego de, *Yucatan before and after the Conquest* (trans. William Gates), Producción Editorial Dante, Merida, Mexico, 1990.

Langway, C. C. and Hansen, B. Lyle. *The Frozen Future: A Prophetic Report from Antarctica*, Quadrangle, New York, 1973.

Lee, J. S., *The Geology of China*, London, 1939.

Lemesurier, Peter, *The Great Pyramid: Your Personal Guide*, Element Books, Shaftesbury, 1987.

- *The Great Pyramid Decoded*, Element Books, Shaftesbury, 1989.

Lewin, Roger, *Human Evolution*, Blackwell Scientific, Oxford, 1984.

Lichtheim, Miriam, *Ancient Egyptian Literature*, University of California Press, 1976.

Luss, R. S., *Fossils*, London, 1931.

Mantheo (trans. W. G. Waddell), Wm. Heinemann, London, 1940.

Mason, J. Alden, *The Ancient Civilizations of Peru*, Penguin Books, London, 1991.

Maspero, Gaston, *The Passing of Empires*, 1902.

Mendelssohn, Kurt, *The Riddle of the Pyramids*, Thames & Hudson, London, 1986.

Mexico, Lonely Planet Publications, Hawthorne, Australia, 1992.

Mexico: Rough Guide, Harrap-Columbus, London, 1989.

Miller, Mary and Taube, Karl, *The Gods and Symbols of Ancient Mexico and the Maya*, Thames & Hudson, London, 1993.

Milton, Joyce; Orsi, Robert, and Harrison, Norman, *The Feathered Serpent and the Cross: The Pre-Colombian God-Kings and the Papal States*, Cassell, London, 1980.

Moncrieff, A. R. Hope, *The Illustrated Guide to Classical Mythology*, BCA, London, 1992.

Monroe, Jean Guard and Williamson, Ray A., *They Dance in the Sky: Native American Star Myths*, Houghton Mifflen Company, Boston, 1987.

Montesinos, Fernando, *Memorias Antiguas Historiales del Peru* (trans. and ed. P A. Means), Hakluyt Society, London, 1920.

Morley, S. G., *An Introduction to the Study of Maya Hieroglyphics*, Dover Publications, New York, 1975.

Morrison, Tony, with Hawkins, Gerald S., *Pathways to the Gods*, BCA, London, 1979.

Moscati, Sabatino, *The World of the Phoenicians*, Cardinal, London, 1973.

Murray, H., Crawford, J. et al., *An Historical and Descriptive Account of China*, London, 1836.

Murray, Margaret A., *The Splendour that was Egypt*. Sidgwick & Jackson, London, 1987.

— *The Osireion at Abydos*, Bernard Quaritch, London, 1904.

Mystic Places, Time-Life Books, Virginia, 1987.

Mythology of All Races, Cooper Square Publishers, New York, 1964.

Myths from Mesopotamia (trans. and ed. Stephanie Dalley), Oxford University Press, 1990.

Narratives of the Rights and Laws of the Yncas (trans. and ed. Clemens R. Markham), Hakluyt Society, London, 1873.

New Larousse Encyclopaedia of Mythology, Paul Hamlyn, London, 1989.

Okladnikov, A. P., *Yakutia before Its Incorporation into the Russian State*, McGill-Queens University Press, Montreal, 1970

Osborne, H., *Indians of the Andes: Aymaras and Quechuas*, Routledge and Kegan Paul, London, 1952.

——*South American Mythology*, Paul Hamlyn, London, 1968.

Oxford Dictionary of the Christian Church, Oxford University Press, 1988.

Patten, Donald W., *The Biblical Flood and the Ice Epoch: A Study in Scientific History*, Pacific Merdian Publishing Co., Seattle, 1966.

Pears Encyclopaedia of Myths and Legends: Oceania, Australia and the Americas (ed. Sheila Savill), Pelham Books, London, 1978.

Penguin Dictionary of Religions, Penguin Books, London, 1988.

Peru, Lonely Planet Publications, Hawthorne, Australia, 1991.

Petrie, W. M. Flinders, *The Pyramids and Temples of Gizeh*, (Revised Edition) Histories and Mysteries of Man, London, 1990.

Plato, *Timaeus and Critias*, Penguin Classics, London, 1977.

Popol Vuh: The Sacred Book of the Ancient Quiche Maya, (English version by Delia Goetz and S. G. Morley from the translation by Adrian Recinos) University of Oklahoma Press, 1991.

Posnansky, Arthur, *Tiahuanacu: The Cradle of American Man*, (4 volumes), J. Augustin, New York, 1945.

Prestwich, Joseph, *On Certain Phenomena Belonging to the Close of the Last*

Geological Period and on their Bearing upon the Tradition of the Flood,
Macmillan, London, 1895.

Quarternary Extinctions: A Prehistoric Revolution (eds. Paul S. Martin and R. G.
Kline), University of Arizona Press, 1984.

Reeves, Nicholas, *The Complete Tutankhamun*, Thames & Hudson, London,
1990.
Reiche, Maria, *Mystery on the Desert*, Nazca, Peru, 1989.
Ridpath, Ian and Tirion, Wil, *Collins Guide to Stars and Planets*, London, 1984.
Rig Veda, Penguin Classics, London, 1981.
Roberts, P. W., *River in the Desert: Modern Travels in Ancient Egypt*, Random
House, New York and Toronto, 1993.
Romer, John, *Valley of the Kings*, Michael O'Mara Books, London, 1988.
Rundle-Clark, R.T., *Myth and Symbol in Ancient Egypt*, Thames & Hudson,
London, 1991.

Sabloff, Jeremy A., *The Cities of Mexico: Reconstructing a Lost World*, Thames
& Hudson, London, 1990.
Santillana, Giorgio de and von Dechend, Hertha, *Hamlet's Mill*, David R.
Godine, Boston, 1992.
Scheel, B., *Egyptian Metalworking and Tools*, Shire Egyptology, Aylesbury,
1989.
Schlegel, Gustav, *Uranographie chinoise*, 1875.
——*The Hung League*, Tynron Press, Scotland, 1991.
Schwaller de Lubicz, R. A., *Sacred Science: The King of Pharaonic Theocracy*,
Inner Traditions International, Rochester, Vermont, 1988.
Sellers, Jane B., *The Death of Gods in Ancient Egypt*, Penguin, London, 1992.
Seton-Watson, M. V., *Egyptian Legends and Stories*, Rubicon Press, London,
1990.
Sitchin, Zecharia, *The Stairway to Heaven*, Avon Books, New York, 1983.
——*The Lost Realms*, Avon Books, New York, 1990.
Smyth, Piazzi, *The Great Pyramid: Its Secrets and Mysteries Revealed*, Bell
Publishing Co., New York, 1990.
Sollberger, Edmund, *The Babylonian Legend of the Flood*, British Museum
Publications, 1984.
Spence, Lewis, *The Magic and Mysteries of Mexico*, Rider, London, 1922.
Spencer, A. J., *The Great Pyramid Fact Sheet*, P. J. Publications, 1989.
Stephens, John L., *Incidents of Travel in Central America, Chiapas and Yucatan*,
Harper and Brothers, New York, 1841.
Sykes, E., *Dictionary of Non-Classical Mythology*, London, 1961.

Temple, Robert K. G., *The Sirius Mystery*, Destiny Books, Rochester,
Vermont, 1987.
Thompson, J. Eric, *Maya Hieroglyphic Writing*, Carnegie Institution,

Washington DC, 1950.
——*Maya History and Religion*, University of Oklahoma Press, 1990.
——*The Rise and Fall of Maya Civilization*, Pimlico, London, 1993.
Tilak, Lokamanya Bal Gangadhar, *The Arctic Home in the Vedas*, Tilak Bros., Poona, 1956.
Titchenell, Elsa B., *The Masks of Odin*, Theosophical University Press, Pasadena, 1988.
Tompkins, Peter, *Secrets of the Great Pyramid*, Harper & Row, New York, 1978.
——*Mysteries of the Mexican Pyramids*, Thames & Hudson, London, 1987.

Upham, Warren, *The Glacial Lake Agassiz*, 1895.

Vega, Garcilaso de la, *The Royal Commentaries of the Incas*, Orion Press, New York, 1961.
Velikovsky, Immanuel, *Earth in Upheaval*, Pocket Books, New York, 1977.

Wallis Budge, E. A., *Egyptian Magic*, Kegan Paul, London, 1901.
——*A History of Egypt*, 1902.
——*Gods of the Egyptians*, Methuen & Co., London, 1904.
——*Osiris and the Egyptian Resurrections*, Medici Society, London, 1911.
——*An Egyptian Hieroglyphic Dictionary*, (2 volumes), John Murray, London, 1920.
——*From Fetish to God in Ancient Egypt*, Oxford University Press, 1934.
Ward, John, *Pyramids and Progress*, London, 1900.
Ward, J. S. M., *The Hung Society*, (3 volumes), Baskerville Press, London, 1925.
Warren, William F., *Paradise Found: The Cradle of the Human Racce at the North Pole*, Houghton, Mifflin & Co., Boston, 1885.
Waters, Frank, *Mexico Mystique*, Sage Books, Chicago, 1975.
——*The Book of the Hopi*, Penguin, London, 1977.
Wendorff, Fred and Schild, Romuald, *Prehistory of the Nile Valley*, Academic Press, New York, 1976.
West, John Anthony, *Serpent in the Sky*, Harper & Row, New York, 1979.
——*The Traveller's Key to Ancient Egypt*, Harrap–Columbus, London, 1989.
Wheeler, Post, *The Sacred Scriptures of the Japanese*, New York, 1952.
White, John, *Pole Shift*, A. R. E. Press, Virginia Beach, 1994.
Wilkins, W. J., *Hindu Mythology: Vedic and Puranic*, Heritage Publishers, New Delhi, 1991.
World Mythology (ed. Roy Willis), BCA, London, 1993.
Wright, Ronald, *Time Among the Maya*, Futura Publications, London, 1991.

Index

Page numbers in *italics* indicate line drawings

Also available from Mandarin Paperbacks

GRAHAM HANCOCK

The Sign and the Seal

A Quest for the Lost Ark of the Covenant

'Graham Hancock's obsession has led him to give up nine years of his life to tracking down the exact location of the Ark of the Covenant . . . The obsession is well worth sharing. The excitement is nail-biting'
Sunday Express

'Hancock's book will probably be as popular as the Raiders film. Added to the Holy Grail excitement of his quest, he has invented a new genre: an intellectual whodunit by a do-it-yourself sleuth'
Guardian

'Part travelogue, part sensation, part unravelling . . . a fascinating story'
Catholic Herald

'Eat your heart out, Harrison Ford'
Gerald Seymour

ROBERT BAUVAL/GRAHAM HANCOCK

Keeper of Genesis

A Quest for the Hidden Legacy of Mankind

Guardian of the ancient mysteries, the keeper of secrets . . .
For thousands of years the Great Sphinx of Egypt has gazed
towards the east, his eyes focused on eternity, reading a
message in the stars that mankind has long forgotten. And
today, as our civilisation stands poised at the end of a great
cycle, it is a message that seems to beckon insistently to be
understood.

Robert Bauval and Graham Hancock presents a *tour de
force* of historical and scientific detective work, using
sophisticated computer simulation of the ancient skies to
crack the millennial code that the monuments transcribe,
and presenting a startling new theory concerning the
enigmatic Pyramid Texts and other archaic Egyptian
scriptures.

These texts serve as an ingenious treasure trail and, as the
authors reveal in their shattering conclusion, a covert
treasure hunt has been underway for the last twenty years —
a hunt bringing together senior Egyptologists, high
government officials, wealthy funders, and a strange esoteric
organisation lurking behind the scenes.

The secrets can be kept no longer . . .

A Selected List of Non-Fiction Titles Available from Mandarin

While every effort is made to keep prices low, it is sometimes necessary to increase prices at short notice. Mandarin Paperbacks reserves the right to show new retail prices on covers which may differ from those previously advertised in the text or elsewhere.

The prices shown below were correct at the time of going to press.

All these books are available at your bookshop or newsagent, or can be ordered direct from the address below. Just tick the titles you want and fill in the form below.

Cash Sales Department, PO Box 5, Rushden, Northants NN10 6YX.
Fax: 01933 414047 : Phone: 01933 414000.

Please send cheque, payable to 'Reed Book Services Ltd.', or postal order for purchase price quoted and allow the following for postage and packing:

£1.00 for the first book, 50p for the second; **FREE POSTAGE AND PACKING FOR THREE BOOKS OR MORE PER ORDER.**

NAME (Block letters) ....

ADDRESS ....

....

☐ I enclose my remittance for ....

☐ I wish to pay by Access/Visa Card Number

Expiry Date

Signature ....

Please quote our reference: MAND